Party
Politics
in
Canada

6th edition

edited by

HUGH G. THORBURN

Department of Political Studies
Queen's University, Kingston, Ontario

PRENTICE-HALL CANADA
Scarborough, Ontario

Canadian Cataloguing in Publication Data

Main entry under title:
Party politics in Canada

6th ed.
Includes bibliographical references and index.
ISBN 0–13–650847–2

1. Political parties – Canada.   2. Canada – Politics
and government.   I. Thorburn, Hugh G., 1924–   .

JL195.P37 1991   324.271   C90–095622–4

Prentice-Hall, Inc., Englewood Cliffs, New Jersey
Prentice-Hall International, Inc., London
Prentice-Hall of Australia, Pty., Ltd., Sydney
Prentice-Hall of India Pvt., Ltd., New Delhi
Prentice-Hall of Japan, Inc., Tokyo
Prentice-Hall of Southeast Asia (Pte.) Ltd., Singapore
Editora Prentice-Hall do Brasil Ltda., Rio de Janeiro
Prentice-Hall Hispanoamericana, S.A., Mexico

ISBN 0–13–650847–2

Copy Editor: Elise Levine
Production Editor: Linda Collins
Production Coordinator: Florence Rousseau
Cover Design and Illustration: Monica Kompter
Page Layout: Colborne, Cox & Burns

1 2 3 4 5   JD   95 94 93 92 91

Printed and bound in Canada by John Deyell Company

CONTENTS

PREFACE

This sixth edition of *Party Politics in Canada* is the most thorough revision to date. Of the 35 articles, 21 are new and six are completely revised, leaving only eight veteran survivors from the previous edition.

The new Section Two, *The Setting of Party Politics*, contains eight new pieces. I offer an essay on interest groups and Robert Hackett and Lynne Hissey present one on the role of the media. Martin Goldfarb, a specialist on polls and pollsters, has permitted the inclusion of his introduction to *Marching to a Different Drummer*, the book he co-authored with Thomas Axworthy. Lise Gotell and Janine Brodie have written on women in politics, and Donald C. MacDonald, the Ontario Commissioner on Election Finances, tells us about the problems of this crucial matter. Charlotte Gray shows how the rules governing campaign finance are, in fact, dodged. William Irvine discusses the electoral system and shows how it could best be reinforced; and Sid Noel shows how patronage has changed in Canadian politics.

The third section is also largely new, and examines the party system as a functioning entity. R.K. Carty offers a stimulating analysis of the three different party systems that Canada has experienced since Confederation, and John Meisel presents a new piece on the dysfunctions of Canadian parties, as well as a revised version of his article on the decline of party in Canada. Keith Archer and Alan Whitehorn present a comparison of the views of party activists from the three major parties and H. Donald Forbes writes about parties and voters in Canada. Janine Brodie has updated her article on regionalism and party policy in Canada. George Perlin discusses conventions to select party leaders. Articles by Gad Horowitz and me are retained from the previous edition.

The section on *The Two Old Parties* is entirely new, except for the classic piece by Reginald Whitaker, "Party and State in the Liberal Era." Thomas Axworthy presents a new appreciation of the present Liberal Party and George Perlin does the same for the Progressive Conservatives.

The section on *Third Parties* retains W.L. Morton's essay on the Progressives and includes two new essays by Alan Whitehorn, one on the New Democratic Party, and one on the Canadian Communist Party. Peter McCormick has prepared a new essay on the Reform Party, which has only recently appeared on the political scene in western Canada.

The last section on *Regional Politics* contains the classic essay by Marcel Rioux on Quebec ideologies, and two new pieces on Quebec politics, one by Raymond

Hudon and another by Réjean Landry. Nelson Wiseman has updated his "Pattern of Prairie Politics," as has David E. Smith his essay on "Grits and Tories on the Prairies." The pieces on Ontario (by Robert J. Williams) and on the Atlantic provinces (by Agar Adamson and Ian Stewart) are revised and updated. Allan Tupper presents a new essay on Alberta politics. The sole survivor from the fifth edition is the essay on B.C. party systems by Alan Cairns and Daniel Wong. Of course, the tables on the national election results have been updated, and new appendices listing the federal party leaders and the results of party leadership conventions have been added, as have notes on contributors and an index.

With the inclusion of all this new material, many solid veteran essays have been sacrificed. I regret this, but they remain in earlier editions for consultation. Time goes on, and textbooks must be kept up-to-date, and hard choices made. The book is growing fatter as one edition gives way to the next. I hope readers will find that it retains its vigour nonetheless.

I would like to thank all the authors and, where their work appeared elsewhere, their publishers, for making their essays available here. Also, I am grateful to the colleagues who acted as readers for this sixth edition and who made many useful suggestions for improvement, which have not gone unheeded.

I hope that the students and interested general readers for whom this book has been prepared will find it helpful and insightful in elucidating the mysteries of party politics in Canada.

H.G. Thorburn
1991

NOTES ON CONTRIBUTORS

Agar Adamson is a member of the political science department at Acadia University. A student of Atlantic Canadian politics, he has written and commented upon numerous aspects of regional politics, including federal-provincial relations, development, elections, and leadership contests.

Keith Archer is an associate professor of political science at the University of Calgary. He is the author of *Political Choices and Electoral Consequences: A Study of Organized Labour and the New Democratic Party* (1990), and articles on political parties and voting behaviour.

Thomas S. Axworthy is Executive Director of the CRB Foundation, and an Associate of the Center for International Affairs, Harvard University. He was Principal Secretary to Prime Minister Trudeau, 1981–1984.

Janine Brodie is an associate professor of political science at York University. She is co-author of *Crisis, Challenge and Change* and author of *Women and Politics in Canada* and *The Political Economy of Canadian Regionalism*.

Alan C. Cairns is a professor of political science at the University of British Columbia, a Fellow of the Royal Society of Canada, and Past-President of the Canadian Political Science Association. He has written extensively on Canadian politics. *Constitution, Government and Society in Canada*, edited by Douglas Williams, is a collection of his recent essays.

R.K. Carty is a member of the department of political science at the University of British Columbia. His interests centre on the relationships between institutions and political organizations, especially political parties. He has published widely on electoral systems, Irish political parties, and Canadian political organization.

H.D. Forbes is an associate professor in the department of political science at the University of Toronto. He is the author of a study of political psychology, *Nationalism, Ethnocentrism, and Personality*, and has edited an anthology, *Canadian Political Thought*. He has published articles in several scholarly journals and is a frequent contributor to *The Idler*.

Martin Goldfarb, chairman of Goldfarb Consultants, is a sociologist who has been involved in providing polling and strategic research services to the Liberal party of Canada and various provincial political parties as well as major international corporations for over two decades. He is co-author of the book *Marching to a Different Drummer* (Stoddart, 1988), which examines the ideological evolution of the Liberal and Progressive Conservative parties.

Lise Gotell is a doctoral candidate in the department of political science at York University. She is currently researching the impact of the Charter of Rights and Freedoms on the Canadian women's movement.

Charlotte Gray is Ottawa editor of *Saturday Night*, and writes frequently on people and issues in federal politics for Canadian magazines including *Saturday Night*, *Canadian Business* and *Report on Business*. She has lived in Ottawa for 12 years.

Robert A. Hackett teaches communication at Simon Fraser University. His research interests include social movements and the media, the politics of social democracy, and ideological roles of news and journalism. He has written a number of articles in these areas, as well as forthcoming books on the press and the politics of peace in Canada, and (with Satu Repo and Zhao Yuezhi) on journalistic objectivity as a form of popular culture.

Lynne Hissey teaches communication and women's studies at Simon Fraser University, and has a research interest in women and the media.

Gad Horowitz teaches political science at the University of Toronto, and is the author of *Canadian Labour in Politics* and other studies relating to political theory and Canadian politics.

Raymond Hudon is professor and chairman of the department of political science at Université Laval. He is co-author, with Vincent Lemieux, of *Patronage et politique au Quebec, 1944–1972*, and has written many articles and contributed to many books on Canadian and Quebec politics and political economy. He is currently conducting research on the relations of young people to politics and on the impact of free trade on state intervention.

William P. Irvine is a professor of political studies at Queen's University. He has written on political parties and elections and on electoral systems for the Task Force on Canadian Unity and for the Macdonald Royal Commission on the Economic Union and Development Prospects for Canada.

Réjean Landry is a professor of political science at Univeristé Laval. His principal published works deal with Quebec politics, public policies and public choice.

Donald C. MacDonald has been a part-time lecturer in political science at Atkinson College, York University, since 1971, and has been general editor of the first three editions of *Government and Politics of Ontario*. He was CCF-NDP leader in Ontario, 1953–70; a member of the Ontario Legislature (1955–82); a Skelton-Clark Fellow at Queen's University in 1989; and has been Chairman of the Ontario Commission on Election Finances since 1986.

Peter McCormick is professor of political science at the University of Lethbridge, and a research associate of the Canada West Foundation. His research interests include political parties, Canadian and provincial politics, courts and judges, and political theory.

John Meisel is the Sir Edward Peacock Professor of Political Science at Queen's University and co-editor of the *International Political Science Review*. He has written extensively on elections and parties in Canada, and on the relations between politics and ethnicity, culture and the arts, regulation, broadcasting and telecommunications.

The late **W.L. Morton**, a noted Canadian historian at Trent University and subsequently at the University of Manitoba, wrote extensively on the history of western Canada, and about the Canadian identity. His study *The Progressive Party in Canada* is the definitive work on that subject.

Sid Noel is a professor of political science at the University of Western Ontario. He has written on a variety of topics, including Canadian federal and provincial politics, consociational democracy and South Africa. His most recent work is *Patrons, Clients, Brokers*, a forthcoming study of nineteenth-century Ontario political culture.

George C. Perlin teaches political science at Queen's University, and is the author of *The Tory Syndrome*, co-author with Patrick Martin and Allan Gregg, of *Contenders: the Tory Quest for Power* and editor of *Party Democracy in Canada*.

Escott M. Reid has served as Canada's ambassador to Germany and High Commissioner to India. He has written books about this experience, about the origins of NATO, and about the World Bank. He has also been a professor of political science and was the first Principal of Glendon College, York University.

Marcel Rioux is professor emeritus of sociology at the Université de Montréal. Author of 425 titles, he specializes in critical sociology. His book *Quebec in Question* has appeared in English. *Les Québécois* is well-known in French.

David E. Smith is a professor of political studies at the University of Saskatchewan. His published works deal with political parties and federalism in Canada. Most recently, he is the co-author (with Norman Ward) of *James G. Gardiner: Relentless Liberal*. He is a Fellow of the Royal Society of Canada.

Ian Stewart is an associate professor of political science at Acadia University. He has published in the *Canadian Journal of Political Science, Publius,* and the *Journal of Canadian Studies*. His recent work has focused on the political culture of Maritime Canada.

Hugh G. Thorburn teaches political science at Queen's University, and has written books on interest groups, planning, political parties, provincial politics and competition policy in Canada. He has served as president of the Social Science Research Council of Canada, and of the Canadian Political Science Association, and as head of the department of political studies, Queen's University.

Allan Tupper is professor and chairman of the department of political science at the University of Alberta. A Canadian politics specialist, he has written about such topics as Crown corporations, Alberta politics and industrial strategies. His most recent major work is *Privatization, Public Corporations and Public Policy* (co-edited with G. Bruce Doern).

Reginald Whitaker teaches political science at York University, and wrote *The Government Party* on the Liberals in the King-St. Laurent period. He also writes on political theory.

Alan Whitehorn is former research director for the David Lewis memoirs, *The Good Fight,* and is completing a book on the NDP. He is a professor in the department of political and economic science at the Royal Military College of Canada in Kingston.

Robert J. Williams is associate professor of political science at the University of Waterloo. His research interests include government policies for the arts and culture, the selection of parliamentary candidates and aspects of municipal government. These topics have been pursued in both Canada (and in Ontario in particular) and Australia.

Nelson Wiseman teaches in the department of political science at the University of Toronto. He has also taught at the University of Manitoba and York University, and has worked as a public policy consultant. His scholarly writing has focussed on prairie politics and voting behaviour. He is the author of *Social Democracy in Manitoba*.

Daniel Wong, a graduate of the University of British Columbia, is a specialist in corporate communications and government affairs. He is a member of the Business Council of British Columbia and the author of numerous articles in trade journals and other business publications on business-government relations and international trade policy.

Historical Background

The following essays present different approaches to the growth of national parties in Canada. I have summarized the historical development of our parties from the pre-Confederation period and viewed their platforms as indicators of what they stood for. Escott Reid, in his essay, finds that national parties were slow to develop because parochialism persisted and members of parliament tended to trade their support of the government for local patronage. I have focused on the people and issues at the centre of the political system; Mr. Reid is concerned with the country-wide political conditions during the years of slow party growth before the turn of the century.

1 The Development of Political Parties in Canada

HUGH G. THORBURN

The Canadian party system is largely unique and traces its origins to the pre-Confederation legislative assemblies, particularly to that of the United Province of Canada. From an inchoate politics dependent on local patronage and the extent of the governor's powers, it has developed into a stable two-and-a-half party system, in which the two parties of consensus (the Liberals and the Conservatives) receive between them over three quarters of the votes. The remainder go mainly to the third party, the New Democratic Party (NDP)—so far no more than 20 percent—and the rest to other minor parties. We refer to the Liberals and Conservatives as parties of consensus because they are essentially brokerage parties or parties facilitating élite accommodation, which have no ideological perspective deviating from the status quo.

Historical Development

The beginnings of a party system first appeared in the United Province of Canada (now southern Ontario and Quebec) in the period following the Act of Union of 1840. After Confederation and with the addition of the Maritime provinces, this party system was extended to them, and later to the West. However, a national party system did not exist in Canada until the turn of the century.

The pre-Confederation constitutional system was similar in all of British North America: a governor was sent from Britain to exercise the royal prerogative and actively to head the government. He was supported by a council drawn from the leading figures of the colony. The people were represented by a Legislative Assembly which had the traditional parliamentary budgetary powers to vote or withhold revenues (minus control of such essentials as the civil list and the revenue from crown lands). The elected Assemblymen were at first concerned with obtaining their share of local works, especially roads, and came into conflict with the governor and council over the extent of their powers.

This is a revised and updated version of the essay that appeared in the previous edition of this book.

Their aim was to become another parliament on the Westminster model. Responsible government, according to which the government must resign when it loses the support of a majority of the Legislature, came to most of the colonies in the 1840s.

Members formed groups around the stronger of their number and developed relations with the other groups—some tending to align themselves with the governor's policy and some against. Weak coalitions were developed, crossing the barrier between English and French. The Baldwin-Lafontaine government brought the Reformers together to face the Conservatives. As this developed, the governor became more of a figurehead and power came to be centred in the Assembly and subject to the unstable vagaries of the shifting factions. However, "In spite of the gradual evolution of political groups and the tendency to apply different names to the same political group as it progressed from era to era, there were permanent political parties during the whole Union period (1840–67) and these parties were largely consistent in membership, viewpoint and policy."[1] The government's policies were moderate and there was no "dynamic matter of principle distinguishing the enactments of the Liberal from the Liberal-Conservative governments of the period."[2] The habit of pragmatic moderation, used to appeal to a majority, was formed well before Confederation.

The period of legislative union in the Province of Canada was one of great instability. A more lasting governmental coalition was needed and was supplied by the Liberal-Conservative party, under the leadership of John A. Macdonald. His Tories were the weaker party in Canada West but were more disciplined and cohesive than their Liberal opponents, who were constantly being frayed by new radical movements. The Tories of Canada West and G.E. Cartier's Bleus, along with some moderate reformers from Canada West and big business interests from Montreal, formed the new and lasting coalition that governed both before and after Confederation.

The components of the party were typical of subsequent Canadian parties: Cartier's Bleus, who represented a stable French Canadian majority with the blessing of the hierarchy; the Grand Trunk and other English Canadian business interests, who were seeking an economic empire based in Montreal; Macdonald's Tories with their anti-American bias; Galt's English-speaking Montreal big business supporters with voting strength in the Eastern Townships; and the Hinksite Reformers from Canada West who had followed Robert Baldwin, and who had established connections with the Grand Trunk.[3] The essential components constituted sufficient voting strength and business support to finance the electoral effort.

Pitted against the Liberal-Conservatives were the Clear Grits of Canada West, who drew their voting strength from the Ontario peninsula and their inspiration from George Brown's paper, the *Globe*. They represented frontier agrarian democracy and opposed the Grand Trunk and Galt's protective tariff. In loose association with the Grits were the Rouges of Canada East, whose anti-clericalism ensured their weakness before a dominating hierarchy. They were the most radical group in the Legislature, espousing the republican ideas of France's

1848 revolution and American democracy. They opposed Confederation as "a Grand Trunk job."[4]

This embryonic two-party system was too unstable for orderly government because of the double majority convention, under which the government sought to command a majority in both Canada East and Canada West. Confederation with the Maritime provinces offered an escape from this trap. The French Canadians would clearly be dominant in the new Quebec Legislature, which had control over education, property and civil rights, and local matters. English Canadians, on the other hand, had a clear majority in the new parliament, which controlled the major economic areas.[5]

Macdonald's Conservatives dominated parliament for the first 30 years (except for one parliament when his party was defeated because of the revelation of money passing to the party from railway contractors, known as the Pacific Scandal). His coalition was solidified and extended into the Maritimes and the West as the party of Confederation, the party controlling patronage and therefore the party with the most money at election time. It was a party that made the government a partner with business in developing the economic resources of the country. As sponsor of the transcontinental railway, it worked out the philosophy of development that came to be known as the National Policy, which was implemented in the budget of 1878. Under this arrangement, a protective tariff would shelter the infant industries of central Canada from foreign competition and guarantee them a privileged market in Canada. The revenues would support railway expansion, permitting the opening up of new territory and thereby enlarging the market. The railways, in turn, would service the new areas by bringing in settlers and manufactured goods and carrying the grain, timber and other primary products to Montreal for export.

As long as the Liberals continued to represent the farmers of western Ontario and the rural Rouges south of the St. Lawrence, they were no match for Macdonald's business-oriented and development-minded Conservatives. The Mackenzie government (1874–78), which came to power as a result of the disgrace of the Conservatives in the Pacific Scandal, proved to be an upright but immobile holding operation that could not operate on Macdonald's expansionist basis. Mackenzie failed because he could not bring himself to grant the concessions demanded by the business promoters and the representatives of the outlying provinces. Only when the Liberals abandoned their reformist posture as defenders of the agrarian underdog and spokespersons for reform did they succeed; but once they patterned themselves on Macdonald's Conservatives they beat the Tories at their own game—and they have, until recently, continued to do so.

The "credit" for this transformation goes to Wilfrid Laurier, who took over the Liberal leadership in 1887. He turned his back on the Rouge, republican, anti-clerical tradition and declared himself a Liberal in the British, Gladstonian style. He wooed the clergy and sought their good will and that of the hierarchy (which still eluded him). He made peace with the manufacturers and, in effect, accepted the National Policy. This he accomplished with the brilliant stroke of "Empire Preference," which permitted a protective tariff for Canadian manufactures and discrimination in favour of British goods, which appealed to the low-tariff English Canadian farmers. To gain approval from the business community he chose the more tractable W.S. Fielding to replace Sir Richard Cartwright as Minister of Finance. Thus he was able to combine democratic principles with business-oriented policies.

Prosperity came at the same time as Laurier's government, permitting economic expansion. He built up railway and banking associations for the Liberals (the Grand Trunk with its western dream, the Grand Trunk Pacific, as well as Mackenzie and Mann's Canadian Northern, and the Bank of Commerce). This proved a match for the Conservatives' Canadian Pacific-Bank of Montreal connection. If imitation is the highest form of flattery, the Conservatives were honoured indeed because they remained in opposition for 65 of the next 87 years. With the change in the Liberal party, Canada had a two-party system that resembled the American more than the British. Each party mirrored the other closely and sought the support of all classes, religious and ethnic groups by offering prosperity through programmes of government support of business. Conflicts between classes and regions were handled quietly within the party rather than openly between parties; both parties recognized the value of secrecy for their internal and financial affairs.

It was during the Liberal years that the Prairies were settled and the provinces of Saskatchewan and Alberta created. Naturally, at first, immigrants were loyal to the party under whose auspices they came to Canada and received their lands. However, it was not long before they came to resent the monopoly position of the railway and the high prices of tariff-protected Canadian manufactured goods. This contrasted sharply with the open world market on which their wheat and other primary products were sold. They began to agitate for reform of these abuses. When President Taft was willing to contemplate free trade in natural products between the United States and Canada, Laurier made "reciprocity" his issue in the 1911 election. Like the Empire preference device, this appeared to please everyone. The farmers would have an outlet for their produce, yet the eastern industrialists would keep their protected market. But when Laurier went to the country on this platform, he lost.

How? In retrospect, one can say that he broke the basic rule for success in Canadian politics: he gave priority to the outlying areas. The business community feared that reciprocity in natural products would soon be followed by reciprocity in processed goods, and it did not like the party to cater to the farmer. It backed Borden's Conservatives, enabling them to raise the bogey of American domination. "No truck or trade with the Yankees" was their slogan and they won after an emotional campaign. The Conservative victory was aided by an alliance with Henri Bourassa's Quebec nationalists, who opposed Laurier for not doing more for French Canadian rights. He had opposed the creation of a Canadian navy and favoured a bilingual Canada. Opposition to the Liberals meant alliance with the Conservatives. The Tory victory was built on Ontario, Manitoba and British Columbia, and on Quebec, which provided Borden with 27 of its 65 seats.

The election of 1911 marked a turning point in Canadian party politics. The

old, simple, two-party system was modified by the complexity of regional discontent in both Quebec and the West: the former for cultural reasons and the
latter for economic ones. The empire based on the St. Lawrence valley's great
economic interests had matured and was showing signs of strain: there was the
beginning of significant class, regional and cultural conflict.

The coming of war in 1914 masked these strains for a time. The patriotic call
rallied much of English Canada to the imperial allegiance, but the imposition of
conscription alienated French Canada. Laurier opposed conscription and in so
doing lost many of his English-speaking Liberals, who joined Borden to form the
Unionist coalition. Now the Liberal opposition was predominantly French Canadian and the government English Canadian. The omnibus two-party system
appeared to be in ruins.

The end of the war saw a remarkable change. The unionist government suffered from internal strain and the Liberals rebuilt their forces. The Liberal convention of 1919 confronted the party with the basic choice, between Fielding—the
Nova Scotian who had gone over to Borden during the war, the older man with
the more conservative image— and King, whose absence from the country during the war spared him from involvement in the struggles within the party. He
was therefore acceptable to both French and English Canadians, and he
appeared to be on the left of the party. In choosing King, the party regained its
broad acceptability and made the Conservatives the party of the English and of
conscription. In every general election from 1917 to 1958 (except 1930), the Conservatives got fewer than 10 seats in Quebec,[6] and the Liberals won absolute
majorities there every time. It was the same technique used by the Democrats in
the United States: "waving the bloody shirt" in the South; and it produced a
solid Liberal contingent from Quebec by blaming the Conservatives for conscription. In these 11 elections the Quebec contingent alone constituted more than a
third of Liberal representation in the House of Commons every time but one
(1935).

King was in the Macdonald-Laurier tradition; he fashioned a party drawing
support from all regions, all classes and all cultural groups. As a consequence, he
succeeded in being prime minister longer than anyone else in the history of the
Commonwealth: from 1921 until 1948 (except for a few weeks in 1926 and the
Depression years, 1930–35).

However, it was in the King years that the party system changed from a simple
two-party system to what has been called a "two-and-a-half party system." The
regional, cultural and class disaffection that appeared earlier grew into firmly
entrenched third-party movements, centred mainly in the Prairies, Quebec and
the urban working class. The discontent on the Prairies that Laurier had sought
to assuage in 1911 grew into the Progressive party, the Co-operative Commonwealth Federation (CCF) and the Social Credit party.

Unlike his predecessors, King's government did not have a broad national
development policy—it was much more of an *ad hoc* arrangement. These were the
years of the opening of the forest and mining frontiers. Investment poured in

from abroad (increasingly from the United States) to develop the pulp and paper, base metals and gold mining industries and, most important, secondary manufacturing. Branch plants were set up—mostly in the St. Lawrence drainage basin between Windsor and Montreal—to replicate the U.S. consumers' durables and other industries. Ironically, Macdonald's National Policy of tariff protection was created to fend off American economic domination. Now it served to attract American industry to settle behind the wall and sell in the protected Canadian market, and to export to the rest of the Commonwealth and Empire under the Empire preferences system.

The old east-west trading axis based on the timber and wheat economies (which found its markets in Europe and its transportation in the transcontinental railways and the North Atlantic sea route) was challenged by the new north-south axis (based on pulp and paper, minerals and manufacturing, oriented to the United States, and carried by motor vehicle and aircraft as well as by railway).

The new arrangements, while they "developed" the economy, also inhibited Canada's national independence. Instead of being financed by bonds which, when repaid, would leave a Canadian-owned and operated industry, they tended to be subsidiaries wholly owned or at least controlled by the foreign corporation. As these subsidiaries grew and prospered, the Canadian economy fell more and more under foreign domination. At first there was little concern about the new pattern. Development meant jobs, prosperity and the appearance of national maturity. Only later was the country troubled about the dangers of falling into a new colonial status. All this occurred during the Liberal years, when the country was proud of its growing independence and stature in the world. Its active role in World War II earned it standing and British power declined at the same time. The British connection grew more tenuous and could no longer be used by Canadians to fend off American encroachments. The Liberal leadership, perhaps recognizing the inevitable, cooperated with the Americans at home and abroad. The Liberal party, long seen as the champion of Canadian independence against British imperialism, became the party accepting greater continental integration, and the Conservatives under Diefenbaker, the resisters against "Texas buccaneers."

The omnibus character of the two old parties asserted itself as this distinction became clearer. Walter Gordon led a group of Canadian economic nationalists within the Liberal party and was defeated. Diefenbaker was obligated to desist in his anti-American forays and was replaced by a more cautious and compromising Stanfield.

The policy distinctions between the parties are not great or clear. The major difference has not been between the two old parties themselves, but between the two taken together and the third parties. In fact, it is because the two old parties remained so similar during the years when the regional, cultural and economic groups of the country matured and began to demand more of their government, that the third parties appeared. They entrenched themselves as part of the Canadian party system because the old parties did not, or could not, satisfy the grievances they represented. The Progressive party marks the bridge between the two-party period before World War I and the more recent one that includes third parties.

The discontent on the Prairies that led Laurier to offer reciprocity in 1911 increased during the 1914–18 war period, and appeared in the form of a party of political protest among the farmers, not only on the Prairies, but in Ontario as well. In the decade following World War I, the Progressives or United Farmers formed the government in Ontario, dominated the Prairie provinces and had more seats than any opposition party in parliament, although they refused to become the official opposition. They constituted an agrarian radical reaction against the National Policy and its successors that had built up the commercial empire based on Toronto and Montreal business and given it political power. The revolt lacked discipline and organization and was not agreed on policy or philosophy. Therefore it lacked the staying power to confront the old parties over time. Mackenzie King's flexibility and radical posture succeeded in winning over the key Progressive leaders to the Liberals and the party was largely absorbed.

Western radicalism was not satisfied with King's blandishments and continued in different forms—but the farmers' movement in the East disappeared. The Co-operative Commonwealth Federation (CCF), a socialist movement drawing support from western farmers, the urban working class and university intellectuals, was formed in the Depression of the 1930s. It was the first party in Canadian history to build up an organization, a philosophy and a cadre of leaders in order to offer a sustained challenge to the two omnibus parties. It got nine percent of the votes in the 1935 election and grew vigorously during the next decade of depression and war, winning control of the Saskatchewan government in 1944. Postwar prosperity rolled back its advance. To escape from the trap of inadequate campaign funds and a too-narrow base, the CCF merged with the labour movement in 1958 to form the New Democratic party (NDP). The result so far is a more conspicuous (richer, but less doctrinaire) party than the CCF. Whether it will become more conservative in order to defend trade union interests and privileges is yet to be seen. So far the party constitutes the one major challenge to the old parties in both voting strength and intellectual content.

The other outgrowth of western discontent is the Social Credit movement. When the Alberta variant of the Progressive movement collapsed from incompetence, scandal and the effects of the Depression, the province grasped at a magical solution which would defend existing property relationships but infuse effective demand for goods and services into the economic system by issuing "dividends" to enable people to purchase more. While the party was continuously in power from 1935 to 1971, its philosophy was soon forgotten and the party became the most conservative in the country. Its success in both Alberta and British Columbia reveals the combination of western Canadian prosperity-born conservatism and mistrust or jealousy of the East, which is presumed to dominate the old parties.

The western parties of dissent have generally been more successful at the provincial than the federal level. Every western province has at one time or another been governed by one of these parties, although no eastern or central Canadian province has (except for the one-shot United Farmers of Ontario government in Ontario in the 1920s). Reasons for this situation are difficult to determine, beyond the obvious fact that to be counted among the government or official opposition one must be either Liberal or Conservative in federal politics. Also, westerners could vote for Diefenbaker from 1957 to 1965, which was not the same as voting Conservative when the leader was close to eastern Canadian business.

The other manifestation of localized dissent—French Canadian nationalism—was even more confined to provincial politics. It too can be traced to the pre-1914 period. The use of troops to suppress the two Riel rebellions and the hanging of the leader, the controversy surrounding the disposal of the Jesuits' estates, the bitterness over the New Brunswick, Manitoba and Ontario school questions—all quickened the sensitivity of French Canada to its vulnerable minority situation. Henri Bourassa, politician and founder of *Le Devoir*, became an effective spokesman for French Canadian nationalism in parliament, and did much to bring down Laurier in 1911. However, it was during the Depression that the Liberal establishment was brought down provincially by a new nationalist party under Maurice Duplessis. The *Union Nationale* was built on the electoral organization of Quebec Conservatives, with dissident Liberals and nationalists joining in. Unlike the western third parties, the Union Nationale confined itself to provincial politics and many of its workers remained faithful to the Conservatives federally. Its policies were conservative, with an admixture of nationalist rhetoric. When the nationalist issue sharpened to the separatist option in 1970, the party equivocated and suffered a serious defeat.

In general, French Canadian dissent and western dissent have much in common. Both are reacting to the two-party system, which they see as the instrument of Toronto- and Montreal-based English Canadian, and now American, business interests. They see the old parties as alter egos of each other; to dissent they must rely on a third party. In the West this party appears in both federal and provincial politics, although it has been more successful in the latter. In Quebec, the Union Nationale and Parti Québécois have so far confined themselves to provincial politics, although Social Credit has achieved its modest successes at the federal level. The province, and particularly its French Canadian majority, has preferred to keep its federal contingent on the government side and its representatives in cabinet—a choice that is not only in its interest but favours national unity. If there were no influential French Canadians in Ottawa, the separatist cause would have had additional serious grievances to feed upon. With the emergence of the Bloc Québécois (drawn from dissident Conservative MPs and one Liberal) after the failure of the Meech Lake Accord, the stage may be set for a more successful independent challenge in federal politics.

ENDNOTES

1. P.G. Cornell, *The Alignment of Political Groups in Canada 1841–1867* (Toronto: University of Toronto Press, 1962), p. 83.
2. *Ibid.*
3. F.H. Underhill, "The Development of National Parties in Canada," *Canadian Historical Review*, Vol. 16, No. 4 (1935), p. 367.
4. *Ibid.*
5. See the article by F.R. Scott in *Evolving Canadian Federalism*, A. Lower, F.R. Scott *et al.*, (Durham, NC: Duke University Press, 1958), pp. 54–91.
6. Quebec had 65 seats until 1949 when it got eight more for a total of 73. It had 75 seats from 1953 to 1968, when it lost one, for a total of 74 from 1968 to 1974. Since 1979 it has had 75 seats. With the emergence of the Bloc Québécois (drawn from dissident Conservative MPs and one Liberal) after the failure of the Meech Lake accord, the stage may be set for a more successful independent challenge in federal politics.

2 The Rise of National Parties in Canada

ESCOTT M. REID

To understand Canadian politics during the first quarter century or so of the country's history one must constantly bear in mind certain differences between the conduct of general elections then and now. The two most important points of difference are that in the first three general elections, those of 1867, 1872 and 1874, voting was open throughout all the provinces and the polling in the various constituencies did not take place at the same time. Toronto might elect its member one day and the neighbouring York constituency six weeks later. The grosser abuses of the system of non-simultaneous elections were remedied in 1874 but not till 1878 was the ballot used and simultaneous voting established in all but a few of the constituencies of the five eastern provinces. In 1882 Manitoba voted simultaneously with the East and by 1908 deferred elections had been discontinued in the great majority of the remaining western constituencies. It is also worth noting that open voting was resurrected for use in the first two federal general elections held in the Northwest Territories, those of 1887 and 1891.

Deferred elections and open voting are important in a study of the rise of national political parties in that they make it possible for government to exercise a great measure of control over the results of elections—and the greater this control of government over elections, the weaker the political parties. Under the old system of open voting, civil servants, contractors—anyone who wanted to obtain favours from the government—could not vote against the candidates it supported without losing their jobs or their expectations of favours should the government be returned to power. On the other hand, if they voted for the government and the opposition were successful their fate would be equally unhappy. As a natural consequence they disliked partisan electoral contests. This dislike was shared by many of their neighbours who, though they did not expect to be the direct recipients of government favours, had the interests of the whole constituency at heart and did not want its chances of obtaining a new post office, wharf or railway spoilt by its unintentional support of the weaker party at an election.

Escott M. Reid, "The Rise of National Parties in Canada", *Papers and Proceedings of the Canadian Political Science Associations* IV (1932). Reprinted by permission of *The Canadian Journal of Economics and Political Science* and the author.

Even after vote by ballot was adopted these people continued to disapprove of partisan electoral contests, which committed the constituency to the support of one side or another before they knew which side would constitute the government. The ideal election of these political realists was an uncontested one in which the member was not definitely committed to any party and could therefore make good terms for his constituency in return for giving his support to the strongest party in the House.[1] Such members constituted an important fraction of all the early parliaments; Macdonald called them "loose fish," George Brown, "the shaky fellows" and Cartwright, "waiters on Providence." These appellations are hardly dispassionate enough for us so we shall call them, for want of a better term, "ministerialists," because their politics were not to support a party but a ministry and any ministry would do. These ministerialists were inverted Irishmen. They were always "agin" the opposition. Their counterpart in ecclesiastical politics was the Vicar of Bray.

It was because of the strength of this political realism that non-simultaneous elections threw such power into the hands of the ministry. The government could bring on the elections first in those constituencies in which they were safe, and having carried them, tackle those where they had some chance against the opposition, and leave the dangerous seats till the last. At the close of the election of 1872, The Toronto *Globe* wrote that: "The sole object of this nefarious trickery was to enable the Ministerialists to raise a grand howl over their pretended success and cheat the people into the belief that the Opposition were being awfully beaten."[2]

The *Globe* knew that if the people believed the opposition were being awfully beaten many of them would rally to the government camp and the opposition would be badly beaten. The illusion of victory would create victory. For if the voting in a ministerially minded constituency, in our sense of the word, were deferred until it seemed pretty clear which party would form the government, that constituency need no longer return an avowed "loose fish"; it could return a proper party candidate. Nevertheless that would not mean that it cared at all for parties—that parties had any real existence in that constituency.

National political parties certainly did not exist under the Macdonald government from 1867 to 1873. Confederation saw group government established at Ottawa. The dominant groups or parties in the coalition government were the several branches of Ontario conservatism under Galt, Macdonald and others, and the French Conservative groups under Cartier. This dual alliance was supported by the Ontario Liberals under McDougall, Howland and Blair, the English minority in Quebec under Galt, and a large group of ministerialists mostly from eastern Ontario, Quebec and New Brunswick. The Ontario coalition Liberals and the Cartier followers were not members of a coalition party because they owed their allegiance entirely to their own sectional leaders. They appear to have been willing to support an alternative administration which would have excluded Macdonald and his supporters, and Macdonald in 1871 had to use all his cunning to prevent a successful alliance arising out of the "coquetting", as he called it, which was going on between his French followers and the two wings of Ontario liberalism.[3] By 1872 the coalition Liberals had returned to the Reform party or had been swallowed up by one of the Conservative groups, and consequently the government followers in Ontario were slightly more homogeneous, though the number of parties which made up Ontario conservatism was still great if we can judge from the events of 1873. Certainly in that year it appeared as if the Conservative sectional leaders in Ontario could transfer their personal following to the support of another administration at their own mere pleasure. If Galt, for example, had entered Mackenzie's cabinet, as at one time seemed likely, he would have brought over the Conservative members from the Cobourg district and this, according to his adviser (the conservative editor in Cobourg), would have given him "the strongest personal following of any member of the Cabinet."[4]

The members from New Brunswick in the first two parliaments were either ministerialists or independents. The election of 1867 in that province was fought not between an anti-government party and a pro-government party but between so-called anti-unionists under Smith and Anglin and so-called unionists under Mitchell and Tilley. These terms apparently meant nothing and, when the respective groups got to Ottawa, the former did not consistently vote with the opposition nor the latter with the government. As a group they gave a "fair trial to the administration" (that over-worked phrase of early Canadian politics) but occasionally they would show their complete independence as, for example, when they voted unanimously in favour of an amendment to the first national tariff debated in parliament.[5] In the election of 1872 only one successful candidate appears to have committed himself to the support of the government or opposition. The others professed varying degrees of independence of party ties.

The Nova Scotians in 1867 constituted a separate political party and its very *raison d'être*, opposition to confederation, signified that it owed no loyalty to any party or leader outside Nova Scotia. According to Howe, even the beaten Tupper party had not taken sides in the party politics of Ontario. "No man in this country," said Howe in the first session of parliament, "went to the hustings pledged to any side of any question in the politics of Canada."[6] When Howe entered the cabinet his followers became still another group within the coalition, for they continued to owe their allegiance to their sectional leader, not to Macdonald. In 1872 in Nova Scotia as in New Brunswick, the issues were mainly personal and the candidates were unpledged to any party. Their general attitude was that they had no affection for the government but that the Reformers were even less likeable for they were a selfish Ontario party.[7]

It follows from this analysis of the government supporters in the first two parliaments that there was then no national Liberal party. The Brownite Liberals of Ontario possessed the unity of adversity—all who were not truly loyal had deserted to join the winning side—but they, like the Conservatives, did not even extend over the whole province, for Ontario east of Kingston was a hotbed of ministerialism. Members from that district might call themselves Liberal or Conservative but they almost unanimously supported the government. There was also a Liberal or Rouge party in Quebec but the Ontario and Quebec Liberal parties were not united. There was between them little more than an *entente cordiale,* at most a dual alliance. Not until 1872 were they able to draw close enough together to choose a common leader in parliament. This dual alliance of Ontario and Quebec Liberals did not even have an entente with the New Brunswick independents or the Nova Scotian party. The leaders of the Liberals, Mackenzie and Dorion, tried to cooperate with the Maritimers but they could carry only about half their supporters with them on a division.[8] The Liberals did not even possess enough cohesion to pursue a tactically sound policy.

The election of 1872 increased the number of votes the Liberal alliance could muster on a division but it did this by increasing the number of groups (and perplexed ministerialists who attached themselves to its standard) rather than by adding to the strength of the real party. The reason for ministerialists supporting an opposition party was that, as the returns came in during the long six weeks of polling, they were so close that both parties claimed the victory and the ministerialists were not certain on which side of the fence to jump. The wiser of them concluded that even if Macdonald had won, his was but a temporary triumph and his tenure of office would be brief. Consequently it was good policy to support the opposition so that they would be remembered when the opposition came into its own. In Quebec there were interesting developments which showed how thin was the veneer of party unity which had covered the fissures between the various groups under Cartier, now weakened by the intrigues of church politics, by the Riel rising and the New Brunswick school law. He lost support on the right to the Ultramontanes or Programmists and on the left to the Parti National, and both dissident groups attached themselves to the Rouges. Thus the Quebec oppositionists constituted no longer a fairly united party but a heterogeneous collection of groups. The parallel with 1896 is interesting.

After the downfall of Macdonald over the Pacific Scandal one coalition government succeeded another. The dominant groups in the new coalition were the Ontario Liberals and the Quebec Rouges. They were supported by a few Ontario Conservatives who had left their party because of the scandal, by the Parti National and the Programmists, by the usual assortment of ministerialists from eastern Ontario and Quebec and by almost unanimous ministerial groups from the Maritimes and the West. The personnel of the cabinet gives convincing evidence of the coalition's heterogeneity. The Ontario members were Mackenzie, Blake, Cartwright, D.A. Macdonald, Scott and Christie. Of these, Cartwright and Scott had been avowed Conservatives as late as two years before and D.A. Macdonald was an eastern Ontario "wobbler". The original Quebec representation of three were all Rouges but not one of the five Maritime members could have been called a Mackenzie supporter in the previous election. A.J. Smith of New Brunswick had declared at his nomination meeting that he had said to Sir John Macdonald and Sir George Cartier, that even if he had the power he would not turn them out for the sake of office, for he thought no other could do any better than they.[9] Burpee, the other cabinet minister from that province, had denounced the Liberal opposition because they were engrossed by the sectional interest of Ontario.[10] Ross of Nova Scotia had not even supported the remonstrance to the Governor General on August 12, 1873, when a dozen of the usual government supporters had bolted, and though Coffin of Nova Scotia had joined in the remonstrance he had previously supported Macdonald in the two-party divisions on the charges of corruption. Laird of Prince Edward Island had not taken part in the campaign of 1872 since the Island was not then a member of Confederation. Thus even counting D.A. Macdonald as Liberal, the Liberals constituted only half the Mackenzie cabinet.

It was only by 1878 that the Ontario-Quebec parties had conquered most of eastern Canada. That was the election, it will be remembered, in which the ballot was introduced and elections were held simultaneously in all but four of the eastern constituencies. Of the 141 eastern members of parliament who sought re-election, all but one did so as supporters of that leader whom they had supported in the first session of the parliament of 1874, and the great majority of the other candidates committed themselves in their election speeches to following one of the two party leaders. The result was that the Toronto *Globe* and the Montreal *Gazette* disputed over the party affiliations of only five members-elect instead of the 35 of 1872, and it was possible to discover the approximate strength of the parties in the House as soon as the ballots were counted, whereas previously that knowledge could only be gained after the first party division had taken place. There flowed from this the establishment of a constitutional precedent, for Mackenzie resigned before meeting the new parliament. This break with tradition did not go uncondemned. The *Dominion Annual Register* for that year summed up the criticism which was directed against his action: "To count up the results of an election according to the success of certain candidates who were represented to hold certain views on public affairs and to accept that result as the will of the people constitutionally expressed was ... a dangerous approach to the plebiscite."[11]

The critics were right. General elections were becoming dangerously like plebiscites but the reason was not Mackenzie's break with constitutional precedent but the establishment of the two-party system in eastern Canada. Every advance towards national political parties was to mean a further step towards making general elections plebiscites.

We must not think of the two parties as being as firmly established in eastern Canada in 1878 as they were by 1896. The Conservative party in Quebec in 1878 was still made up of a union of groups and it is possible that the only loyalty which a member of one of these groups owed was to his own sectional leader. Certainly in 1887 the ultramontane members did not seem to experience any violent conflict of loyalties when they broke with Macdonald and sought to destroy him in revenge for the murdered Riel; they were so nearly successful that Macdonald was only saved by the extra seats his gerrymander had given him in Ontario. It would appear, however, that from 1891 on the federal Conservative party did possess a measure of sovereignty in Quebec, for Chapleau was not certain enough of the loyalty of his followers to risk an open break with Macdonald. Instead he kept one foot in each camp.

Partisanship had been making no progress in the western provinces in the 1870s. The politics of Manitoba and British Columbia in the three general elections of that decade can be explained as the result of two forces: their desire for the Pacific Railway and the holding of their elections some weeks after the results in the East had been declared. Until the railway was completed the West could not afford the luxury of party politics. It had to be ministerialist. And as it always knew which party had been sustained by the East, it could be ministerialist without difficulty. All parliamentary candidates in the West in the 1870s were unanimous in their opposition to the opposition. Opposition candidates did not appear in Manitoba until 1882 nor in British Columbia until 1891. Western ministerialism was, however, of a different nature from the *politique de pourboire* of the eastern ministerialists. The westerners did not sell their support in return for the petty favours of the patronage machine and the pork barrel but only in return for the railway, the whole railway and nothing but the railway. This attitude of political realism, dictated by the economic needs of the frontier, did not triumph in Manitoba without a struggle against the partisan political attitudes of the Ontario settlers. The struggle was short and not severe. The economic necessities of the present triumphed over the political institutions of the past.[12] The British Columbians had no such struggle, for few of them had any interest in the party politics of the East until the completion of the railway in 1885 brought eastern immigrants and with them eastern political ideas. This difference in the composition of the population of the two provinces meant that Manitoba declared its allegiance to the eastern parties as soon as it was safe for it to do so, that is in 1882 or 1887, while British Columbia delayed till 1891 or 1896. The Northwest Territories did not swear loyalty to the parties till 1896 in spite of a false appearance of partisanship in 1887—the result of perplexed ministerialism. The *Globe* told them that the Liberals had won and the *Gazette* that the Conservatives had again triumphed.

With the conquest of the West completed in 1896 the Conservative and the Liberal parties had at last become national and thus a national two-party system was established in Canada for the first time. In becoming national the two parties did not lose all their old characteristics. 1878 and 1896 do not mark breaks in the evolution of political parties in Canada, for the development of such extra-legal political institutions is a gradual process. Consequently it is not surprising to find today sectionalism in parties, heterogeneity in cabinets and ministerialism in constituencies—veiled and modified as they are by the party system. Bargaining between sectional groups still takes place but nowadays more often in caucus and cabinet than on the floor of the House of Commons. In caucus the party is sectional. In public it is homogeneous. In reality it is federal.

What is the force which has made out of the loose coalitions of Macdonald and Mackenzie the federated unions of sectional groups that have constituted the national parties from 1896 to the present day? The loose coalitions had as their core dual alliances of Quebec and Ontario groups. Whichever of these alliances proved to be the more powerful ruled with the assistance of the Maritime and western groups, which remained neutral until the struggle in the central provinces had been resolved and then made as good terms as possible with the victors. There came a time when the neutral groups had to choose before the struggle of the rival dual alliances which one they would support. As some chose one and some another, the dual alliances would have become quintuple had not other forces been working to make them two federations of five or more groups. For when allied and associated powers are fighting a war for supreme power— and political combinations are always fighting a war for supreme power—the alliance tends to itself become the direct object of the devotion and loyalty of the citizens of the separate powers or, in other words, there is a tendency for the alliance to acquire sovereignty and so become a super or federal state. The other force making for closer union is the result of the actions of the leaders of the groups who find from bitter experience that an alliance is most effective in attack or defence when it is united under a supreme command. These two forces meet, the force of individual devotion pushing up from the bottom and the force of political strategy pushing down from above, and what was once a loose dual alliance is compressed into a federal union. The cement which made this union durable is furnished from non-political sources. Better means of communication bind the sections together; inter-migration breaks down sectional differences; new territories are settled as a common enterprise; a national feeling struggles into existence. Out of the alliances of sectional parties are created the federations of sectional groups—the national Conservative and the national Liberal parties.

ENDNOTES

1. An example of such an election is that in the constituency of Cornwall (eastern Ontario) in 1872. Candidates of both parties were nominated but the Conservative, who was a son of John Sandfield, withdrew and allowed the nominal Liberal, Bergin, to be elected by acclamation. In withdrawing, Macdonald said that "he believed that when Dr. Bergin got into Parliament he would throw over all ties and follow the crowd if the Government had a majority in the House. He thought that he would show good judgment in doing so, because he would get more favours by going with the majority than he could from the minority." The Toronto *Globe*, 24 August 1872.
2. *Ibid*. 8 August 1872.
3. Sir John Macdonald to Hon. Alex. Morris, 21 April 1871, in Sir Joseph Pope, *Correspondence of Sir John A. Macdonald* (Toronto: Doubleday & Co., Inc., 1921), p. 145.
4. H.J. Ruttan to Sir Alex. Galt, 17 November 1873, in O.D. Skelton, *Life and Times of Sir A.T. Galt* (Toronto: Oxford University Press, 1920), pp. 465–466.
5. Amendment of McDonald (Lunenburg) of 14 December 1867, "for the purpose of placing wheat and rye flour, cornmeal and corn in the free list," *Journals of the House of Commons* (Canada), 1867–68, p. 92.
6. *House of Commons Debates* (Canada), 8 November 1867.
7. For example, Killam, the member of Yarmouth from 1867 to 1882, said in his campaign, according to an editorial in the *St. John Daily Telegraph*, 17 August 1872: "I have not had much confidence in the Government in many respects; but am sorry to say that I have no confidence in the Opposition. They ... have attempted to treat the interests of these Maritime Provinces as mere makeweights in the scale, to further the selfish aims of great parties in Ontario."

8. Examples of such divisions are those on the amendment of McDonald (Lunenburg) of 14 December 1867, mentioned above, and on the Holton amendment of 29 April 1868, moving the House into Committee of the Whole "to consider the alleged grievances of [Nova Scotia]". *Journals of the House of Commons* (Canada), 1867–68, pp. 92, 249.

9. *St. John Daily Telegraph*, 6 August 1872.

10. *Ibid.*, 5 August 1872.

11. H.J. Morgan, *Dominion Annual Register 1878* (Montreal: Dawson Brothers, 1879), p. 211.

12. This struggle is reflected in the editorials of *The Manitoba Free Press*, 10 January, 17 January and 7 February 1874.

The Setting of Party Politics

This section outlines the environment of parties and the structures within which they operate: the interest groups, the media, the pollsters, the pervasive political patronage, and the institutions recently created to control campaign finance. Special problems are discussed, such as how the electoral system might be reformed to become more democratic and functional, and the status of women in the Canadian political system.

3 Interest Groups and Policy making in Canada

HUGH G. THORBURN

Canada had its beginnings in a situation of close relationships between private interest groups and the colonial governments. In the United Province of Canada, before Confederation, commercial capitalist interests sponsored the development of railways and canals, which formed the infrastructure for the developing colony. A desire to expand the horizons of the colonies west into the prairies and east to the Maritimes, combined with fear of the United States after the Civil War, were major incentives for the enlargement of the colonies into the new Dominion of Canada via Confederation. Representatives for such interests as the major banks, railways, shipping interests and trading companies had, from the very beginning, ongoing relations with the governments in British North America. Policy making was shared between these people and the elected politicians sitting in the cabinets of Canada and the provinces. Therefore, the pattern of what was later known as élite accommodation, or pressure group politics, was a thriving arrangement from the very beginnings of Canada's history as a nation. Governments were closely involved in the financing and planning of railways and other major projects of development. Connections were forged between these capitalist interests and the political party leaders of Canada, and through them with the governments, provincial and federal. Such well-known events as the Pacific Scandal in the 1870s bear witness to the close collaborative or patronage arrangements that existed at that time.

With the passage of time, the relatively informal personal relations that developed between leading politicians and their higher civil servants, on the one hand, and the business leaders, on the other, hardened into a more bureaucratic relationship. As governments built up larger administrative structures in order to deliver services to the community, interest groups in the areas of activity that were closest in relation to these governmental initiatives were called into being. Close clientele relations developed between individual departments of govern-

From Hugh G. Thorburn, *Interest Groups in the Canadian Federal System* (Volume 69 of the Research Studies for the Royal Commission on the Economic Union and Development Prospects for Canada), pp. 3–15. Reprinted by permission of the University of Toronto Press.

ment and the communities they served, typified by the close collaboration existing between the Canadian Federation of Agriculture and the federal and provincial departments of agriculture. Similar relationships developed in other major sectors, such as forestry, mining and secondary manufacturing. Policies relating to the support of these industries and their protection through tariffs and import regulations of various kinds were elaborated through consultation by government representatives with the spokespersons for these substantial interests. Relations with other major concentrations of capital in such institutions as the banks, insurance companies, railways and grain trading companies were established with governments in order to influence policy as it affected individual private concerns.

Businesses saw the advantage of organizing associations, permitting them to collaborate in their consultation with governments. Permanent organizations with specialist staff were built up to carry on liaison with government in the most propitious manner possible.

These representations were carried on not only with government leaders, such as ministers and their senior civil service associates, but also extended to committees of parliament and the provincial legislatures and often involved representations to private members of parliament, both on government and opposition sides. It was generally conceded that the groups had a right to be heard before policy affecting them was finalized by either order of government, provincial or federal.

Communities of interest developed, composed of politicians, bureaucrats and interest group representatives organized along functional lines. Associations, some pan-Canadian, some regional or local, each devoted to advancing the substantive concerns of its members, worked together where their interests coincided, and in opposition to one another when they diverged. Their concern was to influence policy along with other matters: legislation, the formulation of regulations, day-to-day administration and the general attitudes of government. Government came to rely for information upon these groups as a major input in the policy making process. Their relationship, therefore, was not an adversarial one but one of collaboration in a common enterprise. The support of the groups could at times extend beyond the supply of information and advice to other considerations affecting the well-being of the political parties and personalities concerned.

The result was a kind of parallel process in government. On the one hand, there was the representative system which saw members of parliament elected in their constituencies to sit in the legislative assemblies and hold the government responsible. While legislation was usually government-initiated, the majority party would have to give its assent if it was to be enacted. The opposition soon developed the habit of systematic criticism of and at times obstruction to these initiatives. The dynamics of the system involved a continuous campaign by the opposition to show up the inadequacies of the government, and a corresponding attempt by government members, under cabinet leadership, to show up the opposition as incompetent, irresponsible and ill-informed. The electors were called upon at fairly regular intervals of about four years to decide which side would form the government in the ensuing period.

Parallel to this was the government to private interest relationship, which was much less widely known but was nonetheless important. Through this arrangement, advice, supplemented by at times considerable pressure, was focused upon the government to induce it to adopt the policies favoured by individual groups. The government, therefore, was subjected to these two processes of advice and pressure, and it had to make its way between them. At times the representations would be parallel and consistent; at other times they would go in two or more directions, and the government would either have to reconcile the various positions in some kind of compromise or make hard choices between them. The task of the government then was a more difficult and complex one than appeared to the casual eye of the citizen, who was much more aware of the representative, official structures than of the more informal and less conspicuous interest group process.

Interest groups began to receive serious scholarly attention in the mid-1960s, and since that time the body of interest group literature has grown. Most of this work, however, is made up of case studies, with very little theoretical work to support it.

Most definitions of interest groups stress the link between a socially based interest and the attempt to influence public policy. David Truman's oft-cited definition saw interest groups as a "shared attitude group that makes certain claims through or upon other groups in society. . . . If and when it makes its claims through or upon any of the institutions of government, it becomes a political interest group."[1] A more useful definition for analytical purposes is provided by A. Paul Pross: "Interest groups are organizations whose members act together to influence public policy in order to promote their common interest."[2]

The major concern of political scientists has been with the extent of these groups' influence over government policy making. This "communication function" is determined by the structure of the group, the functioning of the group and its access to government. Structure refers to the degree of organizational sophistication. A group that is highly institutionalized will possess the resources to establish a permanent staff that can seek to influence government on a continual basis and offer advice on a wide variety of issues. On the other hand, groups with only loose and volatile structures are more likely to have to resort to public confrontational approaches. This is the case especially for issue-oriented groups. This approach helps to compensate for small and fluctuating memberships.

Interest groups provide a forum where their members can compare and exchange information about common problems and about the effects of proposed government action or changing social conditions. Shared attitudes emerge about the suitability of various government actions and the need to influence government in these directions. Finally, a precondition of influence is the communication of these shared attitudes to the appropriate decision makers. Therefore, securing access is a vital part of exercising influence on government. Access can occur at a number of points in the political system: the bureaucracy, the cabinet, members of parliament, and officials of political parties. Not all access points are valued equally, but groups will try to maintain as many contacts as their resources will allow.

Access alone will not ensure that a group will be successful in influencing government. The communication of group concerns is of little impact unless decision makers can be induced to accept the interest group recommendations and support them. For their part, governments have two primary interests in pressure groups. They value the information that groups are able to provide, and they seek out the legitimacy that interest group support can give to their policies. Continued access to the centre of power depends on the degree to which a group can fulfill these needs reliably and well. The size of the membership, the control of financial resources, the monopoly of technical knowledge, the prestige of the group's leaders and the willingness of the group to cooperate and avoid outright confrontation are important elements in gaining recognized status within government. David Kwavnick observes that within the labour movement, the competition for recognition from government is at least as important to the major labour unions in Canada as defending the immediate interests of their members. The process has led some analysts to conclude that groups closely involved with government eventually become dependent on the state:

> Group involvement in the policy discussions not only expands the range of information available to government—it can be used to neutralize group objections to proposed legislation and to engage support for it. Government thus finds in the pressure group system a device for testing policy proposals and a means of eliciting support for them.[3]

This close relationship, according to Pross, can enhance the position of cooperative groups since they are guaranteed a measure of collaborative influence over policy decisions that affect their interests, but the groups must be willing to accept short-term defeats for continuing favourable relations in the long run. Appeals to parliament, especially the opposition, or to the public at large, could jeopardize their privileged position with government. This arrangement may also serve the important function of keeping the political system abreast of changes within the social system, thereby promoting political stability:

> The successful performance of this last function, however, will depend on the sensitivity of the governmental and pressure group sub-systems to changes in their own immediate environments. Closed and captive agencies and groups through their failure to absorb external demands, may compound rigidities existing elsewhere in the system.[4]

Pross offers a useful conceptual approach to understanding the role of interest groups in the political system. He ranges them on a continuum from institutionalized groups to issue-oriented ones. The underlying assumption of this approach is that "the organizational characteristics of a given group may have a great deal to do with the extent to which it performs recognized functions." His model incorporates the interrelationship between the structure and functioning of a group.

Institutional groups are:

> Groups that possess organizational continuity and cohesion, commensurate human and financial resources, extensive knowledge of those sectors of government that affect them and their clients, stable memberships, concrete and immediate operational objectives that are broad enough to permit each group to bargain with government over the application of specific legislation or the achievement of particular concessions, and a willingness to put organizational imperatives ahead of any particular policy concerns.[5]

Issue-oriented groups, as one would expect, have the reverse characteristics:

> Groups whose primary orientation is to issues, rather than to organizational continuity and cohesion; minimal and often naïve knowledge of government; fluid membership; a tendency to encounter difficulty in formulating and adhering to short-range objectives; a generally low regard for the organizational mechanisms they have developed for carrying out their goals; and, most important, a narrowly defined purpose, usually the resolution of one or two issues or problems, that inhibits the development of "selective inducements" designed to broaden the group's membership base.[6]

The implication of this approach is that the

> . . . capacity to act in pressure group politics is determined by the interaction of large-scale political forces and the internal characteristics of individual groups. That is, the nature of the policy process in a given political system, its political culture, power structure, and so on, define the general conditions of pressure group behaviour, but the actions of a specific group depends on the group's capacity to utilize internal resources.[7]

The advantage of the organizational base model is that it allows us to compare how different groups respond to different environments and to relate this behaviour to the structures and process of the policy system. At the theoretical level, the model shows that institutionalized groups have the financial and human resources necessary to participate in a system that encourages sustained collaboration between government agencies and their "recognized" client groups; on the other hand, issue-oriented groups can be effective in a competitive and open decision-making situation in which they can compensate for their insignificant size and lack of cohesion by rallying public opinion behind them. Their weak organizational base and narrow scope make them less valuable to governments as a steady and reliable source of information and legitimation, but they do serve an important warning function in any political system:

> In general systemic terms, issue-oriented groups enhance the adaptive capacity of the overall system, permitting a responsiveness to emergent issues that is not easily achieved by more cumbersome mechanisms of political communication. . . . Their chief advantage lies in their flexibility. Because they develop extremely quickly and are unencumbered by institutionalized structures, they are excellent vehicles for generating immediate public reaction to specific issues. Because their stake in the future is usually limited, they can indulge in forms of political communication that institutional groups are reluctant to use. This is particularly true in Canada where established groups tend not to resort to publicity for fear of disturbing relations with administrative agencies.[8]

In this sense, issue-oriented groups can act as a social barometer which forces decision makers to recognize the legitimacy of socially divisive issues that would otherwise be neglected. For example, the present increased political willingness to address the problem of drinking when driving is primarily due to the public concern generated by the efforts of the families of accident victims.

Pross's model can also be employed to analyse how the relationships between interest groups and government change over time. For example, a shift from a closed and secretive political system to one that is open and competitive would enhance the organizational advantages of issue-oriented groups. This, in fact, appears to be happening in Canada (as well as other Western countries) since the 1970s.

Prior to 1975, writing on Canadian pressure group politics demonstrates a general acceptance of the élite accommodation model as an accurate and complete description of pressure group behaviour. Essentially, this model posits a system of mutual accommodation between government and interest groups, in which social and economic élites alone determine the interest of society in informal, secretive, face-to-face contact between the upper echelons of government (ministers and their bureaucracies) and interest groups. Robert Presthus describes the Canadian political process as one in which "political leaders, including the senior bureaucracy, could and did define and seek the public interest without much need for explanation of their actions or for participation by the general public." Pross attributes this situation to two main factors: (1) the closed, hierarchical nature of Canadian political structures, especially the bureaucracy and the party system; and (2) the limited extent to which the Canadian political system is based on a pluralistic, competitive approach to decision making:

> Some competition exists, of course—intergovernment rivalry arises out of the current exercise of power or the unclear definitions of jurisdiction—but within each government there is relatively little of the functional rivalry which typifies interagency competition in the United States. Similarly, the fact that the executive operates within a cabinet and parliamentary system of government means that rivalries between legislators cannot be readily exploited.[9]

As a result, access to key decision makers has played a more important role in interest group activity than popularizing issues:

The Canadian political system, then, tends to favour élite groups, making functional accommodative, consensus-seeking techniques of political communication, rather than conflict-oriented techniques that are directed towards the achievement of objectives through arousing public opinion.[10]

Obviously, such a system of decision making strongly favours institutionalized groups over issue-oriented ones. Presthus outlines the most significant features of élite accommodation: (1) a built-in disposition toward support of the status quo because it restricts meaningful participation to established groups with a direct substantive interest in the process; (2) the tendency to define problems as essentially technical with the implication that political considerations are illegitimate and certainly divisive (the result is the uncoordinated incremental expansion of governmental and private programs without adequate direction by government); and (3) the crystallization of existing patterns of resource allocation, "which makes the introduction of new scientific, technical and economic directions difficult as they strike against established influence structures, based largely on long-standing, functionally determined, agency-clientele relationships."[11]

James Gillies argues that a relationship of mutual accommodation, where business and government worked together to plan the economy, was facilitated during the 1940s, 1950s and 1960s by their shared belief in how the goals of society (i.e., economic growth and prosperity) could be achieved. Since World War II, the issue-by-issue approach has been the most frequent strategy used by business to influence government. This approach is one in which:

> . . . business reacts to individual initiatives of the government as those initiatives are introduced. The ones that are perceived to be detrimental to the corporation or an industry—and the public interest—are opposed. It implies no grand strategy; it is simply, as it states, an approach that calls for dealing with issues as they develop.[12]

This approach rests on three major assumptions: first, that a close interrelationship with the bureaucracy, the executive and the legislature is the most effective means of influencing government and preventing the formulation of policies that are hostile to the interests of business:

> Indeed, trade association officials stress that one of their major duties is to keep close to the members of the bureaucracy so that they may spot the early evolution of ideas and inform their members about any developments that may influence their activities.[13]

Second, it assumes policy flows from the bottom up and that the transmission of appropriate and useful information will stop an inappropriate policy from being enacted. Finally, it assumes that government accords business a special, privileged position over other interests, and therefore that the exercise of persuasion is a sufficient instrument for achieving its policy goals.

During the 1940s and 1950s, élite accommodation was facilitated by the growth of the bureaucratic state. Politicians took an incremental approach to the expansion of government activity after World War II, so responsibility for the planning and implementation of the massive intervention of the state was mainly left to the experts within the line departments. Government expansion occurred in an incremental, uncoordinated fashion, as each of the government agencies distributed resources according to its own professional norms. Therefore, the most important groups during this period were special interest groups whose concerns corresponded to the functions of separate government agencies. The special interest groups could offer officials the expertise and information necessary for the development of policy initiatives in return for policy input. Because most shared the same professional values as the government officials, cosy "clientele" relationships developed, where groups and government officials mutually agreed upon the appropriate form of action.

Despite this fundamental change in the role of the state in society, the policy making structures of government remained relatively uncomplicated and informal:

> There were no committees of cabinet, except for the Treasury Board which was established by statute, and individual ministers operated in a highly independent manner. Any coordination that had to be undertaken was handled by deputy ministers in a very informal fashion and in those days of less complex government, the system worked effectively. Individual ministers were powerful and ran the departments without advice, let alone interference from anyone.[14]

Strong ministers such as C.D. Howe worked with their constituencies (in Howe's case the industrial community) and developed policies in collaboration with the groups and, it was assumed, in the interests of the country. No conflict was perceived between the private and the public interest. However, by the end of the 1960s, broad social changes and the continued growth of government led to a fundamental rebuilding of the policy making structures at the federal level and in some of the provinces.

Pross cites three factors as the source of the emergent pattern in which institutionalized groups are "exposed to heightened public scrutiny and are more dependent on public opinion": (1) changes in the government policy making structure designed to bring about central control over policy making; (2) the proliferation of interest groups, especially citizens' groups, in response to the growth of government and the increased exposure of the activities of institutionalized groups; and (3) the advent of television, which allowed groups to mobilize public support for their cause.

Changes in the policy making structure began on a small scale in the early 1960s as governments became dissatisfied with the lack of political control over the growth of their expenditures and activities. However, the major restructuring of the system came after 1968, when Prime Minister Trudeau introduced a centralized cabinet committee system as a means of directing policy making within the cabinet as a whole. Hugh Faulkner observes that these structural changes give the appearance that ultimate power is highly concentrated within the policy process when, in practice, it is highly dispersed. One reason for this is that policy making from its earliest stages now involves coordination between a number of departments:

> The new policy and expenditure management system . . . ensures that ministers must process any initiative that involves expenditures (which includes tax expenditures) through their cabinet colleagues. This process integrates policy decisions into the government priorities framework, tightens up decision making by juxtaposing policy options and expenditures and strengthens the pattern of collegial authority over policy development and expenditure management. The effect is to limit the capacity of an individual minister to respond to interest groups. To take an initiative in one area means that another area is going to be affected. Trade-offs will be required, so that the other area has to be massaged as well. Consequently, interest groups must now be prepared to deal with the whole range of cabinet, including the cabinet committees, the membership of which has only recently become public information.[15]

This, of course, spreads a group's resources even thinner than before, as more contacts are necessary to petition government effectively.

The problem for groups is compounded because the federal example was followed at the provincial level. Ontario and Quebec adopted the same type of committee structure a few years later, and the other provinces too made similar adjustments in their structures.

Perhaps more important than the cabinet committee system itself has been the concomitant growth and development of central agencies. The Privy Council Office and its close affiliate, the Federal-Provincial Relations Office, have become crucial to the policy making process, having assumed responsibility for advising Cabinet on the integration of policy recommendations into the general framework of government objectives. Gillies and Pigott argue that the shift in influence from departments to the central agencies of government has seriously affected the ability of established groups to penetrate the decisionmaking process. Despite the important policy making role played by the Privy Council Office, its officials "simply do not see their function as dealing with individual legislative thrusts, but as coordinating various inputs into the policy-making process." While the traditional channels of involvement are no longer adequate:

> . . . special interests do not have a satisfactory method of inserting their input into the determination of the public interest in anything like as meaningful a fashion as was once the case.[16]

Finally, the increased complexity of the policy making process, due to the increasing speed and unpredictability of social and technological change, has meant that government has had to try to improve its mechanisms for interest group involvement and employ new techniques to facilitate the process. Since the 1970s, there has been a formalization of consultative devices, as the government attempted to augment its information coming from society to adapt to changing conditions. One such development was the increase in the use of white papers. Audrey D. Doerr observes that since the advent of the Trudeau administration, the white paper has been used by the federal government "to promote and stimulate broad public debate among interested groups and individuals, so that the government can receive direction from those people who will be most affected by the policies." However, she notes that examples of public responses, by and large, represent the articulate and financially well-endowed sectors of the community which have an enhanced capacity to participate and perceive a sense of efficacy in participation. Government has addressed this problem of underrepresentation with some success through financial assistance to groups with limited resources, such as welfare groups and consumer associations. The formalization of the process has had the twin advantages of opening-up the process to anyone determined enough to participate and, exposing who the vested interests are in a given policy area by making them operate through public structures.

This development of central agencies has been paralleled by similar arrangements at the provincial level, especially in Quebec and Ontario. Also, coloured papers (white papers, green papers, etc.) have been employed at that level to facilitate public discussion of policy issues with groups. This has, of course, greatly added to the burden of groups, just as it has increased their opportunities—opportunities more easily exploited by the larger and richer institutionalized groups.

A larger problem cited by Doerr is the lack of appropriate machinery to conduct debates with the general public. One promising step taken recently to improve this situation was the appointment of seven special parliamentary committees, or parliamentary task forces, which travelled the country providing early access to government policy proposals for the public, special-interest groups and parliament. Hugh Faulkner claims that the crucial issue in dealing with government overload is the absence of a legitimate process for defining the public interest in an ongoing manner, not the excessive control of big business. He considers the introduction of the parliamentary task force mechanism the most progressive change to date.

A major consequence of these changes in consultative mechanisms is that groups are now expected to prepare formal presentations and to formulate detailed recommendations in a form that allows the government to compare the demands relating to government priorities of one group with those of another. All groups and individuals are now on a more equal footing in that greater emphasis is placed on the quality of group management, rather than on size or economic resources. This enhances the opportunities for smaller groups and individuals to participate in the policy making process. As Faulkner, an ex-federal cabinet minister, has observed:

> ... one of the ironies of the contemporary pressure group scene is that the influential interest groups today seem to be less satisfied with the results of their efforts than some of the less powerful.[17]

The combined impact of the insularity of the Privy Council Office and the need for agencies and their associated interest groups to compete for scarce resources through open structures has forced institutionalized groups into the public arena and increased the public awareness of their activities. As a consequence, there has been a proliferation of citizens' groups established to counter the demands of vested interests. This has been especially true in those sections of the community that previously had no means of organization:

> ... both agencies and groups discovered that by going public they have alerted other interests to the nature of the debates that are in progress and so have encouraged their participation and perhaps the formation of new groups.[18]

In many cases, the formation of these groups has been facilitated by government funding.

In 1981 the Institute of Public Administration held a seminar on interest groups and government. As *rapporteur*, Paul Pross outlined the two schools of thought into which explanations for the proliferation of groups fall. There are those who support general environmental explanations, and those who argue that the expansion of group activities constitutes a "reactive spiral." The latter claim that the development of relations between groups and government has occurred incrementally and disjointedly and, in the process, has expanded both state activity and the constellation of formal groups which surround the state. Khayyam Paltiel, as reported by Pross, argued that:

> ... the state itself is progenitor and prime mover in both the fostering of intervention and the formation of groups. Étatisme ... is inspired from within the machinery of government, but must be buttressed and made legitimate by individuals and groups who are part of the general public. Hence the emergence of bureaucratic patronage and the fostering of supportive groups—to which other groups respond from a more traditional, individualistic ideological base.[19]

Others attribute an active role to the state but steer clear of the *dirigiste* tendencies of Paltiel's explanation. Here the state is seen as fostering group activity in response to the public's expectation that certain groups should not be excluded from the process, rather than as a means of promoting support for its own initiatives. Women's groups and native groups, for example, are said to have been sponsored because government needed to hear from these sectors of the community before determining its policies.

These explanations are in many ways compatible with the environmentalist argument, which also views the proliferation of groups as an incremental response to both state activity and involvement of other pressure groups. The crucial difference is that environmentalists claim that the elaboration of government-group relations is not merely an extension of past relations but represents a fundamental change of the Canadian state into what is called the *dirigiste* state. Dominique Clift, in the same seminar, asserted that the Canadian state, now dominated by a "dynamic" public sector, co-opts what elements of the public it can and destroys those that oppose it. Clift describes it as a state in which "the kind of consensus that guides contemporary society comes not from the people, but is sponsored by the state itself."

Paltiel's moderately *dirigiste* argument seems particularly persuasive. The need for government to deal with increasingly rapid and complex social change appears to have outdistanced the capacity of existing consultative mechanisms. As a result, there has been a tendency for such devices to become political tools for building the necessary support for decisions that have already been made for government. This is not entirely manipulative, for government may not always get the support it is looking for. However, as Doerr suggests, society will have to learn quickly if it is to participate meaningfully in policy formulation in the future.

A third factor that has influenced the environment within which pressure groups must now operate is the social impact of television. Television solved the problem of communication between interest groups and people in densely populated areas and gave groups the opportunity to mobilize a more general public reaction to political issues. Issue-oriented groups have benefited most from this development; they have been able to compensate for their small and loosely organized membership by attracting public support. In fact, television can destabilize the position of established groups, which have always been able to rely for their strength on their firmly grounded status. Now, established groups are compelled to cater to public opinion, as well as to the views of their membership in couching their demands. For example, Paul Pross commented:

> A.E. Diamond, president of the Canadian Institute of Public Real Estate Companies, recently offered an illustration of this process when he asserted that the CIPREC must "make the public more aware of the difficulties faced by developers" in order to challenge the power that various pressure groups have captured over the development process.[20]

While television can focus public attention on an issue, it cannot act as a source of detailed demands. The complexity of most public policy and the resources needed to monitor the process mean that institutionalized groups are still in a better position to participate effectively in the complex structures of policy making. However, as indicated above, even institutionalized groups are experiencing great difficulty influencing government. Overall, a consequence of the recent changes in the policy making environment of pressure groups seems to be an opening up of the process to greater public debate, though this has not necessarily been translated into policy outputs. There is reason to believe that this increased group activity masks the greater autonomy of the state to decide the course of government action.

ENDNOTES

1. D. Truman, *The Governmental Process* (New York: Knopf, 1951), p. 37.
2. A.P. Pross, "Pressure Groups: Adaptive Instruments of Political Communication," in Pross, ed., *Pressure Group Behaviour in Canadian Politics* (Toronto: McGraw-Hill Ryerson, 1975), p. 2.
3. *Ibid.*, p. 6.
4. *Ibid.*, p. 7.
5. A.P. Pross, "Pressure Groups," in D.J. Bellamy, J.H. Pammet and D. Rowat, eds., *The Provincial Political Systems* (Toronto: Methuen, 1976), p. 133.
6. *Ibid.*
7. *Ibid.*
8. Pross, "Pressure Groups: Adaptive Instruments," p. 12.
9. *Ibid.*, p. 18–19.
10. *Ibid.*, p. 19.
11. R. Presthus, *Elite Accommodation in Canadian Politics* (Toronto: Macmillan, 1975), p. 351.
12. J. Gillies, *Where Business Fails: Business-Government Relations at the Federal Level in Canada* (Montreal: Institute for Research on Public Policy, 1981), p. 48.
13. *Ibid.*
14. J. Gillies and J. Pigott, "Participation in the Legislative Process," *Canadian Public Administration*, Vol. 25 (1982), p. 261.
15. J.H. Faulkner, "Pressuring the Executive," *Canadian Public Administration*, Vol. 25 (1982), p. 243.
16. Gillies and Pigott, "Participation in the Legislative Process," p. 263.
17. Faulkner, "Pressuring the Executive," p. 245.
18. A.P. Pross, "Governing Under Pressure: The Special Interest Groups," *Canadian Public Administration*, Vol. 25 (1982), p. 177.
19. *Ibid.*, p. 172.
20. A.P. Pross, "Canadian Pressure Groups in the 1970s: Their Role and Their Relations with the Public Service," *Canadian Public Administration* (1975), p. 127.

4 Polls and Pollsters in Canadian Politics

MARTIN GOLDFARB

One of the most controversial figures in the constellation of contemporary political life is the public opinion pollster. Yet the role of the pollster in today's political arena is expanding continually. Like any seer or oracle, the pollster plays a role that is viewed with a combination of respect, fear, intrigue and controversy. We must reflect briefly on the role of the pollster in Canadian politics.

We live in the world of the information blitz. Information, constant but ever-changing, comes so quickly that to absorb it all is impossible. But for the ordinary citizen to feel involved in this process, he or she must absorb, analyse and apply this information. It is in this context that the pollster has been thrust forward as a notable figure in the new political arena.

Polls provide an instant means for the individual to identify herself or himself on the scale of public opinion. Polling belongs to the world of universal democracy. The process enables citizens to understand where their opinions and values fit in the range of attitudes about issues that affect their lives and their country. Polls are not plebiscites, but function in a similar manner: they provide instant feedback on the most important issues.

Polls create an involved citizenry. For the voter, polls may make the political process more gratifying, challenging and thought-provoking. As a result of polls, the individual is able to become more knowledgeable about issues confronting society and the institutions and processes that serve it.

Polls put pressure on politicians. In the shadow of public opinion and public accountability, politicians cannot lead blindly. Polls help politicians to understand public opinion and thereby to develop strategies.

In the information age, the pollster has taken on a new role, which has evolved over the last 20 years to make him or her a force in the machinery of idea generation in modern society. In politics and public policy, in product development and subsequent promotion, in image crafting and positioning, the pollster has become a quintessential contributor.

From Martin Goldfarb and Thomas S. Axworthy, *Marching to a Different Drummer: An Essay on the Liberals and Conservatives in Convention* (Toronto: Stoddart, 1988), pp. xi–xxiii. Reprinted by permission of Stoddart Publishing Co. Limited. This essay has been edited to suit the needs of this volume.

Edward L. Bernays was the founding father of American advertising, the very first presidential media advisor and—curiously—Sigmund Freud's nephew. The fundamental principle of Bernays' conceptual thinking, which he succinctly and provocatively called "The Engineering of Consent," was, in his words, "the application of scientific practices and tried practices in the task of getting people to support ideas and programs." *Engineering* implies the use of scientific methods, and *consent* means the public must be won over, not an easy task since the appeal must be constant. Consent also denotes choice—a crucial yet volatile element. It implies that people can choose to change their minds and withdraw their consent. This applies equally to selling products and to winning elections.[1]

To put it simply, Bernays wanted to translate insight into action. This is the essence of the role of polling in today's society. Unlike his uncle, Freud, who was happy to acknowledge insight for its own sake, Bernays wanted to use insight as a way of making things happen. But more than anything else, he knew that a pollster's work is an art form—not just a profession.

Rarely do people reflect deeply about what pollsters do; what roles they play in the evolution of our society; what ethics they uphold. Pollsters are seen paradoxically—simultaneously revered and reviled, praised and blamed, and mostly misunderstood by both their clients and the public.[2]

In a society insecure about the nature of political power, pollsters seem to possess a mystique. In point of fact, the techniques pollsters use to collect information are relatively simple: to collate data and generate numbers, one needs a devotion to procedure and a commitment to established practice. Similarly, there is little mysticism involved in statistical manipulation of the information that has been generated. And while the results may be startling, the process of arriving at them is not. Pollsters simply ask what they consider to be pertinent questions, then analyse and interpret the answers.

It is the interpretation of results—not the collection of data—that sets a good pollster apart from an ordinary one. There is no magical formula. As any capable cultural anthropologist knows—and a capable pollster is a sophisticated student of cultural behaviour—deciphering the nuances of attitudes, opinions and behaviours in a context of cultural complexity is a difficult task. It requires intellectual instinct, intuition and an immense amount of experience. It requires a genuine intimacy with culture and sensitivity to a generation. Cultural artifacts change quickly in our age, and pollsters must be equally quick to anticipate, recognize and analyse these changes.

All pollsters, whether or not they admit it (and the good ones do!) have a value system. This is not simply a matter of personal ethics, but of awareness of the value systems of clients and of society, whether the values in question are political, corporate or any other. It is a spurious argument for pollsters to try to deny this reality. Good polling, like good art, demands and propagates certain values as opposed to others.

And so it should be! For a good pollster concludes his or her work by recommending or advocating certain courses of action which will either promote or prevent certain outcomes. It is also vital, however, to recognize that ethics demand that pollsters portray the reality their research has made apparent. Frequently, such a portrait may not be the one clients expect, or even want to see. That, however, is a secondary consideration. What is consistently important is that pollsters adhere to the reality, perceptions and interpretations evoked by their results.

Pollsters do not change society's behaviour: this is neither their role, nor their function. They are essentially private figures who are unlikely to have any *direct* influence on the public's behaviour. This is not to say, however, that a pollster's findings do not potentially influence the decisions of other individuals who do wish to affect public behaviour.

There are, however, ethical questions that all pollsters face. Should we know? Should information gleaned from polling be made available? Should we find out what we don't want to know? These are questions crucial to the ethics of polling. Should politicians, for example, have access to the results of polls taken during election campaigns? Should polls form part of the context of decision making? Indeed, the formative and abiding commitment of the pollster is to discern reality, not to withhold or change the findings. Information may be used, or it may not be, depending on the individual or the situation. Pollsters, however, must be true to the portrait of reality that has emerged from their work.

The questions do not stop here. Can anyone become a client? In my view, the answer is no, and for two reasons. First, the pollster-client relationship is a very intimate one. To do a good job, a pollster must understand the perceptions, requirements, problems and difficulties of the client. If there is a fundamental clash of values between them, the results will benefit neither. Second, a pollster should never warp the results for anyone's benefit—even for a client. There must be some fundamental empathy—shared values, if you like—between pollster and client. Only with this commonality can a pollster tell a client "the way it really is," while also enabling the client to appreciate the significance and the implications of the results.

The Pollster and the Politicians

There is a crucial, and very private, relationship between the pollster and a politician, the pollster and the government and between a pollster and the governing political party. It is a truism to say that today, if you are going to succeed in securing and maintaining political power, part of the accoutrements of power is the pollster. Polling today is to the politician what the stock market is to the financial analyst. It is impossible to think of the conduct of political affairs without the art and science of the pollster.

We tend to think of this relationship as a direct consequence of the information age. However, in another sense, the parallel is with the traditional and historically specific role of the advisor to the court. Throughout history, every court had a soothsayer, a prophet, a court jester or a fool. These individuals served at the pleasure of the king or the leader. They were appointed by the king and they lived, and frequently died, with the success or the failure of the king.

Historically, these figures stood as the voice of wisdom, the independent source of truth. They offered the king their views of reality, regardless of whom these revelations might offend. They stood as interpreters of public sentiment to a court and a class of nobility which was in most cases far removed from what the masses thought or felt. The court jester watched the spectacle of politics and the often bloody infighting among the nobility, and he interpreted these spectacles for the king, admonishing, counselling, advising and even warning him. Each court jester, history tells us, had his own style, his own insights, and his own unique characteristics. The fool in Shakespearian plays, for example, was the metaphysician of the court, revealing the world for what it really was. The fool always retained a measure of objectivity in court matters, for his primary duty was to speak the truth. He could never be punished for telling the truth.

It was the dynamic between the fool, or jester, and the court that made a sense of balance or justice prevail in the affairs of men. If the king simply succumbed to the nobility, naked power would prevail in court affairs. In many of Shakespeare's plays, in fact, the fool was the central character and has exerted a long-lasting fascination. We understand the king by understanding the fool.

The modern equivalent to this historical figure is the pollster. Like the historical fool, he assumes his office at the bequest of the court, or the decision makers who hire him. His fate is tied to the success or failure of those individuals, for his star rises and falls with the success or failure of the "court" he serves. He is the court confidante and knows more about the inner machinations of his court than anybody else—maybe even more than the leader.

Today, however, there are many new dimensions to this already complex relationship. Democracies are built on the assumption that the citizen makes decisions, usually electoral decisions, based upon information, formulating attitudes and opinions which affect the behaviour patterns of the public at large.

Politicians today believe that they understand these complex patterns of attitudes, opinions and beliefs. Their confidence in a pollster's ability to identify the consensus of society gives them the impetus to rely so heavily upon polls and the individuals who create them.

But it goes even further. Politicians come to pollsters not only to find out what the public wants or thinks or feels, but also to ask the pollster what to do. The pollster, as a result, becomes involved in strategic development, action plans, guidance for poltical rule and even governing.

Moreover, since the issues and the agenda of public action change so quickly today, the politicians make increasing demands upon the pollster. Politicians may want to know where the public stands on issues on a day-to-day basis, and the technology of day-to-day polling is available to provide that information. It is not difficult to discern where the consensus rests on any issue. Presidents, prime ministers and others have availed themselves of this information.

The ethical question, however, remains: given poll-derived information, what course of action is legitimate? Political leaders still do, and always will, face this question: while we may know this or that, what should we do? Herein lies the art of politics. What makes the art of politics even more difficult today is the fact that more information is available. We can know more, know it more accurately and know it in greater detail! It is increasingly difficult for politicians to ignore public opinion on any given issue. The dissonance between what we know and what we should do, therefore, becomes more extreme.

The art of the pollster has made the life of politicians much more difficult, not easier. The pollster has added a new dimension of responsibility to the decisions of the politician. The crisis politicians frequently face is that while they know what may be *popular*, they want to act on the basis of what they think is *right* and the two are often in conflict. This is a crisis which the art of the pollster has intensified.

There is another dimension to this problem. The public, through broadcast and print reporting, is becoming increasingly aware of the results of polling. They read or hear continually about what pollsters report as the consensus on a given issue and they use this information as a basis on which to make political decisions. Voters judge politicians on the basis of this public knowledge and frequently they make some harsh and educated judgments. Hence, the growing independence of voters or the increasing volatility of the electorate may be a direct result of the pervasiveness of polling information in our society.

The information that polling provides, by means of the media, does two things. On one hand, it generates a more involved electorate. On the other, it creates a more volatile and pressure-ridden political system.

Today's politicians have access to very little information that is not also available to the public. Voters, therefore, can judge politicians' decisions on the basis of what they themselves think or might do about any political issue. As a result, they are better able to evaluate decisions made by their politicians. Voters today, by means of poll-generated information, are far better critics of the political decision-making process than those who came before.

Furthermore, politicians can no longer hide behind private information. In a world dominated by an instant and massive communications network, steered by pollsters and the media, the public now has access to information right on the heels of the politicians. This has fundamentally changed the nature of politics in our society. No longer do we see ourselves electing, or hiring, politicians as wiser, more knowledgeable sages to protect us with their deeper insight into the means of attaining the public good. They have become instead our public representatives, our public relations spokespeople. We elect our politicians to represent our values, attitudes and interests to the country and to the world at large.

Polling signals to politicians and to the public that they are playing in the same ballpark. What one knows, the other knows. What one wants, the other can engineer.

The Influence of the Pollster

As the pollster becomes a more public figure, the extent of his or her influence reaches far beyond the confines of the pollster-patron relationship. In political affairs, for example, the pollster now operates not only in the context of elections and electioneering, but also in relation to the formulation of policy and the implementation of policy. The pollster is a major player in all levels of government policy making. The politician, and even the civil servant, consults the pollster on an ongoing basis. While the pollster has not eclipsed more traditional instruments and institutions of policy making (in other words, members of parliament, the caucus, the bureaucracy, the opinion leaders of society), we now have, to a degree, "government by pollster."

The pollster is also a significant figure in the legitimization of policy. He or she is frequently consulted for advice and counsel as to how government can sell or market its policies to the public. This process of legitimizing public policy is becoming an increasingly important and sophisticated aspect of governing. Here again, the pollster's influence is increasing.

However, the extension of the influence of the pollster in the political process, in the policy making process and in the legitimization of policy raises some very serious questions. First, the pollster is a unique, non-elected player in the political arena. As we begin to recognize this fact, we must begin to rethink the way in which the pollster fits into the political apparatus governing our society. At the moment, neither pollsters nor politicians have given much thought to this problem but it is probably the single most revolutionary innovation in the nature of government. The pollster contributes information which is used as leverage in decision making by those with the power to do so. This is fundamental to the future of the polling profession and presumably fundamental to the future development of the political process. All must begin to consider and debate it.

There is another vital aspect to this problem. Can we say that this phenomenon, the extension of the influence of the pollster in our political process, is beneficial or detrimental to individual freedom? Does it mean that our democratic institutions are more—or less—democratic than they were, say, 30 years ago? Does it make the individual voter a more responsible citizen?

The extension of the influence of the pollster has fundamentally shifted the balance in our political system to enhance and make more difficult citizens' political choices. As the pollster becomes established as a political institution in our society, and voters become more detached from traditional partisanship, they become more independent and more volatile. The problems of governing successfully become more—not less—difficult. We are entering a phase in the development of democratic citizenship where people armed with much more sophisticated information are making harsher and more analytical judgments of their politicians.

The Pollster and Political Leverage

Public opinion does change, but as all political polls show, it changes rather slowly. Frequently, this rate of change is much too slow for the likes of politicians. Barring unforeseen calamities or catastrophes from which politicians cannot disassociate themselves, their ability to affect the nature of public opinion is limited. In our society, you cannot control all events, all news, nor all the ways in which the public forms opinions about its political leaders.

In spite of this, politicians can and do affect the nature of public opinion. Though this is only part of their mandate, it is becoming increasingly important. Indeed, politicians now have become *more* fixated upon affecting public opinion than upon doing what they think is right.

Politicians accomplish their manipulation of public opinion today through the notion of *leverage*. In an open-market society such as ours, individuals and groups are under enormous cross-pressures, factors which seek to affect their behaviour, thoughts, attitudes, values, political preferences and so forth. One should not underestimate this vast complex of cross-pressures. (Leverage is the ability to determine the point at which, and the mechanism by which, one is able to affect an individual or group's behaviour, thoughts, attitudes and values.) Timing, the medium and the message are crucial in order to lever someone's attitudes. Politics today is, more and more, the seeking out of leverage.

The one commodity increasingly at the disposal of government and politicians is information. And this information is used, more and more, as a basis of leverage in our political system. Someone who has information which another person or the electorate does not have uses this information as a basis of levering that other person toward a particular position or decision.

Polling has increasingly become the art of acquiring that vital piece of information that the other person or group does not have. This then enables the politician or party to lever public opinion in certain directions. Both the timing and the medium by which that information is communicated and the content of its messages become critical. The pollster provides the basic information from which levering strategies are fashioned.

Politicians increasingly act defensively. They do not want to do anything that may come to be considered a mistake. Ongoing paralysis of political action is one of the most perplexing realities of our politics. Politicians might readily admit that they think they know what should be done to alleviate a problem, but the fear of making a mistake, fear of a crippling error, frequently deters them from taking such actions.

The pollster, today, functions frequently to help reduce the risk of untoward actions. By providing vital information about the likely public receptivity to political policy and behaviour, the pollster defines the costs and benefits of political action.

Are polls detrimental to the public good? This question has now become an ongoing preoccupation of many. Some would ban polls altogether. Others would ban polls at election time. Still others demand that all polls conducted at public expense should be made public immediately.

Society indeed has a right to know the means by which decisions made in the public interest are taken. I believe in freedom of information and public access to government documents. Hence, I believe that polls conducted as a basis of collecting information and polls used in the decision-making process of government should be made public.

Equally important in our political life, however, is the notion of responsibility. We elect politicians to conduct the affairs of our nation, province, or municipality.

Politicians assume that public trust, and with it they must assume the burden of responsibility for acting in the public interest.

The increasing public posture of pollsters and the opening of access to polled information should not become a foundation for the shirking of responsibility by public officials. Politics means judgment—judgment about actions conducive to the public good. Elections are institutional mechanisms whereby we are able to define the nature of that responsibility—to heap praise and to assign the burden of blame. The pollster is not, nor should he or she ever become, the focus of this process of responsibility.

I believe that polling and the increased use of polling in our political life has increased the capacity of elected officials to make wise decisions. Wisdom means mature intelligence, common sense, sound judgment, perception and discretion. The pollster has provided a vehicle for pursuing, interpreting and directing action for the public good, based upon this notion of wisdom.

The Pollster and the Changing Nature of Democracy

Information is power and political information is political power—or so goes an adage of our age.

Democracy has changed—from small-scale participatory democracy, through representative democracy, to information democracy. While we retain the institutional structures of representative democracy, it is clear that new forces, new figures and new, evolving institutions are changing our democratic processes. Information—issue specific, time specific—is now the life-blood of the political process and the policy making process of our society. The pollster is the gatekeeper of political information.

We must now begin to discuss the problem of how the pollster has affected the nature of contemporary democracy. Have we moved irrevocably away from representative democracy to a pollster/information-based democracy? What does that mean? How has the pollster transformed the elements of traditional politics: i.e., values, ideologies, personalities? Can the nature of political life be the same after the advent of the pollster? In realistic terms, to what degree is the pollster, as the gatekeeper of information, the instrument of political manipulation and control?

My experience suggests to me that the consumer and the voter bases his or her decisions on a combination of experience, fact and intuition. Individual decision making, either for consumer goods or for political leaders and parties, is becoming increasingly evaluative. People today are taking the time to make hard choices. Choice—whether to drink Pepsi or Coke, whether to vote for leader X or leader Y—is a given throughout our society. Nobody should assume that winning over a person from one soft drink to another is an easy task. It is not. Nor is winning over a person for leader X or leader Y. The process of winning individual choice today is an ongoing process. This done, it is a constant struggle to maintain a person's allegiance.

The process of winning over an individual and acquiring his or her allegiance is exactly what consent involves. Consent implies choice. And today, in an extremely competitive environment, winning over someone to a product or a leader is a precarious business. People are constantly being asked to change their minds and to evaluate what they are doing. They are constantly being seduced or challenged to consider the alternatives.

The pollster can help us understand how individuals make decisions and help us understand the process of choice. He or she may even be able to predict the stages in the decision-making process, but cannot predict the actual choice. By explaining to the politicians the decision-making process and its stages, a pollster can reduce the risks to the politician and increase the leverage the politician may have. But a pollster can neither determine the outcome of the political process nor predict how the voters will decide. If voters sense a lack of leadership, for example, a very rapid process of rejection sets in. One cannot predict, nor even control, what will trigger off the sense of lack of leadership.

The Pollster and the Canadian Voter

Polling has taught me many things. But probably the most important thing, the fact that all good pollsters must always keep in mind, is that the source of wisdom rests always with the consumer and the voter. The consumer and the voter react from a fundamental and deeply rooted base of common sense. In the final analysis, people vote from self-interest. They evaluate the political world and make their decision on the basis of what they think and know is best for themselves and their families. This does not mean that people are egotistical, narrow, or selfish, but rather that citizens in our society participate in a community where they recognize that choosing always means choosing the best for themselves, for their children and families, and for their community. This is what common sense means. It is a sense of what is best or what is common to all people in a community, the collective wisdom of the voter and the consumer. The fundamental responsibility of the pollster is to seek out, understand, and to make apparent what that collective wisdom is all about.

ENDNOTES

1. Probably the best source of the ideas and character of Edward L. Bernays is found in *Biography of an Idea: Memoirs of Public Relations Counsel Edward L. Bernays* (New York: Simon and Schuster, 1965).
2. The literature of pollsters is, indeed, expanding. Many pollsters are now becoming more public figures and they are beginning to write for journals, magazines, etc. However, there is still a lack of self-reflection in most of the work of the pollsters. A valuable source of ideas is found in the journal, *Campaigns and Elections*.

Who Sets the Agenda? Perspectives on Media and Party Politics in Canada

5

ROBERT A. HACKETT AND LYNNE HISSEY

Few would disagree that the mass media—particularly television, radio and newspapers—have gained increasing prominence in Canadian political life. But what is the nature of their role? Do they operate merely as vehicles through which politicians communicate with citizens? Or, do they determine or shape the contours of the political world? We outline and assess the most common answers to these questions below. First, however, we examine some general characteristics of Canadian media as they relate to the political scene.

Media as Part of the Political Environment

What are the politically relevant functions of the mass media? In a very general sense, some sectors of the media (notably television) are important agents of political socialization, contributing to the long-term process, begun in childhood, by which people in a given society acquire political values, orientations and knowledge. Even media content that is not explicitly about politics, such as television entertainment programmes, can convey politically relevant themes or messages. Such programmes may, for example, present attitudes about authority figures, about the nature and values of the society to which we belong and about threats to "our" way of life.

However, the more immediate, day-to-day impact of the media derives from the capacity of news in particular to help set the political agenda. Such influence can be seen in two ways. First, by directing audience attention towards some aspects of reality and away from others, the news media help *define* reality for their audiences and to structure the public's perception of the political world. Contrary to popular belief, news does not simply "reflect" reality: the mere necessity of selecting some events to cover while ignoring others, and choosing language and frameworks in which to describe these events, makes such a goal

An original essay written especially for this volume.

impossible. Thus, by structuring public perceptions of the political world, media can indirectly influence public opinion. For instance, the focus of news coverage, whether it be on scandals, internal dissension, policy achievements or leadership, can affect the level of public support for competing parties in the short term, and help create long-term public images of each party.

Research has established that the issues stressed in news coverage tend to become those that the public regards as most important. As Bernard Cohen puts it, the media may not be successful in telling us what to think, but they are "stunningly successful" in telling us "what to think about."[1]

Second, the media also affect the decision-making schedules of policy makers.[2] For example, by giving prominent coverage to particular events or issues, the media can force governments and politicians to address issues they may have preferred to avoid. The abortion debate and legislation provides an example of this phenomenon: intensive media coverage of related legal decisions spurred recalcitrant politicians to address this political "hot potato."

It should be noted that the media do not typically exert whatever agenda-setting influence they possess deliberately or in accordance with partisan biases. Rather, this influence is a by-product of the media's newsgathering and reporting routines. News is the product of organizations which have their own institutional imperatives and their own routine ways of processing information. As well, the environment of a complex, liberal-democratic, industrial society within which media operate in Canada conditions their political influence. We return to these points later in this essay.

Media Characteristics

We turn to an examination of some of the most important politically relevant characteristics of the mass media in Canada.

As in most liberal-democratic political systems, the Canadian media are formally independent of the state and not generally subject to state censorship. On the contrary, media autonomy is reinforced by the widely held norms of freedom of the press and of expression—principles now enshrined in the Charter of Rights and Freedoms. Such formal independence, however, co-exists with informal constraints (discussed below) which potentially limit the range of perspectives and information conveyed by the media.

The Canadian media scene is also characterized by a French-English duality. The extent to which French- and English-speaking Canadians live in separate media worlds is a matter of some debate. It is not likely that many Canadians read or watch news in both languages. Most media corporations tend to publish or broadcast in one of the other language, not both. In terms of content, substantial differences in press coverage of both foreign affairs[3] and domestic politics[4] have been found between French and English media. Some contrary evidence suggests a common news agenda, at least during federal election campaigns.[5] However, significant blockages to communication between the two linguistic/national groups remain. This renders even more difficult the task of parties seeking to build national coalitions. The tensions within all three major federal parties over the Meech Lake Accord exemplifies this point.

The French-English duality is matched by a duality of parochialism and centralization in the production and dissemination of news.[6] The segment of the news media reaching audiences nationwide (e.g., *The Globe and Mail*, CBC radio, CBC and CTV network television news) is both small and severely limited in the ability to establish a national news agenda. Most news agencies with the largest audiences, such as daily newspapers and private TV and radio stations, are based in particular cities and regions, and their editors are important gatekeepers, tending to select items of local interest. Furthermore, the national news media tend to reflect the sensitivities of editors and audiences in the Montreal-Ottawa-Toronto axis, contributing to regional alienation elsewhere (and sometimes to the growth of protest parties, such as the Reform party).[7]

An important characteristic of Canadian media is their dependence on American media content; this is especially true of English-language media. While this phenomenon is most prominent in TV entertainment programming (itself not without political implications, as we note above) it is also evident in news. Canadian media rely heavily on U.S.-based news agencies and TV networks to cover foreign affairs. The reasons for this reliance are principally economic: it is cheaper to purchase American material than to produce Canadian equivalents. The constant presentation of the world through American eyes has potential cumulative political consequences.

Another distinguishing feature of Canadian media is the absence of distinct partisan orientations. While the recent emergence of tabloid dailies with a populist style and right-wing politics is an exception to this tendency, Canadian media generally maintain a formal "neutrality." The historical partisanship of newspapers has steadily declined in the twentieth century, due in part to competition from the broadcasting industry and economic pressure to become "omnibus" journals appealing to the widest possible audience. The legal and regulatory framework of broadcasting is intended to ensure independence from the government of the day, relative neutrality in the access and coverage accorded to the major parties and reasonable balance in the presentation of viewpoints on public issues.

As with the news media in other Western countries, the occupational culture of Canadian journalism emphasizes certain "news values" which shape the presentation of the news. These news values lead to a focus on events and individuals (rather than processes or structures), authoritative spokespersons, drama, conflict, the violation of societal norms (such as scandals), and electoral/parliamentary politics, at the expense of other centres of social power (notably, corporate boardrooms and government bureaucracy) and extraparliamentary socio-political movements. These characteristics of news discourse have been accentuated by the growing importance of television as a news medium, with its emphasis on personalities, entertainment value, images rather than issues, broadest common denominator (or least objectionable) programming, photogenic events and brief speech clips. Later in this essay, we discuss some of the ways in which television may affect political parties.

Finally, and perhaps most importantly, the Canadian media are in various ways governed by the logic of a capitalist economy and market relations. Most media organizations are in the business of making money; and, on the whole, both daily newspapers and broadcasting companies are quite profitable relative to other industries. Ownership of mass media outlets tends to be concentrated in the hands of a small number of corporations. The Royal (Kent) Commission on Newspapers reported in 1981, for example, that just 12 companies produced 88 of Canada's 117 daily newspapers, with just two of those "chains" (Southam and Thomson) accounting for three fifths of English-language circulation.

As well, newspapers tend to enjoy a monopoly in most markets, for economic and other reasons.[8] Only a few Canadian cities have dailies that compete meaningfully. Broadcasting outlets generally do not possess such monopolies; the industry is characterized by regulated competition and the emergence of new pay-TV and cable services. Only a few of these new services, such as CBC's Newsworld, carry programming that is directly pertinent to politics. Although the electronic media, apart from the CBC, still do not rival the daily press in the depth or diversity of political coverage, more and more people rely on television for political information.

A further economic characteristic of the Canadian media scene is the trend toward conglomeration—ownership of media by companies with extensive non-media holdings. The archetype of this phenomenon is the Thomson family's corporate empire, which has held interests in wholesaling, retailing, real estate, oil and gas, insurance and financial and management services.[9] Moreover, media owners are likely to be tied to the rest of the business community through shared social interest and milieu, as well as through interlocking corporate director-ships.[10]

No discussion of the political economy of the media can ignore their financial dependence upon advertising which accounts for over three quarters of the revenue of daily newspapers, and over half of the broadcasting industry's reve-nue, including almost all of the revenue of private radio and TV stations. Thus, the basic economic purpose of most Canadian media organizations is to make profits by attracting audiences whose attention can be sold to advertisers. This imperative has some subtle but pervasive and important implications for news reporting. News oriented towards the mass market (as distinct from specialized or affluent segments of the market) tends to address the reader/viewer as a taxpayer, a consumer, and a passive spectator of politics-as-entertainment, rather than as a worker or an active participant in political life. If people are encouraged to view themselves as consumers rather than as workers, for example, they are less likely to identify with a party claiming to represent "working people," as the NDP has done in the past.[11]

This integration of the mass media with capitalist economic rationality is widespread but not total in Canada: the major exception is the public sector Canadian Broadcasting Corporation. The CBC's original mandate included such tasks as providing programming for minority audiences and offering national programmes to assist in the development of a Canadian identity, tasks which were often unprofitable and hence unattractive to private broadcasters. CBC's early dominance has, however, steadily shrunk, a process accelerated by recent funding cuts. Morever, CBC TV is a kind of hybrid of commercial and public broadcasting systems: CBC television networks are partly dependent upon commercial revenues and privately owned affiliate stations. In short, with the partial exception of its radio services, the CBC does not provide a strong alternative to the logic of commercialism which now dominates Canadian broadcasting.

In the view of its defenders, the capitalist and commercial nature of Canada's media system ensures that media are independent of government, economically efficient and responsive to audience values and tastes. Critics, however, see a potential contradiction between the media as industries, and their social responsibilities as vehicles of democratic political communication. In this view, concentrated and corporate control may pose new kinds of threats to an independent and diversified press—threats such as homogenized editorial content, penny-pinching journalism and a "basic commitment to the business community's views on public issues rather than to a wider range of interests."[12] It can even be argued that the advertising basis of media revenue has acted historically as a kind of informal censorship of the press, since journals espousing radical views or appealing disproportionately to the economically dispossessed are of little interest to advertisers seeking to reach affluent or mass markets.[13] This position argues that parties that radically challenge capitalism are likely to be treated coldly by the media.

The divergent interpretations of the role and implications of the political economy of the mass media for news reporting have their counterparts in broader debates, discussed below, about the nature of the relationship between the media and politics.

Parties and the Media

Having considered some pertinent characteristics of Canadian media as part of the political environment, we turn now to an examination of more direct relationships between parties and the media, focusing on their relative power to set the political agenda. As noted in the introduction, there are various perspectives on this issue.

One view, perhaps dominant in North America, may be described as *pluralistic*. It regards the relationships between media, parties and other political forces as variable and contingent. In this view, election campaigns can be seen as contests between the parties, and between the parties and the media, to set the agenda.[14] This would also apply to the disputes over political issues *between* elections. The pluralist position holds that each "side" has its own power base and resources, the "edge" shifting back and forth from one to the other.

Media "weapons" in this struggle include oligopolistic access to mass audiences, the credibility and trust accorded by audiences, the ability to expose, ridicule and/or embarrass politicians and the respect accorded in liberal philosophy to freedom of the press.[15] The arsenal of electorally successful parties includes the financial resources and expertise to engage in media image-making, and their legitimacy and newsworthiness as presumed representatives of broad segments of the public and as major players in parliamentary politics and electoral competition. As well, governing parties can have recourse to the weapons of "economic and judicial harassment, competing enterprises, withdrawal of patronage, monopoly control of information, legal *force majeure*, and, occasionally, appeal to the civic emotions of patriotism and 'the national interest.'"[16]

The liberal version of this pluralist perspective sees all of this as a "fair fight," a reflection of the way in which all power groups operate in democratic societies and as insurance that no single group wields excessive power over the others for any sustained period. A conservative variant of the pluralist view sees the media as not just independent, but also as power-seeking institutions which have adopted an unduly adversarial and cynical approach to parties, government and political leadership. This approach, it is said, can be traced to the lasting influence on journalism of both television and the 1973 Watergate scandal and to the emergence of a generation of journalists who want to oppose "the system" itself.[17] In this view, politics and politicians are held hostage by journalists' anti-authority bias.

The conservative pluralist perspective receives very little support from the scholarly literature, however. While some news coverage of parties is undoubtedly "negative" to parties, particularly those in government, it tends to be ritualistic, superficial and focused on individual power-holders, rarely offering fundamental critiques of the overall political or economic system.[18] There is little reason to believe that such coverage is the result of journalists' oppositional mentality or biases; certainly strong organizational and economic forces, such as those mentioned earlier, militate against news coverage which consistently offends majoritarian values. Indeed, counter-examples can be cited which suggest that journalists' personal beliefs and attitudes (of whatever political stripe) have little systematic influence on the overall news coverage of specific events and issues. We can point, for instance, to the increasingly tarnished public image of B.C. Premier Bill Vander Zalm: there has been a perceptible shift in media coverage, from media-darling in the 1986 election campaign to increasingly negative coverage in subsequent years. Yet there is no reason to believe that journalists shifted their political values *en masse* in such a way as to account for Vander Zalm's later problems with the media.

The pluralist perspective, in each of its manifestations, has another fundamental problem. It ignores the many ways in which media actively reinforce dominant political values and power-holders. It is precisely this absence which is challenged by a contrary, *critical* view, wherein the media, far from being adversarial or even independent, are indirectly but systematically subordinate to the state and other established institutions, including the leadership of the dominant parties. Much of the news consists of statements by or about events, policies, or issues by official or political "sources" who strongly influence what journalists regard as credible facts and newsworthy events. Moreover, such sources, in this view, function as "primary definers," setting the terms of debate and the definitions of reality which the media use as raw material in describing the world of politics.[19]

Various factors are cited as contributing to such media dependence on official sources. First, the occupational ethic of objectivity, as journalists understand it, leads them to attempt to anchor their stories with statements attributed to relevant, authoritative and accredited sources. Second, the historical focus of Western journalism on electoral politics reinforces the choice of politicians as sources. As well, journalists have a social and cultural proximity to their sources, including politicians; journalists and party officials share an occupational milieu that rewards political "savvy" and the articulate manipulation of language. Finally, political and official sources are organizationally convenient for news media, since they supply information "which is freely available, can be attributed to an authoritative source, does not have to be chased, and has been produced with generous resources."[20] It could be argued that the increasing reliance of politicians and parties on media-wise image-makers, including extensive budgets for TV advertising and staged photo opportunities, further increases this dependence.

This explanation of news perhaps applies more to relationships between media and goverment rather than media and parties as such. But it can be argued that the dominant political parties do establish the boundaries of what the media regard as relevant issues and legitimate policy options. From this viewpoint, it is not surprising that the available research shows that one of the major parties, not the media, set the agenda during recent federal election campaigns; due to the lack of resources or incentives to initiate independent analysis of issues, news media have been vulnerable to manipulation by parties.[21]

Countering this view of a thoroughly manipulated media is a *media determinist* position which regards the media not only as autonomous, but as the dominant force in political life, setting the institutional pace and "logic" to which parties and politics must adapt.[22] Although the media determinist position has some important limitations, sketched below, it does suggest two important insights. First, it suggests that news does have a certain "logic" or "relative autonomy"; it is not simply putty moulded in the hands of external forces. Second, this position implies that the characteristics of the media system do indeed influence the political functions, electioneering style, resource allocation, leadership recruitment and organizational control of political parties.

To illustrate this, we point to the growing dominance of national television networks in the flow of political information and images. This phenomenon has been held (at least, partly) responsible for numerous trends. The most often cited of these is television's reduction of politics to entertainment, of parties to personalities and of issues to events or snappy one-liners. The "logic" of television—economic, organizational and technological—requires that it present its information in an entertaining and engaging manner. It also leads to a focus on leaders, leaders who must, furthermore, have certain media-genic characteristics and skills. Former Conservative Prime Minister Joe Clark and former B.C. NDP leader Bob Skelly provide examples of politicians with a negative media image which possibly contributed to their lack of electoral success. On the other side of the coin, B.C. Premier Bill Vander Zalm, arguably one of Canada's least qualified senior politicians, self-avowedly ran his successful 1986 election campaign on "style" not substance. The requirements of television news have led the political parties to hire legions of media strategists; policies and procedures are more and more determined not by political experts, but by media consultants. The media tend, as well, to cover elections (and leadership conventions) as if they were horse-races: the focus is on winners and losers rather than on more substantive issues. Accordingly, polls often receive a great deal of attention by the media; indeed, media often commission political polls, thus creating their own news. It has been argued that polls are often self-fulfilling insofar as, for example, people may vote for the candidate of the predicted "winning" party in order to ensure that their own regions are represented in the governing party. The media, particularly television, may also exercise an agenda-setting function beyond the realm of elections proper. For instance, the commercial and entertainment imperatives of television may influence not only the content but also the amount of political information available to the public on an ongoing basis. Television coverage itself may become a political issue, sometimes competing with the parties' attempts at publicity. The CBC "bugging" of participants in the 1989 NDP leadership convention, for example, attracted much media attention in the post-convention coverage. Finally, we point to television coverage of parliament. Such coverage may very well encourage the manifestation of politics-as-theatre; and the televising of Question Period, in which the government is necessarily placed on the defensive, has been viewed as a boon for opposition parties.[23]

While we may gain important insights from each of the above points, the media determinist position itself does have severe limitations. In particular, this perspective tends to ignore political and social relations of power which structure the development of media technology and the nature of media content.[24] Also ignored are continuities in Canadian political life which have remained relatively constant for decades. These features include corporate power, the logic of capital accumulation, a powerful U.S. influence, French-English dualism, regional cleavages, and social stratification based on class, gender and ethnicity. If media are indeed as much a determining factor as this argument claims, why have such structural conditions remained substantially constant? A more fruitful approach sees media organizations not as unidirectional determinants of politics, but as entering into reciprocal relationships with political actors, including parties and protest movements—relationships which are, however, bounded and constrained by such relatively stable interests and power dynamics as those mentioned above.[25] This perspective, unlike the pluralist position, recognizes structural inequalities; it acknowledges that structural differences effectively privilege some groups while simultaneously disempowering others. It also escapes an extreme position in which media are seen either as virtually inconsequential in-and-of themselves, or as the prime determinants of the political world.

Conclusion

Media are clearly a significant part of the political terrain: political parties have had to adapt to functioning within a mass-media environment. It is important to remember, however, that both media and parties operate within the context of a broader social and political system. In some ways, media and parties perform similar political and ideological work: both institutions engage heavily in verbal activities and the manipulation of language and symbols; both engage in competition to attract voters or audiences; and both are highly dependent on particular social and economic interests yet speak in a popular idiom and claim to represent a general public interest. Such similarities help account for the rivalry and intensity of the relationship between parties and the media.

Brodie and Jensen, for example, argue that parties provide the electorate with a definition of politics, helping to shape "the interpretation of what aspects of individuals' lives should be considered political, how politics should be conducted, what the boundaries of political discussion most properly may be, and what kinds of conflicts can be resolved through the electoral process."[26] They argue that at the federal level, Canada's party system has inhibited the politicization of social class cleavages; indeed, a critical or neo-Marxist interpretation of the party system regards it as an institutional means of minimizing conflict and maintaining stability in a society characterized by both structural inequalities and the mass franchise.

Much the same could be said of the mass media. As a by-product of the routine of gathering and presenting the news, resulting in apparently neutral descriptions of reality, media actually help construct particular mental "maps" of the social and political world. Such maps generally tend to naturalize and legitimize the dominant ideology of liberalism and, conversely, to marginalize or delegitimize parties and other political forces advocating fundamental alternatives. That does not imply that there is no room for dissent in the media,[27] or that the process is a deliberate and manipulative one. Rather, it is a consequence of some of the media characteristics discussed above: traditional definitions of news, routine reliance upon a relatively narrow range of sources, and dependence on advertising revenue and the logic of commercialism.

ENDNOTES

1. Bernard C. Cohen, *The Press and Foreign Policy* (Princeton: Princeton University Press, 1963), p. 13.
2. Edwin R. Black, *Politics and the News* (Toronto: Butterworths, 1982), ch. 7.
3. Gertrude Joch Robinson, "Foreign News Conceptions in the Quebec, English-Canadian, and U.S. Press: A Comparative Study," *Canadian Journal of Communication*, Vol. 9, No. 3 (Summer, 1983), pp. 1–32.
4. Arthur Siegel, *Politics and the Media in Canada* (Toronto: McGraw-Hill Ryerson, 1983); Marc Raboy, *Movements and Messages*, David Homel, trans. (Toronto: Between the Lines, 1984).

5. Walter C. Soderland, *et al., Media and Elections in Canada* (Toronto: Holt, Rinehart and Winston, 1984).

6. Frederick J. Fletcher and Daphne Gottlieb Taras, "The Mass Media and Politics: An Overview," in Michael S. Whittington and Glen Williams, eds., *Canadian Politics in the 1980s*, 2nd ed. (Toronto: Methuen, 1984), p. 202.

7. *Ibid.*

8. Arthur Siegel, *Politics and the Media in Canada*, pp. 109–10.

9. Robert Hackett, Richard Pinet and Myles Ruggles, "From Audience-Commodity to Audience-Community: Mass Media in B.C." in Warren Magnusson, *et al.*, eds., *After Bennett* (Vancouver: New Star Books, 1986), p. 231.

10. Wallace Clement, *The Canadian Corporate Elite* (Toronto: McClelland and Stewart, 1975).

11. Robert A. Hackett, "Remembering the Audience: Notes on control, ideology and oppositional strategies in the news media," in Richard Gruneau, ed., *Popular Culture and Political Practices* (Toronto: Garamond, 1988), p. 91.

12. Paul Audley, *Canada's Cultural Industries* (Toronto: James Lorimer/Canadian Institute for Economic Policy, 1983), p. 27.

13. James Curran, "Capitalism and Control of the Press, 1800–1975" in James Curran, Michael Gurevitch and Janet Woollacott, eds., *Mass Communication and Society* (Beverly Hills: Sage, 1977), pp. 195–230.

14. William O. Gilsdorf, "Getting the Message Across: Media Strategies and Political Campaigns," in Liora Salter, ed., *Communication Studies in Canada* (Toronto: Butterworths, 1981), pp. 52–67.

15. Black, *Politics and the News*, p. 206; Michael Gurevitch and Jay G. Blumler, "Linkages between the Mass Media and Politics: A model for the analysis of political communications systems," in Curran, *et al., Mass Communication*, p. 275.

16. Black, *Politics and the News*, p. 206.

17. Anthony Westell, "The Press: Adversary or Channel of Communication?" in Harold D. Clarke, *et al.*, eds., *Parliament, Policy, and Representation* (Toronto: Methuen, 1980), pp. 25–34.

18. W. Lance Bennett, *News: the Politics of Illusion*, 2nd ed. (New York: Longman, 1988), pp. 124–27.

19. Stuart Hall, *et al., Policing the Crisis* (London: MacMillan Press, 1978).

20. Len Masterman, *Teaching the Media* (London: Comedia, 1985), p. 122.

21. Frederick J. Fletcher, "The Mass Media in the 1974 Canadian Election," in Howard R. Penniman, ed., *Canada at the Polls: The General Election of 1974* (Washington, D.C.: American Enterprise Institute for Public Policy Research, 1975), p. 288; Frederick J. Fletcher, *The Newspaper and Public Affairs* (Ottawa: Vol. 7, Research Publications, Royal Commission on Newspapers, 1981), pp. 97–99; and Gilsdorf, "Getting the Message Across."

22. David L. Altheide and Robert P. Snow, *Media Logic* (Beverly Hills: Sage, 1979).

23. For further discussion of points raised in this paragraph, see Colin Seymour-Ure, *The Political Impact of Mass Media* (London: Constable, 1974); Frederick C. Engelmann and Mildred A. Schwartz, *Canadian Political Parties: Origin, Character, Impact* (Scarborough: Prentice-Hall Canada, 1975), esp. pp. 119–140; Jay G. Blumler and Michael Gurevitch, "The Political Effects of Mass Communication," in Michael Gurevitch, *et al.*, eds., *Culture, Society and the Media* (London: Methuen, 1982), pp. 236–67; John Meisel, "The Decline of Party in Canada," ch. 15 of this volume; and Austin Ranney, *Channels of Power: The Impact of Television on American Politics* (New York: Basic Books, 1983).

24. Dallas W. Smythe, *Dependency Road: Communications, Capitalism, Consciousness, and Canada* (Norwood, N.J.: Ablex, 1981), ch. 10.
25. For an example of this type of analysis, see Todd Gitlin, *The Whole World is Watching* (Berkeley: University of California Press, 1980).
26. M. Janine Brodie and Jane Jenson, "The Party System," in Whittington and Williams, *Canadian Politics in the 1980s,* p. 255.
27. Robert A. Hackett, *News and Dissent: The Press and the Politics of Peace in Canada* (Norwood, N.J.: Ablex, forthcoming, 1991).

6 Women and Parties: More than an Issue of Numbers

LISE GOTELL AND JANINE BRODIE

The Country is yours ladies; politics is simply public affairs. Yours and mine and everyone's. The government has enfranchised you but it cannot emancipate you, that is done by your own processes of thought.

Nellie McClung, 1917

Introduction

Many analysts of Canadian politics have heralded the 1980s as the long-awaited watershed for Canadian women in federal party politics. Beginning with the 1984 federal election, each of the major political parties scrambled to nominate a record number of women candidates and, for the first time in Canadian electoral history, the party leaders participated in a nationally televised debate which was devoted exclusively to political issues of special concern to women. In that year, 27 women were elected to the House of Commons—nearly double the record set in 1980, and six women were appointed to the federal cabinet, again twice the previous record. Women continued to make impressive representational gains later in the decade. The 1988 federal election brought 39 women to parliament, six of whom were appointed to Cabinet. Importantly, a woman also was included in the Cabinet's powerful and Strategic Operations Committee. Women still constituted only 13.4 percent of Canada's federal parliamentarians in 1988, but their numbers were approximately four times greater than only 10 years before. (See Table 1.) From the perspective of numbers alone, women finally appeared to be making significant inroads into the traditional male preserve of Canadian federal politics.

Paradoxically, the 1980s have also posed a serious challenge to the Canadian women's movement. At the same time as more women are entering the ranks of the Canadian political élite, the state appears to be increasingly unsympathetic, if

An original essay written especially for this volume.

TABLE 1 **Number of Women Elected to Parliament 1921–1988 Federal Elections**

Year

	0	10	20	30	40	50
1921....1						
1925....1						
1926....1						
1935......2						
1940....1						
1945....1						
1949...0						
1953.........4						
1957......2						
1958......2						
1962...........5						
1963.........4						
1965.........4						
1968....1						
1972...........5						
1974................9						
1979..................10						
1980......................14						
1984...27						
1988..39						

Source: Elections Canada

not hostile, to the policy goals of the women's movement. The primary challenge to women has been the growing popularity of a new theory of governing—neo-conservatism—which has found a place in the platforms of both the Liberal and Conservative parties. Its most articulate and committed partisan proponent, however, is the federal Conservative party, under the leadership of Brian Mulroney, which earned stunning electoral victories in both 1984 and 1988. Since its election, the party's record on women's issues demonstrates clearly that the policy demands of the women's movement are fundamentally incompatible with the political objectives of neo-conservatism.[1]

By most indicators, women are a subordinate group in Canadian society; their improved status is dependent upon governmental intervention both in terms of regulating the private sector and in providing often costly social programmes. Despite bold promises to women voters in 1984 and 1988 and despite a record number of women in the ranks of the governing party, the goal of deficit reduction has tended to dominate the Tory policy agenda. Little effort has been addressed to the conditions that continue to hold women in a subordinate position within Canadian society. In fact, some feminists have concluded that the Mulroney government has in many cases reduced some of the modest gains that the Canadian women's movement achieved in the previous decade.[2]

Current governmental resistance to the demands of the women's movement poses a curious and disturbing problem for feminist analyses of women and party politics in Canada. In the past, studies of women and politics in Canada have focused principally on the issue of women's representation (or lack thereof) in party politics and in Canada's legislatures. Research agendas have been guided by questions such as "Why so few women in politics?" or "What if there were more?" The principal assumption guiding many of these studies was that the marginal presence of women among the political élite helped explain why successive Canadian governments have responded minimally, if at all, to the policy demands of the women's movement.[3]

In this essay, we will argue that the contradictory status of women in Canadian politics in an era of neo-conservatism begs a reappraisal of the issue of women's numerical representation in the corridors of political power. The neo-conservatives' goal of reducing government provides little motivation and decreasing means of ameliorating women's subordinate status in Canadian society. Yet, paradoxically, this may mean that even greater numbers of women will be recruited as political candidates and elected to the House of Commons. We will argue here that mainstream parties can avoid hard programmatic commitments to the women's movement while being seen to be appealing to a women's constituency by recruiting highly visible and usually like-minded women to the parties' legislative ranks. In other words, the future may very well see the election of increasing numbers of women because it enables mainstream parties to symbolically respond to women without any commitments to costly or interventionist social programmes. The 1984 and 1988 elections may well mark the beginning of such a trade-off in which marginal increases in women's numerical representation within partisan politics is being served up by the Liberal and Conservative parties as a kind of fast food substitute for action on the substantive demands of the women's movement. Before elaborating on this argument, however, we will briefly recount the past condition of women in the Canadian party system.

Women and Party Politics in Canada— From Past to Present

The Canadian party system developed within the context of a very rigid and popular ideology about the roles of men and women in society. This ideology revolved around the notion of separate spheres: men were equated with the public sphere of paid work and politics, women were relegated to the private sphere of the family. As in other liberal democratic states, this notion had a number of negative implications for women and politics. First, it influenced the determination of legitimate political actors. Women were effectively barred from politics by legal restrictions on their right to vote and hold property and later by the pervasive expectation that politics was a "man's game." Women interested in public affairs were judged to be decidedly unfeminine.

Equally important, the notion of separate spheres determined the legitimate boundaries of political discourse as the Canadian party system took shape.

Politics came to be equated with public activity beyond the realm of the domestic sphere. This range of discussion effectively excluded issues most relevant to women's lives (childrearing, domestic labour, and so on). Consequently, Canada's political parties did not recognize women's concerns as part of the realm of legitimate politics.[4]

The Canadian suffrage movement did little to challenge a definition of politics constructed within these terms. This is not the place for a detailed history of the suffrage movement in Canada.[5] A brief overview of some of its characteristics, however, helps clarify why women did not emerge as a significant political force immediately after they gained the vote. The Canadian suffrage movement, unlike its British and American counterparts, was slow to develop, regional and somewhat subdued.[6] This "first wave" of Canadian feminism contained many ideological currents but maternal or social feminists dominated the movement.

These women (and some men) accepted and propagated the widespread patriarchal assumption of the period that women, by virtue of their reproductive capacity, were more moral, caring and pure than men and thus would help "clean up" politics and society, if granted the vote. Except for the immediate goal of the franchise, women's rights and subordinate social status were of secondary concern. The historical circumstances associated with the granting of women's suffrage only further marginalized the gender factor in Canadian politics. Suffrage was achieved within the context of the war effort and the conscription crisis. And, in the end, women's formal democratic rights were achieved without a theory or even much recognition of the subjugation of women, without demands to ameliorate the subordinate social status of women and without an agenda for future action. It is not surprising, then, that the suffrage movement soon disappeared from the public stage.[7]

After women's suffrage, Canada's political parties integrated women in such a way as to reinforce an ideology of sexual difference and political inequality. It was fairly common to find women performing many of the menial and housekeeping chores of party organizations. Their formal recognition in the party structure came with the establishment of women's auxiliaries, appendages to the main party organization. The first women's auxiliary was established in 1913, while the first national organization, the Federation of Liberal Women of Canada, was launched in 1928. Shortly after, the Conservative party established a similar organizational appendage.[8]

Women's auxiliaries were initially conceived as educational forums for newly enfranchised women and quickly expanded to the constituency organizations of both the Conservative and Liberal parties. It was not long, therefore, before a sexual division of labour was firmly entrenched in the organizational structure of both major parties. Women's auxiliaries provided a ready pool of dedicated volunteers during election campaigns and succeeded in impeding women's participation within the mainstream of party organizations.[9] By contrast, separate women's organizations were never established on a national scale in either the Co-operative Commonwealth Federation (CCF) or later in the New Democratic party (NDP). Regardless of partisan stripe, however, every Canadian political party has consistently reflected *the higher the fewer rule*: the higher up the party echelon one goes and the more electorally competitive the party, the fewer women are to be found. This phenomenon has always limited women's access to the resources and contacts necessary to secure party nominations to winnable ridings.[10]

From the time of suffrage, then, Canadian political parties have been instrumental in marginalizing women within conventionally defined politics. It was not until the rise of "second wave" Canadian feminism, however, that the gendered practices of parties were subjected to scrutiny. Like its predecessor, second-wave feminism, which dates from the mid-1960s, embodied many ideological streams. Nonetheless, its major currents challenged the rigid dichotomies of "public-male/private-female," the ideological rationale for women's marginalization within conventional politics. Liberal feminism constituted the public face and the mainstream of Canadian second-wave feminism. Its political agenda centred on identifying and challenging the barriers that restricted women's entry into the public world of paid labour and politics. Dominated by an equality of opportunity framework, Canadian liberal feminists identified women's unequal representation in conventional politics as an organizational priority and singled out the discriminatory practices of Canadian political parties as a key impediment to political change.

While liberal feminists challenged the public/private divide in terms of women's access to the public sphere of politics and argued persuasively that women should be included on an equal basis to men, they have remained committed to the notion that politics is something that takes place within the formal political process. Consequently, they have been less stringent than socialist or radical feminists in their examination of the politics of daily life in the private sphere and in their analysis of sexual power and privilege. Both socialist and radical feminism constitute significant streams within the Canadian women's movement.[11] In contrast to liberal feminism, these currents of second-wave feminism assert that the problem of women's political marginality cannot be solved by the simple removal of barriers to equality of opportunity and the increased presence of women in the so-called "public sphere." Instead, they assert that women's oppression is rooted in social structures which span both the public and private sphere. Socialist and radical feminists have attempted to show how the organization of and ideologies dominating the household, personal and sexual relations, childrearing and non-market work are crucial determinants of the distribution of power in society. In the process, they have helped broaden the policy agenda of the women's movement beyond questions of access and representation to include issues such as sexuality, childcare, reproductive freedom, sexual violence, domestic labour and so on.

Second-wave feminism in Canada, then, has been crucial both in politicizing the issue of women's unequal access to the public world of politics and in challenging the social structures which reproduce women's political marginality. Moreover, this challenge has had important implications for the study of political science in Canada. Until the rebirth of the women's movement, political science had very little to say about women. By the 1970s, however, a few Canadian academics (usually women) began to expose the pervasive problem of women's political marginality. This literature has been useful in highlighting the role that Canadian political parties have played in limiting women's political participation, particularly at the élite level. Influenced by liberal feminist assumptions, these studies focused on the question of women's political representation in electoral politics and attempted to identify the barriers which restrict women's participation in all forms of democratic politics.

There is now an impressive body of research documenting how the structures and discriminatory practices of Canadian political parties have inhibited women's chances of obtaining positions of power. By the early 1970s, the gender gap at the level of mass or citizen political participation had all but disappeared; however, women continued to be grossly underrepresented at the élite level where political power is concentrated.[12] A number of studies have identified political parties as crucial gatekeepers guarding the doors of political power for women. They found that women's experiences both with constituency work and within the party's organizational hierarchies have been shaped by a fairly rigid intra-party sexual division of labour. Specifically, women invariably performed housekeeping duties rather than participated in policy and financial decision-making structures.[13]

Of course, as we have argued, the organization of the Liberal and Conservative parties, in many respects, entrenched this division of labour with the establishment of women's auxiliaries.[14] Responsibility for election strategy, policy development, the dispersal of funds—the élite roles of the party—were assumed by men in the main party structure. Largely in response to the pressures exerted by female partisans, the federal Liberals replaced its auxiliaries with the Liberal Women's Commission in 1971; the Progressive Conservatives followed suit with women's caucuses in 1981. These organizations are formally committed to improving the status of women within the main party apparatus. Yet most research continues to indicate that women's partisan activity is still circumscribed by an implicit sexual division of labour. Without exception, studies of Canadian party organizations have reported that far fewer female than male party activists serve élite roles or are identified as influential by their fellow partisans.[15] Admittedly, more women have moved into executive positions, especially at the constituency level, but as Sylvia Bashevkin discovered, these women usually assume "pink collar" positions. In 1981, for example, approximately two thirds of the riding secretaries of Ontario's three major parties were women. But, they comprised less than one quarter of the riding presidents. Moreover, women were most likely to be promoted to riding president in constituencies where their party was inactive and electorally uncompetitive.[16]

Similarly, research on the experience of women candidates confirms that political parties are a significant factor in terms of women's election to legislative office. Canadian political parties have tended to nominate women only in ridings where they are uncompetitive.[17] While there was a steady increase in the number of women candidates in the period from 1964 to 1975, most were on the fringes of the party system as independents, Communists, etc. In fact, during the 1970s, the majority of women contesting federal office did so for a minor party; most of the women who contested election for one of the major parties during this period were lost-cause candidates. Few women were nominated to ridings where their party had a tradition of competition or success—a fact illustrated by the comparative success rates of men and women candidates during the period. As late as 1979, only 5.1 percent of all female candidates for federal office were elected compared with 22 percent of male candidates. During the 1980s, when women achieved their greatest electoral gains, the chance for election among male candidates was almost twice that of female candidates. (See Table 2.)

The standard response of party spokespersons to this dilemma has been that there is a shortage of qualified women to nominate to winnable ridings. However, the results of statistical analyses have indicated that a woman candidate's educational or occupational status was irrelevant to securing a competitive riding. Although rarely secured, competitive ridings were granted most often to women with a long history of party service.[18]

The research on the gender biases of Canadian political parties has been instrumental in directing our attention to the historical role of political parties in reproducing a gender-biased system of political representation. But the question remains as to whether this focus is too narrow. Certainly the issue of women's numerical representation is an important one in its own right, raising fundamental questions of equality and democracy. But our questioning of women's political marginality should perhaps extend beyond an examination of numerical representation and the barriers posed by liberal democratic institutions for women climbing the political ladder.

There is an implicit, if not explicit, assumption in most of the literature on women and party politics in Canada that if more women achieved political power, the political system will necessarily be more responsive to women's issues and concerns. Many authors have posed a positive correlation between the numerical representation of women and the substantive representation of women's issues in party platforms and government policy agendas. Sandra Burt, for example, argues that governmental commitment to breaking down gender roles is unlikely without a proportional representation of women in legislative bodies.[19]

Similarly, Sylvia Bashevkin argues that women partisans are generally more

TABLE 2 **Success Rates among Male and Female Candidates for Federal Office, 1972–1988**

Year	Percentage of Female Candidates Elected	Percentage of Male Candidates Elected
1972	7.6	25.6
1974	7.2	20.4
1979	5.1	22.1
1980	6.4	20.0
1984	12.8	20.6
1988	12.9	20.1

supportive of feminist issues than their male colleagues and urges a strategy of partisan engagement on the Canadian women's movement. Bashevkin believes that the advancement of women in politics depends on an increased feminist presence within political parties, particularly in parties of the left. She notes that feminist partisanship has resulted in progressive internal party reforms. These have included the establishment of pro-feminist women's organizations in the Liberal and Conservative parties and the passage of an affirmative action resolution in the federal NDP in 1981 which ensures both gender parity in élite bodies and the fielding of highly visible women leadership candidates. Such reforms, Bashevkin argues, are necessary if women are to have a greater collective voice and policy input in Canadian politics.[20] However, the link between women's numerical representation in party politics and the political system's responsiveness to women's substantive policy concerns is more complicated than such analyses suggest. The representation literature often argues by implication rather than elaboration, i.e. it is assumed but not demonstrated, that the insertion of more women into the ranks of the political élite will result in general improvements in women's status.

Unfortunately, this hypothesis rests on rather naive assumptions about the nature of political parties. It ignores the practical obstacles confronting female partisans who attempt to alter male-defined agendas. Political parties, especially Canada's brokerage variants, are pragmatic institutions. Their logic is defined by the objective of capturing political power and, thus, they respond to social movements only when they anticipate electoral pay-offs. For most of the history of the Canadian women's movement, this condition has been absent. Women have not figured largely in the arithmetic of Canadian partisan politics and policy making because they have rarely been mobilized in elections as a distinct political constituency. So-called "women's issues" have been treated as private rather than political matters and, thus, women have engaged in partisan politics in much the same way as have men—on the basis of family tradition or regional, religious, ethnic and class affiliations. Unless feminist struggle within a party is able to link its objectives to a tangible electoral constituency, it is unlikely to achieve policy gains in the party platform; it is more likely that such struggle will be marginalized and feminist partisans forced to subordinate their principles to electoralist logic. Women's representation and even feminist struggle within political parties cannot in and of themselves assert a fundamental shift in the boundaries of partisan politics.

The representation literature is also flawed in that its analytic framework is too narrow. The literature which highlights the role of political parties in restricting women's access to élite roles usually ignores more fundamental causes of women's political marginality in society at large. Although there have been some advances in the social status of women, the fact remains that, in our society, women are not valued as much as men. Occupations that are characterized as "women's work" pay less than those that are typically considered male; men continue to earn more than women who perform the same work, let alone work of equal value; and the gap in pay between the sexes is as large today as in the

1930s, with the average female wage approximately 35 percent less than the average male wage. In 1985, for example, the difference in the average earnings of men and women was $11,613.[21] Women also remain stuck in the same job ghettos—60 percent of employed women are in the clerical, sales and service sectors. These and other factors mean that poverty is increasingly a women's issue. Elderly women and single-parent families headed by women are among the poorest of the poor in Canada.

These are significant variables in the competitive game of liberal democratic politics. As Black and McGlen's findings demonstrate, lack of professional employment inhibits women's political participation at the élite level.[22] In particular, women's generally lower earnings have meant that they have less access to the large sums necessary to secure party nominations. (It is estimated that the average woman seeking a party nomination would have to put at least 40 percent of her disposable earnings towards her campaign.)[23] In addition, the enduring division of labour within the home has constituted a major barrier to women's advancement in liberal democratic politics. Women may aspire to public office but they are usually delayed or fully inhibited from crossing the threshold from "private" to "public" life by gender-role constraints.[24]

Given that the representation literature focuses on the role of parties at the threshold, it tends to reflect liberal feminist premises, challenging the "public-male/private-female" distinction solely in terms of access. It assumes that only the actors of liberal democratic party politics must change in order for Canadian women to assume political power. In other words, it argues that the eradication of gender-biased discrimination within political parties can solve the problem of women's political marginality. Its focus is on parties as the metaphorical fence between the "private" sphere and the "public" world of politics and de-emphasizes how the structures of the "private" sphere prevent many women from reaching the fence in the first place.

In effect, an emphasis on parties and women's representation as the pivotal factors determining the political status of Canadian women is simply too narrow. There is indeed a complex relationship between numerical representation and responsiveness. As we shall argue below, increases in women's representation and policy responsiveness to the demands of the women's movement can easily be disarticulated by mainstream political actors. Political parties can respond to women's demands for representation as a form of symbolic legitimation and simultaneously eschew feminist demands for tangible public policies. In contrast to what the representation literature suggests, then, there can be a negative relationship between women's representation and political responsiveness to the women's movement.

Canadian political parties are increasingly accessible to women's representation such that the practices and structures of parties no longer present formidable barriers to women's political participation. Yet, women's partisan activities remain constrained by factors external to the formal boundaries of partisan politics. At the same time, the mainstream parties are becoming more hostile to the policy demands of the women's movement, demands which, if addressed, would ameliorate women's subordinate position within society. This somewhat paradoxical situation challenges much of the conventional wisdom about women and party politics in Canada.

Women and Politics in the 1980s

The 1980s have been characterized by two distinct political phenomena which are especially relevant to the issue of women and politics in Canada. The first has been the rise of neo-conservatism—a new theory of governing with the expressed aim of reducing both the size and role of government. For most of the post-World War II period, Canada's three major political parties devised policies within the context of a shared consensus about the proper role of the state in society. This consensus revolved around Keynesian demand-management techniques and the expansion of social welfare programmes. By the early 1980s, however, consensus no longer existed; Keynesianism and the welfare state had been discredited by a decade of slow economic growth, massive unemployment and spiralling inflation. The Keynesian orthodoxy was soon replaced with the doctrine of neo-conservatism, embraced by Britain in 1979, the United States in 1980 and Canada, especially by the Progressive Conservative party, in the mid-1980s. Neo-conservatives argued that the economic crisis of the 1970s and 1980s was caused by the practice of Keynesianism in the post-war era. Governments, through social welfare programmes and the associated growth of the public service, had become too large, fiscally irresponsible and deleterious to capital investment. The neo-conservatives' solution was simple: minimize the role of the state, cut back on social welfare programmes, reduce governmental intervention in the economy and return the responsibility for economic growth to the private sector.

The other significant political development of the 1980s—the politicization of the women's movement—occurred simultaneous to the development of this new consensus on a reduced role for the state. Since the mid-1970s, second-wave feminists had been active both within political parties and through women's groups, such as the National Action Committee on the Status of Women (NAC), in lobbying government for policy action on women's issues. The policy demands of the Canadian women's movement, however, implied an increased rather than decreased role for the state. More specifically, universal and affordable day care as well as income security for single mothers and elderly women required a significant expansion of social welfare programmes and state expenditures; affirmative action for women in the workplace demanded increased state regulation of the private sector; curbing sexual and family violence as well as family law issues meant that the state had to consider the personal as political and intervene in the domestic sphere. All of these demands became increasingly incompatible with the emerging neo-conservative philosophy which both sought to reduce the definition of what constituted the legitimate realm of public affairs and to re-establish a sharp division between the public and private spheres of Canadian society.

Second-wave feminism, however, was successful in forming a growing consensus among Canadian women about the need to preserve and expand the welfare state and to redress social problems created by the sexual division of labour. Throughout the late 1970s and 1980s, public opinion polls showed Canadian women to be more sympathetic than men to social welfare issues.[25] More importantly, the early 1980s witnessed a previously undocumented shift in the behaviour of women voters—the emergence of a gender gap. What is significant about a gender gap is not so much that men and women perceive the political issues of the day differently, but that these policy preferences translate into votes, potentially providing the margin of victory for one party or another.

The emergence of a gender gap in voting was first observed in the United States in 1980 when an estimated 3.3 million women voters rallied against Ronald Reagan's neo-conservative platform and his voiced opposition to the Equal Rights Amendment (ERA).[26] The following two years saw a similar constitutional struggle in Canada which, after a series of setbacks and a massive mobilization of Canadian women, culminated in the entrenchment of a sexual equality clause in the Charter of Rights and Freedoms.[27] By 1983, Canadian public opinion polls also were monitoring a significant gender gap in the Canadian electorate. Women appeared to be mobilizing in federal politics as a distinctive bloc of voters favouring the Liberal party by a margin of almost 10 percent.[28]

These two factors—the growing popularity of neo-conservatism and the politicization of Canadian women—provide a crucial backdrop to understanding the fate of Canadian women in the politics of the 1980s. As we have already noted, the 1984 federal campaign appeared to be a watershed for Canadian women. Each of the three major parties doubled its number of women candidates and a few were nominated to priority ridings. Moreover, the majority of women candidates, 129 in all, were affiliated with one of the three major parties. And, in the end, more women than ever before were elected to the House of Commons and appointed to cabinet. Also important, all of the parties talked more about women's issues, included specific policies for women in their respective platforms and debated these policies on national television.

Yet, all of this attention only seemed to underline how unfamiliar and uncomfortable the leaders of the Liberal and Conservative parties were with the demands of the women's movement. Turner and Mulroney assumed virtually the same stance on all of the issues raised during the televised debate ranging from affirmative action to day care to the feminization of poverty; the grand Canadian tradition of Tweedledum and Tweedledee was raised to an art form during the 1984 campaign. Few of the policy pledges extended by the victorious Conservatives found their way to tangible legislation during the party's first term in office. Indeed, the Conservatives entered the 1988 campaign with a questionable record: an unsuccessful attempt to de-index old age pensions for even the poorest of the elderly who are disproportionately women, the de-indexing of family allowance payments, an increase of taxes for the poor, little tangible progress made in affirmative action for women and the failure to pass its promised "comprehensive national system of childcare."[29]

Nevertheless, the 1984 campaign provides us with a number of valuable lessons. The first is that our parties will respond to the women's movement when they perceive electoral pay-offs. What distinguished the 1984 campaign was that for the first time since their enfranchisement, many Canadian women appeared to be ready to choose between the parties on the basis of what they were doing for and saying about women. And, it was this possibility that motivated the two major parties to change their electoral strategies toward women during the campaign.

Nevertheless, on the downside, the 1984 campaign also testifies eloquently to the fact that electoral constituencies can be organized and *disorganized* relatively quickly in federal party politics. Although each of the parties scrambled to appeal to the "women's vote," in the end a gender gap did not materialize. Only three weeks before the election, males favoured the Conservatives by a margin of 8 percent and females favoured the Liberals by 13 percent. But, a week before the election and after the celebrated debate, the Gallup poll showed that both men and women were swept up in the Tory tide in roughly equal proportions. The virtually identical positions of the two mainstream parties on so-called women's issues had effectively diffused the threat of a women's vote. The lack of any clear choice made the women's vote volatile and ultimately susceptible to traditional electoral appeals. Indeed, only the NDP appeared to benefit from women's politicization. This is in part because this party had targeted women as a potential electoral constituency as early as the mid-1970s, hiring a full-time organizer to develop an electoral appeal to women voters. But, more importantly, the NDP remained committed to fundamental principles of social democracy and the welfare state. Therefore, in 1984, it could offer women job-creation funding, mandatory affirmative action programmes, affordable day care and more liberalized access to abortion, without compromising the party's basic principles. And, for the first time since national election studies have recorded gender differences in party preferences, the NDP's support base was no longer disproportionately male (a trend which persisted in 1988).

Perhaps the most difficult lesson to be gleaned from the 1984 campaign and subsequent developments is that the demands of the women's movement and the reigning philosophy of neo-conservatism are fundamentally incompatible. Canadian women are a subordinate majority in our society; their improved status is dependent upon government intervention. Nevertheless, the governing Tory party cannot simultaneously pursue its neo-conservative goals and deliver on its substantive promises to women. Within the present climate of smaller government, reduced government spending and reliance on so-called "neutral" market forces, women invariably lose out. Women require concerted government action to free them from traditional job ghettos, to provide support for childcare and to cushion them from poverty. These needs are contrary to the goals of the current generation of political decision makers who are much more concerned with reducing the size of government and withdrawing the state from the economy.

The fact remains that the two major parties are largely out of touch both with the organized women's movement and with the Canadian public on the question of women's equality. This credibility gap is readily observable when we compare the opinions of ordinary Canadians and party delegates attending the 1983 Conservative and 1984 Liberal leadership conventions. A CBC poll conducted in the summer of 1984 revealed that 85 percent of Canadian women and 80 percent of Canadian men agreed that more should be done to promote women's equality in Canada. Among party influentials, however, only 63 percent of Liberal women and 38 percent of Liberal men and 46 percent of Conservative women and 28 percent of Conservative men expressed the same sentiment.[30]

Yet, as we suggested earlier in this paper, the conflicting goals of government and the women's movement may, in fact, result in the recruitment of more women to prominent political positions. Parties with neo-conservative leanings can avoid tangible policy commitments to women and, at the same time, be seen to be appealing to a women's constituency by recruiting highly visible women to its legislative ranks. In other words, the future may very well see the election of increasing numbers of women because it enables mainstream parties to symbolically respond to the women's movement without antagonizing neo-conservative ideologues either within the party hierarchy or the Canadian business community. Indeed, the women recruited can be and often are antagonistic to the goals of the women's movement.

A significant gender gap also emerged in the 1988 federal campaign—Canadian women were far less supportive both of the Conservative party and of the Mulroney government's Free Trade Agreement, the single most important issue of the election. Women's organizations such as NAC warned that the deal would disproportionately affect women's jobs and threaten key social security programmes. These and similar criticisms angered the Tories who perceived them as partisan attacks rather than the voice of the legitimate concerns of the women's movement. Subsequently, Mulroney refused to participate in a NAC-sponsored televised debate similar to the one held in 1984. All parties, however, increased their efforts to nominate and elect more women. For the first time in Canadian electoral history, all three major parties set aside funds specifically designed to help women candidates get elected. And, in the end, 39 women were elected to the House of Commons.

Nevertheless, it is unlikely that the women returned in 1988 will advance the feminist cause in parliament. The election saw the defeat of many important women's advocates such as Flora McDonald, Lucie Pépin, Aideen Nicholson and Marion Dewar. More importantly, the governing party for the most part recruited like-minded neo-conservative women to join its ranks. As one observer of Parliament Hill has reported, among both men and women within the Conservative caucus, feminism has become the new "F" word.[31] Moreover, there is growing resistance on the part of the governing party to consult with the organized women's movement. In 1989, for example, the minister responsible for the Status of Women refused to meet with representatives of NAC during their annual lobbying campaign on Parliament Hill. And, in a recent round of budget cuts, the Secretary of State's programme for funding women's groups has been singled out for a 50 percent reduction over the next three years. This will have a profoundly detrimental effect on the Canadian women's movement ability to lobby against the neo-conservative agenda of the Tory government. As one new woman member of the Tory caucus explained, "The whole organization [NAC] should be eliminated. Why subsidize a lobby that slams our politics?"

With the advent of the 1990s, women continue to make impressive symbolic gains in federal politics. In December, 1989, the NDP elected Audrey McLaughlin, a relative newcomer to the House of Commons, as its leader. Although McLaughlin is an avowed feminist, this dimension of her leadership bid was downplayed during her campaign or subsumed under ambiguous labels, such as "a new generation of leadership." Also, for the first time in the history of the Liberal party, a woman, Sheila Copps, has sought the leadership position. Moreover, the Liberals have allocated one half of voting delegate spaces at the 1990 leadership convention to women.

Despite dramatic increases in women's numerical representation in the House of Commons and in party hierarchies, it is clear that Canadian women and the women's movement face severe challenges during the 1990s. The Tory government's cost-cutting and revenue-gathering programmes (such as cuts to day-care funding, to unemployment insurance and to federal transfer payments, as well as its proposed value-added tax) place burdens on Canada's poor, most of whom are women. At the same time, provisions of the Meech Lake Accord dealing with shared-cost programmes will limit the federal government's ability to establish new social programmes with national standards, thus diminishing its capacity to respond to the plight of Canadian women and other subordinate groups. Moreover, the new free trade regime promises to close down precisely those sectors of the economy in which women workers are "ghettoized."[32] The experience of the past decade underlines that the substantive representation of women's issues is more than an issue of numbers. Regardless of which political party prevails in the future, the visibility and priority attached to women's concerns in the partisan realm still depend on the strengthening of a distinct women's constituency in the federal electorate.

ENDNOTES

1. M. Janine Brodie and Jane Jenson, *Crisis, Challenge and Change* (Ottawa: Carleton University Press, 1988), p. 319.
2. Louise Dulude, "The Status of Women Under the Mulroney Government," in A. Gollner and D. Salée, eds., *Canada Under Mulroney* (Montreal: Véhicule Press, 1989), p. 253.
3. Sylvia Bashevkin, *Toeing the Lines* (Toronto: University of Toronto Press, 1985), p. 160; Sandra Burt, "Legislators, Women and Public Policy," in Sandra Burt, *et al.*, eds. *Changing Patterns: Women in Canada* (Toronto: McClelland and Stewart, 1988), p. 155.
4. Isa Bakker, "The Political Economy of Gender," in Wallace Clement and Glen Williams, eds., *The New Canadian Political Economy* (Montreal: McGill-Queen's, 1989).
5. For an elaboration see Catherine Cleverdon, *The Women's Suffrage Movement in Canada* (Toronto: Oxford University Press, 1950); C. Bacchi, *Liberation Deferred* (Toronto: University of Toronto, 1983).

6. Ramsey Cook and Wendy Michinson, *The Proper Sphere* (Toronto: Oxford University Press), p. 255.
7. Bacchi, *Liberation Deferred.*
8. Bashevkin, *Toeing the Lines*, ch. 5; Canada, *Royal Commission on the Status of Women* (Information Canada, 1970), pp. 345–350.
9. Bashevkin, *Toeing the Lines*, pp. 100–105.
10. *Ibid.*, p. 69.
11. See Nancy Adamson, Linda Briskin and Margaret McPhail, *Feminist Organizing for Change* (Toronto: Oxford University Press, 1988).
12. J.H. Black and Nancy McGlen, "Male-Female Political Involvement Differentials, 1965–1974," *Canadian Journal of Political Science*, Vol. XII (1979).
13. Bashevkin, *Toeing the Lines*, p. 57.
14. *Ibid.*, pp. 100–105.
15. See Alan Kornberg, Joel Smith and Harold D. Clarke, *Citizen Politicians—Canada* (Durham: Carolina Academic Press, 1979), ch. 8; Sylvia Bashevkin, "Women's Participation in the Ontario Parties, 1971–1981," *Journal of Canadian Studies* (Nov., 1982); Sylvia Bashevkin, "Social Background and Political Experience: Gender Differences Among Ontario Party Élites," *Atlantis* (Fall, 1983).
16. Bashevkin, "Women's Participation."
17. See M. Janine Brodie, *Women and Politics in Canada* (Toronto: McGraw-Hill Ryerson, 1985).
18. *Ibid.*, p. 114.
19. Sandra Burt, "Women, Legislators and Public Policy," in Sandra Burt, *et al.*, eds. *Changing Patterns: Women in Canada* (Toronto: McClelland and Stewart, 1988), p. 155.
20. Bashevkin, "Political Parties and the Representation of Women," in Alain Gagnon and Brian Tanguay, eds. *Canadian Parties in Transition* (Toronto: Nelson, 1989), p. 458.
21. Dulude, "The Status of Women," p. 253.
22. Black and McGlen, "Male-Female Political Involvement Differentials."
23. Canadian Advisory Council on the Status of Women, *Women in Politics* (Ottawa: November, 1987), p. 7.
24. Brodie, *Women and Politics*, ch. 6; Barry Kay, *et al.*, "Gender and Political Activity in Canada," *Canadian Journal of Political Science*, Vol. XX (1987), pp. 851–863.
25. See Brodie, "The Gender Factor in National Leadership Conventions," in G. Perlin, ed., *Party Democracy in Canada* (Scarborough, Ont.: Prentice-Hall Canada, 1987).
26. Zillah Eisenstein, *Feminism and Sexual Equality* (New York: Monthly Review, 1984), p. 18.
27. See Lise Gotell, "The Canadian Women's Movement, Equality Rights and the Charter," *Feminist Perspectives*, No. 16, Canadian Research Institute for the Advancement of Women, Ottawa (1990).
28. Brodie, "Reflections on the 1984 Campaign," *The Facts*, Vol. 7, No. 3 (May, 1985), p. 69.
29. See Dulude, "The Status of Women."
30. See Brodie, "The Gender Factor."
31. Charlotte Gray, "The New 'F' Word," *Saturday Night* (April, 1989), p. 17.
32. Marjorie Cohen, *Free Trade and the Future of Women's Work* (Toronto: Garamond Press, 1987).

7 Election Finances Legislation in Canada

DONALD C. MACDONALD

In July 1986 the Ontario Legislature updated the province's decade-old election finances legislation. That fall, I was visited by an Oxford University professor who was observing election finances legislation in North America. As I outlined the highlights of Ontario's amended legislation, he began to shake his head. "In Britain," he observed, "we're back in the Dark Ages." Britain, the original model of parliamentary democracy, in the Dark Ages on as important an element of democracy as assuring "a level playing field" for those seeking to serve the public through elective office! The comment was arresting.

The fact is, however, that Canada is more advanced than any other country in establishing public accountability—along with limits on contributions and spending, and a measure of public funding—in the increasingly worrisome field of escalating election costs. Not all of Canada, however, has achieved the same progress. The situation varies in the federal, provincial and territorial jurisdictions. And it is interesting to note how both Ottawa and the provinces have played a role in the evolution of the legislation.[1]

How the Legislation Evolved

At the time of Confederation, Canadian election law dealt only with the prohibition of corrupt practices, such as treating (entertaining) and bribery. The first reforms in 1874 arose out of the Pacific Scandal, which involved the solicitation and acceptance of a large donation by the governing Conservative party from private interests seeking a railroad contract. The Dominion Elections Act of 1874 established the doctrine of agency, by which an individual must be given the legal responsibility for the use of campaign funds. But the 1874 Act did not acknowledge that political parties are the main conduit of campaign funding. Moreover, the absence of any control mechanism or meaningful sanctions weak-

---

An original essay written especially for this volume while the author was Skelton-Clark Fellow at Queen's University. Opinions expressed are not necessarily those of the Election Finance Commission of which the author is chairman.

ened the effectiveness of the legislation. There were amendments to the Act in 1891, 1906, 1908 and 1920, but there was no political will to clean up the process. On April 5, 1953, for example, *Maclean's* magazine published an article by Blair Fraser, its Ottawa editor, called "Our Illegal Elections." "Most of our lawmakers become lawbreakers in the very act of getting elected," it stated, because the major contributors to election funds were contractors who did business with the government.

In fact, concern over the undue influence of business in election funding was acknowledged early in this century. Federal law banned contributions by corporations in 1908, but the law was not enforced and the ban was lifted in 1930. In 1924, the province of Manitoba prohibited corporate election funding, but dropped the prohibition in 1980, ostensibly because corporate contributions were being laundered through individuals; therefore, the law was unenforceable.

Interestingly, Quebec has been able to enforce a ban on contributions by corporations and trade unions. Quebec legislation during the Quiet Revolution of the early 1960s gave great impetus to provincial electoral reform. Quebec pioneered the imposition of spending limits and the provision of public subsidies, and gave formal recognition to political parties for their role in funding. Nova Scotia enacted parts of the Quebec plan and Manitoba followed with comprehensive disclosure provisions.

These sweeping provincial reforms gave impetus to a growing concern at the federal level. Five election campaigns between 1957 and 1965 had strained party funds, and the rise in the cost and importance of television in election campaigns compounded the problem. As a result, a federal Advisory Committee on Election Expenses was appointed on October 17, 1964. Chaired by Alphonse Barbeau, a Montreal lawyer, the committee's other members consisted of M.J. Coldwell, former national leader of the Co-operative Commonwealth Federation; Gordon R. Dryden, a Toronto lawyer, and secretary-treasurer of the Liberal Federation of Canada; Arthur R. Smith, a Calgary businessman and former Conservative MP; and Dr. Norman Ward, a professor of political science at the University of Saskatchewan. Through this membership the interests and concerns of all parties were brought to bear on a common problem.

The Barbeau Committee reported in October 1966. Its recommendations included bringing parties under the law as responsible bodies; broadening the base of political participation through a system of subsidies; reducing overall election costs by instituting shorter campaign periods and media spending limits; requiring complete disclosure by candidates; enforcing statutory requirements; and the publishing of audited financial statements.

Parliament didn't respond to the Barbeau recommendations immediately. During the following six years, they were reviewed by the House of Commons Special Committee on Election Expenses and, eventually, they were included in Bill C-203 following the 1972 general election. Two more years passed before that bill became the Election Expenses Act of 1974. Its content and passage were influenced by the public's awareness of the questionable fund-raising practices of the Watergate scandal in the United States. Equally important, the provinces were leading the way: prior to 1974, Nova Scotia, Manitoba and Saskatchewan had implemented spending controls in provincial contests and, in 1972, following the revelation of a $50 000 contribution to the Conservative party by a contractor seeking a government agency contract, the Ontario government asked the (Camp) Commission on the Legislature to study campaign financing reform.

Passage of the federal Election Expenses Act of 1974 opened wide the floodgates of reform. In 1975, in response to the Camp Commission recommendations, the Ontario government passed the Election Finances Reform Act, which duplicated the federal legislation, with one significant exception: whereas Ottawa limited election expenditures, it placed no limit on contributions; conversely, Ontario limited contributions, but placed no limit on expenditures. (When the Ontario legislation was amended in 1986, limitations were placed on expenditures as well as on contributions.)

Alberta patterned its new law on the Ontario legislation. Concurrent with the passage of the Alberta legislation in 1977, the Parti Québécois government in Quebec passed extensive amendments banning corporate and union contributions and instituting the most comprehensive system of public funding. In British Columbia, reform was advocated by a Royal Commission report in 1978, but the only change involved tax credits for political contributions. Likewise, Newfoundland only incidentally addressed the problem of election financing; in 1982, a bi-partisan committee held public hearings, and its reform proposals were included in a draft bill in November 1983, but it was never passed.

Throughout the 1980s, most provinces amended their legislation, extending its jurisdiction and/or tightening its enforcement. The most significant changes were that Quebec and Manitoba abolished the separate administrative bodies originally set up to deal with election finances, and placed the responsibility with the Chief Electoral Officer or an official appointed by him or her. Ontario alone retains a separate Election Finances Commission. Furthermore, Quebec and Ontario extended financing legislation to municipal elections, and Ontario has done the same for party leadership contests.

Staged Achievement of the Objective

From the outset, advocates of election finances legislation have pursued the elusive goal of establishing equal opportunity for competing candidates. In recent years, that goal has increasingly involved efforts to check skyrocketing election expenditures which create the greatest disparity among candidates. The most effective mechanism for achieving equal opportunity is by fixing limits for expenditures and contributions, by providing tax credits for contributors. Prohibiting large contributions and encouraging smaller ones represents a democratization of the election financing process, particularly when it is subjected to public disclosure and effective enforcement. In order to cope with disparities in the amounts of money available, this basic mechanism has become supplemented with subsidies to candidates and to parties.

A wide variety of stages has emerged in implementing the many components of financing legislation and in the regulations which strengthen their enforcement. There is only one characteristic common to the legislation in all Canadian jurisdictions: when candidates and/or parties file a campaign financial statement of contributions and expenditures, it is a public document, open to inspection. Otherwise, as will be seen from the following summaries, legislation ranges from the rudimentary to the comprehensive.

Atlantic Provinces

In Nova Scotia and Prince Edward Island, parties and candidates must register. They are subject to expenditure limits and must file campaign financial statements. Neither province places a limit on contributions and both provide tax credits; but while Prince Edward Island requires disclosure of contributions in excess of $250, Nova Scotia requires no disclosure of contributions. Both provinces provide reimbursements to candidates in receipt of 15 percent of the vote, and Prince Edward Island provides an annual subsidy to parties with at least two seats in the Legislature.

New Brunswick has the most comprehensive legislation of the Atlantic provinces. Local associations as well as parties and candidates must register. There are limits on contributions and tax credits for contributors, with disclosure of all contributions over $100. There are limits on expenditures by both candidates and parties. Candidates in receipt of 15 percent of the vote are subsidized. Parties are also subsidized on the most generous basis of any Canadian jurisdiction—an indexed figure ($2.07 in 1989) every year for each vote received in the previous election. It is noteworthy that New Brunswick's legislation encompasses not only election financing, but the activities of political parties *between* elections. Some other provinces do the same, in varying degrees, though New Brunswick's nomenclature is the only one which acknowledges it. The administration rests, not with the Chief Electoral Officer, but the Supervisor of Political Financing.

In 1990, Newfoundland moved from having the most rudimentary election financing legislation to having the most comprehensive. The Legislature is considering a Bill which is modeled on that of Ontario's, with limits on contributions and spending, but without including party leadership contests. On the issue of subsidies, however, Newfoundland has opted for the more generous provisions of New Brunswick, which provide party subsidies not only for elections, but for every intervening year as well.

Canada

The Chief Electoral Officer maintains a registry of political parties which have met a series of criteria, including the fielding of 50 candidates at a general election. Such parties must have an official agent through whom all income and expenses are reported. To be officially nominated a candidate must file a witnessed nomination paper, along with a deposit of $200. Each candidate must also have an official agent through whom all income and expenditures are reported. However, local associations are not registered and have no legal status.

Contributions are not limited, but the names of contributors in excess of $100 must be reported. There are expense limits for parties, based on the number of voters in ridings where they are fielding candidates, and expense limits for candidates, based on the number of voters in his or her riding. There are restrictions on media advertising which must be confined to the last four weeks of the campaign, excepting polling day and the day before.

Parties must file annual reports of donations and expenditures, and must file campaign reports within six months of polling day. Candidates must file a financial statement in which expenses of $25 or more are disclosed. There is a graduated tax credit for contributions to both parties and candidates, up to a maximum of $500. A candidate in receipt of 15 percent of the vote is entitled to a refund of the $200 deposit and a reimbursement of up to 50 percent of the actual election expenditures, provided it is no more than 50 percent of the expense limit. Registered parties are also entitled to a reimbursement of 22.5 percent of their election expenses provided the party has spent more than 10 percent of the maximum limit. Campaign surpluses must be turned over by candidates to the national party or riding association and by independents to the Receiver-General of Canada.

Progress in federal legislation has stalled over the past five years. The traditional consensus on amendments, arrived at by representatives of all parties, has not been acceptable to the Cabinet. Government amendments were finally tabled on June 30, 1987, in Bill C-79, but it was never passed. However, none of the amendments dealt with election finances, and the vagueness of the language of the statute has opened the door to extensive campaign spending which is not subject to any limits. It is a loophole which well-financed parties can readily exploit. In his 1989 annual report, the Chief Electoral Officer of Canada stated: " . . . a clear distinction must be made in the Canada Election Act between *election expenses* and other types of campaign expenses, in order to avoid the kind of uncertainty which has been prevalent since 1984 and which led to a parliamentary inquiry in 1988."

Western Provinces

As in the Atlantic region, the Western provinces range widely in the comprehensiveness of their legislation. In British Columbia, there is no limit on contributions or expenditures. Parties and candidates must file financial statements after each election, but no verifying documentation is required. There is no disclosure of contributors, but tax credits are provided.

Alberta is only marginally more demanding in its requirements. There is no statutory limit on expenditures by either parties or candidates, although each, as well as constituency associations, must file audited financial statements. There are contribution limits with a graduated tax credit up to a maximum of $750, but there are no subsidies or reimbursements to either parties or candidates.

Saskatchewan's statutory requirements are more comprehensive. Political parties must register before they can receive contributions or incur expenses. Candidates do not register, nor do local associations. There are no specific contribution limits though the name and category of contributors over $100 must be disclosed.

The allowable limit for party expenditures is 40 cents per elector in the ridings where registered candidates are fielded; and for candidates, a graduated amount based on the number of electors for the average-sized constituency, the limit is approximately $45 000 (with an extra $5000 for certain northern ridings).

Contributions from whatever source are limited to $4000 a year to parties, and $750 a year to single constituencies up to an aggregate of $3000. This $7000 limit can be repeated in an election year. However, a candidate is limited to $750 like any other contributor. Parties and local riding associations must submit audited financial statements to the commission by May 31 for the previous calendar year, including the names, addresses and amounts for all contributions over $100. Parties, candidates and local associations must submit similar audited statements of contributions and expenditures within six months of polling day. In addition to tax credits for individual contributors, there is public funding. Parties in receipt of 15 percent of the vote receive five cents for each elector in ridings where they fielded candidates; and candidates in receipt of 15 percent of the vote receive the lesser of 20 percent of the maximum expenditure limit, or their actual expenditures.

Municipal elections are subject to regulations roughly comparable to those at the provincial level. However, the municipal elections become the responsibility of the commission only if a municipal council or other municipal body (school board or public utility) opts for providing tax credits for contributors; otherwise, the administrative and enforcement responsibility rests with the clerk of the municipality.

Ontario is the first Canadian jurisdiction whose legislation covers party leadership contests. All candidates must register with the commission and file audited financial statements of revenues and expenditures, including the identification of contributors of over $100. However, there is no limit on contributions or expenditures and there is no tax credit. The legislation also forbids a prospective leadership candidate from raising or spending any money until the race has officially been launched—a requirement which is unrealistic and, therefore, will likely be changed.

Overall Assessment

Has election financing legislation been effective? In general terms, the answer is: very much so. Admittedly, where the legislation requires only minimum public accountability through filing of financial statements (sometimes unaudited) on contributions and expenditures, the regulations are not onerous. But even where the legislation is comprehensive, as in Quebec and Ontario, parties and candidates have not experienced any insurmountable difficulties.

Some observers harbour the suspicion that election spending regulations are a facade behind which much of the traditional hanky-panky in election spending continues. This is not necessarily the case, though there is an interesting contrast in enforcement procedures. In most jurisdictions other than Ontario, if the law is contravened, a charge is laid, and the courts are left with the responsibility of deciding whether there were mitigating circumstances and, therefore, what proportion, if any, of the statutory penalty should be imposed. The Ontario Commission on Election Finances has taken a more lenient approach. In view of the fact that most of the people responsible for fulfilling the Act are volunteers—the foot-soldiers who maintain our party operations—they should not be treated as criminals when contraventions are either minor or inadvertent. On only four occasions in 14 years have contraventions been considered so serious as to merit prosecution. In effect, the staff of the Ontario Commission on Election Finances works with the volunteer in the field to correct contraventions (which is possible in the majority of cases) or, where the contravention is not correctable (as with a late filing), the Commission has traditionally accepted late filings with a reprimand but, in 1989, it strengthened enforcement procedures by deregistering a party or constituency association for such a contravention.

In Ontario, a public inquiry involving political funding was launched in September 1989 under Mr. Justice Lloyd Houlden. The inquiry focused on the relationship between a major developer, Tridel Corporation, and a charity directed by Patti Starr, in their use of political contributions in lobbying officials and elected members of the Legislature. Certain conclusions emerged from the early testimony: first, that the problem lies not so much in flawed legislation as in the ethical standards of those determined to circumvent and/or violate the law; and, second, that the review procedures involving chief financial officers, their auditors and the commission, in combination with the public disclosure of financial filings to opposing candidates, parties and the media, provide a guarantee that wilful violation of the law will ultimately be caught.

Another facet of election financing regulation is its capacity to check the disturbing escalation of election spending. For example, in the 1985 general election in Ontario, candidate expenditures ranged as high as $150 000. The new 1986 legislation fixed a ceiling related to the number of electors, which was about $45 000 for the average-size constituency. In the subsequent election, no candidate exceeded this limit. In fact, the average expenditure for Liberal candidates was $36 000; for Progressive Conservative candidates, $27 000; and for New Democratic Party candidates, $18 000. And yet, with these significantly lower expenditures, there was no evidence that the electoral appeal had been inhibited.

One of the consequences of escalating election costs is that rarely does a party come out of an election without the burden of a deficit. To cope with this situation, the 1986 legislation in Ontario provided for a subsidy to parties. In the subsequent general election the subsidies were relatively low: $303 368 to the Liberals; $252 993 to the New Democrats as Official Opposition; and $232 083 to the Progressive Conservatives. The Ontario subsidies are given only once, contrasting with the party subsidies in New Brunswick, which are paid on an annual basis at an indexed figure (now $2.07) per vote received by the party in the previous election.

Many of the Canadian jurisdictions provide for the registration of constituency

associations (as well as parties and candidates), and extend to the local association the privilege of accepting contributions for which the contributors receive a
tax credit. There is some feeling that this results in monies being siphoned off
from the central party funds, thereby contributing to the deficits with which they
are burdened. There may well be some substance in this contention, but it is
compensated for by the involvement of far more of the citizenry in the whole
election process—surely a desirable objective.

The elimination of large contributions removes the serious bias and distortion
of the election process traditionally created by large contributors, and the provision of tax credits results in thousands of voters making small contributions, and
thereby becoming more involved. These factors, in combination with the total
public disclosure of election financial returns, results in a more open system,
more widely participated in by the electorate. Once again, this is a highly desirable objective in a democracy.

Unregulated Areas

The political financing legislation of Canada's central provinces is
the most advanced—arguably in the world—but there remain areas in which the
objective of establishing equality for all candidates seeking public office has not
yet been achieved. Four such areas in Ontario will serve as illustrations.

First, expenditure limits are restricted to the campaign period, between the
calling of the election and polling day. But if candidates are nominated months,
even years, in advance of the election, there is no limit on the expenditures which
their riding association may make on their behalf before the election is called.
There is no logic to leaving these pre-writ expenditures unregulated. They are as
much an election expenditure as the regulated post-writ spending.

Second, polling and related research through focus groups to try out ad copy
and speech themes on "ordinary citizens" are a key element in modern campaigning. They represent an ever-increasing component of election spending,
yet they are excluded from the statutory limits.

Third, expenditures resulting from the seeking of a nomination are not subject
to any limit or public accountability. In hotly contested nominating conventions
in the Toronto area before the 1987 provincial election, these expenditures were
known to have run as high as $30 000. In one instance, a contestant distributed a
piece of literature to every household in the riding, not simply to the party
members who were eligible to vote at the nominating convention. In this way, a
candidate who has won the nomination has a significant head start over other
candidates when the election is called.

Fourth, is the question of "third party" intervention in a campaign in behalf of,
or in opposition to, a party or candidate. If third-party activities are carried out with
the knowledge and consent of a party or candidate, then the expenditure must be
included in their financial statement, and is subject to the campaign limits.

But, usually, third-party activities are performed without the official consent of any party or candidate, and are subject to no limits or public accountability.

The result is a highly unfair situation: registered parties and their candidates are subject to statutory limits on contributions and expenditures, whereas third parties are not. When the United States Congress passed legislation limiting contributions and expenditures, the Supreme Court in 1976 upheld the former but struck down any limit on expenditures as being a violation of the constitutional right of free speech unless it is voluntarily accepted as part of a programme of public funding. The result has been a proliferation of Political Action Committees (PACs) now numbering nearly 5 000, organized by corporations, unions and independent interest groups, who raise more money than the committees of the parties—indeed, who have become major players in the election game, sometimes overshadowing the traditional parties.

Except for Quebec, the legal position of third parties is unresolved. The federal election law banned them, but on the eve of the 1984 general election the National Citizen's Coalition challenged this section of the law as a violation of the Charter of Rights and Freedoms, and their action was upheld by a lower court in Alberta. The Alberta lower court decision was not appealed and has, in effect, become the law of the land in federal elections.

In contrast, the Quebec legislation has banned third-party activities. When the law was challenged as a violation of the Quebec Charter, the courts, both at the lower and appeal level, upheld the ban. The Quebec decision was that freedom to spend is not equivalent to freedom of expression.

We were forewarned about this kind of development as far back as the Report of the Barbeau Committee in 1966. It stated (page 50):

> The Committee has no desire to stifle the actions of such groups (third parties) in their day-to-day activities. However, the Committee has learned from other jurisdictions that if such groups are allowed to participate actively in an election campaign, any limits or controls on political parties or candidates become meaningless . . . . Such committees (PACs or third parties) make limitations on expenditures an exercise in futility, and render meaningless the reporting of election expenses by parties and candidates. The Committee recognizes that restrictions on all such organizations during election periods may encroach to some extent on their freedom of action but, without such restrictions, any efforts to limit and control election expenditures would come to nothing.

If third-party election activities are to be unregulated, the purpose of existing election finance legislation will be nullified. Contribution limits on registered parties and candidates have been imposed to eliminate the distortion of the electoral process by large contributors, and the names, addresses and amounts of all contributors of over $100 must be disclosed; these requirements, in combination with tax credits to contributors, have been designed to democratize election financing. Expenditure limits have been imposed to establish a "level playing field" for all candidates. Public subsidies have been provided for candidates and parties to ease the growing financial burden of campaigning. Advertising has been limited to certain periods in advance of election day. All these elements of election financing law will be rendered futile if third parties on all accounts— contributions, expenditures, advertising black-out periods and public accountability—are free to operate outside the law.

The situation is an open invitation to a duplication of the American experience. Once registered parties or candidates have reached the limits imposed upon them by the law, their ideological friends can be encouraged to establish third-party organizations whose expenditures can double or treble the expenditure limits to which they are held. The whole objective of reining in escalating election expenditures will be defeated.

In short, the integrity of election financing legislation is being fundamentally threatened. There is an urgent need for this issue to be resolved by the Supreme Court. If the decision of the Alberta court, rather than that of the Quebec courts, remains the effective law of the land, then freedom of speech in Canada will be less important than available money.

ENDNOTE

1. In sketching the evolution of election finances legislation in Canada, and in detailing the current status of that evolution in Canadian jurisdictions, I have extracted and synopsized from *A Comparative Survey of Election Finances Legislation 1988*, published by the Ontario Commission on Election Finances, and from *Campaign Finance Legislation and Litigation in Canadian Federal, Provincial and Territorial Jurisdictions 1988*, published by the Chief Electoral Officer of Canada. The added commentary is mine.

   For more information, see these two publications and the statutes and scholarly writing on the subject, which are listed in the footnotes of the Ontario Commission's survey.

8 Ways Around Expense Accounting Rules

CHARLOTTE GRAY

The 1988 Canadian election was far and away the most expensive election in Canadian history. Officially, each of the three major parties will claim disbursements just below the legal limit of $8 million when it makes its declaration to the Chief Electoral Officer in May. (The Liberal limit was slightly lower since the party did not run a candidate in one riding.) Unofficially, each spent more. But the Liberal and NDP "soft spending" (election expenses not covered by the Election Expenses Act) is chicken feed compared to what the Tories spent—and spent legally. The PC victory cost the party at least $18 million. But we will never discover the precise bill. As Harry Near, director of operations for the 1988 campaign, says with a triumphant grin, "That's none of your business, sweetheart."

Canadian elections are not meant to be multimillion-dollar extravaganzas. The 1974 Election Expenses Act put a ceiling on the amount that parties can spend to win votes during the seven weeks of an election campaign. The purpose of these limits (updated in 1983) is to reduce any unfair advantages to the wealthiest parties and candidates and to encourage broader participation. In addition, the Act imposed strict time limits on the most expensive element in modern campaigning: advertising. Parties are allowed to advertise only in the last four weeks of the campaign, but not within 48 hours of voting day.

However, the Act's reporting requirements are extraordinarily vague. Parties can spend all kinds of money outside its limits, which simply restrict the amounts spent during the campaign directly to win votes. Parties need not declare any money spent before the election writ is dropped. They need not disclose how much they spend on "research" during the election; this includes polling and "focus groups"—the guinea-pig groups of "ordinary citizens" on whom party strategists try out ad copy and speech themes. And they can "shield" many of the party's administrative costs (telephone, party workers' travel, salaries, printing) by not including them as election expenses.

Charlotte Gray, "Purchasing Power," *Saturday Night* (March 19, 1989). Charlotte Gray is the Ottawa Editor of *Saturday Night* magazine. Reprinted by permission of the author.

The vagueness of the Act's wording has been particularly useful for the Progressive Conservative party because it is so much richer than its two rivals. Since 1980, the party has streaked ahead of the Grits and New Democrats in the technology of fundraising. Thanks to advice and technical help from the Republican party machine in Washington, it has profited enormously from the possibilities opened up by the tax-credit system, modern sampling, electronic data processing and direct mail. Between 1980 and 1984, the party secured a threefold increase in income. In the same period, neither the Liberals nor the NDP could match this bonanza: Liberal income rose 55 percent and NDP income 72 percent.

The first election in which the redesigned Tory machine roared into action was in 1984. The party began its campaign 13 months before the election was called. Khayyam Zev Paltiel, professor of political science at Carleton University, who until his death last year was the acknowledged expert on election spending, interviewed several party officials after the 1984 election, and was told that at least 50 percent of total PC election spending occurred pre-writ. The Tories also excluded most of their party running costs from the national office expenses that they reported for the campaign period to the Chief Electoral Officer. The undisclosed expenses included the bulk of their rent, salary, travel, telephone, and fundraising costs. (What was really going on is revealed by their annual operating costs. These zoomed up to $18 million in 1984, compared to $11 million in 1983 and $10 million in 1982.)

Pushing all these run-of-the-mill expenses outside their official election expenses meant the Tories had more "official" money for television advertising, consultants, organizers (they spent eight times as much as the Liberals on professional services), and the leader's tour. (Reporters from the 1984 Mulroney campaign still talk about the dinner they were served in a private room in Montreal's Ritz-Carlton Hotel by waiters in white gloves.) A close examination of the Tories' 1984 spending prompted Professor Paltiel to conclude in 1985 that "the actual, as against the 'official,' costs of the Conservative party's 1984 campaign might well be the highest in Canadian history." Nevertheless, the Conservatives managed to squeeze under the legal limit on spending by a $2500 margin.

The Liberals came within $100 000 of their legal limit; the NDP fell $1.6 million short. Both parties were clearly more candid about the true costs of their campaigns—hardly surprising, since both were church mice compared to the fat-cat Tories. (The New Democrats, indeed, have their own "creative" approach to election financing. As the poorest party, their problem is to reach the legal limit on spending in order to get the maximum reimbursement of 22.5 percent under the Election Expenses Act. Their suppliers are therefore rumoured to charge top-dollar prices for services, then make generous donations to the party—donations for which the supplier gets an additional tax credit.)

There is every reason to suppose that the Tories ran their 1988 campaign the same way. "We didn't do much different this time round," purrs Harry Near. "We didn't really have any more money than in 1984." Tories treat questions about their campaign budget as industrial espionage, but some facts are obvious. They embarked on the election with a well-stocked war chest: in 1987 they had raised $12.8 million, compared to the $8.8 million raised by the debt-ridden Liberal party and $6.7 million raised by the NDP, which was scrambling to put together its first national campaign. And once again, they got a lot of their spending out of the way before the election was called.

Senator Norman Atkins's strategy group was established in 1986 and from then onwards the campaign buzz words were straight out of a military strategy handbook. Senior organizational meetings with headquarters staff and volunteers who were to work on the campaign began in January 1988. All three parties ran training schemes for candidates, riding presidents, and party workers before the election was called, but the Tory schools were the most elaborate. The bulk of the PC campaign literature was ready before the election was called, and much of the work on more than 30 television commercials had been done. (Each opposition party prepared fewer than half that number.) The party was in a state of campaign readiness from June 1 onwards. In the late summer, at government expense, the prime minister did a dry run of his electoral tour through the regions, trying out speech themes such as "managed change" and fine-tuning his "statesman" image. How the Tories handled the operating costs of their office once the writ was dropped won't be known until they file their 1988 fiscal return, but they will probably follow their 1984 blueprint and simply exclude the bulk of administrative expenses.

The enormous advantage that Tory wealth and the larger margin for "official" spending gave the party during Canada's most unpredictable election was soon evident. From Day One, reporters on the leader's tour felt they were travelling first class, in a rock band's entourage. The Tory bus had a fridge full of beer and a microwave oven; reporters agreed that the best food was served in the Tory trough (although there were no white gloves this time); there were up to 25 staffers on No Commentair, the campaign plane, to keep everything rolling smoothly and reporters smiling. The two opposition leaders, in contrast, travelled economy class. On DespAir, the Liberal plane, dyspeptic reporters signed a petition for better food. On Air Apparent, the NDP plane, Lucille Broadbent and the leader's RCMP guard served the sandwiches. News organizations paid the parties around $2000 per reporter per week on the tours. The two opposition parties broke even; at least one third of the tab for the prime minister's tour, admit insiders, will be picked up by the party.

The major expense of an election campaign is advertising—particularly on television. According to Professor Fred Fletcher, a York University political scientist who monitors the political impact of the media, TV commercials "in normal circumstances are the best way to reach uncommitted voters, because viewers cannot avoid them." The NDP's initial advertising budget was $2 million; the Liberals' budget was $3 million; the Tories never revealed how much they planned to spend. However, when Turner's bravura performance in the debate caused the election to skid off the tracks that the Tories had prepared so carefully, all three parties rushed to redirect their campaigns. "It is very expensive to switch strategies mid-campaign," points out Professor Fletcher. "Only the Tories could afford a complete relaunch." The Tories spent at least $2 million in the final week, bringing their total spending on radio and television to an estimated $4 million—half their permitted expenses. The two opposition parties, in contrast, each had only the $1 million allocated in their campaign budgets for a final media blitz.

The Tories spent the money two ways. First, they abandoned two thirds of the commercials they had brought to pre-production stage in the pre-writ period (the costs of which they now do not need to declare) and produced new commercials with unrivalled speed. "We went from concept through production to distribution in 18 hours," recalls the Tory strategist Hugh Segal of two ads aimed at undermining confidence in Turner's competence and his team's strength. The Liberals, according to the Grit adman David Morton, took four days to create a new commercial and couldn't afford to abandon any of the ads they had prepared pre-writ.

Second, the PCs snapped up all available TV and radio slots in a "saturation buy" for the campaign's final week (the week in which they had already decided to concentrate their spending). "We bought 'The Young and the Restless,'" the Tory pollster Allan Gregg told *Maclean's* magazine. "We were in 'Romper Room.'" When the Liberals and NDP went back to look for more slots, almost none were left. "In the final week," estimates Robin Sears, deputy director of the NDP campaign, "the average TV viewer would have seen 10 or 12 of our ads, the same for the Liberals, but at least 20 Tory ads. I'd say the Tories spent three times what we did on their TV and radio campaign." The Tory ads, now focused on destroying John Turner's credibility, worked. Their polls showed belief in Turner's sincerity dropped 28 percent in 10 days. "There was no Liberal disaster in that period," argues Professor Fletcher, "so the drop had to be the result of the Conservative campaign." The Liberals recognized they were outspent and outgunned. "If we had had more money, we could have produced some commercials to counter their negative stuff," says Martin Goldfarb, the Liberals' pollster and communications adviser. "But we didn't."

The parties don't have to reveal what they spent on polling during the election since it is not covered by the Act. But Allan Gregg's company, Decima Research, had gotten a head start on the process with weekly polls for the government during the summer. During the election, Decima conducted regular polls in 25 "representative" ridings plus cross-country "rolling polls" based on samples of 500 a night. As well, Decima conducted four national polls with a sample of 1500. After the debates, when the Tories nose-dived, Decima's polling increased "a lot," admits Near. The total cost, opponents such as the NDP's Sears estimate, was probably "millions." The NDP allocated $250 000 for election polling by their pollster Vic Fingerhut of Fingerhut/Madison Opinion Research in Washington, D.C.: this bought them rolling polls of 200 a night but no riding polls. Liberal spending on polls conducted by Martin Goldfarb was somewhere in between. Polling was crucial in this election because of the volatility of the electorate (more than one quarter of respondents to a *Maclean's*/Decima poll said that they changed their minds at least once during the campaign). The Tories had the edge on the other two parties because they were always the first to know of shifts in opinion. "Knowing which message to pitch, and how to pitch it, made an enormous difference," says Tory insider Bill Neville.

By the start of November, the public began to focus on the millions that were being poured into the election. But it was not party expenditure that aroused the outcry. It was the lavish "third party," or lobby group, spending—another area of election spending over which there is no control. The 1974 Act had confined campaign spending to registered parties and candidates, and outlawed spending by anyone else to "promote or oppose" a candidate or party. But in 1984 the National Citizens' Coalition challenged the Act. It argued that these restrictions breached the Charter of Rights' guarantee of freedom of speech. The court upheld the challenge. Since the Election Expenses Act was never subsequently repaired, the 1988 election was open season for lobby groups, which were now permitted to advertise throughout the campaign, including at the start and finish when official parties were gagged. The National Citizens' Coalition plunged into the 1988 election with its own $842 000 campaign, promoting free trade and suggesting that Ed Broadbent was "very, very scary." Other groups entered the fray to protest abortion and nuclear submarines.

But the megadollars gushed on the big issue: free trade. The cost of advertising campaigns by groups for and against the trade deal probably topped $10 million during the campaign. The biggest single spender was the Canadian Alliance for Trade and Job Opportunities, the blue-ribbon corporate lobby leading the business push for the Mulroney trade deal. Before the campaign began, the Alliance spent $2.5 million to promote free trade. It spent a further $2 million during the campaign. Three weeks before polling day, the Alliance published the 4000-word, four-page supplement, "Straight Talk on Free Trade," which appeared in newspapers across Canada.

"Straight Talk" was only the beginning. Mid-election panic at the prospect of a Liberal victory and the death of the free-trade deal loosed an additional torrent of endorsements from groups as diverse as IPSCO steel in Regina, Artists and Writers for Free Trade in Toronto, and The Coal Association of Canada in Vancouver. Estimates of the total cost of the private sector's November advertising splurge range from $4.2 to $5 million. (The *Toronto Star*, flagship of the anti-deal forces, increased its advertising revenue by approximately $550 000, thanks almost entirely to pro-free-trade ads.) Several companies had already embarked on internal lobbying efforts—letters to employees, "educational sessions"—that the NDP's Sears estimates could have cost as much as $4 million over a 14-month period.

On the other side of the debate stood the Pro-Canada Network, the nationalist coalition of 35 unions and women's, cultural, and church groups. Before the election was called, opponents of the trade deal, including the Network and various labour organizations, had nearly matched what the Alliance spent on lobbying. During the election, the Network produced one enormously effective piece of propaganda. Their "What's the Big Deal?" pamphlet, written by the Toronto playwright Rick Salutin and illustrated by the Montreal *Gazette*'s

Aislin, was to "Straight Talk" what a Doonesbury cartoon strip is to a *Business Week* editorial. Hugh Segal admits grimly: "People in our focus groups would parrot lines out of the comic book as straight fact."

But the Pro-Canada Network couldn't match the $8 million onslaught in November from the private sector and the Tory party. The Network's war chest for the election period was only $750 000. After it papered the country with 2.2 million comic books early in the campaign it was broke. Network member Maude Barlow says, "We felt that if we could have got another million comic books out after the TV debates, we could have held the Tories to a minority. But we were forced to peak too early, and then couldn't afford to counter-attack. They outspent us four or five times. Big business bought this election."

But how much impact the "third-party advertising" had during the election remains a point of bitter controversy. There are several reasons for thinking that it was far less effective than Barlow and others claim. Most of the literature produced by the winning pro-free-trade side was like "Straight Talk"—incredibly turgid. When Harry Near saw the four-page newspaper supplement last November, he rolled his eyes. "This is tough sledding!" he groaned. "Who's going to read it?"

Most of the campaign was conducted in newspapers and, according to Professor Fletcher, "Print is an extraordinarily ineffective way of reaching undecided voters, because people only read what reinforces the views they already hold." The sheer volume of the pro-free-trade advertisements probably had impact, but the content was irrelevant. Martin Goldfarb, the Liberal pollster, admits he's not convinced anybody was influenced by them, "though my gut instinct is that the media weight maybe persuaded a few people." Tory insiders insist that they always had a majority government in the palm of their hands. Big business probably wasted a lot of money.

But if the Daddy Warbucks of the private sector didn't buy the election through lobbying, did it win through its generous donations to the Tories? Those on the losing side are happy to suggest that sheer wealth won the public-opinion battles, but the argument is tenuous. The Tories not only had a gold-plated electoral machine; they could also boast a better track record and make a more convincing case. Historian Michael Bliss of the University of Toronto warns: "This time the people with the most money won, but it's pretty naive to assume cause and effect. Advertising is useful if you are selling a good product, but no amount of money can sell a lemon."

There will be noisy debate in the new parliament on reforms to the 1974 Election Expenses Act, which all parties agree are necessary. The issue of how to control lobby-group campaigning will probably dominate discussion, along with other elements of the electoral system that have aroused public indignation—the cost of nominations (where nasty fights erupted for Liberal nominations in Toronto in 1987–88, the price tag on victory was estimated at $50 000 to $100 000), and the "Marcel Masse" loophole on what constitutes a personal expense for candidates.

But "third-party advertising" was only a sideshow in 1988. A much more fundamental problem with the Election Expenses Act was demonstrated last November: the ineffectiveness of its controls on party spending. The controls now verge on legalized hypocrisy. The fundamental principle of Canadian elections—that parties should campaign on a roughly equal financial footing— has been lost. Robin Sears, who was a member of the committee monitoring the implementation of the Act between 1974 and 1981, argues that "the Act is based on the assumption of good faith on the part of the principals. We never antici- pated wholesale, wilful deception."

Controls on "soft spending" won't be a priority for the Conservative govern- ment. But they will be for the two opposition parties which cannot compete with a party rich enough to buy "Romper Room."

The Electoral System: The Laws of Political Science as Applied to the 1988 Federal Election

9

WILLIAM P. IRVINE

Unlike many elections in Canada, the 1988 federal election offered voters a clear policy choice between the government and the official opposition. The Progressive Conservative party, elected overwhelmingly in 1984, campaigned for a mandate to sign the Free Trade Agreement (FTA) which had been concluded with the United States. The Liberal party and the New Democratic party, however, rejected the Free Trade Agreement.

What was predictable was that, despite the fact that the majority of the Canadian electorate was not persuaded of the merits of the FTA, the election did return a parliament in which the FTA had majority support. Political scientists have known for a long time that, with our electoral system, pluralities can almost miraculously be transformed into majorities. More specifically, almost as a law of gravity, we know the following about our plurality electoral system:

1) The leading party is very well-fed—it gains more seats than votes from electors (the Progressive Conservative party received 57 percent of the seats in the House of Commons for 43 percent of the votes).
2) The opposition party is undernourished—it obtains fewer seats than votes from electors (the Liberal party won 28 percent of the seats for 32 percent of the votes).
3) The remaining parties are devastated as far as seats in parliament are concerned—so, if small parties or individual candidates have no cause or doctrine, they don't survive very long. However, with 15 percent of the seats for 20 percent of the votes, the NDP is a first or second party in many parts of the country, but the system worked as predicted for the Libertarian party, the Christian Heritage party, the Reform party and the Rhinoceros party, among other small parties.

An original essay written especially for this volume.

TABLE 1 **Proportion of Votes Obtained by the Three Major Parties in the 1988 Canadian Federal Election**

Province	PC	Liberal	NDP	All Other	Total
Ontario	38	39	20	3	100
Quebec	53	30	14	3	100
Nova Scotia	41	47	11	1	100
New Brunswick	40	45	9	5	99
Manitoba	37	36	21	5	99
British Columbia	34	21	37	7	99
P.E.I.	41	50	7	1	99
Saskatchewan	36	18	44	1	99
Alberta	52	14	17	17	99
Newfoundland	42	45	12		99
Yukon	35	11	51	2	99
N.W.T.	26	41	28	4	99
Canada	43	32	20	5	

TABLE 2 **Seats Obtained by the Three Major Parties in the 1988 Canadian Federal Election**

Province	PC	Liberal	NDP	Total
Ontario	46	43	10	99
Quebec	63	12	0	75
Nova Scotia	5	6	0	11
New Brunswick	5	5	0	10
Manitoba	7	5	2	14
British Columbia	12	1	19	32
P.E.I.	0	4	0	4
Saskatchewan	4	0	10	14
Alberta	24	0	1	26*
Newfoundland	2	5	0	7
Yukon	0	0	1	1
N.W.T.	0	2	0	2
Canada	168	83	43	295*

*one seat vacant

4) There are predictable anomalies in the results. In the Northwest Territories and the Yukon, the Liberal party won two seats, the NDP won one, while the Progressive Conservative party won none. These results were almost the reverse of the overall vote, which was PC 33 percent, the NDP 37 percent, and the Liberals 30 percent; the PCs had under 1 percent less of the valid vote in Ontario than the Liberals, but won three more seats; the PCs did dominate Quebec with 77 percent of the seats, but with only

53 percent of the vote; while the Liberals won only 16 percent of the seats for 30 percent of the vote. The PCs had almost the same vote as the Liberals in Manitoba, but won two more seats.

Free Trade carried in only two provinces: Quebec and Alberta. If this seems unfair, it is predictable in a "first-past-the-post" or "winner-take-all" electoral system. Before the 1984 election, the Liberal governments of Trudeau and Turner were elected mainly by Ontario and Quebec, though the Liberals did have the majority of the seats in New Brunswick and Newfoundland as well. It is an open question whether our electoral system made possible a mass decision. More people, but not a majority, voted for the Progressive Conservatives, but most provinces voted against them.

The results of the 1988 election were typical of past Canadian elections. But did they permit a collective decision that conformed to what we would call democratic norms? In an electoral system rewarding party pluralities, the 1988 Canadian election neither conformed to a democratic decision nor did it overcome regionalism in the Canadian society. Rather, it distorted the democratic norms, and exacerbated the regionalism.

In the past, I have recommended a proportional representation (PR) electoral system similar to the one in the Federal Republic of Germany[1] that would be composed of members of parliament sitting for 60 constituencies. But these might comprise no more than roughly 60 percent of the total members. The remaining 40 percent would be the provincial representatives who would assure proportionality. This would not result in an excessively large legislative body that would overflow the present chamber. In the hypothetical example in Table 3 (page 90), the size of the parliament is exactly the same as now (297), but only 177 of these would be constituency seats; the other 120 would be provincial seats.

To see how this proposal might have worked in 1988, consult Table 3, which simulates the actual results in a PR system with the contests being decided as at present in constituencies comprising 60 percent of the present House of Commons. Clearly, new boundaries would have to be drawn. However, the simulation attributes 60 percent of the seats to each of the parties victorious in 1988. In Alberta, the Progressive Conservative party would possibly have won more constituencies than it would have been entitled to in a PR House. As in Germany, the directly elected members would be entitled to take their seats, and Alberta would have been over-represented by two seats (and the House of Commons would have had to hold 297 members) until the next election.[2]

The allocation of the 120 provincial seats (in Table 3C) would be less arbitrary. The provincial seats would be allocated disproportionately among the parties to offset the effect of the plurality electoral system at the constituency level. The main beneficiary would be the Liberal party, which would have gained 49 of the 120 provincial seats. The NDP would get 36 seats. Of the smaller parties, only the Reform party in Alberta would pass a barrier similar to that erected in Germany to exclude small parties. The barrier assumed in this simulation is that only parties winning at least five percent of the vote in a province would be entitled to

TABLE 3 Simulation of Seats Possibly Obtained under Proportional Representation by the Parties in the 1988 Canadian Federal Election

3A. ALL SEATS

Province	PC	Liberal	NDP	Other	Total
Ontario	39	40	21		100
Quebec	42	23	10		75
Nova Scotia	4	5	1		10
New Brunswick	4	5	1		10
Manitoba	6	5	3		14
British Columbia	11	8	12		31
P.E.I.	2	2	0		4
Saskatchewan	5	3	6		14
Alberta	15	4	4	4	27
Newfoundland	3	3	1		7
Yukon	0	0	1		1
N.W.T.	1	2	1		4
Canada	132	100	61	4	297

3B. CONSTITUENCY SEATS

Province	PC	Liberal	NDP	Total
Ontario	28	26	6	60
Quebec	38	7	0	45
Nova Scotia	3	4	0	7
New Brunswick	3	3	0	6
Manitoba	4	3	1	8
British Columbia	7	1	11	19
P.E.I.	0	2	0	2
Saskatchewan	2	0	6	8
Alberta	15	0	0	15
Newfoundland	1	3	0	4
Yukon	0	0	1	1
N.W.T.	0	2	0	2
Canada	101	51	25	177

3C. PROVINCIAL SEATS

Province	PC	Liberal	NDP	All Other	Total
Ontario	11	14	15		40
Quebec	4	16	10		30
Nova Scotia	1	1	1		3
New Brunswick	1	2	1		4
Manitoba	2	2	2		6
British Columbia	4	7	1		12
P.E.I.	2	0	0		2
Saskatchewan	3	3	0		6
Alberta	0	4	4	4	12
Newfoundland	2	0	1		3
Yukon	0	0	0		0
N.W.T.	1	0	1		2
Canada	31	49	36	4	120

compensatory seats to enhance their parliamentary representation. All other minor parties, such as the Christian Heritage party, would be excluded from the House of Commons. The Progressive Conservative party would have won 31 provincial seats. In Alberta, of course, the Progressive Conservative party would have no seats. It would have four provincial seats in Quebec, the other province where it did disproportionately well.

The main argument *for* our plurality electoral system is that it produces majority governments that can move decisively in new, perhaps necessary, areas of policy. For example, under a PR system Canada could not have ratified a Free Trade Agreement with the United States, even if such an agreement were necessary in a more protectionist world. However, it is not true that our electoral system naturally produces majorities. In fact, the 1984 and 1988 elections were the first two successive majorities since 1949 and 1953.[3]

Given that only a completely proportional electoral system would conform to the democratic norms for collective decision making, would a system of proportional representation have prevented the country from taking a necessary step, that is, from accepting "free trade"? It is worth reflecting on the fact that five of the six countries that formed the original European Community (EC) were countries with proportional representation electoral systems. Of the newer members of the EC, only the United Kingdom has a "first-past-the-post" electoral system like Canada's. To be sure, the 1988 FTA with the United States could not have been enacted had Canada had proportional representation. But what would this mean? Perhaps it would mean only a renegotiated agreement. For the defenders of the FTA, the world is becoming a more hostile one with primary resources losing their place to artificially produced materials, with nations competing to "add value" to manufactured products and supporting the basic science required by dominating a large domestic market, protected against outsiders. If, in such a world, Canada did find itself becoming isolated in a small market in a protectionist world, then any government, whatever its preferences and campaign platform, might be compelled to accept free trade. Would the resulting deal be less favourable to Canada? Would a PR system in Canada in 1988 have induced the country to miss an opportunity? This decision can't be made. We can't know whether a new agreement, negotiated by a coalition government would have been better, worse or even possible. All we could say is that it would have been negotiated by representatives of a majority of the population and by spokespersons of a broader range of interests.

One of the other predictable laws of political science is that two-party systems are natural under the "first-past-the-post" electoral system, and that three (or more) party systems are unstable.[4]

But doesn't Canada have a three-party system, and wasn't it reinforced in the 1988 federal election? Until the 1988 election, Canada had overlapping two-party systems: Liberals versus Progressive Conservatives east of the Ottawa River and Progressive Conservatives versus NDP west of Lake of the Woods. The only multi-party system has been in Ontario. At one point in 1987–88, it seemed that the NDP might establish itself in Quebec and the Liberals might establish themselves in Manitoba. In fact, as William Riker has shown, our electoral system enables a multi-party system to regenerate itself periodically; nevertheless, there is a tendency towards a two-party system.[5] (In fact, the NDP never did establish itself in Quebec: their 1988 vote was about 14 percent, similar to what they had in 1984, and then they elected no MPs.)

Manitoba was different from Quebec, but still in conformity with Duverger's Law (that two-party systems are natural under "first-past-the-post" electoral systems): the Liberals replaced the NDP as the second party. The vote in Manitoba in 1988 was PCs 37 percent, Liberals 36 percent and NDP 21 percent and the 14 Manitoba seats divided 7, 5, 2. Again, the usual pattern re-asserted itself. The Progressive Conservatives were over-represented, the second-place Liberals slightly under-represented and the third-place NDP badly under-represented. So Canada still has two, two-party systems. It used to be more symmetrical: now the Liberals have replaced the NDP as the second party in Manitoba, but Ontario is still the exception. It remains a three-party system in both federal and provincial politics.

As a final point of predictability (also associated with William Riker) there is a *third law*: governments eventually become minimum winning coalitions.[6] The 1984 federal election resulted in a Progressive Conservative government that was oversized: an unwieldy 211 seats in the House of Commons versus a combined opposition one-third that size. Not all members of the government could obtain their preferred policy, play a significant role or hope to obtain a substantial share of patronage. So, deliberately or not, what resulted in 1988 was a much smaller winning coalition: a government of 170 versus a combined opposition of 125.

Prospects for Electoral System Reform

Electoral system reform is important for Canada to assure that collective decisions conform to democratic principles. A proportional electoral system need not have prevented Canada from taking a necessary step (as FTA proponents argued was true for Canada) but might have encouraged a more favourable agreement (as opponents of the FTA argued). However, the prospects for such reform in Canada now seem small.

When such reform was broached in the late 1970s and early 1980s, Canada seemed to have a permanent majority party, whose support was narrowly based, and an opposition party whose support was also narrowly based. The last two elections, however, indicate that this situation has changed, at least as concerns the governing party. Though its majority may be narrowly based (in Quebec and Alberta), its representation is quite broad (the caucus has MPs from all parts of Canada, except Prince Edward Island and the North). Therefore, the problem addressed may have vanished. Moreover, although the reform proposals made the governing party more representative, the proposals also did the same for the opposition parties. In 1990, the government can ask: "Why should we give the opposition parties more seats and make them more representative?"

ENDNOTES

1. William P. Irvine, *Does Canada Need a New Electoral System?* 2nd ed. (Kingston: Queen's University Institute of Intergovernmental Relations, 1980); William P. Irvine, "Reforming the Electoral System," in Hugh G. Thorburn, ed., *Party Politics in Canada*, 5th ed. (Scarborough: Prentice-Hall Canada, 1984), pp. 128–39.
2. In fact, the hypothetical example was designed to parallel the present House of Commons, but the Progressive Conservative near-"sweep" necessitated an enlarging of the House. This occasionally happens in West Germany as well, where it is referred to by the evocative term *überhangsmandat*.
3. For more discussion, see A.C. Cairns, "The Electoral System and Party System in Canada, 1921–65," *Canadian Journal of Political Science*, Vol. 1, pp. 55–80.
4. Maurice Duverger, *Political Parties*, rev. ed., trans. Barbara and Robert North (New York: John Wiley Science editions, 1965), pp. 216–28.
5. William H. Riker, "The Number of Political Parties," *Comparative Politics*, Vol. 6, pp. 93–106.
6. William H. Riker, *The Theory of Political Coalitions* (New Haven: Yale University Press, 1962), chs. 2–4.

Dividing the Spoils: The Old and New Rules of Patronage in Canadian Politics

10

SID NOEL

I

In any era, one of the most nagging problems of political life is to find some dependable means of linking the energies and aspirations of one individual to those of another; to find, in other words, a political cement that is not prone to come unstuck. Virtually everything has been tried, either alone or in combination, from brute force to more subtle forms of psychological coercion, from promises of human betterment to out-and-out bribery and corruption, from appeals to the mystic bonds of race, language or religion to appeals to the pure light of reason. But of all such linkages, from ancient times to the present, from organizations ranging from the Roman *clientela* to the modern political party, by far the most successful and probably the most prevalent has been the relationship of patron and client. It is not the perfect solution, however, because it is not foolproof: its effective use always requires a certain measure of skill, an awareness of potential hazards and, above all, an understanding of the rules, both legal and prudential, which regulate its application. My aim in this essay is to account for its enduring utility in Canadian politics, to trace its adaptation to changing institutional forms and styles of politics and to distinguish the old rules, especially those of a prudential nature, from the new ones which (amid much confusion) appear to be emerging.

Since the terms "patron" and "client" are variously defined it is as well to make clear that I am using them here in their generally recognized anthropological sense to denote roles within society which interact in a particular pattern. The essence of that interaction is a type of reciprocity: an exchange of mutually valued goods and services between those who are in some way unequal. Less abstractly, a patron is typically in a position to bestow upon a client some tangible benefit—

S.J.R. Noel, "Dividing the Spoils: The Old and New Rules of Patronage in Canadian Politics," *Journal of Canadian Studies*, Vol. 22, No. 2 (Summer, 1987). Reprinted by permission of the *Journal of Canadian Studies* and the author. This essay has been edited to suit the needs of this volume.

such as employment or other material reward, or (less tangibly) security, information or the opportunity to profit. In return, a client is typically able to offer loyalty, personal service and acclaim in some context where these are of value to a patron—as in politics, where they may take such forms as fundraising, organizing, campaigning, "getting out the vote" or, at the very least, voting for the patron or the patron's chosen candidate.

Finally, it should be noted that under certain circumstances two-person patron-client linkages ("vertical dyadic alliances") lend themselves readily to incorporation into more complex clientele chains and pyramidal structures in which each patron is also the client of some more powerful patron, with the sole exception being the patron at the very apex. When structures of this kind develop it usually signifies that the state has become the most important, if not the only, source of benefits channelled downward to clients, and political support the most important benefit reciprocally channelled upward. Regardless of how the patron might initially have acquired his role, it then becomes his contacts with those above him in the hierarchy that enable him to sustain it, for it is through those contacts that he obtains access to the scarce public goods that his clients want. And if a measure of representative democracy is present in the state, electoral support inevitably becomes a crucial element in the exchange. Patrons are thus forced to place a high premium on the reliable delivery of the vote, since without it their own positions are in jeopardy; and clients will more readily support a patron who is a reliable provider of the benefits they seek.

The classic example of an instrument designed precisely to foster (and as far as possible, impose) a reliable system of exchange is, of course, the political machine. In Canada, party machines developed soon after Confederation. Their primary focus was upon provincial or federal office, and they were generally more solidly entrenched in rural than in urban areas (though the latter were not neglected).

First, their membership was drawn broadly from all sections of society, native-born as well as immigrant, the upper and middle classes as well as the lower. At the bottom of the hierarchy, cab drivers, saloon-keepers and others in daily contact with the public formed a cadre of essential manpower, but at other levels important roles were often filled by lawyers, notaries and other professionals. At the very top the leader was typically one who had risen out of the latter group or who belonged to a traditional provincial élite. Moreover, the leader invariably held high office himself, being typically the premier of the province or, in some instances, an important federal cabinet minister.

Secondly, they tended to operate exclusively in the political arena. That is to say, they confined themselves almost entirely to electoral objectives and sustained themselves almost entirely on political patronage—in effect, flourishing on the multifold jobs, appointments, contracts, concessions, honours, favours and opportunities that in Canada constituted the more-or-less legitimate spoils of office. While no strangers to payroll-padding, contract-rigging, influence-peddling and various similar misdemeanours, or to vote-buying, treating, personation and other forms of electoral illegality ("there are Canadian experts," wrote André Siegfried in 1906, "who have carried the science of handling votes to a dangerous perfection"),[1] they nevertheless remained remarkably undistracted by the pursuit of criminal sidelines.

In spite of their generally acknowledged prevalence and importance, party machines have received curiously little attention in Canadian political studies. Escott Reid's famous essay, "The Saskatchewan Liberal Machine Before 1929,"[2] first published in 1936, has been more widely cited and reprinted than emulated. The great original prototype—the Liberal machine of Oliver Mowat in Ontario[3]—was built and perfected in the nineteenth century and few refinements were ever subsequently made in it. It served as the model of some of its successors, worked better than any of them, and the rules of patronage it established remained the Canadian standard well into the modern era. The demise of most machines (including its own demise, ironically) resulted from breaking those rules. It is to the rise—and the rules—of the Mowat machine that we must now turn.

II

It should not be surprising that the Canadian party machine developed first in the most populous province, nor that its rise paralleled the progressive extension of the franchise toward universal adult male suffrage. The creation of electorates that were too large to be reliably managed by the old local methods of dyadic clientelism created new and problematic conditions for those intent on the acquisition of political power and, ultimately, new opportunities. At the same time, however, the massive shake-out of patronage that took place at Confederation (with all of the richest spoils falling into the federal maw) had seemingly left the provincial level of politics with too few resources with which to build or sustain a more appropriately complex form of party apparatus.

The critical factor was Oliver Mowat himself. His sudden accession to the premiership in 1872 (at the invitation of a tiny cabal and without an election) was an event of profound importance. It injected into the previously devalued and murkily defined realm of provincial politics a politician of the very first rank: a superb administrator, a clever and tenacious in-fighter, a leader who could inspire fear in his followers, but also confidence and affection. It injected into national politics a new and nominally Liberal force that would soon counterbalance Macdonald's Conservative, Quebec-based federal ascendancy. And above all, it injected into the old political process, with its extreme decentralization, its dependence upon local patron-client ties, its endemic factionalism, and its weakly cemented parliamentary alliances, a new and ultimately transforming instrument: a cohesive, hierarchical party organization that was without peer in the efficient use of patronage. Thereafter Mowat could not be dislodged. He remained premier of Ontario for an unequalled span of 24 years, until 1896, winning election after election. It was not until 1905, long after his departure, that the machine he had built finally disintegrated and went down to electoral defeat. But by then it was ineptly led and rotted with corruption.

How did Mowat build such a machine in the first place, and how did he operate it so successfully for so long?

At the most general level, the answer to both of these questions is the same: through the systematic centralization of power and patronage. Beginning in 1873, with the Municipal Loan Fund Act, there poured forth from his ministry a stream of centralizing Acts and regulations, in such diverse areas as health, education, liquor licensing, and agriculture, which cumulatively amounted to a redefinition of the role of the provincial government. For Mowat, centralization was always justified on grounds of greater administrative efficiency. But it also meant projecting the presence of the Ontario government *directly* and *formally* into the local constituencies on a scale previously unknown. Provincially appointed commissioners, inspectors, agents and trustees multiplied in number, many replacing municipal officials in fields taken over by the province. And all were appointed on a strict patronage basis.

In 1876 legislation was enacted which effectively stripped the municipalities of their longstanding power to license and regulate the sale of alcoholic beverages and transferred jurisdiction to the province. The *number* of such licences that could be granted was restricted by means of a formula based on population (a device Mowat frequently employed). It thus went some way toward mollifying the temperance movement. But note the effects: at a stroke a cadre of loyal Liberal office-holders was created, distributed across the province in careful parallel to the electoral system, who would fill the crucial intermediate positions as the machine expanded to its full pyramidal shape; and liquor licences were turned into valuable assets which the machine controlled. The holders of such assets were thus necessarily placed in a clientele relationship with the Liberal district bosses who filled the commissionerships, with predictable consequences:

> The liquor regulations were tempered to the behaviour of licence-holders. An adequate display of zeal for the Government was a fair guarantee of security when licences were renewed. Inactivity was tolerated. Open rebellion was often punished.[4]

Their ties to the machine, moreover, were further reinforced and placed on a continuous face-to-face basis by a new corps of provincially appointed liquor inspectors (lower level Liberal party operatives) who replaced the local officials who had previously been responsible for the enforcement of liquor regulations.[5]

The basic blueprint of the Mowat machine is thus plain: it was designed specifically to facilitate central control. And the ultimate controller was Mowat himself, whose position as premier was thereby immeasurably strengthened. Unlike earlier premiers (including those under the old regime of the United Canadas), he had no need to bargain in the lobbies of the legislature with capricious independents and local patrons who would never lend more than their conditional or nominal support to any leader. Instead, for the first time, "The most influential Liberals in the Province and the humblest were subject alike to the will of the Premier."[6] The suppression of factionalism was also dramatic, for his pre-eminence in cabinet as in party was beyond challenge.

The expert construction of a machine, however, is no guarantee that it will be expertly driven. As many party leaders since have found, construction is the easy part; the more difficult task is to keep it operating smoothly. In actual practice the administration of patronage is always fraught with peril. Patronage-fuelled machines, especially, are notoriously prone to backfire upon their operators. Therefore, the fact that Mowat was able to manage patronage so effectively for so many years is all the more remarkable, and more difficult to explain. Part of the answer no doubt lies in his fabled prudence and his indefatigable attention to detail; but beyond such personal qualities, which after all were not unique, there lies a more important factor: namely, the modest and sensible rules he instituted to govern its allocation. These were essentially threefold and may be summarized as follows.

1. Do not offend the disappointed.

In the nineteenth century, no less than today, Canadians were keenly interested in patronage. Everyone held some opinion on it. A few were opposed in principle. Many hoped to be among the recipients of it, but since there was never enough to go around, most of the latter were bound to be disappointed. Its use was consequently always open to harsh scrutiny: by those opposed in principle, by party opponents and, not least, by those who believed themselves deserving of reward but who had been passed over. The only group that truly mattered, however, was the latter. The first would suffer offence, and the second feign it, in any case. But the disappointed made up the broad base from which the machine had to draw its future members; they were inclined to be politically active; if they were offended they might very well cross over and work for the other side. It was vital, therefore, to keep them at least grudgingly satisfied. But this was no easy task. To accomplish it a second rule was required.

2. Patronage should be deserved, and seen to be deserved.

While ideally, perhaps, every patronage recipient would be indisputably deserving—a tireless party worker and a paragon of competence and civic virtue—the actual standard inevitably fell somewhat short of the ideal. Yet there was a standard that had to be observed, and it was nowhere more realistically reflected than in the attitude of the disappointed. (They, after all, had the most at stake in seeing that it was observed and that it was not set unrealistically high.) In Ontario there was a line drawn between patronage and corruption that was generally understood and accepted—even if its precise location was often hotly disputed in particular cases. Where the controversy arose was usually over whether this or that individual who had been given a post or other reward was an honest and competent recipient or a mere "boodler." But if there was room for disagreement on *cases* it was at least agreed *in principle* that rewards ought not to be given to corrupt or incompetent party hacks solely on the basis of services rendered—or still less, services claimed or services promised. On this Mowat was adamant, and there were no exceptions. The typical grassroots operation of the machine may be seen in Elgin county:

> James Coyne, after his defeat by Andy Ingram (a Tory) in 1886 became the manager of patronage in the riding until he pulled out a plum for himself: county registrar. Coyne followed very definite criteria in sifting applicants: *capability, proven party service, proven support from party colleagues.* As well he was careful to make a fair distribution across all areas of the riding.[7]

These were not just the Elgin criteria: they applied everywhere across the province. And Coyne's own plum was likewise not his for the picking: it had to be vetted by those above him in the hierarchy.

Then as now, the use of patronage—like the use of alcohol—was constrained not only or even mainly by the law but also by the values of the community. A party machine which offends those values through flagrant abuse or excess is liable to do itself serious and perhaps irreparable damage. One of Mowat's greatest political assets was his sensitivity to those values and his willingness to work always within the limits set by them; he seemed to know instinctively where the boundaries of patronage lay.

3. Do not waste patronage.

It is in the nature of patronage that there is never enough of it, and increasing the supply serves only to increase the demand. Also, the more there is of it the greater the risk that it will get out of control, that the first two rules will be broken. This has been the undoing of many party machines: in the end they become unable to say "No." It was a danger that Mowat understood perfectly, and his efforts to counteract it were as ruthless as they were ingenious.

In general, there are two ways in which patronage may be wasted. The first, which is annoying to party bosses but not publicly offensive, is if those who receive rewards subsequently slack off in their service to the party. A certain amount of this is inevitable, or in some cases (such as high judicial appointments) fully expected and indeed required. But in the awarding of most jobs, contracts, honours and other benefits there is the expectation of continued service, if not of greater service; otherwise the operation of the machine becomes impaired. It begins to suffer from carrying the added weight of "hangers-on." The natural temptation is not to remove them but to try to make the machine strong enough to carry them by making it larger, in spite of the attendant hazards. But this was something that Mowat would rarely do. Equally importantly, it was something he prevented others from doing. For although in the *allocating* of patronage there was a considerable degree of discretion allowed at all levels of the party hierarchy, from cabinet to township secretary, it was he and he alone who controlled the *volume* of patronage flowing through the system. A typical request for additional patronage (even if made to another senior party figure) was therefore likely to end up receiving this typically Mowatian reply:

> Your letter of the 25th June to Mr. Hardy (Provincial Secretary) about new Magistrates has been transferred to me. I find there are already 49 Magistrates . . . for Southwold, or one for every 106 of the population, while the ordinary rule is that of Magistrates acting and not acting one for every 250 is sufficient.[8]

Note the routine invocation of a seemingly impartial formula (without a hint that the "ordinary rule" was in fact of his own devising) and the implicit judgment that province-wide standards ought to prevail over local particularisms.

The second and more serious way of wasting patronage is if those who receive it continue to serve the party but neglect or abuse their official positions. Nothing is more likely to stir public resentment and weaken the machine's ability to deliver the vote; it is also likely to embarrass and discredit the leader. Patronage so expended is wasted, whatever the devotion to the party of the recipient, and can be dangerous. Obviously, since not every appointee or contractor will be blessed with outstanding competence and sterling character, the only way to ensure that acceptable standards will prevail is by rigorous enforcement—and that was a task from which Mowat did not shrink. There was an undeviating insistence that public duties be faithfully and honestly performed, that contractors give value for money, that the party not be embarrassed. This is not to say that there were no infractions—but when they came to light punishment was swift and severe, and the same standard applied at every level.

Mowat was the most systematic, vigilant and original manager of patronage in Canadian politics, and the most successful. No party boss has ever been more effective in ensuring that patronage was used efficiently and productively. In nearly a quarter of a century in the premiership "the little Christian Statesman"—as his more shameless acolytes were fond of referring to him, no doubt to the annoyance of Tories and other skeptics—was never seriously tainted by the whiff of corruption. His model of the political party became, and long remained, the dominant Canadian model; even today its shadow may still be seen in the amorphous and generally ineffectual organizations that have replaced it. But if the Mowat-style machine has largely vanished, patronage has not: it has merely been tapped from different sources, converted to other uses and directed through other channels. And if the old rules are no longer adequate, they are not irrelevant: those who disregard them are still likely to suffer the consequences, as both John Turner and Brian Mulroney may perhaps have discovered.

III

Before attempting to analyse the role of patronage in the modern Canadian political system, there are two persistent myths that must be dealt with. The first is that the progressive professionalization of the bureaucracy (beginning with the federal Civil Service Act of 1917, followed by various imitative provincial acts down to the 1970s) has drastically diminished the spoils of office, thereby devaluing patronage as a motivator and cementer of political organizations. While superficially plausible, in my view neither of these inferences is correct. The confusion, I would argue, stems from concentrating too narrowly on the eradication of what, in the days of machine politics, had been the primary patronage resource—while overlooking the equally obvious growth in the supply of patronage that has taken place in other areas. Indeed, even in the period immediately after 1917 the supply was reduced only at the federal level (with the unintended consequence of greatly enhancing the value of provincial patronage),[9] and in the more recent past it has increased exponentially at both levels. For the well-charted expansion in the size and range of modern government has produced not only a larger professional bureaucracy: as well, both provincially and federally, it has produced a cornucopia of political patronage—patronage so rich and various as to astound a Mowat or a Macdonald.

Some of it comes from the ancillary growth of old sources that, by tacit agreement between the parties, have never been removed from the spoils system: judicial appointments, legal work ($16.4 million in 1985–86),[10] and, above all, the creative enrichment of the contracting process—"personal service" contracts worth as much as $1000 a day, "contract-splitting" to avoid legislated tendering requirements, and (according to the Hon. Ray Hnatyshyn) the "long-standing tradition" that contracts of any kind under $30 000 be exempt from tendering.[11] A confidential Treasury Board report compiled in 1985 (and leaked to the press) estimated that 84 percent of federal government service contracts in the period 1981–84 were awarded without competition.[12] The most dramatic growth of patronage, however, has come from the opening up of new sources, particularly in the ever-expanding realm of quasi-government: in the appointments, perks, per diems, legal and consulting fees, "research" grants, advertising and polling contracts, and a host of similar awards that flow forth from the Crown corporations, agencies, boards and commissions that have so hugely proliferated in the modern era. The most lucrative of these exceed even Senate seats in value (and in some cases rival them in security, through the use of multi-year terms that are legally difficult to terminate). The chairman of Via Rail, for example, receives a salary in the $114 000 to $135 000 range, the chairman of the National Capital Commission between $81 890 and $96 300, members of the Canadian Transportation Commission between $63 230 and $88 930.[13] Others, across an almost infinite range of regulatory, advisory, (allegedly) ameliorative and therapeutic bodies, vary from the Livestock Feed Board (chairman: $63 230–$74 410) to the National Parole Board (full-time members: $58 520–$68 990), and from the Montreal Port Corporation (chairman: $15 000 plus $300 per day) to the National Advisory Council on Aging (members: $100 per day).[14] On top, all receive "expenses" and many receive additional perks (members of the board of Air Canada, for example, receive free passes for unlimited first-class air travel). Some even acquire pension rights.[15] Every province, moreover, has developed an array of new patronage sources of a similar kind—and the more economically developed the province the wider the range and the more lucrative the rewards, with Ontario naturally leading all the rest. The Ontario Conservative party of the period 1943–85 (possibly the last of the province-wide political machines) was largely built and maintained by such means. Finally, it should be noted, the "spin-off" and indirect patronage generated by these sources is also huge, and in some cases may exceed even the value of direct patronage. The overall result has been to put in place a new spoils system that is richer by far than the old.

It is possible, with difficulty, to track the allocation of direct patronage, and even to determine the broad patterns of indirect patronage. Hence, despite the understandably obscurantist tendencies of both patrons and clients, there is really very little mystery surrounding its downward flow. Where the mystery arises is in trying to identify the reciprocal benefits that (supposedly) flow upwards. It is here that a second myth arises: namely, that the shift to "rational" government policy making, with its bureaucratically administered, programmatic outputs, has made patronage unimportant because party organizations no longer have anything to offer in return for it—in other words, they can no longer "deliver the vote." While undeniably half true, this analysis is also misleading. For, even leaving aside the corresponding rise in the phenomenon that I have elsewhere identified as "bureaucratic clientelism" (the taking over by bureaucrats of patron-like roles once occupied by politicians),[16] it is manifestly clear that the decline in the electoral capacities of party organizations has not in fact restricted the flow of patronage: if anything, indeed, it has had precisely the opposite effect.

On the face of it, this is puzzling: why, it must be asked, does so much patronage still go to the support of party organizations? There can be no doubt that the latter have had their usefulness sharply curtailed, perhaps to the point of marginality, by the rise of mass, leader-oriented, television-dominated electoral politics.

Part of the answer, I would suggest, is that the practice of party patronage has long been so pervasive in the Canadian political system, and clientelism so deeply entrenched in the political culture, that it survives out of sheer inertia: that is, in the absence of any more compelling idea, it simply remains the "longstanding tradition" of those who are most intimately involved in the political process—and is reinforced by that process, which continues to revolve overwhelmingly around issues of a basically allocative or distributive nature. There is, after all, no very great separation between such questions as "Who gets the CF-18 contract?" or "Who gets the National Space Agency?" and "Who gets the board of Air Canada?" or "Who gets the chair of Via Rail?" Part of the answer, also, is that the parties, through their televised leadership conventions, play a vital role in the selection, legitimation and presentation of both national and provincial leaders—which compensates to some extent for their loss of electoral efficacy, and accounts for a good deal of the patronage that continues to be directed toward them. At the same time, however, it alters the criteria of reward, since the most valuable services are now performed not for the party as such but for the various leadership candidates. Accordingly, some of the choicest patronage plums are now reserved for those who manage, finance and otherwise support the campaign of the eventual winner (including, when necessary, a campaign to dump the previous leader).

Finally, the decline in the ability of party organizations to deliver the vote does not mean that patronage has lost its effectiveness in the democratic arena. On the contrary, it means only that to be effective it must now be used in different ways, and particularly to create and support new (but supra-party) political organizations that have as their object the influencing of the mass electorate. For the rise of media-dominated politics has brought forth a critical new element in the electoral process which has taken over precisely where the old party machines left off: namely, the patronage-fuelled advertising agencies, polling firms, media consultants and influence brokers whose sole claim to reward is that they—not the party organizations—are now essential instruments in the struggle for political power, that they alone possess the expertise required to mount successful election campaigns. It is from them that party leaders, and those who aspire to be party leaders, now recruit the teams of advisers, fundraisers and campaign designers upon whom they believe their political fortunes rest.

It is not surprising that the growth of this vital, sophisticated and technically advanced "tertiary" sector of the political process has been costly, nor, given the nature of its business, that its rise exactly parallels the growth of government advertising, polling and consulting expenditures, for these are the sources of patronage that above all sustain it.[17] The result has been to inject huge amounts of public money into the opinion-making and opinion-measuring industries, not only at election times but on the steady basis required to sustain large-scale organizations. The federal government has thus become by far the largest single advertiser in Canada, with spending in 1986 of $63.7 million (putting it far ahead of its nearest rivals, Procter & Gamble Inc. at $51.1 million and John Labatt Ltd. at $37.6 million).[18] This vast expenditure is currently allocated through Media Canada, a Conservative-controlled consulting firm (whose own fees, reportedly $125 000 *per month* in 1985,[19] are not included in the above figure), to a network of agencies which serve as national or regional providers of personnel and services to the party and the party leader. Foremost among them is the firm of Camp Associates, which first rose to prominence at the provincial level, mainly through its pathbreaking campaigns on behalf of Premier William Davis in Ontario. It is in many respects the prototypical example of the new supra-party organizations that have since proliferated. In other sub-specialties such firms as Decima Research and Goldfarb (polling) and various "consulting" firms, such as Public Affairs International (lobbying), add their complement to the reservoir of top political talent.[20] The latter, while not averse to direct patronage, thrive especially on the indirect variety through their role as brokers, in effect, receiving money and deference from clients in return for their known connections to the centres of political power. The circularity of the process is nowhere better illustrated than in the case of the government's own Crown corporation, Petro-Canada, which became a client of Government Consultants International (a firm headed by Mr. Frank Moores, a former premier of Newfoundland who is reputedly "a close friend and political adviser to Prime Minister Mulroney")—presumably in order to receive advice on dealing with the government![21]

At the provincial level, too, the most significant development in the use of patronage, at least since the early 1970s, has been the shift toward fostering the growth of the tertiary sector. The provinces, for example, have become major advertisers and employers of pollsters and consultants, with Ontario once again leading all the rest by a wide margin. Its advertising expenditures alone amount to $26 million (putting it only slightly below General Motors and well ahead of McDonald's, Ford and Coca-Cola),[22] while its polling and consulting contracts are of legendary number and generosity. The organization centred on Camp Associates and known as the "Big Blue Machine," which took over the design and management of the Ontario Progressive Conservative party's election campaigns in the 1970s, was pre-eminently the product of this new trend. Residents of that province, at first puzzled, have now become accustomed to periodic floods of agency sustaining "travel" advertising (usually urging them, somewhat redundantly, to "visit Ontario"). Predictably, following the change of government in 1985 this lucrative business was promptly switched to an agency with strong Liberal party connections.[23]

IV

Given the altered environment of patronage in the modern era, the pressures that exist to extend its role beyond traditional party uses, and the attendant hazards, it is evident that the old prudential rules, while still eminently sound, are no longer sufficient. The administration of patronage has never been easy, but the number and extremity of the problems that have plagued every prime minister since Pierre Trudeau—the incessant swirl of scandal, dissention and public uproar that has come to surround its use, the inflation of rewards, the glaring disparity of value between reward and service, the generally nervous handling of it, and the often counter-productive results—suggest that the structural changes which have taken place in the system are so profound as to require a major adaptation in the traditional approach. Are there, then, new supplementary rules of patronage emerging? While as much honoured in the breach as in the observance, the following may be tentatively suggested.

1. Do not offend the media.
There are still certain public standards that governments must observe in awarding patronage, just as in the nineteenth century, only today the true bearers of those standards are not the workers in the party machine: they are the reporters in the media, and above all in television, who have become the dominant providers and interpreters of political information at all levels of the political system. Most strikingly, in 1987 television is the primary source of information on national politics for fully 69 percent of the Canadian public, up from 48 percent less than two decades ago.[24] Governments are now inescapably dependent upon it for the downward projection to the electorate of their images, postures and policies, and increasingly dedicate their patronage resources to the support of organizations whose professional expertise lies precisely in the management of

such matters. Yet, with astonishing frequency, the best efforts of the latter are nullified by the handling of traditional party patronage in a way that takes no account of the media reaction.

The latter, however, is nearly always predictable. A wave of appointments, for example, will be routinely headlined "Mulroney pulls out plums for 54 Tory friends,"[25] while television reporters will bore in with deadly accuracy on the "connections" of those rewarded (the unspoken assumption, communicated none too subtly by inflection and gesture, being that such "connections" are inherently corrupt). It must be stressed, however, that there is no reason to believe that the media either exaggerate the public's curiosity about patronage (which in Canada has always been understandably high) or invent the standards and attitudes which they apply to it. On the contrary, they obviously play to that curiosity and serve as the popular articulators of standards and attitudes that would otherwise remain largely inchoate. The reductionist nature of television reporting, moreover, seems to favour reporters who are adept at projecting "man-in-the-street" attitudes. There is now no piece of patronage in the government's gift that is worth the risk of incurring their displeasure.

How, then, can their displeasure be avoided, or at least neutralized? The experiences of recent governments suggest some possible answers. First, the awarding of patronage in monsoon-like torrents is in itself offensive: a great deal of the media's reaction to the Mulroney government's handling of it, for example, has been provoked by the habit of releasing it in this inexplicable fashion. (It is possible only to speculate on the reasons. One possible suggestion is that the elaborate network set up to dispense it—which itself consisted of patronage appointees—was too cumbersome and inept. This was perhaps Mr. Mulroney's conclusion, since it was eventually dismantled.)[26] In contrast, the Peterson government in Ontario has gradually and unobtrusively sifted out the remnants of the old Conservative machine from the province's array of agencies, boards and commissions and inserted its own appointees. Care has been taken to announce appointments singly or in small batches, to spread the rewards widely among ethnic groups, to avoid the appearance of favouring the premier's personal friends, and to allocate a few well-publicized plums to party opponents.[27] The result has been a notable absence of offence or even comment by the media.

Second, there have now been enough cases to suggest at least the hypothesis that patronage awarded to members of the media generally causes less offence than patronage awarded to others. For example, the extraordinary organization built up by former Liberal minister Lloyd Axworthy, both in the Department of Transport in Ottawa and in his home riding in Winnipeg, largely through advertising, public relations and other "personal service" contracts, was distinguished by its employment of former journalists in key roles; it functioned without attracting unfavourable media attention until, *ex post facto*, the incoming Conservatives (purporting to be "shocked and offended") decided to make an issue of its allegedly lavish size and overspending.[28] More recently, no appointment of the Mulroney government has provoked less hostility or even notice than the appointment of Bruce Phillips, a former Ottawa bureau chief of CTV (and a waspish critic of patronage), to a position first in the Canadian Embassy in Washington and subsequently in the Prime Minister's Office.[29] In Ontario, in proportion to their number in the population, probably no other group has been as showered with honours and rewards by the Peterson government as the media, from owners and directors to reporters,[30] and all without arousing a whisper of controversy. If the hypothesis stated above is correct, governments in future might find that starting out with a similar priority in patronage allocation will significantly diminish the later risks.

2. Maximize the symbolic value of patronage.

One of the most paradoxical trends in modern patronage is the seemingly irrational weakening of the connection between performance and reward. Thus, to take but the most conspicuous example, the heads of the major political advertising agencies are understandably given the highest rewards that their patrons can bestow (Senate seats, for example, are normally theirs for the asking), but—incomprehensibly to those who still view patronage in old-fashioned machine terms—so too are clients whose services are undistinguished or even trivial. From Senate seats to Citizenship Court judgeships, at every level of the patronage system, a bizarre capriciousness now seems to prevail. It is not, however, an altogether accidental outcome.

The only place where the proven record of service that was once so important to party machines remains important is in the tertiary sector, for the management of both leadership and election campaigns has become too technically complex to be entrusted to any but the ablest and most experienced specialists—who are invariably well-rewarded. Elsewhere, by contrast, the careful balancing of reward against service that so preoccupied the old machines is now virtually pointless and has been all but abandoned. The effect, startlingly accelerated by Pierre Trudeau, has been to convert the bulk of the old clientele system to a variety of new uses as leaders struggle to find some reciprocal benefit to justify its continued existence and compensate for its extravagant cost. Their efforts have been erratic, but two main thrusts may nevertheless be discerned. These are, first, the return to a simpler, more straight-forward, basically pre-Confederation form of dyadic clientelism, built upon friendship, and manifesting itself institutionally in the creation of personal entourages and information networks; and second, the disposition to use patronage for calculatedly symbolic purposes, the object being to disarm critics and to create a favourable climate of opinion, mainly (but not exclusively) among ethnic groups.

Every recent government, federal and provincial, has to some extent followed both approaches, but each has usually shown a clear preference for one or the other (except for Mr. Trudeau's, which fluctuated rather wildly between them). Of those favouring the first approach there are a few successful examples, notably the governments of Peter Lougheed in Alberta and William Davis in Ontario, but the experiences of the first Bourassa government in Quebec, the last Trudeau government, and the Mulroney government all suggest that it leads too often to the breaking of new Rule One (see above). The case of the Mulroney government is particularly instructive, for in many respects it has followed the first approach in exemplary fashion—only to bring down upon its head a truly spectacular barrage of criticism. It would appear, therefore, that although friendship as the basis of patronage is hardly new, it has come to be seen as tasteless, or even a *cause de scandale*, and hence counter-productive.

On the other hand, the experiences of the first Trudeau government, the Levesque and second Bourassa governments in Quebec, and the Peterson government in Ontario all suggest that there is more to be gained by the symbolic approach. Even Mr. Mulroney's limited use of it, as in his appointment of former Ontario NDP leader Stephen Lewis as Ambassador to the United Nations, has been effective (even if somewhat compromised by a too-hasty reversion to the first approach). But it is undoubtedly the Peterson government that has extracted the maximum value from patronage of this kind. Its well-timed handing out of plums to former Conservative minister Robert Elgie (appointed chairman of the Worker's Compensation Board) and former NDP leader Donald C. MacDonald (appointed chairman of the Commission on Election Expenses)[31] stifled both opposition and media criticism and bolstered its image as a fresh alternative to the previous regime. It also allowed the more normal distribution of patronage to proceed in an atmosphere remarkably free of suspicion.

Maximizing the value of patronage used to curry favour with ethnic and other minority groups, however, which in the Trudeau era was relatively easy, is now problematical and potentially a minefield. The theory is that each client so favoured will, in effect, act as a surrogate; that is, if an Italian or Greek Canadian, for example, is given a patronage post the other members of his or her respective community will also be duly grateful. Typically, in such cases the patron-client bond is weak, since it is not the old criterion of proven party service that counts; rather it is the client's symbolic worth. But as long as the symbolism is genuine—that is, as long as the community in question responds favourably to the awarding of patronage to one of its members—the return on the investment of such patronage is generally quite high.

The trouble is, the theory is beginning to break down, mainly because Canadian minority groups have grown too diverse, and in some cases too well-established and well-informed, for any one approach to work for all. In consequence, the opportunities for disaster have multiplied—as the recent problems in the distribution of Citizenship Court judgeships, for example, make only too clear.[32] These used to be low-risk, high-return pieces of symbolic patronage, and indeed were probably invented specifically for this purpose, but now they have acquired a double-edged symbolism—and the wrong edge can cut sharply (as the Mulroney government has no doubt discovered). The problem lies not just in the filling of some of these posts with egregious partisans, although that has certainly contributed, but also in what such posts themselves have come to symbolize: namely, that members of minority groups are given some types of patronage but not others—ersatz judgeships but not real ones, the Citizenship Court but not the Federal Court. Symbolic patronage is still potentially productive, but to maximize its value in such circumstances is no easy task.[33]

3. Do not mix patronage with pork-barrelling.

Observers have always been struck by the relentlessly distributive nature of Canadian politics. Occasionally some non-distributive issue may briefly rise *fortissimo*, but it is the ongoing clatter of competing regional, provincial and local interests over the allocation of government benefits that remains the national political *obbligato*. As André Siegfried put it, exaggerating only slightly, "In the absence of ideas or doctrines to divide the voters, there remain only questions of material interest, collective or individual."[34] Today the debate over such questions is likely to be cloaked in the language of programmes, projects, incentives to development or equalization and other similarly thin veils of bureaucratic neutrality, but the essence of the matter is still "Who gets what?" Or, expressed less crassly, perhaps: "Which city (province, region) gets Project A and which Project B, and what is the value in jobs and other benefits of each?"

For a government to make such allocations with a view to maximizing its electoral support is, of course, the familiar practice of pork-barrelling. The theory is that local communities will respond favourably to diffuse rewards: for example, a national defence contract for a local industry, a new prison, a new wharf, a high technology research centre, a subsidy for a faltering steel mill, a development grant for this, a modernization programme for that, and so on. While some individuals will profit more directly than others (for instance, through jobs, subcontracting, professional fees, or real estate sales), the subsidiary benefits are supposed to trickle into the community at large and produce a general firming up of electoral support for the government. It may also have the valuable supplementary effect of enhancing the government's image of being actively concerned with the welfare of local communities, of not just talking but of "doing things"— of "jobs, jobs, jobs."[35] Little wonder, therefore, that ministers and government members are anxious to attach themselves to the distributive process, even in cases where they have had little or nothing to do with the actual decision making or where the amounts are small. Provincially there appears to be no minimum, with even minor lottery fund awards being subject to political attachment, while federally the general rule is for MPs to be given advance notice of all contracts over $100 000 awarded in their constituencies (though with some exceptions: in six Conservative constituencies in eastern Quebec the current minimum is $25 000.[36]

In spite of its popularity, however, pork-barrelling (and the appearance of pork-barrelling) can be politically hazardous. It is most obviously effective when the allocation of a particular piece of pork is approvingly noted in the recipient community and either passes unnoticed outside it (a condition likely to obtain if, for instance, enough similar pieces are spread around to make any one piece seem unremarkable) or, if noticed, can be plausibly defended as being "in the national interest." But if for any reason these conditions do not obtain, the whole process easily becomes self-cancelling. Thus, to be perceived as acting without due regard for the "national interest" (which, though a fairly elastic concept, can be stretched only so far) is to lose more support than can possibly be gained.

But by far the commonest danger of pork-barrelling arises from the adding of patronage to form a highly volatile mixture—for example, by using the side-benefits produced by a project to reward party supporters. The result is often an explosion of community dissension, hostile inquiries by the opposition and the national media, and even, in certain circumstances, police investigations and criminal charges. For the use of pork-barrel projects as patronage resources is not, it must be stressed, the same as using such legal and system-sanctioned resources as the boards of Crown corporations and regulatory agencies or government advertising contracts. The rewards are far too likely to be covert or illegal: it is to risk crossing the line between patronage and corruption.[37]

Yet in spite of the risk, and in spite of what must be the implacable resistence of party leaders to the treating of pork-barrel projects in such a fashion, it continues undeterred. It is also, on the whole, a more serious problem at the federal level than the provincial—which, again, should not be considered an accidental outcome. One of the reasons the federal patronage structure is so unstable is that over the years it has grown increasingly top-heavy, an army with more generals than privates. The rewards have grown richer but are concentrated at the national level in great indivisible lumps, a situation made worse by the practice of awarding long-term appointments (a 10-year stint on the Canadian Transportation Commission, for example, can be worth upwards of a million dollars in salary and benefits). At the same time, the supply of reasonably rewarding and legitimate federal patronage at the local level has been drastically reduced, with the best of it being confined to the legal profession, even though the number of claimants shows no sign of diminishing. In these circumstances it is perhaps not surprising that pork-barrel-related patronage remains irresistibly tempting. Yet if it is not checked pork-barrelling itself, the most time-honoured of all the distributive principles of Canadian government, will inevitably be threatened. Not just its effectiveness but its very survival depends upon a stricter separation between the two. Mr. Mulroney's severe treatment of alleged offenders in the Oerlikon affair is perhaps indicative of how seriously this rule is now taken.[38]

V

In any era, the prudential rules of patronage will be evident in the behaviour of those political actors who are in a position to measure the gains and losses arising from its use. But their experience will necessarily be conditioned by the surrounding political environment: the size and composition of the electorate, the relative effectiveness of local organization versus mass communication, and, in general, the legal and ethical standards, and popular expectations concerning patronage, which prevail in the society at large.

For approximately the first century of Confederation the party machine had a clear utility, and patronage was undoubtedly the most effective means of building such an instrument and holding it together. The Mowat machine, for example, was deliberately structured upon a broad base of local appointees and was thus well integrated into the social and economic fabric of nineteenth-century

Ontario. Its operatives at all levels were subject to scrutiny and discipline from those immediately above them in the hierarchy, and ultimately from the premier; there were performance criteria that had to be met, and which could be measured; and punishments in the form of firings and demotions were as much a part of the system as rewards. On the whole, it possessed remarkably few rich plums—but it did possess a sufficient supply of lesser ones to support a pyramidal organization with appropriate rewards at every level. While not a perfect reflection of Ontario society, it was nevertheless fairly representative: the rewards it offered were not beyond the reach of ordinary citizens who wished to become activists in the political process; and it was possible to start at the bottom and rise through the ranks.

There are still a few surviving remnants of old-style machine organizations, but their presence in the modern political system is incidental, a mere curiosity: the form itself is dead. Hence the extraordinary chaos in the Canadian administration of patronage during the last quarter of a century: a new system was struggling to be born.

What has emerged is now reasonably clear, and is perhaps best described as a form of "élite clientelism." Huge and rich though the clientele system has become, ordinary citizens now have few significant points of entry into it, for the simple reason that their services are no longer required. And insofar as they continue to perform certain minor services in the expectation of reward—for example, in party organizations, or as the foot-soldiers and banner carriers in leadership campaigns—they may well have become a nuisance. Or, when they expect the pork-barrel to provide them with rewards, they are unquestionably a menace (see new Rule Three above). The points of entry are now restricted for the most part to members of the political élite and the business and professional classes, with a sprinkling of others who are believed to possess valuable reputational or symbolic qualities (see new Rule Two above). The expectations of such appointees, however, are inevitably high: hence the progressive enrichment and concentration of patronage sources at the top, creating, in effect, an inverted pyramid.

Such a structure is manifestly less representative of Canadian society than the old machines, and many times more costly. But it is also manifestly better adapted to the maintenance of strong supra-party organizations and entourages, with their skill and experience in the use of the mass media and their emphasis on the professional management of the political process. What remains to be seen is whether it is not also too unstable, too lacking in reciprocity, and too divorced from the mass of the people not to topple over at the first stiff democratic breeze that blows.

ENDNOTES

1. A. Siegfried, *The Race Question in Canada*, Carleton Library Edition (Toronto: McClelland and Stewart, 1966), p. 128.

2. *Canadian Journal of Economics and Political Science,* Vol. 2 (Feb. 1936), pp. 27–40, and reprinted in the first, third and fourth editions of Hugh G. Thorburn, ed., *Party Politics in Canada.*

3. See S.J.R. Noel, *Patrons, Clients, Brokers: Ontario Society and Politics, 1791–1896* (Toronto: University of Toronto Press, 1990), pp. 275–93.

4. Sir John Willison, *Reminiscences Personal and Political* (Toronto: McClelland and Stewart, 1919), p. 93.

5. There is some suggestion that vestiges of this system still survive a century later. In 1985 David Peterson, then Leader of the Opposition, complained that "Ontario's liquor licence inspectors have been pressing restaurant and tavern owners to contribute money to the Conservative Party." He also alleged that even the clerks in the retail outlets "have to go through Tory riding presidents to get their jobs" (*The Globe and Mail,* 19 April 1985).

6. J.E. Middleton and F. Landon, *The Province of Ontario: A History 1615–1927* (Toronto: Dominion, 1927–28), Vol. 1, p. 447.

7. Barbara A. McKenna, "Farmers and Railwaymen, Patronage and Corruption: A Volatile Political Mix in Turn of the Century Elgin County," *Ontario History,* Vol. LXXIV, No. 3 (September 1982), p. 225 (italics added).

8. University of Western Ontario, *Coyne Papers,* Mowat to J.H. Coyne, 29 September 1888.

9. See John English, *The Decline of Politics: The Conservatives and the Party System, 1901–1920* (Toronto: University of Toronto Press, 1977), pp. 222–29.

10. *The Globe and Mail,* 2 September 1985.

11. *London Free Press,* 17 May 1986.

12. *Toronto Star,* 21 January 1985. Later, Public Works Minister Roch LaSalle released figures showing that the figure for all contracts under $30 000 was "about two-thirds." According to Canadian Press calculations the figure is "about 70 percent," but with wide regional variations, with the Ottawa-Hull area leading the nation at 96 percent (*London Free Press,* 26 June 1986).

13. *The Globe and Mail,* 4 September 1985.

14. *Ibid.*

15. When Mr. Bryce Mackasey, briefly chairman of Air Canada, was fired by the incoming Clark government in 1979, it was revealed that he had acquired a pension right to $25 000 a year (*The Globe and Mail,* 4 August 1984).

16. S.J.R. Noel, "Leadership and Clientelism," in David J. Bellamy, *et al., The Provincial Political Systems* (Toronto: Methuen, 1976), pp. 197–213.

17. For an invaluable account of the early growth of political advertising agencies see Reginald Whitaker, *The Government Party* (Toronto: University of Toronto Press, 1977), pp. 216–63.

18. *London Free Press,* 24 March 1987. These figures are compiled by Media Measurement Services Inc. of Toronto, and are here rounded to the nearest decimal.

19. The nation, however, is now receiving a bargain. The Liberal firm it replaced took a commission of $144 000 per month (*The Globe and Mail,* 24 January 1985).

20. See Jeffrey Simpson, "How Old Pols Turn a Profit," *The Globe and Mail Report on Business Magazine* (October 1985).

21. *The Globe and Mail,* 27 December 1985. This was apparently too much for Mr. Mulroney; he shortly thereafter ordered all Crown corporations to cancel such contracts. This, however, was interpreted by Mr. Mulroney's assistant press secretary to mean that Petro-Canada could still hire Mr. Moores' firm "as long as it is not being used to lobby the federal government" (*The Globe and Mail,* 7 January 1986).

22. *London Free Press*, 24 March 1987.

23. *The Globe and Mail*, 19 December 1985. The agency awarded the contract is Vickers and Benson. The Chairman of the Management Board claimed a saving of $471 000 and denied that political affiliation had played any part in the decision of the Advertising Review Board.

24. *The Globe and Mail*, 26 March 1987.

25. *London Free Press*, 27 December 1986.

26. *Ibid.*, 6 March 1986.

27. *The Globe and Mail*, 2 January 1987.

28. *Ibid.*, 4 December 1984.

29. *Ibid.*, 13 March 1987.

30. Eric Dowd, "Peterson Master at Recruiting Media," *London Free Press*, 27 June 1986.

31. *The Globe and Mail*, 7 September 1985; *London Free Press*, 1 May 1986.

32. "The long-standing quiet tradition of judgeships for party supporters has become an embarrassment for the Conservative Government, which was particularly directing the largesse toward loyalists in the ethnic communities but has been embarrassed by accusations of blatant bias or incompetence among some of its recent appointees" (*The Globe and Mail*, 12 January 1987).

33. The problem is particularly acute in Metro Toronto. The Conservative Metro Caucus has prepared a report complaining that the party's "stated objective" for Metro patronage appointments "of 30 percent women and 20 percent from ethno-cultural backgrounds is not being met. . . ." It goes on to identify the reciprocal benefit that should be the aim of such a distribution: "Ethno-cultural communities must be made to understand precisely why they should give their ballots to the Government rather than to the Opposition" (*The Globe and Mail*, 9 October 1986).

34. A. Siegfried, *The Race Question in Canada*, Carleton Library Edition (Toronto: McClelland and Stewart, 1966), p. 113.

35. Even then, there are no guarantees. When Port-Cartier, in Mr. Mulroney's riding of Manicouagan, was favoured with a new federal prison, the mayor's response was hardly an outpouring of gratitude: "All he gave us was this stupid prison . . . I'd rather have 220 Ph.D.s in my area than 220 inmates. I asked for a military base or research centre" (*The Globe and Mail*, 31 October 1986).

36. *London Free Press*, 5 March 1987.

37. Kenneth M. Gibbons defines pork-barrelling itself as a type of corruption, but to do so is to blur an important legal (and popularly perceived) distinction. See Kenneth M. Gibbons and Donald C. Rowat, eds., *Political Corruption in Canada* (Toronto: Carleton Library, McClelland and Stewart, 1975), pp. 9–10.

38. *The Globe and Mail*, 19–24 January 1987. For an account of the local dissension provoked by the affair see the *Toronto Star*, 25 January 1987.

The Functioning Party System

This section examines the dominant elements of the political party structure in Canada: the ways in which parties relate to one another to form a party system, the ideological bases of the major parties and the interests they stand for, the élites they relate to, the choosing of party leaders, the regional dimension and, finally, the dysfunctions of parties. The picture emerges of a liberal, business-oriented society composed of large bureaucratic structures that have grown ponderous, complex and unresponsive. Interest groups that once dominated have grown increasingly frustrated as they observe the parties they influence fumbling with the new and complex issues that confront government. Overwhelmed by fiscal crisis, chronic unemployment and threatening inflation, the political parties soldier on, unable to deal effectively with mounting problems. The federal system and electoral arrangements combine to sustain this situation. However, recent developments suggest a decline in the salience of parties themselves, as society grows more bureaucratic and complex. Important decisions tend to be made by the prime minister and his coterie in consultation with senior bureaucrats and interest-group representatives. The amateur politician is becoming a "thing of the past."

11 Interpretations of the Canadian Party System

HUGH G. THORBURN

Over the years the Canadian party system has been interpreted in innumerable ways by many observers: party activists, historians, political scientists, sociologists, journalists and interested laymen. Most have been casual, simplistic views, but a few have been stimulating and insightful interpretations. Of the significant analyses, two basic approaches stand out. One sees the system shifting around a basic norm of two rather similar parties. This is examined first under the title "The Two-Party System." The other, which sees the norm as one dominant party with other parties jostling about it, is discussed under "One-Party Dominance."

The Two-Party System

Tories versus Reformers

The oldest perception of the Canadian party system dates back to the early nineteenth century colonial period when our forebears struggled over responsible government. This dispute was most clearly fought out in Upper and Lower Canada, where it culminated in rebellion. The governmental system relied upon the British governor for leadership and control and he, in turn, worked through a small élite of placemen or patronage appointees and privileged economic and social leaders assembled into the Executive Council of the colony. The Legislative Council or upper house also included most of the same Tory faces of the governing clique. The government was a highly restricted power monopoly, which no doubt was acceptable to those of conservative and loyalist mind who feared the rise of popular power lest it lead to revolution. However, many of the excluded people resented their situation and they elected members to the Legislative Assembly who were pledged to reform. In these early days before responsible government was conceded, there was a political party system in embryo, which was to grow into the two-party system of the post-Confederation period.

This is a revised and updated version of the essay that appeared in the previous edition of this book.

At first the governor, most conspicuously Sir Francis Bond Head of Upper Canada, openly campaigned against the reformers, thereby putting the state apparatus, including the crown, on one side of a political dispute. The reformers were then led to rebel not only against the Family Compact but also against the governor and the imperial system for which he stood. Therefore the demands of the reformers took on a seditious appearance, and open armed rebellion, albeit on a small scale, was the result. While the rebels were easily scattered, the British government sent Lord Durham ("Radical Jack", as he was familiarly known in England) to investigate the affairs of British North America. Lord Durham recommended responsible government for the colonies, which would mean the governor would take advice from his council only so long as it was supported by a majority in the assembly, and the combining of the two colonies of Upper and Lower Canada into one to assure an overall British majority.

Once responsible government was conceded, the governor was largely removed from the political arena, leaving the politicians to settle matters between themselves. While different groups appeared in the assembly of the United Province of Canada and in the other colonies, the basic division between Tories and Reformers of earlier times remained in the minds of all as the basic touchstone of political distinction.[1] When the party system settled down to the classic Anglo-Saxon two-party dichotomy after Confederation, this older distinction between the parties was not forgotten: the Liberals continued to remind the electorate of their heroic antecedents and depicted the Conservatives as the successors of the Tories of the Family Compact and the Château Clique. One still encounters this interpretation of the party system, especially from Liberal campaign orators, long after it has lost all relevance to Canadian political life.

The Ins versus the Outs

The most widely accepted of the older interpretations of the Canadian party system is the one which sees two similar parties, each seeking to appeal to the many interests, classes, regions and ethnic groups that make up the country. The parties are depicted as Tweedledum versus Tweedledee, the Ins versus the Outs: two brokerage parties or teams of office-seekers who rival one another in mounting and presenting programmes calculated to attract the support of a majority of the electorate. Alexander Brady describes the relationship:

> Each party is loosely attached to formal attitudes and ideas, and is supported by the social groups and regions which, out of long habit or temporary interest, favour the stand taken. . . . Within a decade the parties may unblushingly interchange programmes. Sir John Williston wrote out of an extensive if cynical knowledge of Canadian affairs that "no man in Canada has been more inconsistent than the man who has faithfully followed either political party for a generation." This circumstance derives inexorably from the internal necessity of the parties to make a universal appeal, to dramatize the fact that they stand for a synthesis of interests within the nation, and to alter their programme with the shifts of opinion throughout the country. As one party or the other manoeuvres into a fresh position, the partisan

battleground changes. The leaders who succeed in making the widest national appeal are those who rule. This is the bedrock of democratic politics in a country constituted like Canada. From it there can be no escape as long as the parties seek to win office by the liberal procedure of debate and persuasion.[2]

Professor Brady admitted that the parties had their differences, especially in their traditional supporters. "The social groups least interested in close relations with the United States are most commonly Conservatives; those least sympathetic to an imperial outlook are usually Liberals."[3] He cited Lord Bryce approvingly: "In Canada ideas are not needed to make parties, for they can live by heredity and, like the Guelfs and Ghibellines of Medieval Italy, by memories of past combats."[4]

One can discern a mixture of two interpretations in Brady and the other prewar writers on the two-party system:[5] a system of two identical parties, totally devoid of theory, that alter their policies like shopkeepers changing their window displays; and a system of a liberal or progressive party versus a conservative or traditional one that exchange office as the mood of the country shifts, from, for example, optimism to pessimism, imperialism to continentalism, free trade to protectionism. In the latter case, each party has a traditional rhetoric and engages in opportunistic posturing (which often contradicts its theory) in the scramble to out-manoeuvre its rival. These two interpretations are vastly different, but there is much evidence in the history of the Liberal and Conservative parties to support each of them. Most casual observers have settled for a mixture of both as the best explanation of the two old parties and most academic observers start with this as the basic set of assumptions from which subsequent refinements can be drawn.

The Shifting National Mood Theory

Professor J.R. Mallory sees the parties as the Ins versus the Outs; yet he explains:

What is important is that at any given time only one party is in tune with a national mood—and that party is likely to stay in power until the mood changes and leaves it politically high and dry. Macdonald was, in his way, the perfect expression of the national spirit in the nineteenth century—raffish, careless, tough and pliable. Laurier expressed the character of the new Liberal Party which he was able to create out of what had been merely a series of doctrinaire and local provincial parties. Laurier combined an elegant and eloquent idealism with the embodiment of a spirit of compromise—of healing the scars of conflicts of race, religion and region which had grown up since the seventies. The time came when much of the glamour of the Liberal position wore off, when compromise appeared merely the inaction of old, tired men in office. The earnest, precise Borden represented the reaction in a time of deep national trial. Again, Mackenzie King, with his earnest preaching about the virtue of conciliation, represented the tortured doubts of an age of national frustration; when constitutional difficulties, the baffling new problems of an industrial age and a shattered world combined to create an atmosphere of cautious despair. With Louis St. Laurent a new look came to the Liberal Party: tough-minded, bland, sophisticated and confident in managing a growing society bursting at the seams with growth. But mere prosperity and competent government is not enough. There is plenty of evidence that the pace of modern living produces a host of frustrations and a mixture of guilt and insecurity. Into this atmosphere was skillfully projected the personality of John Diefenbaker, solemnly intoning evangelical phrases about a national vision and a national dedication. It does not matter whether these 'thoughts' have much meaning—they did catch a mood.[6]

Interest Group Theory

This interpretation suggests that major interest groups, particularly business, are largely determinant in the formulation of policies of the major parties, especially when in office.

Professor Frank Underhill was the Toronto historian who provided much of the intellectual backing for the early CCF, but who later served as the curator of Laurier House, where Mackenzie King lived, and where his memorabilia are kept.

In a well-known article, Underhill wrote:

The real function of the two-party system since the Laurier era has been to provide a screen behind which the controlling business interests pull the strings to manipulate the Punch and Judy who engage in mock combat before the public. Both parties take for granted that their first duty in office is to assist the triumphant progress of big business in the exploitation of the country's resources. . . . A party system which depends for success (i.e. for office) upon the different and often contradictory appeals which it must make to different sectional interests will inevitably in course of time become mainly dependent upon and responsible to those interest groups which are themselves best organized and most strategically located for applying effective pressure upon party leaders. In Canada there are two such groups who have always held a dominating position in our politics because of their superior internal organization—the French Catholic Church in Quebec and the interlocking financial, industrial, commercial interests which we usually refer to nowadays as big business. . . . Big business depends primarily upon campaign contributions, also upon constant official and unofficial lobbying, and upon the complex economic and social relationship between business and political leaders.[7]

With the increasing costs of modern elections, the parties are becoming more dependent upon wealthy interests for funds to finance the campaigns, which in turn rely more on costly image-building in the media than on rational argument. While the public benefits from a modern social security system, the corporate interests have retained much of their influence, although deepening problems are preventing governments from responding as they used to in prosperous times. The largest and most dynamic sector of the business community is under foreign control, and this makes the previously harmonious relationship of élite accommodation between business and government more difficult. Foreign head offices find their interests more likely to clash with Canadian governmental priorities, leading at times to plant closures and the shifting of production out of Canada. Since both leading Canadian political parties have long-standing relationships with the major business interests, they now find themselves torn between this loyalty and the pull of events suggesting policies that some of these interests will oppose. Even the third party, the NDP, is caught in a cross-fire between the international trade union movement which, since its founding in the early 1960s, has provided much of its funding and campaign workers, and the recently expanded, purely Canadian unions based mainly in the public service sector.

The Two-and-a-Half Party System

A more contemporary interpretation takes the minor parties, and particularly the radical CCF-NDP, into account. This party's spokesmen accept the Tweedledum versus Tweedledee theory and see the NDP as the party offering the only real alternative to the Canadian people. This view holds that the Liberals and Conservatives are the agents of the giant corporations and that the NDP is the voice of the people struggling to be heard over the din of the old parties expensive advertising campaigns.[8] T.C. Douglas has argued that both old parties are "committed to maintaining our present unregulated and unplanned economy"[9] with consequent poor economic performance and the permitting of the takeover of the Canadian economy by giant U.S.-controlled corporations. Solutions to the nation's unemployment problem that might adversely affect business are ruled out.[10] The NDP has come to a more nationalistic position than the others because of its opposition to big business, which in Canada is largely controlled from abroad.

Essentially this interpretation seeks to convert the Tweedledum versus Tweedledee party system into one in which the two old parties merge into one defender of big business while the NDP takes up the position of advocate of the "ordinary Canadian"—a familiar analogy is the Conservative versus Labour situation which prevails in Great Britain.

There is an important consequence of the working of this system. If the two brokerage parties monopolize office and the official opposition, the reformers and persons with new ideas will tend to be drawn off to the NDP and other minor parties, where they have virtually no chance of participating in government. Therefore the implementation of reforms is even more remote than if reformers had to remain in the two omnibus parties, although the public agitation for reform will be substantial. People will therefore be led to expect changes that are not forthcoming—a situation that is bound to engender frustration and cynicism among the electorate.

In addition, the NDP (unlike its predecessor, the CCF) is not a pure party of reform. It depends heavily for financial and other support on one of the vested interests of the country, the Canadian Labour Congress (CLC), and is therefore in many ways a conservative force.[11] This fact is enhanced by its affiliation, or rather that of its member unions, with the American labour movement, the AFL-CIO. The importance of this connection was especially obvious at the time of the leadership conventions at both the federal and Ontario levels in the early 1970s. Then, with the separation of the Canadian Auto Workers Union (CAW) from its U.S. parent, the United Automobile Workers, and the rise to prominence of CAW leader Bob White in NDP leadership circles, the party came to be identified with both Canadian and international unions.

A less partisan variant of this theory is that since the two old parties offer so little choice to the disenchanted elector, the third parties supply the needed breadth of choice. Professor Mallory argues:

> The innovator role is explained by the state of monopolistic competition which confronts major political parties—similar to that facing the industrial giants which produce soap or motor cars. Like them, the parties adhere to the principle of minimum differentiation of the product, warily peddling the same set of ideas and policies which have worked for them in the past. They are disposed to be afraid of new ideas, for fear of making costly mistakes which may lose support they already have, without making compensating gains.
>
> Third parties, with nothing to lose, can afford to experiment with new ideas, for ideas are the only working capital they have. In the process the public will be gradually educated to an awareness of the need for a new policy or a new program. Then, in the fullness of time, the larger parties will take over the more durable of the reforms advocated by third parties and enact them into law.[12]

This is the notion of a two-and-a-half party system in which the minor party (the half) supplies the innovating quality to an otherwise static system.

The Communist View: Parties in the Interest of Big Business

Another partisan perspective that is given relatively little attention is the Communist one, for which Tim Buck, long-term leader and virtual personification of the Canadian Communist party, was the best source. In his view, "the actual competition between Liberals and Tories . . . was solely as to which party could serve Canadian capitalism best. There was no difference in their attitudes towards the profit system."[13]

Elsewhere, Buck stated:

> The traditional terms and slogans which until recently distinguished the two parties of Canadian capitalism, have lost their original meanings. In the past the Liberal and Conservative parties represented the competing interests of different sections of capitalism and the rival imperialist interests of Britain and the U.S. Those differences are now completely over-shadowed.[14]

Far from being considered the left-wing innovator, the CCF-NDP is viewed as sharing the same anti-Communist, pro-capitalist goals as the other parties. In reference to J.S. Woodsworth, Buck pointed out:

> His aim was a reform party—a party which could secure support from sections of the capitalist class, from well-to-do farmers and urban middle-class people, and from some workers. He did not pretend that he advocated socialism. His political philosophy was summed up in the following sentences which he repeated hundreds of times: "The state should own and control certain essential public utilities. That is all".[15]

Buck went on to note NDP retreats from the 1933 CCF Regina Manifesto, which stood forcefully against "participation in imperialist wars," to a position of support for the government "in its preparation for an aggressive imperialist war—to make the world safe for capitalism."[16] In short, the Communist critique sees both the major parties and the minor parties (including, in a qualified sense, the NDP) as the servants of the capitalist system and of reactionary positions generally. It proposes itself as the real alternative.

> To stop U.S. domination of our country and to bring about the sort of policies that are needed now in domestic affairs requires the bringing together of a political force which is not hamstrung by ties with U.S. imperialism, as both the Liberal and Tory parties are. It must represent the interest of the masses of the people and be able to unite them at the polls.[17]

The Complex Cleavages Trap Theory[18]

Professors F.C. Engelmann and M. Schwartz present an interesting interpretation in their study of the Canadian party system.[19] They emphasize the role of the media in party politics:

> Technological innovations increase the media's capacities for spreading vast amounts of information to more people more quickly, thus altering the style in which party politics is conducted. Among the consequences is a need for extensive financial resources in order to fully use the media. Parties with insufficient funds from membership contributions must thus rely on large donations from a few contributors. By doing so, they make themselves vulnerable to the pressure which such contributors are then able to exert, a consequence which the new Election Expenses Act hopes to avert. A further consequence has been the utilization of personnel skilled in the exploitation of the media, which tends to turn parties away from volunteer workers and party strategists concerned with issues, to highly paid experts primarily concerned with techniques for electing candidates, regardless of the issues involved. These trends further contribute to the professionalization and rationalization of politics."[20]

While the increased role of the media affects all parties, it most affects those receiving large donations from wealthy corporate interests, which are also the ones least concerned with policy or doctrine. The electorate is skillfully manipulated through the media by the gimmickry of the professional public relations and advertising counsel, drawing their attention away from the serious problems, the solution to which would be against the interest of their clients and their backers.

Engelmann and Schwartz predict the continuation of the "two parties plus" system in which "electoral success, rather than fixed principles has been the focus of so much of Canadian party politics." The many cleavages (generally regional-ethnic and regional-class) in Canada would break up a party that tried to commit itself to broadly-based principles "unless it switches its focus to the attainment of office as an end in itself." In short, we are stuck with a politics based on opportunism because our problems are too complex for a principled party or parties to succeed and tackle them seriously.

We might call this the "complex cleavages trap" theory of Canadian parties. It has been applicable from Mackenzie King's time to the present, but it has not been proven that the reason for obfuscation by politicians is in the cleavages themselves; it may be in the nature or character of the people directing the governing parties. Does the situation really demand that there be more brokers or compromisers than problem-solvers?

One-Party Dominance

The Centrist Party Theory

Professor Frank Underhill commented in 1958: "What Mackenzie King established was a one-party domination at Ottawa with two or three splinter parties as opponents of the leviathan in office." His party, "which called itself Liberal," monopolized the centre of the political spectrum and "spread out so far both to the left and to the right, that the opposition groups seemed to become more and more ineffective."[21] The Liberal defeats in 1957 and 1984 did not signal a basic change of system, but rather its continuance under Tory auspices. The existence of three large parties and the single-member constituency plurality vote electoral system favour a one-party dominance arrangement in Parliament, even though actual popular majorities have occurred only twice in history (1958 and 1984).

For a party to be successful in forming the government over a long period it must come to be considered the government party, as the Liberals were from 1940 until just before their defeat in 1957, and from 1968 until 1978. It must attract the best talent, especially of an administrative and business kind, to serve as candidates, élite party officers and supporters, by appearing to offer the rewards of electoral success. This leaves the other parties to act as poles to attract the protest vote.

After 1958 the Conservatives under John Diefenbaker failed to do this. They alienated the public service by showing that they did not trust it, and they failed to retain the support of the business community by recruiting leaders among it or by following policies that commanded its support and respect. They remained only six years in office, when the Liberals experienced a quiet restoration that lasted (with the 1979–80 Tory minority government interval) until 1984. Then the Conservatives, under Brian Mulroney, preaching neo-conservative philosophy, won the first majority of the popular vote since the 1958 Diefenbaker sweep. The Liberals paid the price of their nationalistic policies (the Foreign Investment Review Act and the National Energy Program) which, along with the accentuated budgetary deficits, forfeited the support of business. The Tories have consolidated their position as the government party by two handsome parliamentary majorities. In late 1990, it appears highly unlikely that they can maintain this position.

The Quasi-Party Theory

Professor C.B. Macpherson presented a variant of the one-party dominance theory with his theory of the quasi-party system, a conclusion to his study of Alberta under Social Credit (which he suggested may be applied to Canadian federal politics).[22] Stated briefly, the theory is that a community like Alberta with a homogeneous population of petit-bourgeois independent producers in a quasi-colonial relationship to, and forming a subordinate part of, a mature capitalist economy, will normally reject the orthodox (two) party system in favour of a "quasi-party" system, i.e., one in which there is a dominant local party outside the two orthodox parties which attract majority support in the country. This system "can, to a limited degree, express and moderate the conflict of class interests in which such a society is involved." Here "the conflict of class interests is not so much within the local society as between that society and the forces of outside capital."[23] The system is essentially a plebiscitary one as "the independent producer resists the subordination imposed upon him by the capitalist economy, yet accepts the fundamentals of its property institutions."[24] In short, he accepts the private property basis of society "because he is himself a small proprietor, yet he supports the local quasi-party to resist the domination of powerful outside interests." However, this resistence is *within* the established economic system, and does not challenge it. The quasi-party system does not provide fully democratic government but does offer a means of covering over class conflict and of preventing or attenuating the arbitrary use of power.

Professor Macpherson suggested that this theory had some applicability at the federal level, where some parallels to the Alberta quasi-party situation are evident. (He was writing in 1953 and noted that opposition parties appeared to be developing into regional parties.) "As Canada becomes increasingly overshadowed by the more powerful economy of the United States, her position approximates the quasi-colonial; the characteristics of independent-producer assumptions about the nature of society are very widespread in Canada."

He saw these to be the basic preconditions for a quasi-party system, which offers "the most satisfactory answer to the problem of maintaining the form and some of the substance of democracy".[25] It is "either the final stage in the deterioration of the capitalist democratic tradition, or a way of saving what can be saved of liberal-democracy from threatening encroachment of a one-party state."[26]

In the 36 years since the writing of *Democracy in Alberta* the two orthodox parties have moved in the direction of their older relationship of alternative governments to each other. However, the conditions of the quasi-party system are even more applicable now than in the past. The theory of the quasi-party system remains a stimulating tool for the analysis of the Canadian party system.

One-Party Dominance as a Cause of the Rise of Third Parties

Another stimulating interpretation of one-party dominant situations is offered by Professor Maurice Pinard.[27] His analysis centres on Quebec and deals with the rapid rise of Social Credit prior to the 1962 federal election.

Quebec was in a situation of one-party dominance in federal politics. Because they were not a realistic alternative to the Liberals, disgruntled voters would be inclined to support another party if one existed.

There were other factors which favored Social Credit, including what Pinard calls "strain within the system" (large-scale unemployment and privation, especially in the rural areas), plus the fact that the leaders of the protest chose to organize their own party rather than to support the Conservatives.

In summary, when a conventional two-party system is subjected to structural cleavages within the society, or when attachments arise linking one party to the local community, or when flagrant corruption discredits one of the two parties (especially under a single-member constituency electoral system), there is alienation from one of the two parties and the emergence of a one-party dominance system. When the voters seek an alternative to the party in power, the opportunity arrives for the rise of a third party.

Pinard does not suggest the applicability of his theory to the Canadian federal government. Indeed, he pointed out that Social Credit was likely to decline because it had no prospect of winning a national election. "The voters do not want to exchange their vote for nothing, and there is not much of a return if the party has no chances of forming a government."[28] However, if Canadian federal politics are, in fact, in the situation of the one-party dominance Pinard refers to, or drift into it, then the road should be open to the rise of a third party, provided the existence of the other conditions of stress and conduciveness are present.

Ideological Continuum Theory

While seldom elaborated in detail, some writers make an analogy between the Canadian party system and a continental European one of an ideological continuum from left to right: Communist, NDP, Liberal, Conservative, Social Credit. While it is easy to agree to put the NDP on the left, the rest of the construct rests on flimsy, if not contradictory, evidence. There is virtually no Communist party, and the evidence of an ideological difference, in a left-right sense, between the Liberals and Conservatives is subject to change over time. Indeed, if preference by the business or capitalist interests is a guide, then the federal Liberals were the more right-wing party until the mid-1970s. As for Social Credit, its distinctive ideology does not fit the left-right continuum, although its period in office in Alberta would align it with the Liberals and Conservatives as a party commanding the confidence of business. Nevertheless, this view of a left-right dichotomy has been put forward, either as fact or desideratum, by leading students of Canadian politics.[29] However, Canadian political dynamics continues, as far as the parties with any chance of governing are concerned, to be a scramble for the centre.

These theories are constructs in the minds of the respective authors, to give meaning to Canadian parties. Students of parties should be aware of these theories if they are to discuss the party system seriously because they assist us in reaching our own interpretations of the party system.

ENDNOTES

1. For a discussion of these events, consult any good history of Canada, notably A.R.M. Lower, *Colony to Nation* (Toronto: Longmans, Green & Co., 1946); D.G. Creighton, *The Commercial Empire of the St. Lawrence, 1760–1850* (Toronto: Ryerson, 1937), pp. 302–3, 331, 336; D.G. Creighton, *Dominion of the North* (Toronto: Macmillan of Canada, 1962).
2. Alexander Brady, *Democracy in the Dominions* (Toronto: University of Toronto Press, 1947), p. 94.
3. *Ibid.*, p. 97.
4. *Ibid.*, p. 103.
5. See the writings of R.A. MacKay, R. MacG. Dawson and H. McD. Clokie.
6. J.R. Mallory, "The Structure of Canadian Politics," in *Canadian Politics* (Sackville, N.B.: Mount Allison University Publications, No. 4, 1959).
7. Frank Underhill, "The Party System in Canada," *In Search of Canadian Liberalism* (Toronto: Macmillan of Canada, 1961), p. 168.
8. See, for example, the speech by T.C. Douglas in Windsor, Ontario, 25 May 1962, as reported in NDP press release in Documents Department, Douglas Library, Queen's University.
9. Text of broadcast "The Nation's Business," 8 January 1962, CBC television, *ibid.*
10. Michael Oliver, President of NDP, Halifax, N.S., 26 April 1962, *ibid.*
11. See speech by Ed Finn, "Nationalism and the NDP," to the National Party Convention, Winnipeg, 28–31 October 1969, *ibid.*
12. J.R. Mallory, *The Structure of Canadian Government* (Toronto: Macmillan of Canada, 1971), pp. 201–2.
13. Tim Buck, *30 Years: The Story of the Communist Movement in Canada* (Toronto: Progress Books, 1952), p. 106.
14. Tim Buck, *Our Fight for Canada: Selected Writings, 1923–1959* (Toronto: Progress Books, 1959), p. 191.
15. Buck, *30 Years*, p. 112.
16. *Ibid.*, p. 115.
17. Tim Buck, *Our Fight for Canada*, p. 185.
18. This awkward title is mine.
19. F.C. Engelmann and M. Schwartz, *Canadian Political Parties: Origin, Character, Impact* (Scarborough: Prentice-Hall Canada, 1975).
20. *Ibid.*, pp. 137–38.
21. Frank H. Underhill, "The Revival of Conservatism in North America," *Transactions of the Royal Society of Canada* LII, Series 3 (June 1958), pp. 1–19.
22. C.B. Macpherson, *Democracy in Alberta* (Toronto: University of Toronto Press, 1953).
23. *Ibid.*, p. 246.
24. *Ibid.*, p. 247.
25. *Ibid.*, p. 249.
26. *Ibid.*, p. 250.
27. Maurice Pinard, *The Rise of a Third Party: A Study in Crisis Politics* (Englewood Cliffs, N.J.: Prentice-Hall, Inc., 1971).
28. *Ibid.*, p. 253.
29. R. MacG. Dawson, *The Government of Canada*, 5th ed. (Toronto: University of Toronto Press, 1970), p. 414.

12 Three Canadian Party Systems: An Interpretation of the Development of National Politics

R.K. CARTY

From the beginning, Canadian party politics has been dominated by Conservatives and Liberals. However, there is little about the contemporary parties that their founders would recognize, for virtually all aspects of them have been reshaped. The process of change has not, however, been either smooth or constant. Twice, the long-established practices of party life have been overthrown, leading to the emergence of wholly new patterns of organization and behaviour. An analysis of Canadian political parties must start by recognizing that three quite distinctive party systems have marked the country's political development.

Such sharp changes in the party system are the result of major alterations in the role of political parties in the governing process. While parties have continually played a central part in managing the electoral process and in organizing parliamentary life (including structuring legislative-executive relations), their latent functions emerged when the country's dominant political formula changed. As David Smith recently argued, three different models of party government, each characterized by different approaches to political leadership and the mobilization of support, have informed Canadian experience. Here, the analysis of parties as organizations reveals clearly how each of these "governing approaches" required distinctive party forms to articulate its principal modalities and encompass its primary political relationships.

This chapter sketches the three-party systems that have existed over the past 120 years, describing and comparing the party types in each and briefly considering the forces and processes that drove the systemic transformations. The periods identified parallel those of Smith's party-in-government model of Canadian

R.K. Carty, "Three Canadian Party Systems: An Interpretation of the Development of National Politics," in G.C. Perlin, ed., *Party Democracy in Canada* (Scarborough: Prentice-Hall Canada, 1988).

politics, supporting the theory of intimate links between political parties and changes in the functional requirements of governing.

Patronage Politics and Caucus Parties (1867–1917)

During the first half-century after Confederation, parties created and dominated Canadian politics. Canada had a small, rural society essentially devoid of aristocrats, large capitalists and organized workers. A professional middle class rooted in parochial communities dominated public life, and government was one of the few institutions (aside from the church) that provided a channel for personal mobility and the opportunity to exercise power. This made elections, which determined who would monopolize government power, high stakes events. Thus, André Siegfried would be led to observe that while "Liberals and Conservatives differ very little really in their opinions on crucial questions, and their conception of power seems almost identical . . . there [can] be few countries in the world in which elections arouse more fury and enthusiasm than in Canada."[2]

These contests took place within a set of rather fluid, pre-democratic institutional arrangements. The country was expanding from four to nine provinces, and the terms on which it evolved were being contested. The prime ministers of the day did not hesitate to take partisan advantage of the political developments. Although open voting and staggered elections ended in the 1870s, governmental control of the electoral administration, blatant gerrymandering, and manipulation of the franchise were regular features of the party battle over most of the period. Corrupt practices flourished and few elections went by without some MPs being unseated for illegal activities. At the same time, party competition was conceived as a series of discrete constituency contests. Acclamations were a persistent, if declining, element of every election, because parties could not always nominate candidates in hopeless situations.

Canada's system of "purposive federalism"[3] and Canadian parties were designed to achieve practical results in governing. For Macdonald, and then Laurier, party-building was simply the necessary political dimension of state-building.[4] The Conservative party emerged as a coherent political entity well before the Liberal opposition because it was in office first and so was able to exploit the prerogatives of power. Patronage was the life-blood of the parties, and partisanship pervaded the state. In his determination to build a lasting political coalition, Macdonald insisted that no government position, from senior bureaucrat or judge down to humble wharfmaster, be given to anyone who had not established a record of service to the party. The entire civil service came to be regarded as a partisan bailiwick, the parties emerged as the principal channel of recruitment for the state, and electoral turnovers quickly led to the replacement of vast numbers of civil servants.[5] In power, the party consumed the state.

As organizations, the national parties were little more than coteries of political notables. The parliamentary caucus was the party; the Liberal convention in 1893 was the only instance in 50 years of a national gathering of extraparliamentary partisans. Despite national rhetoric, party politics focused on the constituency and the parochial and personal claims of individual voters. Parties were vote-gathering machines. Local partisan associations and their supporters were linked through their MP, or defeated candidate, to the leadership at the centre. This structure put an enormous burden on the party leader because he assumed most of the responsibility for party organization, strategy, tactics, management, finance and policy. There was little room in this sort of party for mass participation and few were concerned with notions of internal democracy.

Elections demanded the full attention and participation of all local partisans. Although practices varied widely, it appears that public conventions were commonly used to nominate candidates. They allowed local associations the prerogative of determining who their standard bearer would be, while limiting the forum in which supporters might participate in party decision-making.

It took time to discipline local political notables so that parties could emerge as genuinely national organizations. Early parliaments contained a large number of "loose fish," and governments could not routinely count on the votes of their supporters. During the first decade after 1867, the incentives of office welded Conservatives from across the country together, while the Liberals remained an ill-matched alliance of regionally based opponents of Macdonald's governing coalition. As late as the fifth general election in 1882, the Liberals "had not yet become the truly national party that the Conservatives had. . . . Not only was the Liberal leadership still Ontario-oriented, but the issues they stressed often had little attraction outside of Ontario." It would take Laurier's leadership to "[complete] the forging of a loose alliance of provincial parties into a coherent, national organization."[6]

With 95 percent of the vote between them, the two great parties easily monopolized electoral competition during this first-party system. The record suggests that they were remarkably successful at knitting the country's diverse regions together, for the variation in their vote shares across the provinces was remarkably low.[7] In addition, as one would expect of a territorial system rooted in a politics of patronage, the support base of the party in power was normally even more balanced and geographically representative than that of its opponents.

Partisanship was no cloak to be put on or discarded as the weather changed, and little distinction was made between party activity in federal or provincial arenas. Men served in both, and rewards could come from either the national or provincial government, depending upon the party's position. As Reid noted in his analysis of the Saskatchewan Liberal machine "It [was] the give and take of patronage that [bound] together in an apparently indissoluble union federal and provincial politics."[8] This union was necessary for politicians in opposition as they had to depend upon colleagues in power at the provincial level to produce the resources necessary to nurture and sustain a party organization. Thus Laurier defeated the Tories in 1896 with the support of several provincial Liberal machines, and was in turn defeated in 1911 when Conservative premiers helped return Borden.

Local party organizations normally operated at both levels of competition, with members of constituency associations treating federal and provincial political activity as indistinguishable (see English for evidence from Ontario).[9] Certainly, party notables treated the system as one, moving from one level to another as opportunity allowed or party need demanded. The best-known instances involved premiers, or their nominees, being drafted into Laurier and Borden's new national governments, but men such as George Ross also moved down into provincial politics. Not surprisingly, the evidence suggests that the electorate responded to these parties by being fairly consistent in its voting behaviour across successive federal and provincial elections.[10]

These two cadre parties revolved around their leaders. This was true both of their organization and their appeal. Siegfried was particularly struck by the extent to which electoral contests in turn-of-the-century Canada revolved around leaders "whose mere name is a programme in itself." They did so because successful leaders personified the party, in parliament and in the country.

Leadership selection was the business of the caucus. It was concerned with finding someone who could direct the party in the daily parliamentary battle, and so sought a leader among its own membership. The process was informal and private, and involved weighing opinions as to who was most suitable. Not all opinions counted equally, for senior members of the caucus would inevitably have more influence than younger men. Out of these discussions one man would emerge as most acceptable, and then be designated leader. The governor-general would be involved in the choice of leader for the party in government, as the leader would become the prime minister. For the party in opposition, the problem would likely be to persuade the favourite to take on the burden his colleagues had assigned him.[11]

The lines of leadership responsibility in this system were clear, for what the caucus had given it could also take away. In both parties there were instances of leaders being forced to give up their position when they lost the confidence of the parliamentary party. This practice allowed for fairly quick transfers without a prolonged, semi-public washing of party laundry. It also enabled a caucus to select a temporary, compromise candidate who could serve until one of the strong men appeared to command wide enough support that he could safely be installed. This was the point of Sir John Abbott's ("I am here very much because I am not particularly obnoxious to anybody") short leadership of the Conservatives in the wake of Macdonald's death. That a governing caucus could twice choose a senator to lead it in the 1890s is a useful reminder of the pre-democratic character of this first-party system's politics.

Naturally enough, those who rose to lead their fellows were men of the party. They had generally served a long parliamentary apprenticeship and their experience in office had demonstrated their leadership and managerial abilities.[12] This was a closed leadership politics because there was no way an outsider, or a man not perceived as broadly representative of the party's ideology, might capture the leadership. The system was also a stabilizing force because, with the support of his caucus, a leader could go on indefinitely—no Conservative or Liberal since has managed to lead his party for as long as Macdonald or Laurier. However, such lengthy service inevitably meant that these men came to shape and personify the parties that had raised them to power. Writing of Laurier's leadership, John Dafoe noted: "It is in keeping with the genius of our party system that the leader who begins as the chosen chief of his associates proceeds by stages, if he has the necessary qualities, to a position of dominance; the republic is transformed into an absolute monarchy."[13]

In the absence of any formal or informal extraparliamentary organization, the party leaders had to assume much of the work of building and managing a party machine. Personal attention had to be paid to an endless river of particular requests flowing out of each constituency. One has the impression that the business of patronage overwhelmed their mail. Not the least onerous of a leader's tasks was financing party and electoral activity. In an era characterized by what we would call massive corruption (legislative, administrative and electoral), party politics was inordinately expensive—probably more than it has ever been since. For example, a successful candidate in 1904 might need to spend somewhere between $15 000 and $20 000 to win a riding that had but 8000 voters, at a time when a dollar was equal to a day's pay for a labouring man. This apparently insatiable demand for party money existed even though some public service funds were also directly used in the interests of party-building.

As a consequence, party leaders were driven to recruit relatively well-off local men who had influence in their constituencies and could be expected to help subsidize their own political careers. But at the same time parties were forced to attach themselves to corporate interests (railroads and banks) in Montreal and Toronto that were in a position to supply funds and had some incentive to do so. The result was a series of scandals that plagued parties throughout the period, the most famous being the great Pacific Scandal, which brought Macdonald's government down in 1873. After the turn of the century, western farmers would increasingly come to focus on this eastern money as the symbol of why the system was failing them and demand that parties be reformed.

The practice of leaving important aspects of party finance in the hands of the leader probably had a modest centralizing and disciplining effect at a time when leaders had few other organizational tools at their disposal. There was no control or accountability in the use of party resources, but then there was no national organization or party membership to which the politicians might answer.

The letters of the great party chieftains of this system reveal that they also spent a good deal of time and energy trying to manage and direct the press. All democratic politicians in open societies do so, but in early Canada particularly intimate relationships bound journalism and party together.[14] A great majority of the weekly and daily newspapers, which existed in far greater numbers than they do today, were little more than partisan instruments. Even as late as 1900, the circulation of the party papers exceeded that of the growing independent press. Politicians wanted and expected subservience, not objectivity, from the media.

Parties needed to have their own newspapers in a community to get their message across locally. Where none existed, parties were often driven to help supporters establish a paper. Macdonald himself was involved in starting Conservative papers in Toronto, on three separate occasions, in an attempt to counter the influence the *Globe* gave the Grits. In return, the newspapers and their proprietors received government patronage in the form of advertising and printing contracts. Parties rewarded their friends and punished their enemies. As early as 1876, official lists of papers "deserving" government business were in existence. Journalism came to be one of the common routes into parliament because, in a constituency-based politics, local journalists often came to be important partisan actors.[15]

When party and paper were working well together, three important political tasks were accomplished. First, the party had a communication system that tied its supporters together and kept them informed of its policies and activities. This was vital when no other mechanism existed to link partisans across constituency boundaries. Second, the papers were constant boosters of the party leader and the policies emanating from the caucus. When necessary they could provide an intellectual gloss on party positions, or explain away unpopular or unexpected decisions. Finally, party papers provided an endless critique of the opposition in all its manifestations. As Rutherford concluded: "All in all, a network of newspapers seemed essential to give the party substance, to make it a community of ideas and interests as well as a formidable foe able to compete in the game of politics."[16]

The first party system was stable, well integrated and predictable. The parties were well suited to the rural social order whose governing institutions they designed and managed. But the practices and institutions of half a century's party competition would be swept away by the administrative reform, social mobilization and political realignment that flowed from World War I. New governing approaches would require new parties.

Brokerage Politics and Ministerialist Parties (1921–1957)

Canadian society was beginning to change in the early years of the twentieth century. It began to urbanize and industrialize, to think in modern and self-consciously national terms, and to fill up: modern Canada's set of complex cross-cutting cleavages was developing. However, it took the war to crystallize and accelerate these forces and to stimulate new styles of governing, and hence quite different kinds of political parties.

Party politicians faced a transformed environment after 1918. The West had quickly emerged as a significant and distinctive political region by a process which began at the turn of the century, but was substantially completed by the end of the second decade. This region's socio-economic base put it fundamentally at odds with the industrial interests of central Canada. The protection of these interests had been entrenched in the National Policy by the two old parties, and therefore western farmers perceived that they would have to change the parties before they could alter government policy. The Progressive movement, which coupled that discontent with rural claims in Ontario and the Maritimes, was thus an attack on the first-party system[17] and it created a degree of political uncertainty in the opening years of the second-party system not unlike that the loose fish had provided Macdonald.

At the same time, the country had just gone through its first electoral realignment. Conscription shifted almost a quarter of Quebec's voters to the Liberals, leaving that party in an almost unassailable position in the country's second largest province and ending the possibility of genuine national party competition. But political élites, especially in English-speaking Canada, were beginning to adopt self-consciously national perspectives. The Unionist experiment brought into active politics a modern political class whose informal networks were tying the society together and who rejected the piecemeal politics of constituency patronage.[18]

Progressives and Unionists alike articulated profound shifts in the political culture. Mirroring and responding to these shifts were two important institutional changes. The first was the acceptance and adoption of democratic electoral arrangements. Provision was made for impartial electoral machinery, attempts to gerrymander the constituency map *en bloc* were abandoned, and politicians implicitly decided to stop manipulating the franchise by adopting universal suffrage. Modern party competition began with the 1921 general election.

The second change, civil service reform, constituted a direct blow to the parties. The abolition of widespread patronage deprived the party organizations of the glue that held them together, and which had tightly bound federal and provincial partisan interests. The parties also lost the power to dominate the administrative machinery of the state. This major institutional change ended party life as Canadians had known it for 50 years.

The central task of governing during this second period soon emerged as one of "accommodating the factions and divisions in Canadian society."[19] The country had divided in response to Borden's attempt to establish a national politics. Political cleavages, partially caused by the working of the electoral system were defined in regional terms.[20] This left the parties to operate as regional brokers preoccupied with the delicate balancing act required of nation-building. The Liberals had an inherent advantage in balancing the regions because only they could incorporate Quebec. Mackenzie King's intuitive understanding of what was required allowed him to absorb the West and build a winning cross-region electoral coalition that eventually turned the Liberals into the "Government Party." So successful was their political formula that eventually the state consumed the party.[21]

The focus of party politics in the second system shifted from constituency to region. With a deliberately federal approach to party organization, strong linkages developed between the grass roots and powerful regional bosses. Those men were responsible for the vitality of the party in their regions and, when the party was in power, for articulating regional claims in a way that promoted the emergence of a national consensus. This "ministerialist party"[22] was presided over by a leader who reserved to himself questions of political tactics and timing,

and who, standing above his associates, could defend the integrity of the brokerage process.

Parties, as organizations, grew well beyond the confines of the parliamentary
caucus during this period. In many ways the real organization was the set of
informal political networks trailing down from the regional chiefs, but formal
extraparliamentary national party associations were also established to provide
some continuity with organizational work and to link partisans together. Central
offices were opened in Ottawa but they were meagrely staffed, underfunded and
occasionally closed. The politicians were never clear on what they expected of
these bodies, other than to help win elections while refraining from voicing their
opinions on questions of public policy. Although these national party councils
did not play an important role, they did mark a stage in the institutionalization of
party life, legitimating the notion that the party belonged to its members, and not
just those elected to public office.

The federal character of party organization and the considerably increased
geographic variation in party support were evidence of the lower levels of national
integration that characterized the brokerage parties of this period. The electoral
data also suggest that the parties' capacity to integrate national and provincial
politics within individual provinces was coming under strain.[23] But the regionalization of the country's politics was showing up even here: in the Maritimes and
Quebec (until the emergence of the Union Nationale) the Liberals and Conservatives continued to structure political competition, while west of the Ottawa River
the traditional two-party system lost its grip. Much the same pattern of organizational separation appeared in the career paths of party politicians.[24]

To even casual observers, the changed structure of competition in the second-
party system stood in distinct contrast to its predecessor. Gone was nation-wide
competition, but also gone with it were the balance between the two historic
parties and their once easy mastery of Canadian politics. After their defeat in
1930, the Liberals created an enduring electoral predominance while protest
parties established themselves as permanent fixtures. This was an inherently
asymmetrical system: only the Liberals could build an organization capable of
embracing the regions' diverse interests.

A demand for regional brokerage seemed guaranteed to produce Conservative defeats. That in turn prevented the party from developing a working ministerialist organization, perpetuating its inability to practise party brokerage. The
one time they won a majority during the period was in 1930, when the direct
personal appeal of the leader, R.B. Bennett, could be used to circumvent the
otherwise winning brokerage mode. Although this was recognized as a new and
potentially significant development in the nature of party leadership (Chubby
Power noted: "Beginning with Bennett, I think it could reasonably be said that
the party was his rather than he was of the party"), charisma could not be
institutionalized and the party was left in chaos after the leader proved incapable
of reconciling all the competing regional claims in his own person. Significantly,
the only other time the Conservatives managed to win in the second system was
when they duplicated the experience of the early 1930s. Diefenbaker's charisma

brought the party to power, only to have his government end in much the same disarray as Bennett's. By then, the system of party brokerage was itself passing.

In almost every election of the period considerable numbers of voters rejected both the Liberals and the Conservatives. Although the vitality of other political movements and parties seemed a regular part of the system, three quite distinct phenomena were involved. First there were the farmers of the Progressive movements in the early 1920s. Essentially, they were heralds of the politics of regional brokerage springing up in opposition to the old politics of prewar Canada. Their absorption by the Mackenzie King Liberals, in Saskatchewan and Manitoba, defined the character of the second system. Their continuing alienation in Alberta revealed the limits of that politics.

Social Credit represented a second kind of protest party. It expressed the claims and grievances of those who felt their region had been left out of the accommodative package assembled by the Liberals. It was perhaps inevitable that not all interests could be incorporated in an attempt at nation-wide brokerage, and that as a result a regionally based party would arise to exploit the resulting competitive opportunity. Thus it is hardly surprising that Social Credit's national appeal was limited to Alberta, the very province that had resisted Mackenzie King in the 1920s. As a party of protest it did not survive the system that spawned it.

Socialists, in the form of the Co-operative Commonwealth Federation (CCF), constituted the third variety of protest party. It rejected brokerage politics in principle. Believing in an explicitly ideological politics, the CCF sought to reshape both the definition of Canadian party politics and the national political agenda. In fact its appeal was always highly regional, never really crossing the Ottawa River, and it was soon cast as a Western party. The Liberals, demonstrating the same policy flexibility that they had in the 1920s, moved to pre-empt popular CCF positions on welfare and government management of the economy. Unable to establish a national working class constituency in the face of successful Liberal government brokerage, the CCF went into steady decline after World War II, finally ceasing to exist as a separate entity just as the second-party system was ending.

The CCF was committed to democratic politics. Its organization was designed to allow party members, many originally politicized by the Progressives' democratic critique of Canadian practices, an opportunity to discuss and participate in the making of party policy. This participation was certainly far more than either the Liberals or Conservatives permitted their supporters. As the party was never in power nationally, it is impossible to judge whether the caucus would have felt bound to implement policies that party conventions had passed, but there is little doubt that the CCF considered internal party democracy one of its most important distinguishing features.

The one area in which the two major parties responded to the new ethos and became more democratic was their leadership selection process. Party leaders in this second-party system were chosen by national conventions in which the majority of delegates were representatives from local constituency associations.

Conventions emerged to ensure that the national leader, who had to stand above all the interests gathered into the party, was chosen by a regionally representative assembly rather than a regionally unbalanced caucus.

The first leadership conventions, attended by about 1200 delegates, were managed affairs in which the party notables played an influential role in determining the outcome. There were rarely many serious candidates. Only once (the first time) did it take more than two ballots to determine a winner, and no extensive pre-convention campaigns were conducted by rival candidates. Although the conventions were relatively closed affairs, the process did allow men who were outside the caucus to stand for and win the party's leadership. As a result, parliamentary service and experience became less important qualities.[25]

The decision by the parliamentary caucuses to allow extraparliamentary conventions to choose party leaders divided authority and responsibility within the parties. How any serious leadership conflict might have been resolved was unclear for, as Mackenzie King is reported to have told his colleagues, a leader not chosen by the caucus was not responsible to it. On the other hand, conventions to choose new leaders were only called into being when a leader himself resigned. The potential contradictions in this bifurcated definition of party never became an issue, given the general weakness and timidity of the extraparliamentary organization throughout the period.

Although it occurred in the context of general organizational quiescence, the move towards a more open, democratic leadership selection process did not lead to more active constituency level parties. Indeed, though the evidence is sketchy, it appears that a vigorous local party life was in decline as even the nomination process came under the sway of established regional party élites.

Problems associated with party finance had bedeviled party leaders all during the first-party system. In an attempt to prevent elected politicians from continually being tainted by money scandals, the tasks associated with the raising and spending of party funds were divorced from other party activity and assigned to a small number of individuals who kept very much to the back rooms and the Senate. On the whole, the relative costs of electoral politics were probably lower during this period than they had been before World War I, though definite regional differences existed. East of the Ottawa River, traditional (corrupt) electoral practices flourished.

Although all of the parties appear to have been perennially broke, there were vast differences in their relative poverty. The CCF depended on the contributions of its members, and so lived on a shoestring. Conservative fortunes were very uneven.[26] Bennett himself generously funded much of the party's activity during his leadership, while his successor faced a financial boycott from Montreal supporters due to differences over railroad policy. The party became so strapped that it had to close its national office in 1940. The Conservatives began to make a slow financial recovery only after they were returned to power in Ontario and Toronto business interests decided that a stronger national party was necessary to help counter the socialist threat of the CCF.

The Liberals had far fewer financial worries.[27] Being in office gave them access to the private sector, and they took advantage of it. Reversing the usual case of special interests supporting the governing party in order to win influence, Liberal bagmen instituted a system of kickbacks. Government contractors or suppliers were expected to make a contribution to the party that was proportionate to the amount of government business they were doing. These funds were supplemented by monies raised from large national corporations in private appeals. Together they gave the Liberals a comfortable advantage.

All the parties faced a dramatically changed media environment which altered the basic patterns of political communication. The partisan press was dead, killed by new economic realities and the greater appeal of independent and less political newspapers. Unlike their predecessors, these new papers did not take their cues from politicians as to what and how they should report, and they would not carry partisan messages for free. During election periods many papers charged more than normal advertising rates (a political rate often set only after the ad had been placed), knowing that the parties would have very little option but to pay. Radio emerged as an important communication tool during the 1930s, and parliament began to regulate party access to and use of the airwaves. Although several provincial parties were able to exploit the radio to advantage, national party organizations paid it less attention and as late as the 1950s continued to devote the largest part of their media budgets to the press.[28]

Perhaps the most significant change was the growth of advertising, both as an industry and as a profession. It was inevitable that advertising and politics would be drawn to one another from the beginning: politicians wanted help selling their message, especially in the absence of a docile press, and ad men wanted work. The war made the government the largest advertiser in the country, so the stakes were substantial. Thus was born the ad agency-party-government *ménage à trois*: advertisers did party work in exchange for government contracts. Naturally the governing party had a significant advantage and therefore this pattern was most developed by the Liberals. For the last decade of the system, the general secretary of the national party organization was actually an employee of one of the leading agencies, on "loan" to the politicians.

For the most part the advertising professionals' role was technical. They gave advice on how to package and deliver political messages but were not deeply involved in broader questions of party strategy and policy. The impact of these changes seems to have been to force the parties to clarify the message they wanted to communicate to the electorate, and to lift the substance of political debate from a preoccupation with local patronage. Both were prerequisites to the development of national, issue-centred campaigns.

This party system was well-adapted to meeting the brokerage demands of regional accommodation. As organizations, the parties reflected the imperatives of the system, but when it became clear that the brokerage function was being institutionalized in another part of the political system, the stage was set for the emergence of yet a third pattern of party competition.

Electronic Politics and Personal Parties (from 1963 on)

The Diefenbaker revolution and realignment ended four decades of Liberal brokerage. It opened up Canada to a new, modern, national politics. The country had developed an urban, industrialized, educated, plural society stretching across five distinctive political regions. The electorate was growing quickly, forcing the parties to find ways to socialize and incorporate large numbers of new voters. The parties abandoned the pretense that they were merely informal private groups, and during the 1960s began a process that defined their position and rights in parliament and law.[29]

Provincial governments were growing quickly and provincial politicians took the role of principal regional spokesmen, articulating grievances and pressing demands on the national government. The important political mechanisms for regional accommodation, which had been the life-blood of the parties for 40 years, shifted to the first ministers' conference, and were institutionalized in a complex system of federal-provincial executive relationships. Deprived of the function that had driven them, the parties developed a new style of politics, a new basis for political mobilization.

Parties responded to the new context by shifting the focus of their attention from region to nation, to build an electoral constituency for their policy preferences. This new focus has produced what Smith calls a pan-Canadian style of political leadership and governance.[30] Parties direct their appeal to individual citizens and seek to engage their support for particular definitions of the political agenda and appropriate patterns of public policy. The national parties compete for individual support with one another and with their provincial counterparts.

Dramatic changes in the organization of the two major parties have been produced by the new politics. On one hand, the parties have become more than ever an extension of the leader, a personalized machine to build and sustain a coalition of support for the leader's policies. On the other hand, they have become open, participatory institutions in which the caucus and the extraparliamentary organization often seem to be quite separate, unrelated bodies. These two features have created a continuing internal tension within the parties that has largely focused on leadership issues and personalities.

In order to create a consistent national appeal, party leaders have taken personal control of the campaign machinery across the country. Appointments to all critical party positions are now made from the Leader's office, and if necessary are even made in defiance of powerful regional politicians.[31] This system of appointments guarantees a far more centralized control of electoral strategy, but also makes the party the creature of the leader. Independent regional bosses no longer exist; position and influence are no longer derived from being representative as they are the gift of the leader. The personalization of the entire party organization has an inherent propensity to stimulate the growth of national factions and to transform policy disputes into leadership conflicts.

At the same time, as part of their mobilization strategies, the Liberals and Conservatives have strengthened and institutionalized their extraparliamentary wings. The national party now meets regularly in convention and debates questions of organization, policy and leadership. The national officers it chooses have become increasingly important figures in party life and its committees and agencies are vital parts of the organization. These new structures now constitute a central forum for internal party struggles, and provide party activists with an opportunity to impose their views on the caucuses. By continually bringing together party militants from across the country, these conventions help to establish the parties as national communities of partisans. With the centralization of the electoral machine around the leader has come a significant nationalizing effect within the parties.

Changes in the organization and activities of national political parties have severely strained their ability to integrate politics within the provinces. The result has been the separation, or often formal divorce, of the provincial and federal wings of the same party. As with much in Canadian politics the extent of this internal party disintegration has varied across the regions; it has proceeded furthest in Quebec, while it has been resisted in Atlantic Canada where traditional loyalties and practices still hold the two levels together. On the west coast the two old national parties have simply disappeared from provincial politics, leaving British Columbians to live in "two political worlds."[32]

National electoral competition was reshaped by the realignment of the prairies. As the West deserted the Liberals for the Conservatives and the New Democrats (a development more pronounced at the level of parliamentary seats than of votes), Quebec became the least Tory province for the first time. A system emerged in which there was no genuinely national party, national, that is, in the geographic sense of the term, a definition fostered by the territorially based electoral system. Competition was being structured by parties representing national coalitions of voters not spread evenly across the country. The Liberals sought to align the young, the ethnics, the French-speakers, women, and the urban middle class; the NDP sought to unite trade unionists, the poor, and small farmers. Now that the party system no longer carried the major burden of accommodating regional differences in the governing process, the geographically unbalanced character of the parties' support bases and of party competition was not an inherent threat to the working of the Canadian polity.

Perhaps the clearest evidence of the strength of the new coalitions was the withering of the parties of protest that had been such a visible part of the second-party system. Those parties had come into existence as a response to the workings of brokerage politics. In its absence they no longer had any purpose. The Ralliement des créditistes did disrupt party politics throughout the 1960s, generating the same parliamentary uncertainty that had marked the first decade of each of the two previous party systems, but it was essentially a party in protest against the second system's treatment of its constituency. Like the Progressives of the 1920s, the Créditistes proved to be the harbinger of a new system, but not a part of it.

As the period started, the CCF, with the support of the five-year-old Canadian Labour Congress, transformed itself into the New Democratic Party. The formation of the NDP was a deliberate attempt to escape the regional cast that had settled on the CCF. The provision that trade unions might affiliate themselves was an attempt to tie the party to a distinctive national interest. But the very strength of the party in three of the four Western provinces has made it difficult for its national organization to rise above its provincial roots.

The party has increased its share of the national popular vote to about 20 percent, but because of the single-member constituency system, it has so far been unable to translate that vote into a proportional share of seats in parliament.

The Liberals managed to dominate the first two decades of this third-party system not only because their continuing pre-eminence in Quebec made it easier for them to establish a winning coalition, but also because the Conservatives' ongoing leadership conflict had a debilitating effect on its capacity to compete.[33] And, as in each of the previous party systems, leadership has been a central dimension of party activity.

Mr. Diefenbaker's leadership of the Conservative party ended badly. A majority in the extraparliamentary party moved to depose the leader against the wishes of the caucus. Although procedures by which the national convention might regularly hold the leader accountable were instituted, this did not resolve the question of where final authority in the party lay. Joe Clark lost his leadership, despite a two thirds convention vote, when he proved unable to command the loyalty of the caucus. The bifurcation of party between caucus and convention has proved profoundly destabilizing for party leadership, especially when in opposition, and has opened the parties up to being captured and controlled by highly personalized factions.

Leaders are now chosen in large, competitive conventions. In order to maximize their chances, contestants must engage in extensive pre-convention campaigns to have as many of their supporters as possible selected as delegates and to persuade others to vote for them. This requires the creation of a highly personalized national network capable of penetrating and capturing the wider party. Thus leadership contests now force the building of parties within the party on the basis of winner-take-all. As the direction of the parties can then be set by the leaders through their control of the organization, these contests become struggles over the political agenda and the kind of coalition the parties will seek to mobilize.

In leadership contests there is no premium on parliamentary experience. Some might even suggest, on the basis of the Clark, Mulroney and Turner victories, that outsiders offering a fresh, unsullied face have a distinct advantage. Most important is the capacity to build a sophisticated political machine that, using the modern electronic technologies of polling, communicating and constant monitoring, can mobilize a national constituency.

Much the same pattern of open competition is now typical of the constituency nominating process. Surprisingly large numbers of friends and neighbours are being brought to meetings to support particular candidates. The rather wholesale, almost casual recruitment of individuals for a single meeting may be debasing the notion of party membership, but it has stimulated local political participation. In areas of one-party dominance it is providing a real contest for office.

Early in this third-party system, the parties confronted the problem of their own relative poverty and instituted sweeping changes in the laws governing party income and electoral expenses.[34] The net effect of these developments was to make the parties' financial affairs public, to set limits on the amount of money they could spend and to make it much easier for the parties to raise funds from individual citizens. Some of the provisions have accelerated the drift from the print media to television and most of them have made the parties comparatively rich.

Generous tax credits for small political donations have provided the parties with a major opportunity to raise money from their supporters. They have learned to exploit the electronic technology of direct mail which allows them to connect the party centre directly with individual voters. Appeals typically invite individuals to support a particular leader in implementing his vision for the Canadian future. Not only does this reinforce a personalized definition of party, but it also frees the party from dependence on formal members for financial support. Mailing lists need not correspond with membership lists, and may come to be seen as a representation of the real party to which the leadership needs to respond. This technology also makes possible the organized factionalism that is at the heart of the politics of leadership within the parties.

These changes do not discriminate between the parties, so one of the major consequences has been the equalization of resources available to the three national parties. Indeed, in the last years of the Trudeau regime, both the Conservative party and NDP were able to raise more money than the governing Liberal party. Whether this foreshadows a politics in which the opposition is better financed than the government remains to be seen, though that would certainly represent a major reversal from the earlier systems. A secondary consequence has been the enrichment of constituency associations, many of whom now appear to have more money than they know how to spend. Wealthier constituency associations seem certain to shift some of the traditional internal organizational balances towards increasing local autonomy and weakening party discipline and coherence.

At the same time, the rapid growth in party resources has stimulated the emergence of permanent national headquarters with million-dollar operating budgets. With the establishment of these headquarters has come an increase in the number of professional political technicians who have taken over electoral decision making and campaign management. Instrument of the leadership that appoints it, this new coterie of partisans does not fit easily with the parties' new participatory structures or assertive local associations and so its power is another source of internal conflict.

The character of the third-party system has most obviously been affected by the electronic mobilization of information. As the system started, television was revolutionizing the patterns of communication between party and voter. Television, with its emphasis on personality, and its structural bias towards gathering a national audience, reinforced the imperatives in the system that were producing new forms of party. In this environment the advertising expert evolved from being a technician to being a central advisor and strategist responsible to the leader. As the medium became defined as a potential tool of the opposition, these experts had to learn to manipulate television and to use it to communicate a highly personalized image of the party. What was essentially new about television was the technology, and the premium it put on new kinds of skills.

Even more significant than television are the remarkable advances in attitude and opinion polling that have been part of this third system. They now allow for a systematic upward flow of information that permits party politicians to discern with remarkable accuracy what the concerns and interests of the public, or selected publics, are.[35] These are both catered to and manipulated by the image makers: they are rarely ignored. With a scientific reading of public opinion now available to the leadership, the traditional feedback role of party members and even MPs has become superfluous. Therefore, the hired pollster has replaced the newspaper editor of the first system, and the public relations consultant of the second, to become one of the key figures in the entourage of the successful party leader, and in the electronic politics of the third-party system.

By the end of the 1970s, this third system had begun to crystallize. Like its predecessors it appears to have developed a kind of stable equilibrium in which the various aspects of the parties are well-integrated, and which serve the functional requisites of the wider political system.

Three Canadian Party Systems

Seen in terms of three distinctive systems, the changes in Canadian political parties assume a pattern that might not otherwise be obvious. What is striking is not the fact that many aspects of the parties have changed, but that these changes in organization, leadership, finance and communication have twice come together in short periods to form quite new politics.

The first years of each system were marked by considerable electoral and parliamentary fragmentation and uncertainty. Macdonald faced the loose fish, Mackenzie King the Progressives and Pearson the Créditistes, in their struggles to establish new patterns of party organization and electoral politics. The strategies of political mobilization and incorporation each adopted proved to be characteristic of the system of governance that followed. At the same time one can see forces at work in the last years of each of the first two systems, during the Borden and St. Laurent governments, that were signalling the end of the system and the nature of what would follow.

The periods of party system transformation followed considerable social and demographic change in the basic structure of the electorate. Both periods of change helped break old electoral alignments and patterns of political organization, making it easier for new systems of partisan mobilization to emerge. In both

TABLE 1 **A Summary of Variations in Canadian Parties during the Three-Party Systems**

	I *1867–1917*	*II* *1921–1957*	*III* *1963–*
Dominant Politics	patronage (state-building)	brokerage (nation-building)	electronic (agenda-building)
Focus	constituency	region	nation
Parties	caucus	ministerialist	personal
Leadership	caucus choice proven parliamentarians	managed conventions known politicians	open competition outsiders
Finance	civil service private capital	kickbacks corporations	public funding mass appeals
Media	party papers editors	independent press/ radio P.R. consultants	TV/polling pollsters
Transitions	confederation loose fish	civil service reform 1917/farmers	federal-provincial diplomacy 1958/Créditistes

cases, the Liberals were then left best placed to establish and epitomize the new system.

These party systems, so well-adapted to their political environment, persisted only as long as they served the functions for which they had been called into being. They changed when the basic Canadian political formulae changed, for "the heart of Canadian politics" has always been "party government."[36] Whatever other social or ideological changes were altering Canadian society, the first-party system ended when civil service reform deprived the parties of their state-building role; the second-party system ended when the nation-building tasks of regional accommodation were absorbed into the system of federal-provincial diplomacy. This is not to suggest that those tasks were no longer performed. They had been institutionalized in new ways, and in other parts of the political system. The parties continued to play at patronage, and talk of regional interests, but neither drove party competition as they once had.

Canadian parties have reflected the demands imposed by the structure and character of the relationship between the state and society. They have primarily been shaped by the politics of party governance: party system change has flowed from political change, and most directly from changes in the institutional arrangements for governing, within which the political parties have had to operate.

Writing of the first-party system, André Siegfried pointed to the absolute centrality of the leader in all aspects of party activity. The leader was the entire central organization and policy making apparatus as well as the focus of electoral appeal. Although the modalities of party leadership have changed as the politics of Canadian parties shifted focus from constituency to region to nation, party leaders have remained the hub around which the parties revolve. Siegfried would have recognized in the party leaders who gathered powerful regional chieftains around them, or who personalized the party organization to pursue a national agenda, a continuity that wove a distinctive historical experience through the three systems. This continuity makes the issue of leadership selection—how and whom the parties choose—one of the central issues of Canadian politics, and explains why the study of leadership selection provides one of the most fruitful avenues for studying the country's parties and its policies.

ENDNOTES

1. D. Smith, "Party Government, Representation and National Integration in Canada," in P. Aucoin, ed., *Party Government and Regional Representation in Canada* (Toronto: University of Toronto Press, 1985).
2. A. Siegfried, *The Race Question in Canada* (Toronto: McClelland and Stewart, 1906, 1966 edition), pp. 114, 117.
3. Smith, "Party Government," p. 82.
4. G. Stewart, "Political Patronage Under Macdonald and Laurier, 1878–1911," *The American Review of Canadian Studies* 10.1 (1980); "John A. Macdonald's Greatest Triumph," *Canadian Historical Review* 63.1 (1982).
5. R.M. Dawson, *The Civil Service of Canada* (London: Oxford University Press, 1929), pp. 73–74, 81–82.
6. J.M. Beck, *Pendulum of Power* (Scarborough: Prentice-Hall Canada, 1968), pp. 43–73.
7. R. Johnston, "Federal and Provincial Voting: Contemporary Patterns and Historical Evolution," in D.J. Elkins and R. Simeon, eds., *Small Worlds: Provinces and Parties in Canadian Political Life* (Toronto: Methuen, 1980).
8. E. Reid, "The Saskatchewan Liberal Machine before 1929," in H.G. Thorburn, ed., *Party Politics in Canada*, 4th ed. (Scarborough: Prentice-Hall Canada, 1979).
9. J. English, *The Decline of Politics: The Conservatives and the Party System 1901–20* (Toronto: University of Toronto Press, 1977).
10. Johnston, "Federal and Provincial Voting."
11. J.C. Courtney, *The Selection of National Party Leaders in Canada* (Toronto: Macmillan of Canada, 1973).
12. Courtney, *ibid.*, pp. 142–43.
13. J.W. Dafoe, *Laurier: A Study in Canadian Politics* (Toronto: McClelland and Stewart, 1922, 1963 edition), p. 83.
14. P. Rutherford, *A Victorian Authority: The Daily Press in Late Nineteenth-Century Canada* (Toronto: University of Toronto Press, 1982).
15. N. Ward, "Patronage and the Press," in K.M. Gibbons and D.C. Rowat, eds., *Political Corruption in Canada* (Toronto: McClelland and Stewart, 1976).
16. Rutherford, *A Victorian Authority*, p. 221.

17. W.L. Morton, *The Progressive Party in Canada* (Toronto: University of Toronto Press, 1950).
18. M. Prang, "Networks and Associations and the Nationalizing of Sentiment in English Canada," in R.K. Carty and W.P. Ward, eds., *National Politics and Community in Canada* (Vancouver: University of British Columbia Press, 1986). English, *The Decline of Politics.*
19. Smith, "Party Government," p. 21.
20. A.C. Cairns, "The Electoral System and the Party System in Canada, 1921–1965," *Canadian Journal of Political Science* 1.1 (1968).
21. R. Whitaker, *The Government Party: Organizing and Financing the Liberal Party of Canada, 1930–58* (Toronto: University of Toronto Press, 1977).
22. Whitaker, *ibid,* p. xxii.
23. Johnston, "Federal and Provincial Voting."
24. Whitaker, *The Government Party,* Part B.
25. Courtney, *The Selection of National Party Leaders.*
26. J.L. Granatstein, *The Politics of Survival: The Conservative Party of Canada, 1939–1945* (Toronto: University of Toronto Press, 1967).
27. Whitaker, *The Government Party.*
28. Whitaker, *ibid.*
29. J.C. Courtney, "Recognition of Canadian Political Parties in Parliament and Law," *Canadian Journal of Political Science* 11.1 (1978).
30. Smith, "Party Government."
31. J. Wearing, *The L-Shaped Party: The Liberal Party of Canada, 1958–1980* (Toronto: McGraw-Hill Ryerson, 1981), ch. 2.
32. D.E. Blake, *Two Political Worlds: Parties and Voting in British Columbia* (Vancouver: University of British Columbia Press, 1985).
33. G.C. Perlin, *The Tory Syndrome: Leadership Politics in the Progressive Conservative Party* (Montreal: McGill-Queen's University Press, 1980).
34. F.L. Seidle and K.Z. Paltiel, "Party Finance, the Elections Expenses Act, and Campaign Spending in 1970 and 1980," in H.R. Penniman, ed., *Canada at the Polls, 1979 and 1980* (Washington, D.C.: American Enterprise Institute, 1981).
35. R. Graham, *One-Eyed Kings: Promise and Illusion in Canadian Politics* (Toronto: Collins, 1986), pp. 284, 307–8.
36. Smith, "Party Government," p. 2.

Opinion Structure among Party Activists: A Comparison of New Democrats, Liberals and Conservatives

13

KEITH ARCHER AND ALAN WHITEHORN

Introduction

The degree to which Canadian partisan politics reflect distinctive ideological choices and perspectives continues to enjoin lively debate among political scientists. Empirical studies have generally confirmed that Converse's[1] findings demonstrating a lack of high relevance of ideological constraint in the United States can apply to Canada as well.[2] In the most recent contribution to this debate, Donald Blake, drawing upon surveys conducted by George Perlin, examined ideological differences between delegates to Liberal and Progressive Conservative leadership conventions. Blake found that Liberal and Conservative party activists held significantly different opinions on most matters of policy. However, the variation within each party produced a substantial overlap in the positions held on various issues.[3] Richard Johnston took the argument a step further, demonstrating that ideological cohesiveness explained only a small part (25–30 percent) of the difference in attitudes of Liberal and Conservative activists.[4] Johnston concluded that the lack of agreement on ideology among party activists leaves both parties with considerable latitude for political brokerage.

This article extends Blake's analysis by including New Democrat delegates in a comparison of the attitude structure of party activists. A survey was conducted among delegates attending the NDP federal convention held in Montreal in March 1987, the first federal NDP convention in Quebec.[5] The data indicate that the positions of New Democrats on issues differ from those of Liberals and

Keith Archer and Alan Whitehorn, "Opinion Structure among Party Activists: A Comparison of New Democrats, Liberals and Conservatives." This is a revised version of a paper presented at the 1988 Annual Meeting of the Canadian Political Science Association. A shorter version of this essay was published in the *Canadian Journal of Political Science* (March 1990).

Conservatives in two ways: activists in the NDP hold positions on issues that are further from both Liberals and Conservatives than are the latter two from one another, and New Democrats display a much higher degree of attitude consensus than do activists in either of the other major parties. Bearing in mind the important role of conventions in forming policy for the NDP, the data suggest that NDP leaders may have less latitude than Liberal and Conservative leaders in shaping party policy and brokering competing political interests.

Analysis of Specific Issues

Any survey researcher is confronted with the dilemma of which questions to pose to respondents: questions are based on time constraints, analytical frameworks, the hypotheses being employed and, of course, the norms of the political party under study. The 1987 NDP survey did not always pose the same questions as those presented to the delegates at the 1984 Liberal and 1983 Progressive Conservative leadership conventions[6]; consequently, comparisons of the different surveys are at times difficult to make. Nevertheless, we have striven to offer as many comparisons of policy items and indexes as possible and have indicated where the items in question differ.

Using Blake's Table 1, we have located 30 variables[7] from the Liberal and Conservative convention surveys which are either identical to or seem comparable with those of the 1987 NDP data. We have proceeded to offer a revised version of Blake's table. Some items from his table could not be replicated from the NDP survey and are not included in our newer analysis. Our updated version of the table now includes equivalent statistics for the NDP in terms of the percentage agreeing with the specific statements and the index of difference[8] between the NDP and each of the other two parties (see Table 1).

There are 31 comparable attitudinal statements clustered into 11 policy areas. They include attitudes towards continentalism, hawkishness on defence and foreign affairs, social security, privatization, areas for increases in government expenditures, anti-big business, moral conservatism, civil liberties, minority equality, constitutional powers and, lastly, bilingualism and Quebec.

We explored the frequently postulated hypothesis that the NDP is a party somewhat different from the two older parties. This is a theme posed not only by political scientists but also by political activists on both the left and right. It certainly is an image frequently presented by NDP activists who also often tend to dismiss the differences between the Liberals and Conservatives. We conjectured that our hypothesis would be invalid if the policy differences between the Liberals and Conservatives are on the whole greater than either the differences between New Democrats and Liberals or between New Democrats and Conservatives.

First we compared Liberal-Conservative differences with Liberal-NDP differences on the 31 items. The difference was calculated as the percentage agreeing with a statement in one party minus those agreeing in a second party. Drawing

TABLE 1 **Liberal, Conservative and NDP Attitudes on Selected Policy Items**

Variable I	Variable	(Percentages) Agree			Difference (rounded)		
		Lib.	Cons.	NDP	L/PC	L/NDP	PC/NDP
	Continentalism:						
150	favour freer trade with U.S.	63.9	53.7	14.1	10	50	40
143	foreign ownership threatens independence	51.5	27.3	95.8	24	44	69
144	independent Canada even if income decline	58.1	33.3	76.8	25	19	44
	Hawkishness:						
155	refuse Cruise testing	28.7	18.3	94.0	10	65	76
151	more aid to underdeveloped countries	35.1	15.4	79.7	20	45	64
245	increase defence spending	44.7	75.3	21.9	31	23	53
	Social Security:						
100	too much abuse of social programmes	21.9	37.7	11.4	16	11	26
091	means test for some social programmes*	54.4	74.1	28.6	20	26	46
	Privatization:						
260	less public ownership—rail	13.6	36.5	2.3	23	11	34
261	less public ownership—airlines	22.5	54.2	3.4	32	19	51
267	less public ownership—radio/TV	13.4	38.3	3.8	25	10	35
259	less public ownership—oil/gas	13.8	61.8	2.0	48	12	60
	Spending Increase:						
246	foreign aid	35.1	15.3	76.7	20	42	61
247	education*	71.4	55.1	90.0	16	19	35
254	arts	31.2	23.9	65.5	7	34	42
255	develop new technology	90.2	89.6	75.8	0	14	14
253	welfare payments to poor*	48.5	32.3	87.0	16	39	55
245	defence**	44.7	75.4	21.9	31	23	54
	Anti-corporate Power:						
071	big business has too much political influence	57.4	46.6	98.2	11	41	52
	Moral Conservatism:						
176	abortion private matter*	47.3	44.0	85.9	3	39	42
186	reintroduce capital punishment	48.9	79.9	5.6	31	43	74
190	legalize marijuana possession	47.3	43.2	51.5	4	4	8
196	society too permissive	54.7	64.1	17.1	9	38	47

Continued . . .

TABLE 1 *(Continued)*

	Civil Liberties:						
188	restrict rights to reduce crime	48.8	53.7	18.5	5	30	35
089	right to strike be restricted*	32.7	30.8	36.6	2	4	6
	Minority Equality:						
149	take immigrants from all groups	79.1	67.3	90.8	12	12	24
	Constitutional Powers:						
238	more power to federal government	38.8	9.1	26.6	30	12	18
239	more power to provincial government	7.9	47.1	18.6	39	11	29
129	monarchy essential	54.0	69.0	22.4	15	32	47
	Bilingualism & Quebec:						
166	bilingual federal government*	79.7	38.3	88.4	41	9	50
163	special status for Quebec	33.7	36.9	66.6	3	33	30
			Total			18+	29+
						11−	2−
						2=	0=

Note: **30 sets of items, with one survey item (defence spending) appearing twice in Blake's analysis and also in this table. Index of difference is calculated by subtracting percentage agreeing
with a statement in one party from percentage agreeing in another party. This method is
slightly different than that used by Blake and thus accounts for some recalculations and
some adjustment in the numbers for the Liberal-Conservative differences from those
reported by Blake.
*denotes survey items which are comparable but questionnaire wording differences may be
salient.
+denotes difference greater than Liberal/Conservative pairing.
−denotes difference less than Liberal/Conservative pairing.
=denotes difference equal to Liberal/Conservative pairing.

from the data found in Table 1, we are able to offer the following findings: The
differences between activists in the NDP and those in the Liberal party were
greater than differences between Liberal-Conservative activists on 18 items, less
so on 11 items, and identical on two. We found the difference between NDP and
Liberal convention delegates was greater than that between Liberals and Conservatives, but not as often as initially expected. For either all or most of the items in
the areas of continentalism, hawkishness, spending increases, anti-big business,
moral conservatism and civil liberties, the differences in positions between the
Liberals and New Democrats were greater than the differences in Blake's data
between Liberals and Conservatives. In two areas (privatization and constitutional powers), however, the NDP-Liberal differences were on the whole less
than those between the Liberals and Conservatives. In three other areas (minority equality, social equality, and bilingualism and Quebec) the differences in the
pairings balanced out.

We also compared Liberal-Conservative differences with Conservative-NDP differences for the same questions. The differences between NDP and Conservative delegates were greater than those between Liberals and Conservatives on 29 items, and less on two. For all items in each policy area except one (constitutional powers), the differences in positions between the Conservatives and New Democrats were greater than the differences in Blake's data between Liberals and Conservatives. The gulf between the NDP and Conservatives seems substantial and the consistency of these findings significant.

The data seem to suggest that the gulf between the NDP and the Conservative party is far greater than other pairings (i.e., between Liberals and Conservatives or between the NDP and Liberals). This suggests that the ideological placement of the NDP to one side of the political spectrum (presumably the left) and the Conservatives on the other side (presumably the right), with the Liberals somewhere in the middle, seems once again to have empirical confirmation. It also seems to belie the arguments of the "end of ideology" school of thought[9] in any comparisons between the NDP and Conservatives. On almost every policy item the NDP-Conservative differences are significant.

We also explored the question of the propensity of the NDP respondents to have the highest or lowest level of internal agreement of the three parties on the issues in question. If we assume that the NDP exhibits an ideological distinctiveness, then we would expect the NDP to occupy one of the polar positions (i.e., to have the highest numbers agreeing or disagreeing with a particular policy statement). Note that a random distribution of the three parties would have any one party appearing in the middle range of agreement versus disagreement (i.e., between the other two parties) on average one in three occasions.

Of the 31 occasions explored, the NDP responses appeared in the middle (i.e., between the Liberals and Conservatives) on only two occasions (6.5 percent); this is far less than the 33 percent one would expect with a random distribution. Thus, yet again we see evidence to suggest the NDP is distinctly on one side of the political spectrum. This can be seen more specifically in the 11 policy areas where the NDP delegates indicated stronger feelings than the two other parties in the following ways.

On the issue of continentalism, NDP delegates were least likely of all three parties to favour freer trade with the United States and most likely to feel that foreign ownership threatens Canadian independence. In the area of foreign affairs, NDP activists were least committed to increases in defence spending and were strongly opposed to Cruise missile testing. Reflecting their internationalism, NDP convention delegates were far more tolerant of accepting immigrants from all groups. In the area of social security, the NDP was the least inclined to see abuses in social programmes and most opposed to means tests imposed upon such programmes. Not surprisingly, New Democrats were the most unsympathetic to efforts at privatization. In the area of spending increases, New Democrats most favoured education, payments to the poor and foreign aid; they least favoured defence. Reflecting socialist beliefs, New

Democrats were almost universal in their perception that corporations have too much political influence.

New Democrats were least likely to exhibit features associated with moral conservatism. They were not predisposed to see society as too permissive, nor to favour a reintroduction of capital punishment; in addition they saw abortion largely as a private matter. While New Democrats were the least willing of activists in all three parties to accept restrictions on human rights, they were surprisingly most sympathetic to some restrictions on the right to strike.[10]

In one area only did the NDP cease to take a polar position. Unique to the area of constitutional powers, New Democrats tended to be midway between the Liberals' desire to give more power to the federal government and the Conservatives' desire to grant more power to provincial governments. However, returning to a polar position on other items, New Democrats were the least inclined to see the monarchy as essential and the most inclined to favour both a bilingual federal government and a special status for Quebec.

To examine further the cohesion within and the division between parties, we next combine the positions of party activists into issue indexes and examine the relationship between these indexes.

Analysis of Issue Indexes

In the preceding analysis we compared the position of NDP delegates on a number of policies with the position of Liberal and Conservative delegates. In this section we extend that analysis by grouping positions on related policies into issue indexes. Our indexes are based on those in Blake, and we attempt to replicate his analysis as closely as possible. (See the Appendix for the questions used in the indexes for the NDP. For the Liberal and Conservative indexes, see Blake, Endnote 3., pp. 49–50).[11]

Through our examination of the attitudinal differences within and between the convention delegates in Canada's three major parties we wish to gauge the spatial dimension to those issue positions. Are the parties' positions, as reflected by the attitudes of convention delegates, arrayed along a consistent left-right dimension, with New Democrats farthest left, Conservatives farthest right and Liberals occupying the middle ground? Or is there a multi-dimensionality to the locations of party positions in issue space, with some issues arrayed along a left-right cleavage and others along a dimension independent of left-rightness? To the extent that spatial distances between parties can be mapped along a given ideological dimension, does that distance remain constant across issue domains, or does it vary, with party activists being farther from one pole in some issue domains than in others?

In addition to the relationship between parties, we examine the degree of consensus within the parties. To what degree do party workers agree among themselves on a given issue area? Is one party consistently more consensual than the others, or one consistently less consensual? Does the parties' degree of consensus remain constant for all issue domains, or are the parties more consensual on some issues than on others? Our answers to these questions should provide a fuller understanding of the nature of attitudinal divisions among the activists in Canada's major parties.

The data in Table 2 enable us to explore the differences between parties on a number of issues. The first portion of the table lists the names of the indexes, the range for that index and the direction in which it is measured. For example, in the first index each item relates to the respondents' view of the relationship between Canada and the United States on economic matters. The index was constructed using four questions and it was scored in a pro-continentalist direction. One point was added to a respondent's score for a response of agree or strongly agree to the statement, "Canada should have freer trade with the United States." Three other questions similarly tapping continentalist attitudes also were included. (See the Appendix for a complete listing of the items used in each index.) The respondents' pro-continentalist responses to the four items were summed, thus producing an index ranging from 0 to 4. To the right of the table are the mean scores and standard deviations for Liberal, Progressive Conservative and New Democratic convention delegates. The data for the Liberals and Conservatives are taken directly from Blake, although we use standard deviations instead of the coefficient of variation[12]; and data on the New Democrats are from our 1987 survey. On the right side of the table we include the difference in means for each of the three pairings of parties.

Several trends emerge from the data in Table 2. A comparison of the means[13] indicates that, on almost all items, party delegates are aligned on similar patterns. This suggests a single overarching, and presumably left-right, dimension with the New Democrats and Conservatives occupying the polar positions of left and right, respectively. In addition, the New Democrat delegates are closer to the left pole than are the Conservatives to the right pole.[14] For example, on the four-point continentalist index, New Democrats (0.3) are one third of a unit away from one pole, whereas Conservatives (2.9) are a full point from the right pole and the Liberals (1.8) are close to the centre. Likewise, on the six-point hawkishness measure, New Democrats are on average less than one unit from the left pole and Conservatives are almost two units from the right. Once again Liberals are located near the centre. This general finding holds for the indexes measuring attitudes towards social security, moralism, privatization and, to a lesser extent, anti-corporate power.

In contrast to these divisions are issues in which the parties either array themselves differently on a left-right axis or for which the party alignment is not so obviously based on a left-right dimension. These differences relate to the issues of bilingualism and civil liberties. With respect to bilingualism, the attitudes of Liberals and New Democrats are almost indistinguishable and are toward the "pro-bilingualism" end of the spectrum, whereas Conservatives are near the midpoint. On the matter of civil liberties, New Democrats were the most strongly opposed to restricting civil liberties, Liberals were least opposed to restrictions, and Conservatives were at the midpoint of the range.[15]

TABLE 2 Attitudinal Differences Within and Between Parties

Index —direction	(Range)	Party						Difference		
		Liberal		Progressive Conservative		New Democrat		Lib–PC	Lib–NDP	PC–NDP
		$\bar{x}$	s	$\bar{x}$	s	$\bar{x}$	s			
Continentalism: (pro-continentalist)	(0–4)	1.80	1.22	2.90	1.16	0.32	0.59	−1.10	1.48	2.58
Hawkishness: (pro-hawkishness)	(0–6)	2.65	1.41	4.17	1.42	0.87	1.14	−1.52	1.78	3.30
Social Security: (pro-welfare)	(0–5)	2.63	1.34	1.67	1.25	4.06	1.09	0.96	−1.43	−2.39
Moralism: (restrictive)	(0–3)	1.65	1.14	2.16	1.04	0.58	0.76	−0.51	1.07	1.58
Anti-corporate Power: (restrict corp. power)	(0–3)	1.98	1.01	1.58	1.11	2.64	0.69	0.40	−0.66	−1.06
Bilingualism: (pro-bilingualism)	(0–2)	1.71	0.58	1.01	0.85	1.76	0.65	0.70	−0.05	−0.75
Civil Liberties: (anti-restriction)	(0–3)	1.22	1.01	1.51	1.06	1.92	0.85	−0.29	−0.70	−0.41
Privatization: (pro-privatize)	(0–6)	2.21	1.79	4.00	1.72	0.17	0.75	−1.79	2.04	3.83

The dispersion of data as measured by standard deviation also illuminates aspects of the ideological nature of delegates to the three major parties. In general, the data indicate greater attitudinal consistency and consensus among New Democrats than among the other parties. On every index except bilingualism, New Democrats had the greatest consistency (i.e., the lower standard deviation score). The Liberals and Progressive Conservatives were barely distinguishable in their degree of consensus in all instances except bilingualism. Typically, the Liberals and Conservatives have very similar standard deviation scores, with the marginally greater consistency going to the Conservatives. The exception is with bilingualism, where the greatest consensus is shown by the Liberals, and the least by the Conservatives.

Thus, a comparison of means and standard deviations indicates that New Democrat delegates tend to be more ideologically distinctive and internally more consistent than delegates of the other major parties. In addition, on most issues the Conservatives occupy a position near the right pole, although not quite so near as are New Democrats to the left pole. Internally, however, Conservative delegates are less unanimous in their views than are New Democrats and, instead, display as wide a range of views as Liberals.

In order to make comparisons *between* as well as *within* indexes, we adjusted for the range of the index. We did so by dividing the absolute difference in means between each pair of parties (from Table 2) by the range for that index. The resulting "standard difference in means," which ranges from 0 to 1, appears in Table 3.[16] In addition, the standard deviations from Table 2 are not directly comparable across indexes because they are based on different ranges. Therefore, we adjusted the standard deviations by dividing by the range of the index. The "adjusted standard deviations" therefore are also based on indexes ranging from 0 to 1. Thus, we are able to compare the division and cohesion among the parties across each of the issue areas.

The data illustrate the ideological divides in Canadian politics, at least at the level of political activists. The greatest differences are between Conservatives and New Democrats, especially on the issue of the economic relationship between Canada and the United States (continentalism) and on the question of the role of the government in managing a mixed economy (privatization). Furthermore, since the data on the Conservatives and Liberals were gathered prior to the Conservative government taking office in 1984—before the free trade initiative and the policy of privatization were introduced—the differences today may be even greater. In addition, the Conservatives and New Democrats are sharply divided over the issue of Canada's foreign policy (hawkishness), moral issues such as the right of homosexuals to teach in schools, the legitimacy of the welfare state (social security), bilingualism and attitudes towards corporate power.

The divisions between Liberals and Progressive Conservatives, by contrast, are weaker and have a considerably different focus. The major area that divides them is their attitude towards French-English relations, such as bilingualism. The data also suggest that the New Democrats are in harmony with the Liberals

TABLE 3 **Standardized Attitudinal Differences Within and Between Parties**

Index	Standardized Absolute Differences Between Parties			Adjusted Standard Deviation		
	Lib–PC	Lib–NDP	PC–NDP	Lib	PC	NDP
Continentalism	0.28	0.37	0.65	0.31	0.29	0.15
Hawkishness	0.25	0.30	0.55	0.24	0.24	0.19
Social Security	0.19	0.29	0.48	0.27	0.25	0.22
Moralism	0.17	0.36	0.53	0.38	0.35	0.25
Anti-Corporate Power	0.13	0.22	0.35	0.34	0.37	0.23
Bilingualism	0.35	0.03	0.38	0.29	0.43	0.33
Civil Liberties	0.09	0.23	0.14	0.34	0.35	0.28
Privatization	0.30	0.34	0.64	0.30	0.29	0.13

on this issue. However, whereas this issue provides the greatest distinction between Liberals and Conservatives, it is of more modest importance in separating Conservatives from New Democrats. Other issues are more salient. The difference between the Liberals and Conservatives on a number of other issues, such as privatization, continentalism and hawkishness are important, but the differences are less than between the Conservatives and New Democrats. This observation is reinforced when comparing Liberals and New Democrats, where in most instances the differences are similar to those between Liberals and Conservatives.

Examining the adjusted standard deviations, we find that the greatest internal consensus exists for the NDP. A strong opposition to increased privatization, increased economic ties with the United States and militarization in foreign policy are among the key issues that unite New Democrats. Indeed, New Democrats were more united on each of these issues than were the delegates of the other major parties in agreement on *any issue area.* The Liberals find their greatest agreement on the issues of hawkishness, social security and bilingualism, and Conservatives find theirs on hawkishness, social security, privatization and continentalism.

As noted previously, however, there is reason to suspect that some of these findings result from the different periods in which the surveys were administered. Since coming to power in 1984, the Conservative government has undertaken important initiatives in a number of areas, especially free trade (continentalism) and privatization. We would expect to see both a greater distance between the Conservatives and the other parties on both issues today, as well as a greater consistency in the attitudes of Conservatives. It is not possible to know whether the attitudes of the Conservatives on free trade and privatization would be as consensual as the attitudes of the New Democrats. It is clear, however, that over the range of indexes examined, New Democrats display an ideological clarity and a degree of consensus considerably stronger than do Liberals and Progressive Conservatives.

Conclusion

Much of the debate on the nature of Canadian political culture, and of the role of ideology in shaping political culture, has taken place without benefit of individual-level attitudinal data. Survey research methodology designed to measure the attitudes of the general public and of the political élite—which has included surveys of party workers, parliamentarians and, increasingly, delegates to party conventions—have proven useful in illuminating the content and importance of ideology in Canadian politics.

Our analysis of convention delegates indicates that there is a considerable difference in the attitudes of party activists towards major issues. In addition, the divisions were stable across issue areas. On most issues, the New Democrats were clearly on the ideological left and the Progressive Conservatives on the ideological right. Furthermore, the Liberals had a remarkable facility for locating themselves at the ideological centre. In general, Liberals were closer to the Conservatives than they were to New Democrats, but clearly the Liberals and Conservatives were not as indistinguishable as some have suggested.[17] However, it is also clear that analyses that group both the Liberals and New Democrats together on the ideological left, and contrast them with the Conservatives are misplaced—at least, when based on the attitudes of convention delegates.[18]

Findings on the content of differences between the parties provide an interesting perspective on the nature of ideological divisions between parties. We found, for example, that attitudes regarding the bilingualism issue were most pronounced between Liberals and Progressive Conservatives. As long as partisan conflict is centred on a choice between Liberals and Conservatives, then political debate will be strongly affected by non-economic issues.[19] This finding helps explain the relative unimportance of economic performance in conditioning levels of support for the parties.[20] This is not to suggest that Liberals and Conservatives are not distinguishable on other factors as well. For example, significant differences exist in attitudes towards continentalism, privatization and other issues. Also, we suspect that some of these differences have likely increased since the 1984 federal election. Nonetheless, the issue of greatest importance in distinguishing Liberals from Conservatives was bilingualism.

Although attitudes towards bilingualism also distinguished New Democrats from Conservatives, this item paled in comparison with other more significant factors, primary among which were attitudes towards continentalism and privatization. Although traditionally there has been a regional component in attitudes towards the United States—with Westerners much more amenable to forging closer economic links than many of those in the rest of the country—nonetheless, these issues cut across provincial and regional boundaries in a way that is not possible with the bilingualism issue. A shift in political debate from one centred on the Liberals and Conservatives to one centred on the New Democrats and Conservatives would likely coincide with the downplaying of linguistic issues and a rise in the importance of issues surrounding the division of the economic pie and the underlying structure of the Canadian economy.

Lastly, our examination of the cohesiveness of the party activists revealed a much higher level of ideological consistency among New Democrats than among the delegates to the conventions of the other parties. On almost every index, the New Democrats demonstrated a substantial degree of consistency across issues, whereas the agreement among the Liberals and Conservatives was considerably less. One of the implications of greater consensus within the NDP is that the positions which the party adopts on most issues will remain relatively stable.

The greater ideological diversity among both Liberal and Conservative delegates suggest that the parties' positions on issues are much more subject to shift with a change in leadership. Since there is a wide range of opinion within the party (even at the level of political activists) new leaders, as champions of one policy position or another, have greater latitude in taking the party in new and different directions, while at the same time maintaining the support of large sections of the party.

The substantial degree of ideological clarity that we have observed among the convention delegates, especially from the New Democratic and Conservative parties, does not lead us to conclude that political choice in Canada is based on a model of minimizing the perceived distance between one's own ideological positions and those of the various parties, as postulated by Downs.[21] One of the prerequisites of Downs' model is that the parties organize their positions on issues in an unambiguous way. There are many ways of measuring the degree to which parties are successful in being both internally coherent and externally distinguishable from one another. Examining the attitudes of convention delegates, as we have done, leads to the conclusion that there are considerable differences between Canada's major political parties as well as relative cohesion within each party. In examining the broader question of the role of ideology in structuring choices at Canadian elections, our observations suggest that, for party activists, the ideological divisions are clear and straightforward, even if those perceptions might not extend to the mass public.

ENDNOTES

1. Philip Converse, "The Nature of Belief Systems in Mass Publics," in David Apter, ed., *Ideology and Discontent* (New York: Free Press, 1964).
2. Roger Gibbins and Neil Nevitte, "Canadian Political Ideology: A Comparative Analysis," *Canadian Journal of Political Science* 18 (1985), pp. 592–97.
3. Donald Blake, "Division and Cohesion: The Major Parties," in George Perlin, ed., *Party Democracy in Canada: The Politics of National Party Conventions* (Scarborough: Prentice-Hall Canada, 1988), pp. 47–48.
4. Richard Johnston, "The Ideological Structure of Opinion on Policy," in Perlin, *Party Democracy in Canada*, p. 65.
5. The NDP survey consisted of a post-convention mailed questionnaire sent to all 1391 registered delegates, 738 of whom responded. The 54 percent response rate was one of the largest obtained from a study of federal party convention delegates. Demographic information on the survey is available directly from the authors.

6. Surveys of the 1983 Progressive Conservative and 1984 Liberal conventions were undertaken by George Perlin. For analyses based on these earlier surveys, see Perlin, *Party Democracy in Canada*.

7. We have 30 distinctive items, although the table displays 31. One item on defence is included under two separate categories (hawkishness and spending increase), thus accounting for the 31 items included in Table 1.

8. For an explanation of the term *index of difference* see Blake, "Division and Cohesion," p. 34. It should be noted that we use the index a little differently and in a less complex manner than Blake. Our index of difference is a straight difference between the percent in one party who agree on one item subtracted from the percent who agree on the same item in another party. We recalculated the index of difference between the Liberals and Conservatives. In the overwhelming majority of cases, there is little or no difference in the results obtained by our less complex method of calculation and we have applied the same method to all three parties.

9. D. Bell, *The End of Ideology* (New York: Free Press, 1962).

10. Questionnaire wording difference may account for some of this result.

11. We have adjusted our indexes to have the same range as Blake's. In most instances, we have done so by including in our index the same number of items as are included in Blake's indexes. In those instances when sufficient comparable items were not available (i.e., anti-corporations, bilingualism and privatization) the values on the indexes were adjusted to produce a range equivalent to Blake's. For example, Blake included six items in his privatization index. Since individuals score one point for each "pro-privatization" response, the index has a range of 0–6. With our measure, however, we had only four comparable items. The resulting index was multiplied by 1.5 so that its range also was 0–6. This procedure enables us to compare directly the means within, but not across, indexes. The standard deviation, if affected, is likely increased under this procedure.

12. We have used standard deviation rather than the coefficient of variation (CV) because we feel the former is a more accurate measure of dispersion in this instance. CV is obtained by dividing the standard deviation of each distribution by its mean. With these measures, however, the size of the mean is heavily dependent upon the direction of the index. Furthermore, the decision on the direction of the index is arbitrary. It does not matter whether continentalism is measured in a pro-continentalist or an anti-continentalist direction, as long as it measures feelings toward continentalism. However, since CV divides the standard deviation by the mean, the direction in which the index is measured (itself an arbitrary decision) has a large bearing on the perceived dispersion.

   The use of CV led Blake to infer (p. 41) that "continentalism and hawkishness came closest to reflecting a consensus within Conservative ranks, but were a source of considerable disagreement with the Liberal party." Note that when standard deviation is used as a measure of dispersion, we find identical consensus with the two parties on each issue. Had the index been measured in the opposite direction (i.e., anti-continentalism) resulting in a reversal of means (Liberal = 2.20, Conservative = 1.10), CV would change dramatically and standard deviation would remain the same. To compare dispersion across indexes, one should adjust the standard deviation according to the range, rather than the mean, a procedure we use in Table 3.

13. We have computed the difference in means differently than Blake. Whereas Blake took into account the percentage of respondents in each category of the dependent varia-

ble, we used the less complex method of subtracting the mean for one party from the mean for another.

14. This finding may be owing to the way in which we operationalized our measures of left and right, which as noted are based upon answers to a series of policy questions. Respondents in the NDP survey were asked to place Canada's parties on a seven-point, left-right scale, with 1 indicating farthest left and 7 farthest right. The mean score in left-right placement for the New Democratic party was 3.4. They also placed the Liberal party at 5.3 and the Progressive Conservative party at 6.2.

15. It should be noted that part of the discrepancy of this item is likely owing to the inclusion in the civil liberties index of a question concerning the imposition of the War Measures Act in 1970—a question that likely has provoked a response directed toward the Liberal government's imposition of the Act.

16. This is an attempt to standardize the 'standard deviations' which are based upon indexes of different ranges. Note that standard deviation is in part range dependent.

17. See, for example, Frank Underhill, *In Search of Canadian Liberalism* (Toronto: University of Toronto Press, 1960); M. Janine Brodie and Jane Jenson, *Crisis, Challenge and Change: Party and Class in Canada* (Toronto: Methuen, 1980).

18. Compare Robert Alford, *Party and Society: The Anglo-American Democracies* (Chicago: Rand McNally, 1963).

19. See Brodie and Jenson, *Crisis, Challenge and Change*, for an explanation of this finding which centres on explicit strategic decisions with the Liberal and Progressive Conservative parties.

20. See Kristen Monroe and Lynda Erickson, "The Economy and Political Support: The Case of Canada," *Journal of Politics* (1986); see also Keith Archer and Marquis Johnson, "Inflation, Unemployment and Canadian Federal Voting Behaviour," *Canadian Journal of Political Science*, Vol. 21 (1988), pp. 569–84.

21. Anthony Downs, *An Economic Theory of Democracy* (New York: Harper and Row, 1957).

Appendix

Each index was produced by counting the number of variables in which the individual's response corresponded to the direction of the scale. Note that most of our variables for the NDP are measured with a 5-point scale ranging from (1) strongly disagree to (5) strongly agree, with (3) signifying uncertainty. The items which are identical or very similar to those used by Blake are identified with an asterisk (*). For the operationalization of the Liberal and Conservative respondents' scores, see Blake, "Division and Cohesion," pp. 49–50.

Continentalism
(scored in a continentalist direction)

*1. Canada's independence is threatened by the large percentage of foreign ownership in key sectors of the economy. (DISAGREE OR STRONGLY DISAGREE)

*2. We must ensure an independent Canada even if it means a lower standard of living for Canadians. (DISAGREE OR STRONGLY DISAGREE)

*3. Canada should have freer trade with the United States. (AGREE OR STRONGLY AGREE)
4. We ought to seek greater American investment in Canada. (AGREE OR STRONGLY AGREE)

Hawkishness
(scored in a hawkish direction)

1. Canada should seek closer relations with communist countries. (DISAGREE OR STRONGLY DISAGREE)
2. Canada ought to devote much more effort and money to aiding the under-developed countries. (DISAGREE OR STRONGLY DISAGREE)
*3. Canada should refuse to permit the testing of the Cruise missile on Canadian soil. (DISAGREE OR STRONGLY DISAGREE)
4. Soviet communism is no longer a threat to Canada. (DISAGREE OR STRONGLY DISAGREE)
*5. The spending on foreign aid should be (SLIGHTLY DECREASED OR GREATLY DECREASED).
*6. The spending on defence should be (SLIGHTLY INCREASED OR GREATLY INCREASED).

Social Security
(scored in a pro-welfare direction)

*1. There is a great deal of abuse of social security and welfare programmes in Canada. (DISAGREE OR STRONGLY DISAGREE)
2. Social security programmes, like old age pensions and family allowances, should be based on family income needs, and people who don't need this type of assistance should not receive it. (DISAGREE OR STRONGLY DISAGREE)
*3. Government-sponsored child care services should be greatly expanded. (AGREE OR STRONGLY AGREE)
4. More money should be spent on social services. (AGREE OR STRONGLY AGREE)
*5. The spending on welfare payments to the poor should be (SLIGHTLY INCREASED OR GREATLY INCREASED).

Moralism
(scored in a restrictive direction)

*1. Abortion is a private matter which should be decided between the pregnant woman and her doctor. (DISAGREE OR STRONGLY DISAGREE)
*2. The possession of marijuana should be legalized. (DISAGREE OR STRONGLY DISAGREE)
*3. Our society has become too permissive. (AGREE OR STRONGLY AGREE)

Anti-Corporate Power
(scored in a restrict corporate power direction)

*1. Big business has too much influence in Canadian politics. (AGREE OR STRONGLY AGREE)

 2. The government ought to take stronger measures to break up monopolies and create competition in the economy. (AGREE OR STRONGLY AGREE)

(This index was multiplied by 3/2.)

Pro-Bilingualism

*1. A bilingual federal government is necessary. (AGREE OR STRONGLY AGREE)

(This index was multiplied by 2.)

Privatization
(scored in a privatizing direction)

With regard to public ownership in different sectors, how much do you think there should be?
*1. oil and gas (LESS)
*2. railroads (LESS)
*3. airlines (LESS)
*4. radio-television (LESS)

(This index was multiplied by 3/2.)

Civil Rights
(scored in a pro-civil rights direction)

*1. Certain restrictions on civil rights would be acceptable if it would help police reduce crime. (DISAGREE OR STRONGLY DISAGREE)

 2. People who are homosexuals should be permitted to teach in schools. (AGREE OR STRONGLY AGREE)

 3. Racists should not be allowed to hold public meetings and rallies. (DISAGREE OR STRONGLY DISAGREE)

Conservatism, Liberalism and Socialism in Canada: An Interpretation

14

GAD HOROWITZ

Introduction: The Hartzian Approach

In the United States, organized socialism is dead; in Canada, socialism, though far from national power, is a significant political force. Why this striking difference in the fortunes of socialism in two very similar societies?

... It will be shown that the relative strength of socialism in Canada is related to the relative strength of toryism, and to the different position and character of liberalism in the two countries.

In North America, Canada is unique. Yet there is a tendency in Canadian historical and political studies to explain Canadian phenomena not by contrasting them with American phenomena but by identifying them as variations on a basic North American theme. I grant that Canada and the United States are similar, and that the similarities should be pointed out. But the pan-North American approach, since it searches out and concentrates on similarities, cannot help us to understand Canadian uniqueness. When this approach is applied to the study of English Canadian socialism, one discovers, first, that like the American variety it is weak, and second, that it is weak for much the same reasons. These discoveries perhaps explain why Canadian socialism is weak in comparison to European socialism; they do not explain why Canadian socialism is so much stronger than American socialism.

The explanatory technique used in this study is that developed by Louis Hartz in *The Liberal Tradition in America*[1] and *The Foundation of New Societies*.[2] It is applied to Canada in a mildly pan-North American way by Kenneth McRae in "The Structure of Canadian History," a contribution to the latter book.

The Hartzian approach is to study the new societies founded by Europeans

Gad Horowitz, "Conservatism, Liberalism and Socialism in Canada: An Interpretation," the *Canadian Journal of Economics and Political Science* XXXII, No. 2 (May 1966). Reprinted by permission of the *Canadian Journal of Economics and Political Science*. This essay has been edited to suit the needs of this volume.

(the United States, English Canada, French Canada, Latin America, Dutch South Africa, Australia) as "fragments" thrown off from Europe. The key to the understanding of ideological development in a new society is its "point of departure" from Europe: the ideologies borne by the founders of the new society are not representative of the historic ideological spectrum of the mother country. The settlers represent only a fragment of that spectrum. The complete ideological spectrum ranges—in chronological order, and from right to left—from feudal or tory through liberal whig to liberal democrat to socialist. French Canada and Latin America are "feudal fragments." They were founded by bearers of the feudal or tory values of the organic, corporate, hierarchical community; their point of departure from Europe was before the liberal revolution. The United States, English Canada and Dutch South Africa are "bourgeois fragments," founded by bearers of liberal individualism who have left the tory end of the spectrum behind them.

The significance of the fragmentation process is that the new society, having been thrown off from Europe, "loses the stimulus to change that the whole provides."[3] The full ideological spectrum of Europe develops only out of the continued confrontation and interaction of its four elements; they are related to one another, not just as enemies, but as parents and children. A new society which leaves part of the past behind it cannot develop the future ideologies which need the continued presence of the past in order to come into being. In escaping the past, the fragment escapes the future, for "the very seeds of the later ideas are contained in the parts of the old world that have been left behind."[4] The ideology of the founders is thus frozen, congealed at the point of origin.

Socialism is an ideology which combines the corporate-organic-collectivist ideas of toryism with the rationalist-egalitarian ideas of liberalism. Both the feudal and the bourgeois fragments escape socialism, but in different ways. A feudal fragment such as French Canada develops no whig (undemocratic) liberalism; therefore it does not develop the democratic liberalism which arises out of and as a reaction against whiggery; therefore it does not develop the socialism which arises out of and as a reaction against liberal democracy. The corporate-organic-collectivist component of socialism is present in the feudal fragment—it is part of the feudal ethos—but the radical-rationalist-egalitarian component of socialism is missing. It can be provided only by whiggery and liberal democracy, and these have not come into being.

In the bourgeois fragment, the situation is the reverse: the radical-rationalist-egalitarian component of socialism is present, but the corporate-organic-collectivist component is missing, because toryism has been left behind. In the bourgeois fragments, "Marx dies because there is no sense of class, no yearning for the corporate past."[5] The absence of socialism is related to the absence of toryism.

It is *because* socialists have a conception of society as more than an agglomeration of competing individuals—a conception close to the tory view of society as an organic community—that they find the liberal idea of equality (equality of opportunity) inadequate. Socialists disagree with liberals about the essential meaning of equality because socialists have a tory conception of society.

In a liberal bourgeois society which has never known toryism, the demand for equality will express itself as left-wing or democratic liberalism as opposed to whiggery. The left will point out that all are not equal in the competitive pursuit of individual happiness. The government will be required to assure greater equality of opportunity—in the nineteenth century, by destroying monopolistic privileges; in the twentieth century, by providing a welfare "floor" so that no one will fall out of the race for success, and by regulating the economy so that the race can continue without periodic crises.

In a society which thinks of itself as a community of classes rather than an aggregation of individuals, the demand for equality will take a socialist form: for equality of condition rather than mere equality of opportunity; for cooperation rather than competition; for a community that does more than provide a context within which individuals can pursue happiness in a purely self-regarding way. At its most "extreme", socialism is a demand for the *abolition* of classes so that the good of the community can truly be realized. This is a demand which cannot be made by people who can hardly see class and community; the individual fills their eyes.

The Application to Canada

It is a simple matter to apply the Hartzian approach to English Canada in a pan-North American way. English Canada can be viewed as a fragment of the American liberal society, lacking a feudal or tory heritage and therefore lacking the socialist ideology which grows out of it. Canadian domestic struggles, from this point of view, are a northern version of the American struggle between big-propertied liberals on the right and petit-bourgeois and working-class liberals on the left; the struggle goes on within a broad liberal consensus, and the voice of the tory or the socialist is not heard in the land. This pan-North American approach, with important qualifications, is adopted by Hartz and McRae in *The Founding of New Societies*. English Canada, like the United States, is a bourgeois fragment. No toryism in the past, therefore no socialism in the present.

But Hartz notes that the liberal society of English Canada has a "tory touch," that it is "etched with a tory streak coming out of the American revolution."[6]

Take as an example the central concern of this study—the differing weights of Canadian and American socialism. . . . The CCF failed to become a major party in urban Canada, but it succeeded in becoming a significant minor party—a success denied to the American socialist. . . .

The most important un-American characteristics of English Canada, all related to the presence of toryism, are: (a) the presence of tory ideology in the founding of English Canada by the Loyalists, and its continuing influence on English Canadian political culture; (b) the persistent power of whiggery or right-wing liberalism in Canada (the Family Compacts) as contrasted with the rapid and easy victory of liberal democracy (Jefferson, Jackson) in the United States; (c) the ambivalent centrist character of left-wing liberalism in Canada as contrasted with the unambiguously leftist position of left-wing liberalism in the United States; (d) the presence of an influential and legitimate socialist movement in English Canada as contrasted with the illegitimacy and early death of American socialism; (e) the failure of English Canadian liberalism to develop into the one true myth, the nationalist cult, and the parallel failure to exclude toryism and socialism as "un-Canadian"; in other words, the legitimacy of ideological diversity in English Canada.

The Presence of Toryism and its Consequences

Many students have noted that English Canadian society has been powerfully shaped by tory values that are "alien" to the American mind. The latest of these is Seymour Martin Lipset, who stresses the relative strength in Canada of the tory values of "ascription" and "élitism" (the tendency to defer to authority), and the relative weakness of the liberal values of "achievement" and "egalitarianism."[7] He points to such well-known features of Canadian history as the absence of a lawless, individualistic-egalitarian American frontier, the preference for Britain rather than the United States as a social model and, generally, the weaker emphasis on social equality, the greater acceptance by individuals of the facts of economic inequality, social stratification, and hierarchy, . . . belief in monarchy and empire unity, greater stress on "law and order," revulsion against American populistic excesses, different frontier experiences and so on. One tory touch in English Canada. . . is the far greater willingness of English Canadian political and business élites to use the power of the state for the purpose of developing and controlling the economy. . . . Canada is not a feudal (tory) fragment but a bourgeois (liberal) fragment touched with toryism. . . .

Let us put it this way: pre-revolutionary America was a liberal fragment with insignificant traces of toryism, extremely weak feudal survivals. But they were insignificant in the *American* setting; they were far overshadowed by the liberalism of that setting. The revolution did not have to struggle against them; it swept them away easily and painlessly, leaving no trace of them in the American memory. But these traces of toryism were expelled into a *new* setting, where they were no longer insignificant. In this new setting, where there was no pre-established overpowering liberalism to force them into insignificance, they played a large part in shaping a new political culture, significantly different from the American. As Nelson wrote in *The American Tory*, "the Tories' organic conservatism represented a current of thought that failed to reappear in America after the revolution. A substantial part of the whole spectrum of European. . . philosophy seemed to slip outside the American perspective."[8] But it *reappeared* in Canada. Here the sway of liberalism has proved to be not total, but considerably mitigated by a tory presence initially and a socialist presence subsequently. . . . In

Canada, the Family Compacts were able to maintain ascendancy and delay the coming of democracy because of the tory touch "inherited in part from American Loyalism, which restrained egalitarian feeling in Canada."[9] The early power of whiggery serves to emphasize the importance of the tory touch in English Canada....

In the United States, the masses could not be swayed by the Federalist-Whig appeals to anti-egalitarian sentiments. In Canada, the masses *were* swayed by these appeals; the role of the Compacts was to save "the colonial masses from the spectre of republicanism and democracy."[10] What accounts for this is the tory presence in English Canadian political culture—the "greater acceptance of limitation, of hierarchical patterns."[11]

The next step in tracing the development of the English Canadian political culture must be to take account of the tremendous waves of British immigration which soon engulfed the original American Loyalist fragment.... These British immigrants had undoubtedly been heavily infected with non-liberal ideas, and these ideas were undoubtedly in their heads as they settled in Canada. The political culture of a new nation is not necessarily fixed at the point of origin or departure; the founding of a new nation can go on for generations. If the later waves of immigration arrived before the *point of congealment* of the political culture, they must have participated actively in the process of culture formation....

Between 1815 and 1850 almost one million Britons emigrated to Canada. The population of English Canada doubled in 20 years and quadrupled in 40. The population of Ontario increased 10-fold in the same period—from about 95,000 in 1814 to about 950,000 in 1851.[12] ... Is it not possible that the immigrants, while they were no doubt considerably liberalized by their new environment, also brought to it non-liberal ideas which entered into the political culture mix and which perhaps even reinforced the non-liberal elements present in the original fragment? If the million immigrants had come from the United States rather than Britain, would English Canada not be "significantly" different today?

The difficulty in applying the Hartzian approach to English Canada is that although the point of departure is reasonably clear, it is difficult to put one's finger on the point of congealment. Perhaps it was the Loyalist period; perhaps it was close to the mid-century mark; there are grounds for arguing that it was in the more recent past. But the important point is this: no matter where the point of congealment is located in time, the tory streak is present before the solidification of the political culture, and it is strong *enough* to produce *significant* "imperfectionist" or non-liberal, un-American attributes of English Canadian society. My own opinion is that the point of congealment came later than the Loyalists....

The indeterminate location of the point of congealment makes it difficult to account in any *precise* way for the presence of socialism in the English Canadian political cultural mix, though the presence itself is indisputable. If the point of congealment came *before* the arrival of the first radical or socialist-minded immigrants, the presence of socialism must be ascribed primarily to the earlier presence of toryism. Since toryism is a significant part of the political culture, at least part of the leftist reaction against it will sooner or later be expressed in its own terms, that is, in terms of *class* interests and the good of the community as a corporate entity (socialism) rather than in terms of the individual and his or her vicissitudes in the competitive pursuit of happiness (liberalism). If the point of congealment is very early, socialism appears at a later point not primarily because it is imported by British immigrants, but because it is contained as a potential in the original political culture. The immigrants then find that they do not have to give it up—that it is not un-Canadian—because it "fits" to a certain extent with the tory ideas already present. If the point of congealment is very late, the presence of socialism must be explained as a result of *both* the presence of toryism and the introduction of socialism into the cultural mix before congealment. The immigrant retains his or her socialism not only because it "fits" but also because nothing really *has* to fit. Socialism is not un-Canadian partly because "Canadian" has not yet been defined.

Canadian liberals cannot be expected to wax enthusiastic about the non-liberal traits of their country. They are likely to condemn the tory touch as anachronistic, stifling, undemocratic, out of tune with the essentially American ("free", "class-less") spirit of English Canada. They dismiss the socialist touch as an "old-fashioned" protest, no longer necessary (if it ever was) in the best (liberal) of all possible worlds in which the "end of ideology" has been achieved. The secret dream of the Canadian liberal is the removal of English Canada's "imperfections"—in other words, the total assimilation of English Canada into the larger North American culture. But there is a flaw in this dream which might give pause even to the liberal. Hartz places special emphasis on one very unappetizing characteristic of the new societies—intolerance—which is strikingly absent in English Canada. Because the new societies other than Canada are unfamiliar with legitimate ideological diversity, they are unable to accept it and deal with it in a rational manner, either internally or on the level of international relations.

The European nation has an "identity which transcends any ideologist and a mechanism in which each plays only a part."[13] Neither the tory, nor the liberal, nor the socialist, has a monopoly of the expression of the "spirit" of the nation. But the new societies, the fragments, contain only one of the ideologies of Europe; they are one-myth cultures. In the new setting, freed from its historic enemies past and future, ideology transforms itself into nationalism. It claims to be a moral absolute, "the great spirit of a nation."[14] In the United States, liberalism becomes "Americanism"; a political philosophy becomes a civil religion, a nationalist cult. The American attachment to Locke is "absolutist and irrational."[15] Democratic capitalism is the American way of life; to oppose it is to be un-American.

To be an American is to be a bourgeois liberal. To be French Canadian is to be a pre-Enlightenment Catholic; to be an Australian is to be a prisoner of the radical myth of "mateship"; to be a Boer is to be a pre-Enlightenment bourgeois Calvinist. The fragments escape the need for philosophy, for thought-about values, for "where perspectives shrink to a single value, and that value becomes the universe, how can value itself be considered?"[16] The fragment demands solidarity. Ideologies which diverge from the national myth make no impact; they are not understood, and their proponents are not granted legitimacy. They are denounced as aliens, and treated as aliens, because they *are* aliens. The fragments cannot understand or deal with the fact that *all* people are *not* bourgeois Americans, or radical Australians, or Catholic French Canadians, or Calvinist South Africans. They cannot make peace with the loss of ideological certainty.

The specific weakness of the United States is its "inability to understand the appeal of socialism" to the Third World.[17] Because the United States has "buried" the memory of the organic medieval community "beneath new liberal absolutisms and nationalisms,"[18] it cannot understand that the appeal of socialism to nations with a predominantly non-liberal past (including French Canada) consists precisely in the promise of "continuing the corporate ethos in the very process" of modernization.[19] The American reacts with isolationism, messianism and hysteria.

English Canada, because it is the most "imperfect" of the fragments, is not a one-myth culture. In English Canada ideological diversity has not been buried beneath an absolutist liberal nationalism. Here Locke is not the one true god; he must tolerate lesser tory and socialist deities at his side. The result is that English Canada does not direct an uncomprehending intolerance at heterodoxy, either within its borders or beyond them.(What a "backlash" Parti-Pris or PSQ-type separatists would be getting if Quebec were in the United States!) In English Canada it has been possible to consider values without arousing the all-silencing cry of treason. Hartz observes that "if history had chosen English Canada for the American role" of directing the Western response to the world revolution,"the international scene would probably have witnessed less McCarthyite hysteria, less Wilsonian messianism."[20]

Americanizing liberals might consider that the Pearsonian rationality and calmness which Canada displays on the world stage—the "mediating" and "peace-keeping" role of which Canadians are so proud—is related to the un-American (tory and socialist) characteristics which they consider to be unnecessary imperfections in English Canadian wholeness. The tolerance of English Canadian domestic politics is also linked with the presence of these imperfections. If the price of Americanization is the surrender of legitimate ideological diversity, even the liberal might think twice before paying it. . . .

Non-liberal British elements have entered into English Canadian society *together* with American liberal elements at the foundations. The fact is that Canada has been greatly influenced by both the United States and Britain. This is not to deny that liberalism is the dominant element in English Canadian political culture; it is to stress that it is not the sole element, that it is accompanied by vital and legitimate streams of toryism and socialism which have as close a relation to English Canada's "essence" or "foundations" as does liberalism. English Canada's "essence" is both liberal and non-liberal. Neither the British nor the American elements can be explained away as "superstructural" excrescences.

Un-American Aspects of Canadian Conservatism

So far, I have been discussing the presence of toryism in Canada without referring to the Conservative party. This party can be seen as a party of right-wing or business liberalism, but such an interpretation would be far from the whole truth; the Canadian Conservative party, like the British Conservative party and unlike the Republican party, is not monolithically liberal. If there is a touch of toryism in English Canada, its primary carrier has been the Conservative party. It would not be correct to say that toryism is *the* ideology of the party, or even that some Conservatives are tories. These statements would not be true even of the British Conservative party. The primary component of the ideology of business-oriented parties is liberalism; but there are powerful traces of the old pre-liberal outlook in the British Conservative party, and less powerful but still perceptible traces of it in the Canadian party. A Republican is always a liberal. A Conservative may be at one moment a liberal, at the next moment a tory, and is usually something of both.

If it is true that the Canadian Conservatives can be seen from some angles as right-wing liberals, it is also true that figures such as R.B. Bennett, Arthur Meighen and George Drew cannot be understood simply as Canadian versions of William McKinley, Herbert Hoover and Robert Taft. Canadian Conservatives have something British about them that American Republicans do not. It is not simply their emphasis on loyalty to the crown and to the British connections, but a touch of the authentic tory aura—traditionalism, élitism, the strong state, and so on. The Canadian Conservatives lack the American aura of rugged individualism. Theirs is not the characteristically American conservatism which conserves only *liberal* values.

It is possible to perceive in Canadian conservatism not only the elements of business liberalism and orthodox toryism, but also an element of "tory democracy"—the paternalistic concern for the "condition of the people" and the emphasis on the tory party as their champion—which, in Britain, was expressed by such figures as Disraeli and Lord Randolph Churchill. John A. Macdonald's approach to the emergent Canadian working class was in some respects similar to that of Disraeli. Later Conservatives acquired the image of arch reactionaries and arch enemies of the workers, but let us not forget that "Iron Heel" Bennett was also the Bennett of the Canadian New Deal.

The question arises: why is it that in Canada the *Conservative* leader proposes a New Deal? Why is it that the Canadian counterpart of Hoover apes *Roosevelt?* This phenomenon is usually interpreted as sheer historical accident, a product of Bennett's desperation and opportunism. But the answer may be that Bennett was not Hoover. Even in his "orthodox" days Bennett's views on the state's role in the economy were far from similar to Hoover's; Bennett's attitude was that of Canadian, not American, conservatism. Once this is recognized, it is possible to entertain the suggestion that Bennett's sudden radicalism, his sudden concern for the people, may not have been mere opportunism. It may have been a manifestation, a sudden activation under pressure, of a latent tory-democratic streak. Let it be noted also that the Depression produced two Conservative splinter parties, both with "radical" welfare state programmes and both led by former subordinates of Bennett: H.H. Stevens' Reconstruction party and W.D. Herridge's New Democracy.

The Bennett New Deal is only the most extreme instance of what is usually considered to be an accident or an aberration—the occasional manifestation of "radicalism" or "leftism" by otherwise orthodox Conservative leaders in the face of opposition from their "followers" in the business community. Meighen, for example, was constantly embroiled with the "Montreal interests" who objected to his railway policies. On one occasion he received a note of congratulation from William Irvine:"The man who dares to offend the Montreal interests is the sort of man that the people are going to vote for."[21] This same Meighen expressed on certain occasions, particularly after his retirement, an antagonism to big government and creeping socialism that would have warmed the heart of Robert Taft; but he combined his business liberalism with gloomy musings about the evil of universal suffrage[22]—musings which Taft would have rejected as un-American. Meighen is far easier to understand from a British than from an American perspective, for he combined, in different proportions at different times, attitudes deriving from all three Conservative ideological streams: right-wing liberalism, orthodox toryism and tory democracy.

The western or agrarian Conservatives of the contemporary period, John Diefenbaker and Alvin Hamilton, who are usually dismissed as "prairie radicals" of the American type, might represent not only anti-Bay Street agrarianism but *also* the same type of tory democracy which was expressed before their time by orthodox business-sponsored Conservatives such as Meighen and Bennett. The populism (anti-élitism) of Diefenbaker and Hamilton is a geniunely foreign element in Canadian conservatism, but their stress on the Tory party as champion of the people and their advocacy of welfare state policies are in the tory democratic tradition. Their attitudes toward the monarchy, the British connection and the danger of American domination are entirely orthodox Conservative attitudes. Diefenbaker conservatism is therefore to be understood not simply as a western populist phenomenon, but as an odd *combination* of traditional Conservative views with attitudes absorbed from the western Progressive tradition.

Another aberration which may be worthy of investigation is the Canadian phenomenon of the red tory. At the simplest level, the red tory is a Conservative who prefers the CCF-NDP to the Liberals, or a socialist who prefers the Conservatives to the Liberals, without really knowing why. At a higher level, the red tory is a conscious ideological Conservative with some "odd" socialist notions (W.L. Morton) or a conscious ideological socialist with some "odd" tory notions (Eugene Forsey). The very suggestion that such affinities might exist between Republicans and Socialists in the United States is ludicous enough to make some kind of a point.

Red toryism is, of course, one of the results of the relationship between toryism and socialism which has already been elucidated. The tory and socialist minds have some crucial assumptions, orientations and values in common, so that from certain angles they may appear not as enemies, but as two different expressions of the same basic ideological outlook. Thus, at the very highest level, the red tory is a philosopher who combines elements of socialism and toryism so thoroughly in a single integrated *Weltanschauung* that it is impossible to say that he or she is a proponent of either one as *against* the other. Such a red tory is George Grant, who has associations with both the Conservative party and the NDP and who has recently published a book which defends Diefenbaker, laments the death of "true" British conservativism in Canada, attacks the Liberals as individualists and Americanizers and defines socialism as a variant of conservatism (each "protects the public good against private freedom").[23]

The Character of Canadian Socialism

Canadian socialism is un-American in two distinct ways. It is un-American in the sense that it is a significant and legitimate political force in Canada, insignificant and alien in the United States. But Canadian socialism is also un-American in the sense that it does not speak the same language as American socialism. In Canada, socialism is British, non-Marxist and worldly; in the United States it is German, Marxist and other-worldly.

I have argued that the socialist ideas of British immigrants to Canada were not sloughed off because they "fit" with a political culture which already contained non-liberal components, and probably also because they were introduced into the political culture mix before the point of congealment. Thus, socialism was not alien here. But it was not alien in yet another way: it was not borne by foreigners. The personnel and the ideology of the Canadian labour and socialist movements have been primarily British. Many of those who built these movements were British immigrants with past experience in the British labour movement; many others were Canadian-born children of such immigrants. And in British North America, Britons could not be treated as foreigners.

When socialism was brought to the United States, it found itself in an ideological environment in which it could not survive because Lockean individualism had long since achieved the status of a national religion; the political culture had already congealed and socialism did not fit. American socialism was alien not only in this ideological sense, but in the ethnic sense as well; it was borne by foreigners from Germany and other continental European countries. These foreigners sloughed off their socialist ideas not simply because such ideas did not "fit" ideologically, but because as foreigners they were going through a general process of Americanization; socialism was only one of many ethnically alien characteristics which had to be abandoned. The immigrant's ideological change was only one incident among many others in the general process of changing his or her entire way of life. According to David Saposs, "the factor that contributed most tellingly to the decline of the socialist movement was that its chief following, the immigrant workers, . . . had become Americanized."[24]

A British socialist immigrant to Canada had a far different experience. The

British immigrant was not an "alien" in British North America. The English Canadian culture not only granted legitimacy to his or her political ideas and absorbed them into its wholeness; it absorbed the immigrant into the English Canadian community, with relatively little strain, without demanding that he or she change a way of life before being granted full citizenship. He or she was acceptable to begin with, by virtue of being British. It is impossible to understand the differences between American and Canadian socialism without taking into account this immense difference between the ethnic contexts of socialism in the two countries.

The ethnic handicap of American socialism consisted not only in the fact that its personnel was heavily European. Equally important was the fact that it was a *brand* of socialism—Marxism—which found survival difficult not only in the United States but in all English-speaking countries. Marxism has not found the going easy in the United States; nor in Britain, Canada, Australia, or New Zealand. The socialism of the United States, the socialism of De Leon, Berger, Hillquit and Debs, is predominantly Marxist and doctrinaire, because it is European. The socialism of English Canada, the socialism of Simpson, Woodsworth and Coldwell, is predominantly Protestant, labourist and Fabian, because it is British.

The CCF has not been without its other-worldly tendencies: there have been doctrinal disagreements and the party has always had a left wing interested more in "socialist education" than in practical political work. But this left wing has been a constantly declining minority. The party has expelled individuals and small groups—mostly Communists and Trotskyites—but has never split. Its life has never been threatened by disagreement over doctrinal matters. It is no more preoccupied with theory than the British Labour party. It sees itself, and is seen by the public, not as a coterie of ideologists but as a party like the others, second to none in its avidity for office. If it has been attacked from the right for socialist "utopianism" and "impracticality," it has also been attacked from the right and left for abandoning the "true" socialist faith in an unprincipled drive for power.

Canadian Liberalism: The Triumphant Centre

Canadian Conservatives are not American Republicans; Canadian socialists are not American socialists; Canadian Liberals are not American liberal Democrats.

The un-American elements in English Canada's political culture are most evident in Canadian conservatism and socialism. But Canadian liberalism has a British colour too. The liberalism of Canada's Liberal party should not be identified with the liberalism of the American Democratic party. In many respects they stand in sharp contrast to one another.

The three components of the English Canadian political culture have not developed in isolation from one another; each has developed in interaction with the others. Our toryism and our socialism have been moderated by liberalism. But, by the same token, our liberalism has been rendered "impure," in American terms, through its contacts with toryism and socialism. If English Canadian liberalism is less individualistic, less ardently populistic-democratic, more inclined to state intervention in the economy and more tolerant of "feudal survivals" such as monarchy, this is due to the uninterrupted influence of toryism upon liberalism, an influence wielded in and through the conflict between the two. If English Canadian liberalism has tended since the Depression to merge at its leftist edge with the democratic socialism of the CCF-NDP, this is due to the influence which socialism has exerted upon liberalism, in and through the conflict between them. The key to understanding the Liberal party in Canada is to see it as a *centre* party, with *influential* enemies on both right and left.

In English Canada, Liberal Reform, represented by King's Liberal party, has had to face the socialist challenge. Under socialist influence, it abandoned its early devotion to "the lofty principles of Gladstone, the sound economics of Adam Smith, and the glories of *laissez-faire*."[25] King's *Industry and Humanity* and the Liberal platform of 1919 mark the transition of English Canadian Liberalism from the old individualism to the new Liberal Reform.

King's Liberal Reform, since it had to answer attacks from the left as well as from the right, projected a notoriously ambivalent conservative-radical image:

Truly he will be remembered
Wherever men honour ingenuity
Ambiguity, inactivity and political longevity.

When he faced Bennett and Meighen, King was the radical warrior, the champion of the little people against the interests. When he turned to face Woodsworth and Coldwell, he was the cautious conservative, the protector of the status quo. He

. . . never let his on the one hand
Know what his on the other hand was doing.[26]

Hartz points out that the "pragmatism" of the New Deal enabled it to go farther, to get more things done, than European Liberal Reform. "The freewheeling inventiveness typified by the TVA, the NRA, and WPA, the SEC"[27] was nowhere to be found in Europe. Defending itself against socialism, European Liberal Reform could not submerge questions of theory; it had to justify innovations on the basis of a revised liberal ideology; it had to stop short of socialism openly. The New Deal, since it was not threatened by socialism, could ignore theory; it "did not need to stop short of Marx openly"; hence it could accomplish more than European Liberal Reform.

King had to face the socialist challenge. He did so in the manner of European Liberal Reform. . . . The similarity of socialism and Liberal Reform could be acknowledged; indeed it could be emphasized and used to attract the socialist vote. At the same time, King had to answer the arguments of socialism, and in doing so he had to spell out his liberalism. He had to stop short of socialism openly. Social reform, yes; extension of public ownership, yes; the welfare state, yes; increased state control of the economy, yes; but not too much. Not socialism. The result was that King, like the European liberals, could not go as far as Roosevelt. . . . Like the European liberals, and unlike Roosevelt, he had to defend private property, he had to attack excessive reliance on the state, he had to criticize socialism as "impracticality" and "utopianism." "Half radical and half conservative—a tired man who could not make up his mind"—is this not the living image of Mackenzie King?

"In America, instead of being a champion of property, Roosevelt became the big antagonist of it; his liberalism was blocked by his radicalism."[28] In Canada, since King had to worry not only about Bennett and Meighen and Drew, but also about Woodsworth and Coldwell and Douglas, King had to embark upon a defence of private property. *He* was no traitor to his class. Instead of becoming the antagonist of property, he became its champion; his radicalism was blocked by his liberalism.

An emphasis on the solidarity of the nation as against divisive "class parties" of right and left was "of the very essence of the Reformist Liberal position in Europe." "Who," asks Hartz, "would think of Roosevelt as a philosopher of class solidarity?"[29] Yet that is precisely what Roosevelt would have been if he had had to respond to a socialist presence in the American political culture. And that is precisely what King was, in fact, in Canada. His party was "the party of national unity." One of the most repeated charges against the CCF was that it was a divisive "class party"; the purpose of the Liberal party, on the other hand, was to preserve the solidarity of the Canadian people—the solidarity of its classes as well as the solidarity of French and English. . . .

The Liberal party has continued to speak the language of King: ambiguous and ambivalent, presenting first its radical face and then its conservative face, urging reform and warning against hasty, ill-considered change, calling for increased state responsibility but stopping short of socialism openly, speaking for the common people but preaching the solidarity of classes.

In the United States, the liberal Democrats are on the left. There is no doubt about that. In Canada, the Liberals are a party of the centre, appearing at times leftist and at times rightist. As such, they are much closer to European, especially British, Liberal Reform than to the American New Deal type of liberalism.

In the United States, the liberal Democrats are the party of organized labour. The new men of power, the labour leaders, have arrived politically; their vehicle is the Democratic party. In English Canada, if the labour leaders have arrived politically, they have done so in the CCF-NDP. They are nowhere to be found in the Liberal party. The rank and file, in the United States, are predominantly Democrats; in Canada at least a quarter are New Democrats, and the remainder show only a relatively slight, and by no means consistent, preference for the Liberals as against the Conservatives.

In the United States, left-wing "liberalism," as opposed to right-wing "liberalism," has always meant opposition to the domination of American life by big business, and has expressed itself in and through the Democratic party; the party of business is the Republican party. In Canada, business is close to both the Conservatives and the Liberals. The business community donates to the campaign funds of both and is represented in the leadership circles of both.

The Liberal party in Canada does not represent the opposition of society to domination by organized business. It claims to be based on no particular groups, but on *all*. It is not against any particular group; it is for *all*. The idea that there is any real conflict between groups is dismissed, and the very terms 'right' and 'left' are rejected. "The terms 'right' and 'left' belong to those who regard politics as a class struggle. . . . The Liberal view is that true political progress is marked by . . . the reconciliation of classes, and the promotion of the general interest above all particular interests."[30]

A party of the left can be distinguished from parties of the centre and right according to two interrelated criteria: its policy approach and its electoral support.

Policy Approach

The policy approach of a left party is to introduce innovations on behalf of the lower strata. The Liberals, unlike the liberal Democrats, have not been a party of innovation. As a centre party, they have allowed the CCF-NDP to introduce innovations; they have then waited for signs of substantial acceptance by all strata of the population and for signs of reassurance against possible electoral reprisals, before actually proceeding to implement the innovations. Of course, by this time they are, strictly speaking, no longer innovations. The centre party recoils from the fight for controversial measures; it loves to implement a consensus. Roosevelt was the innovator *par excellence*. King, though he was in his own mind in favour of reform, stalled until public demand for innovation was so great and so clear that he could respond to it without antagonizing his business-sponsored right wing. He rationalized his caution into a theory of democratic leadership far different from Roosevelt's conception of the strong presidency:

> Mackenzie King's conception of political leadership, which he often expressed, was that a leader should make his objectives clear, but that leadership was neither liberal nor democratic which tried to force new policies . . . on a public that did not consent to them.[31]
>
> He believed that nothing was so likely to set back a good cause as premature action.[32]

This was the official Liberal explanation of King's failure to embark on any far-reaching programme of reform until 1943. King himself undoubtedly believed that his caution was based at least in part on a "democratic" theory of leadership. But his diaries suggest that the reforms came when they did because CCF pressure became so threatening that it could no longer be ignored by King's right-wing colleagues—so threatening that King felt able to surrender to it without jeopardizing the unity of his party. The bare facts are these: In August 1943, the CCF became the official opposition in Ontario. In September 1943, the CCF overtook the Liberals in the Gallup poll (Canada: CCF 19 percent, Liberals

28 percent; Ontario: CCF 32 percent, Liberals 26 percent; The West: CCF 41 percent; Liberals 23 percent).[33] King's reaction is summed up in the following quotation from his diary: "In my heart, I am not sorry to see the mass of the people coming a little more into their own, but I do regret that it is not the Liberal party that is winning the position for them. . . . It can still be that our people will learn their lesson in time. What I fear is we will begin to have defections from our own ranks in the House to the CCF."[34] Almost immediately after the release of the September Gallup Poll, the Advisory Council of the National Liberal Federation, meeting at King's request, adopted 14 resolutions "constituting a programme of reform . . . of far reaching consequences."[35] King wrote in his diary: "I have succeeded in making declarations which will improve the lot of . . . farmers and working people. . . . I think I have cut the ground in large part from under the CCF. . . ."[36]

The Liberal slogan in the campaign of 1945 was "A New Social Order for Canada." The election of June 11 returned King to power with a drastically reduced majority. The CCF vote rose from 8.5 percent to 15.6 percent, and its representation in the Commons from 8 to 29. But King's swing to the left had defeated the CCF's bid for major party status. The CCF's success was much smaller than it had expected. The success was actually a defeat, a disappointing shock from which socialism in Canada has not yet recovered.

The Liberal-CCF relationship in 1943–45 is only the sharpest and clearest instance of the permanent interdependence forced upon each by the presence of the other, a relationship which one student describes as "antagonistic symbiosis." The Liberals depend on the CCF-NDP for innovations; the CCF-NDP depends upon the Liberals for implementation of the innovations. When the left is weak, as before and after World War II, the centre party moves right to deal with the Conservative challenge; when the left is strengthened, as during the war and after the formation of the NDP, the centre moves left to deal with the challenge.

In a conversation between King and Coldwell shortly before King's death, King expressed his regrets that Coldwell had not joined him. With Coldwell at his side, he would have been able to implement reforms which were close to his heart; reforms which had either been postponed until the end of the war or not introduced at all. He said the CCF had performed the valuable function of popularizing reforms so that he could introduce them when public opinion was ripe. Coldwell replied that it was impossible for him to join King, especially in view of the people who surrounded King.[37] There, in a nutshell, is the story of the relationship between the Liberal party and the CCF-NDP. The Liberals, says King, are too conservative because the left has not joined them. The left has not joined them, replies Coldwell, because they are too conservative.

King wanted to show the people that he was "true to them." He was saddened that the CCF and not the Liberals were fighting the people's battles. But he could not move from dead centre until CCF power became so great that the necessity of moving was clear, not only to himself but to all realistic politicians. King's best self wanted to innovate; yet he saw the Liberal party not as a great innovating force but as the party which would implement reforms once they had been popularized by the CCF. Yet he wanted to absorb the CCF. The lot of the centrist politician is not a happy one.

The absence of Lockean "monotheism" strengthened socialism in Canada. Socialism was present in the political culture when liberalism began to concern itself with the problems of the industrial age; liberalism was therefore forced to react to the socialist challenge. In doing so, it was cast in the mold of European Liberal Reform (centre) parties—ambivalent, radical and conservative, alternating attacks on the status quo with defence of the status quo. Socialism had sufficient strength in English Canada to force liberalism into the European rather than the American position—centre rather than left. King's liberalism was therefore not capable of reacting to the Depression in the Rooseveltian manner. As a result, socialist power grew.

Socialism was not powerless, so there was no New Deal. There was no New Deal, so socialism grew more powerful. Socialism grew more powerful, so King reacted with "A New Social Order for Canada." The centre and the left dance around one another, frustrating one another and living off the frustration; each is locked into the dance by the existence of the other.

I have been stressing the strength of Canadian socialism in order to make clear the differences between the Canadian and the American situations. Of course this does not mean that the differences between Canada and Europe can be ignored. Canadian socialism has been strong enough to challenge liberalism, to force liberalism to explain itself, and thus to evoke from it the same sort of centrist response as was evoked in Europe. But socialism in Canada has not been strong enough to match or overshadow liberalism. The CCF became a significant political force but, except for the years 1942–45, it never knocked on the gates of national power.

In Europe, the working person could not be appeased by the concession of Liberal Reform. The centre was squeezed out of existence between its enemies on the right and on the left. In Canada, the centre party's concessions were sufficient to keep the lower strata from flocking en masse to the left. The concessions were not sufficient to *dispose* of the socialist threat, but they were sufficient to draw the socialists' sharpest teeth. In Canada the centre party emerged triumphant over its enemies on the right and on the left. Here, then, is another aspect of English Canada's uniqueness: it is the only society in which Liberal Reform faces the challenge of socialism *and* emerges victorious. The English Canadian fragment *is* bourgeois. The toryism and the socialism, though significant, *are* "touches."

Electoral Support

There is a dearth of information about the influence of class on voting behaviour in Canada, but there are strong indications that the higher strata are more likely than the lower to vote Conservative, the lower strata are more likely than the higher to vote CCF-NDP, and that both groups are about *equally* attracted to the Liberals. This would, of course, confirm the picture of Conservatives as the right, NDP as the left and Liberals as the "classless" centre.

This is in sharp contrast to the situation in the United States, where the lower strata prefer the Democrats, the higher prefer the Republicans and there is no centre party.

Although this picture of the relationship between class and voting is broadly true, it is also true that class voting in Canada is, generally speaking, overshadowed by regional and religious-ethnic voting. In some parts of Canada (e.g., Ontario) class voting is as high as in the United States or higher. Nevertheless, in Canada *considered as a whole* class voting is lower than in the United States; non-class motivations appear to be very strong.[38] Peter Regenstrief suggests that one factor accounting for this is the persistent cultivation by the Liberal party of its classless image, its "abhorrence of anything remotely associated with class politics,"[39] its refusal to appeal to any class *against* any other class.

What this points to again is the unique character of English Canada as the only society in which the centre triumphs over left and right. In Europe the classless appeal of Liberal Reform does not work; the centre is decimated by the defection of high-status adherents to the right and of low-status adherents to the left. In Canada, the classless appeal of King centrism is the winning strategy, drawing lower-class support to the Liberals away from the left parties and higher-class support away from the right parties. This forces the left and right parties themselves to emulate (to a certain extent) the Liberals' classless strategy. The Conservatives transform themselves into Progressive Conservatives. The CCF transforms itself from a "farmer-labour" party into an NDP calling for the support of "all liberally minded Canadians." The Liberal refusal to appear as a class party forces both right and left to mitigate their class appeals and to become themselves, in a sense, centre parties.

Class voting in Canada may be lower than in the United States, not entirely because regional-religious-ethnic factors are "objectively" stronger here, but also because King liberalism, by resolutely avoiding class symbols, had *made* other symbols more important.

> He blunted us.
> We have no shape
> Because he never took sides,
> And no sides,
> Because he never allowed them to take shape.[40]

ENDNOTES

1. Louis Hartz, *The Liberal Tradition in America* (New York: Harcourt, Brace and World [Toronto: Longmans], 1955).
2. Louis Hartz, *The Founding of New Societies* (New York: Harcourt, Brace and World [Toronto: Longmans], 1964).
3. *Ibid.*, p. 3.
4. *Ibid.*, p. 25.
5. *Ibid.*, p. 7.
6. *Ibid.*, p. 34.

7. Seymour Martin Lipset, *The First New Nation* (New York: Basic Books, 1963), esp. ch. 7.
8. William Nelson, *The American Tory* (Oxford: Clarendon Press, 1961), pp. 189–90.
9. Hartz, *New Societies*, p. 91.
10. *Ibid.*, p. 243.
11. Lipset, *The First New Nation*, p. 251.
12. Hartz, *New Societies*, p. 245.
13. *Ibid.*, p. 15.
14. *Ibid.*, p. 10.
15. Hartz, *Liberal Tradition*, p. 11.
16. Hartz, *New Societies*, p. 23.
17. *Ibid.*, p. 119.
18. *Ibid.*, p. 35.
19. *Ibid.*, p. 119.
20. *Ibid.*, p. 120.
21. Roger Graham, *Arthur Meighen*, Vol. II (Toronto: Clarke, Irwin, 1963), p. 269.
22. *Ibid.*, Vol. III (Toronto: Clarke, Irwin, 1965), pp. 71–74.
23. George Grant, *Lament for a Nation* (Toronto: McClelland and Stewart, 1965), p. 71.
24. David Saposs, *Communism in American Unions* (New York: McGraw-Hill, 1959), p. 7.
25. Bruce Hutchison, *The Incredible Canadian* (Toronto: Longmans, Green and Co., 1952), p. 6.
26. F.R. Scott, "W.M.L.K.," in *The Blasted Pine*, F.R. Scott and A.J.M. Smith, eds. (Toronto: Macmillan, 1962), p. 28.
27. Hartz, *Liberal Tradition*, p. 271.
28. *Ibid.*, p. 267.
29. *Ibid.*
30. J.W. Pickersgill, *The Liberal Party* (Toronto: McClelland and Stewart, 1962), p. 68.
31. *Ibid.*, pp. 26–27.
32. J.W. Pickersgill, *The Mackenzie King Record* (Toronto: University of Toronto Press, 1960), p. 10.
33. *The Globe and Mail*, 29 September 1943.
34. Pickersgill, *Record*, p. 571.
35. National Liberal Federation, *The Liberal Party*, p. 53.
36. Pickersgill, *Record*, p. 601.
37. Interview with M.J. Coldwell, 28 March 1962.
38. R. Alford, *Party and Society* (Chicago: Rand McNally, 1963), ch. 9.
39. "Group Perceptions and the Vote," in Meisel, ed., *Papers on the 1962 Election*, p. 249.
40. Scott, *The Blasted Pine*, p. 27.

15 Decline of Party in Canada

JOHN MEISEL

Some years ago, the Royal Winnipeg Ballet gave a command performance at the National Arts Centre in Ottawa to honour the King and Queen of Belgium. Balletomanes found it hard to buy tickets, however, because a very large proportion had been obtained by the Canadian and Belgian governments for free distribution to special guests. *The Globe and Mail's* comment on this event struck a note which is increasingly evident in Canadian coverage of politics:

> The ballet gala ... provided an unintended demonstration of who really rates around Ottawa. The elected politicians—Canadian MPs and visiting legislators were invited to come (in lounge suits) for the ballet. ... Guests invited by External Affairs and the Governor General—mostly bureaucrats and diplomats—were invited to come in black tie and dinner jacket and stay for a champagne party.[1]

The incident is trivial and may be explainable in terms of an administrative slip-up or in some other harmless way, but it does provide a picturesque reminder of the declining role of parliament and hence of party politics in Canada's political system.

Anthony King, in a searching paper analysing the role of parties in liberal democracies, summarizes much of the relevant literature by listing six usually cited functions of parties: (1) structuring the vote; (2) integration and mobilization of the mass public; (3) recruitment of political leaders; (4) organization of government; (5) formation of public policy; and (6) aggregation of interests.[2] He notes that there is a good deal of imprecision in the manner in which political scientists deal with the roles of parties and that the importance of their functions tends to be exaggerated. Nevertheless, he concludes, parties are critical components of the political process and they need to be studied, albeit with greater precision than is often the case.

This essay was written for the fourth edition of this volume and revised slightly for the subsequent edition. It attracted considerable attention and controversy. Although some of the arguments no longer apply, it is of enduring interest and is reproduced here with a number of recent commentaries by the author.

This article shares King's view and, although it focuses on the relative decline of political parties in Canada, it should not be interpreted as arguing that the parties and the party system are insignificant. Parties clearly still influence critical aspects of politics and, most notably, they influence who occupies the government benches in parliament and who heads the various departments and ministries. The emphasis in this article is on federal politics, although many of the observations also apply to the provincial arena.

Parties still perform the first function listed: they structure the vote in most elections, except at the municipal level. They, to some measure, present options to the electorate about current issues and so can be said to organize mass opinion, although one is often tempted to conclude that they disorganize it. As for the related role of mobilizing the public, a remarkably high proportion of Canadians participates in elections in one way or another, and by no means just by voting. The preparation of electoral lists, staffing the polling booths, and organizing the campaigns on a polling division by polling-division basis all takes a great deal of effort, most of which is provided by volunteer activists. This not only enables the electoral process to function, it increases the public's knowledge of political questions and facts. It is well-established that a greater sense of partisan attachment is associated with a greater knowledge of politics.

Nevertheless, an increasing number of Canadians have sought to participate in politics and public life outside the framework of parties—in tenants' or neighbourhood organizations or through voluntary associations, from unions to environmental or anti-nuclear groups. There was an upsurge of such "unconventional" politics in the 1960s in the United States and to a lesser extent in Canada, but there is some uncertainty about the degree to which non-partisan politics has continued to flourish in North America in the 1970s. Although the situation in Canada is a little ambiguous, there is no doubt that the proportion of people in the United States who identify with politcal parties in the sense that they think of themselves as Democrats or Republicans is steadily declining.

Parties also recruit politicians, although many question whether, in general, politics attracts a sufficiently high calibre of individuals. Data are unavailable on this point but some speculate that other careers appeal to the ablest Canadians and they conclude that we could do with a good deal more talent in the parties. This question raises another, also imperfectly understood puzzle: what characteristics make for a good politician? Indeed, what is a good politician?

By deciding which partisan team forms the government and who is in opposition, parties do organize government in an important way. But there is little doubt that a great many decisions—about what is placed on the public agenda and at what time—are forced on political parties by events, non-political decision makers and very often the preferences of powerful civil servants, whose responsibility to the politicians is increasingly more formal than real. Even the organization of the government—the way in which legislation is drafted and considered by the cabinet and its committees, the extent to which outside interests are consulted, the manner in which policies are administered—is more likely to reflect the wills of a small number of senior civil servants than the decision of senior party officials, including the ministers. It is indeed questionable whether the government party leader—the prime minister—continues to function as a party person after accession to power or whether the party role and influence are maintained as a successful administration becomes accustomed to power and develops close relationships with senior civil servants.

In short, one must ask whether the parties really play the central role liberal democratic theory ascribes to them in organizing government and in the formation of public policy. And, given the changes in communication and the importance of voluntary associations and interest groups, one wonders about the relative unimportance of parties in the processes which aggregate the interests of various individuals and groups into satisfactory policies.

In seeking to identify the main manifestations of, and reasons for, the decline of party, relative to other political factors, this essay distinguishes between long-run factors, most of which are universal in liberal democracies and appear to a greater or lesser extent in most highly industrialized and post-industrial societies, and those which are of more recent origin and are uniquely Canadian.

Long-Run Reasons for Party Decline

Rise of the Bureaucratic State

Modern political parties evolved from small cliques of power-wielders when the extension of the franchise necessitated the organization of mass electorates. The greater participation of the public in political life led, in conjunction with other factors, to the emergence of the positive state—one which increasingly participated in virtually every aspect of the human experience. But the "ancestors" of our political institutions and the political parties serving them evolved at a time when governments were dealing with a limited range of problems, and when only a small minority of the population was politically active. Under these conditions parties were able to act as suitable links between the small electorate and the even smaller number of political decision makers.

The continuous expansion of governmental activities has created mounting problems for the legislative and representative system. Up until World War I, the Canadian parliament dealt with only a small number of issues, met seldom and required little specialized and technical knowledge to operate. Now the number and complexity of the areas in which the federal government operates are so vast that it is quite impossible for MPs to be abreast of what is going on. At best, each can become reasonably well-informed about one or two areas.

The expansion of government activities and the increasingly complicated nature of government decisions have reduced the capacity of elected officials to deal with many important public issues and necessitated the restructuring of many governmental institutions. Thus MPs and even cabinet ministers are often incapable of fully understanding the problems and options confronting them, and the normal structures of ministries are being supplemented by a large number of quasi-independent administrative, regulatory and judicial boards and commissions not directly responsible to the elected representatives of the public or to party politicians. In short, an important shift has occurred in the focus of power of liberal democracies, from elected politicians to appointed civil servants, whose links to political parties are indirect and increasingly tenuous. This means that parties, supposedly in control of the political process and responsible to the public for its performance, are often little more than impotent observers of processes they cannot control and the results of which they can only rubber stamp.

A good illustration is the case of irregularities in the sale of reactors by Atomic Energy of Canada Ltd., a crown corporation, to Argentina and Korea. There were strong suspicions that bribes had been paid and that the foreign exchange regulations of some countries had been violated. Enormous commissions were also allegedly paid to shadowy foreign agents. One of the reactors was sold at a loss of over $100 million. The Public Accounts Committee of the House of Commons held extensive hearings and questioned closely Mr. J.L. Gray, president of Atomic Energy of Canada at the time of the sales. His stonewalling of the issue, and that by everyone else connected with the matter, was so effective that the House of Commons committee failed to shed light on the sales and finally had to let the case rest.

Pluralism and the Rise of Interest Group Politics

Before the expansion of governmental activities and the increase in their complexity, the usual pattern of lawmaking was relatively simple. Ministers or the whole cabinet, with or without prompting by their civil servants, decided on the broad outlines of what needed to be done. Civil servants, drawing on expert knowledge and advice, prepared the necessary background papers and draft proposals. These were discussed by the ministers, in the absence of their civil servant advisors, and ultimately presented to parliament for enactment. The basic decisions were essentially those of politicians and their officials. More recently, a more involved process of legislation has evolved, partly because of the need to deal with problems having enormous ramifications, partly in an effort to make government more participatory, and partly in response to the claims of a market-oriented, pluralist society in which political parties depend on the financial support of powerful economic interests or of unions. Before any law or important administrative decision is decided upon, an intense consultation between officials and representatives of various vested interests takes place. There has been a striking increase in lobbying by interest groups who have the resources and capacity to do so. Many important decisions are arrived at through private consultations between civil servants and spokespersons for various vested interests, during which politicians play no role. By the time ministers enter the decision-making process, the die is cast and only minor changes, if any, can be made. The *general* interest, therefore, as aggregated by political parties, tends to receive scant attention and parties are left with little choice but to approve what has already been decided by others. The process of consultation is for the most part totally non-partisan and most ministers engaged in it act as governmental decision makers, far removed from their party personas. For the government party caucus to disown government policies already decided on after considerable negotiations would be politically harmful and is hardly ever heard of. Convincing testimony to the relative impotence of parties is found in Robert Presthus's study of Canadian interest groups, which shows that the latter spend considerably more time and effort lobbying bureaucrats than members of parliament.[3] Furthermore, it is clear that having recourse to pressure group participation in policy making is not a feared or temporary phenomenon. The Canadian government, like many others, has institutionalized the practice by appointing large numbers of advisory committees and other bodies designed to ensure the pressure of interested parties in the policy process.

Incipient Corporatism

A related phenomenon received wide attention during the ill-fated, mid-1970s anti-inflation programme of the federal government. Although the case is derived from Canadian experience, the phenomenon is not unique to this country. Efforts to control prices and wages required the cooperation of both management and labour. The idea was that federal economic policy would emerge from regular consultations between the government and representatives of labour, industry and business and that a group comprised of these interests would become institutionalized as a permanent consultative body. In the end, this structure was never established. It is difficult to see how this kind of change in the governmental process could have been made without undermining the power of parliament and hence of political parties. Compromises delicately wrought by a tripartite council would not likely be upset by the House of Commons even if members of the majority party wished to repudiate the deals made by their leadership.

Recourse to the tripartite consultative process reflects a tendency toward a new form of corporatism—a process of arriving at collective decisions through the efforts of representatives of the main "functional" interests in the country rather than of its territorial delegates. Because corporatism is usually associated with facism, it is viewed with suspicion; but there is nothing inevitably authoritarian in it. There are corporatist elements in the usually highly regarded Swedish politico-economic system. But whatever its general merits, corporatist institutions supplement the legislature and reduce the importance of political parties.

A more recent example of a variant of the corporatist approach concerns the Trudeau government's so-called "Six and Five World." This policy designed to reduce inflation was conceived and launched entirely without any involvement of the Liberal party and its success depended very heavily on the government's ability, in private conversations and negotiations with industry, to ensure voluntary compliance by the private sector with the guidelines. While decidedly non-partisan, it diverged from the corporatist model by not resting on the collaboration of government, business and industry, as well as labour. The latter was bitterly hostile to the programme and vigorously repudiated it. It should, however, be noted that in the execution of the scheme, Senator Keith Davey, the quintessential Liberal party activist, played a key role on the committee guiding the implementation of the "Six and Five" programme. But he was asked to perform this task because of his personal qualities and not because of his party connections.

Federal-Provincial Diplomacy

Another and increasingly threatening cause of the decline in the importance of parties lies in the changing nature of Canadian federalism. Accommodation between the various regions of the country (and to some extent, between special interests which happen to be in part regionally based) is taking place more and more through two mechanisms which are largely unrelated to party politics. The first of these is the federal-provincial prime ministerial conference, where Ottawa and the provinces hammer out compromises touching virtually every aspect of human experience. Most of these are the result of delicate bargaining on the part of 11 governments which sometimes cannot help but take positions imposed by other negotiators and which therefore cannot be anticipated by legislative caucuses, let alone by party supporters.

The second procedure through which policies are agreed upon by the federal and provincial governments is the regular meeting and consultation among federal and provincial officials. There are now thousands of such encounters annually and hundreds of formally established committees, task forces and work groups in which decisions are made that bind the participating governments. As with prime ministerial meetings, these encounters reach decisions which can be reversed or altered only at great cost—one not likely to be risked by rank-and-file members of political parties.

It can be argued that governments, at the ministerial level, are composed of leading party politicians and that their actions are in a sense those of political parties. This is technically correct, but the infrequent and unfocused expression of party opinion and the almost nonexistent party activity between elections deprive elected officials of any viable contact with their party organisms. There is, in contrast, a striking frequency and intensity of contacts between office-holding politicians and civil servants and spokesmen for vested interests. It is no exaggeration to argue that although ministers, and through them, the officials who serve under them, formally reflect party interests, they do not do so in any meaningful way. Between elections, except for occasional and exceedingly rare party gatherings, the cabinet *is* the party, insofar as the government side of the equation is concerned. Thus, such major policy changes as the introduction of wage control in the 1970s and Trudeau's 1983 resolve to play a mediating role between the superpowers were introduced without any party involvement of any sort.

The Rise of Electronic Media

Until the advent of radio and particularly of television, politicians were the most effective means through which the public learned about political events. In many communities across the country the political meeting was not only an important means of communication but also prime entertainment. Political issues were personalized by politicians who, in addition to adding colour to the consideration of matters of public policy, lent the political process a gladiatorial dimension that heightened its public appeal.

Television has, to a great extent, changed all that. The average Canadian spends several hours a day watching all manner of programmes among which political material plays a relatively minor role. The entertainment value of face-to-face politics has declined since there are so many other exciting things to watch. And the public perception of the political process and of political issues that remains is derived from television treatment of the news and of political personalities. Public taste and public opinion on almost everything is being shaped by television programmes and television advertising. Politics and politicians are filtered by a medium in which the primary concern is often not enlightenment, knowledge or consciousness-raising but maximal audiences and profits. This has meant that even major political events like the choosing of national party leaders are dominated by the requirements of television. The organization and scheduling of meetings are arranged so that the most appealing events are broadcast during prime time, and all other aspects, even the quality of discussion and the time spent on critical issues, are made subservient to the demands of the electronic media.

Television has to some extent wrested the limelight from party politicians; but, on the other hand, it provides a matchless opportunity for the public to witness the party game. Its coverage of the most colourful political events—leadership conventions, elections, and so-called debates between party leaders—furnishes unprecedented opportunities for parties to be seen in action. The problem is, of course, that the exposure is chosen by the media largely for entertainment value, rather than as a continuous in-depth exploration of the dominant political issues and partisan strategies. The focus tends to be on the people who report and comment on political news rather than on the political actors themselves. One result of this tendency is that public opinion on political matters is shaped as much by media intermediaries as it is by the protagonists representing the various parties. Furthermore, the key role of television is changing the character of political leadership. It is now virtually impossible for anyone who is not "telegenic" to be chosen as party chief. His or her presence and style on television can make or break a politician; yet these are only some (and not the most important) attributes of an effective political and governmental figure.

Investigative Journalism

Although television has come to occupy a key position in the manner in which the public perceives political and party life, it has not eclipsed the more traditional ways of reporting and analysing news and of entertaining the public. Newspapers and periodicals still receive considerable attention, particularly among the politically most active members of the public. Partly, no doubt, in response to the competition provided by TV and partly because of the intense rivalry among some of the major printed media, newspapers and magazines have recently resorted to numerous ploys designed to attract attention and a wider audience. Among these, investigative journalism—a return of sorts to the old muckraking days—has been particularly important. Many of the major papers and some of the periodicals have sought to discover governmental lapses and to reveal wrongdoing on the part of local, provincial and federal authorities. These efforts at exposing flaws and shortcomings, errors, dishonesty and inefficiency perpetrated by governments have often led to the establishment of judicial and quasi-judicial inquiries and to the corroboration of the sins unearthed by the sleuthing journalists. The watch-dog function of the print and electronic media is important to the present argument because it can be seen as an encroachment upon, or at least a complement to, the role of opposition parties. They, of course, are the agents par excellence, according to conventional theory, for keeping governments on their toes and for publicizing their misdeeds.

Although opposition politicians and investigative journalists no doubt derive mutual benefit from one another's activities, the recent increase in the role of the media as agents unearthing governmental malfeasance, regardless of how beneficial it may be, detracts from one of the most essential roles of opposition parties—that of criticizing the government. This is not to say the activities of the journalists inhibit or hamper opposition politicians; on the contrary, the latter exploit them; but the relative importance of government debate is reduced when much of the combat occurs outside the party arena—on the printed page or the television screen. One of the questions presented by the new or, perhaps, revived emphasis in the media on tracking down governmental errors of commission or omission is, in fact, whether the often vigorous reportorial initiative of the media does not reflect a decline in the energy and resourcefulness of opposition parties. Like many of the arguments presented above, this is a question requiring systematic research.

Whatever the reasons, a considerable challenge of, and check on, governments today originate outside the realm of political parties and tend to reduce the effectiveness of the party system. The media may be able to report governmental failings, but they cannot provide alternative governments—one of the functions of opposition parties. By sharing with others the task of exposing and criticizing official actions (and by often being outdone by them), opposition parties lose some of their credibility as alternatives to the current power-holders.

Opinion Polling

Increasingly widespread use of opinion polls by the small groups of officials and cronies working with the party leader has diminished the need to rely on the knowledge of public attitudes by local militants and elected politicians. The vast, sensitive network of contacts, reciprocal favours, and exchanges of information which characterized the relationship between party leaders and their followers has to some extent been attenuated by the use of scientific sampling, sophisticated interviewing techniques and subtle statistical analyses. While the results are in some respects more reliable, there is also a decided loss: the interplay between public opinion and the leadership exercised by politically informed and concerned activists is substantially reduced. There is likely less debate and argument, since local party people are no longer encouraged to take the pulse of their "parishioners" and to mediate between the grass roots and the leadership. Public opinion, as defined by pollsters, guides political decisions more and political decision makers are less involved in forming public opinion. Two consequences, at least, are relevant for our purposes: the character of political leadership and of political styles has changed and the party organization is no longer needed as an essential information network.

The Domination of Economic Interests

There is little agreement among scholars about the exact role of economic factors in the sociopolitical realm. Are the forces and relations of production basic causes of all other aspects of social organization or can social organization be manipulated through political means? Whatever one's judgment, one does not need to be an economic determinist to acknowledge that governments have frequently found it difficult to resist certain kinds of economic pressures or to work against certain economic realities. This vulnerability is enhanced by the greatly increased number and power of multinational corporations. These vast, globe-girdling enterprises are rarely dependent on their operations in any one political jurisdiction and are adept at playing one interest against another. The behaviour of the oil companies before, during and after the oil crisis of the 1970s is a case in point. Even those who doubt that Canadian industry and business can withstand governmental pressure cannot ignore the fact that the multinationals, recognizing no loyalties other than to their balance sheets, can obviate, ignore, influence and even dominate Canadian governments. A striking example came to light in the autumn of 1977 when Inco, a Canadian-based multinational, which has benefited from lavish tax and other concessions, announced that it would lay off 3000 employees in Canada. Against arguments to the effect that the company was at the same time using funds provided by Canadian taxpayers to expand productive capacity overseas, a senior vice-president indicated that "fears of government takeover and other economic recriminations in Indonesia and Guatemala forced Inco . . . to cut back production in Canada where massive layoffs could be made with little prospect of serious political interference."[4] This episode provides an illuminating vignette illustrating the impotence of the Canadian government[5] and of Canadian political parties in the face of economic pressure from industry. This subservience of the political realm to the economic is related to the prevailing value system and dominant ideologies: when parties and governments buckle under economic pressure, they do so because they do not believe in interfering with private enterprise.

One-Party Dominance

Finally, among the general long-run factors leading in the decline of party in Canada is the very nature of the Canadian party system. Its chief feature during this century has been that it is a one-party dominant system, in which the important alternation is not between different parties in office but between majority and minority Liberal governments.[6] Increasingly, the line between the government and the Liberal party has become tenuous: leading Liberals have become ministerial politicians and the opposition parties have been out of office for so long that they are seldom perceived as being capable of governing, sometimes (according to one scholar) even by themselves.[7]

Canada has long been in a situation in which there has been a serious loss of confidence in the government and in the government party and, at the same time, there has been no corresponding or compensating sense that the opposition might do better. The latter was perceived as inexperienced, fragmented and disposed to attack on principle everything and everyone who had anything to do with the government. Public opinion polls taken after the 1975 Conservative leadership convention showed a major decline in Liberal support and a corresponding upsurge in Conservative fortunes, but the election of a Parti Québécois government in November 1976 reminded Canadians of the woefully weak position of the Conservatives in Quebec and of the fact that, in the past, only the Liberals (among the major parties) have tried to find a satisfactory accommodation between French and English Canada. The fear of national disintegration drove many voters back towards the Liberals, albeit with very little enthusiasm. Despite extensive doubt about the Liberal's capacity to provide adequate government (particularly west of the Ottawa River), the Conservatives were able, after the 1979 election, to form only a minority government which was toppled a few months after coming to power by the combined vote of the Liberals and the NDP.

This reinforced the already strong sense, among most leading Liberals, that they are indispensable and (since the Canadian public seems to recurrently favour them), nearly infallible in dealing with Canadian problems. The sense of self-assurance—an increasingly important element in the party's physiognomy[8]—has itself contributed a great deal to the decline of party in Canada.

Among the many other consequences of one-party dominance, one requires special notice in the present context. The less favoured parties (unless they are essentially doctrinaire organizations which attract ideologues regardless of electoral opportunities) experience great difficulty in attracting candidates of top quality. Highly successful and ambitious individuals do not, for the most part, wish to foresake promising careers in exchange for a difficult electoral campaign and, at best, an almost permanent seat on the opposition benches. In a system in which parties in power alternate, able deputies know that part of their career is likely to be spent in the cabinet and they may therefore be attracted to a political career even if their preferred party does not, in the short run, seem to stand a good chance of election.

Short-Run Causes: The Liberal Style

Disdain of Parliament

Prime Minister Trudeau is not, as has often been noted, a House of Commons man. He seems to hold parliament in low esteem and is on record as questioning the intelligence of his opponents. He seldom uses parliament as the platform for important pronouncements, preferring to deliver policy statements or general reflections on the state of the country in public speeches, television interviews or press conferences. Having entered politics relatively late in life, and having been strongly critical of the Liberals, Pierre Trudeau's personal circle appears to be outside the ranks of the party he now leads, and outside of parliament. The two intimate colleagues who entered politics with him, Jean Marchand and Gérard Pelletier, were also not at home in the House of Commons milieu and have retired from it.

A significant decision of Mr. Trudeau, in the present context, was his move in 1968 to establish regional desks within the privy council office, which were designed to keep abreast of developments and ideas in the regions. A more party oriented prime minister would have relied on his party contacts and on colleagues in the House of Commons rather than on civil servants, and there was much criticism of the prime minister's move in the House of Commons and, privately, among Liberal back-benchers. The desks as such have been abandoned but the government continues to bypass the House of Commons on some critical issues.

Examples abound of the Trudeau government wishing to bypass parliament, presumably so as to escape unfavourable or contentious publicity. After the first election of the Parti Québécois, for instance, opposition spokespersons sought an extensive House debate and the establishment of a parliamentary committee which would engage in a searching and continuous consideration of Canada's crisis of unity. The government provided for a three-day parliamentary debate and refused to establish the requested committee. Instead, the prime minister created special national unity groups of officials in the privy council office and established a task force on national unity under Jean-Luc Pépin, a former cabinet minister, and ex-Premier John Robarts of Ontario. Important government decisions, like those dealing with the testing in Canada of the Cruise missile or with the abandonment of Via railway lines, are announced when the House is recessed. Frequently, news likely to embarrass the government is released late on Friday, thereby precluding its receiving the immediate attention of the House. These moves bespeak a lack of enthusiasm for using parliament as an instrument for fashioning—as distinct from merely legitimizing—national policy. And to play down parliament is to play down political parties, since their chief national arena is the House of Commons.

Confusing the Public

A certain amount of sophistry is indigenous to politics when it comes to governments justifying their failure or unanticipated changes in their policies and strategy. But the public is not likely to maintain respect for either its government or the whole political system when it is confronted by an administration which, after an election, completely repudiates a major policy stand or when it welcomes into its ranks a former opposition member who had been a vociferous leader against one of its most important pieces of legislation. The Liberal party has done both, thereby weakening confidence in the integrity of our political parties and of their practitioners.

One of the principal differences in the platforms of the Liberal and Conservative parties in the 1974 election was the question of how to combat inflation. The Conservatives advocated a temporary price and wage freeze (pending the development of a permanent policy), for which the Liberals excoriated them, arguing that the public would never accept such controls. Having done much to undermine confidence in officially sanctioned constraints, and having given the impression that Canadians could not be trusted to cooperate in such a programme, the government in 1975 introduced its own anti-inflation programme, which froze wages and tried (unsuccessfully) to control prices. Not surprisingly, the government that campaigned on a vigorous anti-controls platform encountered considerable opposition when it tried to apply them.

The general language policy of the Official Languages Act of 1969 is one of the most important Liberal government attempts to promote national unity. Robert Stanfield, then Conservative leader, succeeded in persuading his party to follow him in supporting the language bill, but he was challenged and about 20 of his followers broke party ranks. None of them was more implacably opposed to efforts designed to assure that both French- and English-speaking Canadians could deal with the federal government in their own language than Jack Horner, the member for the Crowfoot constituency in Alberta. Mr. Horner had consistently been one of the most savage opponents of efforts to protect the French language and to create in Canada an ambience agreeable to francophones. However, after unsuccessfully contesting the Tory leadership, Mr. Horner became disillusioned with the leadership of his successful rival, crossed the floor of the House and ultimately became a Liberal cabinet minister.

It is not always easy to distinguish between our two old parties but some basic diverging orientations do, in fact, divide them.[9] One is the attitude they adopt towards French Canada. Although the official leadership of the Conservative party has, under Robert Stanfield, Joe Clark and Brian Mulroney, been sympathetic to the aspirations of French Canada, the party has always been plagued by a bigoted wing of members who lacked comprehension of and sympathy for Quebec. Mr. Horner, as a leading member of this group, was a strange bedfellow for the Liberal MPs, the former targets of his venom. While this move gave the Liberals a much needed prairie seat and Mr. Horner a cabinet post long before he might otherwise have received one (if ever), it made a mockery of what our political parties allegedly stand for.[10]

Decline in Ministerial Responsibility

It has been a cardinal principle of the cabinet system of government that individual ministers are responsible for anything that is done by the ministries and departments for which they are responsible. The civil service is supposed to be an anonymous body without political views, obediently carrying out the commands of its masters, the politicians. This has always been something of a fiction, of course, since senior civil servants must provide useful advice and so there is no point in their totally ignoring the partisan and political constraints impinging on the ministers. The tendency for ministers and deputy ministers to see the world in like fashion is particularly pronounced in a one-party dominant system in which the collaboration between a minister and his or her deputy may continue for many years. All this notwithstanding, the principle of ministerial responsibility has had a long and respected tradition in Canada, at least in the sense that ministers, as politicians, have assumed complete responsibility for the actions of their civil servants and their departments. The political party in office has thus been the beneficiary of all the popular things done by the public service and the victim of its failings.

Recent developments have altered the once well-established principle of ministerial responsibility. First, there is a rapid turnover in the various ministries. The result is that few ministers have a chance to master the complex business of their ministry before they are assigned a new portfolio. While an alert and hard-working minister can be briefed fairly quickly by his new subordinates, it takes a prodigious amount of work and insight, and a great deal of time, to be able to become the effective head of a department and to lead it. Until this happens—and many ministers, of course, never gain the upper hand—the politicians are in a sense the captives of their officials. Ministers may, under these conditions, take formal responsibility for what is done in their name but the real power lies elsewhere.[11]

The Trudeau government went further than any of its predecessors in accepting ministerial *lack* of responsibility for the actions of officials and in so doing has brought about an important revision in our constitutional practice. Trudeau's ministers steadfastly refused to resign when consistently harrassed by opposition members, sometimes for the excellent reason that the bloodthirsty cries of their opponents were unjustified and irresponsible. But there were several instances when, under previous custom, ministers would have backed down. However, members of the Trudeau cabinet, supported by their leader, refused to assume responsibility for the actions of people working under them. The most notorious and, on other grounds, exceedingly troubling instance of this concerns revelations, made in 1977, about RCMP break-ins and other illegal acts in 1972 and 1973. The government's cavalier manner of responding to this situation need not detain us here, although it is another case of the government undermining public trust in the political process. The relevant point is that the government defence was simply that the then solicitor-general (the "responsible" minister) had not been informed of the RCMP's actions and since the particular minister had been moved to another department, the principle of ministerial responsibility was no longer applicable. The former solicitor-general at first failed even to make a statement to the House about the whole affair, although he later did deliver one. Members of the RCMP repeatedly broke the law and no minister took responsibility for these extremely serious transgressions. If a party holding office is no longer accountable for what is being done by officials under one of its ministers, the party system cannot ensure that governments are responsible to the electors. This state of affairs makes a mockery of democratic procedures and further diminishes the credibility of political parties.

Plebiscitary Tendencies

All of the short-run causes for the decline of party mentioned so far were laid at the doorstep of the Liberals. While that party has been an important cause of the process of party attenuation, it should not, of course, be assumed that it is the sole culprit. The opposition parties have been unable to present an acceptable alternative and have failed to convince the public that they could remove some of the ills currently afflicting the country. Nor can party politicians of any stripe be held responsible for the fact that much of the political decision making has shifted from the conventional sites to federal-provincial negotiations, where parties do not fit neatly.

A recent factor that might possibly further impair the viability of parties is also not the Liberal's making, although Mr. Trudeau's reaction to it might exacerbate its effect on the place of parties in our system. The Parti Québécois' insertion of the referendum into our political process takes away from the monopoly enjoyed by parties in deciding certain issues. The PQ is of course not the first to introduce direct consultation of the public to Canadians. W.L. Mackenzie King had recourse to this device during the conscription crisis in World War II, and two referenda were held before Newfoundland became part of Canada. But the commitment of the PQ government to conduct a referendum to decide whether Quebeckers wish to break or redefine their relationship with the rest of the country has brought forth an indication that Ottawa might itself conduct a similar vote.

Referenda normally ignore political parties and emphasize policy options, thereby diminishing the importance of parties in the political process. If they are held very infrequently, and only with respect to such fundamental issues as the nature of the country and its constitution, then they are unlikely to do much damage to the role of parties. But once they are used in one case, it may be impossible to prevent them from being applied to other issues—for example, the reintroduction of capital punishment, or language legislation—and they might slowly usurp some of the functions performed by parties. Any federal recourse to referenda is therefore seen by some opposition members as a potential further encroachment on the traditional role of parties.

Conclusion

The above catalogue of factors and developments reducing the relative importance of parties touches only some of the highlights; it is a partial and superficial look at a very complex phenomenon. This article's emphasis on federal politics has, for instance, led it to neglect the all-important provincial sphere and the interaction between federal and provincial party organizations. And our skimming of the high points has led to a neglect of some serious questions posed by these developments. We might have asked, for instance, whether the reason for the Liberal party's role in reducing the importance of parties is to be found in the fact that it is a quasi-permanent government party or in some special characteristics associated with Canadian liberalism at the federal level. Does the Ontario Conservative party play a similar role in the decline of party in that province?

Our purpose here is not to answer these kinds of questions, important though they are, but to indicate that significant changes are occurring which alter the role played by political parties. If a series of limited advantages is allowed to reduce the overall effectiveness of a major mechanism for decision making without producing at least an equally useful alternative, then the cost to society may be unexpectedly high. One is reminded in this connection of one of R.K. Merton's celebrated "theories of the middle range":

> Any attempt to eliminate an existing social structure without providing adequate alternative structures for fulfilling the functions previously fulfilled by the abolished organization is doomed to failure.[12]

Now it is true that no one is consciously trying to eliminate Canadian parties or even to reduce their importance, and that Merton was thinking of the return or rebirth of a structure whose function was needed. But the parties' sphere of influence and effectiveness is being reduced, by design or not. It may be to the country's advantage to reassign the functions of parties if they are being neglected: society might find other ways of performing these needed functions. There is a danger, however, that the alternatives may be less satisfactory and in other respects—in the field of individual freedom, for instance—potentially very harmful.

The Canadian party system is far from being perfect, but the world is full of examples showing how appalling some of the alternatives can be. That considerable reform is needed is clear. We can benefit from some of the changes occurring now and from ones which could be instituted. Students of Canadian parties need to decide which features deserve preservation and which require change. And before they are in a position to do that, they must undertake more extensive study of the issues raised here.

Notes on the Decline of Party in the 1990s

The appearance of the sixth edition of *Party Politics in Canada* provides an opportunity to reassess briefly the above arguments about the decline of party, first formulated over 10 years ago, and to take note of some recent developments.

Before exploring these aspects, however, it is necessary to address a misconception occasioned by the original piece. Comments on it by two highly reputed scholars suggest that its main thrust may have been expressed with less clarity than was intended. The late Professor Khayyam Z. Paltiel[13] and Frederick C. Engelmann[14] somewhat differently ascribed to me the view that parties are no longer important. Paltiel's article shows that parties can still raise substantial sums of money for their electoral activities and concludes that this challenges my argument. Engelmann agrees with part of what I wrote but questions, among other things, my assigning the blame for some of the reasons for the short-run causes of party decline to the Liberal style under Trudeau, and my point about the growing political importance of the new journalism. Who, Engelmann asks, manipulates whom? Do the media exploit parties, or is it the other way round?

Paltiel was, of course, right when he noted that substantial funds can still be generated by parties. This, however, is not inconsistent with my conclusions and does not conflict with my assertion that parties are now relatively much less important than they once were. Likewise, Engelmann's observations reveal that I gave the impression of having downgraded the parties all too categorically. The parties are *declining* in importance, I argued. I did not say they are becoming *extinct*.

Although I see many areas in which various nonparty institutions have come to usurp or invade some of the parties' roles, parties are, of course, still very much at the centre of our political life. Although complemented and partially replaced by other institutions, political parties determine who is to form the government, select party leaders and candidates, mobilize citizens for political action, provide an ongoing link between the government and the public (through the government caucus), structure political opinion and still play a nation-building role.

* * * *

Turning now to the original argument, it is easy to see that several factors that once deprived the parties of their previous influence no longer prevail. Not surprisingly, most (although not all) of these were listed as "short-run". Thus, the "disdain for parliament" argument applies much less than it did 11 years ago; and the points made under the "plebiscitary democracy" and "confusing the public" headings no longer apply. Similarly, a factor identified as being long term—one-party dominance—is no longer applicable, although some of the habits of thought it engendered occasionally still surface.

One of the items in the short-term category has proven to be much more enduring than expected, and more far-reaching: federal-provincial diplomacy which, along with executive federalism, has become a permanent and increasingly manifest feature of the political landscape. The Meech Lake Accord was only the most dramatic of a growing number of instances in which governments of diverse party stripe decided matters without enabling the parties themselves to play an active role in the decision-making process. It is noteworthy in the present context that the failure of the accord is likely to change Canadian federalism dramatically and, while leaving federal-provincial diplomacy intact, may attenuate executive federalism.

* * * *

Some tendencies identified earlier continue to affect the role of parties more or less as before, while others are becoming more intrusive and complex. The lavish pluralism and the accompanying vigorous political involvement of interest groups, and the impact of the electronic media are fixed elements of Canada's political life, just as they were in the 1970s. The bureaucratic state, on the other hand, is becoming even more noticeable and is undergoing further transformations that affect political parties. Among the features of this development is the increasing politicization of the public service. This is manifested particularly in two domains: (1) the blurring of the line between the world of nonpartisan officials and the performance by civil servants of partisan roles; and (2) the activities by government departments of acts which have unmistakable political (i.e., partisan) consequences.

The partisan "contagion" of the most senior reaches of the public service occurred first during the Trudeau years. Michael Pitfield who, as Clerk of the Privy Council was the most senior civil servant, met regularly with Jim Coutts and Keith Davey—Trudeau's most political (i.e., party linked) advisors—and consulted them on a great many highly sensitive issues. Although Pitfield had no visible ties to the Liberal party, he was universally seen as being so strongly identified with the Liberal prime minister's political fortunes that he was unacceptable as the senior public servant advisor to Joe Clark, Trudeau's Conservative successor. Brian Mulroney continued the process of dragging the senior civil service into the partisan arena when he appointed Dalton Camp to a most senior position in the Privy Council Office (PCO) and thus to one of the top jobs in the civil service. Mr. Camp had been President of the National Progressive Conservative Party Association, a Conservative parliamentary candidate and a widely publicized advisor to a number of Conservative leaders at the national and provincial levels. Later, Mulroney moved Derek Burney—a seasoned, high-ranking diplomat—to the Prime Minister's Office (PMO) where he became the Conservative leader's key advisor, not only on most of the burning policy issues confronting the government, but also on partisan political tactics and strategies.

While these reversals between the traditional roles of nonpartisan civil servants and partisan personnel by no means permeated the whole federal civil service, they occurred at the highest and, therefore, most influential levels. It is significant, as will be seen below, that the choice of the individuals concerned was exclusively that of the prime minister and in no way involved the party organization or machinery.

The other encroachment by the public service into the sphere previously occupied by parties concerns the bureaucratic invasion of the domain of partisan opinion formation. It is now commonplace for government departments to conduct vast advertising campaigns, ostensibly to inform the public about the details of proposed policies but, in fact, to sell the policy of the government party. Similarly, expensive opinion polls, the results of which are used for partisan purposes, are frequently conducted by government departments. The findings are, of course, not available to the opposition in time to be useful in the political battle.

The two developments just described further enhance the encroachment of the bureaucratic state on the sphere of the parties, noted in my original article.

* * * *

As for investigative journalism, the media are becoming increasingly aggressive about prying into the private lives of people in public life. While this practice, like so many others, is more muted in Canada than in the United States, it is nevertheless clearly noticeable. One result is that people contemplating a political career must be prepared to have their past and present life, and that of their family, scrutinized in minute detail. Health records, past academic performance, youthful peccadillos, friendships, family life, holiday activities, entertainment preferences and all else are now fair game in North American journalism. This may serve a useful purpose in keeping undesirable individuals from being elected but it also deters potentially excellent politicians from seeking public office. People of talent, capable of making a valuable contribution to our political parties, may not wish to expose themselves to the fish-bowl world of the new journalism even if they do have a blameless past. Although it is too soon to reach firm conclusions here, it is likely that as a consequence, the overall quality of politicians is declining, and may decline further as the result of the intrusion of the media into matters they formerly avoided. This deprives political parties of the opportunity of drawing on the most promising pool of talent and so weakens their competitive position in relation to other institutions in society.

* * * *

A new dimension has emerged in the manner in which economic interests encroach on the domain of political parties. During the concluding phase of the 1988 general election, so-called "third-party advertising" flooded the media in an effort to influence voters' attitudes to the free-trade issue and, hence, to the return to power of the Conservatives. The term "third party" in this context no longer refers to minor political parties but to normally non-political interests who became involved in the campaign. Unions, and a coalition of nationalist groups, advertised to oppose the trade agreement between Canada and the United States and, consequently, the Conservative government. The business community, on the other hand, bought media time and space to support the government's espousal of the trade pact. The latter groups substantially outspent the anti-free trade groups, and many observers concluded that the outcome of the election was materially affected by the massive infusion of these resources into the campaign. The funds involved in this advertising were not, under the then existing laws, subject to any of the restrictions on electoral expenses or requirements for disclosure applying to the parties and candidates.

While the involvement of non-political groups in an election does not necessarily encroach on the role of the parties, it nevertheless means that various vested interests engage in electioneering. They therefore compete with the parties for the attention of the public and do influence public opinion. The political information they convey may not reflect the priorities or even the perspectives of the parties and may, therefore, deflect the latter from the courses they had sought to pursue. Electoral choices may, as a result of third-party advertising, be influenced by nonparty agencies grinding their own axes.

Third-party advertising raises other problems which are not relevant to our concerns here but, because of these problems, it is likely that legislation will emerge regulating it. At the time of writing, however, this phenomenon comprises a new (although not major) challenge to the parties and so constitutes a factor additional to the ones I noted in my original paper chronicling the decline of party in Canada.

Three New Developments

In addition to the changes noted so far, some of which either weakened or removed factors contributing to party decline, there are three new developments that deserve notice as Canada enters the 1990s.

First, that senior public service appointments were made by two prime ministers without any involvement of their respective parties illustrates an important development in our political system that has implications for the role of parties. This development can be characterized as the "imperial prime ministership." The term is an adaptation of a phrase used in the United States to describe the immense rise in power of the president. This new style and might of the prime minister manifests itself at two levels: the actual power exercised and the ceremonial features of the office.

The aggrandisement of the prime minister evolved slowly but took an immense leap forward with the advent of television and the consequent personalization and nationalization of politics, the stress on short news clips and the popularity of leadership debates. But the process was also aided by the management style and the personalities of Trudeau and Mulroney.

Trudeau outshone his ministers in many respects and provided strong leadership in areas he considered important and congenial. Under him, decision making became firmly located in cabinet committees and, particularly, the Committee on Priorities and Planning over which he presided. The Treasury Board and the powerful coordinating ministries of state (such as that responsible for social development) vetted policies proposed by ministers and often second-guessed the work previously done by government departments. The Privy Council Office (PCO) and the Prime Minister's Office (PMO), both under the prime minister, were immensely influential and towered over the other departments, partly as the result of direct influence and partly because of the informal network of their senior personnel embracing, *inter alia*, the other central agencies and ministries of state. As a result, the power of the ministers slipped to that of the central agencies and, particularly, to those closest to the PCO, the PMO and, through them, to the prime minister. The remarkable growth in the size and budget of the PMO during the Trudeau years represents the degree to which the prime minister's power had increased. Another quantum leap occurred under Mulroney.

Insofar as the ceremonial aspects are concerned, Trudeau had a more patrician manner than his immediate predecessors. Whether because of his personal preferences or because of the changing times, the prime ministership under him became more aloof and august. A small, possibly insignificant but, nevertheless, telling example is that it was during his occupancy of 24 Sussex Drive that the practice was established of providing Canadian prime ministers with bullet-proof limousines.

Mulroney's chosen instrument for the domination of the decision-making process was the PMO which came to be dreaded by ministers and government departments alike. Its involvement in every facet of decision making has become legendary and is among the most characteristic features of Mulroney's governing style.

Mulroney also acquired the habit of making statements about policies falling under the immediate jurisdiction of his ministers. This was nowhere so evident as in the field of foreign policy where he, on many occasions, not only upstaged but also contradicted Joe Clark, the Secretary of State for External Affairs. Mulroney also enlarged the sphere of his office at the expense of the Governor-General. This was particularly evident during the first Canadian visit by President Reagan. It would have been normal and customary for the American Head of State to be greeted by his Canadian counterpart, the Governor-General. But, although there is a vice regal official residence in Quebec City, the site of the first Reagan-Mulroney summit, Jeanne Sauvé was nowhere to be seen. The prime minister, on the other hand, constantly occupied centre stage.

Brian Mulroney not only enlarged the scope of the prime minister's role but also added considerably to the trappings associated with it. On his numerous trips, he has been unfailingly accompanied by a massive phalanx of aids, including his own photographer, and preceded by a troop of advance people who ensure that the prime minister will be treated in a manner befitting an august personage and that he would be displayed in the most flattering setting and manner. At international gatherings it was not unusual that the hotel suites and floors graced by the prime minister and his staff rivalled in size and splendour those occupied by the heads of delegations of the United States and other world powers obsessed by a mania for security and an affinity for ostentation. Prior to the Trudeau era, the Canadian pattern was similar to that prevailing in the Scandinavian countries, where even first ministers behave, and are treated, like any other citizen. Particularly under Mulroney, the prime minister's style and ceremonial manner have become quite ostentatious and substantially more exalted than that of ordinary mortals, including other ministers.

An exalted prime ministership has important consequences for the role of parties. In a sense, the prime minister is, of course, every millimeter a party person and everything he or she does can be seen as a party act. But much depends on the degree to which the prime minister's decisions are reached with the involvement of the party, and to what degree they reflect contributions of non-party forces, such as various interests, personal cronies or hired gun consultants. The network of daily contacts and influences enmeshing a prime minister may include so many non-party forces that the party's role in the decision-making process becomes narrowly circumscribed.

*   *   *   *

Second, one significant non-party force is reflected in the rise in number and influence of highly specialized advisors, particularly in the field of opinion formation and manipulation. The grand strategy of parties, their conduct during elections, their contacting the public and their conducting so-called media events are now influenced by specialists who are not associated with a party but who act as consultants for a fee. A relationship of deep and complete trust must obviously develop between the party leaders and the special advisors, many of whom actually tend to sympathize with the cause of their clients, but the consultants are nevertheless independent of the party.

One of the consequences of this process is that the ideas and preferences of party members, as embodied in the leadership of the party organization, tend to be played down in favour of the expert's advice. The latter is held to be more reliable and electorally rewarding. The fact that the public relations advisors and other spin doctors have access to secret daily polls conducted during a campaign further diminish party positions and party views. Decisions, not only on *how* the party's case is to be presented but also on *what* is put forward, are made on short notice on the basis of the latest shifts revealed by opinion polls. Thus, the stance espoused by parties during a campaign is to some extent the result of the close interaction between party strategists and the powerful experts on public opinion and its management. As elsewhere, expert opinion tends to triumph over that of people considered to be amateurs.

*   *   *   *

Third, a new set of circumstances rooted in the political environment also diminishes the influence of parties. It is not only parties and the political game which are being modified but also the overall environment in which they operate. Relevant in this context are two features that did not exist or were not evident 11 years ago. They are the adoption in the 1982 constitution of the Charter of Rights and Freedoms, and changes in the nature of the Canadian community.

The Charter, as has been widely observed, has considerably enhanced the powers of the courts and has consequently contributed to the relative reduction in the importance of political, as distinct from judicial, decision making.[16] Political parties, like other political institutions, therefore cede some of their previous sphere of influence to that exercised by judges.

The impact of changes in the Canadian community is more complex and still only very imperfectly understood. During the last third or quarter of the twentieth century, new ways emerged in the manner in which many Canadians defined themselves and their role in the larger community. Previously, the salient reference points followed by most Canadians in thinking about themselves and the place they occupied in their community were religion, ethnic origin and the geographical setting they called home. A Canadian would, consequently, think of himself or herself as, say, a Catholic, a French Canadian and an inhabitant of Montreal. More recently, a new set of categories became important to many of us, which often diminished the old attachments and either replaced or augmented them with new ones. Some of these new ways of thinking are reflected in parts of the Charter.

The most salient of these new links are those of sex and a different conception of ethnicity. Feminism has made many Canadians aware of the manner in which society has been largely blind to a critical distinction in humankind, and of the manner in which society's structure and the allocation of its values discriminate in favour of one sex at the expense of the other. A growing number of people consider the redress of this neglect to be among the most critical issues on the public agenda.

Religion has been largely (although not completely) privatized and removed from public discourse. Ethnicity used to, at one level, centre on one's attachment to the French or British families. Those Canadians whose ancestry was not among what the terms of reference of the Royal Commission on Bilingualism and Biculturalism called "the founding peoples", thought of themselves as belonging linguistically to one of the two dominant groups. Ethnicity was generally considered to be a private matter more or less unrelated to the public agenda. With Canada's growing multicultural population, this has changed, and many "new" Canadians or their descendants now see themselves not only as Canadians speaking one of the official languages, but also as members of an ethnic group whose interests are of relevance to the public agenda.

Native peoples, who have traditionally been considered a very special problem with only certain vestigial limited rights, came to be recognized as falling into a number of communities whose identity and rights deserve specific recognition not only in public policy but also in constitutional guarantees.

Before the redefinition of how Canadians identified themselves, the structures, programmes, and activities of political parties had been designed to respond to the linguistic and territorial context of Canadians by focusing on regions and constituencies. The new identities evoked by considerations such as sex, multiculturalism and native rights have so far had a very limited impact on the way in which parties attempt to respond to the emerging needs of Canadians. If the abortion issue—one of the most important "women's issues"—is taken as an example, it appears that parties are experiencing great difficulty in accommodating themselves to the new identities and the resulting cleavages in society and in playing an effective role in finding solutions to the problems posed for the country by the changing composition and definition of its constituent communities.

It is largely non-party organizations that have addressed the challenges of the "new Canada" and have become deeply involved in the resolution of resulting tensions. Parties have so far failed in becoming the principal players in the emerging politics affecting the new claims of groups and interests which had for so long lain dormant. In this way, too, their influence can be seen as having declined relative to other political players. It is too soon to say whether this situation is likely to endure or whether parties will manage to adjust to the new circumstances and recover some of the lost ground.

*   *   *   *

This brief review and extension of the analysis of the changing role of parties developed 11 years ago may not convince all readers that the influence of parties is diminishing, but it is most likely to persuade them that the contribution parties make to our political world and the manner in which they go about it is changing, and that these alterations have far-reaching consequences.

ENDNOTE

1. "Getting in Cheap with the Aristocrats," *The (Toronto) Globe and Mail,* 26 September 1977, p. 8. See also "Another Chapter in the Propaganda War," *The (Toronto) Globe and Mail,* 3 October 1977.
2. Anthony King, "Political Parties in Western Democracies," *Polity,* Vol. II, No. 2, (Winter 1969), pp. 111–41.
3. Robert Presthus, *Elite Accommodation in Canadian Politics* (Toronto: Macmillan, 1974).
4. Roger Croft, "Safer to Fire Canadians Inco Admits," The *Toronto Star,* 29 October 1977, p. A3.
5. There is little difference between the federal and provincial spheres here: *The Globe and Mail,* 28 October 1977, p. 3, ran a story entitled "Davis Cautions Critics of Inco Layoffs," with a sub-head reading "Cites threat to investment climate." Similarly, even more reform-minded regimes have floundered in the face of industrial pressure.
6. For a fuller description and analysis, see John Meisel, "The Party System and the 1974 Election," in Howard R. Penniman, ed., *Canada at the Polls* (Washington: American Enterprise Institute for Public Policy Research, 1975).
7. For a recent analysis of this phenomenon within the Conservative party, see George Perlin, *The Tory Syndrome* (Montreal: McGill-Queen's University Press, 1980).
8. See John Meisel, "Howe, Hubris and '72," in J. Meisel, *Working Papers on Canadian Politics* (Montreal: McGill-Queen's University Press, 1975).
9. See John Meisel, "Recent Changes in Canadian Parties," in H.G. Thorburn, ed., *Party Politics in Canada,* 2nd ed. (Scarborough: Prentice-Hall Canada, 1967).
10. Horner's subsequent career is instructive. He was repudiated by his electors in 1979, but not abandoned by the Liberal government. In 1982 he was appointed Chairman of the CNR by the Trudeau government.
11. An interesting and possibly path-breaking departure from the traditional pattern occurred when Ian Stewart, the then Deputy Minister of Finance, resigned and in a letter to the Prime Minister took responsibility for Allan MacEachen's ill-fated 1980 budget. See J.E. Hodgetts, "The Deputies' Dilemma," *Policy Options,* Vol. IV, No. 3, (May/June 1983), pp. 14–17.
12. R.K. Merton, *Social Theory and Social Structure* (Glencoe, Ill.: The Free Press, 1949), p. 79.
13. "Political Marketing, Party Finance and the Decline of Canadian Parties," in Alain G. Gagnon and A. Brian Tangay, eds., *Canadian Parties in Transition* (Scarborough: Nelson Canada, 1989).

14. "Canadian Political Parties and Elections," in John H. Redekop, ed., *Approaches to Canadian Politics*, 2nd ed. (Scarborough: Prentice-Hall Canada, 1983).

15. Donald V. Smiley, *Canada in Question: Federalism in the Seventies*, 2nd ed. (Toronto: McGraw-Hill Ryerson, 1976).

16. Michael Mandel, *The Charter of Rights and the Legalization of Politics in Canada* (Toronto: Wall & Thompson, 1989).

16 Leadership Selection in the PC and Liberal Parties: Assessing the Need for Reform

GEORGE C. PERLIN

Among parties in cabinet-parliamentary systems Canadian parties are unique in their use of the leadership convention as the method of selecting their leaders. Leadership conventions replaced leadership selection by the parliamentary caucus as a means of compensating for regional imbalances in caucus and of strengthening the democratic legitimacy of the parties. While the convention method has now been in use for 70 years, it remains subject to recurring criticism and frequent attempts at reform. This essay will assess the convention in the context of recent scholarly debate about its performance and will focus on the experience of the two principal competitors for federal office—the Liberal and the Progressive Conservative parties.

In scholarly literature much of the debate concerning conventions reflects a wider controversy in democratic theory. One ideal model of leadership selection can be related to the élite theory of democracy which stresses the values of political and social stability. The élite theory holds that in their day-to-day conduct of public affairs élites should be insulated from the pressures of mass participation because most citizens are not well-informed about politics, lack the self-restraint necessary to make responsible decisions, and have both a limited understanding of liberal-democratic values and a limited commitment to them. It is only because élites are committed to the system's values and understand its operating principles that democracy is preserved. The citizen's role in politics should be limited to participation in periodic elections to choose among élites seeking office through the mechanism of competitive party politics. This competition is sufficient to ensure political accountability and responsiveness.[1] From this perspective, leaders are best chosen through conventions in which the delegates are political "professionals"—that is, elected and organizational élites. These delegates will make the wisest choices because they are better informed,

This is a revised version of a paper presented at a conference at the University of British Columbia in May 1989.

recognize the need for accommodation and compromise and better understand the requirements for building an electoral majority. The ends of democracy are ultimately satisfied because party élites are primarily interested in winning power and will try to choose leaders who can create and hold the broadest possible base of public support for their parties.

A second ideal model of leadership selection can be related to the theory of participatory democracy. The proponents of this theory believe that if large numbers of citizens are not well-informed about politics, do not act responsibly in pressing their political claims, and lack commitment to liberal-democratic values, it is because the political system has not provided mechanisms for effective participation in its decisions. This theory holds both that democracy is meaningless if it does not facilitate broadly based citizen participation in politics, and that popular understanding of and commitment to liberal-democratic values can only be achieved if citizens are actively involved in making the decisions that affect them.[2] Since parties are at the centre of the democratic process, they have a critical role in facilitating the development of a citizenry that is informed, responsible and committed to the principles of democracy. Leaders, therefore, should be chosen by a method that provides for the widest possible participation and that is thoroughly consistent with democratic norms.

Reflecting these different theories, some critics of the convention have argued that it is too democratic, others that it is not democratic enough. But the two ideal models are not completely at variance with one another. Proponents of the participatory theory would not deny the importance of preserving political and social stability, while proponents of the élite theory would not deny the importance of creating a citizenry that is better-educated in the requirements of democracy, better-informed about public policy and more committed to liberal-democratic values. Thus, both ideal models of the convention identify criteria that should be considered in evaluating the convention's performance.

Criticisms of the convention from the perspective of élite theory have raised questions about the effect of the convention on the stable exercise of leadership, its ability to provide for informed and competent decision making in the selection of leaders and its effectiveness in promoting social consensus through the accommodation of conflicting interests. Criticisms from the perspective of participatory theory have raised questions about the convention's openness to non-élite participation, the extent to which it is representative of social interests, its contribution to the informed discussion of public policy and the extent to which its processes conform to democratic norms. These two sets of questions will provide the framework for the following discussion.

Canadian conventions have clearly developed in the direction of the participatory model. While early conventions preserved a major role for party élites, recurring amendments to apportionment rules have extended the representation accorded the parties' mass membership. *Ex officio* delegateships continue to be used to provide voting rights to members of the parties' parliamentary and organizational élites, but the balance of voting power in both parties now lies with elected representatives of the constituency associations and local units of affiliated student and women's organizations. Delegates from the constituency associations, which are the basic units of mass participation in the two parties, made up 56 percent of the PC convention in 1983 and 57 percent of the Liberal convention in 1984. This proportion was substantially larger at the 1990 Liberal convention because the party constitution had increased the number of delegates assigned to each constituency association from six to 12.

Both parties have adopted procedures to facilitate broad participation in conventions through the delegate selection process. The rules for voting at delegate selection meetings have been so minimal that these meetings are open to participation by any person who chooses to be declared a party member. Both parties have allowed the constituencies to decide when and where delegate selection meetings will be called, although the parties have tried to ensure fairness in the process by establishing minimum standards of procedure for these meetings.

The only significant constraint on the openness of this process has been the adoption of affirmative action rules designed to ensure representation from the constituencies for women and young people. Under the terms of the Conservative constitution, one third of the delegates from each constituency must be women and one-third must be under 30. The Liberal party follows the same practice for young people and in 1984 followed the same practice for women. But in 1986 the Liberal constitution was amended to require equal representation for men and women from each constituency. In addition, both parties have added further weight to their affirmative action policy for young people and women through the apportionment of delegates to local student and women's organizations.

The balloting procedure at conventions also reflects a participatory perspective. In contrast to the process of bloc voting by state delegations used in American conventions, in Canada delegates vote by individual, secret ballot. Thus, the delegate is an autonomous actor who should be able to form preferences free of any organizational or other group pressures.

The requirement for election is a simple majority of all the voting delegates. If that is not achieved on the first ballot, successive ballots are held. Candidates who do not meet a minimum threshold of votes or are at the bottom of the poll are dropped from succeeding ballots.

As the base of participation in the convention has widened, its fundamental character has changed. Since 1967, as Courtney[3] points out, conventions have become institutions of mass politics. The number of voting delegates at the 1983 Conservative convention and at the 1984 Liberal convention exceeded 3000 and the number of people who attended meetings to elect delegates may well have been as large as 50 000 in each of the parties. As well, the conventions were the focus of months of coverage by the media (thus reaching a vast audience), millions of dollars were spent on convention campaigns, and the leading candidates employed the technologies of general election campaigns to try to mobilize delegate support. The development of the "mass politics" convention has fundamentally altered the character of leadership selection in Canadian parties with important consequences for both the parties and the process of government as a whole. The debate about conventions turns on the interpretation and assessment of these consequences.

In reviewing this debate I will first examine the issues that flow from the values stressed by the élite model.

The Élite Model

Stable Leadership

The convention has been a problematic device for providing stability in the transfer and exercise of leadership. The convention method of leadership selection does not fit naturally with the cabinet-parliamentary system of representative government. The convention has led to the anomalous situation in which the authority of the leadership flows from one institution which functions intermittently and has no public responsibility or accountability but can be exercised only through another institution which functions continuously and whose members owe their positions to their ability to retain public confidence. This is a system in which divisions over the leadership are bound to occur, particularly since the two institutions, because of the very design of the convention, are likely to represent different sets of social as well as institutional interests.

Courtney[4] argues that the development of the mass politics convention, in which the parliamentary party has little influence, has made it all the more likely that there will be a divergence between the leadership preferences of the parliamentary caucus and the party outside parliament. As Courtney points out, severe strains are imposed on the system when the parliamentary party is forced to work with a leader which it does not want.

There is ample evidence to support Courtney on this point. It is clear that the Conservative caucus did not want Robert Stanfield in 1967 or Joe Clark in 1976 and the result was a serious impairment of the leaders' effectiveness,[5] while after the 1984 election John Turner's leadership of the Liberal party was seriously disrupted by his difficulties in managing a hostile caucus.

The parties have not dealt very effectively with the problems inherent in the leader's dual line of accountability. The conflict in the Conservative party over John Diefenbaker's leadership lasted nearly four years because the party did not have an accepted, effective procedure of leadership review. With a substantial majority of the caucus behind him, Diefenbaker was able to resist repeated attempts from the extraparliamentary party to force him to resign. The effects from that conflict were felt in the Conservative party for two decades and contributed significantly to the party's ineffectual performance during this period. Diefenbaker's acceptance of the decision by the 1966 biennial meeting of the party's national association to call a leadership convention had seemed to establish that the extraparliamentary party was the legitimate final arbiter of the leader's tenure, but both Clark's experience in the Conservative party in 1983 and Turner's in the Liberal party from 1986 to 1988 suggest neither party has actually settled this issue. Because of his weakness in the parliamentary party, Clark felt compelled in 1983 to accede to the calling of a leadership convention despite the fact that two thirds of the delegates to the party's biennial meeting had voted to support him. Turner, having won the support of 76 percent of the delegates at the biennial meeting of the Liberal party on 1986, was thought to have freed himself from challenges from his opponents in the parliamentary party but they continued to attempt to dislodge him up to the very eve of the 1988 election.

The Clark and Turner episodes make clear that the parliamentary parties will not accept the legitimacy of a procedure of accountability that denies their special role at the centre of Canada's system of cabinet-parliamentary democracy. Their reasons are not difficult to understand. It is, after all, only through parliament that the ultimate end of the parties—the achievement and exercise of power—can be realized. They can make the claim to a continuing right to call the leader to account on the ground that a decision to confirm a leader taken at intervals of two or more years is not consistent with the principle of continuous responsibility, which is the essence of executive responsibility to parliament. Just as the leader, because of this principle, claims independence from the extraparliamentary party in the ability to determine in caucus what party policy will be, members of caucus can claim to have a right to hold the leader accountable to them as well as to the extraparliamentary party.

Compounding this fundamental difficulty is the fact that the parties lack stable procedures for leadership review. Reflecting the fact that the principle of review is not accepted as legitimate by all party members, there have been frequent amendments to the review procedures to make them more or less difficult to apply. The Conservatives have had four different sets of leadership review procedures since the concept of review was accepted in 1966, and the Liberals have had three.[6]

Another problem is that the parties have not dealt with the case in which a very large minority instead of a majority of convention delegates vote for a convention. Some people within the parties have argued that since the electoral system works on a simple majority principle it is unfair to impose a higher standard in a test of confidence for a party leader, but it is clear that the nature of party leadership does require a higher standard. The leader's ability to command public confidence is seriously weakened if he or she can be portrayed as lacking the confidence of a significant number of his or her own party's members. Neither party has attempted to establish what level of support should be deemed sufficient. For Clark, 66.9 percent was not enough in 1983 because he had told his caucus in 1981 that he would resign if he did not do better than the 66 percent he had received at the 1981 biennial meeting. Clark's decision established a standard by which many commentators suggested Turner's leadership would be tested at the Liberal review vote in 1986. But other commentators speculated that the appropriate threshold to secure Turner's leadership should be higher (or lower). This speculation only served to add to the perception of confusion in the party.

Quality of Convention Decision Making

Another set of criticisms from the perspective of élite theory focuses on the quality of decision making in the contemporary convention. It is argued that the contemporary convention contains defects which weaken its ability to produce leaders with the skills and experience required to give competent direction to public affairs.

One criticism in this vein centres on the effect of parties' affirmative action rules for young people. These rules have had a significant impact on the representation of young people. The number of delegates under 30 attending Conservative conventions grew from 20 percent in 1967 to 27 percent in 1976 to 40 percent in 1983. The rate of growth in the Liberal party—which before the rules changes of 1986 had less generous affirmative action provisions for young people—has been slower but, by 1984, the number of delegates under 30 had reached 30 percent. Young people, therefore, appear to have attained numerical representation at conventions disproportionate to their representation in the population at large. Courtney[7] warns that the consequence of this growth in the number of younger delegates at conventions is to bring into the process a large number of people with little or no previous experience in politics. For example, he cites data that show the number of delegates with less than five years experience in politics increased from 11 percent at the Conservative convention of 1967 to 31 percent in 1976. Reinforcing Courtney's concern on this point is evidence that at least some young people may not be motivated by an appropriate level of concern for the public-serving ends of politics. Interviews with student activists who participated in the 1983 and 1984 conventions, and data from the surveys of delegates to those conventions[8] indicate that young party members see politics primarily as a means to personal ends and that they take little opportunity to involve themselves in discussions involving public policy.[9]

Adding weight to these criticisms of the rules for representing young people is the fact that the vote of young delegates has become an important factor in convention outcomes. Clark built his victory at the Conservative convention in 1976 from a strong base among young delegates[10] while Mulroney's victory at the 1983 Conservative convention was assisted by a big bloc of youth delegate votes that put him in the strategically important position of second place on the first ballot.[11]

From the parties' perspective, affirmative action for young people is of singular importance. The protection of their role is defensible not only on the ground of interest representation, but also on the ground that a strong youth organization is essential to ensure a continuing supply of energetic workers in the campaign organizations of the parties, to preserve the appeal of the parties to first-time voters, and to recruit new members into their élites. But these arguments do not justify the expansion of youth representation without regard to the principle of proportional balance in the overall structure of the convention. Under the rules now in effect, there is every reason to expect that young delegates will acquire an even larger role in future conventions. The constitutions of both parties now permit the establishment of hundreds of new campus clubs because a political club can be established at any recognized post-secondary educational institution. If these opportunities to create new clubs were to be fully exploited, conventions could literally come under the dominance of the parties' youth wings.

The enlarged role of the mass media in contemporary conventions is a second source of concern about the quality of convention decision making. The convention has become a media spectacle rivalling a national election in the attention it attracts. The parties have welcomed and attempted to facilitate the media role in conventions because the publicity that conventions generate has been shown to have the dramatically beneficial effect of raising party standing in public opinion polls, at least in the short run, by as much as 15 points.

One effect of the enlarged role of the media is that journalists have come to play an important part in leadership selection. Their role is particularly important in establishing the viability of candidates. Fletcher argues that in doing this journalists are guided by the existing public profile of candidates, the evidence of committed support from party notables, the apparent national appeal of the candidates, the capacity of candidates to raise funds and certain personal characteristics of candidates.[12] But there is wide latitude for journalists to interpret the information from these sources, which gives journalists an independent capacity to influence how the candidates are perceived. Fletcher points to evidence that suggests journalists may have their own agendas in advancing a candidate. He cites Graham's comment that Turner's candidacy was kept alive in the media through his nine-year retirement from public life in part because of the desire of journalists to have a "device with which to hammer Trudeau."[13] More generally, it seems reasonable to suppose that journalists have a disposition to view candidates in terms of factors or attributes that will create an interesting or exciting story.

Partly for this reason it has been argued that, in the era of television politics, candidates who are new to the central arena of politics have a distinct advantage in comparison to more seasoned candidates. The value of novelty over experience is illustrated by the most recent conventions. When Mulroney was chosen as Conservative leader in 1983, he had been a candidate for the leadership in 1976, but had never run for public office. When Turner won the Liberal convention in 1984, as has already been noted, he had been out of active politics for nine years.

Fletcher also points to three benefits from the increased media role in leadership selection. First, it provides delegates with more extensive and more independent information about the candidates. In the open campaign of the modern mass convention, candidates cannot avoid the critical scrutiny of journalists, particularly since the candidates need media coverage to develop credibility as serious contenders and to convey their message to the delegates. Second, the open campaign tests the ability of candidates to withstand the pressures they will face if they win the leadership. Thus, what Fletcher calls the "media trial by ordeal" is valuable not only for the substantive information it produces but also for what it reveals about the inner resources of the candidates—their ability to act effectively under stress. Third, the requirements of this kind of campaign provide delegates with an opportunity to assess the effectiveness of candidates as communicators. As Fletcher has noted elsewhere,[14] the ability to communicate effectively is an important criterion of leadership in modern government.

Another criticism of the convention focuses on the effects of mass communications on the way in which delegates make their voting decisions. It is argued that, under the conditions of the modern convention, delegates have become increasingly like voters in the mass electorate. Their ability to secure accurate information is limited by their need to rely on mass communications. In addition, the messages conveyed through mass communications are subject to manipulation and tend to operate most effectively by eliciting emotional responses to a candidate's image. In this view, delegate decision making in contemporary conventions is unlikely to be an informed and deliberative process of rational assessment of the character and ideas of candidates. Leaders are likely to be chosen not on the basis of their competence or their ideas but on the basis of their success in creating images that appeal to delegate emotions.

One questionable element in this critique is the extent to which delegates rely on the mass media for information about candidates. In 1983 and 1984 the leading candidates made personal contact, directly or through a worker, with 90 percent or more of the delegates. Moreover, the delegates were "bombarded with candidate materials through the mail (including everything from newsletters, computer-produced 'personal' letters and pamphlets, to books and cassette tapes)."[15] In fact, when asked to identify their primary source of information about the candidates—news reports or materials from the candidates—only 16 percent of the Conservatives and 17 percent of the Liberals said *news reports*, 41 percent of the Conservatives and 42 percent of the Liberals said *both equally*, and 42 percent of the Conservatives and 40 percent of the Liberals said *materials from the candidates*. It is not surprising in light of these figures that only 34 percent of the Conservatives and 46 percent of the Liberals said news reports had either some or a great deal of influence on their opinions of the strengths and weaknesses of the candidates.

Nonetheless, evaluations of the candidates' television images were an important factor in delegate decision making in 1983 and 1984. Delegates had been asked in pre-convention surveys to rank the candidates on several attributes. In both parties the best predictor of final ballot vote was the delegates' ranking of the candidates for their appeal on television.

While this evidence suggests that the contemporary convention may devalue the competence and ideas of candidates, it should be noted that delegate rankings of candidates on attributes related to competence also significantly affected delegate voting behaviour. It seems that delegates were not willing to vote for a candidate they thought deficient in these attributes simply because they believed that that candidate had a more attractive television image. Thus, the portrait of the delegate as a person manipulated by the process of mass communications would appear to be an exaggeration. In fact, most delegates are not just passive actors, responding to the messages they receive through the mass media or from candidate materials; most are active participants in the process of communications and persuasion within the convention. For example, 39 percent of the Tory delegates in 1983 and 31 percent of the Liberal delegates in 1984 said they were part of a candidate's organization and an additional 48 percent of the Tories and 48 percent of the Liberals said they had tried to persuade other delegates to vote for a candidate. By acting and interacting in the process of persuasion, delegates may be expected to acquire a sophisticated understanding of the issues at stake, the required attributes for effective leadership and the merits of the candidates contesting the leadership.

Balloting procedures at conventions have also been criticized for their impact on the quality of convention decision making. One argument is that the process of calling successive ballots, without delay, until a result is produced inhibits deliberative and informed choice.[16] A response to this criticism is that delegates do not need extended intervals during the balloting to decide their alternative preferences. The pre-convention surveys in 1983 and 1984 show that most delegates in both parties had formed a preference ranking well before the convention met. The effect of the delegates' prior ordering of their preference is reflected in ballot outcomes. Delegates who had formed alternative preferences and who voted for candidates who dropped out were likely to follow their pre-convention preference ranking—even when the candidate they had originally supported attempted to direct them to another candidate.

An additional criticism of balloting rules is that the procedure of dropping the candidate who places last on each ballot may deny delegates the opportunity to choose a compromise candidate who represents the "best choice" of a convention. The argument against this rule has been convincingly made by Levesque.[17] At the 1983 Tory convention, John Crosbie won a higher score than either of the other leading candidates in the sum of his first and second rankings on several of the attributes on which the delegates were asked to rank the relative merits of the candidates. Moreover, Crosbie was ranked as a second preference by so many delegates that the sum of his first and second preferences was greater than that for any other candidate. On the basis of this evidence, Levesque argued that Crosbie would have been the best choice for the party but the balloting procedure forced him out. It has been argued elsewhere[18] that, in fact, Crosbie was not the party's "best choice" because of his unacceptability to francophone delegates. However, with the current system of balloting, it is quite possible that a party which is polarized between deeply divided factions could be forced to choose a leader who is unacceptable to a significant proportion of its members. It is also possible with this system that superior candidates may be passed over because they do not have the organizational resources to develop a strong enough base to be able to stay in competition.

Promotion of Social Consensus

Elite theory emphasizes the role of political parties in promoting the achievement of social consensus. It has been argued in analyses of American conventions that the widening of participation has opened the parties to the danger of adopting ideologically narrow or extreme positions which will make them less effective in performing this consensus-building function.[19]

Open membership rules for delegate selection meetings in the constituencies have made Canadian conventions vulnerable to the same danger because they permit the penetration of conventions by extremist or single-issue groups. The success of supporters of Peter Pocklington in using the Amway sales network to win constituency delegateships at the 1983 Conservative convention exposed the weakness of the present system to this form of penetration.[20] The opportunities for the capture of delegate selection meetings are extensive because attendance at meetings in many constituencies is still very small. In 1983 and 1984 more than half the meetings were attended by fewer than 200 party members.

Evidence concerning the ideological content of delegate opinions suggests that people with extreme views have not been very successful in penetrating conventions. There is some ideological cleavage in delegate opinion in both parties but it is not very strong. Few delegates hold ideologically consistent positions across more than two issue dimensions and even within particular dimensions, when multiple items have been used to test opinion, the number of delegates whose positions are ideologically consistent across every item is relatively small.[21] Even in locating themselves within their parties on a left-right scale, delegates tend to take moderate positions. Only about 10 percent of delegates are prepared to identify themselves as being on the far left or the far right.

Perhaps an even more compelling piece of evidence on this point is the fact that convention outcomes show that delegates have consistently rejected candidates who take extreme positions or use extremist rhetoric. For example, the three candidates who were identified in this way at the 1983 Conservative convention—Peter Pocklington, John Gamble and Neil Fraser—*collectively* won only 129 out of 2991 first-ballot votes.

Far from contributing to the polarization of social differences, it is arguable that conventions have been remarkably effective in promoting the achievement of accommodation across deeply divisive cleavages in national politics. In fact, the need to compensate for regional and linguistic imbalances in the leadership selection process was a key factor in inducing the parties to adopt the convention method and, in both the Liberal and Conservative parties, the convention has performed this function well. Its importance in this respect is clearly demonstrated by the experience of the Conservative party over the past two decades. From 1963 to 1984 the Conservative parliamentary élite was almost exclusively anglophone and contained many members who were hostile to the language-based concerns of francophones. However, the party's leadership conventions provided francophones from Quebec a substantial role in the selection of party leaders and thus permitted them to act as an effective counterweight to the minority of anti-French anglophones who sought to impell the party towards their own extremist views. The choice of Mulroney as the Conservative leader in 1983 and the party's subsequent electoral break-through in Quebec are directly attributable to the regional balance which the convention has provided in the process of leadership selection.

The Participatory Model

Representation

From the perspective of the participatory model one of the most important criteria for evaluating conventions is their effectiveness in performing the function of representation. In this respect, no characteristic of the conventions is more striking than the class bias in the backgrounds of delegates. Every study of Liberal and Conservative conventions has found that two-thirds or more of the delegates come from the wealthiest, best-educated and highest-status occupational groups in the Canadian population. Thus, convention politics in the Liberal and Progressive Conservative parties is dominated by high-status groups.

All studies of political participation have found higher levels of activism among the better-off and better-educated. Contributory factors include the fact that these people have higher levels of interest in politics and more time to devote to public affairs. But there are also structural barriers to political activism by people of lower socio-economic status. In the case of conventions, the obvious structural barrier is the cost of participation. Travel, subsistence and registration expenses for the average delegate exceed $2000. The parties provide some support to equalize disparities in travel costs, but otherwise have failed to deal with this problem.

Stewart[22] casts new light on the significance of status bias in convention structure. Studies of earlier conventions had found no evidence of a relationship between status cleavage and convention decision making. However, Stewart found that status cleavage did make a difference at the Liberal convention in 1984. It seems likely from his analysis that a convention proportionately representing the lower middle class and working class would have chosen Jean Chrétien, not John Turner, as the Liberal leader in 1984.

It is not in this area only that conventions have failed to be representative. Affirmative action has increased the proportion of women participating in conventions, but there is still gender imbalance in both parties. Between 1967 and 1983 the number of women participating in Conservative conventions increased from 19 to 37 percent, while between 1968 and 1984 the number of women participating in Liberal conventions increased from 18 to 40 percent. The under-representation of women has had a clear impact on the balance of opinion in conventions, as reflected in attitudes on issues and in voting behaviour.[23]

One reason the parties have not achieved gender balance in past conventions is that few constituency associations have exceeded their minimum quotas for women—set at two in six delegates for the Conservative convention in 1983 and two in seven for the Liberal convention in 1984. Another reason is that party élites, represented through *ex officio* delegateships, remain predominantly male. Only about 10 percent of the *ex officio* delegates to the 1983 Conservative convention and 11 percent of the *ex officio* delegates to the 1984 Liberal convention were women. The effects of this imbalance were partially offset in the Liberal party by the provision of representation for women's clubs.

The Liberal party has now instituted regulations that require gender equality among all delegates selected by constituency associations and youth clubs. Coupled with the representation accorded women's clubs, this should ensure gender parity in future Liberal conventions.

The Conservative party, however, does not provide for representation from women's clubs, it has reduced the quota for women among constituency delegates to two out of seven, and it has not imposed a gender quota on representation from campus clubs or a newly established category of youth constituency clubs, each of which is entitled to elect three delegates.

The Educative Function

From the perspective of participatory theory another criterion by which the convention should be judged is its contribution to the creation of an informed citizenry. It has been widely argued that public opinion is insufficiently informed to make rational choices about alternative courses of public policy. In the view of advocates of the participatory theory the only way this problem can be overcome is if there is the widest possible debate about policy among the competitors for public office and if citizens are directly engaged in the process of policy making. Thus, conventions can perform an important function in creating an informed public by encouraging leadership candidates to discuss and debate public issues and by providing party members an opportunity to take an active role in the discussion of policy.

Early convention campaigns were relatively private affairs, conducted on a limited scale through intermediaries, with few public appearances by the candidates and little coverage by journalists. These conventions were ill-suited to provide a forum for the debate of public policy. The contemporary campaigns of the mass politics convention are much better suited to this purpose. Candidates travel extensively across the country, holding open meetings with delegates, meeting journalists at press conferences, making speeches at joint meetings with other candidates and making elaborate use of techniques of mass communications to attract attention. But this change in the style of convention campaigning has done little to create a public opinion that is better informed about policy, mostly because few candidates debate the substance of policy. The campaigns of 1983 and 1984 were typical. The major candidates tried to avoid comment about issues which were potentially divisive. They used surveys to assess delegates' priorities concerning issues and to calculate their appeals in order to express sympathy with delegates' concerns while avoiding specific commitments. For the most part, candidates made declarations about their goals at a level of generality that did not admit debate. The enlarged role of the mass media in convention campaigns reinforced this tendency. Fletcher[24] shows that media coverage gave little attention to the substance of policy, being weighted towards reporting and commenting on the process itself—on who was ahead and on how the campaign was being conducted. The effect of this form of campaign is to focus delegate decision making on the personal attributes and popular appeal of the personalities of the candidates rather than on choices between alternative policy directions.

At the same time, the opportunities for delegates to have a direct voice in policy have been reduced. At earlier conventions delegates participated in the discussion of policy, adopting resolutions at local meetings and forwarding them to a national resolutions committee for presentation to the full convention when it assembled.[24] In the conventions of 1983 and 1984, delegates were denied any opportunity to initiate policy. Formal discussion of policy during the convention campaigns took place in carefully managed appearances by the candidates in forums that provided limited opportunities for participation from the floor. In this system, the delegate is limited to responding to the candidates' declarations of policy and expressing his or her judgment in the silence of the polling booth. In effect, participation by party activists in policy making has been completely separated from leadership selection.

Democratic Norms

One further set of criticisms raises questions about the extent to which convention processes conform to democratic norms.

An issue of particular importance is the role of money in convention campaigns. Campaign costs have grown rapidly with the development of the mass-based convention. Candidates conduct surveys, make national tours, involve themselves in delegate selection meetings, make direct appeals to delegates by telephone, distribute literature, subsidize delegate expenses and pay for elaborate entertainment and demonstrations when the convention meets. Some candidates in the 1983 and 1984 conventions spent in excess of $1.5 million and the cost of a campaign on the same scale in the 1990s could easily exceed $2 million. Having access to such sums is important, not just because they are needed to ensure that the candidate can get his or her message through to the delegates. One of the criteria by which journalists and delegates are likely to measure the viability of a candidacy is the candidate's ability to conduct an effective national campaign. Indeed, as Fletcher[26] observes, simply having "the capacity to raise funds" is one of the indicators journalists use in judging the seriousness of a candidacy. Thus, while a substantial campaign treasury may not be a sufficient condition for success, it is necessary if a candidate is to have a serious chance at contesting the leadership.

The large amount of money required clearly limits access to the competition and makes it difficult for candidates to compete on an equal footing. For one thing, few candidates are likely to be able to raise campaign chests of $2 million.[27] In addition, candidates are unlikely to have large enough numbers of supporters to be able to raise much money in the form of donations from people able to make only small contributions. Thus, only those candidates who are able to secure contributions from wealthy individuals or corporations are likely to be well-enough financed to be able to wage competitive campaigns. It has been argued that this is particularly discriminatory against women candidates because they are not well-connected to the interests which are the parties' principal contributors.[28] It also clearly discriminates against candidates whose opinions do not conform with those of the principal contributors.

Candidates have been able to obtain some relief from the financial pressures of the system through a ruling by Elections Canada which permits contributions to candidates to be considered, for tax purposes, as if they were contributions to their parties. This means that donors can deduct part of their donations from their taxable income. While this makes it easier to raise money, candidates still remain dependent on wealthy donors.

To try to neutralize the effects of money on convention outcomes, some people within the parties have urged the establishment of low limits on campaign spending; these proposals, however, have been rejected on the grounds that such limits are unrealistic. In fact, such limits are probably unenforceable because the parties are outside the authority of public law, and have no effective internal sanctions they can impose to secure compliance with the regulations.[29]

Delegate apportionment has also been criticized for failing to meet democratic norms. It has been pointed out that the parties' affirmative action rules violate the principle of one-person one-vote: "An 18- to 29-year-old female university student in the PC party, for example, ... is entitled to vote for four different categories of delegates—constituency youth, constituency senior, university and women's association. A male, 30 years or older, can vote for one category of delegate only (constituency senior)."[30]

It is impossible to determine how many party members actually avail themselves of their opportunities to vote for different categories of delegates but anecdotal evidence, from student activists and from complaints to party officials, suggests that multiple voting is a fairly common practice. The effect on party morale is reflected in the complaints to party officials. These complaints also turned up in comments to journalists during the 1983 Conservative convention campaign and in notes appended to questionnaires from participants in the 1983 delegate survey.

Multiple voting is at variance with the most fundamental of democratic principles. Moreover, in the form it takes, it unfairly weakens the role of party members with established records of service because it discriminates primarily against older party members and distorts the representation of opinion from the party's grass roots.

Another source of concern about the democracy of convention processes arises from the increasing resort to the packing of delegate selection meetings in the constituencies with "instant" party members. This practice undermines the effectiveness of, and is likely to discourage, participation by citizens who have a serious commitment to the process. Television pictures of a bus disembarking men recruited from a hostel for the homeless to vote at a Conservative delegate-selection meeting provided dramatic evidence of this practice during the 1983 convention campaign. There were complaints as well during the 1983 and 1984 campaigns that new immigrants, who knew little or nothing about the events in which they were taking part, were recruited to vote at delegate selection meetings through networks in their ethnic communities—entirely on the basis of affective ties within those communities.

The extent of the use of such techniques to pack meetings has probably been exaggerated. Only about one quarter of the constituency delegates at the 1983 and 1984 conventions said they had run for election on a slate pledged to support a particular candidate and there is no reason to suppose all of these slates were backed by meetings packed with "instant" members.[31] However, the openness of the current rules for delegate selection leaves the parties vulnerable to the widespread use of this practice.

Proposals for Reform

Most of the pressure for the reform of conventions continues to come from advocates of further democratization. Indeed, the pressure for reform along "more democratic" lines has become so relentless that the place of the convention itself is now being called into question.

Some critics advocate the replacement of the convention—with its delegate system of leadership selection—by a process in which all party members would vote directly to choose the leader. The Parti Québécois and the Ontario Conservative party have adopted this method, and it has been proposed for consideration by the federal Liberal party. While at the provincial level this process may be effective, its adoption by the federal parties may be criticized on several grounds.

First, this form of leadership selection would be more vulnerable to penetration by organized interests from outside the party and to such abuses as the creation of instant memberships to win votes. Only by moving to an American-style system of state-regulated voter registration in which voters are required to declare a party affiliation could there be any reasonable hope of avoiding problems of this kind.

Second, the use of a system of direct membership voting, with votes apportioned on a one-person one-vote principle, would undermine the principle of constituency representation, which is fundamental to the Canadian system of parliamentary-cabinet government. It would therefore increase the tendency towards the "presidentialization" of leadership in government which, without the checks and balances built into the presidential-congressional system, would contain serious dangers for Canadian democracy.[32]

Third, this approach would make leadership campaigns much more expensive because it would require even greater reliance on mass communications. Money would become a bigger factor in limiting competition and in influencing the outcome of the process.

Fourth, a mass-membership voting system would add more weight to the pressures towards image-style campaigns and thus further diminish the role of policy in leadership selection.

Fifth, at the same time it would further limit the ability of party members to participate effectively in the discussion of party policy.

Sixth, if there is one way in which the convention method of leadership selection has clearly proved its usefulness, it has been in the promotion of accommodation and compromise among diverse and conflicting interests. The Conservative party's success in restoring its credibility among francophones is a dramatic demonstration of the effectiveness of the convention method in this respect. It is difficult to see how a mass-based selection process could be as effective.

Seventh, related to this last point, a mass-based process would vitiate the significant accomplishment of the existing system in achieving proportional representation for regional interests in the selection of leaders. The ability of the parties to compensate for regional weakness, which the present system provides, would be completely undermined by a one-person one-vote system.

While, for these reasons, the convention method of leadership selection may seem more preferable than a process of direct election, the criticisms of the convention outlined in this paper point to significant defects in the present system. From the perspectives of both élite theory and participatory theory, there is need for reform. The following proposals indicate some directions reform might take.

(1) The instability created by the leader's dual line of accountability is among the most difficult of the problems that flow from the selection of leaders by convention. No set of procedures can solve these problems, but two kinds of reforms would help contain them. First, the parties could eliminate the uncertainty in their procedures for leadership review by requiring that review votes be held at every biennial meeting of their national associations and by establishing the size of the majority needed to confirm confidence in the leader. Second, the parties could recognize the separate line of accountability of the leader to the caucus by giving the caucus the right to invoke the calling of a test of confidence in the leader. The parties' constitutions could enable a leadership review vote to be initiated upon a formal request from a majority of the caucus. To protect the leader from continuous harassment from dissidents, the use of this procedure could be limited to one occasion during the interval between biennial meetings.

(2) The parties should discontinue the open-ended system of representation for youth delegates by assigning a fixed number of delegates from campus clubs for each province. To ensure the maintenance of regional balance within the convention this limit should be made proportional to the province's population.

(3) To widen the range of choice among candidates and to extend the opportunities for compromise in the selection of leaders, balloting procedures at conventions should be amended to eliminate the requirement that the candidate with the smallest number of votes be dropped at the end of each ballot. The danger that candidates with small blocs of votes could use this change to obstruct a convention could be avoided by requiring a candidate to have a minimum percentage of the total number of votes cast to be allowed to remain on a ballot.

(4) To promote effective discussion of policy, the parties should restore the practice of having conventions debate and adopt policy resolutions.

(5) To remove structural barriers to participation in conventions by

status groups, the parties should require local party organizations to pay all convention expenses for constituency delegates.

(6) The Progressive Conservative party, to work more effectively towards the achievement of gender balance among delegates, should adopt the Liberal party's requirement of equal representation for men and women in constituency and youth organizations.

(7) Given the importance of the role of leadership in Canadian politics, it seems reasonable to extend the application of electoral expense and party financing legislation to the process of leadership selection. One purpose would be to permit candidates to obtain reimbursement from the state for a portion of their expenses. A second purpose would be to establish sanctions in public law to enforce spending limits.

(8) The rules for participation in delegate selection meetings should be tightened to prevent the packing of meetings with "instant" party members. This could be done by closing membership lists at a fixed date following the calling of a convention. A period of four to six weeks would be long enough to permit interested individuals to be listed, and short enough to make it difficult for candidates to manipulate the process.

(9) Apportionment rules should be amended to eliminate multiple voting. Party members eligible to vote for different categories of delegates should be restricted to voting for just one category. This could be implemented by issuing a single party membership card covering all forms of party membership.

ENDNOTES

1. See, for example, Thomas R. Dye and L. Harmon Zeigler, *The Irony of Democracy, An Uncommon Introduction to American Politics* (Belmont, CA: Wadsworth, 1972), ch. 1.
2. For a discussion of this theory, see Carole Pateman, *Participation and Democratic Theory* (Cambridge, U.K.: Cambridge University Press, 1970), chs. 1 and 2; and Terrence E. Cooke and Patrick M. Morgan, *Participatory Democracy* (New York: Harper and Row, 1971), ch. 1.
3. John C. Courtney, "Leadership Conventions and the Development of the National Political Community in Canada," in R. Kenneth Carty and W. Peter Ward, eds., *National Politics and Community in Canada* (Vancouver: University of British Columbia Press, 1986).
4. *Ibid.*
5. See George C. Perlin, *The Tory Syndrome: Leadership Politics in the Progressive Conservative Party* (Montreal: McGill-Queen's University Press, 1980); and Patrick Martin, Allan Gregg and George Perlin, *Contenders: The Tory Quest for Power* (Scarborough: Prentice-Hall Canada, 1983).
6. The most recent constitutional amendments (made in both parties in 1986) only provide for a review vote. In the Liberal party, this occurs at the first biennial meeting following a general election; in the Conservative party it occurs at the first biennial meeting following a general election in which the party has failed to form the government.

7. Courtney, "Leadership Conventions."

8. The author conducted surveys before and after the 1983 and 1984 conventions. Data from these surveys were used by contributors of papers in George Perlin, ed., *Party Democracy in Canada* (Scarborough: Prentice-Hall Canada, 1987). Where reference is made to data from these surveys without citation of a specific paper in Perlin, *Party Democracy in Canada*, the reference is to analysis conducted independently by the author. Some references have also been made to data from surveys of the 1967 and 1968 conventions (conducted by J.K. Lele, H.G. Thorburn and George Perlin) and the 1976 PC convention (survey conducted by George Perlin).

9. George Perlin, Allen Sutherland and Marc Desjardins, "The Impact of Age Cleavage on Convention Politics," in Perlin, *Party Democracy in Canada*.

10. Robert Krause and Lawrence LeDuc, "Voting Behaviour and Electoral Strategies in the Progressive Conservative Leadership Convention of 1976," in *Canadian Journal of Political Science*, Vol. 12 (1978).

11. Perlin, Sutherland and Desjardins, "The Impact of Age Cleavage."

12. Frederick J. Fletcher, with the assistance of Robert J. Drummond, "The Mass Media and the Selection of National Party Leaders: Some Explorations," in Perlin, *Party Democracy in Canada*.

13. *Ibid.*, p. 106.

14. Frederick J. Fletcher, "The Prime Minister as Public Persuader," in Thomas A. Hockin, ed., *Apex of Power, The Prime Minister and Political Leadership in Canada* (Scarborough: Prentice-Hall Canada, 1977).

15. Fletcher, "The Mass Media and the Selection of National Party Leaders," p. 109.

16. Donald D. Smiley, "The National Party Leadership Convention in Canada," in *Canadian Journal of Political Science*, Vol. 14 (1968).

17. Terrence H. Levesque, "On the Outcome of the 1983 Conservative Leadership Convention: How They Shot Themselves in the Other Foot," *Canadian Journal of Political Science*, Vol. 16, No. 4 (1983).

18. George C. Perlin, "Did the Best Candidate Win? A Comment on Levesque's Analysis," in *Canadian Journal of Political Science*, Vol. 16, No. 4 (1983).

19. See Jeane Kirkpatrick, *The New Presidential Elite* (New York: Russell Sage Foundation and the Twentieth Century Fund, 1976) p. 330.

20. See Martin, Gregg and Perlin, *Contenders*, pp. 148–153.

21. See Perlin, *The Tory Syndrome*; Donald Blake, "Division and Cohesion: The Major Parties," in Perlin, *Party Democracy in Canada*; and Richard Johnston, "The Ideological Structure of Opinion on Policy," in George Perlin, ed., *Party Democracy in Canada*, 1987.

22. Ian Stewart, "Class Politics at Canadian Leadership Conventions," in George Perlin, ed., *Party Democracy in Canada*, 1987.

23. M. Janine Brodie, "The Gender Factor and National Leadership Conventions in Canada," in Perlin, *Party Democracy in Canada*.

24. Fletcher, "The Mass Media and the Selection of National Party Leaders."

25. Smiley, "The National Party Leadership Convention in Canada."

26. Fletcher, "The Mass Media and the Selection of National Party Leaders."

27. Only three of the Conservative candidates in 1983 and two of the Liberal candidates in 1984 raised sums in excess of $1 million.

28. Joseph Wearing, "The High Cost of High Tech: Financing the Modern Leadership Campaign," in Perlin, *Party Democracy in Canada*, p. 81.

29. *Ibid.*, p. 78.

30. Courtney, "Leadership Conventions," p. 8.
31. Carty, *National Politics and Community in Canada*.
32. Denis Smith, "President and Parliament: The Transformation of Parliamentary Government in Canada," in Thomas A. Hockin, ed., *Apex of Power: The Prime Minister and Political Leadership in Canada* (Scarborough: Prentice-Hall Canada, 1977).

17 Tensions from Within: Regionalism and Party Politics in Canada

JANINE BRODIE

Introduction

Conventional wisdom has been that our two major parties do not offer the electorate distinct policy options, especially in economic matters, because they are too preoccupied with mediating the often intense regional and ethnic divisions in Canadian society. Recent developments in federal party politics, however, may call this conventional wisdom into question. The dual federal elections of 1979 and 1980, as well as the 1983 Progressive Conservative leadership campaign, suggest that there is a growing cleavage in party positions on such fundamental questions as the power of the federal state and the proper role for government in the economy. The Progressive Conservative party appears to be staking out a unique position on the right of the political spectrum through its advocacy of greater provincial power and greater reliance on the private sector for economic growth. The Liberals, in contrast, have maintained their commitment to a strong federal state and, if anything, envision a greater activist role for the state than they have in the past. The present period, therefore, represents one of the rare instances in Canadian party politics when the electorate has been asked to choose between quite distinct party platforms.

Two questions about the apparent diversity in the platforms of the major federal parties will concern us here. The first is whether the inter-party debate on federalism and economic strategy which was so clearly evident in the campaign rhetoric and party platforms of the late 1970s was reflected in the electorate. Second, if Canadian voters were divided over these issues, did their party loyalties or their regional orientations underlie their disagreement? These questions will be examined below with survey research data collected from Canadian voters

This is a revised and updated version of the essay that appeared in the previous edition of this book.

in the spring of 1979. First, however, we will briefly trace the history of Liberal-Conservative consensus and disagreement on the questions of federal power and economic strategy.

Federal Parties and Development Strategies

Fundamental disagreements between the Liberal and Progressive Conservative parties over questions of state power and economic development have been relatively rare in our political history. The BNA act provided for a strong federal government and, from the beginning, it was an active participant in Canada's economic development. For example, under the so-called "National Policy," first unveiled by Macdonald's Conservative party, the federal government underwrote large, capital-intensive infra-structural projects, such as a national railroad system; it also sponsored immigration and discouraged the free-flow of continental trade by placing prohibitive tariffs on imported manufactured goods.

While in opposition in the early years of Confederation, the Liberals were viewed as the party of provincial rights and sometimes toyed with a free trade platform. Nonetheless, when the Liberals replaced the Conservatives as the dominant federal party in 1896, the distinctions between their platforms gradually disappeared. Except for a brief and unsuccessful flirtation with trade reciprocity in 1911, the Liberals also adhered to the economic development strategy designed by their Conservative predecessors. Both parties offered the electorate an essentially similar policy of developing a national economy through tariffs, though the Conservatives broke ranks briefly in the 1930s and again, in 1942, after the Port Hope conference.

The apparent consensus on economic policy among federal party élites during Canada's first half-century was not, however, clearly reflected in the electorate. Voters in the prairie provinces, especially farmers, grew increasingly disaffected with the economic policies of both federal parties. They argued that tariffs on manufactured goods such as farm machinery were excessive, and freight rates, which imposed a higher toll on goods shipped in the West than in the East, were discriminatory. Farmers' organizations pressed both parties to reconsider their economic platforms, but neither responded favourably. The economic alternatives advocated by the western farmers' movement were not voiced in the federal party system until it launched its own political party, the Progressives, in 1921.

The typical practice in federal politics has been that alternative economic development strategies have been introduced to the electorate by third parties rather than by one of the two major parties. The Progressives faded from the federal political landscape in the mid-1920s after they had extracted a few concessions from a minority Liberal government. They were quickly succeeded in 1933 by the Co-operative Commonwealth Federation (the CCF) which advocated a radically different role for the state. As a self-defined socialist party, it raised the option of direct state participation in the marketplace through public ownership of key sectors of the economy. More important, it advocated state economic planning to ensure economic stability and a wide net of social legislation for the general welfare. Each of these goals became part of the postwar Keynesian consensus.

The CCF's strong showing in the public opinion polls during the war years may have encouraged the Liberals and later the Conservatives to adopt a new perspective on economic policy. Both parties maintained an overriding commitment to capitalism in their postwar economic platforms, but both advocated state intervention and social welfare programmes. The "new national policy" was based squarely on the Keynesian imperative that the chief economic role of the national government was to ensure appropriate levels of aggregate demand through fiscal and monetary policies and through lowering barriers to international trade and investment.[1] Taken together these currents in economic thought provided the foundations for the contemporary Canadian state and the integration of the Canadian economy into the greater North American one.

With the possible exception of the Diefenbaker years, the two major parties offered the electorate essentially the same development strategy throughout the 1950s, 1960s and most of the 1970s. Thus, it is hardly surprising that survey research conducted during the period found that the public perceived only minor, if any, differences between the two. Analysis of voter perceptions indicated that the electorate tended to place both the Liberals and Conservatives at the centre of a left-right continuum while the NDP was perceived to be to the left of both.[2] The conclusion drawn from these studies was that the two major parties simply did not conform to the conventional classificatory schema of parties of the left and parties of the right.

It has been argued that the late 1970s witnessed an uncharacteristic, if incomplete, polarization in Canadian party politics. The Progressive Conservatives became the party of free enterprise and decentralization while the Liberals became the party of state intervention in the economy and federal power.[3] We cannot be certain whether the current debate in federal partisan politics constitutes the long-term agenda in Canadian politics. At the very least, however, the 1979 and 1980 federal elections represent one of the rare periods in Canadian history when the two major parties offered the electorate different economic development strategies.

The Liberals and Progressive Conservatives appear to be in fundamental disagreement over three broad policy questions. The first is whether the federal or provincial governments should have more power in the determination of economic priorities and policy. The postwar interparty consensus was that the federal government should have priority in setting economic policy. In many ways, the new consensus necessitated an overarching federal power because the key governing instruments of the Keynesian state, money supply and taxation, rested within federal jurisdiction. Moreover, the federal government had both the will and the requisite spending power to initiate a welfare state when most of the provinces did not.

The movement for decentralization of federal power did not come initially from the federal Tories but rather from western provincial governments which throughout the 1970s came in conflict with the federal government in their attempts to gain control over economic development and diversification within their respective jurisdictions. In 1979, however, the federal Conservatives, perhaps reflecting the influence of their western support base, raised the option of provincial power with the rather ambiguous phrase, "community of communities." They argued that federal programmes and constitutional powers involving lotteries, fisheries, resources, culture and communications should be turned over outright to the provinces or shared by both levels of government. That Canada should draw its strength from building strong provinces was anathema to the Liberals, who stressed that Canada was more than the sum of its parts and that the strategic role of the federal government in economic and other policy fields should not be relinquished to the provinces.[4]

The proper role for government in the economy was the second point of dispute between the two major federal parties during the late 1970s. The Liberals and New Democratic parties did not deviate much from the postwar consensus about the propriety of an activist state in the social and economic policy fields. The Progressive Conservatives, however, increasingly adopted the "buzzwords" of neo-conservatism, a philosophy which already had attracted adherents not only in the United States and Britain, but also in the western provinces and among members of the Canadian business community. At the heart of the neo-conservatives' analysis of the ongoing economic malaise was the proposition that the postwar state had failed to nurture economic stability and growth. It was too large, wasteful, inflationary, overly burdensome on the average taxpayer and restrictive of free enterprise. Reflecting this new orthodoxy, the Conservatives argued that the state should not participate directly in the economy but simply provide favourable conditions for the private sector to achieve. The new direction of Conservative economic policy would place far greater faith in the free market and put more onus on individual Canadians' own initiatives to create a better life for themselves.[5] The Conservatives, therefore, offered to cut taxes, reduce the size of the federal civil service, minimize government regulatory activity and turn numerous crown corporations over to the private sector.[6] The Conservatives promised nothing short, in the words of John Crosbie, of "a new era in the economic and financial affairs of this country—an era of new realism and an economic climate to provide improved opportunities and incentives for Canadians."[7]

The Petro-Canada issue, in particular, demonstrated the fundamental differences in the economic approaches of the parties. Petro-Canada had been established by a minority Liberal government under pressure from the NDP, which proposed that a public corporation in the petroleum industry was a necessary counterbalance to the power of giant multinational oil companies and a means to achieve Canadian ownership in a vital resource sector. While at first resisting the idea, the Liberals became increasingly reliant on the crown corporation as a means of penetrating the provincial jurisdiction over petroleum resources and opening new projects for the possible participation of Canadian capital. These goals were later firmly enshrined in the National Energy Programme. For the

Conservatives, however, Petro-Canada seemed to embody all that was wrong with the drift in postwar economic strategy—federal dominance over provincial jurisdiction and an unnecessary intrusion by the state into a field best left to the private sector. Thus, even though public opinion polls favoured the retention of the corporation in the public sphere, the Tories were determined to "privatize" it.

In addition to federal power and state intervention, the Petro-Canada issue also reflected the third major area of interparty disagreement—the issue of economic nationalism. For most of the postwar period the Liberals had actively encouraged foreign, especially American, investment in Canada. This policy had facilitated the growth of a branch-plant manufacturing sector in central Canada and large-scale ownership of key resources by U.S. interests. The Liberal party's continentalism was opposed by the NDP and by the Tories under the leadership of John Diefenbaker. By the late 1970s, however, the Liberals appeared to reverse their familiar continentalist orientation in favour of economic nationalism. Whether because of pressure from the political left, the force of public opinion or, more likely, the failure of the branch-plant economy to sustain employment, they adopted policies and established agencies designed to improve investment opportunities for Canadian capital. In contrast, the Conservatives perceived such regulatory instruments as the Foreign Investment Review Agency (FIRA) as unnecessary restrictions on the private sector. Discouraging foreign investment, they argued, was a luxury the economy could ill-afford.

Political parties constantly sort through issues, championing some and ignoring others, in order to gain electoral advantage. It is more difficult to explain why political parties change their orientations on such fundamental questions as the proper balance of federal power, the role of the state and economic nationalism. In the case of the Progressive Conservatives, their new direction may be viewed as part of the revival of conservatism in many western democracies and the rejection of the Keynesian state because of its apparent failure to live up to its promise of economic growth. This shift, however, cannot be separated from the politics of Canadian regionalism and the party's western support base. Western premiers, in recent years, have been major proponents of decentralization of the federal state's economic prerogatives, the free market system and foreign investment. The "twinned moods" of regionalism and conservatism have been manipulated by many western politicians, especially in Alberta, to protect provincially oriented and often provincially directed development strategies, strategies which often relied heavily on American investors and consumers, from the advances of the federal government.[8] Indeed, the Liberals were not beyond intimating that the new economic orientation of the federal Tories was simply a capitulation to the demands of the province-builders and resource exporters.

It is not uncommon for political parties to give greater weight in their policy calculations to regions or groups from which they draw their electoral strength. The Liberal party, for example, is careful to adopt platforms which, at the very least, do not alienate their Quebec support base. Similarly, the Conservatives' new orientations may reflect their reading of the demands and aspirations of what is increasingly their bastion of electoral support, the prairies. The question is whether the partisan policy differences observed at the élite level in recent years also characterize the electorate.

Policy Cleavages Between and Within the Major Federal Parties

There is little research examining the policy preferences of the Canadian electorate. Perhaps this is because early voting studies found the electorate confused about the respective policy positions of the federal parties and far less issue-oriented than political élites.[9] These findings, however, may have reflected the lack of coherent policy options presented to the electorate in a typical federal election. A more recent analysis of public opinion polls in the 1949–1975 period indicates that policy cleavages exist in the Canadian electorate and, more relevant to our present discussion, partisan disagreement over economic and social policy has increased during the postwar period while regional differences have declined.[10]

In this brief analysis of Canadian public opinion we will be concerned with the questions of whether the current debate over economic strategy among party élites is reflected in the electorate and, second, whether mass policy preferences are primarily partisan or regional in origin. These questions are explored with survey data collected from 3475 Canadians in the period between April and July of 1979.[11] The questionnaire incorporated a number of items which relate to the issues discussed above. In particular, a question concerning whether the federal or provincial governments should have more power in Confederation addresses directly the issues of decentralization of federal powers. Two questions pertaining to inflation and two questions referring to government intervention in the private sector tap the neo-conservative undercurrents of the 1979 and 1980 federal campaigns. Finally, there is an item concerning American investment which will serve as a partial measure for the economic nationalism issue.

The degree to which Liberal and Conservative voters disagree on each of these issues is displayed in Table 1. The survey results indicate a substantial degree of conformity between the positions put forward by party élites at the end of the decade and the policy preferences of their supporters.[12] While the depth of the policy cleavages among the voters vary by issue, those favouring the Progressive Conservatives in 1979 were more likely than Liberal voters to agree that provincial governments should have more power, that inflation is the most serious economic problem and that government policies are inflationary. They also were more likely to adopt a free enterprise position, agreeing that government should leave big business alone and energy in the hands of the private sector. The only inconsistency with expectations was that Liberal voters were more likely than Conservatives to agree that foreign investment is good for the economy. The Liberal party's recent foray into the unfamiliar terrain of economic nationalism, it would seem, was not clearly reflected in its electoral constituency in 1979.

The survey results indicate an approximate organization of Canadian voters

TABLE 1 **Partisan Differences in Mass Attitudes Toward Selected Economic Issues**
(% in Agreement)

	(Federal Party Support)	
	Liberal	*Conservative*
1) Provincial governments should have more power.	31.5% (346)	43.8% (345)
2) Inflation is most serious economic problem.	34.9% (434)	46.0% (403)
3) Government policies cause inflation.	39.7% (459)	57.4% (467)
4) Government should leave big business alone.	22.3% (251)	28.7% (229)
5) Government should leave energy to the private sector.	28.0% (323)	36.6% (295)
6) Foreign investment is good for the economy.	52.2% (597)	44.0% (362)

along a left-right continuum with the Liberals to the left of the Conservatives. The fit, however, is not perfect. While Conservative voters were more likely than Liberals to endorse positions consistent with the political right, the majority of Conservative voters do not appear to accept the fundamental tenets of neo-conservatism. For example, only 29 percent of Conservative voters rejected out-right government regulation of big business and a minority, 37 percent, felt government should withdraw from the energy sector. Similarly, less than half felt provincial governments should have more power. These findings, then, lend some support to the argument that the Clark administration did not have a solid electoral foundation from which to pursue some of its more conservative policy initiatives, especially those with a free enterprise orientation.[13]

We have found that Conservative voters tend to take more conservative pos-tures than Liberal voters in the issue areas examined here, areas where one might expect more Conservative support. Our previous discussion, however, suggests that voters in different regions of the country might also take different positions on these items. To what extent, then, is region more important than party prefer-ences in determining the policy preferences of Canadian voters? The relative importance of region and partisanship in explaining variations in policy prefer-ence can be inferred from the measures of association displayed in Table 2. Their magnitude indicates the degree of disagreement among the sample on each item: first, on the basis of their party preference, and second, on the basis of their region of residence.[14] While neither party nor region explain a great deal of the variation in the sample, region appears to take precedence over party in most cases. Party preference is marginally more important than region in explaining which voters are most likely to endorse a free enterprise orientation, but region is more important in understanding the sample's disagreement over the question

TABLE 2 **Strength of Partisan and Regional Differences in Mass Attitudes Toward Selected Economic Issues (Cramer's V)**

Issues	Party	Region	Issues	Party	Region
1) Provincial Power	0.14*	0.21*	4) Free Business	0.13*	0.09
2) Inflation	0.09	0.29*	5) Energy	0.08	0.11*
3) Government Inflationary	0.12*	0.14*	6) Foreign Investment	0.11*	0.12*

*p. < 0.05

of provincial power, inflation and government activity in the energy sector. Thus, while the statistics are not as conclusive as we might like, these findings suggest that there are regionally based cleavages within both parties.

The measures of association in Table 3 are approximate indicators of the degree to which each party's electoral support base is riddled with regional policy cleavages. Liberal supporters are more divided among themselves than Conservative voters on the question of whether inflation is the most serious economic problem facing Canada and slightly more divided on the provincial power option. Regional cleavages within each party's electorate are more or less of equal strength with respect to government as a source of inflation, government involvement in the energy sector and foreign investment. Both parties, in short, house regional policy cleavages.

Space does not permit us to examine the region by region responses of both party electorates on these issues. On the question of increased provincial power, however, voters from Quebec and the prairie provinces, regardless of party preference, were more likely to endorse the provincial power option. Western voters were more likely to worry about inflation and see government as inflationary while Quebec voters were least likely to agree that government should not intrude on big business or the energy sector. Overall, the orientations of Quebec voters and, to a lesser extent, prairie voters, account for much of the regional variation within each party's electorate.

Since regionalism is a pervasive force in Canadian politics, it is hardly surprising to note that the electorate houses geographically based policy cleavages. Nevertheless, the nature of these cleavages pose unique dilemmas for the strategists of each party. The different policy orientations of Quebec voters, for example, are not too threatening to the Progressive Conservatives, at least in the short run, because of the party's electoral weakness in the province. Parties can and often do "write off" the demands of regions which hold no promise of electoral momentum. Party unity and electoral fortunes can be jeopardized, however, when two or more regions from which a party draws the bulk of its electoral strength disagree about fundamental policy objectives. To what extent, then, do the regional constituencies upon which each party is dependent for electoral survival disagree in their policy preferences?

In order to address this question, we will exclude Liberal voters in the prairie provinces and Conservative voters in Quebec from our calculations.

TABLE 3 **Regional Divisions Within Partisan Electorates on Selected Economic Issues (Cramer's V)**

Issues	Party Supporters		Issues	Party Supporters	
	Liberal	P.C.		Liberal	P.C.
1) Provincial Power	0.20*	0.17*	4) Free Business	0.05	0.09
2) Inflation	0.34*	0.20*	5) Energy	0.10*	0.12*
3) Government Inflationary	0.11*	0.12*	6) Foreign Investment	0.11*	0.10*

*p. <0.05

Table 4 shows how much, on average, (in percentage) Liberal and Conservative voters residing in regions where their party is electorally competitive disagree among themselves on key policy issues. The results of this analysis give us a quite different impression of the nature of regionally based policy cleavages within each party's electoral constituency. Progressive Conservative voters in regions of that party's strength are quite similar in their policy preferences. PC voters in the prairie provinces differ from those in Ontario, in particular, on the question of provincial power, but the average deviation in percentages across all regions excluding Quebec is only 5.7 percent.[15] Most of the remaining issues examined here have been interpreted as a basis for conflict between Ontario and the West. It is noteworthy, therefore, that Conservative voters do not demonstrate much disagreement on them cross-regionally. Although we found little basis for a rigid neo-conservatism among Conservative voters in 1979, clearly there are electoral foundations in the electorate outside Quebec for a moderate cross-regional conservative coalition.

Liberal voters are more deeply divided among themselves than Conservatives on each of the six policy questions even when the responses of prairie Liberals are excluded. As might be expected, the source of this disagreement is Quebec. Liberals in that province were much more likely than Liberals elsewhere to support the options of provincial power and foreign investment but less likely to be concerned about inflation or to see government as its cause. These findings point to a possible strategic dilemma for the Liberal party. It has successively won decisive electoral battles in Quebec by appealing to its uniqueness in its ethnic composition and cultural concerns. This electoral tactic is perhaps most feasible when the two major parties agree on fundamental developmental policies. When

TABLE 4 **Mean Regional Variations in Partisan Attitudes Toward Selected Economic Issues (In %)**

Issues	Party Supporters		Issues	Party Supporters	
	Liberal	P.C.		Liberal	P.C.
1) Provincial Power	9.9	5.7	4) Free Business	1.8	1.2
2) Inflation	12.6	5.3	5) Energy	3.7	3.7
3) Government Inflationary	8.2	4.9	6) Foreign Investment	7.0	5.3

the two major parties disagree on the country's economic future, however, cultural appeals may be less effective. While the Liberal party captured Quebec in the 1980 federal election, it is also evident that many of the province's voters do not share the party's centralized and nationalist visions for the future. The Liberal party in the late 1970s appears to have been in the difficult position of countering the Progressive Conservatives' policies favouring decentralization and foreign investment, even though their major voting block favoured these options.[16]

Summary

This brief analysis of public opinion data indicates that the supporters of the Liberal and Conservative parties in 1979 were marginally divided on the questions of federal power and the proper role of the state in the economy. While Conservative voters were more likely to endorse decentralist and neo-conservative postures than were Liberals, the data also show that the Progressive Conservative party has not cultivated a solid electoral constituency for its more neo-conservative, anti-Keynesian policy proposals. The majority of Conservative voters surveyed did not believe that government should leave big business alone or vacate the energy sector. Moreover, the majority did not think that provincial governments should have more power within Confederation. The Clark government, therefore, may have misread its mandate in 1979.

This analysis also indicates that region is more important than party preference in explaining, if only partially, the different positions of Canadian voters on these issues. In this respect, the Conservative party's distinct positions on the questions of decentralization, the proper role for the state in the economy and foreign investment appear to be most compatible with the preferences of western Canadian voters.[17] Quebec voters also favour decentralization and foreign investment but they also are in substantial agreement about the propriety of government intervention in the economy. This latter position is much more compatible with the Liberal party's rhetoric. Only the future can tell whether this point of agreement as well as more traditional electoral appeals will be sufficient to maintain the Liberal party's historical bastion of support in Quebec.

Epilogue

Canadian politics and the federal party system have witnessed a number of dramatic changes in the decade since this article first appeared. These years brought both the collapse of a strongly nationalist and interventionist development strategy and the embrace of an alternative strategy based on continental economic integration and the primacy of the market. They saw an intensification of the ideological and policy differences between the two major parties, changes in party leadership and a fundamental realignment in the federal party system. The federal Liberal party lost to the Progressive Conservatives its long-standing status as the governing party and its deep well of electoral support in

Quebec. Nevertheless, the nature of the political debates and electoral struggles of the 1980s were defined during the crucial period examined in this article. The drama of the politics of the past decade is, in many ways, a chronicle of how the Conservative party succeeded in forging new regional alliances in order to displace the Liberals and thereby realize their vision of a decentralized, continentalized and market-driven economy.

After the defeat of the short-lived Clark government in 1980, the federal Liberal party, under the revived leadership of Pierre Trudeau, introduced a new development policy which embodied its position on the three areas of difference in policy between the parties. The Charter of Rights and Freedoms, the National Energy Policy and an ambitious "mega-project" industrial strategy were combined to reflect the primacy of a centralized federalism, government intervention in the economy and economic nationalism. The combined forces of a global recession and plummeting oil prices, however, doomed the Liberal's economic initiatives and Quebec refused to endorse the new constitutional order. It appeared that the party's new vision and bold initiatives had only succeeded in alienating significant parts of the capitalist class and both the western and Quebec electorates. Bereft of ideas about how to restructure the failing Canadian economy or soothe a deepening sense of regional malaise, the Liberal government appointed the Royal Commission on the Economic Union and Development Prospects for Canada (the Macdonald Commission) and selected John Turner as its new leader.

In the meantime, the Conservative party was steadily consolidating its position in the federal party system as the representative of decentralization and neoconservatism. After several years of effort, the right wing of the party finally succeeded in replacing Clark with Brian Mulroney. In him, they found a charismatic leader who favoured a decentralized federalism, private enterprise and foreign investment. More than that, he was a fluently bilingual native son of Quebec. Although the 1984 federal election did not reflect the clear party differences evident in the previous two elections, this combination proved sufficient to provide the Tories with the largest landslide ever before recorded in a federal election.[18]

The 1984 election had not made clear to the electorate the future agenda of the new Conservative government. The Mulroney administration, like the Clark government before it, had not received public endorsement for a radical restructuring of the economy or the welfare state. Nevertheless, its actions with respect to foreign investment, crown corporations, energy, the deficit and taxation soon made it apparent that the Tories' approach to economic development would conform to the principles it had increasingly espoused over the past decade. Their approach would eschew economic nationalism and state intervention and promote market-driven decentralized development.

The new Conservative government did not articulate a coherent development strategy based on these premises until after the release of the Report of the Macdonald Commission in 1985. In it, the Conservatives found theoretical justification and nonpartisan legitimization for their new agenda. The commission concluded that a decentralized and market-driven approach combined with a free trade agreement with the United States was the only viable development strategy left to Canadian policy makers. Moreover, the contingencies of a free trade agreement promised to wind down Canada's increasingly expensive welfare state because some forms of government assistance to individuals, economic sectors or regions could be challenged by the Americans as unfair subsidies.[19]

The combined appeals of economic decentralization and free trade promised to forge a new regional coalition in the federal electorate. It potentially could draw both the western provinces and Quebec into a firm and enduring alliance with the Conservative party. To ensure this outcome, the Conservatives initiated constitutional negotiations with the provinces to resolve Quebec's outstanding grievances. The hastily constructed Meech Lake Accord recognized Quebec as a "distinct society," a provision that the Trudeau government would have been loath to concede. The accord also provided constitutional recognition for decentralization by allowing all provinces to develop their own social programmes without risk of financial penalty from Ottawa.

The 1988 federal election nominally fought over the "free trade" issue proved the wisdom of this strategy. The Conservatives won Quebec with the dual appeals of free trade and the Meech Lake Accord while western support was further consolidated with appeals to decentralized, continentalized and market-driven development. The Liberals' vision of economic development so clearly articulated at the beginning of the decade had finally been silenced and the party which had dominated the federal electoral terrain since the turn of the century was set adrift in an electoral realignment.

ENDNOTES

1. Donald V. Smiley, "Canada and the Quest for a National Policy," *Canadian Journal of Political Science*, Vol. III, No. 1, p. 47.
2. For a discussion see Rick Ogmundson, "On the Measurement of Party Class Positions: The Case of Canadian Federal Political Parties," in R. Schultz, O. Kruhlak and J. Terry, *The Canadian Political Process*, 3rd ed. (Toronto: Holt, Rinehart and Winston, 1979), pp. 192–203, esp. p. 194.
3. James Laxer, *Canada's Economic Strategy* (Toronto: Lorimer, 1980), p. 9.
4. John Courtney, "Campaign Strategy and Electoral Victory: The Progressive Conservatives and The 1979 Election," in H. Penniman, ed., *Canada at the Polls, 1979 and 1980: A Study of the General Elections* (Washington: American Enterprise Institute for Public Policy Research, 1980), p. 148.
5. Michael Prince, "The Tories and the NDP: Alternative Governments or Ad Hoc Advocates," in B. Doern, ed., *How Ottawa Spends: The Liberals, the Opposition and Federal Priorities* (Toronto: James Lorimer, 1983), p. 45.
6. William Irvine, "Epilogue: The 1980 Election," in Penniman, *Canada at the Polls*, p. 342.
7. John Crosbie, Budget Speech, as quoted in Jeffrey Simpson, *Discipline of Power* (Toronto: Personal Library, 1980), p. 19.
8. Laxer, *Canada's Economic Strategy*, p. 21.

9. John Meisel, *Working Papers in Canadian Politics* (Montreal: McGill-Queens University Press, 1972), ch. 2.

10. R. Simeon and D. Blake, "Regional Preferences: Citizen Views of Public Policy," in R. Simeon and D. Blake, eds., *Small Worlds: Provinces and Parties in Canadian Political Life* (Toronto: Methuen, 1980), pp. 77–105.

11. A complete description of the data collection project is in Bryn Greer-Wootten and Bharat Patel, *Sampling the Quality of Life in Canada: A Design Report for the National and Panel Studies* (Toronto: Institute for Behavioural Research, York University, 1978). The survey was administered by the Survey Research Centre of the Institute for Behavioural Research at York University in cooperation with the Centre de Sondage at the Université de Montréal.

12. Party supporters were determined by the following question: If a federal election were held today, which party's candidate do you think you would favour?

13. Simpson, *Discipline of Power*, xii.

14. The sample was divided into five regions—Atlantic, Quebec, Ontario, Prairies and BC.

15. Some 50.7% of PC voters in the prairies endorsed provincial power compared to 34.4% in Ontario.

16. Among Quebec Liberals, 43.1% favoured provincial power and 57.8% saw foreign investment as good.

17. Among prairie PCs, 51% supported the option of provincial power; 53% saw inflation as the most serious economic issue and 56% saw government as inflationary. Some 43% thought government should leave energy to the private sector.

18. See M. Janine Brodie and Jane Jenson, *Crisis, Challenge and Change: Party and Class in Canada Revisited* (Ottawa: Carleton University Press, 1988), pp. 319–22.

19. See M. Janine Brodie, *The Political Economy of Canadian Regionalism* (Toronto: Harcourt, Brace, Jovanovich, 1990), pp. 217–23.

18 The Dysfunctions of Canadian Parties: An Exploratory Mapping

JOHN MEISEL

"Political scientists are not new to functionalism, but it seldom plays a sufficient part in their analysis. It is in the vocabulary but seldom in use. . . . "[1]

Introduction

The study of political parties, like that of other subjects, is from time to time jolted by the appearance of seminal works so enriching and transforming that they elevate it to a new plateau. The books by Ostrogorskii,[2] Michels,[3] Key,[4] Schattschneider,[5] Duverger,[6] McKenzie,[7] Eldersveld,[8] and Sartori,[9] among others, comprise such milestones on our road to the mastery of the party phenomenon. A potentially similar formative flashpoint burst on the scene in 1949, when R.K. Merton's "Manifest and Latent Functions" (a revision of an earlier paper) appeared in the first edition of his essays, *Social Theory and Social Structure*.[10] Although the article examines concepts and methodologies appropriate to sociology as a whole, one brief illustration, dealing with political machines in the United States, shed radically new light on our understanding of parties and also sketched an uncommonly rewarding way of analysing them.[11] Merton's approach and resulting insights were widely acclaimed and disseminated, and his analysis became a classic of party literature.

Author's Note: The ideas in this paper were first presented to my students in Politics 210 at Queen's. They were then put before the First Annual Workshop of the Working Group on Elections and Parties of the Committee on Political Sociology (IPSA/ISA) in Paris in April 1989. Subsequently they were reworked for a Conference and Festschfrift, Alain Gagnon and Brian Tanguay, eds., *Democracy With Justice* (Ottawa: Carleton University Press, 1991), honouring Khayyam Paltiel. I am grateful for comments on earlier drafts to Ed Black, Sylvia Bashevkin, Ned Franks, Bill Irvine, Al Kornberg, Jean Laponce, Leo Panitch, George Perlin, Paul Pross, Hugh Thorburn, Cynthia and Doug Williams, as well as an anonymous reader. I responded to many but, alas, not all of the suggestions I received. Much help was provided by Margaret Day and Patrick McCartney.

In an effort to explain why periodic efforts to reform corrupt political machines were repeatedly ineffectual and why the machines embraced such seemingly incompatible elements as respectable business people and members of the underworld, Merton subjected party machines to an analysis of both manifest functions ("those objective consequences contributing to the adjustment or adaptation of the system which are intended and recognized by the participants in the system") and latent ones ("those which are neither intended nor recognized").[12] Distinguishing between these two kinds of functions enabled Merton to conclude that the notorious machine met the needs of diverse subgroups in American society that were not taken care of by culturally approved and more conventional structures. Reform could succeed only when alternative structures emerged that fulfilled the neglected functions.[13] An equally important element of Merton's approach focused on the fact that social phenomena also exhibit dysfunctions, the consequences of which "lessen the adaptation or adjustment of the system."[14]

Many of the most useful items in the literature on political parties which have appeared since Merton published his important essay dwell on the functions of parties.[15] Thus Anthony King, in a clarifying, memorable essay, identifies six major functions of parties: (1) the structuring of the vote; (2) the integration and mobilization of the mass public; (3) the recruitment of political leaders; (4) the organization of government; (5) the formation of public policy; and (6) the aggregation of interests.[16] Similarly, the influential work of Gabriel Almond and his various collaborators stressed four key party functions: (1) interest articulation; (2) interest aggregation; (3) political integration; and (4) political socialization.[17] For Sartori, the major party activities perform "a representation function and an expressive function."[18]

The emphasis in much of the relevant literature has been on party functions; the idea of dysfunctions has largely been ignored. A notable exception is provided obliquely by Lawson and Merkl who note that "[I]t may be that the institution of party is gradually disappearing, slowly being replaced by new structures more suitable for the economic and technological realities of twenty-first century politics."[19] This implicit recourse to dysfunctional aspects of parties stands out as the exception that waives the rule: Merton's revealing use of the concepts of latent and manifest functions, and of dysfunctions, while much acclaimed, has not been showered with the flattery of imitation.

Given the promise of rich rewards offered by the trail blazed by Merton, why have few party scholars chosen to pursue it? It is too simple to ascribe this neglect merely to the vagaries of fad and fashion, although these two human foibles no doubt have something to do with it. Functional analysis had come under severe criticism and then became the subject of vigorous controversy.[20] It was argued, *inter alia*, that its practitioners failed to specify precisely the particular system within which functions were assessed; that the approach cloaked an inherent conservative bias; that it lacked an adequate causal explanatory power; that it had been impossible to reach a consensus on what structural-functional analysis really meant; that, in Merton's hands at least, it failed to distinguish between individual and societal functionalism; and that it depended on the acceptance of a systems approach to social analysis—an approach which was itself questioned by some scholars, notably, Homans,[21] Davis,[22] Mendoza and Napoli,[23] and Demerath and Peterson.[24]

Despite the undoubted presence of difficulties in Merton's approach when applied to parties, he demonstrated that there was much to be gained from applying his mode of analysis. Although functional analysis raises a number of complex conceptual and methodological problems, it also holds promise for extending our understanding of social and political phenomena.

In this essay I draw on Merton's idea of dysfunctions in an examination of the role parties play in the Canadian political system. The work is preliminary. Its purpose is to see whether focusing on dysfunctions adds something useful to our understanding of Canadian parties. Before plunging into the substance of my theme, however, it is necessary to clarify a number of points.

First, although my focus is on the dysfunctions of Canadian parties, I do not mean to suggest that these institutions, so central in the country's political system, have necessarily undermined its viability. In many respects Canada is among the most successful of political experiments, having attained an enviable level of civility and stability. While many failings are clearly evident, so are numerous achievements, and it would be unrealistic to deny that political parties have played a major role in fashioning the country's successes.[25] Merton suggests that "[I]n any given instances, an item may have both functional and dysfunctional consequences, giving rise to the difficult and important problem of evolving canons for assessing the net balance of the aggregate consequences."[26] The survival of Canada—not an easy country to govern and hold together—as a reasonably effective polity for much longer than most countries and, so far, without catastrophic internal schisms, indicates that parties have performed effectively in the maintenance of the system. Therefore, the emphasis here on dysfunctions is not a summary accusation of failure but an attempt to add a neglected piece to the mosaic of party studies in Canada.

Second, many scholars have been severely critical both of individual parties and of the party system.[27] To differentiate between the arguments of these critics and those presented here, it is necessary to specify what is meant by dysfunctions and other terms denoting shortcomings or weaknesses. By *dysfunctions* of parties, I refer to the consequences of their activities that weaken or undermine the political system in which they operate or that disrupt its smooth operation. These consequences are inevitable and are a by-product of activities that are otherwise functional.

Dysfunctions must be distinguished from *malfunctions*. The latter do not grow inescapably out of tasks undertaken by the parties in the pursuit of their normal goals, as do dysfunctions, but result from *unnecessary* practices which have harmful effects on the political system. For example, the psychological state of partisanship in an individual inevitably leads to a certain limiting of the political discourse. The degree to which this occurs varies with the individual concerned and the context, but some constraint on one's openness of mind is unavoidable.

This phenomenon is dysfunctional. A malfunction, in our lexicon, occurs on the other hand when an unnecessary activity of a party or of the party system, or a harmful procedure which could be avoided is pursued with deleterious effects on the political system.

The present procedure employed by the national Liberal and Conservative parties in selecting their leaders is an example of a malfunction. The manner in which conventions are organized has, in many instances, led to the selection of delegates in a highly questionable way. These massive gatherings have been in part packed, which has damaged their representativeness of the whole party population. (See Wearing,[28] Bashevkin[29] and Perlin[30].) Furthermore, the procedure has become so expensive that only extremely wealthy candidates or people backed by rich individuals or corporations can contest the leadership. The withdrawal of Lloyd Axworthy from the 1990 Liberal leadership race, because of his alleged failure to raise sufficient funds, illustrates the point. Party practices thus preclude certain interests or groups—such as women, the poor and those not supported by corporations—from being heard effectively in the party. This represents a malfunction because the flawed process of selecting leaders can be avoided. Other procedures are available, as the Parti Québécois and the Ontario Conservatives have shown.

Although the distinction between dysfunctions and malfunctions may, at times, be hard to establish, partly because the causes of party actions are so complex and often intertwined, the critical difference is clear: a dysfunction occurs when necessary and desirable activities have unavoidable sequels that harm the effective operation of the whole system; malfunctions result from activities that are done badly but that could be done in a different, less harmful way.

Most of those cited in endnote 27, who have found fault with Canadian parties focused on the malfunctions of our party system, rather than on its dysfunctions. To find, for instance, that parties have been exceedingly patriarchal and inhospitable to women in terms of the selection of candidates or in the allocation of positions of power, is to identify an area in which parties have performed badly not because this was an inescapable by-product of their activities but because of a failure to be more acute and sensitive.

Third, a notion related to dysfunctions which is sometimes applied to parties refers to their *decline*. The loss of influence of parties, relative to that of other institutions or political actors, *may* be linked to their dysfunctions but often it is not. The decline usually results from a new agency fulfilling the role formerly performed by parties. Parties then become less necessary and are supplanted, partly or completely, by the new institutions' pre-empting their former role.[31] The decline may occur even though the parties' activities were in no way dysfunctional. The idea of party dysfunctions, while related to that of party decline, is thus conceptually distinct.

Fourth, there is merit in distinguishing between the functions and dysfunctions of parties generally, under all circumstances, and those related to the role of parties in a specific context. Thus some of the functions identified by King,

Almond, and Sartori, noted above, are universal; others are performed only under certain circumstances. Ranney and Kendall,[32] for instance, include among the roles of the American party system the democratizing of the constitutional system, while most of the contributors to the well-known collection of studies edited by LaPalombara and Weiner[33] see parties performing functions within a developmental context. Many observers of the Canadian scene (marked by a somewhat fragile sense of national cohesion) have identified a nation-building role as an essential contribution of parties and of the party system.[34] Some of the dysfunctions noted below are specific to the Canadian situation; others are also evident in some or all other sites.

Among the many possible ambiguities that can creep into functional analyses are the questions of: *for whom* and *by whom* are functions performed? The context of the analysis needs to be specified. In the present perspective, we are concerned with the effects of parties on the political system within which they operate at a given time. Their performance is seen as dysfunctional if it undermines the viability of the political system and if it makes the performance of the manifest and latent functions of parties more difficult. With respect to the question of whose functions are under scrutiny, we focus on the party system. Thus, if a party declines and another benefits accordingly, this in itself is not considered dysfunctional. The issue is the performance of the whole political system.

In subjecting parties to a functional analysis, the observer is compelled to identify those functions that appear to be most central to the political system and those, although important, that are nevertheless secondary. This illustrates that a considerable subjective element is present in the exercise. For example, while some Canadian scholars attach particular importance to the parties' nation-building function, others are guided by hierarchies of values in which social justice, feminist goals, civil liberties or any number of other roles are supreme. It would be fascinating to overhear a discussion between Pierre Trudeau and Jacques Parizeau, for instance, on what is functional and what dysfunctional in the role of the Parti Québécois in Canadian politics.

While this aspect of functional analysis can certainly give rise to confusion, it is by no means a fatal impediment. Normally, scholars will quickly agree on the most critical overarching features of any political system and accept that, whatever one's personal preferences may be, the survival of a given political system is a necessary prior condition for the existence of many key political institutions and practices. Even someone committed to the independence of Quebec cannot escape the fact that in the context of Canada, parties undermining the integrity of the polity are dysfunctional. Likewise, a federalist must see that from the independentist's perspective, institutions and processes facilitating the break-up of Canada may be functional. The subjectivity associated with functional analysis poses no problems as long as the analyst's assumptions and analytical framework are specified.

Fifth, a problem with functional analysis arises from the difficulty of distinguishing between consequences of parties themselves and those caused by the context in which they find themselves. Some dysfunctions to be noted, for example, result from the manner in which parties respond to or are influenced by the electoral system. In this instance, is it the electoral system or the party system which is dysfunctional? Analysis would be meaningless if the presence of intervening variables were to permit parties to escape responsibility for their actions. The subject of the inquiry is parties, whatever the reasons which have compelled or induced them to act as they do. We must deal with the parties as we find them.

Sixth, dysfunctions of parties sometimes induce politicians to devise corrections that permit the system to compensate for the disturbing phenomenon. An interesting example arising from the dysfunction of narrowing the political discourse can be found in the reform of parliamentary procedure introduced in the mid-1980s. A number of changes strengthened the House of Commons committees that, in some cases, assumed important policy-making roles.[35] The Standing Committee on Communications and Culture, when discussing a new broadcasting act in 1988, took a different position on some matters than did the minister responsible for the legislation, partly because party lines were much less evident in committee than outside.[36] Eventually, an almost nonpartisan committee confronted the government. Thus excessive partisanship in the political mainstream was compensated for by the creation of a forum in which party lines were attenuated. Since the impetus for the changing role of committees came from a multi-party parliamentary committee, chaired by an independent-minded backbencher, the corrective measures were initiated by party people who were at a certain distance from the party leaderships. The corrective action therefore emanated from within the parties themselves and was implemented through changes in parliamentary procedure. While not banishing a particular dysfunction of parties, therefore, some of their actions can be functional in compensating for the damaging consequences of others.

Seventh, dysfunctional aspects of parties do not manifest themselves uniformly throughout a political system. We shall note below that parties have unwittingly deepened sectional cleavages and that they have had divisive effects, as well as unifying ones. Pross[37] and Bickerton[38] argue that insofar as the Atlantic provinces are concerned, parties play a key role in redistributing income from the centre to the periphery. Since they are perceived to be performing this role, they presumably help bind the poorer regions to the national whole. According to Bickerton:

> [T]he party system elsewhere may have declined relative to other *functional* means of integration and representation (specifically through the mechanism of the capitalist market economy and through the centralized bureaucracy . . .), but on the Atlantic periphery it retained its importance precisely because of the inadequacy of such means to integrate and represent periphery residents. . . .
>
> This is particularly true with regard to the Maritimes, where an historic dependence on state allocations conferred by political élites at the centre has given the individuals and institutional mechanisms that link centre and periphery— especially the party system—a place of central importance in the social, political, and economic life of the region.[39]

Eighth, dysfunctional consequences of party activities occur because of the relationships that prevail between the parties and their environment. As a result, dysfunctions may develop—even though parties continue doing precisely what they had previously done without harmful effects—because of a changing world. For example, the decline of localism and the ever stronger nationalizing forces in the economy strained the capacities of parties to perform adequately their representational functions. The adoption of the merit system in the public service is another example. While the application of nonpartisan criteria to the selection of officials must have had the approval of party politicians running the government, the drive for the change emanated from the logic of management and for the desire for efficiency. It was not, in other words, parties that wished to do away with patronage (although reform elements within some of them may have advocated it) but the larger sociopolitical system in which the parties operate. As a result, however, the traditional reliance on personal clientelism became dysfunctional.

Dysfunctions of Canadian Parties

Turning, at last, to the dysfunctions themselves, 10 are particularly noteworthy. Whatever else it does, Canada's party system also:
   (1) limits political discourse;
   (2) institutionalizes confrontation;
   (3) undermines the legitimacy of the political system;
   (4) attenuates the public philosophy;
   (5) confuses the government mandate;
   (6) encourages wasteful government expenditures;
   (7) ignores some important issues;
   (8) misrepresents political forces;
   (9) weakens the central government;
   (10) neglects the policy role.
Put this starkly, the list looks like a scathing indictment. This impression is misleading—much depends on what is represented by the shorthand headings, on the seriousness of each item and on what else parties do. I have already noted that the quality of the Canadian polity is such that one can conclude that the political system, and its linchpin—parties—must have been doing something right.

Limiting Political Discourse

Although research-based empirical evidence is lacking here, it is hard to escape the conclusion that Canadian federal politicians become increasingly more intolerant of one another on the basis of party distinction.[40] There are exceptions, to be sure, but the continuous mutual denigration in parliament, heightened by the visceral quality of the televised question period, seems to damage many of the members' capacity to endow their opponents with even a modicum of decency or intelligence.

It is rare for an opposition politician to give the government party credit for having done anything right. Every initiative, every statement, every decision of the government is treated as if it was the work of an incompetent and possibly dishonest idiot.[41] By the same token, every concern of opposition politicians is viewed by the government party as a mean, self-serving, petulant part of a mindless filibuster. Constant repetition of mutual attack and recrimination ultimately has a self-hypnotic effect—a great many members become persuaded that their opponents really are as malevolent and stupid as the party rhetoric suggests.

The atmosphere at Westminster is, interestingly, not nearly as bitter; opposing politicians normally show considerably more tolerance and respect for one another. The cause of Canada's seemingly exaggerated partisanship, therefore, may be in part ascribed to the legacy of a one-party dominant system and to the personalities involved, particularly the abrasive manner of two recent prime ministers. This style can be traced partly to the exasperation of the Conservatives during the long years in which they seemed to be doomed to perpetual opposition[42], and partly to the effects on the Liberals of being "the government party."[43] After the massive Tory victory in 1984, the Liberals were as ill-prepared for being in opposition as the Conservatives were to govern. The Liberals simply adopted the manner of the previous opposition—a process that in the guttersnipe antics of the Rat Pack, seriously degraded the atmosphere of the House.

At election time, political pugnacity reaches exceptional lows and also a much wider public. The 1988 contest, because of the deep emotions stirred by the free trade issue and because of changing campaign strategies and personnel, revealed that otherwise reasonable people can come close to losing their senses under the flush of extreme partisanship. While none of the leaders can be said to have done much to inform the public effectively about the nature of the Free Trade Agreement, the Liberal and NDP leaders' "facts" and arguments were so far-fetched as to make both look both silly and dishonest. The prime minister's penchant for hyperbole has had the same effect.

This situation ultimately creates political actors unable to fathom the arguments of their opponents. Political discourse turns into a dialogue of the deaf, and the normally salutary consequences of argument and the interaction among contending parties are lost. Since it is probable that the blinkers bestowed by partisanship become thicker and larger as the victim rises in the party hierarchy, it is likely that the most powerful leaders are particularly prone to impaired vision.

All partisanship reduces the openness of mind of the partisan, of course. No great harm results from this when the attachment to one's own side, and the distrust of the others, is moderate. It is when these become inflated into all-consuming passions that truculence and blindness preclude the creative enrichment expected from the exchange of ideas and from the confrontation of differing interests. The limitations thus imposed on the political discourse sap the effectiveness of political decision making and inhibit the development of effective policies. To the degree that parties contribute to this situation, they exert a negative influence on the political system and they make it harder for themselves to perform their tasks effectively. They are, in part, dysfunctional.

Institutionalizing Confrontation

The factors just noted have other impairing consequences for the political system. They institutionalize confrontation and convey the impression that it is only through adversarial procedures that acceptable decisions are found in the public sector.

The logic of party competition requires a certain level of confrontation and of adversarial politics. What in the language of commerce is called "product differentiation" induces parties to perpetuate differences and disagreements even when the points at issue have become minimal or no longer salient. Similarly, the parties' desire to appear to meet the needs of various constituencies better than their opponents leads them constantly to exploit every conceivable difference. The fostering, aggravation and prolongation of artificial or needless disputes for the sake of party advantage is, therefore, a natural consequence in a system in which the spoils of power are the *sine qua non* of political survival. But when these practices become deeply ingrained and institutionalized, they preclude recourse to other avenues of discourse. Serious consideration of alternative modes of thought and decision making is discouraged and the whole system is deprived of effectively canvassing all available alternatives.[44]

Underming Legitimacy

Mutual denigration, so characteristic of current party politics in Canada and epitomized in the Commons Question Period, reduces the credibility of people in public life. The decline of trust in government and in politics as a whole, evident in Canada as elsewhere,[45] is almost certainly related in part to the vituperative and confrontational style espoused by large numbers of party politicians. The televising of parliamentary debates, and the manner in which TV handles political news generally and elections in particular, heightens the perceived degradation of public life and robs the players in the public domain of the support needed for optimal effectiveness.

Attenuation of Public Philosophy

To define the public interest is among the most vexing and elusive challenges in all politics, although among the functions of political parties in liberal democracies, none is more important. Acceptable definitions of the public interest normally occur when two types of approach are merged. On the one hand, policies are pursued which are deemed to be of general interest to the whole community, such as those dealing with culture, defence or the environment. On the other hand, there are measures intended to satisfy the claims of specific groups, centring on such issues as regional, economic or ethnic demands. Both elements must be satisfied—the trick is to arrive at a balance. If the former predominates unduly, measures demanded by powerful groups or sought by needy ones tend to become neglected and the regime may become endangered; excessive emphasis on the latter is likely to lead to inequitable, unfair decisions, damaging to the well-being of the whole body politic.

Although the Canadian party system has achieved some success in combining both elements[46], one of its dysfunctions results from being biased in favour of specific groups, thus attenuating the application of what Walter Lippman[47] called the public philosophy. Patronage, always the life-blood of the party system, has changed dramatically over the years. From involving mostly individual rewards, the paving of roads and the bestowing of benefits on relatively minor enterprises, it has shifted towards mega-policies and mega-spending. In other words, patronage has changed from being localized, small potatoes to becoming colossal, Guinness Book of Records-sized pumpkins. Government decisions affecting the location of major industries (automobile or aerospace, for instance), the quintessence of political culture (multiculturalism), or centre-periphery tensions (regional development) are made in response to potential impact on voter support for the government party.

Changes in the magnitude and style of lobbying have exacerbated the trend towards the customizing of policy making. "National life," a former leader of the Conservative party has said, "has become a struggle for advantage among large and powerful organizations—not simply trade unions and corporations. Organized pressure groups abound."[48] Furthermore, it has become common for former ministers, MPs and party technocrats to become "consultants"—that is, lobbyists working in large and often powerful firms engaged in influence-peddling. While they seldom if ever descend to anything as crude as greasing anyone's palm, they do grease the progress along the corridors of power for particular interests seeking favourable policy decisions by governments. While some of their efforts are directed at officials, the really big decisions are made by ministers, and it is often here that their former party comrades, turned lobbyists, manage to satisfy their clients.

These links between present and former party people facilitate the buying of specific government favours by vested interests and result in an incrementalist, client-oriented style of policy making in which the general interest is neglected. The notorious failure of governments, both provincial and federal, to protect the environment from profit-seeking extractive and polluting industries provides a classic example.

The old saw that there is no public interest, only public interests is, of course, partly correct. But the fact remains that the government and the party system must define the interest of all, in areas in which the play of particular forces fails to produce system-maintaining policies and decisions. To the degree that party systems encourage processes which lead to the rewards of the faithful, to influence-peddling, and to the "buying" of government largesse by specific groups of electors at the expense of the community as a whole, to that degree parties have dysfunctional effects.

Confusing the Government Mandate

A number of scholars, displeased by what they see as the excessive "brokerage" role of Canadian parties, have criticized them for reasons related to the attenuation of a public philosophy. In this perspective, parties lack sufficient ideological or permanent positions on specific programmes and instead act as brokers mediating as many cleavages as they can. Their position varies from election to election, depending on what concerns the electorate at the time. Among the consequences is the inability of the party system to innovate and to find solutions to new problems. Brokerage politics has also weakened party loyalty and has contributed to the unprecedented importance attached to party leaders. These features result in horse-race elections in which the personalities of the leaders are paramount and where ideological concerns are completely absent. As a consequence, election outcomes provide no guide as to programme priorities and elections fail to bestow a meaningful mandate on the government.[49]

Although this assessment has been challenged[50], it cannot be dismissed altogether. The authors of *Absent Mandate* (Clarke, *et al.*) while perhaps indulging in a utopian dream in yearning for ideological parties in the Canadian setting, do identify some real issues and do make observations which are suggestive in the context of this essay. They assert that "third" parties have ceased being sources of innovation and see "the virtual displacement of policy innovation from the party system altogether."[51] Consequently, "the arena of policy controversy and innovation shifted, moving more and more into the public service and into federal-provincial relations." One of the many consequences of this development is that parties come to be seen as removed from policy making and less accountable for government policy. Clarke and his collaborators consider this to be an important factor in the decline of "political activism as a way of registering disapproval" and relate it to the secular decline in a sense of political efficacy.[52]

Although in this instance the harmful features of party activities are caused in part by malfunctions, dysfunctional features are also evident. Brokerage politics is the natural by-product of a party system performing nation-building functions. The constant preoccupation with building coalitions that ensure parliamentary majorities makes the brokerage approach irresistible: maximizing support, from whatever quarter and for whatever reason, is a logical strategy for a party to adopt in the context of a community marked by deep regional and ethnic divisions and a low level of ideological commitment. A consequence, however, may be that the esteem for, and trust in, parties and the party system is low, and that newly elected governments enter office without a clear mandate from the electorate.[53]

Encouraging Wasteful Expenditures

The parties' approach to attracting votes is dysfunctional in another way as well. The conditions that create brokerage politics also encourage a form of party competition which leads to waste and public debt. To attract votes, politicians attempt to cap one another's promises of new and improved government programmes, frequently involving large expenditures. Competitive largesse of parties with the taxpayers' money contributes to the escalation of public expenditures (and, hence, public debt) and to the allocation of resources not according to need or a coherent national plan, but to electoral expediency. Every region or sub-region, every group, every interest is courted in this way if the number of people involved, or their strategic placing on the electoral map, promises an adequate pay-off. While genuine needs are no doubt often met during this process, unnecessary or badly timed projects are also involved, resulting in the misallocation of resources and the ultimate weakening of the economy and of the credibility of the system. This tendency of parties, therefore, has dysfunctional features, whatever its advantages may be in other contexts.

Sweeping Issues under the Rug

The fragility of the Canadian national community and the slender links binding it together have brought forth a sort of conspiracy among parties, in accordance with which they avoid confronting one another on a few deeply controversial issues.[54] This silence is intended in part to protect each from losing significant political support, but it also has an important latent function in that it forestalls the exacerbation of major cleavages. This tacit accord offers a striking exception to the limiting of political discourse and the institutionalizing of confrontation noted earlier, and so illustrates the versatility and complexity of the party system. While this avoidance of certain topics enhances the system's success in fostering national cohesion, it has also banished certain important topics from polite party conversation.

A recent study of media coverage of elections makes this suggestive comment:

> Although the public has been divided on such issues as official bilingualism, separate school funding [in Ontario] and Quebec's position as a "distinct society," the major parties have taken similar positions to avoid polarizing the electorate. Thus, with the parties producing similar policies and similar statements on many major issues—particularly those involving regional, religious, sexual-orientation or linguistic matters—it is hardly surprising that many of the issues have not been discussed significantly during election campaigns. By neutralizing or restricting debate on many contentious issues, the parties have reduced the role of issues and the ability of the media to report on policy alternatives.[55]

Other consequences follow from the unwillingness or inability of parties to make some of the most contentious national issues the subject of interparty conflict and competition. First, issues which are particularly divisive are not mediated by a political instrument—the party system—which has been reasonably effective in reconciling conflicts and which, because of its diffuse and open-ended concerns, is capable of attenuating extreme views.

Second, the major parties' failure to take competing positions on matters arousing public passion—language policy, abortion, and so on—encourages the emergence of splinter parties and/or single-issue movements reinforcing fanatical commitments to extreme positions. This decreases the chances of ultimately finding acceptable compromises and encourages recourse to extra-political direct action—possibly of an illegal kind.

Third, if the conflicts about which many people feel most deeply are left outside the universe of political parties, the latter appear to be irrelevant. This leads not only to the movement of people animated by intense passions into single-issue ghettoes, but also weakens the parties' ability to fashion coalitions around other issues. Parties are consequently handicapped in performing some of the tasks expected from them.

Misrepresenting Political Forces

Among the tasks expected of parties, none has received as much attention as that of nationalizing Canadian politics, of reducing the fissiparous forces that impede the development and acceptance of national policies.[56] A major revisionist analysis in the 1960s demonstrated, however, that "the party system, importantly conditioned by the electoral system, exacerbates the very cleavages it is credited with healing."[57] A major cause, according to Cairns, is the lopsided regional representation in the caucus of party strength, caused by biases in the electoral system. This factor led to the Liberal party's becoming increasingly insensitive to the needs of the western provinces, and to the Conservatives' failure to sympathize with Quebec. The blind spots existed in part because the viewpoints of the neglected regions were not pressed adequately in the highest party circles. Such popular support as the Liberals enjoyed in the West, and the Conservatives in Quebec (it was often not inconsiderable), was not reflected in the parties' contingent of MPs. These and related factors have, according to Cairns, led the parties unwittingly to deepen sectional cleavages and hence to divide rather than unify the political community.

Realignments of electoral support in the 1980s have corrected some of the flaws identified by Cairns[58]: all regions were represented in the Tory government caucuses under Mulroney. But despite recent election outcomes, the fact remains that at certain periods of Canada's history the party system performed only indifferently as a national unifier. In this instance, the functions performed by parties of structuring the vote, mobilizing the mass public, recruiting leaders, and organizing the government were accompanied by the dysfunction of widening the gap between regions and attenuating national unity.

Weakening the Central Government

Another consequence of the inadequate representation by the party system of regional interests is the relative weakening of the federal government and the corresponding strengthening of the provinces. The failure of the federal government to respond effectively to regional demands has contributed to the growth in importance of provincial governments, both with respect to the scope of their activities and to the degree to which they are considered legitimate representatives for their regions. "Denied what they regarded as effective representation in national institutions," one observer has noted, "Canadians looked increasingly to their provincial governments, acting within the forum of intergovernmental relations, to promote and defend their regional interests."[59] In describing the modern (post-1963) party system, marked by electronic politics and personal parties, Carty finds that "provincial politicians took the role of principal regional spokesmen, articulating grievance and pressing demands on the national government." Parties ceased being the main mechanism for regional accommodation, and were replaced by first ministers' conferences "which were institutionalized in a complex system of federal-provincial executive relationships. Deprived of the function that had driven them, the parties developed a new style of politics."[60]

There are those who argue that this is a desirable tendency within the overall Canadian political system; the point is one which can certainly be argued. But whatever the merits of this argument, one fact is inescapable: the exclusion of federal parties from the process in which demands are converted into outputs weakens their appeal, their influence and their capacity to perform their remaining functions. Parties, Carty notes, "have become more than ever an extension of the leader, a personalized machine to build and sustain a coalition of support for the leader's policies." The modern developments "have created a continuing tension within the parties that has largely focussed on leadership issues and personalities."[61]

No rigorous evaluation of the effectiveness of the new system has yet been made. There is a good deal of evidence, however, that suggests that the extensive diffusion of power in Canada and the growing relative strength of the provinces have made the development of policies required to deal with emerging problems extraordinarily difficult and that the party system is not particularly well-suited to coping with the new challenges. The dysfunctional consequences of party behaviour which have weakened the federal government strengthen the "decline of party hypothesis," which claims that parties are becoming less relevant to political decision making than heretofore and that many of their traditional functions are being assumed by other agencies—bureaucracy, media, interest groups, federal-provincial conferences, and so on.

Neglecting the Policy Role

The historical decline in importance of parties and the rise of interest groups[62] is linked to a dysfunctional effect that is caused in part by the electoral system. Constituencies, which comprise the basic organizational building blocks of parties, are geographical areas. The parties' representation function, performed by parliamentarians[63], is therefore inevitably influenced by the continuous need to reflect geographical areas. But the complexities of modern life have forced governments to satisfy, as often as not, functional rather than territorial claims—that is, claims not of localities but of individuals or groups who share something other than spatial proximity: workers, patients, the elderly, exporters, and so on. Their demands are usually represented better by interest groups than by parties. The emergence of powerful spokespersons for particular, functional interests has lowered the parties' representational role. In a perceptive essay on the subject, Pross finds that Canada has become what he calls, a "special interest State."[64]

This tendency is reinforced by the parties' declining interest in, and capacity for, focusing on issues and generating policy ideas. Pross[65] finds that "party contributions to policy appear to be quite limited and riding associations seem to prefer to direct their energies to delivering the seat and distributing patronage." The contemporary party system, as was noted above, is centred on personalities. It is also heavily influenced by the electronic media, and dominated by public relations, polling and communications. These features have made it less relevant to the origination and adaptation of policies. The policy role has become dominated by officials, think tanks and consultants. "Ministers have become bureaucrats themselves."[66]

In adjusting to their new environment, parties are successful in structuring the vote, mobilizing the mass public and organizing the government. Practices required for the effective performance of these functions are, however, at the same time dysfunctional in that they impair the party system's capacity to form public policy. Current methods of electioneering and of interest aggregation end up distancing parties from the policy process and this, in turn, makes them less effective in representing regional and other interests. It is significant that neither the Meech Lake Accord nor the free trade negotiations—two of the most important policy initiatives of the Conservatives following the 1984 election—can be linked to policy documents or even to the rhetoric generated by the party prior to the election or to inter-party debates before the balloting. Subsequently, during the 1988 contest, they were, of course, very much on the table.

Yet, there is no doubt that both these policy initiatives, as well as some others—the reduction of VIA services and extensive privatization, for instance—reflect the political will of Mulroney's Conservative government. Thus, while modern party leaders *do* occasionally initiate ideologically consistent policies, these programmes emerge from the entourage of the leader and not from the party ranks or party policy deliberations. (It is possible that the Mulroney government has initiated a new, more ideologically driven era in Canadian politics, but this is both doubtful and, at present, unverifiable.)

It is paradoxical that the parties' need to engage in territorial, as distinct from functional, representation has sapped even their capacity to satisfy some of their geographically concentrated constituents. Insistent demands for Senate reform and the institutionalization of first ministers' conferences attest to the sense of some groups that mechanisms other than the traditional party system are needed to ensure the effective articulation and aggregation of certain spatially based interests.

Conclusion

This journey through the highways and byways of the Canadian party scene—on a functionalist vehicle—has shown us enough to be able to conclude whether the views afforded by our conveyance are rewarding enough to compensate for its undoubted hazards. While our approach is prompted strongly by the work of Merton, it only draws on a part of his method (it has not exploited the distinction between manifest and latent functions, for instance, nor specified the nature of the system in which the parties function). The approach is also a far cry from that powerfully advocated by Lowi in his paper applying functional analysis to the innovative role of party systems.[67] Instead, the purpose here has been to ascertain whether the notion of dysfunctions can help us gain a deeper and more realistic understanding than we have had heretofore of the changing role of parties in contemporary Canadian society and in the Canadian state.

The particular functionalist route chosen has compelled us to try to distinguish between functions, dysfunctions and malfunctions, and has led us to consider these notions in relation to the decline of party perspective. It has also directed our gaze to the interaction between parties and their sociopolitical and economic environments and has raised the question of the extent to which one must seek the cause of changing party roles in the parties themselves or in their setting. Although our explorations have in no way diminished the claim parties can make to being central agencies of democratic government, they have nevertheless indicated that parties and the party system are anything but solely functional in the context of the political system housing them.

Our fleeting reconnaissance of the party terrain in Canada indicates that a fully articulated functionalist analysis of the Canadian party system is likely to enable us to identify those aspects of party performance which are attributable to their basic nature and their primary role, those which result from error or exceptional inspiration, and to distinguish lapses or triumphs caused by temporary conditions from those endemic to the nature of the party system. Functionalist analysis also compels the consideration of whether the problems parties experience in performing the tasks expected from them arise from changes in the structure, personnel or folkways of the parties, from their interactions and behaviour, or whether the causes must be sought in the broader context of their environment. Is it necessary to redefine the role of parties in the electronically driven global village, recognizing that many of their traditional services are now performed by others?[68]

Despite the partial perspective taken here, functional analysis permitted us to obtain helpful insights into the parties' difficulties in playing the role John Stuart Mill and similar liberal theorists would have prescribed for them. In conjunction with the rich literature stressing the functions performed by the parties, this approach is capable of rendering significant assistance to anyone attempting to reform parties and the party system, and to propose changes which would enable democratic institutions to be fully congruent with prevailing conditions in society.[69] We can reasonably conclude that despite undoubted problems posed by functional analysis, the perspective it affords does direct attention to features of the party phenomenon all too frequently overlooked or played down by other approaches. A more systematic, extensive development of the notion of dysfunctions therefore strongly commends itself as a desirable item on the research agenda of party scholars.

Merton, as we saw, noted that lasting reform requires that certain functions performed by flawed institutions need to be assumed by alternative structures or procedures. This critical insight points to the direction of the inquiries to be taken by party scholars and parties wishing to minimize the dysfunctional aspects of party activities: new or modified ways must be explored of carrying out some of the tasks parties have performed within Canada's political system.

ENDNOTES

1. T. Lowi, "Toward Functionalism in Political Science: The Case of Innovation in Party Systems," *American Political Science Review*, Vol. 57, No. 3 (September 1963), p. 582.
2. M.I. Ostrogorskii, *Democracy and the Organization of Parties* (New York: The Macmillan Co., 1902).
3. Robert Michels, *Political Parties: A Sociological Study of the Oligarchical Tendencies of Modern Democracy* (New York: Hearst's International Library Co., 1915).
4. V.O. Key, *Politics, Parties and Pressure Groups* (New York: Thomas Y. Crowell Co., 1942).
5. E.E. Schattschneider, *Party Government* (New York: Farrar and Rinehart Inc., 1942).
6. M. Duverger, *Political Parties: Their Organization and Activity in the Modern State* (London: Methuen & Co. Ltd., 1954).
7. R.T. McKenzie, *British Political Parties* (London: William Heinemann Ltd., 1955).
8. S.J. Eldersveld, *Political Parties: A Behavioral Analysis* (Chicago: Rand McNally & Company, 1964).
9. G. Sartori, *Parties and Party Systems: A Framework for Analysis* (Cambridge, U.K.: Cambridge University Press, 1976).
10. R.K. Merton, *Social Theory and Social Structure* (Glencoe, Ill.: The Free Press, 1949).
11. *Ibid.*, pp. 70–81.
12. *Ibid.*, p. 51.
13. *Ibid.*, pp. 79–80.
14. *Ibid.*, p. 50.
15. There is, of course, a world of difference between merely talking of the function of phenomena and explaining their origin and/or consequences in terms of their functions. For pertinent discussions, see G.C. Homas, "Structural, Functional and Psychological Theories," in N.J. Demerath and R.A. Peterson, eds., *System, Change and Conflict* (New York: The Free Press, 1967), pp. 350–56, and K. Davis, "The Myth of Functional Analysis as a Special Method in Sociology and Anthropology," in Demerath and Peterson, *System, Change and Conflict*.
16. A. King, "Political Parties in Western Democracies," *Polity*, Vol. 2, No. 2 (Winter 1969), pp. 111–41.
17. G.A. Almond and G.B. Powell, Jr., *Comparative Politics: A Developmental Approach* (Boston: Little, Brown and Co., 1966), pp. 114ff.
18. Sartori, *Parties and Party Systems*, p. 27. Among Canadian scholars who adopt a functionalist view on parties, Engelmann and Schwartz were early pioneers; see F.C. Engelmann and M.A. Schwartz, *Political Parties and the Canadian Social Structure* (Scarborough: Prentice-Hall Canada, 1967). Carty and Pross also employ a functionalist perspective; see R.K. Carty, "Three Canadian Party Systems: An Interpretation of the Development of National Politics," in G. Perlin, ed., *Party Democracy in Canada* (Scarborough: Prentice-Hall Canada, 1988), p. 24, and A.P. Pross, "Space, Function, and Interest: The Problem of Legitimacy in the Canadian State," in O.P. Dwivedi, ed., *The*

Administrative State in Canada (Toronto: University of Toronto Press, 1982), pp. 120–1. Although Winn and McMenemy are less explicit, their book is structured in accordance with a functional approach; see C. Winn and J. McMenemy, *Political Parties in Canada* (Toronto: McGraw-Hill Ryerson, 1976). By far the most important work utilizing the idea of functions in a central way is that of Vincent Lemieux, *Systèmes Partisans et Partis Politiques* (Sillery, Québec: Presses de l'Université du Québec, 1985), regrettably little-known in English Canada.

19. K. Lawson and P.H. Merkl, "Alternative Organizations: Environmental, Supplementary, Communitarian, and Authoritarian," in K. Lawson and P.H. Merkl, eds., *When Parties Fail* (Princeton: Princeton University Press, 1988), p. 3.

20. One of the most useful compendia assembling major arguments on various aspects of the controversy appeared in 1967 and provides an essential canvassing of the points of issue: Demerath and Peterson, *System, Change and Conflict*. See also Lowi, "Toward Functionalism in Political Science."

21. G.C. Homans, "Structural, Functional and Psychological Theories," in Demerath and Peterson, *System, Change and Conflict*, pp. 350–56.

22. K. Davis, "The Myth of Functional Analysis as a Special Method in Sociology and Anthropology," in Demerath and Peterson, *System, Change and Conflict*, pp. 378–96.

23. M.G. Mendoza and V. Napoli, *Systems of Man: An Introduction to Social Science* (Lexington: D.C. Heath & Co., 1973), pp. 26ff.

24. Demerath and Peterson, *System, Change and Conflict*.

25. David E. Smith, "Party Government, Representation and National Integration in Canada," in P. Aucoin, ed., *Party Government and Regional Representation in Canada* (Toronto: University of Toronto Press, 1985), pp. 1–68.

26. Merton, *Social Theory and Social Structure*, p. 51.

27. Among the works which deal, *inter alia*, with various shortcomings of parties and of the party system, the following discuss the main *types* of failings: C.B. Macpherson, *Democracy in Alberta: Social Credit and the Party System* (Toronto: University of Toronto Press, 1953), John Porter, *The Vertical Mosaic* (Toronto: University of Toronto Press, 1965), M.J. Brodie and J. Jenson, *Crisis, Challenge and Change: Party and Class in Canada Revisited* (Ottawa: Carleton University Press, 1988), David E. Smith, *The Regional Decline of a National Party: Liberals on the Prairies* (Toronto: University of Toronto Press, 1981), G.C. Perlin, *The Tory Syndrome: Leadership Politics in the Progressive Conservative Party* (Montreal: McGill-Queen's University Press, 1980), J. Laxer and R. Laxer, *The Liberal Idea of Canada: Pierre Trudeau and the Question of Canada's Survival* (Toronto: James Lorimer and Co., 1977), H.D. Clarke, J. Jenson, L. LeDuc, and J. Pammett, *Absent Mandate: The Politics of Discontent in Canada* (Toronto: Gage Publishing Ltd., 1984), pp. 50–52, S.B. Bashevkin, *Toeing the Lines: Women and Party Politics in Canada* (Toronto: University of Toronto Press, 1985), Smith, "Party Government," Carty, "Three Canadian Party Systems," and Pross, "Space, Function, and Interest."

28. Joseph Wearing, *Strained Relations: Canadian Parties and Voters* (Toronto: McClelland and Stewart, 1988), pp. 212–23.

29. Bashevkin, *Toeing the Lines*, and "Political Parties and the Representation of Women," in A.G. Gagnon and A.B. Tanguay, eds., *Canadian Parties in Transition: Discourse, Organization, and Representation* (Scarborough: Nelson Canada, 1989), pp. 446–60.

30. G.C. Perlin, *Party Democracy in Canada: The Politics of National Party Conventions* (Scarborough: Prentice-Hall Canada, 1988).

31. There is a great deal of "decline of party" literature, consisting both of analyses of the relative diminution of party influence and of those challenging this view. A leading

American statement can be found in W. Crotty, *American Parties in Decline*, 2nd ed. (Boston: Little, Brown and Co., 1984). Dissenting views are expressed by X. Kayden and E. Mahe, Jr., in *The Party Goes On: The Persistence of the Two-Party System in the United States* (New York: Basic Books Inc., 1985), and L.J. Sabato, *The Party's Just Begun: Shaping Political Parties for America's Future* (Glenview, Ill.: Scott, Foreman and Co., 1988). In a comparative context, J. Blondel, *Political Parties: A Genuine Case for Discontent?* (London: Wildwood House Ltd., 1978) and the collection of papers in Lawson and Merkl, "Alternative Organizations" in Lawson and Merkl, *When Parties Fail* are particularly useful. The most explicit Canadian articulation of the party decline argument is in J. Meisel, "The Decline of Party in Canada" in this volume. Views criticizing or modifying Meisel's analysis are in F.C. Engelmann, "Canadian Political Parties and Elections," in J.H. Redekop, ed., *Approaches to Canadian Politics*, 2nd ed. (Scarborough: Prentice-Hall Canada, 1983), pp. 205–32, and K.L. Paltiel, "Political Marketing, Party Finance and the Decline of Canadian Parties," in Gagnon and Tanguay, *Canadian Parties in Transition*. See also G. Amyot, "The New Politics," *Queen's Quarterly*, Vol. 93, No. 4 (Winter 1986), pp. 952–55.

32. A. Ranney and W. Kendall, *Democracy and the American Party System* (New York: Harcourt, Brace and Co., 1956), pp. 506–7.

33. J. LaPolombara and M. Weiner, eds., *Political Parties and Political Development* (Princeton: Princeton University Press, 1966).

34. See for example A.C. Cairns, "The Electoral System and the Party System in Canada," *Canadian Journal of Political Science*, Vol. 1, No. 1 (March 1968), pp. 55–80, R.W. Jackman, "Political Parties, Voting, and National Integration: The Canadian Case," *Comparative Politics*, Vol. 4, No. 4 (July 1972), pp. 511–36, Smith, "Party Government," and J. Meisel, "Cleavages, Parties and Values in Canada," *Contemporary Political Sociology*, Vol. 6, No. 3 (1974); "Recent Changes in Canadian Parties," in H.G. Thorburn, ed., *Party Politics in Canada*, 2nd ed. (Scarborough: Prentice-Hall Canada, 1967), pp. 33–54; "Conclusion: An Analysis of the National (?) Results," in *Idem, Papers on the 1962 Election*, (Toronto: University of Toronto Press, 1964), pp. 287–88; and "The Stalled Omnibus: Canadian Parties in the 1960s," *Social Research*, Vol. 30, No. 3 (September 1963).

35. C.E.S. Franks, *The Parliament of Canada* (Toronto: University of Toronto Press, 1987), pp. 100, 136–42.

36. J. Meisel, "Near Hit: The Parturition of a Broadcasting Policy," in K. Graham, ed., *How Ottawa Spends, 1989/90* (Ottawa: Carleton University Press, 1989).

37. Pross, "Space, Function, and Interest."

38. James Bickerton, "The Party System and the Representation of Periphery Interests: The Case of the Maritimes," in Gagnon and Tanguay, *Canadian Parties in Transition*, pp. 463ff.

39. *Ibid.*, p. 463.

40. The present comments have no more to support them than unsystematic personal observation and a little reading. It would be highly desirable to launch a rigorous inquiry testing the evolution of partisanship among diverse classes of politicians.

41. The only recent major exceptions are the Conservative and NDP acceptance of Trudeau's 1969 Official Languages Act, and the Liberal and NDP support for the Meech Lake Accord reached under Mulroney in 1987. It is noteworthy, however, that both instances of opposition support for the government caused serious dissension within the opposition parties.

42. Perlin, *The Tory Syndrome*, and J. Simpson, *The Discipline of Power: The Conservative Interlude and the Liberal Restoration* (Toronto: Personal Library, 1980).

43. R. Whitaker, *The Government Party: Organizing and Financing A Liberal Party of Canada, 1930–58* (Toronto: University of Toronto Press, 1977), and J. Meisel, "Howe, Hubris and '72: An Essay on Political Elitism," in Meisel, *Working Papers on Canadian Politics*, 2nd enlarged ed., pp. 230–45.

44. The lack of interest in even considering neo-corporatism as a possible policy making mechanism (more pronounced in Canada than in many other countries) or of experimenting with the devolution of decision making to nonpartisan community bodies can, in part, be ascribed to the mental framework engendered by the institutionalization of confrontation as a "natural" and inevitable process.

45. Clarke, *et al.*, pp. 50–52.

46. For a perceptive view, see Smith's discussion of the historical evolution of the "party in government model" in "Party Government." Smith's argument is complemented by the illuminating analysis of Carty in "Three Canadian Party Systems," which identifies three "distinctive party systems [which] have marked the country's political development."

47. W. Lippman, *The Public Philosophy* (New York: Mentor Books, The New American Library, 1956).

48. R.L. Stanfield, cited by A.P. Pross in *Group Politics and Public Policy* (Toronto: Oxford University Press, 1986). This book provides a trenchant analysis of the phenomena noted here.

49. Clarke, *et al.*, *Absent Mandate*, pp. 10–16.

50. Smith, for instance, refers to the process which has produced the brokerage theory as "blinkered scholarship." See Smith, "Party Government," p. 2.

51. Clarke, *et al.*, *Absent Mandate*, p. 12.

52. *Ibid.*, pp. 178–9.

53. The new era ushered in by the 1984 election and consolidated by that of 1988—in which the Conservative party finds itself firmly entrenched—provides a challenge to some of the traditional interpretations of Canadian politics. Thus, the 1988 election gave the Mulroney government a mandate to proceed with the ratification of the Canada-U.S. Free Trade Agreement and also to seek the ratification of the Meech Lake Accord on constitutional change.

54. Two examples are mentioned in Note 41.

55. J.M. Langdon, *Changing Emphases in Media Coverage of Elections: The Case of Toronto Newspapers, 1930–1984* (Queen's University, Kingston: unpublished master's thesis, 1989), pp. 53–4.

56. The standard formulations, which dominated the thinking of several generations of Canadian students were those of Corry and Dawson. See J.A. Corry, *Democratic Government and Politics* (Toronto: University of Toronto Press, 1946), and R.M. Dawson, *The Government of Canada* (Toronto: University of Toronto Press, 1947). Each of these classics went through numerous editions and revisions, with the assistance of younger colleagues. It is significant, in the present context, that the latest edition of Dawson states: "In Canada, indeed, the role of national parties as a unifying agent bringing together in amity some of the most powerful dissident forces in the country, despite contemporary argument to the contrary, *can hardly be discounted.*" See N. Ward, *Dawson's The Government of Canada*, 6th ed. (Toronto: University of Toronto Press, 1987, p. 7). In a previous edition, the last four words read "could hardly be overestimated."

See R.M. Dawson, *The Government of Canada*, 5th ed. (revised by Norman Ward); (Toronto: University of Toronto Press, 1970), p. 415.

57. Cairns, "The Electoral System," p. 64.

58. J.A. Lovink, "On Analyzing the Impact of the Electoral System on the Party System in Canada," *Canadian Journal of Political Science*, Vol. 3, No. 4 (December 1970), pp. 497–516.

59. P.G. Thomas, "The Role of National Party Caucuses," in P. Aucoin, ed., *Party Government and Regional Representation in Canada* (Toronto: University of Toronto Press, 1985), p. 70.

60. Carty, "Three Canadian Party Systems," p. 24.

61. *Ibid.*

62. Pross, *Group Politics and Public Policy.*

63. Parties "are an instrument, or an agency, for *representing* the people by *expressing* their demands." See Sartori, *Parties and Party Systems*, p. 27.

64. Pross, "Space, Function, and Interest," p. 116.

65. *Ibid.*, p. 109.

66. *Ibid.*, p. 122.

67. Lowi, "Toward Functionalism in Political Science."

68. Paltiel, "Political Marketing, Party Finance and the Decline of Canadian Parties," in Gagnon and Tanguay, *Canadian Parties in Transition*, pp. 332–55.

69. It also, of course, assists individuals in organizing their political perceptions and in structuring their political stance.

19 Absent Mandate '88? Parties and Voters in Canada

H.D. FORBES

According to one widely accepted theory about Canadian electoral politics, Canadian parties practise brokerage politics, Canadian voters see no differences between the parties, and Canadian elections, therefore, fail to produce any clear mandates for policies to deal with the serious problems facing the country. The source now usually cited for this theory is *Absent Mandate*, a survey based study of the 1974, 1979, and 1980 elections by Harold Clarke, Jane Jenson, Lawrence LeDuc, and Jon Pammett.[1] Other authors have said similar things about parties and voters in Canada, but *Absent Mandate* provides the best statement of a theory that deserves careful consideration.[2]

The most recent federal election (1988) helps to clarify the strengths and weaknesses of this theory. Liberals, Conservatives and New Democrats clearly disagreed about an important question of public policy, and there are good reasons for saying that the election yielded a mandate for one particular policy. But readers should not jump to the conclusion, appealing at first glance, that the election simply disproves the theory. Although complicated, the theory is basically sound; simple criticisms of it tend to be misleading.

I

Brokerage theory begins from an observation of Canada's three main political parties: they are not divided by clear differences of principle, nor do they speak for distinct social groups. They are not like the socialist or other doctrinaire parties of the past, with their detailed programmes for broad social change rooted in elaborate ideologies. Nor are they like the farmers' parties or the Catholic parties that still exist in some countries and that limit their electoral appeal to selected voters. Canadian parties are basically similiar "catch-all" parties: they try to offer something to every group in the electorate. They stick to the middle of the road ideologically, swerving right or left with the twists and turns

H. Donald Forbes, "Absent Mandate '88? Parties and Voters in Canada," *Journal of Canadian Studies*, Vol. 25, No. 2 (Summer, 1990). Reprinted by permission of the author and the *Journal of Canadian Studies*.

of public opinion. As the authors of *Absent Mandate* say, the parties constantly compete for the same policy space and the same votes. "Voters are rarely presented with a clear choice between world views and the political projects that follow from them, but more commonly with appeals to narrow interests and proposals that amount to little more than short-term tinkering."[3] In short, they are all "brokerage parties."

Although not beyond dispute, this way of describing Canada's *major* parties has a relatively long history. In *The Race Question in Canada*, published in French in 1906, André Siegfried provided a classic analysis of Canadian politics that emphasized the lack of principled differences between the two parties then contending for power.[4] From its founding in 1932 until quite recently, however, the CCF-NDP has generally been treated as an exception to the "catch-all" pattern. Most students of Canadian party politics have seen it as a party of principle appealing to the underprivileged. Its leaders have been called saints or prophets, and its supporters have been thought to be farmers and workers. The now widely accepted brokerage theory departs from this once standard way of describing Canadian parties by putting the NDP in the "brokerage" category along with the Liberals and Conservatives.

According to the version of brokerage theory in question here, the brokerage pattern of party competition has important implications for policy making and for electoral behaviour. At the beginning of *Absent Mandate*, its authors outline the serious economic problems that developed in Canada during the late 1970s and the early 1980s. They point to regional inequalities, trade imbalances, a falling dollar, a weak manufacturing base, declining productivity, high levels of both inflation and unemployment, and dwindling supplies and rising costs of energy. Faced with these grave problems, bureaucrats and academics put forward various new policies and "industrial strategies." But their policy innovation was not "internal to the process of party competition." No "dynamic" existed within the party system itself which led reliably "toward innovation or the identification of solutions for new problems." The parties, being brokerage parties, were concerned only with electorally saleable "images" and "quick-fix solutions."[5] They had no real interest in long-term policies. The parties fiddled while Canada burned.

Policy innovation shifted, as a result, into the public service and into federal-provincial relations. The real alternatives—"free trade, greater monitoring of the relationship with the [United States], a form of industrial strategy emphasizing new manufacturing [or] resource-based export strategies"[6]—were debated by specialists behind closed doors, and were never translated into terms meaningful for electoral debate.

> Campaigns [during the 1970s] provided the occasion for articulation of concerns and grievances rather than for competition among fundamentally different long-term strategies to ameliorate economic troubles. Elections were fought by parties which were most comfortable making adjustments at the margin and quite uncomfortable with the notion that structural causes existed for problems or that radical

solutions might be needed. . . . [T]he electorate could not act, nor was it asked to act, as an arbiter among competing strategies.[7]

Brokerage competition of this sort necessarily produces a volatile electorate, the authors of *Absent Mandate* go on to say. Voters, unable to see fundamental differences between the parties (because none exist), have no reason to develop long-term loyalties to parties. In fact, the Canadian electorate is unusually volatile. A generation ago studies of the Canadian electorate found levels of partisan instability higher in Canada than elsewhere. More recent studies have confirmed that finding. "The keynote of partisanship in Canada is its volatility."[8]

Brokerage competition also shifts the focus of election campaigns from issues to leadership. Parties become simply the vehicles for their leaders, and electoral politics becomes image politics, not policy debate. "Lacking ideological or continuing policy differences, the parties take on, in a sense, the personality of their leaders."[9] Images and moods are now the most important ingredients of electoral politics, instead of political principles, ideology, or even long-term programmes of incremental adjustment.

Such a pattern of competition makes it very unlikely that an election will ever "deliver a mandate for policy innovation designed to cope with economic problems of a fundamental nature."[10] The brokerage system does not mobilize popular support behind broad policies. "Instead of providing an opportunity for choice among real solutions to important problems, elections [have become] contests among leaders, emphasizing personality and style, or . . . an opportunity to make a statement about the performance of an incumbent government."[11] Victorious parties emerge from elections knowing only that they were better than their rivals at somehow putting together an appealing patchwork of quick fixes, goodies, band-aids and leadership images. It is almost impossible for them to feel or act as if they had a mandate from the public to implement a comprehensive economic policy. "In times of severe difficulty, when a mandate to engage in long-term innovative economic engineering is most needed, it is in fact least likely to be forthcoming."[12]

II

In the general election of 1988, the Progressive Conservative party, led by Prime Minister Mulroney, was returned to power with 169 out of 295 seats in the House of Commons. The main issue in the election had been the trade policy developed by the government over the previous three years and embodied in a bilateral treaty signed 10 months earlier. The speeches of the leaders and the national advertising of the parties concentrated on the benefits and dangers of this policy. The Conservative party, of course, championed "the Canadian-American Free Trade Agreement." The Liberals and the NDP opposed "the Mulroney-Reagan trade deal," promised to "tear it up" if elected and advocated significantly different approaches to economic policy (a mixture of multilateral trade negotiations within GATT and industrial-strategy-style interventions in the domestic economy).

Journalists, politicians and voters all agreed that free trade was the central issue in the election. About 60 percent of respondents to public opinion polls named free trade as the most important issue in the campaign.[13] In fact, seldom has a campaign been as clearly focused on a single issue as the recent campaign was on free trade.

The free trade policy of the government is not easily explained and remains, in part, to be clearly defined. Its aim is to create a single Canadian-American market for goods and services, without unduly limiting the sovereign powers of the two governments. It involves the elimination of tariffs between Canada and the United States over a period of 10 years, the prohibition of new non-tariff barriers, a bi-national panel to advise on the fair application of existing trade legislation, a common definition of unfair subsidies (yet to be negotiated), "national treatment" of the businesses of each country operating within the other and a number of minor provisions to deal with other irritants or barriers in the relations between two large, very complex, mixed economies.

Proponents of the policy presented it as the key to Canada's future prosperity. Prices would go down (due to the removal of tariffs), they said, while wages and profits would go up (due to the opening of markets for Canada's exports). Many new jobs would be created due to the expansion of the Canadian economy. Naturally enough, they said little about the factories that would close and the jobs that would be lost because of the removal of tariffs and other forms of protection. (Any free trade policy deliberately aims to put some inefficient businesses out of business and is thus hard to sell to a democratic electorate.)

The division between supporters and opponents of free trade was not, however, a classic fight between those industries and regions that stood to gain from the removal of tariffs and those that stood to lose. Astonishingly little attention was paid to the narrow interests of potential winners and losers. The Ontario wine industry, a potential loser (needless to say), got some attention, but little was heard about such classic losers as shoes and textiles. Rather, the Free Trade Agreement triggered a debate about the welfare state and economic management. Should social programmes be preserved and expanded or should they be cut back? Should Canada retain its freedom to use various instruments of economic policy—subsidies, taxes, regulations, etc.—to encourage socially conscious and environmentally sound development, or should it trust more to the market (and the American regulatory system)? Should Canada tie itself to the United States, or should it boldly accept the challenge of global trade? If "band-aids" symbolize the character of debate about economic policy in the 1979 and 1980 elections, amputations and genetic engineering better convey the flavour of the most recent campaign.

Opponents of the deal did not neglect the potential loss of jobs in threatened industries, but they spoke even more frequently about the threat to old-age pensions and Medicare. When they spoke about jobs, they tended to stress the jobs to be lost in industries that employ large numbers of women, and the bad effects of the deal, therefore, on women. The heart of their opposition was not the immediate, more or less predictable economic effects of the deal, but its broader political and cultural consequences. Women were the tip of an iceberg, the bulk of which was native people, minorities, the old, the poor, the sick, single mothers, depressed regions, artists, the handicapped, the unemployed—in short, all the dependants of the modern welfare state. Canada, the opponents claimed, is a compassionate society that provides its weaker members with a good safety net; the United States is one of the last havens of *laissez-faire* capitalism, a land of dog-eat-dog competition, where the sick pay up or die. The purpose of the deal, it was said with some justification, is to make Canada more like the United States.

Defenders of the agreement denied that it need have any negative effects on social programmes. They claimed that it would make possible an even better safety net than we can now afford. But they also said, *sotto voce*, that the deal should stiffen the backs of politicians facing demands for a net with a finer mesh and softer springs.

Much was heard about dreams and visions. Would free trade be the end of the Canadian dream? What vision of the country underlay the agreement? The advertising specialists were busy and they enjoyed some success linking the parties' dreamy or visionary differences to simple images. The social democratic vision, which features nurses, planners and safety nets, collided with the neo-conservative vision, which features production managers, markets and the school of hard knocks.

The recent campaign was thus strikingly different from the sort of campaign that one is led to expect by the theory of brokerage politics found in *Absent Mandate*. The parties championed different long-term strategies of economic development, which were thought by many to have profound implications for social programmes.

III

How exceptional was the most recent election? Is there perhaps a trend away from brokerage politics? Have Canada's political parties ceased to be brokerage parties? There is no good reason to think so.[14] It is simpler to say they never were brokerage parties in exactly the sense implied by the contemporary use of the term, but still are the brokerage parties they have always been.

"Brokerage," as the term has been used for many years, suggests, first of all, pragmatism and flexibility. A brokerage party is definitely a *party*, not an ideological movement. It is willing to accommodate changing public opinion. Like a stockbroker who will help investors buy Consolidated Dynamics one day and sell it the next (for a small commission), a brokerage party will help the electorate move left one election and right the next. It is a team for fighting elections and sharing the spoils of office, is not, as Burke said, "a body of men united for promoting by their joint endeavours the national interest upon some particular principle in which they are all agreed." Still less is it a Leninist vanguard determined to lead the people out of their false consciousness. Stephen Leacock caught the spirit of brokerage politics when he said, "pledges first, principles afterwards": "having first decided to agree, [the members of a brokerage party] must next make up their minds what it is they agree about."[15] Brokerage politicians put party loyalty ahead of doctrinal purity or devotion to abstract principles.

The older accounts of brokerage politics emphasized the integrative function of brokerage parties. Politicians like John A. Macdonald, who linked Ontario's fiercest Orangemen with Quebec's bluest *Bleus* in his Liberal-Conservative (or "Union") party, illustrate the point. Macdonald tried to win support in all the main regions of the country; he decried sectionalism; and his pursuit of power was restrained by his devotion to national unity. Defenders of brokerage politics argued that only such leaders can put together coalitions in which all the great forces in a country like Canada will be represented. Brokerage parties were thus treated as important instruments of national harmony and reconciliation. They were commonly credited with knitting together Canada and the United States.[16]

More recent discussions of brokerage politics have been more critical in tone. For the past generation leading writers have been emphasizing the *similarity* of brokerage parties, not just their flexibility or responsibility, and suggesting that similar parties stifle debate on important questions. Their arguments raise the interesting possibility that brokerage parties (and the old brokerage theory) may be parts of an ideological apparatus for suppressing consideration of issues that would threaten the dominant classes of modern society. Brokerage parties, many writers now claim, do not in fact serve as neutral brokers of all legitimate interests. They arrange compromises among established élite groups, neglecting the interests of the masses. Like stockbrokers, they are more interested in the business of the rich than the poor.[17]

The authors of *Absent Mandate,* as noted earlier, stress similarities and share this critical outlook. Canada's three main political parties, they say, adopt practically identical positions on all the important questions of the day. The parties may try to distinguish themselves by taking different positions on minor questions (mortgage deductibility, gasoline taxes, etc.), but they seldom make an appeal to any important group without making equal and opposite appeals to its rivals. To act as successful brokers, the parties believe, they have to avoid alienating any powerful segment of society. Consequently, they tend to compete the way manufacturers of beer or soap are said to compete, by offering the same suds in different packages, endorsed by different stars. Voters can choose between leaders, but they have no way of expressing their opinions about policies, and hence no opportunity to confer a real mandate on government. The result, one gathers, is ideological domination.

The standard criticism of this contemporary brokerage theory emphasizes the persistent *ideological differences* among Canada's three main parties.[18] Christian and Campbell maintain that the parties are divided by *principles,* not just the lust for power, patronage and the spoils of office. Canadian Conservatives, Liberals and Socialists, they say, tend to be conservatives, liberals and socialists. They blame Mackenzie King for setting Canadians on the wrong course politically. He obscured the serious ideological divisions within the country by forcing conservatives and socialists to compete on his liberal brokerage terrain. (He dismissed Bennett's "New Deal" as a fraud and patronized the CCF as "Liberals in a hurry.") "He imposed a style of politics on Canada, which took such deep root that people mistook a way of practising politics for politics itself. Interest group politics and the politics of regionalism became the prevailing orthodoxy, the Canadian way." If he had been more successful, Canada would have become "a country without imagination or vision . . . in danger of atrophy." Fortunately, he ruled for only 22 years. "Since the 1950s, toryism, socialism and nationalism have revealed that they can still make an important contribution to the debate about what kind of country Canada should be. . . . Canada was in its origins and is still a country of rich ideological diversity; and . . . these differences give our country a much greater chance to resolve the question of the kind of social life we wish to share as fellow citizens."[19]

It may be difficult to find a middle ground between these conflicting positions, but the recent election provides some guidance. The main parties clearly differed on an important question of public policy, but not one that had much to do with our theoretical or inherited notions of conservatism, liberalism and socialism. Looking back over past Canadian or American elections, one can find many similar cases.[20] Elections in which the main parties have taken contrasting stands on issues generally considered important have been as common as elections in which only leadership has been in question. In Canada, the competition between the major parties and the CCF or NDP has for 50 years given voters a significant choice of approaches to economic and social policy (whatever exactly it has to do with "socialism"). There is no need to review this history in detail since the recent election illustrates what the currently dominant concept of brokerage politics obscures.

To be sure, in 1988 the Liberals, Conservatives and NDP demonstrated flexibility, ideological moderation, willingness to follow public opinion on most questions and a commendable concern for finding support in all regions of the country. Their flexibility on free trade was especially noteworthy. The traditional party of protectionism and distrust of the Americans, the Conservative party, espoused continentalism. The traditonal party of free trade and the American alliance, the Liberal party, opposed it. The moderation of the parties on questions of principle was equally striking. Both the Liberals and the NDP claimed that free trade threatened Canada's social programmes and violated the caring and sharing philosophy of Canadians, but the old fighting words, *capitalism* and *socialism*, were hardly ever heard. John Turner's opposition was often called "passionate" and "committed"—it was "the fight of his life," he claimed—but all the while he had two children attending American universities. Ed Broadbent was advised throughout the campaign by an American pollster.

On many important issues the three parties took very similar positions. Abortion and Meech Lake best illustrate the point. On state nurseries ("quality day care"), the big-ticket social policy of the next generation, the parties differed only on questions of detail. And they maintained a statesmanlike silence about the knotty problems of immigration and Quebec unilingualism.

Any generalization about similarities and differences between parties must, of course, depend on judgments about which issues are truly important. Academic observers tend to focus on economic policies: contemporary brokerage theory rests on the unstated assumption that the important differences between parties (if any existed) would be differences of economic policy.

It is this unquestioned assumption that makes the 1988 election seem so anomalous: the parties did differ clearly on a basic question of economic policy. Only by dismissing free trade as unimportant can one maintain that the parties competed "for the same policy space and the same votes."

Some observers will argue that free trade was a sham issue hiding the fundamental similarities of all three parties. Let us imagine a voter convinced that abortion is murder. He or she might go beyond noting the flexibility, moderation and national orientation of the three parties, and add something about their all being the same, since they offer voters no real choice on *the* fundamental question of public policy. Such a voter would be attracted to certain formulations—about "essential similarities"—in the recent literature about brokerage politics, but would be puzzled by statements to the effect that "bourgeois parties" think politics should be about "race or religion" and that they therefore emphasize "religious and linguistic differences within the electorate" and practise a "politics of religion and culture."[21] Such a voter might scratch his or her head and mutter something about false consciousness.

IV

On the evening of November 21st, 1988, as the votes were being counted—indeed, even before all the polls were closed—politicians and journalists were saying that Mulroney's Conservatives had a mandate from the Canadian people to proceed with their Free Trade Agreement. There was virtual unanimity on this point. Not just Mulroney, but his rivals, Turner and Broadbent, said that a mandate had been conferred. The next day, even the *Toronto Star*, which had filled its pages with news and opinion hostile to free trade, and which had taken every opportunity to boost the Liberal campaign, said that "the people of Canada have spoken convincingly .... [T]he Progressive Conservatives [have] won a solid majority and received the mandate necessary to push forward with the Canada-U.S. trade deal." Thus, Canada's political parties had differed on a basic question of economic policy, and the competition between them had produced a clear mandate for a specific long-term policy.

Or had it? Perhaps it would be closer to the truth to say that an election campaign dominated by one important issue had nonetheless failed to yield a mandate. In the weeks following the election, various trade unionists, interest group leaders, academics and other writers of letters to the editor denied that a mandate had, in fact, been conferred. What evidence was there, after all, that the Canadian people really agreed with the government's policy of free trade?

The first difficulty—the most obvious—is the fact that Conservative candidates won only 43 percent of the popular vote. The dissenters asked: How is it possible to say that the Canadian people endorsed free trade, when almost 60 percent voted for parties opposed to free trade? If the election is viewed as a referendum on trade policy, then free trade lost.

If the popular vote is broken down by province, then one might say that free trade won in Alberta and Quebec (52 percent and 53 percent of the vote, respectively), but lost badly everywhere else.

If the *shift* in the popular vote between 1984 and 1988 is the measure of support for free trade, then it lost everywhere except in Quebec. Nationally, the Conservative vote went down from 50 percent of the total to 43 percent.

Would a more detailed analysis of voting patterns using survey data throw any light on this question of mandates? Chapter 7 of *Absent Mandate* illustrates one way that such data could be used. In each of its three main surveys, respondents were asked to name the issue they considered most important to them in the recent election campaign. (The surveys were conducted shortly after the elections of 1974, 1979, and 1980.) The answers covered a wide range of topics, but economic issues, like inflation, were mentioned more frequently than any other. The respondents were also asked which parties they had voted for in the most recent election and in the previous election. Depending upon how they answered the question about the most recent election, they were classified as Liberal, Conservative or New Democratic voters. Depending upon how they answered the question about their previous vote, they were classified as having switched, remained with the same party or entered (or re-entered) the electorate. By cross-tabulating these three variables—choice of issues, party supported and switching—habitual partisans were separated from switchers, and the switchers were classified according to the issues they regarded as most important and the direction of their movement. These tabulations clarified whether the winning parties (Liberal in 1974 and 1980, Conservative in 1979) had gained or lost support among voters concerned about each of the main issues in these elections.[22]

The big issue in the 1974 election was inflation and, specifically, the Conservative proposal, which was harshly criticized by the Liberals and the New Democrats, to impose a 90-day wage-price freeze. The Liberal victory in 1974, as the authors of *Absent Mandate* note, was generally understood to be a clear repudiation by the Canadian people of an incomes policy as a way of fighting inflation. Hence, the dismay a year later when the Liberal government adopted wage-and-price controls of their own design: this famous Trudeau "flip flop" was widely seen as a cynical betrayal of clear instructions from the electorate. But there need not have been such dismay, according to the authors of *Absent Mandate*, for the survey method described above reveals how weak the supposed mandate was in the first place. Switching voters concerned about wage-and-price controls (a mere 1.2% of the 1974 sample) were about as likely to switch to the Conservatives

(0.6% "for controls") as to the Liberals (0.4% "against controls"). The electorate, in other words, spoke with two voices, both rather feeble.[23]

These statistically unreliable differences in very small percentages are typical. The same pattern is found in practically all of the similar tabulations presented in *Absent Mandate*. For example, mortgage deductibility in 1979: 1.2% of the sample named this issue and switched their vote between 1974 and 1979. Some of these switched to the Conservatives (0.7% of the sample), but others switched to the Liberals or the New Democrats (0.2% each).[24] In 1980 there was a lot of discussion of a new 18-cent gasoline tax that had been imposed in the budget whose defeat precipitated the election. Those who named oil and gas prices as an issue and also switched their vote amounted to 3.1% of the 1980 sample. Those who switched to the Liberals, the winners, exceeded those who switched to the Conservatives, the losers, by only a tiny margin: 1.2% versus 1.1%.[25]

Following the 1988 election, some of the respondents to the 1984 national election study were re-interviewed and were aked the standard questions about issues and voting.[26] This most recent survey reveals that a surprisingly large number of voters—more than 30% of those who voted in both elections—switched their vote. About half of these switchers (15.7% of the total sample) said that issues were the most important factor in their voting decision and that they were most concerned about free trade. As one might expect, most of these "free trade" switchers were moving in the Liberal direction, but a substantial number were moving towards the Conservatives: 7.5% of the sample switched to the Liberals (and said they were most concerned about free trade) as opposed to only 3.7% who switched to the Conservatives. (An additional 4.5% switched to the NDP or to other parties.) These numbers provide no support for the orthodox interpretation of the election, but practically no support either for the dissenters' suggestion that a mandate *against* free trade should be inferred from the vote totals. With voters moving in all possible directions, for a variety of reasons, and with most voting for the same parties in both 1984 and 1988, no clear message emerges from the statistics.[27]

In short, the electorate never seems to be of one mind on anything, and statistics may be of very little help in determining the meaning of an election, except perhaps to discredit extravagant assumptions about the interest and attention of the electorate.

Much the same conclusion could be drawn from the simpler tabulations provided by pollsters whose results were published in the daily press. Most polls showed less than majority support for the Free Trade Agreement, but also less than a majority opposed to it. There was a trend away from free trade during the campaign, but a swing in its favour in the final days before the election. At the end, the electorate was about equally divided, with about a fifth or a sixth undecided on the merits of the agreement.[28]

The newspaper polls also revealed that a very large number of voters did not feel adequately informed about the agreement (a 315-page document full of legalese, accounting jargon and equations). In surveys conducted at various times before the election, about three out of every four respondents admitted to not understanding it "as well as they would like" (or some similar phrase to maintain rapport).[29] Whatever the exact proportions, most of those who cast their vote on the free trade issue undoubtedly did not really know what they were voting for or against.

V

At the very end of *Absent Mandate*, its authors briefly distinguish four types of mandates—national, directional, policy and performance—and claim that the conditions are almost never satisfied for the first three types. A *national* mandate requires (it seems) that the winning party obtain more or less the same level of support in all regions of the country. A *directional* mandate requires that most vote switchers and new voters move towards the winning party. A *policy* mandate requires that the main positions espoused by the winning party cause significantly more voters to shift to the winning party than to either of its opponents.[30] Finally, a *performance* mandate requires only that the voters put a government in office. "The most that can [normally] be said [when a majority government is elected] is that the winner has a general *performance* mandate, to attack the problems as it sees fit."[31]

Canadians obviously gave the present Conservative government a performance mandate, as they do whenever they return a majority of one party. Plainly they did not give it a national mandate or a directional mandate. They also seem to have denied it a policy mandate, although the tests for such a mandate leave room for differences of interpretation. Nonetheless, the 1988 federal election would seem to illustrate the broad conclusion about "absent mandates" formulated by Clarke, Jenson, LeDuc and Pammett—despite the clear difference between the contenders on a basic question of public policy.

Where does this leave us? With the theory of electoral mandates developed in Great Britain about 200 years ago, long before there were pollsters to confuse commentators in their interpretation of elections.[32] Election interpretation, like any interpretation, relied upon a mixture of simple rules and common sense. If a party announced an important policy, and that policy was disputed by its opponents, but the party still won a majority, then it must be because the people supported the policy: *post hoc ergo propter hoc*. This loose rule of interpretation allowed commentators to insert their own opinions about what the government should do, under the guise of explaining what the people had said it must do.

During the past 50 years the task of interpreting elections has been complicated by polls. It is now possible to know (within a margin of error) what people actually think about particular policies and how their thoughts relate to their votes. This new knowledge was supposed to clarify the meaning of elections but, in fact, it has had the opposite effect. Broadly speaking, all the material and intellectual resources expended on polling in the past 50 years have contributed nothing to extracting politically acceptable meanings from elections. Rather, survey research has clearly raised the question of whether elections normally have any relevant meaning at all, except as a method ("better to count heads than to break them") for bringing a government to office.[33]

What is most debatable in *Absent Mandate* and related Canadian literature is the suggestion that elections would yield clear mandates about how to deal with the big questions of public policy if only the parties would cease to be brokerage parties and would take principled stands on all the issues of the day. People would then be able to control the government, big and complicated as it is, because the parties would give them some real questions to decide.

Although one case can't disprove a complicated theory with deep ideological roots, it can illustrate some of the difficulties with even the most elaborate theory. The case reviewed here suggests that brokerage parties can differ on important questions of economic policy without ceasing to be brokerage parties, and that one such party can win a majority of seats, following a campaign in which one big economic issue was discussed (to the exclusion of practically all others), without some simple conditions being satisfied for inferring some important kinds of mandates.

The details of the case reflect the peculiarities of Canada's regionalized three-party system. Things would look better mandate-wise, if there were only two parties in serious contention, since a majority of seats would then normally be won only with a majority of votes. Whether mandates are really more solid in two-party systems than they are in three-party systems may well be doubted, however. The fundamental problem has to do with the limitations of the electorate as a deliberative body—the multiplicity of issues it must ponder simultaneously, its lack of consensus on the dimensions of conflict and its broad ignorance of the relevant options.[34]

Fortunately, the Canadian system of government is *representative* democracy, not direct democracy along Athenian lines, and not the Swiss system of constitutional legislation by referenda. Representative democracy in Canada operates in the framework of responsible government, with all that this implies for party discipline. In choosing among the candidates who run as the standard-bearers of parties, Canadian voters are influenced, as they should be, by a number of considerations: the many different policy positions of the parties, the kinds of people who pledge themselves to these parties, the qualities of both their leaders and their local candidates and their records in office. With growth of government and the development of television, elections have tended to become simply contests between leaders, emphasizing personality and style, or opportunities to express discontent about the performance of an incumbent government, with complex issues perhaps becoming less important. But issues still play some part in elections, as free trade did in the last one, and when the people put a government in office pledged to enact a certain policy, that government clearly has a mandate to enact its policy. They are right to get on with the job. There is no prospect, in any future worth worrying about, that any Canadian government will ever have a better mandate than the present one has.

ENDNOTES

1. Harold D. Clarke, Jane Jenson, Lawrence LeDuc and Jon H. Pammett, *Absent Mandate: The Politics of Discontent in Canada* (Toronto: Gage Publishing Ltd., 1984).
2. See also M. Janine Brodie and Jane Jenson, "The Party System," in Michael S. Whittington and Glen Williams, eds., *Canadian Politics in the 1990s*, 3rd ed. (Toronto: Methuen, 1990), pp. 249–66; M. Janine Brodie and Jane Jenson, *Crisis, Challenge and Change: Party and Class in Canada Revisited* (Ottawa: Carleton University Press, 1988); and M. Janine Brodie and Jane Jenson, "Piercing the Smokescreen: Brokerage Parties and Class Politics," in Alain G. Gagnon and A. Brian Tanguay, eds., *Canadian Parties in Transition: Discourse, Organization, and Representation* (Toronto: Nelson Canada, 1989), pp. 24–44. The dictionaries and handbooks of political science seem to have nothing on "brokerage parties" or "brokerage politics." John Porter, *The Vertical Mosaic: An Analysis of Class and Power in Canada* (Toronto: University of Toronto Press, 1965), ch. 12, has evidently influenced many recent writers about Canadian party politics. An important earlier source cited by Porter is Pendleton Herring, *The Politics of Democracy: American Parties in Action* (New York: W.W. Norton, 1940). See also the comments on Herring by Frank H. Underhill, *In Search of Canadian Liberalism* (Toronto: Macmillan, 1960), pp. 192–96. Gad Horowitz, "Towards the Democratic Class Struggle," in Trevor Lloyd and Jack T. McLeod, eds., *Agenda 70* (Toronto: University of Toronto Press, 1968), pp. 241–55, like *The Vertical Mosaic*, is an attack on the older brokerage theory and a source of the contemporary theory. There is an excellent brief discussion of brokerage politics and the theories about it in Joseph Wearing, *Strained Relations: Canadian Parties and Voters* (Toronto: McClelland and Stewart, 1988), pp. 227–33.
3. *Absent Mandate*, p. 10.
4. André Siegfried, *The Race Question in Canada*, ed. Frank H. Underhill (Toronto: McClelland and Stewart, 1966). A generation earlier, Goldwin Smith had dismissed Canadian party politics as mere factionalism. "The bane of Canada is party government without any question on which parties can be rationally or morally based. . . . [Since the 1840s] there has been absolutely no dividing line between the parties or assignable ground for their existence, and they have become mere factions, striving to engross the prizes of office by the means which faction everywhere employs." "The Political Destiny of Canada" (1877), reprinted in H.D. Forbes, ed., *Canadian Political Thought* (Toronto: Oxford University Press, 1985), pp. 128–29.
5. *Absent Mandate*, pp. 11–12.
6. *Ibid.*, p. 20.
7. *Ibid.*, pp. 16, 21.
8. *Ibid.*, p. 56.
9. *Ibid.*, p. 14.
10. *Ibid.*, p. 10.
11. *Ibid.*, p. 13.
12. *Ibid.*, pp. 180–81.
13. See the polls reported in the *Toronto Star*, 3 October 1988, 11 October 1988 and 29 October 1988, and in *The Globe and Mail*, 10 December 1987. A post-election poll showed 82 percent of respondents naming free trade as the most important issue in the election. Jon H. Pammett, "The 1988 Vote," in Alan Frizzell, Jon H. Pammett and Anthony Westell, *The Canadian General Election of 1988* (Ottawa: Carleton University Press, 1989), p. 123.

14. Compare Martin Goldfarb and Thomas Axworthy, *Marching to a Different Drummer: An Essay on the Liberals and Conservatives in Convention* (Toronto: Stoddart, 1988), but note the flimsy statistical basis for their contention that the major parties have diverged ideologically in the past 20 years.

15. Stephen Leacock, *Elements of Political Science* (Boston: Houghton Mifflin, 1906), p. 335.

16. For example, Siegfried, *The Race Question*, pp. 113-14, and R. MacGregor Dawson, *The Government of Canada*, 5th ed., rev. Norman Ward (Toronto: University of Toronto Press, 1970), pp. 430–31. Cf. Porter, *The Vertical Mosaic*, pp. 368–69 and 373–77.

17. Cf. David E. Smith, "Party Government, Representation and National Integration in Canada," in Peter Aucoin, ed., *Party Government and Regional Representation in Canada*, Macdonald Commission Studies No. 36 (Toronto: University of Toronto Press, 1985), pp. 1–68.

18. William Christian and Colin Campbell, *Political Parties and Ideologies in Canada*, 3rd ed. (Toronto: McGraw-Hill Ryerson, 1990); William Christian and Colin Campbell, "Political Parties and Ideologies in Canada," in Alain G. Gagnon and A. Brian Tanguay, eds., *Canadian Parties in Transition: Discourse, Organization, and Representation* (Toronto: Nelson Canada, 1989), pp. 45–63.

19. Christian and Campbell, *Political Parties and Ideologies*, p. 3. Any such judgments about the richness of diversity or the chance of resolving political problems must be comparative. The implied comparison here is with the United States.

20. For example, the great debate about nuclear weapons and national independence in 1963, which was preceded by a famous Liberal flip flop, which evoked outrage from a future Liberal prime minister, Pierre Elliott Trudeau, who was then generally thought to be a socialist.

21. Brodie and Jenson, "The Party System," pp. 253, 254, 260. See also Brodie and Jenson, *Crisis, Challenge and Change*, pp. 1–3, 8–11, 39–44, 290–92, and 296–99, and Brodie and Jenson, "Piercing the Smokescreen," pp. 35 and 39.

22. See Jon H. Pammett, Lawrence LeDuc, Jane Jenson and Harold D. Clarke, "The Perception and Impact of Issues in the 1974 Federal Election," *Canadian Journal of Political Science*, Vol. 10 (1977), pp. 93–126, and Lawrence LeDuc, "Political Behaviour and the Issue of Majority Government in Two Federal Elections," *Canadian Journal of Political Science*, Vol. 10 (1977), pp. 311–39, for more detailed discussions of the method than is provided by *Absent Mandate*.

23. *Absent Mandate*, pp. 159–60.

24. *Ibid.*, p. 165.

25. *Ibid.*, p. 170.

26. See Pammett, "The 1988 Vote." There are some difficulties comparing the results of this survey with the results of the earlier surveys, because first-time voters were underrepresented in the 1988 survey and because an additional variable (whether or not issues were cited as the most important reason for the voting decision) was used in the analysis of the 1988 data. Nonetheless, the published tables relating issues, votes and vote switching in 1988 are roughly comparable to the earlier tables.

27. "The results cannot be interpreted as reflecting a clear public statement on the issue [of free trade] .... No pro-FTA policy mandate can be claimed by the Progressive Conservative party, despite the fact that they won the election .... Strictly speaking ... the public judgement on free trade was not clear-cut, supporting yet again the position that elections are a very poor mechanism for genuine public consultation on specific public policy issues." Pammett, "The 1988 Vote," pp. 124–25. An early report on the 1988 national election study, Richard Johnston and André Blais, "A Resounding Maybe," *The Globe and Mail*, 19 December 1988, supports this conclusion.

28. See the polls reported in the *Toronto Star*, 18 November 1987, 9 January 1988, 18 January 1988, 29 July 1988, 3 September 1988, 25 October 1988, 29 October 1988, 8 November 1988, 15 November 1988, 8 December 1988 and 12 January 1989, and in *The Globe and Mail*, 30 December 1987, 3 September 1988, 14 October 1988 and 11 November 1988.

29. See the polls reported in the *Toronto Star*, 18 November 1987, 14 September 1988 and 17 September 1988.

30. See *Absent Mandate*, pp. 159–60, 163, 166, 171, 177 and 182, where the absence of policy mandates is tied to the lack of any "decisive advantage" attributable to the impact of particular issues on vote switching. But Pammett, "The 1988 Vote," pp. 124–25, uses a slightly different test.

31. *Absent Mandate*, pp. 181–82.

32. Cecil S. Emden, *The People and the Constitution*, 2nd ed. (London: Oxford University Press, 1956).

33. Some years ago an eminent American student of public opinion and voting offered a particularly sharp formulation of this point. "The more I study elections, the more disposed I am to believe that they have within themselves more than a trace of the lottery. That, of course, is not necessarily undesirable so long as all concerned abide by the toss of the coin. Be that as it may, the moral for our purposes is plain. Even when the public in manifest anger and disillusionment throws an Administration from office, it does not express its policy preferences with precision. The voice of the people may be loud but the enunciation is indistinct." V.O. Key, Jr., "Public Opinion and the Decay of Democracy," *Virginia Quarterly Review*, Vol. 37 (Autumn 1961), p. 487.

34. The problem of the electorate—if such a problem can be briefly defined—is a combination of the limitations of any method of voting as a way of reaching good decisions and the limitations of ordinary citizens as voters. For general background, see Alfred F. MacKay, *Arrow's Theorem: The Paradox of Social Choice: A Case Study in the Philosophy of Economics* (New Haven: Yale University Press, 1980), and W. Russell Neuman, *The Paradox of Mass Politics: Knowledge and Opinion in the American Electorate* (Cambridge, Mass.: Harvard University Press, 1986), and the literature cited there.

SECTION FOUR

The Two Old Parties

This section examines the traditional party system in Canada, and shows how it has been upset and restructured by the two Conservative election victories of 1984 and 1988. Until this time, Canada had a party system in which the Liberal party was the government party, winning most elections and drawing to itself the predominant support of the business community and the upwardly mobile professional middle classes who sought to undertake political careers or take an active interest in party politics. The Conservatives were the opposition party in the sense that while they usually lost the elections, they could at least count upon forming the official opposition. They too attracted members of the professional élite and some business support, but not as successfully as the Liberals who had a much stronger position as the government party. The Conservatives tended to be more issue-oriented, because it was by manipulating issues that they hoped to dislodge the Liberals from power.

In 1984, however, the Conservatives under Brian Mulroney and a neo-conservative agenda, succeeded in driving the Liberals into opposition. This was such a stunning victory, won with over half of the total votes cast, that many saw it as a kind of landslide, reconstituting the party system with the Conservatives as the government party and the Liberals as the opposition party. This perception was confirmed in the 1988 election when the Conservatives returned to power, this time running on the issue of the Canada-United States Free Trade Agreement.

The essays in this section examine the two parties closely to discover the reasons for change and the dynamics of the new party system in which the Conservatives dominate.

20 Party and State in the Liberal Era

REGINALD WHITAKER

Environmental Constraints

The environmental constraints on the Liberal party would appear to have been dominated by three factors. The Canadian political system is liberal-democratic, which, as C.B. Macpherson has ably argued, is a system characterized by a fundamental or structural ambiguity: the coexistence of the democratic and egalitarian values of the political institutions based on universal adult suffrage and the inegalitarian nature of the liberal capitalist economic structures upon which the political structures arose historically. The Liberal party was operating in an environment in which two sometimes contradictory forces were at work in shaping the party's role. On the one hand, the party had to finance its operations as a party as well as to manage a capitalist economy as a government, both of which left it vulnerable to the demands of the corporate capitalist world. On the other hand, the party had to get votes, which left it vulnerable to the demands of public opinion. Contradictions were not always in evidence between these two forces, but when they were, the party was in a state of crisis. Crisis can mean not only danger but opportunity. The Liberal party demonstrated superior skill at calling in one of these forces to redress the balance when the other became too dominating. In the King period this often meant calling in the force of the voters to compensate for the opposition of the private economic interests, but in the St. Laurent period it more often meant calling in the force of corporate capitalism to restrain and manage public opinion. In either event, both the political power of the voters and the economic power of corporate capitalism were in effect resources with which the party, as an intermediary force, could bargain. The ambiguity of this role was heightened, and even cultivated, by the ambiguous ideological role of the party fashioned by Mackenzie King. That the party never rejected the support of the vested capitalist interests, while at the same time never entirely losing its credibility with the voters as a party of

Reprinted from *The Government Party*, by Reginald Whitaker, by permission of the University of Toronto Press. © University of Toronto Press 1977.

democratic reform, left it precisely the flexibility and freedom of action to "wheel and deal" in the centre of the political spectrum and to make the kind of practical accommodations necessary to maintain its hold on power.

The third environmental factor, this somewhat more specific to Canada, was the regional diversity and political fragmentation inherent in a federal society as decentralized as Canada. This factor is at the same time so obvious as to be almost taken for granted, and yet so important that it can scarcely be overestimated. The relatively weak impact of the dominant *class* cleavages of modern industrial society on Canadian party politics in the face of economic regionalization and cultural divisions not only simplified the role of the Liberals as the centre party exploiting the ambiguities and contradictions of liberal-democracy—rather than becoming a victim of them, as in the case of the British Liberal party—but also gave a very particular cast to the structure of the party. It is no exaggeration to say that the structure of the Liberal party in this era can *only* be understood in the light of the impact of federalism on the inherited political structures of the British parliamentary system.

Party Finance

The relationship between the party and its financial supporters was a complex one, to a degree which rather forbids easy generalizations. The celebrated Beauharnois affair of 1930 was a highly misleading guide to the financial state of the party. The penury into which the party fell following the defeat of that year illustrates two points: first, whatever the motives of corporate donors to political parties, a party which sustained a major defeat was quickly abandoned. This was particularly crucial for the Liberal party, whose traditional links had been more to government contractors than to significant sections of big business whose interests closely related to party policy or ideology. A party which depends heavily on government contractors is in obvious difficulties when faced with a period out of office. The second point to emerge from this period is that the party was clearly unwilling to compromise its policies in return for financial support. In the case of the banks and the mining companies, as well as the railway unification issues and the wheat marketing board, there is evidence that the party—and here the decisive role of the party leader must be emphasized—would not alter policy at the behest of businesspersons armed with financial inducements. On the other hand, the party's own ideological bent, while it might distance itself from some capitalist interests, drew it close to certain sectors of the corporate world. Capitalism is not a monolithic set of interests, except in those comparatively rare moments when it is challenged by other classes from below or external enemies from without. There were always some sectors of the corporate world, even if not the greater part, which were willing to work with the Liberals, particularly where their interests coincided closely with Liberal policy. Even while still in opposition there were those who found such an identity of outlook—particularly, the retail chain stores and the meat packing industry.

Later, the Liberal party in office was able to greatly widen the scope of its friendly relations with the corporate world, as the identity of interests broadened and deepened with the years of power.

The contract levy system which Norman Lambert enforced in the late 1930s was predicated upon the desire of business to maintain good public relations with government as a major purchaser of goods and services from the private sector. This system not only was maintained after Lambert's departure from active party work, but was extended and deepened. Two developments made this consolidation possible. The enormous growth of government intervention in the private sector, arising out of the demands of the wartime economy and the commitment to interventionist Keynesian fiscal policies following the war, along with the maintenance of relatively high levels of defence expenditure in the Cold War period, had a specific meaning for the financing of the government party. A greatly expanded state sector which involved government in continuous interaction with private corporations as sellers of goods and services to this sector enhanced the scope for party finance—on a contract levy system where tenders were in force, or on a straight patronage basis where public bidding was not the practice. That this growth of state activity was expressed initially through the federal government, and that this centralization was closely associated with the policies of the Liberal party, also meant that the position of the federal party was reinforced in relation to its provincial counterparts. Of course, business generally wishes to retain good relations with government parties, especially when government intervention in the private sector becomes less predictable than in the past. There is also the motive of wishing to purchase access to decision makers in case of difficulty. Thus, with or without specific connection of government contracts, the federal Liberal party was able to increase its capacity for financing its activities as a partisan organization through the 1940s and into the 1950s. Another sign of this improved financial position was the growing regularization of funding over the inter-election period, reflected in the growing ability of the party in the 1950s to finance its day-to-day operations on a normal business basis—a condition which had certainly not existed in the 1930s.

Party finance was not an isolated factor: party organization was intimately, even inextricably, bound up with the problem of party finance. Adequate financing was the necessary, although not the sufficient, condition for the vitality of the party as an organization. The genesis of the National Liberal Federation in the early 1930s was as much, if not more, a matter of fundraising as it was a matter of creating an extraparliamentary organization for electoral purposes.

This concentration of the extraparliamentary party on fundraising may indicate an endemic condition of cadre parties with their aversions to mass membership participation in policy making or leadership selection and their extreme vulnerability to a small number of corporate donors, but it also illustrates two specific factors of the Canadian political experience in this era. First, the Liberal party, especially under King's leadership, found considerable political utility in a formal separation of the fundraising apparatus from the parliamentary leadership of the party. There is very little evidence of demands for participation by the rank-and-file membership in policy making or even leadership selection in this era of the Liberal party's history. Nor is there much, if any, evidence of a perception of electoral threat from mass party techniques of campaigning. The move of the Liberal party toward extraparliamentary organization had much more to do with the demands of party finance.

The second major factor forcing the national party's attention on party finance was the divergence between the concentration of economic power in the private sector—both in the corporate and in the regional sense—in a small handful of influential corporations in Toronto and Montreal and the decentralized nature of the formal political system. As a political organization, the Liberal party was based on the constitutional distribution of elective offices into more than 200 local constituencies and nine provinces (10 after Newfoundland's entry into Confederation). However much the central regions might dominate the party as a whole, such centralization could in no way match the centralization of private economic power. Indeed, the autonomy of the local units of the party in a political and electoral sense was one of the characteristics of the Liberal party as an organization, and the very structure of the formal institutional arrangements of election under the parliamentary system of single-member constituency voting ensured that this would be so. Consequently, the scope of such political activities as electoral organization and policy making on the part of an extraparliamentary national office was necessarily limited; on the other hand, the importance of the small number of party donors in two concentrated geographical locations meant that local units of the party at the provincial and constituency level were generally incapable of generating the necessary contacts for fundraising purposes—but for the crucial exception of the provincial units in these areas. With this exception and its consequent problems aside, it is clear that party finance would necessarily be one area of party activity best left to an extraparliamentary wing of the national party. Hence the high degree of concentration on this one activity most relevant to the extraparliamentary national party.

Party Organization

There is no doubt that the Liberal party was a cadre party: parliamentary in origin, small in membership, deriving support from local notables, and so on. Yet I have already suggested that there is little evidence of Duverger's "contagion from the left" as a factor shaping the party's structure. The growth of an extraparliamentary party alongside the parliamentary party did not come about as the emulation of a successful mass socialist party organization on the left—since such never did develop fully at the national level in Canada—but rather as the consequence of electoral defeat, in 1930, or the fear of defeat during World War II. Even when, as in the latter case, it was fear of a leftward trend in public opinion and the possible capitalization of the CCF on this trend that moved the party to change its approach, the specific *organizational* changes introduced in the party were not significant; changes rather took place on the level of policy and party programme. There was no democratization of the party organization or any shift of influence from the parliamentary to the extraparliamentary party; rather the parliamentary leadership skilfully manipulated the extraparliamentary structure to help initiate desired policy changes. Once the next election was won, the organization reverted to its former state.

The point is that a cadre party operating in a federal system is particularly vulnerable in an organizational sense to the loss of office, not only because the fruits of power are useful resources for party organization but also because the party lacks a firm and loyal *class* basis of support in the electorate. Moreover, the fact that the party's provincial bases are not really bases at all, but rather problematic elements in the overall structure of the national party, with different electorates, different concerns and even different sources of party funding, means that a national cadre party out of office cannot rely on the provincial parties as a second, fall-back position for the national party in its hour of organizational need. Conversely, if it does (as in the case of Ontario in the 1930s), it may be creating organizational and political problems for itself in the long run.

The alternative in this situation is for the defeated cadre party to create an extraparliamentary structure to undertake some of the functions normally carried out by the cabinet ministers while in office. This in turn reflects the particular cast which federalism gives to cadre parties in office, which can be called a *ministerialist* system of party organization. This system places a premium on the regional representativeness of the executive and encourages the emergence of regional power-brokers as key cabinet ministers, who thus play a double role as administrators and as political leaders of regions. When the administrative powers of patronage are severed from the political role of regional power-broking, ministerialist organization becomes a liability rather than an asset to the party. Hence the attempt to create an extraparliamentary wing of the party as an electoral alternative, particularly when the party leader, as in the case of King from 1930 to 1935, is unwilling to personally assume the organizational burden.

On the other hand, when the party returns to power the extraparliamentary party diminishes drastically in importance in the face of the return of ministerialism. In the case of the Liberal party after 1935, however, one can see a new factor entering into the parliamentary versus extraparliamentary equation. In the absence of strong class bases to national politics, cadre ministerialist party organization rests most comfortably on what can be loosely called a patron-client model. The regional discontinuities of the country lend themselves to a clientist type of politics in which one sees vertical integration of subcultures and horizontal accommodation among the élites generated by these subcultures. As long as politics revolves mainly around questions of patronage and regional bargaining, ministerialism fits in well with the needs of the party as an organization. Even out of office, as with the creation of the National Liberal Federation (NLF) in the early 1930s, the promise of future patronage considerations is a powerful weapon to line up political support. Yet to the extent that the forces of industrialism and urbanism and events such as depressions and world wars intrude on this somewhat petty little political stage (the provincialism and sordidness of which was noted by earlier outside observers such as Lord Bryce and André Siegfried), the attention of governments is drawn inevitably toward wider problems, which demand universalist, bureaucratic solutions rather than the old-fashioned particularistic solutions of patronage political cultures. Under the pressure of these external forces, ministerialist government becomes administrative government, politics turns into bureaucracy and the Liberal party becomes the government party. Paradoxically, ministerialist organization thus becomes an impediment to the political health of the party as a patronage organization, as well as the source of the necessary instruments of that type of politics. In these conditions there is a continued need for some sort of extraparliamentary wing of the party to maintain the necessary contacts between the party's external supporters and the largesse of the government, to coordinate the patronage side of the party's operations and to remind it constantly of its role as an electoral as well as an administrative organization. Thus the NLF did not disappear entirely after the return to office in 1935, as had happened in 1921. The partisan ceasefire in the war years coupled with the intense and accelerated bureaucratization and centralization of the wartime government led to such a political crisis for the Liberal party that it found it necessary to call the extraparliamentary party back into existence to help get the electoral machine functioning once again. Ministerialism thus generated its own limitations.

The electoral victory of 1945, in which the party's ability to respond to *class* politics as well as regional politics was tested, and the return of prosperity in the aftermath of war, laid the foundations for an apparent reversal of the relationships just indicated. After the war the extraparliamentary party was relegated to the status of a mere paper "democratic" legitimization of ministerialist organization. Even party publicity was in effect "farmed out" to a private advertising agency in return for government business, thus directly linking party publicity with state publicity. The Liberal party's transformation into the government party had reached its logical culmination, with the virtual fusion of party and state. The Liberals won two general elections under this arrangement and convinced most observers that they could continue indefinitely. But they lost the third election, and then suffered a devastating collapse when faced with the necessity of running while out of office, suddenly bereft of ministerialist organization, yet lacking any real extraparliamentary party organization.

Ministerialist organization thus appears a curiously ambiguous factor in party organization. Partly as a result of this ambiguity, the role of the national leader in the Liberal party was of paramount importance. When the party was out of office in the early 1930s the leader was in a very real sense the sole representative of the national party. In the aftermath of defeat, it is no exaggeration to assert that Mackenzie King had become the sole personal embodiment of the party in any significant way. The parliamentary party remained, but without clear responsibilities, and often without either the inclination or the ability to function as a continuing party organization. Hence King's frantic efforts to set up an extraparliamentary organization for the purposes of election planning and especially fundraising, since the responsibility for these activities was forcing an intolerable burden on his own shoulders. It should also be noted that when out of office the potential patronage powers of the leader of the opposition in a future government are almost the only inducements available to the party for organizational purposes. This places the leader squarely at the centre of the political stage, to a degree which would appear to almost match the domination of the party by an incumbent prime minister. There is no doubt that Mackenzie King returned to office in 1935 in a stronger and more commanding position over his parliamentary party and his ministers than that which he had enjoyed before defeat. The circumstances of that period of opposition may have been exceptional, and no attempt should be made to generalize on the role of the leader of a party on the strength of this example. What is clear, however, is that the crucial role of the leader in the party organization was enhanced by this experience, and that the creation of an extraparliamentary party was not a detraction from the role of the leader but rather an instrument of the leader's continued influence over all aspects of the party's operations.

The well-known patronage powers of an incumbent prime minister, his direct relationship with the voters, his prerogative of dissolution and his financial control over the fortunes of individual candidates, all demonstrate that the role of the party leader while in power is of enormous importance. Yet ministerialist organization, as well as the concentration of the prime minister on policy and administrative matters, tended to push the Liberal party in power towards a somewhat more diffuse distribution of responsibilities for party organization than had been the case while out of office. This tendency became quite striking when a new leader, Louis St. Laurent, who showed not the slightest interest in matters of party organization, allowed a still greater degree of devolution of responsibility in these matters to his ministers. Paradoxically perhaps, the greater strength of ministerialism in the St. Laurent years is itself an indication of the discretionary role of the leader in shaping the party organization; Liberal leaders had the capacity to leave their personal stamp on the party structure, even if, as in St. Laurent's case, this stamp was delegation of authority to his cabinet colleagues. Under King's direction the party organization, as well as the cabinet, was under tighter control. Yet it must also be pointed out that this greater control was only a matter of degree. It is clear from the historical record that King's ability to dominate his colleagues was limited, the limits being well-recognized by King himself. Ministerialism was more than a tactic of a certain kind of prime minister; it was a structural feature of cabinet government in a regionally divided society. The historical circumstances and the accident of personality might allow greater or lesser scope for ministerialism, but the *fact* of ministerialism was not subject to these vicissitudes. National party organization when the Liberal party was in office derived its basic structure from the interplay of the leadership of the prime minister and the ministerialist distribution of responsibilities.

The domination of the extraparliamentary by the parliamentary leadership was an inevitable feature of a cadre-ministerialist party in a federal political system. This did not make the administrative task of the extraparliamentary officials an easy one, in the sense of a division of responsibilities and recognition for their work.

That the party leadership expended considerable anxiety and energy at the various advisory council meetings over the question of preventing anything remotely critical of the parliamentary party's policies from being aired is a striking indication of how far parliamentary control over policy went: the extraparliamentary membership was not only to be powerless in deciding policy, but it had to be *seen* to be powerless as well. The smallest hint of disagreement over policy among Liberals—which is to say, the hint of any dissension from the policies adopted by the parliamentary leadership—was to be avoided at all costs. Democratic legitimation of the internal processes of decision making in the party was accepted, but only at the most rarefied and abstract level, that of the mandate of the party leader derived from the majority vote of a party convention at one point in time. The autonomy of the parliamentary party in policy making was justified in rhetorical terms by the invocation of the constitutional supremacy of parliament. Whatever the merits of that argument, it was rendered somewhat problematic by the increasing bureaucratic influence on the policies of the parliamentary leadership, to the extent that by the last years of the St. Laurent period, virtually all Liberal policy was formulated by the permanent civil service. Policy making was delegated to an institution which was, in the formal sense at least, nonpolitical as well as nonpartisan. The exclusion of the extraparliamentary party membership from policy making may thus be viewed as a matter of practical expediency rather than as one of constitutional principle. The party membership was not judged competent to formulate policy.

The 1948 national convention which chose Louis St. Laurent as King's successor best illustrates these relationships within the Liberal party. The extraordinary lengths to which the party leadership went, in this unique example of a national party meeting throughout the period of this study, to prevent any public manifestation of criticism or disagreement within the membership, extended not only to policy questions but to the matter of leadership itself. The evidence clearly indicates that the convention format was manipulated throughout to ensure that King's chosen successor should receive as little opposition as possible. On the other hand, the necessary democratic legitimation seemed to demand that St. Laurent receive some token opposition. Both imperatives were carried out in a remarkable example of stage-management conflict, in which the two genuine opponents of St. Laurent were effectively utilized for maximum public effect and minimum internal impacts. Even in the case of the selection of the party leader, then, the "democratic" mandate becomes highly questionable, and the domination of the party by the parliamentary leadership is seen to be decisive.

Conventions at the constituency level during this era would appear to have served equivalent legitimation purposes for the parliamentary élite. Nomination votes by the constituency association membership were often, although not always, called before elections. Rarely were these exercises more than empty formalities. Sitting members were virtually assured of renomination; defeated candidates from the previous election had the inside track; and if neither of these conditions obtained, the local cabinet minister and his organizers would normally anoint the man they wanted for the nomination. The association would then ratify the choice. It did not happen like this in every instance, but it was the general rule. Observers of contemporary Canadian political culture who have noted the "quasi-participative" nature of Canadian democracy might examine the role of the Liberal party, the dominant party in Canadian politics for well over a generation, in the political socialization of its members and supporters. The Liberal party was certainly no training ground for participatory democracy, however loosely that phrase might be defined. If anything, the dominant values, which it propagated as a mediating institution between the state and the mass of the citizens, were those of deference and unreflective loyalty.

Deference and loyalty are political values appropriate to the clientist web of relationships which formed the basic structure of the party. Clientist relationships, moreover, flourished in the era of one-party dominance, when the Liberals as the government party monopolized the basic medium of exchange in patron-client politics: patronage. But the general condition referred to earlier, the transformation of politics into bureaucracy in the period of one-party dominance, had a double effect on the party as an organization. The use of the state as a reward system for party loyalty effectively drained away the human resources of the party as a partisan organization into levels of the bureaucracy and judiciary where they could no longer be of political use to the party. Second, as an inevitable consequence of the first problem, the party had to rely heavily on direct cooperation from the bureaucracy or the private sector to replenish its parliamentary leadership. Thus it merged more and more intimately with the senior civil service, both in terms of policies and personnel, and with the corporate élite outside the state system itself but in regular contact with government. For these organizational reasons, as well as for the more general ones mentioned earlier, the party became less and less distinct as an entity, its separation from the state system and the private sector more and more blurred. The government party was becoming in a curious sense a non-partisan party, so long as its hold on office was not challenged. Some might prefer to argue that it was a case of the bureaucrats being made into Liberals. Yet however one approaches the question, it seems reasonable to conclude that the Liberal party, as a political party, was growing less distinct, that the party was more a vehicle for élite accommodation, involving not only the élite of the two linguistic and cultural groups in Canada but the bureaucratic and corporate élite as well, than a partisan organization. When partisanship got in the way of élite accommodation it was partisanship which was usually discarded. No better example of this can be found than in the examination of federal-provincial relations within the Liberal party in this era.

Federal-Provincial Party Relations

Quebec, as the homeland of French Canada, held a special status within the national Liberal party, based on tradition and a mild form of consociational tolerance. Yet it was Ontario, with its strong and semi-autonomous economic base, which mounted the toughest challenge to the dominance of the national party in this era. In both cases the federal party ran into difficulties with its provincial counterpart, to a moderate degree in Quebec and to an extreme degree in Ontario. In Quebec, electoral defeat for the provincial party in the mid-1930s gave the federal party, which remained ascendant in its own electoral sphere, the opportunity to control the provincial party, even to the extent of guiding it back into office briefly. Eventually, the federal party settled into a pattern of constituency collaboration with its provincial party's enemy, and more or less accommodative intergovernmental relationships with the Union Nationale in terms of federal-provincial affairs, including acommodations which sometimes drastically undercut the political position of its provincial counterpart. In Ontario, a politically (and even financially) stronger provincial party in the mid-1930s waged open war on the federal party, even extending its campaign to Quebec, both on the intergovernmental and political fronts. This vigorous challenge was finally defeated by intelligent mobilization of the federal party's resources, and the intervention of an external event, the coming of World War II. Following the provincial defeat, the federal Liberals managed very well in Ontario by allowing a much weakened and discredited provincial party to flounder unaided in the further reaches of opposition, while dealing with the Conservative provincial government in federal-provincial relations with little regard to partisan considerations. Thus, in both cases, the long-run result was the same: the federal party prospered in the two largest provinces without a strong provincial wing. Little was done to aid the provincial parties and, in the Quebec case, much was done to damage the provincials. This distant relationship was matched by an emphasis on intergovernmental relations with the provincial administrations of the opposite political colour. In other words, executive federalism overrode federal-provincial party solidarity. The government party at Ottawa preferred to deal with other governments.

Intraparty relationships with the hinterland regions of Canada were not normally troubled by financial competition between the federal and provincial wings. The financial superiority of the federal party was almost always evident. In the Atlantic provinces this financial strength, in conjunction with competitive two-party systems and patronage political cultures, resulted in highly integrated party organizations and low levels of intraparty strains. Newfoundland was a somewhat exceptional case, representing one-man provincial rule in close cooperation with the federal Liberal party and the federal state, but even here there was a close meshing of the two parties, albeit with rather more provincial direction than in the Maritime provinces. Basically, the Atlantic provinces represent a case study of the Liberal party as an integrative device within Confederation, drawing the provincial units into the federal sphere of influence and control, a political reflection of economic and administrative domination of poor and undeveloped provinces by the federal government.

The West presents a striking contrast with the Atlantic region. Although very much in a state of economic inferiority to central Canada, the western provinces resisted a status of political inferiority to the government party at Ottawa, first by giving relatively weak electoral support to the party in federal elections and second by tending to strike out on experimental routes with the party system in provincial politics. Thus, the Liberal parties in Manitoba and British Columbia entered coalitions at the provincial level while maintaining their full partisan identities in federal politics. Even in Alberta unsuccessful moves were attempted in this direction. In all cases severe intraparty strains became apparent. Only in Saskatchewan was a consistently high level of federal-provincial party integration maintained, due to tradition, strong partisan leadership and relative provincial political strength. Yet even in Saskatchewan prolonged relegation to provincial opposition bred growing internal party disunity. The Liberal party at Ottawa during its long period of domination grew further apart from its provincial counterparts in the West, which were either cooperating with its federal party competitors or floundering in opposition. Eventually, a pattern of intergovernmental relations with provincial administrations ranging in partisan colouration from quasi-Liberal to social democratic to Social Credit began to predominate over the kind of intraparty integrations which the Saskatchewan Liberal machine had once represented. The Liberal party's experiences in the West were very different from those in central Canada. Yet the same basic result was reached from different routes: executive federalism proved stronger than federal-provincial party solidarity.

This study in effect constitutes a documentation of the growing confederalization of the Liberal party over a period of almost 30 years. It should be emphasized that this process does not necessarily imply the attenuation of federal dominance over provincial wings of the party. Indeed, in most cases examined, the federal party emerged as the most successful. That this took place in the two central provinces, those best situated in economic, political, and even cultural (in the case of Quebec) terms to mount effective challenges to federal domination of the Liberal party, is a striking indication of the ability of the senior level of the party to maintain its superior position.

Confederalization did mean the separation of the two wings in terms of senior personnel, career patterns, party finance and even ideology. This means that by the 1950s, the government party in Ottawa was loosely linked with unsuccessful opposition parties in Quebec City, Toronto and three western provinces—parties whose weakness was more or less enforced by the very success of the federal party. Nor was this distinctly asymmetrical relationship simply an accident; rather it reflected a crucial problem in federal-provincial relations.

The problem revolves around the inevitable conflict in which two wings of the same party in the same province must engage for the available human resources. An increasing separation and insulation of the two wings at the level of parliamentary leadership was never matched by an equivalent separation of the membership at the constituency level. The critical problem faced by all parties of the mobilization of the party rank and file at election time to perform the multiple organizational tasks necessary for successful electioneering, could become itself a cause of contention and competition between two wings of the party in the same area. Only in the extreme—and in the Canadian context, unlikely—eventuality of complete jurisdictional accord between the province and the national government might political conflict at the governmental level not cause conflict at the party level. Another factor capable of overriding intra-party divisions might be a cross-provincial ideological cohesiveness within the party; in the case of a brokerage party like the Liberals, this was never true in practice, and doubtful in theory. Nor could pure patronage politics serve to override divisions.

In Quebec provincial disputes spilled over into federal constituency politics; the federal party reasserted stability by the subordination of the provincial wing, first by directly placing it in office, later by abandoning it to successive terms of opposition while collaborating with its opponent. The capacity of the federal wing to enforce a permanent opposition status on its provincial counterpart derived from its superior political and financial resources accruing from the national office, and its evident unwillingness—except in the very special circum-stances of 1939—to utilize these resources on behalf of the provincial party. Superior political and financial resources combined to ensure superiority in the attraction of human resources. Yet, in the long run, the provincial Liberals were able to rebuild their strength, not through prior solution of their financial prob-lem, but by generating new and separate organizational structures which could serve as alternative sources for the mobilization of human resources. In other words, political resources were developed independently of the federal party.

To a degree in Manitoba and much more so in British Columbia, coalition arrangements in provincial politics put severe strains on constituency organiza-tion and the loyalties of local party activists. There is definite evidence for British Columbia that the federal Liberals were in a much stronger position when the provincial party went into opposition in the 1950s than when it had been the dominant provincial coalition partner earlier. Saskatchewan, in the period of joint Liberal rule in both capitals from 1935 to 1944, appears to offer a contrast, inasmuch as party integration was smoother than it was later when the provin-cial party was out of office. In this case, Saskatchewan is closer to the example of the Atlantic provinces, when intraparty unity was bought at the price of clear federal domination, exercised in the Saskatchewan case, however, with some autonomy at the level of the federal cabinet by Jimmy Gardiner as the regional prairie power-broker at Ottawa. In other words, federal Liberal domination within Saskatchewan did not preclude regional representation of some signifi-cance within the cabinet, a regional power which was backed precisely by the high level of intraparty integration and the bargaining leverage this placed in Gardiner's hands. Saskatchewan thus represented a model of party politics as a vehicle of regional representation quite different from those adopted elsewhere in the West. The Liberal parties of the Atlantic provinces, on the other hand, did not appear to utilize party integration as a bargaining lever within the federal cabinet to the same extent. Here party loyalty overrode regional discontent and the same local activists could be mobilized equally for either level of electoral politics with the same well-integrated set of rewards backed by the political financing of Montreal and the coordinated patronage inducements of the federal and provincial states. Only in Newfoundland is there real evidence of this Liberal loyalty being translated into any real provincial influence on the federal party, but here the small size of the province and its state of underdevelopment and poverty severely limited its power. The Maritimes aside, it is clear that in the case of Saskatchewan federal-provincial integration as a vehicle of provincial political representation is not without strain when one party loses office. In the late 1940s and in the 1950s it became apparent that a certain tension between two wings at the leadership level was being reflected in problems at the local level.

There is a sense, then, in which federal and provincial wings of a party are often locked into a rather self-destructive relationship. If, as many observers have argued, political parties act mainly as recruitment agencies for the staffing of elective office—and the weakness of the Liberal party as a channel of demands on the political system through extraparliamentary policy formation appears to give added weight to the emphasis—then federal and provincial wings of the same party are necessarily locked into competition for the same pool of human resources. Provincial weakness matched by federal strength guarantees the latter wing against too much competition. Dealing with governments of another political colour at the provincial level, on the other hand, avoids this problem. The claims of other governments can be treated as a matter of intergovernmental negotiation. The claims of party become a complicating factor, adding new levels of conflict which can be avoided when the problem is simply intergovernmental. The intraparty dimension of federal-provincial relations is thus a matter of *additional* complexity. It is difficult to generalize beyond this from the limited time period which has been examined, but it does seem safe to conclude that a government party will prudently seek to avoid such complications. They may opt, as the federal Liberals did in Ontario and Quebec, for underwriting the position of their provincial wings as permanent opposition parties, thus keeping the party name before the provincial voters while at the same time minimizing their impact on the federal level. Thus, the dominant strategy of the federal Liberals in confronting this organizational problem in Ontario and Quebec was to downplay partisanship between levels of government.

In a country as diverse and as decentralized as Canada, and especially in the case of provinces as crucially influential in relationship to the federal government as Ontario and Quebec, a party in power in Ottawa could not afford the intraparty strains involved in attempting to use the party as an integrative device in federal-provincial relations. Instead, the Liberal party reverted to intergovernmental, even interbureaucratic, relations as the major channels of accommodation. This not only helped account for the weak and underdeveloped nature of extraparliamentary national party organization in this era, but also strongly reinforced the tendency already present in the government party to transform politics into bureaucracy and party into state.

Perhaps this may be the final, paradoxical conclusion to be drawn from this study. The curious lack of definition of Canadian parties, which has troubled so many observers of our politics, is only reinforced as the evidence concerning their structures is marshalled. The Liberal party was an organization seeking not so much to consolidate its distinct partisan identity as to embed itself within the institutional structures of government. Its fulfillment was not so much organizational survival as it was institutionalization as an aspect of government: control over recruitment channels to senior levels of office. The deadening of political controversy, the silence, the greyness which clothed political life at the national level in the 1950s, were reflections of a Liberal ideal of an apolitical public life. In place of politics there was bureaucracy and technology. This in no sense meant that Canada stood still. Profound changes were taking place in the nation's political economy. But these changes tended to take place outside the realm of traditional political debate. Instead, it was between the great bureaucracies, whether public (federal and provincial) or private (Canadian and American), that debate and policy refinement took place. The Liberal party had truly become the government party—an instrument for the depoliticization and bureaucratization of Canadian public life. The vision of Mackenzie King in his almost forgotten *Industry and Humanity* had begun to take shape: "whether political or industrial government will merge into one, or tend to remain separate and distinct" was King's question for the future in 1918. He concluded that "the probabilities are that for years to come they will exist side by side, mostly distinguishable, but, in much, so merged that separateness will be possible in theory only."

The Government Party in Opposition: Is the Liberal Century Over?

21

THOMAS S. AXWORTHY

Introduction

As Liberal party activists prepare to meet in Calgary in June 1990 to choose a new leader, they are haunted by a chilling question: Is the Liberal century over? A party that, having governed Canada for 62 of the 88 years between 1896 and 1984, prided itself on being one of the most successful political organizations in the western hemisphere, is now traumatized by the prospect that it has lost its political heartland in Quebec. A party that made loyalty to the leader and discipline in its ranks central tenets of its operating code is now riven by faction. Above all, a party that had a sense of self-assurance so pronounced that, like Lord Denning, "It was occasionally wrong but never in doubt"[1] is now stricken by uncertainty. "Welcome to the 1980s," Pierre Trudeau intoned to a wildly cheering party throng, packed into the ballroom of the Chateau Laurier on February 18, 1980. It is unlikely that the new party leader chosen at Calgary will greet the next decade with quite the same insouciance.

Liberals have just cause to worry. For, not since the legendary Sir John A. Macdonald inflicted back-to-back losses in 1887 and 1891, has the federal Liberal party endured defeats as crushing as the elections of 1984 and 1988. In 1984, for the first time in Canadian history, a party won a majority of seats in every province and territory as the Conservatives cruised to power, gaining 211 seats and polling 50 percent of the national vote. In 1988, the Conservative victory was perhaps even more impressive—if less grandiose—than the previous landslide. Elections are often won because of particular circumstances like 1984's clarion call of "time for a change," but the crucial question is, can the time in office be used to make the gains stand up? By retaining much of their 1984 base, attracting a plurality of first-time voters, establishing dominance in Quebec and winning 169 seats well-distributed from every region, Brian Mulroney's Conservatives served notice in 1988 that a new party era was emerging.

This is an original essay written especially for this volume.

Anguish and relief, in equal measure, tugged at Liberal hearts as the election results rolled in on the evening of 21 November, 1988. Anguish, because most Liberals knew that the Mulroney government could have been beaten. This election was one that got away at least as much due to Liberal ineptitude as Conservative skill. Through much of their mandate the Conservatives had been third in the polls, behind both the Liberals and the New Democratic Party. As late as June 1988, the Liberals enjoyed a comfortable eight-point lead over the Tories according to Gallup and, in August, Gallup had the two parties virtually tied. For a party that deeply believes in the nineteenth-century observation of Sir John Willison that "to be out of office was to be out of the world",[2] to be so close for so long but to end up so far from the prize is especially galling.

Disappointment over what might have been, however, was tempered for most Liberals by relief at what did not come to pass: the party finished a comfortable second, well ahead of the New Democratic Party. Finishing second has not normally been a prime Liberal goal but, in the tumultuous politics of 1984–88, the success of John Turner in ensuring that it was his party that provided the main electoral challenge to the Conservatives was an achievement not to be underestimated.

Politics is about opportunities—how they are missed or seized. The Liberals missed an opportunity to humble Mulroney and to duplicate in 1988 what Lester Pearson and Walter Gordon had achieved against John Diefenbaker in 1962–63. But perhaps even more significantly, Ed Broadbent and the NDP failed to seize the historic opportunity to displace the Liberal party as the official opposition. In the third week of the campaign, Gallup placed the NDP at 29 percent, one point ahead of the Liberals. Broadbent was sufficiently encouraged to opine publicly that Canada some day would see a two-party system and the demise of the Liberals.[3] Many Liberals feared that Broadbent might be right. But Turner's riveting performances in the French and English television debates, which galvanized free trade as *the* issue of the 1988 campaign, briefly brought the Liberals equal to the Conservatives in public support and marginalized the NDP.[4]

Paradoxically, free trade proved to be the salvation of both the Conservatives and the Liberals: it was a sufficiently bold initiative to give 1984 supporters of the Tories reason to continue their allegiance and it was a sufficiently emotional issue to polarize the electorate, thereby giving Turner the opportunity to make himself the leader of the anti-free trade coalition. Although defeated, the Liberals doubled their seats to 83, carried Atlantic Canada, made dramatic inroads in Manitoba and fought the Conservatives to a draw in Ontario. If the Mulroney government proceeds to undermine its popularity, as it nearly did between 1984 and 1988, the Liberal party will be the natural repository for anti-government sentiment. This, too, will be a legacy of the turbulent election of 1988.

The Liberal Century

John Meisel, the dean of Canadian party analysts, uses a compelling nautical metaphor to explain elections. "The causes of electoral outcomes," he writes "can be likened to factors affecting the surfaces of oceans."[5]

Fluctuations in sea levels are determined in the long term by the shrinking of glaciers, in the short term by tides and, in an immediate fashion, by waves. Elections, too, are similarly influenced: long-term historical conditions create the basic environment for the whole process, events occurring since the previous election are like the tides, and the parties' conduct in election campaigns are like waves.

The turbulence of the seas is a fitting metaphor for the political process because no election is ever static. Electoral majorities are majorities of the moment. V.O. Key, the Harvard pioneer in election studies, recognized that "no sooner has a popular majority been constructed than it begins to crumble."[6] Parties must be alert in adapting to basic long-term changes in the political environment, to the short-term events that dominate political agenda and to improvements in campaign techniques or communication technology.

For nearly a century, from 1896 to 1984, the Liberal party of Canada was a master of this process of adaptation and change. It maintained its historic base, it moved skilfully in tandem with changing social and economic realities and it continually introduced into Canada such innovations as leadership conventions and election polling. This near-century of dominance provides the background for an assessment of the Liberal party of today. What did the Liberal party used to do right? What has it been doing wrong recently? And what is the likelihood that it can regain its winning touch?

Canada's first party era was dominated by the Conservative coalition of Sir John A. Macdonald and Sir George Etienne Cartier. This alliance of Tory loyalists, Montreal business interests and ultra-montane French-Canadian *Bleus* swept six of Canada's first seven elections and lost to Alexander MacKenzie's Liberals in 1874 only because of the Pacific Scandal.

The origins of the Liberal party predate Confederation with the parliamentary alliance of the Clear Grits of Ontario and Les Rouges of Quebec. But this was a minority coalition and an uneasy partnership as many Clear Grits were antagonistic to French Canada. In 1887, the Liberals gambled in that age of religious intolerance and racial prejudice, by choosing the French-Canadian Catholic Wilfrid Laurier as party leader. With one stroke, the Liberal party transformed Canadian politics.

Although Laurier lost to Macdonald in 1891, the Liberals greatly strengthened their position in Quebec, increasing their seats from 12 to 37. In 1896, Laurier took Quebec away from the Conservative party when the Liberals won 53 percent of the vote in Quebec, increasing their seats from 37 to 49. Quebec's switch was the critical factor in Laurier's national victory. In 1900, the realignment was complete as the Liberals won 87 percent of Quebec's seats. Laurier's elevation to party leader demonstrates that parties are not mere bystanders to events. They can force the pace of change themselves.

If Laurier's leadership demonstrates the potency of national unity as a theme in Canadian politics, Mackenzie King's carefully constructed consensus on social policy shows how a party can move with the times. Elected in 1919 in Canada's first leadership convention involving the extraparliamentary party, King propelled his party into the twentieth century. On economic and social issues, the

Laurier Liberals had been classic liberals in the Gladstone mould. King was a former Deputy Minister of Labour and he inclined to a more positive view of the role of the state. The 1919 Liberal platform included references to hospital insurance and other welfare measures. King's caution insured that his party was hardly a radical reforming force but, just as Canada was emerging from its agrarian origins into the industrial age, so too the Liberal party was transforming and widening its appeal to include the urban middle and working classes. Under King, the Liberal party founded a consensus based on Keynesian economics and social policy: the state would intervene through fiscal and monetary policies to sustain demand, business would reap the profits and some of that wealth would be redistributed back to the people through unemployment insurance, family allowances and old age pensions. Like the New Deal and Roosevelt's Democratic Party coalition in the United States, Mackenzie King's successive triumphs in 1935, 1940 and 1945 created the basis of the modern Liberal party.

King's policy instincts were progressive but in federal-provincial relations he harkened back to the Laurier past. King governed through the accommodation of Canada's regions both in federal-provincial relations and in internal party matters. His method was to work through powerful regional Cabinet barons such as James Gardiner or Angus L. Macdonald. Regional differences were conciliated, not challenged. In the 1960s, Pierre Trudeau broke with this tradition in fashioning a new pan-Canadian approach "wherein policies were designed to appeal to individual citizens regardless of their geographic location, religion or class."[7] The pan-Canadian philosophy of the Trudeau Liberals took many forms—from economic policies like the creation of Petro-Canada to social policies like the Child Tax Credit and constitutional policies like the Charter of Rights and Freedoms. This national appeal to individuals rather than to regional or sectoral powerbrokers was made possible by the emergence of new instruments of mass communication. Trudeau dominated the electronic age, using television to communicate his ideas directly to the people.

Trudeau's personality, the power of his pan-Canadian appeal, and the expertise of the Davey, Coutts and Lalonde team in running campaigns, added another important element to the Liberal base. Most of the baby-boom generation cast their first vote for the Liberal party. The members of the baby-boom generation—a huge cohort of six million Canadians—first voted in 1968, and the last of the generation first voted in 1984. Under Trudeau, these first-time voters became critical to Liberal fortunes: in the 1974 election, for example, the Liberals suffered a net loss of people switching away from them but, among newly eligible voters, the Liberals led with a plurality of 45 percent compared to the PC's 17 percent. In the swing province of Ontario, 70 percent of the new vote went Liberal.[8] Similarly, in 1979, a Conservative majority was prevented because new voters voted Liberal by a margin of three to two. Laurier brought French Canada. King made the Depression generation a Liberal strength. And Trudeau persuaded the largest generation in Canadian history to begin their political involvement by voting Liberal.

Laurier's championing of national unity, King's skilful response to the pressures of the Depression, Trudeau's mastery of television to connect with individual Canadians: all are examples of how the Liberal party has been able to understand, accommodate and master the historical changes, political tides and campaign waves that determine elections. But, in 1984, the Liberal ship ran aground. Whether Liberals can regain their navigational skills and chart a proper course for the 1990s is the question we will now examine.

Regaining Quebec

In 1988, the Liberal party won only 12 seats in Quebec—its worst showing since 1887 when it won but 13. Quebec's realignment is an historic event that completely transforms the political environment. To have any chance of again becoming the government party, the Liberals must at least become competitive in their former heartland. This priority takes precedence over all others.

In June 1984, the Liberal party still commanded 61 percent in Quebec public opinion polls and Mulroney was behind in his own seat; by September, however, a political earthquake had erupted. In 1988, the realignment was complete as Mulroney solidified his standing: Quebec was the only province where the Conservatives did better in 1988 than 1984. They improved both their share of the vote (from 50 percent to 53 percent) and number of seats (from 58 to 63). According to Allan Gregg, the Conservative party pollster, for the first time in decades the Conservatives now have more party identifiers in Quebec than does the Liberal party.[9]

The current difficulties of the Liberal party are strikingly evident in the decline of the numbers of Canadians who usually identify with the party. (See Table 1.) Throughout the Trudeau era, over 40 percent of Canadians identified with the Liberal party and, as recently as 1980, the Liberals had a commanding 17 percent lead over the Conservatives. Presently, according to a poll published in *Maclean's* magazine, only 29 percent of Canadians identify with the Liberal party and, at 37 percent the Conservatives lead in all regions of the country except Ontario. As the authors of the 1984 national election study have pointed out about this transformation in party loyalties, the advantage this gives the Conservative party is that "it can determine its own political fate rather than having to depend upon the Liberals to make mistakes."[10]

TABLE 1 **Distribution of Federal Party Identification**

	1974	1979	1980	1984	1988
Liberal	49	43	44	34	29
PC	23	28	27	41	37
NDP	10	13	15	14	19
Other	3	4	2	1	1
Non-identifiers	15	12	12	9	13

Figures compiled from "The Character of Electoral Change: A Preliminary Report from the 1984 National Election Study" and the *Maclean's* 2 January, 1989 edition on the aftermath of the 1988 election.

The only good news for the Liberal party in these indicators of decline is that, although the party is now behind the Conservatives in hard-core party identification, only one third of Canadians are such durable partisans. Two thirds of the electorate are flexible—even volatile—in their affections.[11] With most of the electorate making their political choice in reaction to short-term events, current issues or leadership image, parties can assemble winning coalitions by harnessing, in the words of Lawrence LeDuc, "the basically negative attributes and impulses of a de-aligned electorate."[12]

Such a task, however, will be more difficult for the current generation of Liberal leadership than their predecessors because the three pillars of Liberal ascendancy have been so weakened. Laurier brought Quebec into the Liberal fold but French Canada has now spurned the party twice in a row. King created a classic centrist consensus that appealed to a newly urbanized Canada but, in 1984, this coalition fell apart and by 1988 it was only partially rebuilt. Trudeau brought the first votes of young people to the Liberal party but, in 1988, the Liberal party was third in the affection of new voters: the Conservatives scored 41 percent, the NDP 29 percent, and the Liberal party 28 percent.[13] The Conservatives had a net loss of voters switching from their 1984 allegiance but they made up for this deficiency by recruiting a new cadre of support. In 1988, the Conservatives won the replacement game. Canadian voters may be volatile but the 1988 election shows that it takes skill to grasp the opportunities that volatility presents.

Recreating Policy Consensus

The realignment of Quebec fits Meisel's description of an historic change in the political environment: the responses of the Liberal party to the tide of events from 1984–88 demonstrates that Liberals are now confused about their direction and unsure about their values.

Canadian political scientists debate whether our parties have any values at all. The brokerage theory uses the market as its main metaphor. Parties are sellers in the marketplace, dependent upon sensitivity to the consumer but with no particular loyalty to their brands. Janine Brodie and Jane Jenson write that "numbers, not principles or even self-interest, are the currency of electoral politics."[14] Others take a different view: William Christian and Colin Campbell argue that Canadian politics has been characterized by "a system of beliefs which relate to fundamental political aims."[15]

Both sides in this debate capture part of the complex reality of Canadian party politics. Canadian parties do put a premium on winning, as brokerage theory posits. Survey research on the political motivations of Conservative and Liberal delegates to the leadership conventions of 1983 and 1984, for example, demonstrates that a passion to win was the most important motivation of the activists.[16] Winning power, rather than policy purity, is the dominant thrust.

But, while winning is still the name of the game for Canadian parties, the parties play the game for very different ends. The values and policy positions favoured by party activists are quite different. More importantly, such differences matter. The party leadership may make tactical choices based on the brokerage model but, in time, the overall direction of the party reflects the core values of the most committed members. The 1988 debate over free trade is a case in point.

The Liberal consensus on basic principles, however, has become frayed. And confusion within a party eventually becomes communicated to the populace. The Liberal party, as measured by the views of party delegates at the 1984 and 1986 conventions, is a party of the centre left. Two-thirds or more of the delegates were "social welfare" liberals who put a premium on advancing equality of opportunity and were quite willing to use the state to intervene in the market; one quarter to one third of the activists were "business" liberals who opposed state intervention and welfare spending.[17]

Leadership in a political party is a careful balancing act between the interests and values of the parliamentary caucus, the extraparliamentary party and the electorate as a whole. The caucus demands a fighting leader who can lift morale and score points in the cockpit of the House of Commons. The extraparliamentary party will accept tactical moves to win elections but it presses for policies that reflect the clear-cut ideological preferences of the activists. The party supporters in the electorate are less partisan than the caucus, less ideological than the activists and more interested in consensus positions.[18]

These interests must be melded into a coherent party approach. If any one of these three components of a modern party is ignored for too long, or becomes too disenchanted, the leader will be in trouble. The Trudeau policy consensus revolved around a strong commitment to individual rights, including language rights, opposition to special status for Quebec, a strong national government, preservation and expansion of the welfare state, and activist intervention in the economy, especially to control inflation and to promote Canadian ownership. In 1983, these policies were characterized by one observer as the "most coherent assertion of political belief and principle by the Liberals in years."[19] Although key constituencies such as the West and the business community were antagonistic, this approach commanded broad support within the Liberal triangle of caucus, extraparliamentary activists and electorate.

Upon assuming the leadership in 1984, John Turner committed himself to altering the Trudeau priorities: this reflected both Turner's own beliefs and the widespread desire in the country for a change after 21 years of Liberal rule. There is no need to repeat here all the gaffes of the 1984 campaign: Stephen Clarkson has succinctly described the essence of the debacle. While Mr. Turner "needed to reject the style but not the policies of Pierre Trudeau, he was in fact rejecting the policies while endorsing the patronage style, and becoming an object of public derision in the process."[20]

Problems in the transition from Trudeau to Turner were one thing, but most Liberals expected that the upcoming years in opposition would be used to develop a new consensus. Such a process was a Liberal tradition. In 1893 under Laurier, the Liberals held Canada's first national convention, an innovation that helped prepare the way for the successful campaign of 1896. Similarly, in 1919 after the crushing defeat of 1917, the Liberals made use of Canada's first leadership convention to endorse a new progressive platform. In 1960, Lester Pearson called the famous Kingston Conference, composed of non-aligned intellectuals and active Liberals, which laid the groundwork for the expansion of the welfare state when the Liberals again assumed power.

No such policy renewal occurred in the years between 1984 and 1988. In 1986, the party was transfixed by a challenge to Turner's leadership and the convention passed a confusing series of contradictory resolutions. In the two years leading up to the election of 1988, the party sponsored three regional thinkers' conferences. These meetings produced the gist of an expansive 40-point Liberal platform that the Liberals released as a policy manifesto in September 1988, just before the writs were issued. Although many of the individual policies were well-developed, there was confusion in their presentation to the public, and throughout the campaign neither the leader nor anyone else paid much attention to any of the 40 points.

This failure to develop a coherent plan for the 1990s hindered the party in two dramatic ways. First, the absence of a coherent set of policies made it easier for Liberals to fall prey to that bane of opposition parties—factionalism.

Throughout his term as leader, Turner found it difficult to satisfy the competing demands of the caucus and the extraparliamentary party. With no policy vision to inspire them, Liberals became rancorous. In April 1988, only months before the election, half of Turner's MPs took part in an abortive uprising. The Liberal's slide in public esteem during the summer of 1988 was in part due to the spectacle of a party that could not govern itself. Second, after Turner's strong performance in the debates caused Canadians to give the party a second look, there was no ensuing presentation of policy to consolidate the negative blows that Turner had unleashed in the debates. Canadians knew that the Liberal party was opposed to the free trade pact; but they had no idea what alternative economic plan the party would implement to replace it. When there was no positive reinforcement to the Liberal campaign, the Conservative advertising blitz on Turner's credibility worked, and the voters drifted back to their original choice. Turner's masterful debate performance saved the Liberals from oblivion but it could not make up for the policy and organizational failures of the preceding four years.

Revitalizing Campaign Expertise

Electoral volatility may give the Liberal party the opportunity to capitalize on the mistakes of the Conservatives, but it needs a party organization equal to the task. Using Meisel's nautical metaphor one last time, the Liberal party needs sailors who can comprehend the direction of the tides, ride out rough waves and break for the open when the winds are finally good. Such expertise has been lacking in recent campaigns.

In 1984, at the start of that campaign, the Liberals held an 11-point lead over the Conservatives. Never before, in the history of Gallup (over 13 previous election campaigns), had a party gained or lost more than 8 points during an election,[21] so the Liberal lead should have been sufficient for a close contest if not outright victory. However, the 1984 Liberal campaign managed to lose 20 points between the first week of July and the first week of September!

In 1988, from the pre-election Gallup poll in September to the final results in November, both the Conservative and Liberal campaigns increased their standings during the course of the election: the Liberal party improved by 6 percent, the Conservatives by 3 percent, and the NDP suffered a drop of 11 percent.[22] The Liberal campaign had first-rate television commercials and the leader's tour was smoothly conducted. But, like 1984, there was tension between the leader's personal entourage and the national campaign organization and this in-fighting became public, thereby eroding Liberal prospects. Conservative strategists had used the summer of 1988 to give their party a lead by the campaign's start, and their counterattack after the first of the television debates is a model—albeit a negative one—of cool campaign management.

Party organizations cannot be constructed overnight. Personal ties, campaign experience and receptivity to new election technologies are crucial for building a modern campaign staff. But the pre-condition for developing the roots of party strength is frequent watering with money. Resources are crucial for hiring proper staff, carrying out pre-campaign preparations and using sophisticated but expensive modern campaign techniques. The Liberal party is in need of a variety of reforms to give the extraparliamentary party a more relevant organizational structure and a more focused policy role,[23] but the overarching party need is to make the Liberals competitive with their opponents in fundraising.

The 1974 Election Expenses Act which introduced public subsidy and disclosure for Canada's party system was one of the truly significant reforms of the Trudeau era. With this Act the Liberals made the system of campaign finance fairer, but at considerable financial disadvantage to itself. Prior to 1974, as the party usually in government, the Liberals had found it easier to raise money from the corporate sector than their opponents. With public financing and the introduction of the political tax credit in 1974, this advantage was neutralized. By 1979 the Conservatives were equal to the Liberals in income raised and the NDP were not far behind. In 1984, the Liberals raised $11.5 million, the NDP $10.5 million and the Conservatives had doubled the efforts of their opponents by raising $22 million.[24] The pattern repeated itself in 1988: the Liberals raised $13.2 million, the NDP $11.7 million and the Conservatives $23.5 million.

The Conservatives early discovered the use of the political tax credit which made it imperative for the parties to solicit individual donations. The Liberal party, in a classic miscalculation, did not follow suit until 1980. Starting in 1980, the Liberals did a credible job in doubling the number of individual donations to the party—from 17 760 to 33 649 in 1983—but the Conservatives more than tripled theirs from 32 720 to 99 264.

Overspending added to Liberal woes. During the Trudeau era the party usually raised more income per year than was spent. In 1983, for example, the party raised $7.7 million and spent $6.3 million.[25] While these balances were narrow—no large nest egg was left to the Turner forces—party financial controls had been strict and at the June 1984 leadership convention, the President of the party, Iona Campagnolo, complimented Liberals on being debt free. For the 1984 election, however, the party was unable to raise enough money in the campaign to cover the cost of the election. This debt was added to in subsequent years as party expenditure always exceeded party fundraising. By 1988, the Liberal debt was reported to be over $5 million.[26]

To be competitive in the 1990s, the Liberal party will have to retire the debt, match the Conservatives in pre-election spending and raise enough to finance the next campaign. This is a tall order. And unlike creative policy formation or electoral coalition building where the Liberals have a proven track record, the party has consistently been outgunned in fundraising for over 15 years.

Conclusion

Nothing is preordained in politics. Despite back-to-back election losses of major proportions, the Liberal party could well be in a position to resume power in 1992 or 1993. The 1988 election left the party in a solid second position: the anti-free trade campaign gives Liberals the chance to establish enduring links with church groups, the cultural community, environmentalists, and members of the women's movement, who were also opposed to the pact, and Liberal successes in several provinces could give the federal Liberals a cadre of seasoned campaigners to throw into the next election battle.

But the road back will not be easy. Liberal demerits are at least as imposing as Liberal assets. The party has lost its stronghold in Quebec and developing any sort of Liberal appeal in a post-Meech Lake, post-free trade Quebec, is a formidable task. The party failed to develop a new policy consensus during its first term in opposition and, with the national debt ever-growing, simply promising to spend more money on a host of problems is no answer. Few Social Democratic or Liberal parties in the Western democracies have been successful recently; one of the reasons for this is that Conservative thinkers have won the battle over ideas. Lastly, money is the mother's milk of politics, to quote the cliché, and for many years the Liberal party has been undernourished.

Thus, Jean Chétien—the new leader chosen at Calgary in 1990—will have an imposing agenda. The Liberal party must:

(1) restore itself to a competitive position in Quebec;

(2) reduce factionalism by practising the politics of inclusion rather than exclusion;

(3) develop a policy consensus which will command intraparty unity while being relevant to the needs of a Canada approaching the twenty-first century;

(4) create for the first time a truly participatory party able to finance itself by appealing to a mass base of individual donors.

The Liberal party is one of Canada's few enduring institutions. For nearly a century it has been a successful practitioner of the magical political arts of inheritance, conversion and replacement. After two recent defeats, Liberals are certainly sadder. Whether they are any wiser, only time will tell.

ENDNOTES

1. For an impartial observer's obvious distaste for Liberal pride, see John Meisel, "Howe, Hubris and '72" in J. Meisel, *Working Papers on Canadian Politics* (Montreal: McGill-Queen's University Press, 1975).
2. Quoted in David E. Smith, "Party Government, Representation and National Integration in Canada" in *Party Government and Regional Representation in Canada* (Toronto: University of Toronto Press, 1985), p. 122. Willison's comment reflected a nineteenth-century view. For a current assessment of the Liberal party that explains how much Liberal activists value winning over promotion of their policy preferences, see Martin Goldfarb and Thomas S. Axworthy, *Marching to a Different Drummer* (Toronto: Stoddart Publishing Co. Ltd., 1988).
3. For an account of the 1988 NDP campaign, see Alan Whitehorn, "The NDP Election Campaign: Dashed Hopes" in Alan Frizzell, Jon N. Pammett and Anthony Westell, eds., *The Canadian General Election of 1988* (Ottawa: Carleton University Press, 1989).
4. See Stephen Clarkson, "The Liberals: Disoriented in Defeat" in Frizzell, Pammett and Westell, eds., *The Canadian General Election of 1988*, and Gerry Caplan, Michael Kirby and Hugh Segal, *Election: The Issues, The Strategy, The Aftermath* (Scarborough: Prentice-Hall Canada, 1988) for accounts of the Liberal campaign.
5. John Meisel, "Introduction" in Howard Penniman, ed., *Canada at the Polls, 1984* (Chapel Hill, N.C.: Duke University Press, 1988), p. 1.
6. V.O. Key, *The Responsible Electorate* (Cambridge, Mass.: Harvard University Press, 1960), p. 30.
7. Smith, "Party Government," p. 3.
8. Harold D. Clarke, Jane Jenson, Lawrence LeDuc and Jon H. Pammett, *Political Choice in Canada* (Toronto: McGraw-Hill Ryerson, 1979), pp. 361–62.
9. See *Maclean's*, 2 January 1989, "Fickle Voters, New Loyalties."
10. Barry D. Kay, Steven D. Brown, James E. Curtis, Ronald D. Lambert and John M. Wilson, "The Character of Electoral Change: A Preliminary Report from the 1984 National Election Study," a paper prepared for the 1985 Annual Meeting of the Canadian Political Science Association.
11. See Lawrence LeDuc, "The Changeable Canadian Voter" in Frizzell, Pammett and Westell, eds., *The Canadian General Election of 1988*, pp. 103–13. The volatility of the electorate is also demonstrated in the 2 January 1989 *Maclean's* survey. Conservative party identification was at 32% in 1986, fell to 24% in 1987 and rebounded to 37% in 1988. Liberal identification was 33% in 1986, 35% in 1987 and 29% in 1988. The NDP scored 18%, 22% and 19% in the three years. With party identification changing so quickly in response to events, many analysts argue that party identification is of declining relevance and that it is more useful simply to discuss the voting patterns.
12. *Ibid.*, p. 106.
13. Jon H. Pammett, "The 1988 Vote," in Frizzell, Pammett and Westell, *The Canadian General Election of 1988*, p. 129.

14. M. Janine Brodie and Jane Jenson, "Piercing the Smokescreen: Brokerage Parties and Class Politics," in Alain G. Gagnon and A. Brian Tanguay, eds., *Canadian Parties in Transition: Discourse, Organization and Representation* (Scarborough: Nelson Canada, 1989), p. 29.
15. William Christian and Colin Campbell, *Political Parties and Ideologies in Canada: Liberals, Conservatives, Socialists, Nationalists* (Toronto: McGraw-Hill Ryerson, 1973), Preface, p. viii.
16. See Goldfarb and Axworthy, *Marching to a Different Drummer*, pp. 49–61.
17. *Ibid.*, pp. 75–83 and 110–24.
18. *Ibid.*, pp. 92–105.
19. G. Bruce Doern, "The Liberals and the Opposition," in G. Bruce Doern, ed., *How Ottawa Spends 1983* (Toronto: James Lorimer and Co., 1983), p. 12.
20. Stephen Clarkson, "The Dauphin and the Doomed," in Penniman, ed., *Canada and the Polls 1984*, p. 110.
21. Kay, Brown, Curtis, Lambert and Wilson, "The Character of Electoral Change," p. 4.
22. Party standings according to Gallup in September 1988 compared to the results of the November 21 election were:

	Sept. 1988	*Nov. 21*
PC	40	43
Liberal	26	32
NDP	31	20
Other	3	5

23. See Joseph Wearing, "Can an Old Dog Teach Itself New Tricks?: The Liberal Party Attempts Reform," in Gagnon and Tanguay, eds., *Canadian Parties in Transition*, pp. 272–86.
24. W.T. Stanbury, "Financing Federal Political Parties in Canada 1974–1986," in Gagnon and Tanguay, eds., *Canadian Parties in Transition*, p. 358.
25. *Ibid.*, p. 358. According to Liberal party reports filed with the Chief Electoral Officer for 1974–79, the party raised $1.8 million more than it spent; for 1980–83, it raised $2.7 million more than it spent; in the transition year of 1984, there was a deficit of $400 000 during the year, and a deficit of $4.9 million for the election. From 1985 to 1988, the party spent $1.8 million more than it raised.
26. Clarkson, "The Liberals: Disoriented in Defeat," in Frizzell, Pammett and Westell, *The Canadian Federal Election of 1988*, p. 32.

22 The Progressive Conservative Party: An Assessment of the Significance of Its Victories in the Elections of 1984 and 1988

GEORGE C. PERLIN

The electoral history of the Progressive Conservative party before 1984 falls into three periods. In the first period, from 1867 to 1896, the Conservatives dominated federal politics, winning five out of six elections. In the second period, from 1896 to 1921, they competed on roughly equal terms with the Liberals, losing four elections and winning two. In the third period, from 1921 to 1984, the Conservatives became a minority party, winning occasionally but holding office for only brief intervals between long periods of Liberal rule. Over this span of 63 years the party won only five out of 20 elections and held office for a total of only 12 years.

In 1984 and 1988, for the first time in almost 70 years, the Conservatives won two successive elections with an absolute majority.[1] In these brief comments I propose to examine how these victories were achieved and to discuss their significance in the context of the party's electoral history. The paper is divided into three parts: the first reviews the factors in the party's electoral decline, the second analyses how the party achieved victory in 1984 and 1988, while the third discusses the significance of these victories and what they imply for the future of the party.

The Decline

The most important element in the decline of the Conservative party was its alienation of the French Catholic population of Quebec.[2] The Conservatives' early success had rested on their ability to build support across the cleavages of language and religion. Through the first years of Confederation, the party had been able to avoid conflict along these cleavages but, in the 1880s, the issue of the rights of French Catholics in Manitoba and the Northwest intruded into federal politics. The rebellion by the Métis in the Northwest was the turning

---

This is an original essay written especially for this volume.

point. Sir John A. Macdonald's decision in 1885 not to intervene to prevent the hanging of Louis Riel, the leader of the rebellion, inflamed French-Catholic opinion against the Conservatives with the result that in 1887 they were reduced from 51 to 36 seats in Quebec. As the controversies in the Northwest continued, Conservative support in Quebec continued to erode. In 1891 the party won a national majority but it lost Quebec. The party then became entangled in the Manitoba schools controversy. When the government was asked to pass remedial legislation to override a Manitoba law denying support for the separate-school system, members of the government—caught between their desire to preserve the accommodation with French Canada and the threat to their support among the anglophone Protestant majority outside Quebec—procrastinated until it was too late to pass remedial legislation. In 1896 the Conservatives lost additional seats in Quebec and with them their national majority.

Left now in control of an anglophone majority opposed or insensitive to French-Canadian views, the Conservative caucus continued to make decisions that offended French-Canadian opinion. This, in turn, led to further defeats in Quebec.

The party was afforded an opportunity to rebuild in Quebec in 1911 when it regained office with the support of a bloc of Independent Conservatives who carried 27 seats in Quebec. But this opportunity was lost as French and English members of the government came into conflict, first over Canada's commitment to Empire defence; then over demands that the government disallow Ontario legislation which struck at French language instruction in the Ontario school system; and, finally, over the deeply divisive issue of conscription. When conscription was introduced in 1917, even though it was supported by a large bloc of Liberals, it was at the initiation of a Conservative prime minister and the Conservatives bore the blame for it in Quebec. The effect was devastating. In the 1917 election the Conservatives and their Liberal conscriptionist allies won only three seats in Quebec. With conscription, the hostility of francophones towards the Conservative party reached a new level of emotional intensity. In the 1921 election, not one Conservative was elected in Quebec.

From 1891 through 1957 the Conservatives lost 17 successive elections in Quebec. Only three times over that period did their share of Quebec's seats exceed 15 percent. Since Quebec elects one fourth of the members in the House of Commons, the effect was to put the Conservatives at a permanent national disadvantage.

In 1958 the Conservatives won a new chance to rebuild in Quebec when the provincial political machine of the governing Union Nationale, anticipating a major national victory by John Diefenbaker's minority government (elected in 1957), gave the Tories its backing. The Conservatives elected 50 members in Quebec but Diefenbaker, with a huge national majority, failed to take advantage of this opportunity. Francophones were accorded only minor positions in the Cabinet and their special concerns were treated with indifference. In 1962 Diefenbaker, the anglophone populist leader of the Conservative party, was denied a second national majority in large part because a francophone populist,

Réal Caouette, leader of the Quebec wing of the Social Credit party, cut heavily into the Conservative vote in Quebec. This reduced the number of Conservatives elected there from 50 to 14. In 1963, the number fell to eight. Once again, francophones were a small minority of outsiders in the caucus. Diefenbaker's disdain for them was reflected in his treatment of Léon Balcer, his designated Quebec lieutenant and parliamentary seat mate, to whom he rarely spoke. In the debate on the adoption of the national flag in 1964, Balcer called upon the Liberal government to use closure to halt a filibuster staged by Diefenbaker to oppose it. In 1965, the Conservatives again elected only eight members from Quebec.

Robert Stanfield, chosen to succeed Diefenbaker in 1967, represented a new generation of Conservatives who were deeply committed to a policy of making francophones feel at home within the party. Stanfield's initial efforts were frustrated in the 1968 election by the immense popularity of the new French-Canadian Liberal leader, Pierre Trudeau. Stanfield's subsequent efforts were undermined by a group in his own caucus who, led by Diefenbaker, opposed the policy of official bilingualism, voting against the bilingualism bill in the House and attacking the implementation of the policy at every opportunity. While most of the caucus followed Stanfield in supporting bilingualism, it was the activities of this vocal minority which attracted attention. The Conservative party was once again stigmatized as a party which provided a vehicle for the expression of the attitudes of anti-French extremists.

In this context, Joe Clark, who succeeded Stanfield in 1976, could make little headway in Quebec, particularly as that province became absorbed in the debate about separatism. Clark tried but, as opinion polarized around the issue of separation, the Conservative party and its leader could play only a peripheral role.

Under Stanfield in 1972, the Conservatives elected only two members from Quebec and, in 1974, only three. Under Clark in 1979, they elected only two Quebec members and, in 1980, only one. The Conservative share of the popular vote in Quebec in the 1979 and 1980 elections fell to 13 percent, lower than ever before.

The second factor in the party's decline was the breakdown in support among the anglophone Protestant majority outside Quebec which occurred in 1921. Conservative support among this segment of the population began to weaken as conflict developed around divergent class and regional interests. In the 1921 election, as a result of the strains imposed on farmers by the economic crisis that followed the First World War, the Progressives, an agrarian and regional protest movement, cut heavily into the support of both established parties in rural sections of Ontario and British Columbia and throughout the Prairies. The Progressives actually elected more members than the Conservatives, 65 to 50, while the Liberals emerged with the largest group in the House due to their strength in Quebec, where they won 65 seats.

Although the Progressives did not endure, the disruption of the hegemony that the Conservatives and Liberals had jointly enjoyed since Confederation was to become permanent. With the emergence in the 1930s of Social Credit and the

Co-operative Commonwealth Federation, the phenomenon of multi-partyism became an entrenched characteristic of federal politics. As these new parties cut into the support of the two older parties, it was the Conservatives, because of their weakness in Quebec, who suffered most. Without a secure base elsewhere in the country to counterbalance their weakness in Quebec, they became a minority party.

The Conservative party's difficulties in adapting to changes in its competitive environment were aggravated by a persistent problem of internal instability. From the time of Sir John A. Macdonald's death in 1891, the party was subject to recurring conflict that centred on its leadership. The party's ability to deal with external challenges was impaired by challenges to the leader from within. These conflicts occurred whether the party was in opposition or in government. In fact, three of the four Conservative governments in the critical period from Macdonald's death to the important Depression election of 1935 were shaken by major conflicts involving the leader in the final months before the elections in which they were defeated.

The persistence of internal conflict helped create an enduring image of the Conservative party as one that was unable to manage its own internal affairs and that was therefore not to be trusted to manage public affairs. It was an image that the party's rivals played upon constantly.

One reason for recurring conflict over the leadership was the tendency for factional cleavages to persist long after the issues that originally gave rise to them had been settled. This factionalism reflected the infusion of conflict with a high emotional content. Factional loyalties and rivalries tended to be based on affective ties and antipathies. This was both because of the central role of leadership in the party, which has produced a tendency to relate all of the party's successes and failures to the strengths and weaknesses of its leaders, and because affective ties of personal friendship and loyalty to a particular individual have had a special importance in the formation of support networks within the party.

As the party spent longer and longer periods in opposition, conflict over the party leadership was aggravated by the fact that leaders were deprived of the resources of office to use as patronage in building support. Even in opposition, the promise or hope of patronage may be an effective restraint on dissident behaviour if party members have a reasonable expectation that the party can win, but Tory leaders were gradually stripped of the use of this form of potential patronage as the mind-set of defeat settled on the party. As the Conservatives lost election after election, their belief in the possibility of victory was strained— further weakening party leaders and contributing to the process of conflict that made defeat all the more likely.

This tendency was part of a broader set of forces that may affect any party which has been out of office for a long time. An additional element in this set of forces was the fact that the experience of being in opposition for long periods created a culture in the party caucus that shaped the outlook and behaviour of its members. The function of opposition is to criticize the actions and policies of government. Because this was the tenor of their public statements, Conservative

MPs tended to be perceived as having a negative rather than a constructive perspective on public affairs. Moreover, they did not acquire the skills of policy development, which meant that when they did attempt to propose policies they often made mistakes. This added to the impression that they lacked the competence to govern.

Habituation to the role of opposition hurt the party in another way on the occasions when it did manage to win office. In opposition members tend to work independently of one another; they do not acquire the habit of close cooperation required to act effectively in government. As a result, when they assumed office, the Conservatives had difficulty in coordinating and concerting their actions, which tended to create an impression of confusion in the direction of policy. In addition, because of their experience in opposition, many Conservatives were suspicious of the public service, and when they came to office, they had difficulty in establishing effective working relationships with its members. This also contributed to policy mistakes by Conservative governments.

Another problem for the party was that as it became identified as the party of opposition it began to attract people whose political motivation was to express some frustration or special grievance. Many of these people belonged to groups that were experiencing social marginalization—people from rural or small-town backgrounds with limited formal education, in occupations or circumstances vulnerable to the forces of economic change. John Diefenbaker's selection as leader in 1956 signalled the importance of these people in the party. Diefenbaker's populist rhetoric appealed directly to their feelings of social insecurity. He spoke of an anonymous "they" who were trying to frustrate him in his efforts to speak and act for the people.[4] It was language that permitted anyone who felt in any way outside the centres of economic, social and political power in the country to identify with his leadership.

The presence of these groups added a social dimension to factional conflicts in the party, but it also had a wider significance. Anyone who had a neglected cause or special interest to advocate, and who did not choose to join one of the smaller parties, turned instead to the Conservative party; thus, the party became fragmented by diverse interests and outlooks. Although overlapping, three distinct minorities emerged within the party: one clustered around a variety of moral conservative positions; one espousing an ideologically radical, economic liberal view of the role of the state; and one animated by objections to specific policies ranging from metrification to bilingualism. Each of these positions challenged prevailing opinion in the party and made any attempt to build policy consensus impossible. The party could find unity only in what it stood against, not what it stood for. This added to its difficulties, giving it an image of being confused about its direction and often leading it to produce conflicting policies.

The Conservative party's problems with internal conflict were particularly damaging in the 20 years from 1963 to 1983. After 1963 no party was able to command a national base. While the Liberals restored their hold on Quebec, a resurgent regionalism fed a shift in Western Canada toward the Conservatives and the New Democrats. Ontario became the major battleground in federal elections, and none of the parties was able to establish a firm grip on the loyalties of voters there. Voting patterns were becoming highly unstable. In part this volatility was driven by forces of social and economic change, but it also reflected a profoundly important change in the technology of mass communications. This was the period when television became the dominant medium for the transmission of political news and political advertising. While Canadian politics had always been leader-centred, television personalized it in a unique way. Research shows that with the influence of television, leader images have become an increasingly important factor in voting choice. Television thus heightened the impact on the electorate of conflicts over the Conservative leadership. At the same time it exposed these conflicts as never before.

From 1963 to 1983 the party seemed to be in almost continuous turmoil over its leadership. Conflict in the cabinet of Diefenbaker had precipitated the defeat of his government in 1963 and was followed by a protracted struggle to force Diefenbaker to resign. The conflict over Diefenbaker's leadership that occupied the party from 1962 until his defeat at the leadership convention of 1967 created a set of factional cleavages that persisted throughout the tenure of his successor, Robert Stanfield. A hard core of Diefenbaker's supporters, driven into opposition in the party, kept the conflict alive, creating a constant challenge to Stanfield's authority, which contributed to the development of the popular perception that he lacked the competence to govern. After three electoral defeats, under pressure from the factional resistance to his leadership, Stanfield resigned. His successor, Joe Clark, faced opposition from the same group and from defeated rivals at the 1976 convention. The harassment of Clark's leadership had become so widespread by the time of the party's biennial meeting in November 1977, that there was speculation by journalists that he might not be able to win a vote of confidence from the meeting. Just as they had in Stanfield's case, Clark's difficulties in managing the party helped create an image of him as an ineffectual leader. Journalists began to scrutinize everything he did, consciously or unconsciously, looking for evidence that might reinforce this image. Clark's image problems seriously impaired the Tories in the 1979 election. They won the election but were denied a majority and seven months after they came to office they were forced into a new election by the defeat of their budget. In this election the burden of Clark's image and the party's reputation were augmented by mistakes the government had made in its few months in office. Clark had had to reverse himself on well-publicized commitments, ministers had made conflicting statements on major issues and the government had been slow to develop and present its policies. In February 1980, only nine months after it had come to power, the Clark government was defeated.[5]

The loss of power led to new attacks on Clark's leadership. When one third of the delegates to the biennial meeting of 1981 voted to call a leadership convention, Clark was forced to promise his caucus that if he did not do better in the vote on his leadership at the next biennial meeting he would agree to the calling of a convention. Over the next two years, even though the Conservatives overtook and passed the Liberals in public opinion polls, there were persistent attacks on

Clark's leadership and, at the biennial meeting in 1983, he was denied the vote he felt he needed to retain the support of caucus. As a result, he asked the party to call a leadership convention and announced his intention to seek re-election. Six months later he lost the leadership to Brian Mulroney.

The PC Victory in 1984

Mulroney's selection as leader was a significant factor in the Conservative victory of 1984. His first contribution was to bring unity to the party. There were several reasons for his success in this regard. First, in winning the leadership Mulroney had had the support of most of the social outsiders in the party. For the first time since Diefenbaker's removal from the leadership they were in a position of real power and could be counted on to give their loyalty to the leader. Second, since it was in this group that most of the anti-French feeling in the party was located and since he, himself, was a fluently bilingual native of Quebec committed to establishing a base for the party in French Canada, Mulroney was in a strong position to build accommodation across the language cleavage. Third, although his own views were in the tradition of pragmatic toryism, Mulroney had taken a conciliatory attitude towards the party's right wing, and so won most of its support. Thus, he was equally well-placed to build accommodation across the ideological cleavage. Fourth, there was a clear determination by Clark and his backers to avoid the kind of factionalism that had so often harmed the party in the past.

Mulroney also had personal attributes which contributed to the PC victory in 1984. He was a strong and effective performer on television, possessing a magnetism that both of his predecessors had lacked. At the same time his working class background enabled the party to establish credibility with lower status voters. That he was fluently bilingual and a native of Quebec enhanced the party's ability to appeal to francophone voters.

The strength of the party's organization was another significant factor in the Conservative victory of 1984. The party had begun to build an effective modern organization under the leadership of Robert Stanfield in 1970, but its efforts had been frustrated by a lack of financial support. That obstacle had been overcome with the passage of legislation in 1974 that provided tax deductions for contributions to parties and for the reimbursement of party campaign expenses. Under Joe Clark's leadership Conservative organization had been transformed. By 1984, the party had instituted a regular survey research programme, introduced direct-mail fundraising and built national headquarters into a major bureaucratic support structure for the party's continuing organizational and campaign activities. The survey research programme was developed by Allen Gregg who worked first in-house and then established his own firm, Decima Research. Gregg adapted the latest techniques from American political polling to Canada and applied them with a unique conceptual flair. Survey research was given the central role in the development of campaign strategy and became an integral part as well of direct voter mobilization in the constituencies. The party's fundraising achieved unprecedented success. Contributions even during the difficult off-years of 1981 and 1982 when the party was distracted by the controversy over Clark's leadership reached $6.9 million and then $8.1 million, which, even allowing for inflation, was 10 times the sum that had been available at the beginning of Stanfield's tenure. In 1983 the party raised $14.1 million and during the election year of 1984 it raised $21.1 million—twice the amount raised by the Liberals.

A third factor in the Conservative victory of 1984 was the accumulation of discontents against the Liberal government of Pierre Trudeau. The government's efforts had had little effect in ameliorating the conditions of the severe recession of 1981–82; Western antipathy toward the Liberals had reached a new level as a result of the government's national energy policy; Quebec nationalists were embittered because none of their concerns had been met in the constitutional agreement of 1982 in which the amending formula had been located in Canada and the Charter of Rights had been entrenched in the constitution; throughout the country there was a reaction against the conflictive course of federal-provincial relations; and a widespread antipathy existed toward what was perceived as the confrontational political style and personal arrogance of Trudeau. In polls conducted in 1982, Allen Gregg had found a significant decline in the number of people who identified themselves as Liberals. Behind the specific factors in this erosion of Liberal support, Gregg found a deep-rooted and general concern about how the process of government was working. He recommended that the party develop a campaign strategy which focussed on this feeling, emphasizing a more open, less confrontational, and more responsive style of government.[6]

Although they had identified the thrust of their campaign, the Conservatives realized they still had serious problems to overcome. First, the party still bore the burden of its past. Voters continued to entertain considerable doubt about the Conservative party's competence to govern. Second, despite his success in managing the party, Mulroney's own image had not been clearly defined in positive terms as a prospective prime minister. His personal image was not strong enough to compensate for doubts about the party.

The third problem was that much of the discontent with the Liberal party was tied to its incumbent leader, Pierre Trudeau. Thus, when the Liberals changed their leader, public perceptions of the party changed. Most voters expected John Turner to produce the change they wanted.[7] As a result, when Turner was chosen Liberal leader, the Tories lost the lead that they had held in the polls since 1982, with both uncommitted voters and former Liberal identifiers shifting their preferences.

Events in the early stages of the campaign seemed to further weaken the Tory position. An apparent conflict within the party over the cost of Conservative campaign proposals became public, and the party's shadow finance minister, John Crosbie, allegedly leaked figures to journalists showing that the party's promises would add $20 billion to the federal deficit. In addition, Mulroney was forced to retract comments he had made to journalists aboard his campaign plane about Liberal patronage appointments and his own position on the distribution of patronage to Tories. The Tories' rolling poll showed that for the first two weeks of the campaign they continued to trail the Liberals.

The turning point came with the leaders' debates in the third week. In the first debate, conducted in French, Mulroney's fluency in French and his greater sensitivity to the French political culture established his credibility to the Quebec electorate. In the English debate on the following night, a blunder by John Turner undermined the basis of his advantage over Mulroney. When pressed by Mulroney as to why he had agreed to make a widely criticized series of patronage appointments requested by Trudeau, his predecessor, Turner extended his arms in a gesture of seeming futility and said, "I had no option." The image and words, which were to be shown in film clips on national television night after night and evoked in mocking humour by Mulroney in every subsequent speech as he crossed the country, destroyed the stereotyped contrast between Liberal competence and Tory incompetence. At the same time Turner's statement was an admission that he could not produce change; he had had to give in to Trudeau, the prime minister whose political style a majority of Canadians had rejected.

The effects of the debates were immediately apparent in the Tories' rolling poll. The belief that Turner could produce change was held by 60 percent of a national sample polled by the Tories on the day before the English debate and by only 40 percent two days later. And there was a shift of vote intentions from the Liberals to the Conservatives. Three days after the debates the Conservatives overcame the Liberal lead and 10 days later they led by 13 points.[8]

The PC victory in 1984 was striking both for its size and its breadth. The Tories won 211 seats, carrying majorities in every province (something no party had ever done before), and winning large numbers of new voters across all divisions on every politically relevant dimension of social cleavage. The election had provided the Conservatives with an opportunity to establish themselves on a broader base, but their majority rested on a very fragile foundation.

As the volatility of voter preferences right up to the middle of the campaign suggests, short-term forces, not fundamental realignment of partisan preferences, had produced the Tory majority. The critical factor in the election outcome had been a shift to the Conservatives by 1980 Liberal voters with weak partisan attachments. "Outside Quebec, a combination of weak attachment, negative evaluations of John Turner, attraction to PC policies, and the desire for change Turner did not represent seemed to explain the decision to defect to the PCs in 1984. . . . In the province of Quebec . . . the leadership issue dwarfs almost all others in the voting equation."[9] Thus, the Conservative majority rested on votes the party had won from members of the electorate whose continued support was contingent entirely on the new government's performance in office.

The Tories in Office

Eighteen months after the election of 1984 the ephemeral nature of the Tory majority became stunningly apparent when national polls showed the

Conservatives had fallen behind the Liberals in voter preferences and their support continued to decline. By January 1987, they were running third in the polls, a position they were to occupy until the spring of 1988. There appear to have been at least four factors in this dramatic decline in the party's support.

First, the government was forced to deal with a serious budgetary problem which severely restricted its policy choices. Deficits accumulating since the mid-1970s had pushed the cost of servicing the public debt to some 25 percent of total spending, and the size of the deficit had reached such proportions—in excess of $30 billion—that there was no way to bring it quickly under control. The government did not have the resources to meet new commitments. This left it in the position of having to disappoint groups to whom it had made promises of increased support during the campaign. In addition, the deficit was so large that the government felt it had to both increase taxes and curtail existing programme spending.

The size of the government's majority posed a second problem. Its supporters included interests whose claims would inevitably come into conflict. This problem was compounded by the fact that the party had articulated no clear direction in which it wished to take the country. There was no common goal it could use to build support across the diverse range of specific interests embraced by its broad social base.

One set of conflicting interests that posed particular difficulty was created by the party's success in Quebec. Set against its need to consolidate support in Quebec were the expectations of western Canadians who felt they had been on the periphery of national politics throughout the Trudeau period. The western provinces were accorded the largest bloc of appointments in the cabinet they had ever had, and western ministers held many senior portfolios. In addition key western goals, such as the dismantling of the Trudeau government's National Energy Policy, were achieved. But decisions that seemed in western eyes to continue a policy of favouritism toward Quebec at western expense seriously damaged the government's standing in the West.[10]

Voters in the Atlantic provinces were also disappointed. The government created a new regional development policy, but the main change it made was in the structure through which regional assistance was distributed. The level of regional development spending did not increase. In addition, the government's restraint programme limited other forms of transfers from Ottawa and led to some job losses in the region.

The government also disappointed some of its more right-wing supporters, particularly those animated by moral conservatism. The government made some gestures in their direction but there was little substantive change in the policy areas that most concerned them. There was some token support for the anti-feminist group Real Women, but the bulk of funding for women's advocacy groups continued to go to feminist groups; a resolution to restore capital punishment was presented but was defeated with the help of the votes of a large number of Conservatives; and, although the abortion issue was debated, the government refused to endorse the anti-abortion position.

Third, the Tories had been able to win voter confidence in 1984 because, for once, they had been perceived to be more competent than the Liberals, but that perception was shaken by their performance. In part this was because while the government could not fulfil the expectations its election campaign had generated, it tried desperately to avoid creating disappointment—with equally negative consequences. "The most powerful motive underlying the Mulroney style is a desire to be liked, to please—and not give offence. But what that has meant in policy terms is that whenever the Mulroney government finds itself under attack or saddled with an unpopular position, it tends to surrender its position."[11] The government thus very quickly came to be seen as indecisive and directionless. In addition, the new government was plagued by a series of individual ministerial blunders. Between January 1985 and January 1987, six ministers were forced from office because of administrative mistakes or allegations of personal misconduct. A seventh had to resign for a brief period while a charge of a breach of the electoral law, from which he was cleared, was being investigated. In addition, the reputations of several other ministers were damaged by the way they handled problems in their departments or by allegations of patronage excesses. In the words of one assessment of the government's performance, written in mid-1986: "Scandal and misadventure have followed scandal and misadventure and it seems as if a week cannot go by without some further story of a conflict of interest, a ministerial indiscretion, or a judgement that seems to fly in the face of common sense."[12]

Fourth, the image of the prime minister became a problem for the government. In media analyses the government's lack of clear direction was attributed directly to Mulroney's lack of a "strong personal agenda,"[13] and its indecision was explained as "an expression of his own personal desire to be liked."[14] He was blamed for creating problems within the government by centralizing power in his own office while surrounding himself with personal staff who were not competent to exercise it.[15] He was also accused of lying to deflect criticism and of making exaggerated claims in an attempt to build up his personal image.[16]

Some commentaries on the Conservative government's decline in popularity ascribed it entirely to Mulroney's personal conduct and personality. Given the prime minister's central role in the Canadian system this is hardly surprising. The prime minister defines policy, makes all of the principal appointments in government and represents the party to the country. Thus, the prime minister's personal goals, style of leadership and personality have a profound impact on the direction of any government.

But whatever the impact of Mulroney's personality on the government, it is important to recognize that his leadership had to be exercised within the constraints of the character of the party as it was. From this perspective, the Mulroney government's problems need to be seen in the context of the party's long-term problems.

Thus, it may be argued that: (1) the Mulroney government came to office without a coherently defined set of objectives around which to mobilize national purpose because of the internal fragmentation of the party and, in particular, its

internal ideological divisions; (2) the need to represent all of the factional interests and cleavages within the party and the persistence of interfactional suspicions adversely affected the quality of Mulroney's initial ministerial appointments; (3) the pool of ministerial talent was limited, particularly in Quebec,
because the party (because of its historic weakness and its general reputation)
has had difficulty in recruiting people of outstanding ability or with records of
outstanding accomplishment in other fields to run for it; (4) effective cooperation
among members of the government took time to develop because party members
tend to interact on the basis of attitudes bred by persistent factionalism; (5) many
members of the government were slow to make effective use of advice from the
public service or had problems with their departments because, having been so
long in opposition, they were suspicious of the public service; (6) members of the
government, many of whom had never even sat in parliament before, made
mistakes because of their inexperience; and (7) collectively, the government was
overly cautious and tentative in its approach to office because of the obsessive
concern among Conservatives with their failures in the past.

The 1988 Election

Several factors contributed to a reversal in Tory fortunes.

First, in the summer of 1986, the prime minister took steps to reconstitute his
government. The cabinet was completely restructured, the deputy prime minister was replaced and the prime minister's personal staff was reorganized under
new leadership. These changes gave the government a new image and brought a
greater degree of internal coordination and more effective management to the
activities of the government.

Second, in June 1987, the prime minister achieved what at the time was seen
as a major policy success by negotiating the Meech Lake constitutional Accord
with the premiers of the 10 provinces. The Meech Lake Accord benefitted the
Conservatives in two ways. In Quebec it met that province's five conditions for
constitutional change, including its recognition as a distinct society, and so
permitted the Conservatives to secure the support of moderate provincial nationalists and to lay the foundation for a political alliance between Mulroney and the
new Liberal Premier, Robert Bourassa. In the country as a whole it enhanced
Mulroney's prestige because it secured the Quebec government's recognition of
the legitimacy of the constitutional changes of 1982 under which the power of
constitutional amendment had been patriated and the Charter of Rights and
Freedoms had been entrenched in the constitution.

Third, despite the government's other problems, since 1984 there had been a
general improvement in economic conditions and the economy seemed set upon
a course of sustained growth. The government ascribed this improvement to its
"open-for-business" approach which had included a policy of privatization of
public corporations, deregulation and tax measures aimed at encouraging
increased investment.

A fourth factor was the negotiation of a Free Trade Agreement with the United States. The government claimed that the Free Trade Agreement would bring long-term economic benefits for the country, securing access to the American market, creating the opportunity for economic rationalization and creating a mechanism for resolving trade disputes with the United States. Politically, it brought other benefits. The Liberals were divided about the issue. Thus, even though the Liberal caucus finally decided to oppose the agreement, many prominent Liberals publicly supported it. Among them was Premier Robert Bourassa of Quebec. In addition, since both the Liberal federal caucus and the New Democratic party had decided to oppose the agreement, the Conservatives were in a position to mobilize all of the pro-free trade opinion in the country, while the opposition parties had to compete with one another to win anti-free trade opinion.

A fifth factor was probably the most important. The Liberal party was in general disarray. Disagreement about the Meech Lake Accord and the Free Trade Agreement had contributed to this situation, but the issue at the centre of the problem was discontent with the leadership of John Turner. Turner had survived a leadership review in the fall of 1986, but plotting against him continued. Although their party still held a substantial lead in the polls, in the spring of 1988 a large group in the Liberal caucus attempted to force Turner to resign. While Turner succeeded in suppressing this coup, with an election only a few months away the country was presented with the spectacle of a significant group of his own supporters questioning his ability to lead the party and, by implication, the government—a spectacle which reinforced public doubts about Turner's abilities. Ever since polls in Canada first included comparative evaluations of party leaders, no Liberal or Conservative leader has received as low a rating on the key dimensions of competence and leadership ability as Turner was to receive at the outset of the 1988 campaign.

Finally, while the Liberals had seriously damaged themselves, most voters were not prepared to contemplate voting for the only other alternative to the Conservatives—the New Democratic party. Although the NDP leader, Ed Broadbent, was personally popular, polling data show that most of the electorate did not trust the NDP to manage the economy or to provide competent direction to government.[17]

By the summer of 1988 the Conservatives had pulled even with the Liberals and in September, with the help of a series of carefully timed announcements of new projects and policies, they moved ahead. It was in this context that the election was called.

Through the first two weeks of the 1988 campaign the polls suggested the Conservatives were headed towards a victory as substantial as they had won in 1984. But, at mid-campaign, their lead collapsed. Two events appear to have precipitated this change. The first was the beginning of Liberal television and radio advertising. Through the early part of the campaign the Liberals had had to rely on news coverage to put their attack on the Free Trade Agreement before the public, but news coverage had focused on the party's mistakes and internal difficulties. With the beginning of their television and radio ads they were able to get their message directly to the public. The second event was the leaders' debate in the third week of the campaign in which Turner performed well, particularly in an exchange with Mulroney over the Free Trade Agreement. Turner was widely perceived to have won the debate, giving force to his attack on the Free Trade Agreement and establishing his own presence as a credible alternative to Mulroney. Polls over the next 10 days showed a significant increase in the number of voters preferring Turner as prime minister. Although he still ran behind the other two leaders, he had closed the gap—mainly at Mulroney's expense.

While the Conservatives had underestimated Turner, they responded quickly and effectively. Turner had won over marginal voters uncertain about the Free Trade Agreement. To reach these voters the Tories slotted their TV ads in soap operas during daytime TV as well as in prime time, and bought a substantial bloc of radio time. One thrust of their response was to attack Turner's credibility. If many potential swing voters were confused and uninformed about the agreement, the Tory strategists reasoned, they would have to undermine their confidence in the truthfulness of the anti-free trade messenger. Accordingly, the Conservative advertisements accused Turner of lying about the Free Trade Agreement in a desperate attempt to save his political career. The second thrust was to try to restore confidence in the Free Trade Agreement by getting independent authorities to respond to elements of the attack on it. This part of the campaign was reinforced by the activities of members of the business community who had formed a pro-free trade organization. This group stepped up its schedule of public statements and appearances and intervened directly in the campaign by purchasing advertisements arguing the virtues of the agreement.

It was the superb organization of the Tories as much as their deep financial resources and the support they received from the business community that rescued the Conservative campaign. Their research enabled them to identify the effective response and to target it precisely, while their technical skills gave them the adaptability to make the radical change that was needed to put the new strategy into effect.

Reports from daily tracking polls show the effectiveness of this change in tactics. Support for the Free Trade Agreement rose, the relative rankings of Mulroney and Turner shifted again in Mulroney's favour, and the Conservatives regained the lead.[18]

The Conservatives hung on to their lead through the remainder of the campaign, but their victory in the election was on a smaller scale than the one they had achieved in 1984. Their overall share of the popular vote fell from the 50 percent they had won in 1984 to 43 percent and they lost seats in every part of the country except Quebec where they increased their number of seats to 63.

The Conservatives almost lost the 1988 election. Their ultimate victory reflected not their success in converting their support from 1984 into a new national base, but the effect of a number of short-term forces. Among these were the Liberal party's weakness and, in particular, Turner's image as an ineffectual leader; public unwillingness to accept the New Democratic party as an alternative government; the Tories' exclusive hold on the "pro" side of the debate over the Free Trade Agreement; and the technical superiority and strong financial resources of Conservative organization.

Conclusion

At one level it is clear that the Conservative victories of 1984 and 1988 have had no effect on the party's situation. As the volatility of Conservative support in the polls through both campaigns and during the period between the two elections suggests, there has been no increase in the party's core strength. Indeed, the number of committed partisans upon whom the Conservatives can count actually seems to have decreased during this period. The evidence for this is that at both the mid-point between the 1984 and 1988 elections and in 1990 Conservative support in the polls fell to its lowest levels since polls began to be taken in Canada.

To some students of voting behaviour in Canada, the fact that there has not been an increase in the number of Conservative party identifiers in the electorate is not surprising. Lawrence LeDuc has argued that over the past two and one half decades there has been a general pattern of "dealignment" from partisan commitments in Canada. LeDuc estimates that "only one-quarter to one-third"[19] of the electorate has stable party attachments. As a result Canadian election outcomes have become highly susceptible to short-term influences such as economic events, the performance of the government on specific issues and, most importantly, the images of party leaders.[20]

While the outcomes of the 1984 and 1988 elections did not increase the number of Conservative identifiers, there is one obvious dimension of the results of these elections that does represent change of a fundamental kind. That was, the Conservative party's success in winning the support of francophones. Brian Mulroney has reversed 100 years of history by making the party acceptable to francophone voters. The Conservatives are clearly no longer stigmatized as anti-French. Quebec's 75 ridings and the other 20 or so ridings where there is a significant francophone vote are now competitive territory for the Conservative party.

Mulroney has achieved this success at the cost of driving some people out of the Conservative party. Another significant shift in the distribution of the vote in the 1988 election was the increase in support for third parties of the right. The Christian Heritage party won five percent of the vote in the 30 seats it contested in Ontario; the Reform party won 14 percent of the vote, ran second in 10 ridings, and took a seat from the Conservatives in a by-election called shortly after the general election in Alberta; and the Confederation of Regions party won five percent of the vote in New Brunswick. The specific issue agendas and emphases in the approaches of these three parties differ, but they share attitudes of moral conservatism, economic liberalism and opposition to official bilingualism. Many of their supporters are from the socially marginalized groups who had turned to the Conservative party as it became identified as the party of opposition.

There is an irony in the shift of people on the right away from the Conservative party. Mulroney's government is widely perceived to have been the most conservative in Canada since before the Depression. The commitment to free trade, the selling off of public corporations, the capping of social programme expenditures, the tacit abandonment of the principle of universality in the old-age pension system, the reduction in support for regional development, the cutbacks in support to advocacy groups and the deregulation of foreign investment are products of an outlook that reflects a more market-oriented perspective on state-economy relations. Nevertheless, the Mulroney government has clearly sought a position to the centre-right and not to the far-right. Whatever the consequences of their actions, there is no evidence that the Conservatives want to dismantle the welfare state as Margaret Thatcher has attempted in Britain. In fact, it may be argued that the Mulroney government would have been less disposed to cutting back on the role of the state had it not found itself in 1984 facing an enormous budgetary deficit. Thus, for example, in 1988 it was willing to commit itself to both a number of "mega-projects" and an expansion of social expenditures in a nationally funded day-care programme. (After the election the government announced deferral or cancellation of most of these proposed new commitments because of the deficit problem.) In short, the Conservative party in office has been "conservative" but its positions are consistent with the model of a brokerage party that does not want to stray too far from the centre.

The loss of supporters on the far right and among "social outsiders" may hurt the party by splitting its vote. On the other hand it makes it easier for the party to appeal for support among francophones, ethnic minorities, people living in suburban and urban centres and people with liberal views on moral issues. It also makes it easier for the party to develop coherent policies.

In summary, the Conservative party did emerge from the 1984 and 1988 elections in a stronger competitive position. It had ended its disadvantage in Quebec and rid itself of some of those people whose support was most difficult to accommodate in a consensus-building strategy.

Yet, by the end of 1990 the chances of the party winning a third consecutive victory seemed slim. Early in 1989 its popular support across the country had begun to slide and by March 1990, polling firms were reporting that only 15 to 17 percent of the voters who had formed vote intentions said they would vote Conservative. Over the 50 years since the polls were first taken in Canada no governing party has ever fallen so low in public esteem.

Survey data indicate there were two main factors in this dramatic decline. One was a set of adverse economic conditions precipitated by adjustments resulting from the Free Trade Agreement, declining exports linked to a rise in the value of the Canadian dollar, and the effects of a substantial rise in interest rates (created by the Bank of Canada's attempts to control what it believed to be excessive inflation). The other was the introduction of legislation to replace a 13 percent federal sales tax on manufactured goods with a seven percent Goods and

Services tax of more general application. The negative reaction to the GST was particularly harmful. It was attacked from virtually every sector of Canadian society—including small-business and middle-class groups which have traditionally supported the Conservative party. Opposition was especially strong among Conservatives in western Canada where an anti-GST movement ran candidates to win control of Conservative riding executives and tried to force Conservative MP's to vote against the legislation. (Two Alberta Conservative MPs refused to support the new tax and were expelled from the caucus.) Combined with the western regional resentment toward the Conservatives that had begun during the government's first term, anti-GST sentiment produced a substantial shift in support in the polls from the Conservatives to the Reform party. In Alberta, the province that has been most consistent in its support of the Conservatives since 1958, some polls suggested that in an immediate election the Reform party could win a majority of seats.

A further major difficulty for the Conservative party arose in June 1990, when the Meech Lake Accord, which required unanimous provincial consent to be ratified, failed to win approval in the Legislatures of Newfoundland and Manitoba. The defeat of the accord dealt a blow to Prime Minister Mulroney's personal prestige in anglophone Canada, and jeopardized the success he had achieved in Quebec. Even before the accord was defeated Mulroney's Quebec lieutenant, Environment Minister Lucien Bouchard, and two other Quebec Conservative members of parliament had resigned from the party to protest what they saw as potential compromises of its principles.

The failure of the Meech Lake Accord also hurt the Liberals. The Conservative slide in the polls that began in 1989 resulted initially in a shift toward the Liberals, giving them a three-to-one lead in voter preferences across the country by the spring of 1990. However, following the defeat of the Meech Lake Accord, Liberal support in Quebec fell dramatically. Jean Chrétien, chosen as the Liberal leader on the day after the accord's defeat, was seen by Quebec nationalists to be hostile to their views. Two Liberal members of parliament resigned from the party following Chrétien's election and joined with Bouchard and two other Tory defectors to form a new group in parliament, the Bloc Quebecois, to fight for Quebec sovereignty. In August the Bloc Quebecois won a by-election with two-thirds of the vote in a Quebec riding that had been held by the Liberals. An October 1990 CBC-*Globe* poll revealed that while the Liberals, as a result of their support from Quebec anglophones, still held a slight plurality in voter preferences among all decided voters in Quebec, the Liberals, Conservatives, and New Democrats had the same level of support among Quebec francophones. This poll also showed that in evaluations by francophones of Chrétien and Prime Minister Mulroney on four key attributes, Chrétien had substantially lower average scores than Mulroney. In contrast, among Quebec anglophones and outside Quebec, Chrétien had significantly higher scores. Thus, ironically, following a century in which the Conservative party's efforts to build a national majority have been frustrated by its weakness among Quebec francophones, the party's best prospects for the short term now appear to lie in the support Mulroney has developed among this group.

The new situation in Quebec and the rise in support for the Reform party in the west signal a departure in Canadian party politics that goes well beyond the question of changes in the nature and competitive position of the Conservative party. The whole structure of competitive relationships in the party system that has been in place over the past 30 years seems to be in the process of breaking down. If the Conservatives do hold a significant portion of their gains in Quebec and the Reform party can translate its standing in the polls into votes, the next federal election is likely to produce a parliament in which power is divided among five parties, and no party will have enough seats to govern on its own. Beyond that the processes of change now at work in the country are such that the likely direction of party competition is impossible to discern.

ENDNOTES

1. The last time this occurred was in the elections of 1911 and 1917, and in the latter, the Conservatives were running in coalition with conscriptionist Liberals.
2. For a fuller discussion of the events described in this account of the party's decline in Quebec see George C. Perlin, *The Tory Syndrome, Leadership Politics in the Progressive Conservative Party* (Montreal: McGill-Queen's University Press, 1980).
3. *Ibid*.
4. For a discussion of Diefenbaker's leadership and its significance for the party, see *ibid*, chs. 4–6. There is an extensive literature on Diefenbaker's leadership, but see, in particular, the two volumes by Peter C. Newman, *Renegade in Power: The Diefenbaker Years* (Toronto: McClelland and Stewart, 1963) and *Distemper of Our Times* (Toronto: McClelland and Stewart, 1968).
5. For a full account of the Clark government's problems, see Jeffrey Simpson, *Discipline of Power* (Toronto: Personal Library, 1980). The subsequent conflicts over Clark's leadership and the events which brought Brian Mulroney to the leadership are discussed in Patrick Martin, Allen Gregg and George Perlin, *Contenders: The Tory Quest for Power* (Scarborough: Prentice-Hall Canada, 1983).
6. Cited in unpublished notes by Patrick Martin of *The Toronto Globe and Mail*, which Mr. Martin kindly made available to me.
7. *Ibid*.
8. *Ibid*.
9. Steven D. Brown, Ronald D. Lambert, Barry J. Kay and James E. Curtis, "The 1984 Election: Explaining the Vote," paper presented at the annual meeting of the Canadian Political Science Association, June 1986.
10. The most contentious of these was the awarding of the maintenance contract for Canada's CF-18 fighter aircraft to a Montreal firm even though the government's technical experts had said a Winnipeg firm was better able to fulfill it.
11. "The Winning Ways of an Irish Magus," *Maclean's*, 6 May 1985.
12. David Bercuson, J.L. Granatstein and W.R. Young, *Sacred Trust: Brian Mulroney and the Conservative Party in Power* (Toronto: Doubleday, 1986), p. 297.
13. "The Winning Ways of an Irish Magus."
14. See "The Tories Fight Back," *Maclean's*, 9 September 1985.

15. *Ibid*. See also "Mulroney's Uneasy Anniversary," *Maclean's*, 9 September 1985.
16. See "Mulroney Under Fire," *Maclean's*, 7 October 1985, and "The Tories Fight Back."
17. This observation is based on data from the national poll taken by the CBC at the beginning of the campaign.
18. See, for example, Richard Johnston, André Blais, Henry E. Brady and Jean Crete, "Free Trade and the Dynamics of the 1988 Canadian Election," a paper presented to the Canadian Political Science Association meetings, Université Laval, June 1989).
19. Lawrence LeDuc, "The Changeable Canadian Votes," in Alan Frizzel, Jon H. Pammett and Anthony Westell, eds., *The Canadian General Election of 1988* (Ottawa: Carleton University Press, 1989), p. 113.
20. Cf. Harold Clarke, Jane Jenson, Lawrence LeDuc and Jon Pammett, *Absent Mandate*, (Toronto: Gage Publishing Ltd., 1984).

Third Parties

Canadian old-line parties, although vague in their policies, have generally disciplined parliamentary groups, requiring of their members a high degree of conformity. The leader can have great authority and there is little room for dissidence. Protest, then, must occur outside the old parties and, to be effective, tends itself to assume the form of a political party. There have been many such parties in Canadian history, but the essays here refer to only three: the Progressive movement (which has disappeared), the New Democratic party and the Communist party. The first two achieved their greatest success in the West, built upon the structure of voluntary associations already existing among the farmers, and in a time of economic crisis. The Communist party is an ongoing but electorally insignificant mini-party.

The Progressive movement appeared after World War I, as a farmers' party protesting against eastern capitalist domination of Canadian economic and political life. It attracted wide support from the frontier provinces of Alberta and Saskatchewan, as well as from the farmers of Manitoba and Ontario. Eastern support weakened its militant sectionalism and prompted some of its leaders to join the Liberal party. The failure to develop effective leadership and organizational structures, and reliable financing arrangements doomed the party to an early demise. Its place was taken by other radical movements which attracted the support of its members, notably the Social Credit and the Co-operative Commonwealth Federation parties. The latter formed the nucleus of the New Democratic Party.

As the major third party at the moment, the New Democratic Party has had its problems assimilating different streams of radical opinion. This has led it to expel its radical nationalist wing and to form a lasting alliance with the Canadian Labour Congress. The New Democratic Party has always considered that communist association would drive off its more conservative supporters. The Communist party itself remains a tiny, rejected faction.

23 The Progressive Tradition in Canadian Politics

W.L. MORTON

... The Progressive movement was a revolt against a concept of the nature of Canadian economic policy and of Canadian political practice. The concept of Canadian economic policy which the Progressives had formed and on which they acted was that of a metropolitan economy designed, by the control of tariffs, railways and credit, to draw wealth from the hinterlands and the country-side into the commercial and industrial centres of central Canada. The concept of Canadian political practice which the Progressives had formed and on which they acted was that the classic national parties were the instruments used by the commercial, industrial and financial interests of metropolitan Canada to implement the National Policy of tariff protection and railway construction by dividing the vote of the electorate on "political" issues and by the compromises and majority decisions of the legislative caucus.

To what extent did these concepts correspond to actuality, what success had the Progressive revolt against them and what are the consequences of its success or failure in Canadian history?

That the national economic policy of the period was mercantilist in its inspiration and metropolitan in its operation may be affirmed without subscribing to the heated conviction that deliberate greed or malice entered into its formulation, or even that it rested on the blind and selfish inertia of its beneficiaries. Arch Dale's cartoons in the *Grain Grower's Guide* of bloated capitalists siphoning off the hard-earned dollars of the western farmer were effective for their purpose and are amusing comments on an epoch in Canadian history, but they belong to the realm of folklore rather than to that of historical interpretation. The National Policy was designed to make central Canada into a commercial and industrial empire, based on the development of the hinterlands of the West and North by the construction of railways to serve both East and West. During the Laurier boom, conditions were favourable, and great success was enjoyed in exploiting the virgin lands of the continental West. When those conditions passed, an adjustment of the policy was necessary. The metropolitan East was challenged by

Reprinted from *The Progressive Party in Canada,* University of Toronto Press, 1950.

the Frontier West it had called into being; the old National Policy was confronted by the new. The adjustment could be either a modification of the policy towards freer international trade, as by an agreement for reciprocity with the United States, or by the metropolitan area assuming, as part of the whole country, the costs of increased benefits to the hinterland areas.

It was to force such an adjustment that the farmers took political action in 1919. Unfortunately, as the controversy over the Wheat Board revealed, they at once fell into confusion about which alternative they would pursue. They strove for results as far apart as a tariff for revenue, and a system of open and organized lobbying in group government, which would have been in practice a scramble for economic benefits distributed by the state. The farmers in the movement represented conflicting interests themselves and were also responsive to the forces impelling the swift transition from the free economy of prewar years to the economic nationalism of the 1930s. The seeming unity of purpose of 1919 to 1921 was soon dissolved. In federal politics, the agrarian voters of the West for the most part returned to the Liberal party. In economic matters, the great body of farmers found hope in the new cooperative movement which gave rise to the wheat pools. But resentment of the long Liberal domination, and the vision of a stable farm income ensured by government action through a wheat board, remained to drive Conservative voters to support new, anti-Liberal parties, to maintain the United Farmers of Alberta (UFA) in power in Alberta, and to erode the old economic individualism of the farmer with the hope of state action, which would counter the discrimination of the tariff by underpinning the farm economy.

The Progressives, nevertheless, gained certain material benefits for their constituents, especially in the matter of railway rates and communications. The restoration of the Crow's Nest Pass rates, the completion of the Hudson Bay Railway and the proliferation of branch lines in the 1920s were their work or owed much to their effort. "With a split representation from the West," wrote the *Free Press* in 1930, "the Crow's Nest Pass rates would never have been restored. The 'National Policy' on this question, favoured along St. James Street, would have been imposed upon both parties had there not been a parliamentary contingent from the West free from control in caucus by an eastern majority."[1] This was spoken in the authentic accents of progressivism, and it expressed, no doubt, a partial and limited view. If national politics were a struggle for sectional benefits, however, the Progressives had won a measure of success.

At the same time, the Progressives influenced Liberal fiscal policy to the extent of forcing abstention from increases in the tariff and ultimately of actual reduction. The electoral success of 1921 checked a swing towards economic nationalism evident in most countries after the war, even in free-trade Britain, and notably in the United States. After the disappointments of the Liberal budgets from 1922 to 1929, they seemed at long last to be on the threshold of success in the Dunning budget of 1930. Indeed, the Conservatives were able to use the cry of western domination with effect in Quebec in 1930.[2] Otherwise their successes, as the reimposition of the Crow's Nest Pass rates on east-bound wheat and flour and in the construction of the Hudson Bay Railway, were in the nature of sectional concessions won from the dominant metropolitan area. On the whole, the Progressive movement left the metropolitan economy of central Canada unaltered in substance or spirit.

Against the concept they held of Canadian political practice the Progressives revolted with notable results. Again, of course, they were divided. There were those who revolted against the composite party because in caucus a sectional group might be consistently outvoted. These, the Manitoban or Liberal Progressives, sought to force a realignment of parties along the lines of the liberal and conservative elements in the electorate. They wished not to abolish the practices and conventions of party government but to use them in the interests of the primary producers, as a party of liberal principle. The others were the doctrinaire or Albertan Progressives, who rejected party government as such and proposed to replace it and its accompanying conventions by group government.

Both, however, were in revolt against the traditional parties as the instruments of the beneficiaries of the metropolitan economy. Did this concept correspond with actuality? While the Progressive view, undoubtedly, was a caricature of the relations of the national parties and the beneficiaries of the metropolitan economy, the caricature has that grasp of salient features which makes a caricature recognizable. Both parties from 1896 on were the practically indistinguishable proponents of the National Policy, and they acted through the caucus, the party-managed nominating convention and the distribution of campaign funds.

It was these three focal points of party government at which the Progressives struck. That sovereignty had passed from the legislature to the majority in caucus they recognized, and also that that meant the subordination of the weaker to the more populous sections of the country. Henry Spencer said before the United Farmers of Canada (Saskatchewan Section) in 1931: "Of 240 odd members in the Dominion, the great majority went from Eastern Canada, and so it didn't matter which group was in the majority. The Western vote was so absolutely submerged in the caucuses, that however good a man might be, his vote was lost. That was the reason we took independent action."[3] To restore sovereignty to the legislature, and to make sectional views known, the Progressives refused to be bound by decisions taken in caucus. Nominating conventions they proposed to take away from the parties and restore to the electorate. Campaign funds filled by private donations, they wished to replace by public subscriptions and a levy on party members.

The revolt against caucus, however, could only have succeeded by reversing the development of parliamentary government. No modern cabinet in the parliamentary system could undertake the vast work of the annual financial legislative programme without reasonable assurance of the consistent support of its followers. The independence of the legislatures of an earlier day was no longer possible; parliament had become the critic, not the master, of cabinets. The popular control of nomination and provision of campaign expenses depended, moreover, upon a zeal for public affairs the electorate failed to display for any length of time. The Progressives put a challenge to democracy which only the UFA met successfully.

Did the restoration of the old parties in 1930, then, and the rise of the CCF and Social Credit parties, essentially composite parties like the old, mark a complete defeat of the Progressive revolt against the party system? To a great extent it did. Yet the old order of Macdonald and Laurier, when party affiliation was hereditary and party chieftains were almost deified, was not restored. The two-party system did not return in its former strength. The rules and conventions of parliament made provision for more than two parties. The electorate became more independent, indeed, to the point of political indifference. The authority of the whip became lighter, the bonds of caucus weaker, than in the old days. These were effects of the Progressive movement and constituted its mark on Canadian political life.

The mere modification of political conventions and modes was perhaps a slight result of so much effort. Yet where could the sectional and agrarian revolt have led except to secession or class war, or to an acceptance of the composite party once more chastened, no doubt, but essentially unchanged? A free society is an endless compromise between anarchy and authority, union and secession. To compromise, no doubt, is to corrupt—to corrupt the simplicity of principle, the clarity of policy—but if so, then all politics corrupt and federal politics, the politics of the vast sectional and communal aggregations, especially. To this conclusion all purists, all doctrinaires and all Progressives must ultimately come or abstain from power. The logical alternative is Robespierre guillotining the guillotiner.

Yet the Progressive insurgence was not merely a sectional protest against a metropolitan economy, it was also an agrarian protest against the growing urban domination of the Canadian economy and of national politics. As such, it was closely allied to the sectional protest. As an agrarian protest, the Progressive movement was a response to the industrialization of the economy and the commercialization and mechanization of agriculture. In the years of the Progressive movement Canada was undergoing an industrial and urban revolution. To meet the challenge of the coming order, the old, hard-working farmer with his faith in long hours and sweat was ill-equipped. He had to be made over into a manager, a business man and a skilled technician. The work was largely done in the farm organizations from which the Progressive party sprang. The professional men and especially the lawyers whom the old parties put before the voters to elect were inadequate, not so much to make the legislative adjustments required by the transition from manual to mechanized agriculture, but to express the resentment and discontent the farmer experienced in the throes of the transition and to speed the work of adjustment. This task the Progressive movement performed, particularly in the two agricultural provinces it captured and held, Manitoba and Alberta. Its very success caused its passing, for the farmer came into business in the cooperatives, into politics in the parties, old or new, to stay. He stayed, not to protest further, but to get on with the job of looking after the interests of the new commercialized and mechanized agriculture. In this aspect the Progressive movement was the expression of the late phase of the transformation of the old semi-subsistence agriculture into the business of farming. With the Progressive revolt, farming ceased to be a way of life and became simply another occupation. Countryman and city dweller no longer inhabited separate social orders; the city had prevailed over the country, but in prevailing had learned, not a little because of the Progressive movement, to respect the countryman. No one after 1921 would have thought of writing Gadsby's "Sons of the Soil," in which the farmers of the great anti-conscription delegation of 1918 had been ridiculed by a slick and too clever journalist.[4]

In a larger view, also, the Progressive movement marked a profound transformation. Behind the sectional protest lay not only resentment of the National Policy and of its agents, the political parties. Behind it lay also resentment of the inequality of the provinces of the continental West in Confederation. They had been created with limitations, imposed "for the purposes of the Dominion." They entered Confederation, not as full partners or sister provinces, but as subordinate communities, subject to the land, fiscal and railway policies of the metropolitan provinces and the special interests of the French Canadian in the French dispersion in the West. They were, in short, colonies under the form of provinces "in a federation denoting equality."[5] The Progressive party was a full-blown expression of the West's resentment of its colonial status. As such, it was one phase of the development of the Canadian nation.

As such, also, it had a great measure of success. Not since the days of the revolt has the West been subjected to the indifference, the neglect and the fumbling administration which provoked the troubles of 1869, the Rebellion of 1885 and the movement itself. The swaggering hopes of the boom days, that the West would dominate Confederation by holding a balance of power in Ottawa, were happily not realized. But the increase in cabinet representation from the one lone minister of Laurier's day to the minimal three of the present, was not merely an exercise in abstract justice, but a response to the political weight of the West in the Union government and to the force of the Progressive movement. The choice of western leaders by political parties from 1920 on was a similar response to the political power and electoral independence of the West. At the same time, it is to be observed that just as the Dunning budget denoted the beginning of Progressive success in fiscal matters so the transfer of the natural resources in 1930, the purposes of the Dominion having been fulfilled, marked the end of the colonial subordination and the achievement of equality of status by the West in Confederation. This, too, was a response to western pressure embodied in the federal Progressive party and the provincial governments the movement threw up. The progressive movement, in short, marked the achievement of political maturity of the West and the symbols of equality could no longer be withheld.

Yet the resolution of the sectional animosities, of the narrow complacency of the East and the equally narrow assertiveness of the West was to be accomplished not by the bitter exchanges of the 1920s or by enforced concessions. The work of reconciliation, a work of time, of patience, of manoeuvre, the Progressive party advanced by proving that the West, too much tried, would and could resort to independent political action. The work might have been completed in that way. It was, however, completed by tragedy. No sooner had the West, through the

Progressive movement, begun to win a modification of the National Policy and no sooner had it achieved equality of status in Confederation, than depression drove the country into a defensive economic nationalism. Drought ruined the agrarian economy of the West and threatened the great cooperatives and the provincial governments with general bankruptcy. The West was saved by federal action, and from the disaster of the thirties came, in East and West, a deeper sense of interdependence than the past had known. The Rowell-Sirois Commission, the great inquest provoked by the disaster, accepted and elaborated the basic thesis of the Progressive movement, that in a federal union of free citizens and equal communities, there must be such equality of economic opportunity and such equality of political status as human ingenuity may contrive and good-will advance.[6]

ENDNOTES

1. "The Fruits of the Progressive Movement," *Manitoba Free Press*, 6 August 1930, p. 13.
2. *Ibid.*
3. *Minutes of Annual Convention of United Farmers of Canada* (Saskatchewan Section) (1931), p. 317.
4. H.F. Gadsby, "The Sons of the Soil," *Toronto Saturday Night*, 1 June 1918, p. 4.
5. C.C. Lingard, *Territorial Government in Canada: The Autonomy Question in the Old North-West Territories* (Toronto: University of Toronto Press, 1946), p. 251.
6. See R. McQueen, "Economic Aspects of Federalism," *Canadian Journal of Economics and Political Science*, I (August 1935), pp. 352-67 for a sober analysis of these points.

24 The CCF-NDP and the End of the Broadbent Era

ALAN WHITEHORN

An Historical Overview

The New Democratic Party's roots lie in the Depression of the 1930s. In 1932, 131 delegates gathered together in Calgary and decided to form the "Co-operative Commonwealth Federation (Farmer, Labour, Socialist)." A year later, the CCF held its first annual convention in Regina and drafted the Regina Manifesto, a statement of principles and, to many, the touchstone of Canadian socialism. In the 1990s the New Democratic Party, the successor to the CCF, has celebrated almost 60 years of CCF-NDP history. Without a doubt, there is much pride in the party's political accomplishments, but that is also combined with serious reflection and critical self-appraisal of its past and some concern about its future, particularly with the end of the Broadbent era.

Among the questions being posed by party members, press and scholars alike are the following:

(1) Is the NDP stalled as a third party?
(2) Has the NDP in the main failed in its efforts to be more successful than its predecessor, the CCF?
(3) Why, despite its image repackaging, does the NDP in Quebec continue to make so little electoral gain and experience no major break-through?
(4) What are the long-term prospects for the NDP in the industrial heartland of Ontario?
(5) Is the NDP's provincial base in the West still its strength?
(6) Has the NDP ceased to provide a clear socialist alternative to the two old-line parties?
(7) Is the NDP more of a brokerage party and less of an ideologically based movement?
(8) Why, after almost 60 years, has the NDP not made greater gains?

This is a revised version of the essay that appeared in the previous edition of this book.

These questions will be analysed to provide an overall evaluation of the CCF-NDP as it commences the last decade of the twentieth century under its newly elected leader, Audrey McLaughlin.

Support

The CCF vote reached its peak at 15.6 percent in 1945, support for the party dropped consistently in the four subsequent elections to 13.4 percent (1949), 11.3 percent (1953), 10.7 percent (1957) and 9.5 percent (1958). The CCF was clearly on the path to oblivion and might well have gone the way of the Socialist Party of the United States.[1] The birth of the NDP gave new electoral vitality to Canada's socialist movement. In its maiden election in 1962 the NDP polled 13.5 percent of the vote, higher than all but one of the elections contested by the CCF. Electorally, in the years 1962 to 1988, the federal NDP has polled an average 17.2 percent of the votes, versus 11.1 percent for the CCF, a clear gain of 6.1 percent of all votes cast and a 55 percent increase in the percentage of votes cast for the party. In seven of the 10 federal elections since 1962 the NDP has gained a higher percentage of votes than the CCF did in its best year, 1945.

In terms of the percentage of the federal vote, the CCF-NDP has only once (1988) broken through the threshold of the 20 percent barrier,[2] and thus has not become a major party on the brink of power. Nevertheless, it would be a mistake to conclude that the NDP has not shown growth in support in recent years. In the 1988 federal election, the NDP vote nationally was at its highest ever and above its 26-year average (1962–88) in every province or region except Manitoba and Nova Scotia (see Table 1).

Despite these overall gains, it should not be concluded that NDP electoral support has shown improvement over the CCF in all regions equally. Regionalization between and within parties is a fact of life in Canadian politics. The CCF-NDP is no exception. When data are compared regarding the average federal vote by province for the CCF and for the NDP (see Table 1 on page 326), we find that the party's vote in Saskatchewan declined from 34.7 percent to 32.4 percent. Saskatchewan's support faltered most in the years 1962–65, when it returned no MPs—the only years in the history of the federal CCF-NDP that this has been so. Several factors contributed to this: (1) the resentment of the transformation of the CCF into the NDP in the only province where the CCF had formed a government; (2) disappointment by Saskatchewan residents at T.C. Douglas' departure from provincial politics and return to federal politics; and (3) the growing disenchantment with the provincial CCF as it neared the end of its second decade of uninterrupted power.

The NDP was formed in part with urban, labour-oriented Ontario in mind and its greatest increase in support occurred in Ontario, where the vote went from a 10.7 percent average for the CCF to a 20.0 percent average for the NDP. Ontario, a primary NDP target, has seen a virtual doubling of the party's votes, a seven-fold increase in its average number of seats per election (from just over one to eight)

TABLE 1 **Average Percent CCF-NDP Federal Vote By Province (1935–1988)**

Province	CCF (%) (1935–1958)	NDP (%) (1962–1988)	Difference
B.C.	28.0	32.4	4.4
Alberta	10.2	10.6	0.4
Saskatchewan	34.7	32.4	−2.3
Manitoba	23.3	25.0	1.7
Ontario	10.7	20.0	9.3
Quebec	1.5	8.1	6.6
NB	3.0*	8.1	6.6
NS	8.1*	9.3	6.3
PEI	1.7*	12.1	4.0
Nfld.	0.3*	5.1	3.4
NWT/Yukon	22.3*	9.4	9.1
Canada	11.1	24.6*	2.3

*did not contest every federal election in the province/territory. Average is based only on elections contested.

and an equally large increase in the percentage of the party's total seats from that province (from 7.1 percent to 31.1 percent).

The CCF was an electoral disaster in Quebec where it averaged a mere 3.6 percent of the vote. Problems emerged from the start. Few francophones were present at the founding convention. The name Co-operative Commonwealth Federation did not translate well into French. In addition, the party had an image of being atheistic, materialistic and anti-clerical.[3] In policy, the CCF stressed the need for a strong federal government and central planning at the expense of provincial powers and jurisdiction. The heavy anglophone membership of the Quebec CCF reinforced the image of the party being antithetical to French Canadian interests. The NDP was created to a large degree to make a new and better start in Quebec. While a major break-through in that province has not yet occurred during a Canadian general election, the NDP, with an average 8.1 percent of the votes, has fared much better than did the CCF. Overall, Quebec has become the province with the party's third largest increase in votes in the NDP era and the third highest percent of the party's total votes (12.5 percent). The recent 1988 election showed that more than one in 10 NDP voters is now located in the province of Quebec. Still, the party has never elected a single MP from that province during a general election. It has, however, achieved some limited success recently. Between federal elections, the NDP has acquired on two separate occasions a solitary Quebec MP; once, by means of a defection from a rival party (Robert Toupin from 1987 until 1988) and more significantly, through a by-election victory (Phil Edmondston in Chambly in 1990). Whether these small steps are indicative of potentially greater future gains for the NDP in Quebec, particularly during a general election, remains to be seen.

The NDP has been better able than the CCF to establish a presence in all parts of Canada. This can be seen in terms of the greater percentage of candidates the party has run for office over the years (61.3 percent for the CCF versus 96.0 percent for the NDP)[4] and in gaining votes from all regions of Canada. (See Table 1.) For example, the average percentage vote for the NDP in the province in which it has done worst (PEI) is still a vote percentage higher than what the CCF usually received in a number of provinces.

Many writings portray the CCF as a western protest movement.[5] Certainly, the leaders of the CCF came from the West as did the vast majority of its MPs (89.3 percent).[6] (See Table 2.) However, there is a tendency by many to overestimate western and "farmer" input in the CCF vote and to underestimate eastern and "labour" support. The CCF voting base was greater in the West (59.3 percent)[7] but not to the degree often assumed. (See Table 3.) On average, 40.7 percent of the CCF's total votes came from the East. As early as 1949, 12 years before the NDP's founding, Ontario provided more of the CCF votes than did the Prairies.[8]

With respect to total number of NDP votes, the more populous East (i.e., Ontario and Quebec) accounts for the larger proportion. The NDP has collected 60.5 percent of its votes from the East versus 39.6 percent from the West. In terms of total votes, the NDP is very much an eastern party. Votes, however, are not the only criterion. As to seats, the party's representation continues to have a western orientation with 67.3 percent of the NDP's MPs coming from the West. This is a lower rate than the CCF days but still somewhat at variance with its total votes.[9] The 1988 election continues this pattern of asymmetry between total number of votes and seats. Nevertheless, the West continues to provide the NDP with its highest levels of voter support ($X = 25.0$ percent versus $X = 10.7$ percent for the East).[10] For example, the 1988 federal election saw the NDP receive a record high in each of the following provinces: 44.2 percent in Saskatchewan, 37.0 percent in British Columbia and 17.4 percent in Alberta.

In two other very important ways the NDP retains a very strong western orientation. On the one hand, 1987 data on members of the party affiliated indirectly through unions[11] (see Table 5) indicate that the East, in general, and Ontario, in particular, account for the overwhelming majority of the 276 128 affiliated members (79.5 percent and 76.0 percent respectively). In contrast, data on direct individual membership (see Table 4) reveal that 73.0 percent of the party's individual members[12] are found in the West. To a considerable degree this may reflect the strong provincial bases for the NDP in this region since federal party members are also simultaneously provincial party members, with the recent exception of Quebec from 1989 onwards. Until recently, the only CCF-NDP governments to date had occurred exclusively in the West from 1972–75 in British Columbia, from 1944–64 and from 1971–82 in Saskatchewan, from 1969–1977 and from 1981–88 in Manitoba, and from 1985 to the present in the Yukon. Any decline in the party's provincial fortunes in this region, therefore, is likely to have an effect upon the federal party's position in terms of membership and, therefore, finances. Thus, no analysis of the federal NDP would be complete without some discussion of the NDP's key provincial bases in British Columbia,

TABLE 2 **Percent of Party's Total Federal Seats By Region (1935–1988)**

Region	CCF (1935–1958)		NDP (1962–1988)	
	N	%	N	%
Maritimes	4	3.6	4	1.6
Nfld.	0	0	1	0.4
PEI	0	0	0	0
NS	4	3.6	3	1.2
NB	0	0	0	0
Quebec	0	0	0	0
Ontario	8	7.1	80	31.1
Prairies	71	63.4	73	28.4
Manitoba	19	17.0	33	12.8
Sask.	52	46.4	39	15.2
Alta.	0	0	1	0.4
B.C.	29	25.9	95	37.0
NWT/Yukon	0	0	5	1.9
Total	112	100.0	257	100.0
East		10.7		32.7
West		89.3		67.3

Sources: Gibbins; Beck; Penniman, Report of the Chief Electoral Office (various years).

TABLE 3 **Percent of Party's Total Federal Vote By Region (1935–1988)**

Region	CCF (1935–1958) (%)		NDP (1962–1988) (%)	
Maritimes		4.3		5.8
Nfld.	0.0		1.0	
PEI	0.1		0.2	
NS	3.4		3.0	
NB	0.8		1.6	
Quebec		3.6		12.5
Ontario		32.8		42.2
Prairies		38.5		19.9
Manitoba	12.2		6.7	
Sask.	20.8		8.6	
Alta.	5.5		4.6	
B.C.		20.8		19.4
NWT/Yukon		0.0		0.3
Total		100		100*
East		40.7		60.5
West		59.3		39.6

Sources: Cairns; Beck; Penniman, Report of the Chief Electoral Office (various years).
*does not total 100% due to rounding

TABLE 4 **Membership in the NDP in 1987**

Province	N	%	X*
British Columbia	34 225	23.4	1 222
Alberta	12 677	8.7	603
Saskatchewan	38 086	26.1	2 720
Manitoba	21 263	14.6	1 518
Ontario	33 036	22.6	347
Quebec	1 696	1.2	22
New Brunswick	1 136	0.8	113
Nova Scotia	2 456	1.7	223
Prince Edward Island	169	0.1	42
Newfoundland	920	0.6	131
Yukon	227	0.2	227
Northwest Territories	230	0.2	115
Total	146 121	100 **	

Source: Data provided by communication with NDP federal office.
 *average size of federal ridings
**does not total 100% due to rounding

Saskatchewan, Manitoba and, increasingly, Alberta. Of course, the historic NDP victory in Ontario makes that province noteworthy.

In Saskatchewan the defeat of the Blakeney government in 1982 occurred with a forcefulness that is still being felt. The party received only 37.2 percent of the vote, the worst in 44 years. Its fall in seats from 44 to eight was the most precipitous drop ever for the provincial Saskatchewan CCF-NDP.[13] It was, of necessity, a time for renewal but a considerable NDP base remained. With the provincial election of 1986, the NDP received 45.2 percent of the vote, a sizeable increase from 1982. It was the highest vote for any of the parties and higher than in 1975 when the NDP had formed a government. However, the electoral system was

TABLE 5 **Organizations Affiliated With the NDP: 1987 By Province**

Province	Affiliated Locals	Affiliated Members
British Columbia	56	28 874
Alberta	21	4 221
Saskatchewan	34	10 516
Manitoba	37	12 951
Ontario	516	209 748
Quebec	12	3 983
New Brunswick	2	84
Nova Scotia	10	2 096
Prince Edward Island	2	635
Newfoundland	2	3 020
Yukon/Northwest Territories	—	—
Totals	692	276 128

weighted more heavily to the less populated rural ridings and the NDP, while winning the vote tally, lost the competition for legislative seats 38 to 25.[14] The Conservatives, with 44.6 percent of the vote formed the government and stalled the would-be electoral comeback of Allan Blakeney. Still, the prospects for Roy Romanow, Blakeney's successor, in the province that pioneered Canada's socialist programmes, remain excellent. Certainly, the record high NDP 1988 federal vote in Saskatchewan gives party members in that province renewed reason for optimism on the eve of the next provincial election likely to be fought on the issue of privatization.

BC

The failure of British Columbia's provincial NDP to tap the discontent amidst the recession of the 1980s and return to power after more than a decade as the official opposition was also a severe blow to party hopes. Its percentage of the vote, however (at 44.2 percent in 1983 and 42.6 percent in 1986 being down slightly from its all-time previous high of 45.2 percent in 1979), suggests that the British Columbia provincial NDP is still in good health organizationally, despite past provincial election losses. The record high vote and number of seats won by the NDP in the province during the 1988 federal election has done little to dampen party members' enthusiasm. If recent opinion polls endure, newly elected provincial NDP leader Mike Harcourt stands a solid chance of becoming the next premier of British Columbia.

Man

The NDP's success story during the decade of the 1980s was the Manitoba provincial victories in the early and mid-1980s. Not only did the party come back to power in 1981 with its largest number of seats at 34 but also with its highest ever vote of 47.4 percent. The Manitoba election of 1986 saw a reversal of the NDP's fate in Saskatchewan. Despite a decline in the Manitoba vote for the NDP to 40.6 percent (second place to the Conservatives) the party retained a slim majority of seats (30 versus the Conservatives' 26) and continued, albeit precariously, as the provincial government for another two years. By 1988, however, the Pawley government, suffering from defections and dissent, lost a legislative vote and Pawley chose to resign amidst a provincial election. After seven uninterrupted years in power, the Manitoba NDP was ripe for defeat. It received only 23.6 percent of the vote and 12 seats. New NDP leader Gary Doer had to commence rebuilding the party not only from the opposition side of the Legislature but also from the more difficult position of leader of a third-place party. It appears, however, that voter dissatisfaction with the NDP was specific to the 1988 election as the 1990 provincial election in Manitoba saw a partial resurgence of the NDP vote to 29 percent. Still, with 20 seats versus the Liberals eight, the NDP had begun the first step on the road back to power. It is now the official opposition. Nevertheless, the NDP has to contend with a still revitalized provincial Liberal party and deal with the more complex calculations involved in a three-party system. The NDP decline in its federal vote in 1988 is a reminder that the NDP in Manitoba will continue to face obstacles.

Alta

Alberta, historically infertile NDP territory, has seen a significant change in NDP fortunes. In four of the five provincial elections since 1971, the NDP has seen its percentage of votes increase. Since 1982, the NDP has become the second largest party in the Legislature and currently is the official opposition. In 1986, the NDP received its highest ever provincial vote (29.2 percent) and seats (16).[15] In 1989, the provincial NDP vote dipped slightly to 26.3 percent, less than the Liberals at 28.6 percent, but the NDP still retained its record high number of 16 seats, sufficient to remain as the official opposition. Alberta now offers one of the NDP's better hopes for electoral success, despite the rise of the Reform party. The 1988 national election saw the Alberta wing of the party receive its best ever NDP federal vote in the province and achieve an electoral foothold with its first ever MP. This was something the CCF, despite its founding in Calgary in 1932, was never able to achieve.

As the decades-long provincial Conservative dynasty in Ontario came to a close, NDP activists hoped that the NDP might be seen as the vehicle for change rather than the provincial Liberals. These NDP strategists speculated this was to be the long-anticipated electoral break-through in one of the two heartland provinces. In 1943, 1948 and 1975, the Ontario CCF-NDP had displaced the Liberals as the official opposition and expectations were that this feat could not only be repeated but sustained. However, when the Conservative bubble burst in 1985, it was the Liberals who were catapulted to power, first as a minority and then as a majority government in 1987. It seemed like a long road ahead with the Liberals under David Peterson commanding huge leads in the polls. The only consolations members of the Ontario provincial NDP seemed to be able to gather were: first, the drafting of the now famous (and for some controversial) 1985 accord between the minority government Liberals and the NDP concerning the legislative agenda; and, in 1987, what seemed a somewhat precarious displacement by the NDP of the Conservatives as the official opposition. The Ontario political scene had become a competitive three-party system, perhaps a precursor of future federal developments. The Ontario NDP, like its federal cousin, appeared a contender for the opposition role, not that of the government. The immediate prospects for changing this situation seemed slight. However, the sudden summer election of 1990 changed all that. The Peterson Liberals, plagued by scandals, rising taxes, the public's growing concern about the environment, and discontent over the defunct Meech Lake Accord, suffered a stunning setback. The NDP under Bob Rae ran a strong campaign, increasing the party's support to a record high of 38 percent of the popular vote and 74 seats, thereby forming the first-ever social-democratic government in the province of Ontario.

As the 1980s ended, there existed no provincial NDP government in the country. The NDP territorial government in the Yukon, elected in 1985, was the only major Canadian outpost of socialist administration. The 1990 victory in Ontario is a sign that the 1980s are over, and perhaps a new dawn is emerging for social democrats. As far as the federal NDP is concerned, there is disappointment in the current fate of the four western NDP provincial parties but, overall, the western base still seems significant and it is there that most potential future provincial election successes lay. It is at the provincial level in British Columbia and Saskatchewan where the NDP has its best other chances for victory. Given that the federal party has failed in its recent bid for an electoral break-through, federal party strategists may have to content themselves with hoping that provincial successes will be the stepping stones to improved federal prospects in the long run.

Electoral Bias and Distortion

The impact of distortion in the single-member constituency system has been ably analysed in a pioneering study by Cairns.[16] It is particularly a problem for a third party which endeavours to draw votes from across all regions. It is thus not surprising that both the federal CCF and NDP have suffered by our current electoral system. Whereas the CCF averaged 11.1 percent of the votes, it collected only 6.2 percent of the seats, a difference of 4.9. The NDP, despite increasing its overall vote to 17.2 percent, has collected only 9.3 percent of the seats, a difference of 7.9. (See Chart 1.) If one accepts as a fundamental premise that in a democratic polity each vote should count equally, then it seems reasonable to conclude that both the CCF and the NDP should have received a percentage of seats closer to their percentage of vote. As the data suggest, this is not a problem that is likely to diminish in the future. In fact, the bias in the electoral system seems to be operating at least as strongly against the NDP as it did against the CCF even though the NDP has acquired a significantly higher percentage of the vote. On average, the CCF should have received 79 percent more seats and the NDP 85 percent more. In 1988, for example, instead of winning 43 seats, the NDP should have been closer to receiving 60 seats. Modifications in our electoral system which might bring it closer to proportional representation would clearly help the NDP. Curiously, the federal party under Broadbent was not a strong proponent of this idea.

A number of scholars have observed[17] that beyond reducing the representation and importance of a party, electoral distortions can also transform the image of a party. Thus, while 40.7 percent of the CCF's vote came from the East, only 10.7 percent of its seats came from that region. This fostered the impression of the CCF being overwhelmingly a western rural-based party, an image that did not always help the party in its efforts to represent itself as a truly pan-Canadian party.

Much has been made of the CCF-NDP failure in Quebec. There are a number of reasons for this. One reason frequently overlooked is the bias in the electoral system. The CCF-NDP from its birth contested federal elections in Quebec. In total it received 2 371 811 votes but it has never had a single Quebec CCF or NDP member victorious in a general federal election.[18] From 1949 to 1965 the CCF-NDP showed a consistent trend of increasing its vote: 1.1 percent (1949), 1.5 percent (1953), 1.8 percent (1957), 2.3 percent (1958), 4.4 percent (1962), 7.1 percent (1963) and 12.0 percent (1965). Yet no CCF-NDP MP was elected during that period from any Quebec riding. Most recently, in the 1988 election, 487 971 Quebeckers voted for the NDP. Despite the fact that one in seven (14 percent) in Quebec supported the NDP in the last election, not one of Quebec's 75 seats was

CHART 1 **Percentage of Total Votes and Seats Received By the CCF–NDP (1935–1988)**

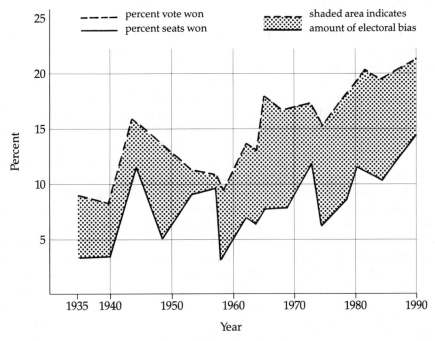

awarded to the party. Yet some MPs from Quebec sit on the basis of having received fewer than 16 000 votes. What would be the outcome if an electoral system was in place that would respond to the growing support for the party? Would the NDP have more articulate voices speaking on behalf of Quebec? Would the NDP be encouraged to try harder in Quebec? Would the Canadian polity be better served by each party receiving adequate representation in each region of the country? One can speculate that perhaps one reason the federal NDP may have been less sympathetic to Quebec's concerns in 1989 was because of the lack of responsiveness of the electoral system to the considerable NDP efforts in Quebec in 1988.

In the 1988 federal election, a party that won over 20 percent of the vote in Canada acquired no MPs east of the Ontario riding of Oshawa.[19] It is hard to imagine that Canada's regional tensions are alleviated by such electoral imbalances. Instead, such a system seems likely to promote parochialism.

Leadership

In the history of the CCF-NDP, there have been seven party leaders: J.S. Woodsworth, M.J. Coldwell, Hazen Argue,[21] T.C. Douglas, David Lewis, Ed Broadbent and the recently elected Audrey McLaughlin, with an average tenure of 9.3 years (versus 11.2 years for the Liberals and 6.2 years for the

Conservatives) in the period 1932–88.[21] All three CCF leaders were from the West as was the first NDP leader. Lewis and Broadbent came from the East. McLaughlin is also from the West.

Perhaps not surprisingly under the tutelage of an eastern leader, Ed Broadbent, the NDP acquired a peak of 13 Ontario seats in 1984, its highest ever. No matter what personalities might have been involved, it seems that a certain amount of tension would be inevitable in a situation in which the leadership has been largely eastern-based, while most of its MPs, 73.0 percent of the party's individual membership, the most successful provincial New Democratic parties and until recently the only NDP governments were western-based. To some, particularly in the West in the early 1980s, fuelled by frustration over Broadbent's constitutional stand and the party's then low standing in national polls, it seemed time to see the leadership revert back to a westerner. Indeed, the rumblings of Saskatchewan NDP-MP Doug Anguish at the 1983 Regina convention suggested such a concern. Nevertheless, Broadbent was re-elected by acclamation at the 1983 convention, although not without a brief moment of doubt.[22] Given that 60.5 percent of the party's vote and 79.5 percent of its affiliated members come from the East (see Tables 3 and 5), the case for a western federal leader is not as strong as many have assumed. Since the nadir of 1983, Broadbent saw his personal popularity and that of the NDP soar to a zenith where both topped the national polls. Broadbent, like earlier CCF-NDP leaders, became one of the most respected politicians in the country. Broadbent led the party to its highest ever vote total (20.4 percent) and number of seats (43) in 1988. Despite Broadbent's hopes for and efforts towards a long-awaited break-through, the NDP emerged from the aftermath of the 1988 free trade election still very much in third place. Despite some gains, the outcome was far short of the heightened expectations. The 1988 election, echoing in an uncanny fashion that of 1945, demonstrated the vulnerability of a social democratic party to a hostile bourgeois press[23] and a big-business financed media campaign. The forces of capitalism when confronted by an ascendant socialist party[24] responded, as in 1945, swiftly and effectively to thwart the challenge. Unable to guide the party to a new electoral plateau, Broadbent, having been a member of Parliament for more than two decades and having served for 14 years and four campaigns as party leader, announced in the spring of 1989 his intention to resign effective as of December. Audrey McLaughlin, the new NDP leader, will have her chance to guide the party out of its seemingly entrenched third-place position.

As the first elected female leader of a major Canadian federal party, Audrey McLaughlin will have a difficult task ahead. She has promised that the NDP will reach out more effectively to women. However, historically, women have not been the strongest supporters of the NDP. It remains to be seen whether the election of McLaughlin as leader and the rise in the number of women in the paid workforce will be sufficient to alter significantly this earlier pattern of gender support. It is also not clear how well a western-based leader will do in the federal NDP's efforts to build a stronger base in central Canada and establish a greater pan-Canadian presence. This is particularly so if constitutional matters remain at the fore. Despite Bob Rae's unexpected victory in Ontario a western-based federal leader may reinforce an image of the federal NDP as a western regional party and may enhance a proclivity by the party to concentrate more energy in the western provinces, particularly after its disappointing Quebec results in both the 1988 federal and 1989 provincial elections. Whether the 1990 Chambly, Quebec by-election victory and the Ontario provincial victory will lessen this tendency remains to be seen.

Ideology and Policy

There has been much written about the alleged CCF-NDP shifts in ideology and policy.[25] More often than not this literature has also raised the interrelated themes of a protest movement becalmed, of ideological decay in a third party and of the "embourgeoisement" of a working-class organization.[26] It may, nevertheless, be useful to raise a few queries and provide some data as a stimulus to thought.

In the history of the CCF-NDP five key statements of principles predominate. The page-long Calgary Programme of 1932 was a provisional outline of the general socialist and humanitarian goals of the CCF and acted as a prelude to the document which followed a year later. The Regina Manifesto of 1933 is by far the most enduring and, given its enunciation at the birth of the CCF in the midst of the Depression, it will always have special significance to most party members. The Winnipeg Declaration of 1956, drafted in the depths of the Cold War and during world-wide debates about the means to achieve socialism, continued the ideological rethinking that ultimately led to the creation of the NDP and the issuing of the New Party Declaration in 1961. In 1983, a new Regina Manifesto, 50 years after the first, was drafted to guide the party in the 1980s. Each document provides a useful insight into the evolution of socialist thought in Canada.

A certain mythology has arisen about the 1933 Regina Manifesto. Because of a few provocative passages, the Manifesto has acquired an image somewhat more radical than the text as a whole conveys. In fact, a content analysis of the text reveals that (see Table 6 on page 336) Underhill and his colleagues certainly did not dwell upon the terms 'socialism' or 'socialist' as self-descriptions. In fact, the solitary usage in 1933 suggests the terms were used 'gingerly' and somewhat timidly, not unlike in the 1950s. The League for Social Reconstruction (LSR) drafters in 1933 preferred to choose words such as 'socialization' or 'social owner-ship' which appeared less intimidating to potential supporters. While the fairly moderate language of the Regina Manifesto became even more so in the 1950s and early 1960s, it seems implausible to argue that the NDP in the 1980s has shied away from a fundamental commitment to socialism. Its 1983 statement of princi-ples is emphatic in its employment of the term—far more than in any other official party statement of principles.

To observe this is not to suggest that the socialism of the 1980s is identical to that of the 1930s. Canadian socialists have realized that any ideology, to be

TABLE 6 **Frequency of Use of Key Terms in CCF-NDP Manifestoes**

Term	1933 Regina Manifesto	1956 Winnipeg Declaration	1961 New Party Declaration	1983 New Regina Manifesto
Socialism/Socialist	1	4	0	13
Social Democracy	0	1	1	0
Class	3	0	0	2

meaningful, must be an evolving doctrine that endeavours to change the environment, but in turn is also changed by the environment. An ideology which fails to interact with the socio-economic base will ultimately recede into quixotic scholasticism and irrelevance, as a number of Marxist-Leninist regimes have discovered.

When compared to the 1933 Manifesto, the 1983 Manifesto is a less centralizing document which stresses "stronger provincial and local governments capable of realizing important tasks of economic and social development ..." and "... the demand of Canadians to decentralize, where feasible, ..." so that they can "participate more directly in the political decisions...." It acknowledges much more readily a "respect for its [Canada's] regionalism, and for its duality" and "the unique and enduring identity of the French Canadian people...." It also reflects a less technocratic view and belief in central planning by asserting that "planning must ... not [be] imposed ... from above" and that "social ownership" does "not simply [mean] the transfer of title of large enterprises to the state" but rather involves "decentralized ownership and control" and the "progressive democratization of the workplace." The document also proceeds to recognize the need to set "ecological priorities" and the danger of the "annihilation of our species in a nuclear holocaust." The importance of the "women's movement" and "aboriginal peoples" are also stressed.

The NDP is now, as was the CCF, a blend of different colours of the political rainbow.[27] It is composed of individuals whose attitudes range from Marxism to reformism.[28] There has always been a 'ginger group' striving to push the party further left. Over the years the names of the ginger groups have changed: the Socialist Party of Canada, the B.C. Socialist Fellowship, the Ontario Ginger Group, the Waffle, or more recently the Left-Caucus. The result is inevitably the same: a militant minority sufficiently strong to provoke lengthy and often intense debate, but rarely able to construct a winning majority. For example, at the 1983 convention, the new Regina Manifesto was approved by a two to one ratio. The Left-Caucus organizational and strategy meetings attracted between 75 and 100 persons; and in the elections to the governing federal council of the party, the Left-Caucus leaders who chose to run averaged about 200 votes (20 percent of the total). This is enough support to be felt, but not enough to achieve any real power within the NDP.

Beyond the commitment to a socialist Canada, the party also shows its distinctiveness from the two other parties[29] by its long-term, and somewhat delayed, goal of Canada's withdrawal from NATO and NORAD, cessation of all Cruise-testing in Canada and call for Canada to become a nuclear-free zone.

At the outset of the 1990s, several issues are the focus of NDP attention. Despite the lengthy and intense debate on free trade during the 1988 federal election, the free trade issue continues to fester both within the party and the country at large. The post-election backlash against Broadbent and his strategists for allegedly abrogating leadership of the opposition to free trade has been partially deflected by the NDP's change in leader. Nevertheless, discussion of the best tactics remaining to reverse the Free Trade Agreement continues. If the Liberal party lessens its opposition to the Free Trade Agreement, this may enable the NDP to reassert a more forceful leadership role among the ranks of free trade opponents. Certainly, previous survey data on party activists[30] suggest that free trade should be a better issue for the NDP than the Liberals, given that the latter have been far more divided on the issue.

During the transition between the Broadbent and McLaughlin leadership, the NDP has been divided on both the process and content of the Meech Lake Accord. Evidence for this can be seen in the lengthy debates on the topic at the NDP's two federal council meetings in the fall of 1989 and its 1989 federal convention in Winnipeg. This development should not be surprising since the country at large is split on the subject. In fact, Broadbent and McLaughlin have differed significantly on the topic—Broadbent voted for the Accord while McLaughlin was one of only two NDP MPs who did not. Another NDP handicap concerning the Meech Lake Accord is the fact that the public generally perceives the NDP as less relevant on constitutional issues than on social programmes or on the environment.[31] The re-emergence of extensive debate upon the twin topics of constitutional matters and Quebec's status is not likely to bode well for the NDP, even with a newly elected Quebec NDP spokesperson in the House of Commons. In the past, it is the Liberals that have benefited when such issues have prevailed.

The decade of the 1980s was one in which neo-conservatives dominated in setting much of the Canadian policy agenda. Issues such as government spending and the deficit have been items on which the NDP has not fared well. The task for New Democrats in the 1990s will be to present more effectively its preferred agenda. Bob Rae's stress on the environment and the populist theme of fairer taxes is an example of a successful strategy that other NDP leaders may seek to emulate.

The Future

After almost six decades what does the future hold for the party? Curiously, while the CCF was born in the midst of the Depression of the 1930s, it was unable to form a federal or provincial government in that decade. It was not until the worst of the unemployment had receded in 1944 that the CCF formed its first pioneering government in the province of Saskatchewan. Similarly, despite the high rates of unemployment in the 1980s, the NDP's progress seems slower than expected.

Contrary to the assumption of many socialists, an increase in economic deprivation does not necessarily lead to a corresponding increase in support for a socialist party.[32] This comes as a paradox to most socialists who expect exploitation and poverty to generate immediate demands for political change. Why have the gains been less than anticipated?

While the NDP was born amidst great fanfare concerning trade union financial support, organizational assistance and votes, there is some evidence to suggest that the support may not be as strong or enduring as many might have hoped. Data on rate of union affiliation to the NDP suggests a fairly steady decline from a peak of 14.6 percent of all unions in 1963 to a low of 8.2 percent in 1981.[33]

A perusal of Gallup data for the past two decades reveals that Canadians as a whole have feared 'Big Labour' (33 percent in 1968 and 30 percent in 1987) far more than 'Big Business' (17 percent in 1968 and 15 percent in 1987).[34] Further evidence of a class-biased culture can also be seen in data showing that more Canadians prefer a right-wing party (28.6 percent) than a left-wing party (9.4 percent).[35] Also, more Canadians have indicated that they prefer to see Canada move away from the ideology of socialism (35 percent) than towards it (23 percent).[36]

Perhaps not surprisingly, the CCF's and NDP's social welfare policies have fostered an image of the party encouraging the growth of government spending and employment. In recent years such a perception has become a greater liability as more Canadians are concerned that 'Big Government' is the greatest threat (23 percent in 1968 and 42 percent in 1987).[37] Certainly, the growth in size and scope of governments in recent decades accentuates this fear. For example, combined government expenditures for all levels amounted to 20.7 percent of Canada's GDP in 1951 but by 1987 had increased to 43.1 percent.[38] It is somewhat ironic that in the decade of the infamous year 1984, 'big brother' rather than 'being my brother's keeper' became the pressing concern of many. The NDP's stress on decentralization is perhaps a recognition of the difficult path ahead towards the cooperative commonwealth and the twenty-first century.

There can be no doubt that the NDP will be confronted with one additional challenge. It will be starting the 1990s without its greatest asset from the 1988 campaign, its leader Ed Broadbent. He was a man who as party spokesperson conveyed a sense of decency and integrity speaking on behalf of ordinary Canadians.[39] In an age where alienation and cynicism seem to thrive, there are too few such voices.

Audrey McLaughlin offers the hope that a female leader may accomplish something that her male CCF-NDP predecessors have been unable to achieve— an electoral break-through at the federal level. Whether she can mobilize sufficiently high levels of support amongst women, residents of Ontario, Quebec and Atlantic Canada and the non-unionized workforce while still retaining traditional levels of support in the West, among males and unionized workers, remains to be seen.

ENDNOTES

1. The Socialist party went from an all-time high of 919 799 votes in 1920 to 6898 votes in 1980. F. Smallwood, *The Other Candidates: Third Parties in Presidential Elections.* (Hanover: University Press of New England, 1983).
2. There have been occasions, however, when the CCF-NDP has also passed this barrier in Gallup polls. The famous CCF example occurred in September 1943 when the CCF polled 29 percent versus 28 percent for the Liberals and 28 percent for the Conservatives. More recently, in July 1987 the NDP polled as high as 41 percent versus 31 percent for the Liberals and 23 percent for the Conservatives. In both cases, the poll results were electrifying to party members and political opponents alike. On each occasion, big business intervened with an unprecedented effort against the socialist hordes. David Lewis's memoirs, *The Good Fight* (Toronto: Macmillan, 1981) documents the earlier campaign.
3. The irony here is that a substantial number of the party activists were recruited from church ranks, for example, J.S. Woodsworth, T.C. Douglas, and Stanley Knowles. See Richard Allen, ed., *The Social Gospel in Canada* (Ottawa: National Museums of Canada, 1975) and Richard Allen, *The Social Passion* (Toronto: University of Toronto Press, 1973). See also G. Baum, *Catholics and Canadian Socialism* (Toronto: Lorimer, 1980).
4. J.M. Beck, *The Pendulum of Power* (Scarborough: Prentice-Hall Canada, 1968) and data from the Chief Electoral Officer. Data on NDP support by ethnicity, class, education and sex can be obtained from H. Clarke, *et al., Political Choice in Canada* (Toronto: McGraw-Hill Ryerson, 1979).
5. S.M. Lipset, *Agrarian Socialism* (Berkeley: University of California, 1968), p. 188.
6. Data derived from R. Gibbins, *Prairie Politics and Society* (Toronto: Butterworths, 1980), p. 115; Chief Electoral Office, various years.
7. Data derived from Beck, *The Pendulum of Power*; A. Cairns, "The Electoral System and the Party System in Canada, 1921–1965," *Canadian Journal of Political Science*, Vol. 1, No.1; H. Penniman, *Canada at the Polls* (Washington, American Enterprise Institute, various years); Chief Electoral Office.
8. Derived from Beck, *The Pendulum of Power*. The League for Social Reconstruction, the CCF's 'brains-trust', was largely an eastern phenomenon. See M. Horn, *The League For Social Reconstruction* (Toronto: University of Toronto Press, 1980).
9. This is a theme so ably demonstrated by Cairns, "The Electoral System and the Party System in Canada."
10. Provincial votes were averaged without weighting for population size.
11. The top three trade unions in 1989 with the largest numbers of affiliated members to the NDP were Canadian Autoworkers (CAW), United Steelworkers of America (USWA) and United Food and Commercial Workers (UFCW).
12. Some care should be taken in the interpretation of the data since members can also belong to the party indirectly through union affiliation. Here, of course, eastern representation is far more significant.
13. P. Fox, *Politics: Canada* (Toronto: McGraw-Hill Ryerson, 1982) pp. 682–84.
14. P. Fox and G. White, *Politics: Canada* (Toronto: McGraw-Hill Ryerson, 1987) pp. 414–15.
15. *Ibid.*, pp. 414–15.
16. Cairns, "The Electoral System and the Party System in Canada."
17. Cairns, *ibid.* and Gibbins, *Party Politics and Society*.

18. Robert Toupin, an elected Conservative, briefly switched over to the NDP in 1987–88, but soon departed from the NDP caucus. In 1990, Phil Edmondston won a seat for the NDP in the federal by-election in Chambly, Quebec. In the period 1962–88, 12.5 percent of the NDP's total federal vote had come from Quebec, yet it had never won a seat in that province in all that time. A similar case could have been made with the province of Alberta until 1988.

19. For more detailed analysis of the 1988 federal election, see A. Frizzell, *et al.*, *The Canadian General Election of 1988* (Ottawa: Carleton University, 1989). The NDP as of 1990 acquired one seat in Quebec due to a by-election victory.

20. In party literature and many of the press accounts, one leader's name is consistently omitted. Hazen Argue, the man who defected to the Liberals and later became a Liberal senator and cabinet minister, has become a virtual non-person as far as the NDP is concerned. While such a partisan view is understandable, analysts should focus more attention on this individual since he is a significant example of co-optation and the calculation that it is more desirable to participate in power immediately rather than waiting for an NDP government. Former Prime Minister Trudeau was another and more prominent example of this phenomenon.

21. For an elucidation on leadership selection at CCF-NDP conventions, see Alan White-horn, "The New Democratic Party in Convention," in George Perlin, ed., *Party Democracy in Canada* (Scarborough: Prentice-Hall Canada, 1988).

22. John Bacher, a young member of the Ontario Left-Caucus, initially chose to run as a leadership candidate. Upon reflection and counsel from colleagues and foes alike, he chose to withdraw his nomination.

23. One is hard-pressed to locate a major urban daily newspaper that supported the NDP in the 1988 federal election. Indeed, the pattern exists for most federal elections.

24. The Chief Electoral Office reports, for example, that in 1988 more persons in Canada donated to the NDP (120 703) than either the Liberals (37 911) or the Conservatives (67 926). Nevertheless, given the mass nature of a party such as the NDP, the total income received was smaller than for the Liberals and Conservatives. The latter two, reflecting their élite and more affluent origins as cadre parties, received larger income from fewer donors. See Report of the Chief Electoral Office, 1989. See Maurice Duverger, *Political Parties* (New York: Wiley, 1963) for an elucidation of the differences between mass and cadre/caucus parties.

25. See M. Cross, *The Decline and Fall of a Good Idea* (Toronto: New Hogtown, 1974); L. Zakuta, *A Protest Movement Becalmed* (Toronto: University of Toronto Press, 1964); W. Young: *The Anatomy of a Party: The National CCF: 1932–61* (Toronto: University of Toronto Press, 1969).

26. For an analysis of the historians' writings on the CCF-NDP, see Alan Whitehorn, "An Analysis of the Historiography of the CCF-NDP: The Protest Movement Becalmed Tradition," in W. Brennan, ed., *Building The Co-operative Commonwealth* (Regina: Canadian Plains Research Centre, 1985).

27. It should be kept in mind that, as in the case of MPs, convention delegates need not be fully representative of the general party membership.

28. For an elucidation of this theme, see R. Hackett, "The Waffle Conflict in the NDP," in H. Thorburn, ed., *Party Politics in Canada*, 4th ed.; R. Hackett, "Pie in the Sky: A History of the Ontario Waffle," *Canadian Dimension*, (Oct.-Nov., 1980), special edition; John Bullen, "The Ontario Waffle and the Struggle for an Independent Socialist Canada: Conflict Within the NDP," *Canadian Historical Review*, No. 2 (1983); J. Brodie, "From Waffles to Grits: A Decade in the Life of the NDP," in H. Thorburn, ed., *Party*

Politics in Canada, 5th ed. Data from Hackett and Brodie are derived from 1971 and 1979 surveys of NDP convention delegates conducted by George Perlin and his associates. Analysis from my own 1983 survey of NDP delegates reveals a break-down very similar to that found by Perlin and associates. The 1983 distribution is as follows: Marxist 3.0 percent, socialist 29.6 percent, social democrat 44.6 percent, ecologist 1.3 percent, social gospel 3.5 percent, populist 1.0 percent, reformer 4.3 percent, liberal 1.5 percent. Other categories and multiple responses account for the remainder of the replies. Some caution should be taken in the interpretation of the data. For many in the NDP the terms socialist and social democrat are interchangeable. See, for example, David Lewis, *The Good Fight*, p. 301.

29. See Keith Archer and Alan Whitehorn, "Opinion Structure Among Party Activists: A Comparison of New Democrats, Liberals and Conservatives," in Hugh Thorburn, ed., *Party Politics in Canada*, 6th ed.

30. *Ibid.*

31. Environics poll, *The Globe and Mail*, 15 October 1988.

32. L. Erickson, "CCF-NDP Popularity and the Economy," *Canadian Journal of Political Science*, Vol. XXI, No. 1 (March 1988).

33. K. Archer, "Canadian Unions, the New Democratic Party, and the Problem of Collective Action," *Labour/Le Travail*, No. 20 (1987). It should be noted that numbers of members affiliated have continued to increase but at a slower rate than that of unionization.

34. CIPO, *Toronto Star*, 16 August 1978 cited in F. Fletcher and R. Drummond, *Canadian Attitude Trends 1960–1978* (Montreal: Institute for Research on Public Policy, 1979) and Gallup Report, 16 February 1987. An August 1990 Gallup poll suggests the greater fear of labour may be diminishing. *Toronto Star*, 10 September, 1990.

35. N. Chi and G. Perlin, "The New Democratic Party in Transition," in H. Thorburn, ed., *Party Politics in Canada*, 4th ed.

36. Gallup Report, 5 December 1988. The coexistence of such public opinion data and radical critiques of the party, which suggest that a more left-wing orientation by the NDP would be a solution to the NDP's lack of electoral break-through, is puzzling. Ideological criticism of the NDP for allegedly being insufficiently socialist seems a plausible argument but to suggest also that a lack of socialist commitment would be a reason for the NDP's insufficient electoral success in Canada seems a far less viable assertion.

37. CIPO, *Toronto Star*, and Gallup Report, 16 February 1987.

38. I. Bakker, "The Size and Scope of Government: Robin Hood Sent Packing?," in M. Whittington and G. Williams, eds., *Canadian Politics in the 1990s*, 3rd ed. (Scarborough: Nelson Canada, 1990), p. 431.

39. Note, for example, the editorial in the *Toronto Star*, 6 March 1989.

25 The Reform Party of Canada: New Beginning or Dead End?

PETER McCORMICK

Through the 1970s and early 1980s, the Canadian political map seemed clearly drawn: Liberal dominance in the centre, Conservative strength in an aggressively alienated West, and a political stand-off in the Maritimes, with the New Democratic party showing persistent but limited strength everywhere west of the Ottawa River. As the Liberals gradually succumbed to the political antitoxins of 20 years in power, a reinvigorated Conservative party with a new leader from Quebec led a powerful sweep of English-speaking Canada, and did so with astonishing penetration into the Liberal fortress of Quebec that had resisted Conservative appeals for a generation. It is too early to tell whether this is a short-term aberration or a permanent turn-around, especially when the free trade issue undercut support in Ontario, and Prime Minister Brian Mulroney seemed to be attempting a 1990s replay of Mackenzie King's formula of building protracted national dominance on the twin pillars of Quebec and the West.

In the centre of these scenarios has been true-blue Alberta, Conservative since 1958, whether its phalanx of MPs sat in government or (more frequently) in opposition. With a strong trio of powerful cabinet ministers (Mazankowski, Clark, Andre), Alberta seemed assured of a prominent place in the Tory party's rosy future. But, by the end of the 1980s, the emergence of the Reform party of Canada (RPC) confused the situation. Buoyed by a strong showing in the 1988 federal election, a by-election victory and a solid win in Alberta's 1989 senatorial "election," it topped the province in 1990 public opinion polls and spilled over into British Columbia, Manitoba and Saskatchewan. Its sudden strength placed large question marks over future federal elections within (at least) Alberta, suggesting a new and more complex political dynamic.

In retrospect, the worm at the core of the Tory apple is obvious. The West, particularly Alberta, felt estranged from and maltreated by the Trudeau Liberal government, and saw the Conservatives as both the spokesman for its discontent and the weapon for its future vindication. The departure of Trudeau, and the

---

This is an original essay written especially for this volume.

1984 landslide Conservative victory, seemed to be the realization of both of these hopes, but the electoral logic quickly became clear: the official opposition in a parliamentary system is the logical focus for those interests that feel themselves neglected by government, but the opposition can displace the government only by broadening its appeal and, in the process, may replicate the very policy priorities and biases of the government it replaced. The resulting frustration in the West, summarized in the "Pierre Elliott Mulroney" stickers, created the opportunity for a movement of protest against both the major national parties, yet one that could not (especially in Alberta) be seized by the NDP. The Reform party can be understood as an attempt, at least temporarily blessed with success, to capitalize on this discontent.

This sudden transformation of western Canadian politics raises obvious questions. What is the Reform party? Where did it come from? Who and what started it? What issues was it created to address and from what segments of the public does it draw its support? What are its prospects for long-term survival? How much damage will it do and to which political parties in the process? With all the obvious reservations appropriate to discussing a recent and possibly temporary political phenomenon, answers can be sketched out for all these questions.

The Emergence of the Reform Party

The Reform party first appeared in the spring of 1987 in the form of the Western Reform Association, jointly founded by Edmonton consultant Preston Manning (son of Ernest Manning, Alberta Social Credit premier, 1942–68), Calgary lawyer John Muir and Vancouver investment counsellor Stan Roberts (onetime Manitoba Liberal MLA, former president of the Canadian Chamber of Commerce and the Canada West Foundation). The catalyst was the CF-18 decision that assigned Canada's major aerospace contract to Quebec despite a cheaper and technically superior bid from a Manitoba-based group. The Conservative government notwithstanding, the West was clearly low on Ottawa's priorities. Also, the bilingualism issue had exploded in the Manitoba legislature[1] and exacerbated feelings across the West.

Under the slogan "The West Wants In!" the association took out large ads in the western Canadian media, announcing its sponsorship of a western assembly on Canada's economic and political future in Vancouver in May, and inviting interested persons to apply for delegate status. The concerns it enunciated were based on criticism of a national government that was fiscally irresponsible, preoccupied with issues such as bilingualism and, by turns, indifferent or hostile to western Canadian interests. The message was explicitly nonpartisan: western MPs and MLAs from all parties were invited to attend, and the assembly would decide whether these concerns would be best pursued through existing parties or through a new party. Three hundred delegates, mostly from Alberta, were selected to attend the assembly, and after several days of workshops and speeches, they voted 76 percent in favour of forming a new political party. The party's first assembly was held in Winnipeg in November, with 306 delegates in attendance (140 from Alberta, 91 from British Columbia, 65 from Manitoba and 10 from Saskatchewan). Preston Manning was acclaimed leader after fellow vice-president Stan Roberts withdrew from the race, alleging irregularities in the delegate registration process.

The resolutions adopted at the convention set the tone for the party. Delegates endorsed the principle of the Triple E Senate, favoured restrictions on the extension of federal bilingualism policies[2] and firmly opposed Meech Lake both for giving special status to Quebec and for creating a roadblock to Senate reform. They voted in favour of entrenching property rights and endorsed the principle of free enterprise. They also favoured a number of direct democracy measures (such as recall petitions for sitting representatives, referenda in conjunction with general elections and looser party discipline) that would make MPs more accountable and responsive to the concerns of their constituents.

The Reform Party: Structure and Organization

According to the party constitution, the highest authority is the party assembly, made up of voting delegates meeting annually. Delegates include candidates from the previous election and are all drawn from the constituency organizations, the numbers varying according to that constituency's number of party members; there are no *ex officio* delegates. Each assembly votes on whether or not to hold a leadership assembly. Workshops discuss policy options, and plenary sessions choose between policy alternatives with the decisions binding the party leadership.

The assembly elects 11 members to an executive council that, together with the party leader, party chair and vice-chair, is responsible in consultation with the constituency organizations for carrying out the policy and organizational directives of the assembly. There is also a chief financial officer appointed by the executive council who is responsible for the party's financial affairs. In practice, the council has tended to be a cohesive group fully supportive of Preston Manning, although there have been a number of floor fights. The leader has authority to overrule a constituency association on the choice of a candidate, a power used in 1989 to reject a British Columbian candidate strongly opposed to federal immigration policy.

In March 1990, the executive council had two elected members each from Manitoba and Saskatchewan, three each from Alberta and British Columbia, and one seat vacant. About half the council members elected at the initial convention in 1987 were replaced at or before the 1989 assembly. Also as of March 1990, the total party membership stood at 30 000 members, 60 percent in Alberta and 30 percent in British Columbia; these figures do not include memberships generated by Manning's spring tours in Ontario and the Maritimes.

The Reform Party and the Voters, 1988 and 1989

The Reform party fielded 72 candidates in the four western provinces in the 1988 federal election and received 275 000 votes; these results are summarized in Table 1. Most candidates placed well out of the running, averaging one twelfth of the riding vote and less than one fifth of the winner's votes. Four (all in Alberta) received more than 25 percent of the riding vote, five (all in Alberta) received more than half the votes of the winner and nine (again, all in Alberta) placed second. Ridings with the strongest showings were scattered all over the province. Support was strongest in the rural areas of the centre and south (average over 18 percent), and lowest in Edmonton (average 10 percent). We can identify a double gradient: Reform party support rises as one moves from north to south, and falls as one moves from country to city.

The results fell far short of the half dozen seats that optimists had dreamed of during the campaign but, for a first campaign, it was a respectable showing. In Alberta, where support was clearly the strongest, the Reform party won over 15 percent of the popular vote, compared with 17 percent for the New Democratic party. In British Columbia, support was much lower, but Reform party candidates played the spoiler in three ridings, receiving more votes than the margin of defeat for the unsuccessful Conservative candidate. In Saskatchewan and Manitoba, Reform party support was negligible.

A footnote to the general election provided more substantive success. The death of the newly elected Conservative MP for Beaver River necessitated a federal by-election in March of 1989. Reform party leader Preston Manning declined to run, allowing Deborah Gray, the candidate in the general election, to run again. She tripled her November vote to double the Conservatives' and win the seat. The turnaround was all the more dramatic in that she had placed fourth in the general election, and the riding included the highest concentration of francophone voters in the province, making it a hard sell for a party unapologetically hostile to federal bilingualism policy. Although by-election support does not easily extrapolate into future general elections, Beaver River added a practical victory to the moral victory of the general election, and gave the party a presence in Ottawa. It also provided a solution to the pressing problem of all marginal political parties—that of maintaining public visibility between elections.

The Reform party's third election opportunity was a Canadian first when Alberta held an election on 16 October 1989 to choose a Senate nominee; the vote was held in conjunction with province-wide municipal elections. In the Meech Lake Accord, it was agreed that future Senate appointments would be made from a list of provincial nominees and that this process was to begin immediately, even before the accord was ratified. After the 1989 provincial election, the Getty government passed legislation for the "election" of a Senate nominee. The Conservatives nominated Bert Brown, a Kathyrn area farmer and founder of the Canadian Committee for a Triple-E Senate. The Liberals ran Calgary lawyer, Bill Code, who had conducted a lengthy high-profile public investigation into the

TABLE 1 **Support for Reform Party Candidates, by Province**
1988 Federal General Election

	Candidates	Average Votes	Average Vote (%)	Average Margin (%)
Alberta	26	6879	15.5	−35.7
B.C.	30	2510	5.1	−37.1
Manitoba	12	1480	3.9	−42.1
Saskatchewan	4	964	2.9	−44.6
All	72	3830	8.6	−37.9

Note: "average margin" = RPC vote − winner's vote

collapse of the Edmonton-based financial services company, the Principal Group. The Reform party chose retired General Stan Waters. Two independents, one a former MP, ran as well, while the NDP chose not to take part.

The Senate campaign focused on a unique mix of personal, provincial and federal issues (including Getty's 30 percent pay increase for MLAs and the proposed federal Goods and Services Tax) as much as on abstract questions of institutional reform. The Senate election started slowly but gradually built up steam and attracted public interest. On voting day over 620 000 electors voted for a Senate nominee. The turnout was estimated at slightly over 40 percent.[3] Waters was the winner by a decisive margin, with more than a quarter of a million votes (41.5 percent); runner-up Bill Code trailed badly and Brown placed a strong but surprising third. To underline the decisive nature of the win, Waters placed first in every urban centre in the province except Medicine Hat; Liberal Code ran second in the cities and Tory Brown placed second in the rural centres.

The focus of the 1988 general election on free trade hurt the Reformers by rallying wavering Conservatives who might otherwise have wished to send the government a message; that is, it probably understated public support in the West for the RPC. In contrast, issues since the election have been precisely those that divided many western Conservatives from their own national party, and that is precisely what the RPC is well-placed to exploit. Political events between 1988 and 1990 clearly played into their hands: a respectable but modest showing in the general election became a springboard for a quick by-election victory and success in the Senate nominee election added another national spokesperson. His profile was enhanced rather than reduced by the prime minister's reluctance to appoint him, which only embarrassed Premier Getty in his unwavering support for the unpopular Meech Lake Accord and placed a ticking bomb of unknown power beneath federal Conservative support in the province.

Who Supports the Reformers?

The regional base of the Reform party's support is in Alberta. Half of the party's members, half of the party's delegates at all the assemblies and two thirds of the votes the party received in the federal general election came from that province. British Columbia is a poor second on all these measures, Manitoba a distant third and Saskatchewan's presence is purely nominal.

The Reform party conducted its own survey of 5000 of its members and reported on the findings to the participants in the 1989 assembly.[4] The largest single category was "retired"—accounting for 38.4 percent of the respondents; concomitantly, 47.9 percent of respondants were aged 60 or over. Another 41.3 percent were clearly middle class (small business 16.7 percent, professional 15.75 percent and management 8.9 percent); 9.5 percent were homemakers and only 4.7 percent identified themselves as involved in labour or trade. Striking by its absence is the agricultural sector; on this profile, the party emerges as solidly urban middle class and not a rural phenomenon at all.[5] Three quarters of the members were born in western Canada; of those born elsewhere, most (15.3 percent) were born outside of Canada.

In response to the question as to which political party "generally received your support" before the Reform party, almost three quarters (73.4 percent) of the party members identified themselves as former supporters of the Progressive Conservative party, and another fifth (21.9 percent) as former Socreds. A survey of the delegates to the 1989 assembly[6] revealed a similar pattern for former partisans, but also found that one third of delegates said they had not previously supported any party. This suggests that the Reform party is not only converting members of other parties (mainly Conservatives) but also reaching out into groups not previously politically mobilized. Given that turnouts in Alberta, in particular, have been very low, especially in provincial elections where they hover around 50 percent, the suggestion of a capacity to mobilize the previously inactive could be very significant.

A survey of 1989 assembly delegates[7] also examined their ideological self-perception (on a 7-point scale, 1 representing extreme left and 7 extreme right), compared with their perceptions of the provincial and federal electorate, and of provincial and federal parties. These results are shown in Table 2 on page 348.

The delegates saw themselves as somewhat right of centre,[8] with the Canadian electorate as a whole at or near the centre and their own provincial electorate somewhere in between. Among the federal parties, the Conservative party was seen to be near the centre, with Liberals and especially New Democrats significantly left. The Reform party is seen as articulating a point of view on public issues to which delegates adhere and which they believe attracts some sympathy from their neighbours, but one that finds little expression among the major parties. The Conservatives come closest, but even they are seen as left of the Canadian electorate and of western provincial electorates. This same table shows the lure of provincial politics in Alberta, but in no other province. Elsewhere, Conservatives or Social Credit are close to the self-perception of RPC delegates; Alberta is the province where the perceived gap is the largest and where the provincial Conservatives are seen as the least right of centre.

TABLE 2 **Ideological Self-Perception of Reform Party Delegates**

Ideology of		*Province*			
(Respondants)	*Alberta*	*B.C.*	*Manitoba*	*Saskatchewan*	*All*
	303	111	30	17	461
Self-Perception	5.101	5.094	4.793	5.143	5.083
Provincial Electorate	4.614	4.123	3.760	3.643	4.409
Canadian Electorate	3.629	3.933	3.962	3.933	3.739
Fed. PC Party	3.440	3.632	3.778	4.571	3.546
Fed. NDP Party	1.768	2.058	1.786	1.800	1.850
Fed. Liberal Party	2.571	2.771	2.500	2.867	2.629
Fed. Reform Party	5.120	5.028	4.966	5.286	5.089
Prov. PC Party	4.208	—	4.480	4.714	4.264
Prov. Liberal Party	3.240	—	3.357	3.600	3.253
Prov. NDP Party	1.851	2.344	2.000	1.867	1.967
Prov. Social Credit	—	5.089	—	—	—

The Reformers: What Lies Ahead?

The first question about the Reform party is whether they will continue to avoid the oblivion that is the normal fate of minor parties. So far, the leader's shrewdness and fortuitous access to the national stage on behalf of Grey and Waters have carried the party through the first half of the inter-election doldrums. If there is no break-through in the next federal election, the chance will clearly have passed, and the RPC will have proven to be yet another dead end. Even in "tomorrow country," there comes a time when people must see results.

As a minor party, the Reformers cannot create their own opportunities, but must rely on others to provide openings that they can exploit. The focus of national politics in the 1990s is very much to their liking. The issue of the Goods and Services Tax focuses on the contrast between the down-to-earth common sense of the average citizen and the perceived financial irresponsibility of Ottawa; it allows the Reformers to identify themselves as the most credible proponents of real change. Bilingualism issues (Quebec sign laws and Meech Lake) remind western Canadians of how unresponsive the major national parties are to their concerns and priorities. The issue of federal multicultural initiatives (Sikh turbans in the RCMP) triggers the assimilationist values of a culturally homogeneous West, which has been more of a melting pot than a mosaic. Only an issue of a different sort (such as free trade in 1988, which rallied the West behind a national initiative) would take the wind out of the Reformer sails.

The other question is the lure of provincial politics, particularly in Alberta where the Getty government has proven to be a surprisingly lacklustre sequel to Lougheed's comfortable dominance. Recent polls suggest a provincial Reform wing would have a serious prospect of nudging past both opposition parties to win a provincial election. As Reformers are aware, polls asking hypothetical questions must be taken with a grain of salt and a lot can happen between now and 1992, but the chance is real.

Several factors, however, hold them back. The first is a reluctance to be distracted from their primary purpose of gaining the federal balance of power to change national politics—a brief window of opportunity that may not come again. The second is a fear of being "suckered," of being drawn into provincial politics only to have the Tories choose an aggressive new leader to pop the Reform bubble once and for all. The third is the fact that many Reform supporters are provincial Tories disillusioned with Mulroney; they would face a difficult choice if the Reformers went provincial, and it is not likely that all would desert the Conservatives. The fourth is the problem of resources: of finding the credible candidates, campaign workers and money that would be necessary for a provincial election and, most critically, of finding an effective provincial leader.

The ambivalence of the Reform party is reflected in the voting at a 1989 Assembly Plenary Session, which defeated a resolution calling for the formation of provincial parties, and then defeated the obverse proposition that the RPC remain exclusively a federal political party.[9] Without question, the Reformers will hedge their bets a while longer. The temptation will increase if Getty still leads the Conservatives as the next provincial election approaches. He is not an effective campaigner: he has a knack for saying the wrong thing at the wrong time and for misreading the public mood so badly that his promises (often echoes of successful Lougheed ploys) become new electoral liabilities. The Reformers may feel that if they do not seize the advantage, someone else will.

Conclusion

Gagnon and Tanguay identify the classic structural elements necessary for the emergence of a minor party of protest. These are: the "non-representation of significant social groups in the traditional party system, a sharp reversal of economic fortunes combined with the systematic blocking of the economic ambitions of important social strata ... and the existence of strong social ties among the disaffected groups" with the added proviso that the success of such parties depends "in no small measure on the quality of their leadership and the attractiveness of their candidates."[10] The Reform party is a textbook example. The non-responsiveness of the major parties was demonstrated by the hated National Energy Policy, and less dramatically but just as importantly by a wide range of federal programmes and policies that favour centre over region[11]; it is persistently reflected as well in policies such as bilingualism that strike few chords in the daily realities of western Canadians ("if Alberta had a second language, it would be Ukrainian"), and therefore become symbolic lightning rods of the gap between region and centre. Resentment is fed by memories of the 1970s resource boom, its demise accelerated (some would still say caused) by short-sighted national policies that in some western minds were either malicious or criminally defective. When 1984 merely substituted Tweedle-Tory for Tweedle-Grit, the crop of resentment was ripe for the harvest, and bespectacled Preston Manning, his droll sincerity the antithesis of charisma and his name a reassurance to Albertans with a political memory, filled the role better than the overtly separatist radicals (Western Canada Concept, Confederation of Regions, Western Independence party) who had tried to work the field before him.

If structural elements provide the opportunity, the ideological content is populism.[12] This is the tradition with which the new movement identifies itself, and the label is clearly appropriate. Populism, as much a mood as a systematic philosophy, responds to the following factors: a common-sense celebration of the average citizen, a preference for the devices of direct democracy (recall, referendum, initiative) to allow direct and ongoing influence by the electors, an identification with small-scale business capitalism, a tendency to blame outside forces (sometimes sinister in nature) for economic and social problems and to see solutions in simple (even simplistic) terms, a strong feeling of community and traditional values that borders on nativism and xenophobia[13] and a project of reform rather than revolution to solve economic and social ills. Although movements built on these sentiments tend to be regional in their origin, they are not necessarily narrowly regional in their appeal, and Manning's trips to central Canada and the Maritimes in the spring of 1990 appear less quixotic in the light of history. For example, one of the three provinces whose governments succumbed to the onslaught of the Progressives—who represented the first major wave of Canadian populism—was Ontario, briefly governed by the United Farmers of Ontario (UFO).[14]

The comparison, however, makes a critical point: the invocation of populism is essentially accurate but carries wishful overtones. The modern replay lacks the angry spontaneity and explosive success of the Progressives in the 1920s, who within a span of five years toppled three provincial governments and briefly displaced the Conservatives as the second largest party in the Commons. The current vituperation against federal bureaucrats and their left-leaning policy advisors is a weak reflection of the passionate hatred for the eastern banks and the sinister financial interests (the "Fifty Big Shots"), just as the GST is a poor substitute for the Depression that generated the second wave of populism in the form of Social Credit and the CCF. As well, urbanization has decimated the agrarian social base exploited so successfully by the earlier varieties of populism. None of this proves that populist Reformism cannot flourish as the Progressives, CCF and Social Credit did before, but it indicates some of the obstacles.

The Reform party dream scenario runs as follows: with a new leader, the Liberals would split central Canada and the Maritimes with the Tories, while the NDP would make at most minor gains in Ontario and the West. Reform party candidates could then sweep Alberta, penetrate British Columbia and pick up a few seats in Manitoba and Saskatchewan to hold a decisive balance of power. Clearly, many things have to break just right for the RPC to do this well. In the horror scenario, the Reformers do little more than serve as spoilers—drawing enough votes from Conservatives to elect Liberals or New Democrats—in a broad swatch of ridings in western Canada; clearly, much would have to go very wrong for the RPC to achieve this little. Its direct electoral impact is likely to be on the two major national parties, drawing votes from the Conservatives in such a way as to prevent the Liberals from benefiting from the swing. Its impact on the New Democrats is likely to be small, and what effect there is will be through the vagaries of the single-member riding.

Politically, national politics has been raining on the West for a long time (or at least Westerners think it has and, in politics, perceptions are reality). The limited successes of the Reform party are rivulets appearing on the dry stream bed. It is clearly premature to decide either that a flash flood is on the way, or that there is no more water coming. The real question, of course, is how long it is going to keep on raining.

ENDNOTES

1. See Russell Doern, *The Battle over Bilingualism: The Manitoba Language Question 1983–85* (Winnipeg: Cambridge Publishers, 1985).
2. There is widespread sentiment in western Canada, which the RPC reflects but did not create, that one can oppose bilingualism without being "against" Quebec. The logic is as follows: bilingualism is a device of national élites (governmental, bureaucratic and media) imposed upon the rest of the country regardless of popular opposition. Quebec's domestic policies, whatever party is in power, resist bilingualism and pro-mote unilingualism, and Quebec's principled support of provincial autonomy creates alliances between Quebec and provinces such as Alberta or Saskatchewan. To reject bilingualism is to reject Ottawa's obsession, but does not preclude reaching past Ottawa to the sentiments and interests of Quebec.
3. Only estimates were possible, because municipal elections in Alberta do not include an enumerated voters' list.
4. Reform Party of Canada, "Summary of Assembly Results" (Memorandum to Mem-bers), 15 December 1989.
5. A survey of delegates to the 1989 convention indicated that 23.1 percent were retired, 47.3 percent middle class, 11.9 percent clerical/sales, 8.5 percent were farmers, and 5.1 percent were homemakers.
6. See Endnote 5.
7. Survey of the delegates to the 1989 Assembly of the Reform Party of Canada, 27–29 October 1989: done by Faron Ellis of the Lethbridge Community College and David Robb of the University of Lethbridge. Analysis is based upon a response rate of 76.5 percent. I am indebted to Ellis and Robb for letting me use some of their results; I expect that a fuller report of their findings will soon be published.
8. The "somewhat" conflicts with some popular impressions of the party as composed of extreme rightist welfare slashers; however, it is consistent with, for example, the Reform criticism of big government and big government spending, which is targeted not on social programmes (only 25 percent thought such services should be cut) but on "top echelons of government" (82 percent), bilingualism (63 percent) and multi-cultural programmes (45 percent). (Figures taken from: Reform Party of Canada: Letter to members on results of questionnaire; 27 October 1989.)
9. Reform Party of Canada, "Summary of Assembly Results."

10. Gagnon and Tanguay, "Minor Parties of Protest in Canada: Origins, Impact and Prospects," in Gagnon and Tanguay, eds., *Canadian Parties in Transition: Discourse, Organization, Representation* (Scarborough: Nelson Canada, 1989), p. 240.

11. The ongoing term for this sentiment is, of course, western alienation. See David Elton and Roger Gibbins, "Western Alienation and Political Culture," in Schultz, Kruhlak and Terry, eds., *The Canadian Political Process*, 3rd ed. (Toronto: Holt, Rinehart and Winston, 1979); and Larry Pratt and Garth Stevenson, eds., *Western Separatism: The Myths, Realities and Dangers* (Edmonton: Hurtig Publishers, 1981).

12. For populism in general, including an attempted typology, see Margaret Canovan, *Populism* (London: Junction Books, 1981) and J.F. Conway, "Populism in the United States, Russia and Canada: Explaining the Roots of Canada's Third Parties," *Canadian Journal of Political Science*, Vol. XI (1978); for a more focused account of Canadian populism, see David Laycock, *Populism and Democratic Thought in the Canadian Prairies, 1910 to 1945* (Toronto, Buffalo and London: University of Toronto Press, 1990).

13. But logically must be differentiated from racism; rather, if we needed a new label, it would be "assimilationalism," less aggressive than racism (in that if "they" stay over "there" there is no problem) and less vicious (if "they" come here, "they" should be willing to become like "us.") In this sense, the RCMP Sikh turban issue perfectly catches the mood, but only as a complete vignette in itself and not as the first step towards something more grim and dangerous.

14. See W.L. Morton, *The Progressive Party in Canada* (Toronto: University of Toronto Press, 1967), and "The Progressive Tradition in Canadian Politics," in this volume.

26 The Communist Party of Canada

ALAN WHITEHORN

Introduction

Maurice Duverger in his pioneering work *Political Parties* set out a classification system of modern parties. He postulated two generic types of parties: the older, élite-based cadre party versus the newer and larger mass party. While Duverger suggested only one analytical example (the caucus) of the cadre party, he listed three examples of the mass party. These three organizational sub-types were the socialist branch, the communist cell and the fascist militia.

During the nineteenth century cadre parties predominated. In Canada, the Liberals and Conservatives were examples of cadre parties controlled by the powerful and wealthy few. Leadership selection was made from within the parliamentary caucus. In the twentieth century, however, as the franchise was extended, mass parties became more prevalent. Accordingly, the Liberal and Conservative parties altered somewhat and acquired selected features of the newer mass party (e.g., leadership election by means of the larger and more representative political convention). In so doing, the Liberals and Conservatives moved more closely to the branch type of mass party. The social democratic CCF-NDP, born first in 1932 and rechristened in 1961, had its origins as a mass branch party. Thus, by the 1990s all three major Canadian parties can be labelled, to varying degrees, as examples of the branch party.

There is another party, even older than the CCF-NDP, that exhibits the features of a mass party. It is, however, an example of a second sub-type—that of the cell structure. The Communist Party of Canada (CPC), like its counterparts throughout the world, is a mass party but of a different type. A case study of the CPC may be useful for the following reasons:

(1) The CPC is a party with a long historical record that predates the social democratic CCF-NDP. One of the explanations for the emergence of the CCF-NDP has been the failure of the Canadian communist movement to

---

This is an original essay written especially for this volume.

build on earlier gains.[1] Accordingly, the organizational history of the CPC is important in contributing to our understanding of the emergence of the modern Canadian party system and the rise of the CCF-NDP.

(2) The CPC has had an influence that is disproportional to its electoral strength and membership size. This is particularly so in the labour and peace movements.

(3) An account of the CPC also offers a stark reminder of the extent the Canadian state has pursued illiberal acts in Canadian political history. It is a history often ignored in school civic texts.[2]

(4) In an age and society often preoccupied with electoral politics, it is sometimes useful to include in our analysis comparisons with parties that operate on different assumptions. Many parties in the world have revolutionary goals. A study of the CPC may offer insights into such parties.

(5) Much of the world has been and, to varying degrees, continues to be ruled by communist parties based on the cell structure. Throughout its history, the CPC shared the aspirations of those parties and their Leninist organizational principles.[3]

Organization

Historically, the CPC has been organized along the lines drawn in Lenin's 1902 book *What Is To Be Done?*[4] Lenin believed that given the revolutionary goals of a communist party operating in a bourgeois society, it was necessary to structure such a party so as to be capable of effective clandestine activities and resist penetration by hostile police security forces. Accordingly, he favoured small units or cells based in the workplace or schools rather than larger units organized on territorial ridings. The smaller cell structure would minimize the number of party members at risk by police agents who might infiltrate. It would also make meetings easier to hold and occur more frequently. Given that the members often saw one another in the workplace, the bonds between members were likely to be stronger.[5] It also made monitoring the performance of individual party members by their communist colleagues easier.

From their birth until the late 1980s the operating organizational code for all communist parties has been democratic centralism and involved four component parts: (1) election of all leading party posts; (2) periodic accountablity of all leadership positions; (3) decisions of the majority binding on all members; (4) decision of higher party levels binding on all lower levels. Needless to say, the latter two centralizing features have proved to be the more significant and the overall effect has been the creation of a hierarchical and disciplined party capable of swift action and responsive to the commands of senior party leaders.

With the creation of the Communist International (Comintern) in 1919, another 21 further conditions were added for all communist parties. Among the traits required of any communist party being created or restructed in 1921 were the following:

(1) regarding social democratic parties:

There was to be "a complete and absolute rupture" with social democratic parties and their unions and a call to "systematically and mercilessly denounce . . . reformists of every shade." In addition, communists were urged to "carry on stubborn struggle against . . . yellow trade unions" and exhorted to "steadily and systematically remove [reformists] from all responsible posts in the labour movement. . . . "

(2) regarding the newly formed communist party:

Communists were told that, in addition to a more public version of the party, they "must everywhere create a parallel illegal apparatus." The communist party was to be "built on the principle of democratic centralism . . . organized in the most centralized manner, . . . [involving] iron discipline, bordering on military discipline, and . . . the party center [was to be] . . . a powerful, authoritative organ with wide powers,. . . . " In addition, the party was to employ "persistent, systematic propaganda" and instructed to "eliminate all unreliable elements." It was recognized that there would of necessity be "periodic cleanings (re-registration) of the members of the party organizations, so as to systematically cleanse the party from the petty bougeois elements. . . . "

Regarding mass and front organizations (e.g. trade unions), these were to be won over to "the cause of communism" and then, "These communist groups should be completely subordinate to the party as a whole." Newly admitted parties were instructed that they "must in the shortest possible time overhaul . . . [their] programs and draw up a new communist program in conformity with" and "ratified by" the Communist International.

(3) regarding membership in the Communist International:

"All decisions of the congresses of the Communist International, as well as the decisions of its Executive Committee, [were] . . . binding on all parties affiliated. . . . " The list of conditions concluded with the assertion that "The Communist International has declared a decisive war against the entire bourgeois world and all the yellow, social democratic parties . . . " and that "Members of the party who reject the conditions and theses of the Communist International, on principle, must be expelled . . . ".[6]

Throughout the world, these 21 conditions became the litmus test of Marxist-Leninist orthodoxy for admission of the newly formed communist parties. The result was, not surprisingly, centralized and bureaucratic control.[7] Any remaining dissent was crushed. Penner has suggested that the various communist parties around the world became subordinate regional units of a "world party".[8] While Lenin designed the system, it remained for Stalin to consolidate it over the next three decades.

While the Comintern ceased to exist in 1943, the CPC still retains many of the above features. Most significantly, at the outset of the 1990s it continues to adhere to democratic centralism and a Moscow-directed policy orientation.

Following Leninist outlines, the CPC operates in both the electoral and non-electoral areas. In many respects, the CPC's performance in the latter realm is more significant and offers a greater contrast to Canada's major parties. The CPC sees itself as a more conscious revolutionary vanguard and thus endeavours to work within a number of larger, often front, organizations to increase the party's impact and membership ranks. Historically, a number of areas have been targeted in communist strategy. Most important are the labour movement, peace movement, youth groups and selected ethnic communities. A great deal of activity and attention by the CPC is devoted to trade unions. The CPC, predating the CCF-NDP and able to tap the initial enthusiasm among many workers for the Russian Revolution, had a head start in the labour movement. The CPC certainly played a significant role in the early attempts to organize (e.g., the "On to Ottawa Trek" of the unemployed) and unionize workers in Canada. This was particularly the case in the efforts to organize the less skilled workers in the mass industrial unions of the Congress of Industrial Organization (CIO).[9] In contrast, the CPC had less success among the more traditional and conservative-oriented craft unions of the American Federation of Labour (AFL). Over the years, however, CPC influence and control of many key unions has waned. The reasons have included internal mistakes by the CPC in tactics and strategy and external reasons such as government (both federal and provincial) harassment, pressures and expulsions from American and Canadian labour federations and actions of international (i.e., American) union headquarters and, lastly, competition from the more successful social democratic CCF-NDP. Today, relatively few Canadian unions show significant communist influence.

In addition to the labour movement, the CPC has been active in the peace movement.[10] Through its main voice, the Canadian Peace Congress (founded in 1949), it participates in a number of peace alliances, hoping to redirect their orientation and recruit potential new members. It has been noted by a number of authors that the CPC has also been strong among several ethnic minorities.[11] Assisting in the recruitment and retention of members from such ethnic communities are organizations such as the Association of United Ukrainian Canadians.

In addition to the use of front organizations, the CPC endeavours to "propagandize" among the public at large. As a vanguard party that strives to be a catalyst for the less revolutionary and not so militant working class, the CPC places great emphasis upon the use of pamphlets and party newspapers as a means to educate and socialize potential recruits into the party.[12] Somewhat paradoxically, the much smaller CPC continues to publish more newspapers than the larger and more affluent social democratic CCF-NDP. Indeed, the CPC continues to publish a weekly newspaper (*The Canadian Tribune*), something that none of the larger Canadian parties does.

History

The first quarter of the twentieth century saw political turmoil both abroad and at home. The Russian Revolution of October 1917 and the Winnipeg General Strike of 1919[13] generated considerable apprehension among the propertied and business classes. The Canadian state reacted to this upsurge of discontent from the working classes with a series of draconian measures. Section 98 of the Criminal Code banned any associations which sought to change Canadian society by "force" or "threats" of force.[14] Section 98,coupled with various immigration department decrees, enabled the deportations from Canada of thousands of political dissenters over succeeding years.[15] Nevertheless, amidst these circumstances new organizations representing the toiling classes were created. The Progressives emerged among the farmers, while the workers organized to form a number of labour parties of varying political stripes. One of the revolutionary groups to emerge was the Communist Party of Canada. The CPC was founded in 1921 in a barn in Guelph, Ontario, as an underground party in accordance with Lenin's and the Comintern's guidelines.[16] A total of 22 attended the party's founding meeting. Despite efforts at secrecy, the party was penetrated almost immediately by at least one undercover police agent, Sargeant Leopold, a.k.a. Jack Esselweir.[17] A short while later, in 1922, a more public version of the party appeared under the less revolutionary sounding label of the Workers' Party of Canada. It was not until 1924 that the secret underground vanguard wing merged with the open version of the party under the name of the Communist Party of Canada (CPC).

Throughout the 1920s the CPC experienced political harassment, threats and actual deportations of its members by the Canadian state. The size of the party ranged from 2000 to 5000 members. During this Stalinist phase, relatively little attention was paid by the CPC to parliamentary politics. As late as the federal election of 1930, the CPC ran only eight candidates and garnered a mere 7034 votes.[18] Despite the small size and electoral strength of the CPC, the Conservative government of R.B. Bennett felt sufficiently threatened that it banned the CPC outright in 1931 and, in a number of sweeping police raids, arrested eight of the party's key officials, including party leader Tim Buck. Even while in jail, ugly incidents occurred such as the firing of shots at Buck in his cell at the Kingston Penitentiary.

The banning of the CPC in the midst of the 1930s' Depression was no accident. It was a way of weakening the working-class opposition to the injustices and suffering under capitalism. It did, however, provide the newly created social democratic Co-operative Commonwealth Federation (CCF) with an opportunity to gain a foothold. It was not until after the CCF's first and successful 1933 Regina Convention that the ban on the CPC was lifted in 1934. While the notorious Section 98, which had been directed at crushing radical political dissent, was deleted in 1936, it was soon followed in 1937 in the province of Quebec by an equally infamous and anti-leftist Padlock Law. Given the illiberal repressive laws in Canada in the 1930s, the CPC, not surprisingly, did quite poorly in elections. For example, in the pivotal mid-Depression 1935 federal election, the CPC ran only 13 candidates and received a comparatively small 31 151 votes as against 387 056 for the new CCF, 384 095 for the recently created Reconstruction party and 180 301 for Social Credit.[19] At a time when it should have been making its greatest advances—during the decade-long Depression of the 1930s—the CPC failed to achieve significant electoral gains. Of the explanations, a combination of state harassment, Stalinist misdirection and the rise of rival parties seems the most germane.

The commencement of World War II and Stalin's 1939 non-aggression pact with Hitler placed the CPC in yet another difficult situation. In addition to membership unrest on the war issue, the Canadian state, employing the draconian War Measures Act (not for the last time against leftist political opponents) chose once again to ban the CPC. A hundred party members were interned[20] while others who could went into hiding in Canada or into exile in the United States (e.g., Buck). While the Nazi invasion of the Soviet Union in 1941 quickly changed the party's stance to one favouring Canada's involvement in the war, it was not until 1942 that party members were freed from internment. The conservative Roman Catholic church hierarchy continued to lobby against the legalization of the atheistic CPC. Nevertheless, the communist party was reborn in 1943, as the Labour Progressive Party (LPP), a name it was to retain until 1959.

With the Soviet Union as a wartime ally against the German Nazis and the heroic battles and hard-fought victories of the Red Army at Stalingrad in 1943, the CPC experienced a surge in popularity. In 1943 Fred Rose became the first communist elected to the House of Commons in Canada,[21] defeating among others David Lewis, national secretary of the CCF. Similar electoral successes occurred in the provincial legislatures of Manitoba and Ontario. Two years later, the CPC ran 65 federal candidates, its then highest ever, for an historic record of 109 078 votes and one MP re-elected. It was to be the party's zenith. Even so, the CPC was still behind the CCF and Social Credit in both votes and seats.

Shortly after the 1945 federal election, Igor Gouzenko, a Soviet Embassy cipher clerk defected and revealed evidence of Soviet espionage operations in Canada. It was one of the opening moves in the Cold War. In 1946, MP Rose was convicted, jailed and eventually banned from Canada. Despite pleas to return, he died an exile in Poland in 1983.

During the late 1940s and throughout the 1950s, the McCarthyite witch-hunts wreaked their havoc in the trade union movement, civil service and even the arts. Communists and their unions were expelled from labour organizations.

In the aftermath of both the 1956 Communist Party of the Soviet Union's (CPSU) Twentieth Party Congress—in which Khrushchev had denounced Stalin—and the subsequent Hungarian revolt against Soviet occupation, the CPC was in intellectual and organizational turmoil.[22] It ran only 10 candidates in the 1957 federal election and received a paltry 7760 votes. The CPC had tumbled to its nadir.

The 1960s saw an upsurge of radicalism and with it a renaissance of Marxist and Leninist thought. It was also the beginning of the Sino-Soviet dispute and the emergence of Maoism and more rival communist parties. The impact of the Sino-Soviet dispute is perhaps analogous to the break-up of Christendom into Roman Catholic and Eastern Orthodox fragments centuries earlier. In the communist split, the Soviet Union under Khrushchev opted for a revisionist path, while China under Mao Tse-tung chose a more doctrinaire line. The consequence of this ideological schism between the two communist superpowers was a shattering of the monolithic unity that had largely prevailed in the international communist movement since the early 1920s.

Echoing the split between the Soviet Union and China, many, if not most, communist parties around the world fractured. A host of new and rival communist parties arose. For example, in Canada several Maoist groups[23] emerged in the 1960s as part of the student New Left (e.g. the Internationalists established in 1963). The Workers Communist Party (Marxist-Leninist), formerly the Canadian Communist League, was founded in 1979 and was pro-Beijing. The Communist Party of Canada (Marxist-Leninist) founded in 1970 initially aligned with Beijing but, with the death of Mao Tse-tung in 1977 and de-Maoization in China, became pro-Albanian in its search for Stalinist orthodoxy. The Marxist-Leninist Organization of Canada-In Struggle/En Lutte, founded in 1972 also defended a Stalinist perspective. Since the 1930s, Trotskyist groups have existed. The Trotskyist factions seem to have a penchant for splintering into ever smaller fragments. More recently, these include the Revolutionary Workers League (founded in 1977 as a successor to the League For Socialist Action),[24] the Trotskyist League and the Forward Readers Group. The consequence of the proliferation of communist parties is that an already weak Canadian communist movement has been divided and weakened still further. Often, energy and resources have been directed at mutual denunciations of fellow communists rather than at capitalists and conservatives. Accompanying such infighting has been a loss of faith among communists. No longer hearing a single and relatively consistent message, cynicism and skepticism have spread. This is particularly so as revelations about abuse of power by communist governments have emerged. Not surprisingly, many former communist party members have drifted away from the movement. A number of the parties, particularly the newer Maoist ones, have recently folded. The result is a profound crisis of confidence and belief within the communist movement. The CPC is not immune to these buffeting winds.

Like several of its rival Canadian communist parties, the CPC endeavours to field a sufficient number of candidates to receive official status as a registered party on the ballot and qualify for free time election broadcasts. In the 1980, 1984 and 1988 elections the CPC ran 52 candidates and received 6022, 7609 and 7180 votes respectively for an average of less than 150 votes per candidate.[25]

Ideology

Since its birth under the tutelage of Lenin's Comintern, the CPC has shown a monotonous consistency in echoing the prevailing ideological line emanating from Moscow. For example, the CPC was pro-Stalinist during the Stalin era, revisionist during the Khrushchev period and returned to a slightly neo-Stalinist emphasis during the Brezhnev administration. In 1990, the CPC once more embraces revisionism during the Gorbachev pro-perestroika period.

In foreign affairs during the 1960s, the CPC sided with the Soviet Union in the Sino-Soviet split and, in so doing, lost many of its members. Despite the party's obsequiousness to the interests of the USSR,[26] the CPC has been able to champion Canadian nationalism to the limited degree it serves the interests of one superpower (i.e., the Soviet Union) against another (i.e., the United States). Accordingly, the CPC has condemned NATO, NORAD, Cruise missile testing, foreign ownership of Canadian industry and the American-Canadian Free Trade Agreement.

The CPC has called for extensive state ownership in the economy. It will be interesting to see the extent to which the Gorbachev-inspired reforms in eastern Europe, which have increasingly called for more privatization and use of the market mechanism, will alter the CPC's ideological stance. If the CPC belatedly embraces features of a mixed economy, it will of necessity move closer to the social democratic NDP and make its uneasy and often bitter relationship with that party even more complex.

Future

At the outset of the 1990s the history of the CPC is largely a history of failure, both in policy and organization. Ideologically, like so many of its counterparts, the party has slavishly echoed the policy zig-zags emanating from Moscow. The result has been missed opportunities in the 1920s and 1930s with the purges of Trotskyists, in the early 1940s over the initial delay in fighting Hitler and fascism, in the 1950s with the internal debates and defections over de-Stalinization and the Hungarian rebellion, in the 1960s with the Sino-Soviet conflict, the subsequent rise of rival communist parties in Canada and, later, the Soviet-led Warsaw Pact invasion of Czechoslovakia with the resultant membership departures. The CPC continues to show its inability to break out fully from its Leninist bureaucratic and hierarchical strait-jacket of democratic centralism. It remains to be seen if the impact of Gorbachev's perestroika in the Soviet Union will shake the CPC sufficiently to emerge from its current ossified state. The replacement of the aging William Kashtan by the younger George Hewison is perhaps the first step on a long and difficult road for the CPC. It is, however, probably too little too late. In Canada, as elsewhere, communist parties are in disarray.

The CCF-NDP has been a benefactor of the organizational rigidity and ideological ineptitude of the CPC. A more dynamic and pluralistic CPC would pose a more significant left-wing challenge to the NDP both in electoral and non-electoral realms. The result in theory could be a significant erosion of the more militant elements of the NDP. How likely such prospects for internal change within the CPC are and, thus, how plausible might be an external challenge to the NDP will depend, as ever, on decisions made thousands of miles away behind the walls of the Kremlin in Moscow.

Events in eastern Europe suggest that the 1990s could be the new dawn of a less centralized and more pluralistic communism which is willing to abandon the ideological rigidities of the past. It could, however, be another false start. Khrushchev's attempt at reform in 1956 and the crushing of the Hungarian revolt later in the same year are a grim reminder to Gorbachev in the 1990s that liberalization of communist regimes is not necessarily an easy, controllable or inevitable process. In any case, the CPC does not take the lead in such changes but continues to merely follow behind. As such, in an ironic international sense, the CPC fails as a vanguard party.

ENDNOTES

1. Norman Penner, *Canadian Communism* (Toronto: Methuen, 1988). See also Norman Penner, *The Canadian Left* (Scarborough: Prentice-Hall Canada, 1977) and Norman Penner, "Communist Party of Canada" in J. Marsh, ed., *The Canadian Encyclopedia* (Edmonton: Hurtig, 1988).
2. Some works do, however, address this issue. See, for example: *Ross Dowson v. RCMP* (Toronto: Forward Publications, 1980); Lita-Rose Betcherman, *The Little Band* (Ottawa: Deneau, n.d.); Merrily Weisbord, *The Strangest Dream* (Toronto: Lester & Orpen Dennys, 1983).
3. See Alan Whitehorn, "Canada" in R. Staar, ed., *Yearbook of International Communist Affairs* (Stanford: Hoover, various years).
4. This is the book that precipitated the split between the Menshevik and the Bolshevik factions in the Russian Social Democratic Labour Party.
5. See Richard Crossman, *The God That Failed* (N.Y.: Bantam, 1950) and Gabriel Almond, *The Appeals of Communism* (Princeton: Princeton University, 1954).
6. Helmut Gruber, *International Communism in the Era of Lenin* (N.Y.: Fawcett, 1967), pp. 287–92. See also Sidney Hook, *World Communism* (Princeton: Van Nostrand, 1962).
7. Rosa Luxemburg offered the following critique of Lenin's organizational structure for communists: "Nothing will more surely enslave a young labor movement to an intellectual élite hungry for power than this bureaucratic strait-jacket, which will immobilize the movement and turn it into an automaton manipulated by a Central Committee." Rosa Luxemburg, *The Russian Revolution and Leninism or Marxism?* (Ann Arbor: University of Michigan, 1961), p. 102. Even the former Menshevik Trotsky warned of the dangers of democratic centralism turning into "bureaucratic central-ism" or worse becoming "totalitarian." See Leon Trotsky, *The Basic Writings of Trotsky* (N.Y.: Vintage, 1963), p. 191 and Leon Trotsky, *The Revolution Betrayed* (N.Y.: Path-finder, 1972), p. 279.
8. Penner, *Canadian Communism*.
9. See Irving Abella, *Nationalism, Communism and Canadian Labour* (Toronto: University of Toronto, 1973) and Gad Horowitz, *Canadian Labour in Politics* (Toronto: University of Toronto, 1968).
10. In one sense the famous Mac-Paps (Mackenzie-Papineau) brigade in the Spanish Civil War could be labelled as a part of the movement against fascist warfare.
11. See Donald Avery, *Dangerous Foreigners* (Toronto: McClelland and Stewart, 1979) and John Kolasky, *The Shattered Illusion* (Toronto: Peter Martin, 1979).

12. By far, the most comprehensive account of CPC publications is Peter Weinrich's epic compendium *Social Protest From the Left in Canada* (Toronto: University of Toronto, 1982).

13. See Norman Penner, *Winnipeg 1919* (Toronto: Lorimer, 1975) and Kenneth McNaught and D. Bercuson, *The Winnipeg Strike: 1919* (Don Mills: Longman, 1974).

14. Thomas Berger, *Fragile Freedoms* (Toronto: Clarke, Irwin, 1981), pp. 132–33. The punishments were up to 20 years in jail and confiscation of property.

15. Berger, p. 135; see also Barbara Roberts, *Whence They Came* (Ottawa: University of Ottawa, 1988).

16. For an account of the early history of the CPC, see Ian Angus, *Canadian Bolsheviks* (Montreal: Vanguard, 1981); William Rodney, *Soldiers of the International* (Toronto: University of Toronto, 1968); and Ivan Avakumovic, *The Communist Party In Canada* (Toronto: McClelland and Stewart, 1975).

17. Berger, p. 131; Penner, *Canadian Communism*, p. 66.

18. Murray Beck, *The Pendulum of Power: Canada's Federal Elections* (Scarborough: Prentice-Hall Canada, 1968).

19. *Ibid.*, pp. 220–21.

20. William Repka and K. Repka, *Dangerous Patriots* (Vancouver: New Star, 1982).

21. At least one other was elected but under a different label. See Penner, *Canadian Communism*, p. 173. See also the Communist Party of Canada, *Canada's Party of Socialism* (Toronto: Progress Books, 1982).

22. This pattern was not dissimilar to the late 1980s with Gorbachev's attempts at restructuring and the subsequent unrest in eastern Europe.

23. Interestingly, many of these newer communist parties were headquartered in Quebec in contrast to the CPC which was based in Ontario.

24. See Roger O'Toole, *The Precipitous Path* (Toronto: Peter Martin, 1977).

25. As in the case of the major parties, so too the minor communist parties have been victims of the regionalization of support. For example, in the 1980 federal election much of the CPC-ML vote came from the province of Quebec, while much of the CPC vote came from Ontario. Another regional anomaly is the somewhat curious observation that the CPC chose not to run any candidates in the Maritime provinces even though this region continues to have the highest unemployment rate in the country.

26. Penner notes that "the first principle of the Communist Party of Canada was loyalty to the Soviet Union." Penner, *Canadian Communism*, p. 265.

Regional Politics

Canadian regionalism is largely a reaction against the domination of Canadian economic and political life by the English-speaking élite of central Canada centred in Toronto. To assuage regional discontent, the federal government has granted the outlying areas increased subsidies for their provincial governments, transfers to individuals such as unemployment insurance and pensions, subsidies for communications and support for specific industries. Reactions to this situation of domination vary. The Atlantic provinces have maintained their cautious conservatism by continuing to support the old parties, hoping for "better terms" in exchange. They have preferred to be on the winning side in national elections and to exploit their advantages within the old party structures.

In Quebec there has been a rapid radicalization since 1960, culminating in the election in 1976 of a Parti Québécois government committed to winning independence for Quebec but with economic association with the rest of Canada. At the same time, the Liberals continued to sweep federal elections in the province until 1984, when the province, sensing a Mulroney victory, favoured the Conservatives, thereby remaining on the winning side. Quebec remains the centre of controversy due to the prolonged crisis surrounding the Meech Lake Accord that sought to gain Quebec's consent to the 1982 constitutional arrangements.

Ten years have passed since the referendum on sovereignty association and the concerns of Quebec are still not satisfied. The classic essay by Marcel Rioux written in 1968 is included here to recall the roots of Quebec's conflicting political ideologies. There follow two essays on current Quebec politics by two Université Laval specialists.

The West has also been a nursery of protest movements. The United Farmers or Progressive movement began there after 1918, as did the CCF-NDP and Social Credit in the 1930s.

Since World War II the resources boom created an optimism in the West that led to "province-building" and a taste for the wielding of power by provincial governments. The recent economic reverses of the resource industries have blunted this thrust. Now the sense of grievance associated with harder times is re-emerging, and with it are new parties of protest. We heard of the Western Canada Concept, a fledgling party of western protest against eastern domination. When it fell into decline, the torch was taken up by the Reform party, led by Preston Manning. It seems to have grown, especially after the Progressive Conservative federal victory of 1984 which left Albertans wth Tory governments for which they had voted massively at both federal and provincial levels. Yet, Albertans still felt frustrated and alienated because of the continuing eastern dominance in political and economic life. If they were to air their protests, it would have to be through a third party since the Liberals and NDP appeared to be either overly eastern or overly left-oriented. The Reform party stepped into this breach and became the champion of western concerns, one of which is a preference for an elected Senate.

The party has yet to elect anyone in a general election, but it did carry a federal by-election in 1989. However, it could be important if, by cutting into the Conservative vote, it prepares the way for local victories of the Liberals or NDP. And, it could soar like Social Credit and the United Farmers of Alberta before it, and become the dominant party. But, this is merely speculation.

This section, then, includes essays on all five regions of Canada and examines how they have coped with recent, rapid changes in fortune.

27 The Development of Ideologies in Quebec

MARCEL RIOUX

Historical Outline

To understand the recent evolution of ideologies in Quebec, it is necessary to establish the historical context. What ideas did the Québécois, that is, the francophone majority, have of themselves and their society? What goals did they, as a group, have and what means did they advocate for attaining them? The interpretation of ideologies proposed here will take two centuries of history into account and will, therefore, necessarily be schematic.

When can we begin to speak of an ideology for the Québécois? Usually, as soon as a group has proved itself to be a distinct group and a strong enough "we" has been formed to oppose other "we's," individuals appear who define the situation and who clearly explain this collective consciousness.

Conquered in 1760, ruined by the war, deprived of their élites, the Quebec peasants spent their first 40 years under English domination just surviving and a new élite slowly emerged from their ranks which assumed the function of defining the Quebec community and representing it politically. This new francophone bourgeoisie, made up of people from the liberal professions, was to oppose the mercantile class which, in turn, was to represent the anglophone minority. This social class made up of the liberal professions took it upon itself to define the Quebec nation; this brings us to our first ideology. Fernand Ouellet wrote that, with the appearance of a national consciousness at the heart of the bourgeoisie, its political vocation was greatly strengthened. From that time on, it no longer defended its class interests or proposed abstract values as far as the people were concerned; it represented the nation and its essential attributes. In 1810, Craig wrote:

The above article originally appeared in French under the title "Sur l'evolution des idéologies au Québec" by Marcel Rioux published in *Revue de l'Institut de Sociologie*, No. 1, 1968. This translation was prepared by Gerald L. Gold for *Communities and Culture in French Canada* (Toronto: Holt, Rinehart and Winston of Canada, Limited, 1973), pp. 260–79. Reprinted by permission of Marcel Rioux and Gerald L. Gold.

In truth, it seems to be their desire to be considered as forming a separate nation. The *Canadien* nation is their constant expression. . . . [1]

What is the relationship between this bourgeoisie and the people? Fernand Dumont gives the following explanation:

The fact that this bourgeoisie was, at first, accepted by the people as their natural spokesman is clear, and can be explained, we feel, quite easily. As sons of the people, its members kept the essential attitudes of the peasantry from which they came. [2]

From the turn of the century to the 1830s, this new bourgeoisie got on well with the clergy; both groups had approximately the same views about Canadiens. But soon a division occurred in the Legislative Assembly: "with Papineau, the dream of an autonomous French-Canadian Republic began to take form." [3] The period known as the romantic period in French Canada was to finish badly: the Rebellion in 1837–38 was soon checked. The Church was seen more and more frequently by many of the bourgeois élite as an ally of the colonizers.

The first ideology of Quebec was formulated by a secular élite who defined Quebec as a nation. Independence was the aim of this nation. In an epilogue to the results of the Rebellion, Etienne Parent, a journalist, wrote in 1839:

There were people, and we were among them, who thought that with the backing and the favour of England, the French Canadians could flatter themselves for having retained and spread their nationality in such a way as to form an independent nation afterwards. . . . [4]

The Rise of the Ideology of Conservation

The secular bourgeoisie which dominated the Assembly from 1820–40 acted like a national bourgeoisie and took upon itself the task of defining the Quebec community and its future. It did not cause a great stir among the people who were afraid of the liberalism, anticlericalism, and anti-British ideas of the *patriotes*. On the whole, the clergy remained faithful to the British Crown. Derbyshire, an envoy from Lord Durham, "also reported the noteworthy observation of the Abbé Ducharme, *curé* of Sainte-Thérèse":

'It was the educated men, the doctors, notaries, and lawyers, who were at the head of the rebellion and were the great seducers of the people, and he seemed to derive from it an argument against educating the lower orders.' [5]

That is why, once the Rebellion had been suppressed and its leaders had fled, the clergy could regain its control over the people, with the aid of the British powers. The British, with the Governor, Lord Durham, as their spokesman, became aware of the prevailing situation in Quebec.

Durham stated that he had come to Canada thinking he would find a conflict between the people and the executive, but instead, he had found

> ... two nations warring in the bosom of a single state: I found a struggle, not of principles, but of races. The national feud forces itself on the very senses, irresistibly and palpably, as the origin or essence of every dispute which divides the community; we discover that dissensions, which appear to have another origin, are but forms of this constant and all-pervading quarrel; and that every contest is one of French and English in the outset, or becomes so ere it has run its course.[6]

Durham's solution was simple: he proposed the assimilation of francophone Lower Canada with anglophone Upper Canada.

> I entertain no doubt of the national character which must be given to Lower Canada; it must be that of the British Empire; that of the majority of British America; that of the great race which must, in the lapse of no long period of time, be predominant over the whole North American Continent. Without effecting the change so rapidly or roughly as to shock the feelings and trample on the welfare of the existing generation, it must henceforth be the first and steady purpose of the British Government to establish an English population, with English laws and language, in this Province, and to trust its government to none but a decidedly English Legislature.[7]

Durham added:

> I should indeed be surprised if the more reflecting part of the French Canadians entertain at present any hope of continuing to preserve their nationality. Much as they struggle against it, it is obvious that the process of assimilation to English habits is already commencing. The English language is gaining ground, as the language of the rich and of the employers of labour naturally will.[8]

The Durham Report and the Act of Union which followed the Rebellion mark a very important turning point in the history of Quebec. Quebec's professional bourgeoisie was descended from the peasantry and had defended the traditional form of culture which had developed in Quebec since the Conquest. Was this, however, through choice or necessity? Being the ruling class of a people who were dominated politically, economically and socially, the liberal bourgeoisie was obliged to defend what existed, and what existed was a people that the Conquest had relegated to agriculture. There is nothing to indicate that the Québécois chose to defend the traditional form of economy they practised. It was the dialectic of the situation which gave it momentum. These people the liberal bourgeoisie wanted to lead to independence, "with the support and favour of England," were, for the time being, poor illiterate farmers. By opposing the dominators and the anglophone mercantile class which represents it, the national bourgeoisie defended a way of life imposed on it since the Conquest and the failure of the Rebellion. There is nothing to lead us to believe that it was this way of life that they had defended. Above all, the liberal bourgeoisie was defending the right of the Quebec people to live as a total society. Papineau and his followers were insisting on the liberty of a majority group, which had been conquered militarily, economically and politically by a minority.

However, everything changed after the 1840s. Despair beset even the most committed Québécois. It was no longer a question of leading the people to independence, but of fighting against assimilation and anglicization. With backing from Durham, the clergy became the main spokesman for the Quebec people; they no longer proclaimed an ideology of independence, but one of conservation. From the point of view of the ideology held in the first few decades of the nineteenth century, the new ideology they were expounding marks a tragic contraction. Sensing quite well that they were to become a minority, the Québécois no longer sought to become an independent society, but strove to preserve their culture. The Quebec group was no longer a nation that had one day to obtain its independence, but an ethnic group with a particular culture (religion, language, customs); this culture would have to be preserved as a sacred heritage. Durham accused the Québécois of having no history or literature; they had to prove to him that they had a past and that it was great—to such an extent that the period to be glorified by those who defined the situation was to become the past. The English soon realized that it was necessary to divide the Québécois, both along the St. Lawrence, and later in Acadia, in order to establish a viable state that the English could control at will. Lord Elgin knew this well when he wrote:

> I believe that the problem of how to govern Canada would be solved if the French would split into a Liberal and a Conservative Party and join the Upper Canadian parties bearing the corresponding names. The great difficulty hitherto has been that a Conservative Government has meant Government of Upper Canadians which is intolerable to the French—and a Radical Government a Government of the French which is no less hateful to the British. The national element would be merged in the political if the split to which I refer was accomplished.[9]

Dumont writes:

> Politics will become a ground on which politicians will periodically defend their nationality; but it will only be one area among others for formulating nationalist ideologies.[10]

The arrival of responsible government enabled the élite in the liberal professions to find employment and to acquire a certain vertical mobility in administration and business. Georges-Etienne Cartier, a businessman and politician, is one of the first examples of a type of Québécois who was to profit from the new regime. He took part in the 1837 Rebellion, but with the backing of the clergy, he and his party were to win all the elections in Quebec until the end of the century. Conservatism was triumphant. Some young people from the cities went to settle in the country, in the heart of traditional society.

Several novels from this period were constructed around the theme of fidelity to agriculture and ancestral values. These romantic works, as well as historical studies, were to propagate the ideology of conservation that the petite-bourgeoisie and the Church were systematically building up.

The Church profited from the liberty that the English were according them as a reward for their loyalist attitude during the Rebellion, and strove to get the people under their influence again. This thoroughly succeeded. From that time on, the Church fulfilled for the nation the role that it had filled for many minority groups: that of compensation. The minority should not be saddened by its existing situation because the rewards would come much later. If the Québécois were to realize themselves fully, to become what they really are, it was out of the question to imitate the material successes of the English. It mattered little that they were conquered and poor, because they had a providential mission to accomplish in North America: to evangelize and civilize the continent. National history, particularly in the person of Garneau, helped the Church greatly to build the new ideology of conservation. Nourished by Voltaire and de Raynal, Garneau advocated prudence and fidelity to traditions. He wrote:

> For us, part of our strength comes from our traditions; let us not separate ourselves from these as we change them gradually. We find good examples to follow in the history of our own mother country. Without laying claim to a similar destiny, our wisdom and our strong unity will greatly ease the difficulties of our situation and will arouse the interest of nations and make our cause appear more sacred to them.[11]

The "Catholic reaction,"[12] in the words of Father Léon Pouliot, s.j., took several years to sweep away all that remained of anticlericalism in Quebec. The greatest battle that the clergy had to wage was against the Institut canadien,[13] several members of which were freethinkers.

It seems best to follow Dumont's interpretation that the predominance the Church acquired was achieved with the consent of

> ... leaders, even nonbelievers, who could not help but recognize that religion was an essential factor in social solidarity and a fundamental element in the differentiation of the French-Canadian nation from that of the English.[14]

The federation of the territories of British North America and the British North America Act, which should have been the constitutional document that consecrated this federation, was bound to accentuate what was embryonic in the Durham Report and in the Act of Union. In 1840, the Act which united English Upper Canada and French Lower Canada was supposed to have the result, in the spirit of Durham and the English lawmakers, of rapidly anglicizing Lower Canada. It had done nothing. But with Confederation, that is, with the union of all British territories in North America, the assimilation process appeared to be unavoidable. As a minority in this new political formation, the Québécois again strengthened their ideology of defence and conservation. Although the

Québécois remained the majority in Lower Canada, they were no longer the majority in Canada as a whole. Even inside Quebec, where they represented nearly 75 percent of the population of nearly a million inhabitants, their economic and social position no longer corresponded to their numerical importance. The large cities, such as Montreal and Quebec, had just acquired a francophone majority. But the English dominated commerce, industry and finance. Thus, even within Quebec, English and Canadiens were opposed to each other on all points: the Canadiens, rural and poor, were Catholics and French in their linguistic tradition; the English, urban and better off economically, were Protestants.

The period of Confederation was one of profound economic malaise in Quebec that was evidenced by a massive emigration to the United States. The Canadian economy was being displaced towards southern Ontario and the Québécois were seeking work in New England. To counter this emigration, the clerical élite and the petite-bourgeoisie began a vast movement of colonization and a return to the land. Quebec followed in detail its ideology of conservation which forced it to remain within its borders:

> . . . relatively sheltered from Anglo-Saxon influences, it (Lower Canada) is entirely taken up with the preservation of its personality which it wishes to keep immutable by time and space, in a sealed vase.[15]

An increasingly accentuated rift developed with France. In 1871, the year of the Commune, Mgr. Raymond wrote:

> The capital of France, centre of these uprisings and of this filth, does not seem to me as more than a soiled land, like that of Babylon or Sodom, and as such calling for the vengeance of heaven.[16]

Gradually, the theory of the two Frances was built up. Thomas Chapais gave it most explicit formulation:

> There are now two Frances, radical France and conservative France, the infidel France and Catholic France, the France that blasphemes and the France that prays. Our France is this second one.[17]

This distancing from France was not compensated for by any rapprochement with the English in Canada.

In the decade of 1880, the Riel affair again seemed to harden the relations between Quebec and Canada. When Laurier, a Québécois, became prime minister of Canada from 1896 to 1911, it seemed to mark a truce in the struggle between the two groups: he was elected as much by Quebec as by Canada.

During Laurier's term of office, the Quebec economy experienced an accelerated growth. Although the movement towards industrialization was mostly directed from the outside and activated in Quebec by the anglophone element, it is possible to date the first decades of this century as those of radical transformation which the traditional lifestyle of the Québécois had to go through. And it was from the perspective of the problem of the worker that Quebec first faced the consequences of its massive industrialization.[18] There, as elsewhere, the ideology of conservation played a strong role. To prevent the Québécois from joining international unions, the clergy strongly encouraged the founding of Catholic unions that would protect them from the religious neutrality of the Americans.

In 1911, when Laurier left the government after 15 years in power, Quebec had changed extensively. In 1871 Quebec was 77 percent rural, but 40 years later, it was half urban. Because of its industrial and commercial development, Montreal had attracted many rural people who increased the ranks of labourers and salaried workers. The anglophone minority continued to hold the wealth and the industrial and financial power. Already, at that time, the Québécois writer Errol Bouchette earnestly advised his compatriots to invest in industry rather than land; for him, the future of Quebec was in industry rather than agriculture. Bouchette stated with bitterness that a francophone population of 1 293 000 inhabitants sent only 722 students to university, whereas the English in Quebec sent 1358 for a population of 196 000. Only 27 francophone students were prepared for scientific careers, whereas there were 250 such students among anglophones in Quebec. A few years later, in the first decade of the twentieth century, the Literary School of Montreal aroused great hopes. But it was necessary to wait 40 more years before the movement really had any momentum.

The encounter between francophones and anglophones that was evident during the Boer War in 1899, when the Québécois refused to participate in an imperialist struggle, continued during World War I. The question of the Ontario separate schools again aggravated the conflict between Quebec and the rest of Canada. In the Legislative Assembly in Quebec, a minister presented a bill aimed at the withdrawal of Quebec from Confederation; the debates lasted for many days. In the end, he withdrew his bill and the premier of Quebec, Lomer Gouin, declared himself against withdrawal from Confederation, invoking the fate of the francophone minorities in Canada and the impossibility for Quebec alone to ensure her economic survival. It was during this period that Henri Bourassa, the grandson of Louis-Joseph Papineau, the leader of the 1837 Rebellion, became the champion of a type of pan-Canadian nationalism. Bourassa pleaded for an international policy that was Canadian and no longer British. Towards 1917, facing the facts as he saw them from the turn of events—conscription for overseas service, persecutions of the francophone minorities in Ontario—he turned to the study of religious problems and published a book, *Le Pape, arbitre de la paix*, and arranged a big conference on "Language, Guardian of the Faith." His influence on generations of Québécois was profound and explains certain positions of traditional nationalists who today still gravitate around *Le Devoir*.

During the early postwar years, Quebec continued to industrialize at an accelerated pace. The United States increasingly expanded its economic and cultural hold on Quebec. In 1921, the francophone population of Canada reached its lowest proportion ever—27.9 percent. For the first time in history the urban population of Quebec, 56.01 percent, was greater than the rural population.

Montreal had 618 506 inhabitants of whom 63.9 percent were francophones. Many important industrial centres were developing: Three Rivers, Hull, Shawinigan, Grand'Mère, Chicoutimi, La Tuque. The national resources of Quebec continued to be exploited by foreigners. The lack of capital and technicians further accentuated the domination of the country. In the 1930s, a separatist movement arose which was directly descended from the traditional nationalist movement. World War II put an end to this movement. Not that the conflict between francophones and anglophones was mitigated; as in 1899 and in 1914–18, the majority of the francophone population of Quebec opposed sending troops overseas. The movement of industrialization and urbanization that was produced by World War II was bound to lay the groundwork for lively days ahead.

A Characterization of Québécois Ideologies 1945–65

We shall use the definition of a global ideology that was developed in the first part of these remarks to describe and characterize the ideologies of Quebec during the last two decades. In summary, a global ideology is a plan for living which is proposed to a society by one of its subgroups and which aims at expressing the total consciousness of the society and sharing its definition of the situation with the whole of the society. In a complex society, the conflict of ideologies expresses, above all, the conflict of subgroups which are competing for the majority's acceptance of their theory of society and, ultimately, to govern that society.

The Ideology of Conservation

When World War II broke out in 1939, the dominant ideology in Quebec was the ideology of conservation that had begun to develop in the second half of the nineteenth century. The majority of those in Quebec who had taken it upon themselves to define the nation and who had directed collective action had rallied to this ideology. For about 100 years, the ideology of conservation had been dominant, and the clergy and many of the liberal professions had been its champions. This does not imply that this was the only definition of Quebec that had existed during this century, but other definitions did not gain the favour of the public and did not guide the behaviour of the majority of Québécois. The clergy and the liberal professions were at leisure to disseminate their ideology since they controlled, for all practical purposes, most of the information media, houses of learning, books and textbooks. It is necessary to add that the Québécois also live in another political entity, that of Canada as a whole, and that they could and can, if necessary, forget the fact that they are Québécois and participate in the ideology of Canada. The Québécois can physically or otherwise escape their nationality and live as though they were Canadians or North Americans. Ideological conflicts cannot be produced for this precise reason. In addition, during all this time national education remained in the hands of the clergy, which was thus able to propagate and impose its own definition of the Québécois group. How does one characterize this ideology? It defined the Québécois group as the bearer of a culture, that is, as a group with an edifying history which became a minority in the nineteenth century and whose task it is to preserve the heritage it had received from its ancestors and which it must transmit intact to its descendants. This heritage is essentially composed of the Catholic religion, the French language and an indeterminate number of traditions and customs. The privileged time of this ideology has passed. At the time when it was worked out, the Québécois were becoming a minority and risking assimilation. It was to be expected that this ideology therefore idealized the traits of Quebec society in the second half of the nineteenth century when it was effectively Catholic, French-speaking, agricultural, and traditional. Threatened with assimilation, this type of society and its principal characteristics were not supposed to change. Thus, it had to be rationalized and justified. This culture was not only that of the Québécois, but the best culture that had ever existed. This ideology took hold over the years; from the end of the nineteenth century, it was transmitted almost intact to the beginning of World War II.

The Université Laval sociologist Gérald Fortin has analysed the contents of *l'Action française*, later called *l'Action Nationale*, one of the principal reviews that transmitted this ideology over the course of years. His analysis extends from its appearance in 1917 until 1953[19] and brings out the principal themes of this ideology of conservation. It praised the merits of the French language, the Catholic religion, the spiritual culture, the national history, rural life and the family; it warned of the dangers of English imperialism, industrialization, urbanization and the means of mass communication; it preached about buying Québécois and respect for the two cultures and the francophone minorities. In the decade 1945–53 an interest in economic and social questions grew and the question of the worker appeared in the review. Fortin wrote:

> If the ends and the means of the ideology are considered, it may be seen that the goals have not changed; they have been more strongly confirmed as new interpretations of the situation have been worked out.[20]

The Ideology of Contestation and Recoupment

After World War II, the ideology of conservation was seriously disputed by other strata of the population: union leaders, intellectuals, journalists, artists, students and some members of the liberal professions. It is obvious that this form of contestation had its historical antecedents; it can, in many respects, be linked to the liberal tradition. This certainly does not question the fact that Quebec possessed a culture different from that of the rest of Canada, the principal elements of which must be brought up-to-date. The ideological movement which arose during World War II was, above all, a movement of reaction against the old ideology of conservation. That is, its negative aspect, which opposed the old, was the most nebulous and almost always remained implicit.

It can be said that the ideology and old power structure in Quebec were becoming anachronistic in face of the demographic, economic and social changes that Quebec went through between 1939 and 1945. Its irrationality was obvious. If, for convenience, we consider the decade between 1939 and 1950, the labour force in Quebec doubled.

Quebec has undergone more important changes on a larger scale during the decade from 1939 to 1949 than in any other decade of its history, except those of the Conquest and the Rebellion. The ideology of conservation which had survived all the other waves of industrialization and urbanization could not successfully resist the last. It must be added that this ideology, which had been dominant for so many years, had largely become inoperative on the level of everyday life. It continued to guide the general policies of the nation, but it no longer directed the behaviour of the more dynamic Québécois who kept to themselves or withdrew into small groups which worked within other frames of reference. The patriotic societies continued to defend French-Canadian culture (religion, language and traditions) while the majority of individuals shared a number of core images concerning their nation; others were ideologically integrated into other North American societies, particularly into Canada.

The challenge to this ideology began in the postwar years. Clearly, the sociologists and economists in the Faculty of Social Science at Université Laval formed the most coherent centre for dispute at the end of the 1940s and during the 1950s. This group was associated with reviews such as *Cité Libre* and movements such as the Canadian Institute for Public Affairs (L'Institut Canadien des Affaires Publiques), which brought together intellectuals, professors, union leaders, journalists and liberal politicians. Drawing their inspiration from the analyses of economists and sociologists from the Québécois milieu and from their knowledge of other Western democracies, these movements and individuals undertook the systematic criticism of the ideology of conservation as well as of Québécois culture.

The 1950s was a decade when social problems were dealt with—when the problems of the workers were recognized. These so-called social themes were even introduced into the pages of *Action Nationale,* which had long been one of the most representative mouthpieces of the ideology of conservation. Already by 1949, the reverberations that were provoked by the asbestos strike had brought about a realization that Quebec was no longer a traditional agricultural society but a society in which the majority of citizens were salaried workers; a few years later, it was said that Quebec society was experiencing a slow proletarianization.

It is quite evident that in criticizing the ideology of conservation and Quebec culture in general, opponents had to criticize not only ideas, values, behaviour and institutions, but also those groups and individuals who, according to them, were responsible for the global orientations that were influencing the direction Quebec was taking. Quite clearly, this was a way of getting at the clergy who had always been responsible for national education in Quebec. Open discussions on education, religion and the traditional interpretation of our history date from these years. There was bound to be criticism of Quebec Catholicism and those who had narrowed, particularized and "Quebecized" its content. This fact is well-expressed by Maurice Tremblay:

> Through this attitude of fierce defence against Protestant influences and French modernism, the Church has no doubt succeeded in keeping French-Canadian culture entirely Catholic; unfortunately, it must be recognized that this has been, to a great extent, at the expense of a narrow sterile dogmatism and an authoritarianism rooted in conservatism. On the whole, this French-Canadian Catholicism thus appears to us to be a canned Catholicism, at the rear guard of the radical changes the world is demanding of Christianity. We have here an example of this narrow and unproductive ultra-montanism that the Church has made its right arm in a general policy of conservation and defence of French-Canadian Christianity.

This Church has always sided with the traditional society for which it has been largely responsible, and has wished to preserve itself in the North American world which is repudiating and overtaking it in every respect. Tremblay further says:

> In effect, in a general manner the Church in French Canada tends to run against the increasing industrialization and urbanization, to maintain the structures and life-styles of a rural civilization that it can dominate and guide in its own ideal of a religious and Christian life for which it has an obvious nostalgia.[21]

The other power that was strongly attacked by this group who were trying to define the situation throughout this period, is the political power that was embedded in Quebec from 1936 until 1960[22] through the Union Nationale and its leader Maurice Duplessis. They put into practice the ideology of conservation that had been perpetuated in Quebec for many decades.

Acting completely pragmatically and distrusting intellectuals and idealogues, Duplessis implemented the most conservative policies in the name of autonomy and peasant good sense. In the best vein of traditional conservatism, he carried out a form of personal politics in which everyone knew one another, and the prince granted his largesse to the good (those who voted for him) and left the wicked to sink (counties and regions which had shown some opposition). This manner of administering Quebec was as anachronistic as the ideology which inspired it. It included many characteristics of pre-industrial society which tallied exactly with those of the ideology of conservation that had been developed expressly to ensure the preservation of the traditional Quebec society as it had been in the middle of the nineteenth century.

The Liberal opposition which was made up of partisans of the Liberal party— and other opponents—took 15 years to defeat these two powers, political and ideological, which were grafted together and worked shoulder to shoulder to rally a majority of electors. The traditionalists leaned on the two fundamental characteristics of the Quebec situation: the fact that the Québécois have their own identity that clearly distinguishes them from other North American groups, and a second corollary conviction: the fact that they have remained a people whose culture is still traditional while living in a society that is largely industrialized and urbanized. In conclusion, the ideological opposition prior to 1960 wished to fill the gap that had formed between Quebec culture (ideas, values, symbols, attitudes, motivations) and Quebec society (technology, economy, urbanization, industrialization). This gap between culture and society in Quebec produced a global gap between Quebec and other North American communities. It can be said that those who opposed the regime (ideology and power) in Quebec during the period 1945–60 not only supported an ideology of contestation but also an ideology of recoupment.

In criticizing the delay experienced by Quebec in almost every aspect of human activity, the opponents have above all criticized the élites whom they held responsible for such a state of affairs. What did the new ideologists want for Quebec? What type of society did they want Quebec to become? It is necessary here, from the perspective of the analysis of ideologies, to make certain distinctions. The ideology of conservation and the political powers had idealized Quebec culture to such an extent that it became an urgent necessity for opponents to deflate the balloons that had been blown up over decades. According to those in power, Quebec had the best educational system, the purest religion, the language closest to that of the Louis XIV era, and the most humanist traditions. On top of that was grafted a messianism which wished to make the rest of the world participate in these cultural treasures. According to the opinion that had been attributed to Duplessis, the Québécois had become improved French. It is not surprising that the first task of the postwar opponents was to criticize what Quebec had become and to compare the miserable reality to the phantasmagorias of the élites.

The opponents agreed over what they opposed, but they were not united over the positive objectives that they laid down for the society which they wished to construct. Furthermore, it seems that when mobilized for combat, they submitted to the rule of force and did not question the positive aspect of their ideology. Opposition to the regime had brought together many individuals and groups who came from very different backgrounds: Catholic and progressive syndicalists, Catholic action leaders, Catholic and progressive intellectuals, members of the Liberal parties of Quebec and of Canada and students from various disciplines. It would not be an exaggeration to say that because of the history of Quebec and its political and intellectual climate, the only other model which the protesters could recognize as comparable was that of other North American societies. The majority of them wanted Quebec to become a liberal democracy. Some of them had been influenced by European currents of thought, particularly French, for example, the review *Esprit*, but, for the majority it was the Ottawa model that consciously or unconsciously prevailed. During this period, a number of professors and students from the Faculty of Social Science at Université Laval openly sided with Ottawa. The most typical example is Maurice Lamontagne[23] who was to rally to Ottawa after 1954. Three of the principal leaders of the postwar opposition movement, Marchand, Pelletier, and Trudeau would join Lamontagne several years later. Others, such as Sauvé and Pepin,[24] also entered the Canadian government. Although many opposed the Ottawa regime during the 1950s, it is clear, after the fact, that their preferences unconsciously lay there and that the positive aspect of their ideology was largely drawn from the model of liberal democracy.

From the point of view of the global ideologism of Quebec, which we have taken here, we have laid out three principal ideologies: the ideology of conservation which was dominant for a century and which largely remained intact at the end of World War II; the ideology of recoupment towards which most of the opposition of the 1950s would turn; and the ideology of development and participation that does not appear to have crystallized until the end of the 1950s. In Hegelian terms, a period of affirmation can be seen in the first ideology; in the second, the negation of the first; and, in the third, the negation of the negation.

The Ideology of Development and Participation

If we examine carefully the issues of *Cité Libre*, an organ of opinion which led the most systematic and coherent fight against the ideology of conservation, it will be seen that this was really a review of contestation against Duplessis, the clergy, the educational system and many other subjects, but it never developed the positive aspect of its ideology in a systematic manner. At the outset, in 1950 and until the beginning of 1960, it fought against the ideology of conservation; beginning with the 1960s, it began to run up against the third ideology; it was only in 1964 that Pierre Elliott Trudeau wrote what seemed to be the most positive statement that the review ever published: "Pour une politique fonctionnelle." We would like now to characterize this third ideology against which *Cité Libre* set itself in the 1960s.

The ideology of recoupment largely contributed to the discrediting of traditional power élites and the ideology of conservation; essentially, it has directed its criticisms against the Québécois themselves as a group; that is, it has been concerned with internal criticism. If one could schematize the thoughts of the principal spokesmen of this ideology, they do not seem to cast doubt on the fundamental postulate of the ideology of conservation: that Quebec forms a culture—that is, an ethnic group which possesses certain characteristics of language, religion and traditions that distinguish it from other ethnic groups in Canada or the North American continent. If Quebec is behind compared to other ethnic groups, it is because of its élites which have misled it into the paths of conservatism, nationalism, chauvinism and messianism. They now want this ethnic group to acquire a more open culture and ideology and integrate itself into Canadian society; according to Lamontagne, it is a question of a clear integration into Confederation. We thus see that this ideology of recoupment retains, for the most part, the essence of the ideology of conservation in that Quebec possesses a distinct culture and that it must accommodate itself to being implicated with Canada. The essential difference between conservation and recovery lies in the type of culture that Quebec should have. The first ideology is directed toward the

Nat

past; the second is resolutely turned toward the present; it demands that Quebec culture be brought up-to-date and that it be reflected in the rest of Canada.

The third ideology also retains certain elements of the ideology of conservation in that it recognizes that Quebec possesses a different culture from other North American groups. Together with the ideology of recoupment, it recognizes that the élites of the past have perverted this heritage, that this culture and the ideology of conservation have become anachronistic and that Quebec must move smoothly into the twentieth century. It recognizes that the lag between the social structure of Quebec and its culture must be filled. But the resemblance to the other ideologies ends there. It reaches back across the years to rejoin the first ideology of Quebec, before Confederation and even before union. Quebec is not only a culture, that is, an ethnic group which possesses certain differences of language, religion and traditions, but is a society that must be self-determined and gain its own independence. Now, because this ideology is set in the second half of the twentieth century and because Quebec has become an industrial society, it must, as any other industrial society, control its economy and polity. For the holders of this ideology, there can, therefore, be no question that Quebec should integrate itself with other societies such as Canada.

How do we explain the birth and development of this ideology? It could be suggested with some justification that it is written into the line of our traditional ideologies. But that is not the complete answer. The adherents of the two ideologies do not come from the same strata of society. The traditional nationalists or the liberals of the ideology of recoupment do not seem to have become, for the most part, partisans of the third and most recent ideology. Other groups in the population who have become active since 1960—workers, members of co-operatives, white-collar workers, teachers, civil servants and students—are the most active contributors to the development and diffusion of this ideology. It is true that there are several strata of the population who were already beginning to make their presence felt in the ideology of recoupment, but other strata have become more important and others, such as the newly unionized, are tending to subscribe, often implicitly, to this new definition of Quebec society.

In a phenomenon as diffuse as the birth of a new ideology, it is difficult to follow all the stages precisely. The criticism to which Quebec society has been submitted since the end of World War II has not happened without heart-rending anguish and profound disequilibrium in a population which traditionally "was in quiet possession of the truth." The most firmly established truths, the most diffused myths, were attacked by more and more individuals and subgroups. Finally, in 1960, what has rapidly become known as the Quiet Revolution began, and the time came to change the ideological climate of Quebec in a global manner. From an ideology concerned with the theory that groups advance of their own accord, it is certain that the first effects of 1960 and the reforms that followed were to reaffirm the image that many Québécois held of themselves and their society. One did not willingly boast about being a Québécois during the dark years. To dethrone Duplessis, it was necessary to attack and denounce all those teachers, politicians and professional élites who were responsible for the fact that Quebec was the only feudal state "north of the Rio Grande." The day that more and more Québécois realized that they could collectively escape from their rut was the day that they acquired a taste for change and began to redefine themselves, set new goals for themselves, and seek the means to reach them. The ideology of recoupment, which wished to bring Quebec onto an equal footing with the rest of North America, served as a generator of many new policies and reforms. Now, in the same way as in the 1960s, it was a problem for the people of Quebec to progress to another stage of thinking and development, so the means available to do this and the direction that this reform should take could not be the same as those which had been used many decades ago by the Anglo-Saxon democracies of North America— the societies to which Quebec was catching up.

There had previously been independentist movements during the Duplessis regime. Although the new generation of independentists admitted almost all the critics who had been opposed to the state of Quebec society, they went further than the *Cité Libre* criticism and asked whether many of the problems of Quebec did not come from the fact that it had always been a dominated society; this explained the narrowing of their culture, their economic inferiority and their morbid fear of losing their identity. They were thus exposing themselves to external criticism. And because on a worldwide scale there was increasing talk of decolonization and of national liberation, these terms quickly came to be used and new goals were set for the collective action of the Québécois. From the beginning, however, these new movements split into two major factions: those who, like the Alliance Laurentienne, on the whole accepted the definition of the Québécois group that the ideology of conservation had established; and those who, like Raoul Roy's *Revue Socialiste*, began to give another definition of the Quebec nation. The first more traditional group placed itself in the line of ideological choices that Quebec had known for decades; the second group was to define the ideology of development and participation which will now be discussed in greater detail.

On account of the homogeneity of the Québécois and their culture (setting aside the anglophone minority), the political options of Quebec since Confederation and the frame of reference of all political parties has always oscillated between certain more or less rightist tendencies. However, a considerable consensus has always existed between liberals and conservatives on the principal political options. It is still striking today to note that the differences between the partisans of the Union Nationale and of the Liberal party are quite minimal. The *Journal des Débats* of the Quebec Legislative Assembly gives the impression of a group whose ideas are interchangeable, who share the same values, and whose members are as thick as thieves. Often the only difference that separates them is the width of the aisle between the party in power and the opposition. Their differences are in tendencies rather than in doctrine. It is only recently that a more important cleavage has appeared between the left and the right. This phenomenon is so new in Quebec that at first it was said that these terms had no place in the political vocabulary of the nation since they did not correspond to any reality. Referring only to the members of the Assembly, it is quite evident that these terms do not mean very much. But with the third ideology which has appeared in the past few years, the terms right and left are beginning to refer to an increasingly clearly marked reality. Certainly, on the one hand, the Québécois have not reinvented socialism, Marxism, self-management, state planning or participatory democracy, but, on the other hand, it is also evident that the logic of the present situation has motivated them to take inspiration from these ideas to resolve problems that are demanding their attention in a very real way. It seems certain that it is above all the ideas of decolonization and national liberation that have awakened echoes among those who were troubled over the destiny and future of their nation. The phenomena of decolonization and of national liberation, which could be found in many nations of the world during the 1950s, brought with them ideas of the good life and the good society, of the role of the economy, and of social classes, which were the same as those in the nineteenth century when the bourgeois classes of most Western nations undertook their national revolutions. Thus, all these ideas finally reached a small part of Quebec youth who became aware that they could be applied to their own situation. But, in explaining the development of ideologies in Quebec, the influence of an international convergence must not be exaggerated; it is rather a case of a primarily local aid to phenomena that are the outcome of several decades of history. It must not be forgotten that the three ideologies are superimposed on each other and that they possess characteristics creating a chain whose links are closely interrelated. The radical falling out of the third ideology is to a large extent developing away from a common understanding about Quebec society.

What precisely is this third ideology? It could be said that the three Québécois ideologies are not mutually distinguishable and that there is no question, as some could believe, of a seesaw game between political parties. Let us first say that the distinguishing characteristic of the ideology of conservation is to consider the Québécois group as a cultural minority within Canada; this group is largely centred in Quebec but has offshoots in other provinces. All these groups constitute the bearers of the French-Canadian culture (religion, language and traditions) that must be preserved and transmitted as intact as possible over the generations. The ideology of recoupment also considers the French Canadians as a minority group spread across the country who must modernize their culture throughout that nation; this is a modern version of the ideology of conservation. There is here a difference between conservatives and liberals: the first want more autonomy for Quebec to ensure the conservation of its culture; the second want Quebec to become more integrated into Canada in order to profit from the advantages of the modern state while still preserving and enriching its culture and allowing it to spread across Canada.

The third ideology seems to be the most radical and from the beginning it was more strongly differentiated from the first two than these are differentiated from each other. It breaks from the other two by defining the Québécois francophone group not only as a culture but as a modern industrial society which has been dominated economically and politically by the rest of Canada; it ceases to speak of French Canadians and speaks of Québécois. For most of the people holding this ideology the minorities outside Quebec participate in French-Canadian culture but not in Quebec society. Of primary importance is that the Quebec nation be saved and liberated. This ideology is in accord with the ideology of recoupment in its fight against the ideology of conservation and in thinking that Québécois culture must be modernized (but not necessarily using North American societies as models). In effect, the greatest mutation that this ideology represents in comparison with the others is that it develops a different idea of people and society in general, and of Québécois people and society in particular. It is here that we return to the Quiet Revolution and the international context in which it came into being.

Not only did the ideology of recoupment borrow its model of a good society from Canadian society, but it can also be said that the ideology of conservation was largely inspired by the same source. These two ideologies, one of which was dominant for many years and the other, long in a minority position, established itself after World War II, have both developed a kind of symbiosis with the dominant culture. It can be said that they borrowed from it their dominant ideas on the subject of life in society; that is, according to these ideologies, of a more or less developed capitalism which, however, fitted well with the philosophy of American society. The ideology of conservation has preserved or acquired some concepts derived from certain social encyclicals and from certain rightist dictatorships (Spain, Portugal) but, at its base, the model remained that of the so-called liberal democracies. In the 1950s nothing could predict that the upsetting of the Duplessis regime would result in this third ideology. Observers predicted that the ideology of recoupment, shared by the members of the Liberal party, would become predominant and would take over from the ideology of conservation. But it happened otherwise.

But the independentist movements which had begun to arise again at the end of the 1950s did much to attract attention to the idea of domination of one society by another. Still, for many it was the question of political independence that was to facilitate the cultural expansion of Quebec. But the logic of the Quiet Revolution as carried out by the liberals must not be underestimated. Not only did their slogan of *Maîtres chez nous* contribute to the reinvigoration of Quebec and the Québécois in their own eyes, but it also contributed to the launching of reform in the two major problem areas of Quebec both on the national level and on the economic level. It has also helped to link these two objectives which have tended to exclude each other: the national objectives remaining the prerogative of the right and the socio-economic objectives being traditionally those of the left. The task of catching up was initiated through a modern civil service, extensive reforms in education, nationalization of electricity, the Société Générale de Financement (SGF), conseil d'orientation économique, régime de rentes, caisse de dépôt et de placement, and the Bureau d'Amenagement pour l'Est du Québec (BAEQ). The Liberals, through their dynamism, succeeded in interesting large sections of the population in their reforms (educators, civil servants, students and underdeveloped regions), and kindling among them the desire to participate in this Quiet Revolution.

From an ideological point of view, challenging society and its myth quickly made the Québécois aware that far from having built their society in its final form in the nineteenth century, it still remained to be built. Part of the population quickly came to see Quebec as a developing nation which not only removed them from their past conservatism but also differentiated them from other North American societies. This is another characteristic that brought them closer to colonized countries on the road to liberation and development. However, as opposed to countries that had developed in the nineteenth century and in the first decades of the twentieth century, the nations of today which are in the first phases of industrialization or, like Quebec, are behind in relation to highly industrialized countries, have many models of development at their disposal. Even the concept of development no longer has the exclusive economic meaning that it acquired at the time of the triumph of capitalism. Not able or not desiring to entrust the problem of developing society to industrial entrepreneurs or financiers, the nations which are today on the path to development or who consider themselves to have already achieved it, must count on the state and on their whole population in order to reach their objectives.

In Quebec there are many intellectuals, youth, members of unions and cooperatives and social activists who have realized that for the Québécois to attain their desire of becoming *maitre chez eux,* there must be planned socio-economic development and the establishment of a participatory democracy. The underdevelopment of Quebec, the relative homogeneity of the population, the exacerbation of national opinion and the shallow roots of liberal democracy in Quebec have all encouraged the diffusion throughout the population of ideas of development and of participation. The powerful Quebec labour movement and the entry of new strata of the population into the unions give this ideology of development and participation great potential.

Must it be added that these ideologies are presently being disputed? Nothing definite has been achieved and there does not seem to be any way of predicting which of the three ideologies will become dominant in the near future. This should soon develop into a struggle between the two most recent ideologies, that of recoupment and that of participation.

ENDNOTES

1. F. Ouellet, *Histoire économique et social du Québec, 1760–1850* (Paris: Fides, 1966), p. 210.
2. F. Dumont, ''Idéologie et conscience historique dans la société canadienne-française du XIXe siècle,'' manuscript, 1965, p. 11.
3. *Ibid.,* p. 16.
4. G. Filteau, *Histoire des Patriotes*, Vol. 13 (Montréal: 1942), pp. 243–44.
5. M. Wade, *The French Canadians, 1760–1945*, Vol. 1 (London: Macmillan, 1967), p. 186.
6. *Ibid.,* p. 197.
7. *Ibid.,* p. 208.

8. *Ibid.*, p. 212.
9. *Ibid.*, p. 252.
10. Dumont, "Idéologie et conscience historique," p. 31.
11. F.S. Garneau, *Histoire du Canada* (1852), pp. 401–402.
12. Léon Pouliot, *La réaction catholique de Montréal, 1840–1841* (Montréal: 1942).
13. The Institut canadien was founded in 1844 and brought together young Canadiens who were interested in arts and sciences. This association, with its liberal spirit, came into conflict with the clergy until its dissolution in about 1878.
14. Dumont, "Idéologie et conscience historique."
15. Viatte, cited in Léon Pouliot, *La réaction catholique de Montréal, 1840–1841.*
16. Mgr. Raymond, *Revue canadienne* (1 January 1871), p. 38.
17. Thomas Chapais, *Discours et conférences* (Québec: 1908), p. 39.
18. See Louis Maheu's thesis on this problem (Département de Sociologie, Université de Montréal, 1966).
19. Gérald Fortin, "An Analysis of the Ideology of French-Canadian Nationalist Magazines: 1917–1954," manuscript, Cornell University, 1956.
20. *Ibid.*, p. 205.
21. Maurice Tremblay, "La pensée sociale au Canada français," manuscript, 1950, pp. 33, 36.
22. With an interruption for the war years, 1939–44.
23. He was to become a minister in the Pearson government.
24. These five men were then ministers in the Pearson government.

28 Ambiguities and Contradictions in Being a Distinct Society

RAYMOND HUDON

By the second half of this century, it had become common to portray Quebec as *la province pas comme les autres*. Accordingly, different groups of people across Canada thought that special institutional and constitutional arrangements had to be agreed on in order to meet the specific demands of the political leadership in that province. The recognition of a special status for Quebec became part of some Canadian political parties' platforms in the late 1960s and early 1970s. At the same time, the Official Languages Act was adopted by Canadian Parliament. The Ontario premier, John Robarts, believed that the Canadian Constitution should be revised so that Quebec could proceed with political and social projects of its own, while keeping full membership in Confederation. The growing support for an independence programme was taken as a seriously impending threat.

These positions by no means indicated a consensus in Canadian society concerning Quebec. The implementation of the Official Languages Act met with strong opposition. For many Canadians, Quebec would remain discontented whatever solutions or accommodations were proposed. The so-called Trudeaumania that characterized the federal campaign in 1968 was profoundly ambivalent: whereas it represented an awareness of the new Quebec reality, it could also be interpreted as a desire by a significant number of Canadian voters to keep Quebec in its traditionally submissive place. Political élites had already recognized the acceptability of Quebec controlling its own pension plan.[1] However, it was thought that the making of concessions to Quebec would prepare a seed-bed for additional claims by Quebec leaders.

In fact, Quebec politicians were anxious to cope with the rising expectations from emerging actors in an evolving society.[2] Bureaucrats were playing an increasingly important role in the definition of Quebec policies and the belief spread that greater control of institutions and political resources was necessary to

---

This is an original essay written especially for this volume.

secure the future development of Quebec. This was to influence the conduct of federal politics. According to Kenneth McRoberts:

> the long-standing contention of Quebec governmental élites that only Quebec could be entrusted with the distinctive interests of French Canadians came to have radically different implications for Canadian federalism when it was combined with a new positive conception of the role of government.[3]

Political platforms and electoral slogans tended to increasingly radical nationalist stands, ranging from autonomy to independence. Following the *Maitres chez nous* that had been promoted by the Liberal government in the 1962 electoral campaign, the leader of the Union Nationale (UN), Daniel Johnson (elected premier in June 1966) clearly stated Quebec's situation: *Egalité ou indépendance*. In the meantime, parties clearly committed to an independentist option had appeared. In 1968, the Parti québécois (PQ) was founded, taking the place of the Ralliement national (RN). Against the unified electoral front of independentist forces, the Liberals, led by Robert Bourassa, defended federalism. Despite the unambiguous victories of the federalist position in two consecutive provincial elections, up to 1973 support for the PQ in the Quebec electorate grew steadily. On November 15, 1976, the separatist party won a majority of seats.[4] Quebec seemed to be behaving like a nation in search of a state—an independent state.[5]

During its two mandates between 1970 and 1976, the Bourassa's Liberal government unequivocally opposed the *souveraineté-association* option promoted by the PQ. Nonetheless, this same government had found it necessary to take a position termed *souveraineté culturelle*. In a sense, if the Quebec government was to remain a provincial government, it needed some special powers in order to secure the future of Quebec society as the heart of the French people on the North American continent. To say the least, this shift was disturbing to English Canada and to the federal government. Many felt that no compromise would satisfy any Quebec government, especially after Quebec's rejection of the Victoria Charter (on constitutional amendment procedures) in 1971. To many, the election of a PQ government created an intolerable situation.

The first reactions were twofold. Some suggested a renewal of Canadian federalism that would render the PQ option obsolete. Others, strongly supported by the Trudeau government in Ottawa, refused to bargain with a government whose ultimate goal was to break up the federation. As the PQ had promised to hold a referendum before the end of its first mandate, no serious negotiation was attempted before that deadline. However, if the Quebec people were to reject sovereignty association, they were given the assurance that constitutional change would be pursued to satisfy legitimate Quebec demands.

The referendum was held on 20 May 1980, and independence was defeated by nearly 60 percent. Constitutional meetings were immediately convened. Plans for a renewed federalism met with the opposition of some provinces in September, 1980. Court decisions and the resumed negotiations led to an agreement between the federal government and all the provinces *but* Quebec. In the meantime, in April 1981, the PQ government had been re-elected with a larger plurality of votes. The 1982 Canadian Constitution was proclaimed with Quebec staying outside. Even the return to power in 1985 of a Liberal government, led by Bourassa again, could not make Quebec sign the new Constitution. Among other conditions, the Quebec government demanded an explicit recognition of the distinctiveness of Quebec society before the Quebec government would be reconciled to the new constitutional order.

> In May 1986 the Quebec government revealed five conditions which must be met in order to secure its accession to the 1982 settlement. These were: constitutional recognition of Quebec as a 'distinct society', a constitutionally secured provincial role in immigration, a provincial role in Supreme Court appointments, limitations of the federal power to spend in areas of provincial jurisdiction, and an assured veto for Quebec in any future constitutional amendments.[6]

In June 1986, the Meech Lake agreement was reached between the provincial premiers and the federal government that would make possible the full partnership of Quebec in the Constitution. Three years later, the commitment of the premiers had not yet been ratified by all of the provincial Legislatures. According to public opinion polls, Canadians seem to be evenly divided on the accord. Moreover, it appears that the more they know of the accord, the more they reject it. In other times, such a political situation could have stimulated nationalist sentiments, and the PQ could have expected a larger share of votes in a coming election. However, what seemed to make sense only a decade ago can no longer be automatically predicted.

One could be tempted, based on these summary observations, to infer a collapse of Quebec nationalism, at least in the form in which it was expressed by the independentist movement of the 1960s and 1970s. In this essay, it will be argued that the apparently quiet reaction of the Quebec people points to some disaffection with politics. Quebeckers are still deeply aware that they form a society radically different from the rest of the country, and they behave accordingly. Thus, while they appear less inclined to support independence, they have not developed a strong sense of "Canadianness." Their favourable attitude regarding Canada-U.S. free trade is an interesting indication of that. Finally, there have been developments within Quebec politics that will affect political parties and party politics in the 1990s. The following developments help explain the apparent ambiguities and contradictions that characterize present Quebec politics.

A Distinct Society within a Different Country

Following the 1980 Quebec referendum, many analysts have emphasized that the outcome by no means signified the end of Quebec nationalism. Pierre Fournier warned:

[It is premature] to bury the national question in Quebec irrespective of the electoral fortunes of the Parti Québécois, [since] the problems and questions which prompted the development of a pro-independence movement in Quebec remain unresolved.[7]

Hubert Guindon came to the heart of the question even more radically:

Many would like to think that [the demise of the PQ] spells the end of the separatist threat. The more naive would even go so far as to think that the Québécois have had a change of heart. More realistically, it can be cogently argued that a political issue cannot be kept in the forefront indefinitely. It either advances or recedes.[8]

Guindon argued that the failure of the independence "dream" can be explained by the PQ having become "a business-like organisation [which] is no substitute for a mass movement."[9] One can fully agree with Guindon about the inevitable effects of an institutionalization process like the one which marked the evolution of the PQ as it came closer to power.[10] This is a process that is commonly observable regarding social or national movements.

One important question is whether Quebec voters still consider the sovereignty association option valid. A recent survey[11] showed that among Quebec francophones 43 percent supported sovereignty association, 36 percent were opposed, 15 percent did not know and 5 percent expressed a qualified reaction ("it depends"). It is surprising to note, from the same survey, that 50 percent of these same people were ready to vote for Robert Bourassa's Liberals as opposed to 38 percent who would have voted PQ.

In fact, this apparent contradiction in political opinions and electoral preferences is partly due to the action of parties. Citizens have the feeling that parties cannot do as much as they promise because they do not control the factors which determine decision making. There is indeed a trend that compels decisions to be made based on market conditions and world competition. Many policies now seem conditioned more by leaders' perceptions of what is going on in other countries or regions of the world that could be or are competitors than by demands and pressures from their own "nationals"[12] (unless they are themselves deeply and directly involved in competitive activities). Of course, this is not to say that pressure politics has become obsolete. Nonetheless, pressure politics itself is significantly influenced by global demands. Although electing different governments does still matter, major differences in policies are linked more to the pace and forms of change than to the nature of change itself. Under these conditions, to support an option and not to vote for a party which promotes that option can partly be reconciled in spite of first appearances.

Voters also are becoming aware that the differences in governmental management are not important. For instance, following the adoption of Bill 178 (requiring the use of French in outside signs), Quebec voters have likely realized that language policies in their province can be almost as radical under a Liberal government as they would be under the PQ. To some extent, Premier Bourassa was correct when he emphasized that his government is the first ever in Quebec to suspend the protection of rights as a means to protect French in the province. To be sure, public demonstrations had reminded the Liberal government how important the question of language is in the minds of many francophones in Quebec.

Finally, one cannot disregard the remarkable ambiguities concerning sovereignty association. In the survey referred to above, one must note that if this option is to mean political separation from the rest of Canada (for example, election of no more members to the House of Commons and Quebec ceasing to be a province), then support for sovereignty association is going to decline. As far as francophone voters are concerned, 47 percent oppose sovereignty association, and only 38 percent favour it. This brings us back to a programme of "reconfederation," as Hubert Guindon termed the option promoted by the PQ under René Lévesque.[13]

Given these considerations, one must question the reality of Quebec as a distinct society. Quebec intellectuals have become more silent politically.[14] Is this because the effect of their action has vanished? Intellectuals in Quebec have played an important role in determining collective attitudes:

> Unlike their counterparts in Quebec, left-wing intellectuals in English Canada were unable to articulate an analysis of Canadian society that expressed the interests of an ascendant class. Social scientists in Quebec, particularly sociologists, succeeded in defining Quebec as a distinct national society, a conceptualization that supported province-building activities which expanded the career opportunities of a growing francophone middle class, and that was successful precisely for this reason. Circumstances in English Canada were substantially different.[15]

The national question seems to have been central in the Quebec political debates of the 1970s[16], but the present political situation looks quite different. Business people have now superseded intellectuals as leaders of society. As shown below, this perception must be qualified. Nevertheless, the change in the political agenda stated by Brooks and Gagnon is correct:

> The political agenda of the 1970s and early 1980s, which included a heavy stress on constitutional reform, linguistic protectionism and social policy, is being replaced by the issues of deregulation, the privatization of state assets and ways to increase the competitiveness of the provincial economy.[17]

Unquestionably, Quebec citizens have become more business-oriented. Recently they have gloried in economic accomplishment more than in nationalist rhetoric and political gain. More accurately, they have come to think of collective assertion through economic action. People like the Lemaires (who control the Cascades paper company), Claude Castonguay (formerly a Liberal minister in the Bourassa government of the early 1970s and now associated with the La

Laurentienne financial and banking institution), and companies like Lavallin, Bombardier and Provigo, represent a new brand of standard-bearers of the Quebec destiny. They are considered to have better credentials than politicians and traditional "national" spokespersons (lay or clergy) used to have. In fact, the search for power and prestige has taken radically new forms.

This is not to say that Quebec voters no longer find it important to have a strong provincial state. After all, economic developments in Quebec have materialized to a great extent because of state intervention over the last 30 years. This is possibly why, as Kenneth McRoberts points out, people in Quebec are reluctant to support the reduction of state powers in the province:

> . . . analysis of public opinion suggests that most Québécois did not share [in 1985] business's urgency to roll back the state. Although few Québécois supported further expansion of the Quebec state, apparently most of them were reasonably supportive of the present scale of state activity.[18]

These observations still apply today. In a survey published in *Maclean's*[19] in mid-1989, it appeared that "Quebec residents were significantly less likely than other Canadians to be willing to see their taxes increased or services cut in order to reduce the federal deficit." The exact figures were 32 percent for Quebec residents while the Canadian average was 48 percent.

One can venture the same argument concerning provincial government activities. Some results from the same survey point out that the state must be held responsible for services. For instance, people in Quebec are more likely than other Canadians (68 percent as against a Canadian average of 50 percent) "to say that child care should be . . . available to everyone who wants it." On the question of a guaranteed minimum income for everyone, "Quebecers were much more likely [75 percent] to agree than Ontario residents [Metropolitan Toronto: 49 percent; the rest of Ontario: 43 percent]" and than other Canadians (Canadian average: 62 percent) to think of it as "an absolute right." Therefore it can be suggested that Quebec residents are more inclined than other Canadians to demand public services even though a budget deficit is thus incurred. Actually, the Liberal government elected in 1985, following nine years of PQ rule, was to leave in place some liberal plans that many of the new members of that government favoured:

> . . . there was a major effort during the first two years of the new Bourassa government to "normalize" Quebec's status relative to other provinces, in effect reversing the predominant trend of Quebec politics over the previous two decades. However, there were major obstacles and constraints to such an effort. Important elements within Quebec society were strongly committed to the social and economic roles the Quebec state had assumed over the last 25 years.[20]

At the same time, Quebec voters strongly support, more than other Canadians and certainly more than Ontarians, options that could entail revisions in state involvement in the economic realm and ultimately in social programmes. In the fall of 1988, the federal election gave voters a chance to express support for or against free trade between Canada and the United States. The opinion of *souverainistes* that the implementation of the Canada-U.S. Free Trade Agreement would eventually help in achieving Quebec political sovereignty can only barely be taken seriously. Yet, one cannot disregard the almost total agreement of *péquistes* and provincial Liberals in regard to the agreement. Though not explicable by this one issue, the electoral problems of federal Liberals in Quebec very likely are partly linked to that situation.

The differing attitudes of Quebec residents regarding the United States were also indicated in the *Maclean's* poll. "Quebecers were more likely [60 percent] than other Canadians [49 percent] to favor a common currency with the United States." In addition, "Quebecers were more likely [23 percent] than other Canadians [Canadian average: 14 percent; Metropolitan Toronto: 14 percent; the rest of Ontario: 9 percent] to favor joining the United States." Of course, it might be interpreted that many Quebeckers simply found an expedient way to settle old scores with English Canada. The future of francophones as Americans would not necessarily be an enviable one. Though Americans know almost nothing about Canadians, one can hardly ignore their opinion (however marginal) about the French presence in Canada. To the question: "What do you like least about Canadians?", American residents gave answers as follows: nothing: 37 percent; do not know Canadians: 18 percent; do not know about them: 14 percent; *French-speaking: 6 percent*[21]; they think they are better: 3 percent; don't know: 4 percent; arrogant: 2 percent.

It is better to look for other explanations than the classic Canadian "two solitudes" thesis if we are to reach a more complete understanding of the ambiguous, even contradictory, opinions regarding the constitutional status of Quebec within Canada. Positions about language policies are also not single-minded. For instance, Bill 101 is still preferred to Bill 178[22], but Quebec residents also believe, much more than other Canadians, that "services should be offered in both official languages" by the federal government (88 percent as opposed to 68 percent in the rest of the country), by provincial governments (72 percent and 52 percent respectively), and by private enterprise (76 percent as opposed to 44 percent).[23] Moreover, on the basis of the survey published by *Maclean's*, it seems that "Quebecers would be less willing [37 percent] than other Canadians [48 percent] to have civil rights removed" in times of crisis.

Thus, Quebec citizens are quite distinct from other Canadians as far as some important political questions (state intervention, social services, free trade) are concerned. But this distinctiveness is certainly not only a matter of opinion and attitudes. For example, the number of poor people is increasing more in Quebec than in other Canadian provinces. Beyond official figures concerning economic growth, the prospects for economic development in Quebec have been deteriorating for 20 years, as data on investments show.[24] The rate of unemployment is steadily higher in Quebec than in the provinces west of the Ottawa river. Under these conditions, it is not surprising that, according to the *Maclean's* poll, Quebec residents appear less likely (54 percent) than other Canadians (60 percent) "to favor shutting down a polluter" that provides many jobs in a community (Canadians in the Prairies are more likely—71 percent—to hold that position).

In summary, Quebec political culture appears to be significantly different from that of the rest of Canada. The difference used to be explained in terms of history and culture. But economic realities are inevitably part of any understanding of the many ambiguities and apparent contradictions that colour the opinions and attitudes of the Quebec people. There is also evidence that the situation of the national movement in Quebec cannot be measured by the level of support for the PQ. Some say the "independence myth is vanishing"; however, one may debate Marc Henry Soulet's hypothesis that this is the cause of the decline of politics in Quebec.[25] Politics has never been an activity revolving only around *national* interests! It could be more easily contended that Quebec nationalism has declined as politics has declined, since many Quebec activists have become less involved because they have been disappointed at the PQ government's record. Guindon seems to believe that the Quebec national movement could turn this to its advantage:

> The retreat from party politics is not a blow, but a welcome change of course for the national movement. The new situation opens up the options and courses of action that can best be carried out away from the glare of the mass media. Rather than attempting another foray into party politics, the energies of the national movement should be devoted to considering and implementing these new courses of action. As, indeed, they once were. And they are not spent. In a quieter, more unified, and mature fashion, the dream of nationhood shall live on.[26]

Guindon's position is not entirely misleading; however, it tends to assume that people now find politics irremediably unimportant. This would be misinterpreting the current retreat from politics. It would be an exaggeration to make retreat synonymous with rejection, though strong political skepticism, not to say political cynicism, may be. Citizens continue to vote, although in smaller numbers, in many Western democracies. But do they still believe it really matters?

An Autonomous State for a Distinct Society?

To understand the relative decline of party politics in Quebec, a general explanation previously proposed is: policies of national and sub-national governments are no longer decided in the context of specific societies but are conditioned by factors found well beyond the boundaries of these states. To a certain extent, "democratic revolutions" in eastern Europe as well as adjustments in Western democracies can be related to that new reality.

This is not to suggest that governments have become powerless. However, it does show how expectations about government actions may be in decline and, as a consequence, why perceptions and visions of political action appear to be changing. Moreover, these perceptions and visions are encouraged by a developing impression that traditional political and interest organizations move to a different position between state and society. Indeed, these organizations, particularly political parties which can realistically think of coming to power, seem increasingly inclined to take account of the new limiting conditions which affect a national government's action. This is true also for interest groups. Thus, it is not surprising that citizens consider political activism less central to the promotion and the defence of their interests and preoccupations. They are more given to offering their support to new issue-oriented organizations such as environmental groups or peace movements and, sometimes, to parties which are bearers of these policies. Furthermore, these orientations are expressed more by younger people, about whom there are some quite pertinent considerations.

Comparisons between the political orientations of younger people and those of the general population tend to make converging observations possible.[27] Data from recent surveys of Quebec[28] and Canadian[29] young people will be referred to as illustrating aspects of new elements in political culture. When asked, in the Quebec survey, if they have confidence in politicians, only 33 percent of young people in that province have confidence either "a great deal" (4 percent) or "quite a bit" (29 percent). This result is further confirmed in a Canadian survey where the special position of Quebec young people on a similar question is revealed. Let us consider first the position of Canadian youth as a whole.

> ... the country's 15–24 year olds were asked how much confidence they have in the people in charge of government at the federal, provincial and local levels. Their response was virtually the same regardless of the level involved. Less than one third (29 percent) indicate they have a high level of confidence ["a great deal" and "quite a bit"] in government leaders.
>
> Variations by age are slight, decreasing only marginally among 20–24 year olds. Differences in confidence by community size are also negligible. Regionally, however, Quebec youth stand out as having the lowest confidence in all three levels of government.[30]

Indeed! Quebec young people are confident in government leaders in a proportion of only 18 percent at the federal and provincial levels and 19 percent at the local level. It is interesting to look at some other figures as they relate generally to young Canadians.

> While they believe in the possibility of influencing government, young people do not express much confidence in Canada's political parties. Just 18 percent say they have "a great deal" or "quite a bit" of confidence in political parties—compared to 67 percent for the police, 35 percent for newspaper executives, and 26 percent for religious leaders.[31]

Civil servants seem to benefit from a comfortable degree of confidence (51 percent) among young Quebecers; while unions had 72 percent. Thus it is possible to conclude from these figures that party politics do not attract young people. In that regard, one must emphasize that among the young Canadians surveyed by Gallup, "a majority of 52 percent agreed with the statement, 'For me, the people running for office are more important than the political party they represent'."

Though a low degree of confidence in politics is expressed by young people in Quebec, the Quebec survey indicates that 41 percent have confidence in religious leaders; journalists score a surprising 73 percent. However, in the survey administered by Gallup, this high degree of confidence in journalists clearly is not transferred into confidence in media leadership.

> Beyond the use and enjoyment of various media forms, we asked young people how much confidence they have in the people who provide leadership in the radio, newspaper and television industries. Just under 40 percent expressed high levels of confidence ["a great deal" and "quite a bit"] in the people in charge of the various media. By comparison, they reported confidence levels of about 60 percent in the case of both schools and the courts, and 30 percent in the case of federal and provincial governments. Media confidence is lowest in Quebec [25 percent for radio; 20 percent for newspapers; and 25 percent for TV] and slightly lower among young women and youth in their early 20s.[32]

It appears that Quebec young people have confidence in people as long as they are not related to official or institutional roles. Teachers are given quite an astonishing score of 87 percent, while business leaders or entrepreneurs have the confidence of 79 percent among the 15-18 year olds in Quebec. So, there is evidence that the level of confidence is radically decreasing as politics begins to colour the activities or roles that are considered. Once again, such statements must be interpreted with some reservation. However, the data presented by the Canadian Youth Foundation inspired observations that are worth quoting in length.

> Whether it involves becoming a candidate in a student election or participating in a demonstration, it appears that politically related activity is the domain for a select few. Certainly, there is acknowledgement that the government and its functions is necessary, but the prevailing temperament is to "let the other person do it."
>
> There is evidence that, if invited to do so, young people will respond and, for example, sign a petition. Two out of three define a good citizen as someone who tries to change a government policy he/she disagrees with—especially if people act together. Overall, however, there is a prevailing mood of political skepticism. Party politics, in particular, is viewed by Canada's young people with disinterest.
>
> The young are more oriented to their personal goals than to collective concerns. They are not rallying around causes. They are giving a higher priority to personal pursuits than social justice issues. Today's youth are a politically quiet generation.[33]

Quietness does not mean approval, if the above figures concerning government policies are accurate, especially regarding Quebec young people's views on citizenship and our system of government. So, while 60 percent of young Canadians agree on the statements, "Despite its many faults, our system of doing things is still the best in the world" and "I feel that you cannot be a good citizen unless you always obey the law," young people in Quebec agree in much smaller proportions (respectively 45 and 47 percent).

Only about 34 percent of young Quebeckers find "being a Canadian . . . very important." The measured average for the whole country is 49 percent (almost the same as in the Prairies), with regional highs of around 60 percent in British Columbia, Ontario and the Atlantic provinces. Thus, it is not surprising to observe that support for sovereignty association in Quebec is still coming most strongly from the 25–34 year olds, but also in an important measure from the 18–24 ones (38 percent, for; 52 percent, against).[34] This cannot be reassuring as far as the future of Canada is concerned, even if it is not immediately disquieting. An evidently low level of identification as "Canadian" is not for the moment driving towards separatism, since that agenda is also accorded a low level of confidence. But in times of crisis, the political quiet alluded to above could potentially be very disturbing.

To examine the Quebec young people's sense of their Canadian identity from another point of view, it is interesting to compare their views on Canada's place in the world with the opinions of the 15–24 year olds in Canada as a whole.[35] While 36 percent of Canadian young people agree that "we ought to worry about our own country and let the rest of the world take care of itself," only 28 percent of Quebec young people agree. On the other hand, if 35 percent of young Canadians believe that "decisions made by politicians in Canada have little or no bearing on the rest of the world," up to 43 percent of Quebec 15–24 year olds acknowledge the little influence Canada has in world politics. These results may point to a strong Quebec identity. But according to the survey administered by SEGMA among the Quebec 15–18 year olds, 71 percent would be ready to live outside Quebec, whereas 62 percent would be ready to emigrate from Canada. It is interesting to look at the results when a similar question was asked of 15–24 year olds throughout Canada.

> In probing satisfaction with life in Canada, 15–24 year olds were asked where they would like to live. Some 75% said if they could live in any country, their first choice would be Canada. The number one competitor to "our home and native land" is the United States and one in ten would choose to move there.[36]

It seems that if Quebec young people had a choice, most would prefer to live in Quebec. Nevertheless, these results might justify the questioning of any thesis about Quebec nationalism being explicable by a minority situation or by language specificity. Furthermore, Quebec young people's apparent readiness to move outside Quebec could not mean a pessimistic vision about the future of French, since 77 percent of Quebec young students believe in the survival of that language in North America. Briefly, young people's Quebec identity is not expressed in a chauvinistic mood. This is not to say that provocation could not produce strong reactions. Because, to come back to a former statement, if young people in Canada and in Quebec may not be rallying around causes, this is not to say that they are indifferent to all causes. Many are even speaking up for causes, as interviews with a number of them show. For the time being, they find themselves in a *cul-de-sac*: when they are presented with causes, they have quite a low level of confidence in people and particularly in organizations which used to be the standard-bearers of political causes.

The attitudes and opinions of young people give a fair indication of what is thought and felt in the rest of a society. Of course, there are differences. For instance, recent surveys[36] show that the support for the federal Liberals is greater among Quebec older people, while younger voters tend to support the Conservatives. Sometimes, one has the impression that Quebec people are dreaming of becoming independent without being politically involved and without seriously looking for a proper state apparatus. There possibly one finds a great measure of wisdom!

According to Gérard Bergeron, it had become natural, though not necessary, that the development of the Quebec state in the 1960s and in the 1970s leads to the *souverainiste* project.[38] It is interesting to recall that, in 1963, Léon Dion thought, to some extent, of old formulations:

> The slogans, key formulae, and themes advanced by nationalists of every inclination have not changed. For example, retracing the roots of a phrase such as *l'Etat du Québec* takes over a full century's history of our social and political thought.[39]

In fact, Bergeron's statement was to be true only up to a certain point. Indeed, at the moment when the *souverainiste* project was apparently getting increasing support, plans for the further development of the Quebec state in an autonomous form began to be obstructed. Many of the considerations above could be recalled at this point. However, one should now apply them in the Canadian context. Since the late 1960s, Canadian governments have become aware of the need to adjust to the new conditions that have arisen in world trade and economy in the postwar period. From the Third option to free trade, economic policies were designed to cope with rapidly evolving situations. Besides, one cannot disregard important changes that were visible in the constitutional realm.[40] Following the modernizing of Quebec, growing aspirations developed in Quebec society, and the state was thought to be crucially instrumental in carrying them out. Different "theories"[41] and plans were promoted of which the "two nations" and the "special status" ones remain the most celebrated. But, as time passed, the federal government and some provinces (Ontario in particular) became increasingly reluctant to give Quebec special treatment, especially regarding powers over the economy. In the constitutional meetings convened immediately after the Quebec referendum, the federal government made it clear that centralizing powers over the economy was on the agenda. In the 1982 Constitution, centralization plans were not as entrenched as was desired. Nonetheless, this was compensated for by an integration process that was more or less perceptibly achieved.[42]

By developing the Quebec state apparatus and by expanding its powers, particularly its economic ones, Quebec political leaders became increasingly conscious of limits unavoidably imposed by new economic realities. The result, as Anne Légaré and Nicole Morf suggest, has been a greater coordination of, or a more coherent approach, to economic issues.[43] These authors conclude that the development of the Quebec state has meant a process of making that province a Canadian *region*, so contributing to its self-negation as a *nation*.[44]

This is not to suggest that the Canadian federal state has now firmly and fully established its social legitimacy as Gérard Bergeron reminds us.[45] This is true particularly since the 1982 Constitution and the increasing intervention by governments in economic activities, beyond the mere impressions created by official rhetoric on deregulation and disengagement. The recent promotion of free trade might be interpreted as a form of intervention aimed at reorganizing production for market expansion and restructuring.

In Quebec this takes on special meaning, as state expansion is still a relatively recent development. Quebec voters have undoubtedly become more business-oriented because they felt it to be socially and economically a necessity.[46] The Bilingualism and Biculturalism Commission stimulated Quebecers' awareness of the need to become more business-oriented that began to develop in the wake of the Quiet Revolution. By doing so, the Quebec people have possibly ceased affirming themselves as a nation. For the time being, all appearances lead to that conclusion, particularly since Quebec voters, like many others in Western democracies, are skeptical about political leaders and parties.

Conclusion

Although an unprecedented proportion of the Canadian population favor the separation of Quebec as shown by a Gallup poll,[47] English Canada should find the apparent retreat of Quebec nationalism disquieting. Saving the integrity of the country does not give any assurance that democracy is fully protected. The caveat of Alan Cairns should be seriously taken:

> Those who govern us may have to relearn the ancient democratic message that they are servants of the people, and learn the new message that the constitution under and by which we all now live does not belong to them.[48]

Cairns should have made his point before 1982. Had he done so, the Quebec people would likely be less distrustful when told they will be taken care of by politicians and government leaders. Voting is important in our liberal democracies.

> At the most general level, voting is the most obvious and manifest connecting link between the actions of a government and the preferences of the citizens of the society that it serves.[49]

But when party politics is in decline, voting may become a weak link, and other forms of action might be thought of as more efficient means of satisfying interests and aspirations. But some of these other means are not necessarily better for democracy, as the 1970 October Crisis should remind us. Nor do other practices, such as patronage,[50] contribute to the improvement of democracy.

Finally, it must be repeated that party politics is not the whole of politics. However, in spite of their weaknesses and their disappointing records, party politics have not always hindered peaceful change, and have from time to time conducted forces unquestionably devoted to positive change, though the institutionalization process may have reduced the scope of initial plans.

While dealing with the issue of the distinctiveness of Quebec society, government leaders in Canada should keep these old lessons in mind. If they do not, they may possibly be undermining the viability of party politics in Quebec. If only politicians would show more courage and integrity in making decisions, rather than being motivated by immediate electoral gain, the practice of politics would rise above mere evasion. In the Meech Lake Accord, specifically regarding the "distinct society" clause, there are fewer profound changes involved than its opponents would have us believe. However, *The Financial Post*'s editorial position makes it clear that the real issue revolves around the assessment of the clause's constitutional impact:

> This newspaper would like it on the record: we favor special treatment for Quebec. That goes beyond merely recognizing the obvious sociological fact that Quebec is "distinct". Quebec has different needs, and these should be reflected in law, up to and including the Constitution.

Opposition to the clause is firmly asserted:

> . . . there is a difference between the explicit constitutional provisos and contractual arrangements through which the Dominion has recognized the particular needs of various provinces, and a constitutional blank cheque of the likes of Meech Lake's "distinct society" clause. Here the range of powers potentially arrogated is unlimited rather than defined, asserted as of right, rather than by statute or agreement, and available to one province alone. To say Quebec is a "*province pas comme les autres*" is far removed from declaring it is not a province at all. Special, yes. Special status, no.[51]

It appears from this that the Quebec question is still bothering English Canada. Although social and political realities cannot be denied, they must not be generally recognized, even only in symbolic terms. In short, English Canada seems unprepared to see the bargaining position it obtained from the results of the 1980 referendum diminished. However, one year after the writing of this essay and shortly after the collapse of the Meech Lake Accord, it is clear that Quebec nationalism is stimulated as it has likely never been before. Political parties, and even possibly Jean Chrétien's Liberals, will merely have to go with the flow.

ENDNOTES

1. For an analysis of the negotiations that resulted in that agreement, see Richard Simeon, *Federal-Provincial Diplomacy: The Making of Recent Policy in Canada* (Toronto: University of Toronto Press, 1972).
2. See the classic analysis of Hubert Guindon, "Social Unrest, Social Class, and Quebec's Bureaucratic Revolution," reproduced in Hubert Guindon, ed., *Quebec Society: Tradition, Modernity, and Nationhood* (Toronto: University of Toronto Press, 1988), pp. 27–37.
3. Kenneth McRoberts, *Quebec: Social Change and Political Crisis*, 3rd ed. (Toronto: McClelland and Stewart, 1988), p. 142.
4. For interpretations of this election outcome, see Raymond Hudon, "The 1976 Quebec Election," in Michael D. Behiels, ed., *Quebec Since 1945: Selected Readings* (Toronto: Copp Clark Pitman, 1987), pp. 274–285.
5. For a general review of the evolution of Quebec politics during that period, see Raymond Hudon, "Québec: une nation en quête d'Etat," *Etudes*, Vol. 356, No. 3 (March 1982), pp. 295–310.
6. Richard Simeon, "Meech Lake and Shifting Conceptions of Canadian Federalism," *Canadian Public Policy* [*The Meech Lake Accord*], XIV supplement (September 1988), p. 9.
7. Pierre Fournier, "The Future of Quebec Nationalism," in Keith Banting and Richard Simeon, ed., *And No One Cheered: Federalism, Democracy and the Constitution Act* (Toronto: Methuen Publications, 1983), pp. 171–172.
8. Hubert Guindon, "The Rise and Demise of the Parti Québécois," in *Quebec Society*, p. 162.
9. Hubert Guindon, "The Referendum: The Lessons of Defeat," in *Quebec Society*, p. 116.
10. This thesis was already developed by Raymond Hudon in "The Parti Québécois in Power: Institutionalization, Crisis Management and Decline," in Hugh G. Thorburn, ed., *Party Politics in Canada*, 5th ed. (Scarborough: Prentice-Hall Canada, 1985), pp. 220–233.
11. The results of this survey by Sorécom for *Le Soleil* (a Quebec City paper) and CKAC (a Montreal radio station) were published in that paper on 6 May 1989. See Michel David, "La souveraineté-association monte sans entamer la popularité de Bourassa," pp. A1, A2.
12. See Lionel Stoleru, *L'ambition internationale* (Paris: Editions du Seuil, 1987).
13. Hubert Guindon, "The Rise and Demise of the Parti Québécois," in *Quebec Society*, p. 156.
14. For instance, see Marc Henry Soulet, *Le silence des intellectuels: Radioscopie de l'intellectuel québécois* (Montréal: les Editions Saint-Martin, 1987), especially pp. 79–102.
15. Steven Brooks and Alain G. Gagnon, *Social Scientists and Politics in Canada: Between Clerisy and Vanguard* (Montreal-Kingston: McGill-Queen's University Press, 1988), p. 108.
16. This is the thesis which is defended by Réjean Pelletier and is very summarily formulated to conclude his recent study of Quebec party politics in previous decades. Réjean Pelletier, *Partis politiques et société québécoise. De Duplessis à Bourassa, 1944–1970* (Montreal: Editions Québec/Amérique, 1989), p. 379.
17. Steven Brooks and Alain G. Gagnon, *Social Scientists and Politics in Canada*, p. 69.
18. Kenneth McRoberts, *Quebec: Social Change and Political Crisis*, p. 409.
19. Let us quote the very brief presentation of this poll from the magazine: "The complete poll of 1000 Canadians and 1000 Americans was conducted by Toronto-based Decima Research." The results are reproduced and commented upon at length in a special report entitled "Portrait of Two Nations," *Maclean's*, 3 July 1989, pp. 23–84. Unless indicated to the contrary, references or excerpts will be taken from the summary in pp. 48–50.

20. Kenneth McRoberts, *Quebec: Social Change and Political Crisis*, p. 214.

21. Emphasis added.

22. This statement relies on data from opinion polls conducted by Serécom following the adoption of Bill 178 in December 1988. For more detailed results, see Michel David, "Les Québécois préfèrent la loi 101," *Le Soleil*, 4 February 1989, pp. A1, A2.

23. These data are taken from a table used by Jean-Louis Gagnon in the article "Bilingualism and the American Challenge," published in a special report (*English and French in Canada*) prepared by the Commissioner of Official Languages and published as a special issue of *Language and Society* (Summer 1989). In spite of that, according to a Gallup poll, 51 percent of Canadians (as compared to 43 percent in 1987) believed in the summer of 1989 that the rights of English-speaking Canadians are not well protected in Quebec, while only 15 percent of Quebec residents shared that opinion. More detailed results are presented in *Le Soleil*, 20 July 1989, p. A8 ("Les tensions linguistiques ont créé un climat d'animosité au pays").

24. Some questions related to that have been developed by Raymond Hudon, "Quebec, the Economy and the Constitution," in Keith Banting and Richard Simeon, eds., *And No One Cheered*, pp. 133–153.

25. This thesis that relates the decline of nationalism and the decline of politics in Quebec is held by Marc Henry Soulet in *Le silence des intellectuels*, p. 88.

26. Hubert Guindon, "The other options of the national movement in Quebec," in *Quebec Society*, p. 170.

27. Analyses of this sort already show that younger people's attitudes and opinions about party politics and politics in general, though not exactly similar, are close to those of the general population. For example, see Raymond Hudon and Patrick Lecomte, "Représentations de la crise de la représentation. Quelques dimensions politiques du mouvement étudiant de l'automne 1986 en France," in Jean Tournon, ed., *Alternance et changements politiques. Les expériences canadienne, québécoise et française* (Grenoble: Les cahiers du CERAT, No. 4, Centre de recherche sur le politique, l'administration et le territoire, Institut d'études politiques, Université des sciences sociales de Grenoble, 1988), pp. 227–271.

28. The survey in Quebec was undertaken by SEGMA, a subsidiary of Lavallin, for the Université de Montréal and the magazine *L'actualité*, a monthly publication by Maclean-Hunter. The principal results and comments on that survey are presented in "Les valeurs des jeunes," *L'actualité*, Vol. 14, No. 6 (June 1989), pp. 28–48. The results are calculated from 1 039 interviews from a sampling of 1 519 students who are between 15 and 18 years old and who are in their fourth or fifth year in secondary school or in their first year in CEGEPs (in the general programme preparing them for university). In the following part of this paper, references will be made without additional specifications.

29. "The interview schedule was constructed by [Reginald] Bibby and [Donald] Posterski and administered nationally by the Gallup organization between 26 October and 22 December 1987. A total of 2033 young people between the ages of 15 to 24 were interviewed" (p. 54). More detailed presentation of the methodology and main results of that survey are reported in: Canadian Youth Foundation, *Canada's Youth. "Ready for Today"* (Ottawa: Ministry of State for Youth), 55 pp. Unless it is needed, further references to that survey will be made without additional specifications.

30. Detailed results can be found in the report published by Canadian Youth Foundation, pp. 34–36 (pp. 36–38 in the French version).

31. *Ibid.*

32. *Ibid.*, p. 39.

33. *Ibid.*, p. 36. Figures that are presented below are taken from the same page.

34. See Michel David, "La souveraineté-association monte sans entamer la souveraineté de Bourassa", *Le Soleil*, pp. A1–A2.

35. Taken from a table in Canadian Youth Foundation, *Canada's Youth*, p. 52.

36. *Ibid.*

37. For more detailed information, see André Forgues, "La chute des conservateurs s'est arrêtée," *Le Soleil*, 2 July 1989, pp. A1, A2.

35. Gérard Bergeron, *Pratique de l'Etat québécois* (Montreal: Coll. Dossiers Documents, Editions Québec/Amérique, 1984), p. 427.

39. Léon Dion, *Québec: The Unfinished Revolution* (Montreal: McGill-Queen's University Press, 1976), p. 32.

40. For some developments on this question, see Raymond Hudon, "Intégration et diversité: Les dilemmes du fédéralisme canadien," *International Political Science Review*, Vol. 5, No. 4 (1984), pp. 455–472.

41. For a review of the variety of "theories" concerning Canadian federalism, see Edwin R. Black, *Divided Loyalties: Canadian Concepts of Federalism* (Montreal: McGill-Queen's University Press, 1975).

42. This point is developed, especially regarding fiscal policies, by Anne Légaré and Nicole Morf, *La Société distincte de l'Etat. Québec-Canada, 1930–1980* (Montreal: Coll. Brèches, Editions Hurtubise HMH, 1989), pp. 149–156.

43. *Ibid.*, pp. 215–216.

44. *Ibid.*, p. 223. "[L'appareil provincial québécois] *matérialise*, par son existence même en tant qu'élément de l'Etat canadien, la constitution tendancielle du Québec comme région et *sa disparition tendancielle comme nation.*"

45. Gérard Bergeron, *Pratique de l'Etat québécois*, p. 245.

46. This statement is inspired by Gérard Bergeron who writes: "L'économique n'apparaît jamais autant prioritaire que lorsqu'il devient socialement déficient," p. 428.

47. The results of this poll show that 28 percent of the Canadian population would favor the separation of Quebec. The highest point previously measured was 16 percent in July 1977. For other and more detailed results, see "28% de la population canadienne souhaite la séparation du Québec", *Le Soleil*, 20 July 1989, pp. A-1, A-2.

48. Alan C. Cairns, "Citizens (Outsiders) and Governments (Insiders) in Constitution-Making: The Case of Meech Lake," *Canadian Public Policy* [*The Meech Lake Accord*], XIV supplement (September 1988), p. 143.

49. Peter Regenstrief, *The Diefenbaker Interlude*, as quoted in *The Archivist* [*Elections*], Vol. 16, No. 1 (January-February 1989), p. 1.

50. For a discussion of patronage and its transformation, see (among others) Raymond Hudon, "Le patronage politique: Rationalités et moralité." *Journal of Canadian Studies* [*Patronage*], Vol. 22, No. 2 (Summer 1987), pp. 111–134.

51. "Yes, Quebec is different", *The Financial Post*, 24 July 1989, p. 22.

29

Party Competition in Quebec: Direct Confrontation or Selective Emphasis?

RÉJEAN LANDRY

Political parties are the crucial links between the voters' preferences and the policies enacted by governments. In a representative democracy, the electorate approves or disapproves the past performances of governments and the proposed policies of parties by voting for a party. A party supports a particular programme in its quest for office, and becomes identified with particular policies through its conduct in office. Political programmes have a symbolic significance. Their philosophy or their tone may be as important as the content of their specific policy proposals in showing that particular parties are conservative, social-democrat, nationalist, or whatever. Moreover, programmes have a substantive significance. The theory of representative democracy posits a set of relationships between the party, its programme and those who vote for the party. On the one hand, it is assumed that a vote for a party constitutes an endorsement of the party programme. On the other hand, parties are expected to see their role as one of carrying out their programmes once they hold control of the government. A party that consistently ignores its pledges confuses voters and generates distrust, to its ultimate detriment.

Either in writing their programmes or in enacting legislation, parties respond to the perceived political demands of the electorate. Parties adjust their policies to the peculiarities of each election, evaluate their past electoral records by comparison to other parties and promise specific policy interventions to identifiable groups. In other words, political parties compete for votes by manipulating policy. There are two alternative views on the nature of competition between parties. The traditional view is that parties compete by offering different policies to the voters on the *same* issues; more recently, Budge and Farlie[1] have demonstrated that parties mainly compete by emphasizing the importance of *different*

This is an original essay written especially for this volume; it draws on two research projects supported by the Social Sciences and Humanities Research Council of Canada.

issues. The first view is referred to as competition by direct confrontation, whereas the second is labelled competition by selective emphasis.

This essay will demonstrate that these alternative interpretations of party competition have generated two alternative explanations of Quebec politics: party competition is either seen as a clash of opposing views on debates such as the independence or the linguistic issue, or as the result of an emphasis on different issues regarding governmental intervention. Common sense leads us to interpret party competition mainly in terms of direct confrontation. According to this interpretation, Quebec politics is explained as a series of theatrical dramas characterized by high peaks and low valleys. This interpretation has two basic shortcomings: first, it is usually based on the consideration of a limited number of issues on the agendas of the political parties; second, it does not sufficiently take into account the fact that small or moderate changes in the electoral support are often drastically amplified by the electoral institutions. In this essay, we advance evidence supporting the thesis of selective emphasis by showing that the political programmes and legislative outputs of the parties are much more convergent than generally supposed. Deciding between the two interpretations is a crucial matter. It is linked to our conception of the functioning of the political parties as well as to our normative and empirical understanding of representative democracy in Quebec. It is now time to pay more attention to the data supporting each of these alternative views.

Direct Confrontation as the Major Form of Competition

According to this interpretation parties argue about the same issues and competition results from the clash of opposing proposals of governmental interventions on the same issues. In assuming that parties must choose specific policy proposals on each issue, the most influential rational choice theories model competition as a direct confrontation of different governmental interventions on the same issues.[2] If the distribution of voter opinions on issues tends to look like a unimodal symmetric distribution, that is a majority of voters adopting a median position on the issues, and if the parties maximize their probability of winning the elections, the policy proposals offered by the parties will tend to converge, or be similar. Conversely, if the distribution of opinions of the voters on issues tends to look like a bimodal symmetric distribution, i.e. a minority in the median position with two strong opposing minority positions; and if the parties maximize the promotion of their programmes and ideologies, the policy proposals offered by the parties will not tend to converge.

Most of the studies of party competition in Quebec pay attention to the debates regarding the role and growth of the state. Here, one usually considers opposing views revolving around three basic issues: the political independence of Quebec, the language issue and the role of the state in promoting economic growth as well as the redistribution of wealth in the society. Parties are associated with specific positions on each issue. In the first half of the 1960s, the Parti libéral

PLQ

du Quebec (PLQ) was associated with fights for increasing the powers of the Quebec government over the federal government, for using the state as a tool of intervention to stimulate economic growth and redistribute wealth in the province, and for supporting the betterment of francophones in the province, especially in the economic domain. The nationalization of the electrical power industry and the enlargement of the role atttributed to Hydro-Quebec to promote the use of francophone engineers and francophone technology can be seen as a forerunner of the interventionist language bills debated since the second part of the 1960s. At the time, the positions of the PLQ appeared so radical that they came to be called a part of the "Quiet Revolution."

The Union Nationale (UN), which was the opposition party in the Quebec Legislative Assembly between 1960 and 1966, sharply opposed the PLQ: the UN opposed the expansion of federal intervention into matters of provincial jurisdiction, and only moderately supported the increase of provincial powers over the federal. Moreover, the UN did not support the fostering of economic growth through the use of state intervention. Lastly, the UN was more associated with the giving away of natural resources to foreign corporations than with the improvement of the standing of francophones in the economic domain.

In addition, the PLQ claimed to have a favorable disposition toward francophone labour organizations, whereas the UN was considered to be favorable to farmers, small regional merchants and small business people. The positions of the Liberal party on state intervention are usually explained by referring to the demands of a loose coalition of the new emerging middle class and organized labour as main supporters,[3] and the emerging francophone business class as moderate and sometimes ambiguous supporters.[4] The UN was also supported by the traditional classes, especially farmers and small business people.

The opposing views of the parties on the role of the state and the alleged coalitions behind them generated a situation of competition conducted on a confrontational model: the PLQ and the UN were offering different or opposite policies on the same crucial issues of the time. Party competition was much like a hockey game, with the fights taking place at the same time in the same arena.

With the return of the UN to office in 1966, competition between parties no longer appeared to be confrontational. The UN administration did not institute a drastic break with the policies implemented by the PLQ between 1960 and 1966. To many, the policies enacted by the UN are similar to those of the previous Liberal government.

Therefore, one could not expect drastic policy changes with the re-election of the Liberals in 1970. In the areas of education, health and welfare, the policies implemented by the Liberal Bourassa government were similar to those of the Liberal government of the Quiet Revolution as well as those of the UN administration. However, the Bourassa government was opposed to *étatisme*, that is, against a systematic use of state intervention as a tool for the fostering of economic growth. This position was in stark contrast to that of a new contender competing for the votes of the electorate. Indeed, the Parti québécois (PQ) was promoting recourse, more than ever in the past, to state intervention for the purpose of promoting economic prosperity and the redistribution of wealth. Moreover, the PQ was clearly identified with the promotion of the French language, whereas the PLQ seemed to adopt an ambiguous position that aimed at pleasing both francophones and anglophones. Finally, the PQ promoted a radically new political option, the *souveraineté-association* of Quebec with the rest of Canada whereas the PLQ stood for the *souveraineté culturelle* of Quebec, an option perceived by many voters as ambiguous and too moderate. Meanwhile, the UN disappeared because there was no room for a third player in a match of party competition played on the direct confrontational mode that was restricted to the great symbolic debates that were taking place in Quebec. The PLQ had come to be associated with status quo positions in the 1970s, whereas the Parti québécois was challenging the PLQ with new policy options. This redefinition of the political options has usually been explained as being the result of the demands of a loose coalition made up of the new middle class and organized labour, in conjunction with a secondary role left to the new emerging francophone business class.

In short, the addition of the PQ to the electoral arena generated confrontational competition, consisting of a clash of opposed views on the debates that characterized the first half of the 1970s.

With the election of the PQ in 1976, one might have expected a new surge of direct confrontation between the PLQ and the PQ. It did not occur to the extent expected. In the 1980s, both parties moved toward the adoption of neo-liberal policies and, by so doing, announced the end of the massive recourse to state intervention in the economic domain, and enlarged the role of individuals, notably entrepreneurs, in the economic domain. The return of the PLQ to government in 1985 has not produced any drastic break with the policies enacted by the preceding *péquiste* regime.

With the coming to an end of these debates, competition between parties seems once more to be moving from direct confrontation toward selective emphases on different issues. As a consequence, some observers have concluded that Quebec society is going through a period of depolitization.

Interpreting party competition in Quebec as direct confrontation is embedded in common sense as well as in some academic studies. Such an interpretation is valid to some extent. First, it provides an explanation based on the examination of three issues: the powers of the Quebec government (from expansion of function to independence), the role of the state in the economy and the betterment of the status of francophones and the French language in Quebec. Although significant and crucial, these three issues do not reliably describe the scope of the policy programmes developed by the parties over the years.

Second, changes in direct confrontation derived from the examination of the three issues studied do not always correlate with changes in the votes and seats gained by the parties. As the data in Table 1 indicate, the percentage of votes obtained by the parties from one election to another varies much less dramatically than the percentage of seats. Small differences in the percentage of votes gained have often generated large changes in the proportion of seats obtained.

TABLE 1 **Votes and Seats Obtained by Political Parties, 1960–1985 (in percentages)**

Year	Votes Gained				Seats Gained			
	PLQ	*UN*	*PQ*	*RC*	*PLQ*	*UN*	*PQ*	*RC*
1960	51.3	46.6	NA	NA	53.7	45.2	NA	NA
1962	56.4	42.1	NA	NA	64.1	32.6	NA	NA
1966	47.2	40.9	NA	NA	46.3	51.9	NA	NA
1970	45.4	19.7	23.1	11.2	66.6	15.5	6.5	11.1
1973	54.7	4.9	30.2	9.9	92.7	0.0	5.5	1.8
1976	33.8	18.2	41.4	4.6	24.7	10.0	64.0	1.0
1981	46.1	4.0	49.2	NA	34.4	0.0	65.6	NA
1985	55.9	0.2	38.7	NA	81.1	0.0	18.8	NA

Paying attention to the changes in seats does not reveal the changes taking place in the competition between the parties. It only reflects the biases of the electoral institutions.

These two shortcomings call for the consideration of the alternative interpretation, that of selective emphasis.

Selective Emphasis as the Major Form of Competition

Unlike hockey teams, political parties are able to ignore each other, for they do not have to fight at the same time on the same issues. In party competition, no agenda is binding: parties do not have to take positions on particular issues at the same point in time. Indeed, the best vote-getting strategy a party may choose is the promotion of issues favouring itself at the expense of those advanced by the contending parties. As a consequence, parties have a lower incentive to debate common issues than to talk past each other as if the other parties did not exist. Parties thus have an incentive to stress particular issues that work to their advantage because they own them. For instance, the PLQ can never pretend to appear more committed to the betterment of the French language than the PQ. In reaction, the Liberals' best strategy is to divert the attention of voters from the need to protect French to the need for economic policies, on which the *péquistes* have not been as credible as the Liberals. Therefore, the decision to support a party depends upon which issues are considered salient by the voters.

We hope to show through two empirical studies that parties compete by concentrating on different issues, and also to indicate the issues on which parties do not directly oppose each other. To do so, we prepared a content analysis of the electoral programmes of the PLQ, the UN and the PQ for the campaigns of 1960, 1962, 1966, 1970, 1973, 1976, 1981 and 1985. We have also done a content analysis of all the public acts adopted by the Quebec National Assembly between 1960 and 1985. We began our investigation of the pertinent documents by searching for a list of topics that could be taken as constant over the 25-year period, and

TABLE 2 **Categories of Interventions**

Area 1: Governmental and Administrative Intervention
- intergovernmental relations
- constitution (distribution of powers)
- political institutions
- ministerial powers
- governmental powers
- electoral institutions
- public morality
- administrative management
- justice
- individual rights
- Native peoples
- municipal and regional matters
- external affairs and defence
- immigration
- emigration

Area 2: Economic Interventions
- fiscal matters
- public finances
- roles played by economic agents
- assistance to economic agents
- crown corporations
- financial institutions
- research and technology policies
- economic policies
- unemployment
- inflation
- public services
- agriculture
- forests
- fisheries
- mining
- energy
- tourism
- international trade
- commercial corporations
- industry and commerce
- natural resources
- immigration
- emigration

Area 3: Social Interventions
- social security
- health and welfare services
- family
- situation of women
- labour relations
- working conditions
- social planning
- consumer affairs
- social integration of individuals
- religious matters
- immigration
- emigration

Area 4: Educational and Cultural Intervention
- French language
- educational services
- culture
- sports and leisure
- media
- immigration
- emigration

finally chose the list of topics used to prepare public accounts. As a consequence our list of topics is actually made up of a list of 58 categories of intervention. This list is presented in Table 2. Each governmental intervention was coded under one heading only. In addition, each proposition was analysed using a closed

TABLE 3 **Importance Given by Political Programmes, 1960–1985**

Category	Party		1960	1962	1966	1970	1973	1976	1981	1985
						(in percentages)				
Governmental and	PLQ		20.8	8.3	18.2	13.9	18.0	18.2	16.7	21.3
Administrative	UN		47.1	17.7	23.8	25.4				
	PQ					29.1	17.6	18.5	16.7	19.3
Economic	PLQ		47.2	80.6	27.9	41.7	36.5	38.2	32.7	41.4
	UN		29.4	45.8	38.6	36.1				
	PQ					29.1	31.7	30.8	25.7	31.7
Social	PLQ		22.4	8.3	36.4	30.9	26.5	27.3	29.2	27.5
	UN		11.8	14.5	16.4	21.0				
	PQ					22.9	32.0	32.5	40.9	33.9
Education and	PLQ		9.6	2.8	17.6	13.5	19.0	16.2	21.4	9.8
Culture	UN		11.8	21.9	21.2	17.6				
	PQ					18.9	18.7	18.3	16.5	15.2
Total	PLQ	n	125	36	165	259	389	450	893	367
	UN	n	17	96	189	205				
	PQ	n				354	584	656	1181	910

questionnaire made up of questions concerning the benefits and costs of the governmental interventions. This procedure is explained at length elsewhere.[5] It provides data to study the variations of selective emphases by parties on the topics of the governmental interventions as well as on their substantive aspects. Let us first deal with the topics of governmental interventions.

One might pay attention to each of the 58 categories of topics discussed in the programmes of each party for every electoral campaign. However, we decided to simplify the task by grouping the topics under four broad categories of governmental interventions used extensively: governmental and administrative, economic, social and, finally, educational and cultural. From 1960 to 1985, the programmes of the parties offered 6 876 proposals for governmental intervention of which 19 percent concern governmental and administrative topics, 33.1 percent relate to economic issues, 30.1 percent deal with social problems and 17.2 percent relate to educational and cultural matters. The data in Table 3 indicate that the parties do not stress equally each broad category of governmental intervention.

Indeed, in every programme but that of the 1966 campaign, the PLQ always paid more attention than its opponents to economic issues (Table 3). Moreover, from 1960 until 1970, with the notable exception of 1966, the Liberal Party (PLQ) laid more stress than the others on social issues. This was true even in the programme of 1970, where the PLQ offered 30.9 percent of its basket of state interventions on social matters, as opposed to 22.9 percent for the PQ. However, since 1973, the PQ has always placed more emphasis than the PLQ on social issues. Contrary to expectation, state intervention in governmental and administrative areas have occupied a larger share of the programmes of the UN than those of the PLQ during the 1960s. Since 1973, these issues have been given nearly equal treatment by both the PLQ and the PQ. During the 1960s, contrary to expectation once again, the political party that was most stressing governmental interventions in the area of education and culture was not the PLQ but the UN. Since 1970, the pattern of emphasis in this area of intervention looks like a jigsaw puzzle: the PQ laid more stress on it than the PLQ in 1970, which led to increased emphasis by the PLQ in 1973, to greater emphasis by the PQ in 1976, which in turn led the PLQ to lay more stress in 1981, as opposed to 1985 when the PQ placed more emphasis on it.

The PQ always stressed more than the PLQ issues such as justice, external affairs, research and technology policies, the situation of women, social planning (including, for instance, low cost housing), the protection of consumers and culture. On the other hand, the PLQ has always emphasized educational services more than the PQ. The pattern of emphasis varies from election to election on other important issues such as the distribution of powers between the federal and the provincial governments, which the PLQ emphasized more than the PQ in 1973, 1976 and 1985; economic policies which the PQ stressed more than the PLQ in 1970 and 1976; health and welfare services which the PLQ emphasized more than the PQ in 1970, 1973, and 1981; labour relations which were given more importance by the PLQ than the PQ in 1976, 1981, and 1985; and finally, working conditions, on which the PQ always placed more emphasis than did the PLQ (but for the notable exception of 1985).

As a consequence, one may conclude that, at the level of the broad categories of governmental interventions, selective emphasis constitutes the main mode of party competition: in the 1960s, the PLQ stressed the economic and social domains, whereas the UN placed more insistence on the governmental and administrative domain as well as on education and culture. In the 1970s and thereafter, the PLQ placed more emphasis on the economic domain, whereas the PQ did so on social matters. The picture is more ambiguous when one examines the specific areas of state intervention, because economic matters are not supported exclusively by the PLQ. And in the areas of education and culture, where parties lay the stress alternatively election after election, neither the PLQ nor the PQ can be sure of gaining an advantage.

What happens when a party forms the government? Does a party's legislation follow the same patterns of selective emphasis? The data in Table 4 indicate that, on the whole, whatever party is in power, much more emphasis is placed on economic intervention in legislation (40.5 percent) than in programmes (33.1 percent), and that less than half the stress is laid on education and culture in legislation (7.2 percent) than was laid in the programmes (17.2 percent). Furthermore, it is easy to note that the legislative output differs much less from one party's government to another than do the programmes. That being said, although the PQ scored well during its last mandate, the PLQ still stands as the champion in the area of economic intervention. Contrary to expectations, *péquiste* legislation contained a smaller proportion of social interventions than did liberal legislation enacted between 1970 and 1976. The UN government emphasized

TABLE 4 **Importance of Legislation, 1960–1985 (in percentages)**

Category	PLQ 60–62	PLQ 62–66	UN 66–70	PLQ 70–73	PLQ 73–76	PQ 76–81	PQ 81–85	Total
			Party in Power and Period					
Governmental and Administrative	18.5	22.6	26.2	17.0	15.1	24.8	21.6	20.8 (1805)
Economic	40.8	41.5	33.0	42.1	47.8	36.0	43.1	40.5 (3511)
Social	22.8	29.7	30.8	36.5	31.0	32.8	28.7	31.4 (2721)
Education and Culture	17.9	6.3	10.0	4.4	6.1	6.5	6.7	7.2 (621)
Total n	530	816	1155	1795	1224	1643	1495	8658

education and culture more than any other party, except the Liberal administration of 1960–1962. One is almost led to think that the reforms of education should not be attributed to the Liberal government of the Quiet Revolution but to the UN government. Furthermore, the PQ governments have laid more stress on legislation regarding education and culture than the two previous Liberal governments. Finally, the relative importance of legislation concerning governmental and administrative areas reached its peak with the UN government, not with the Liberal government of the Quiet Revolution or the *péquiste* governments.

Two general conclusions emerge from our analysis of state intervention in programmes and legislation. The data relating to programmes show that party competition is played on the model of selective emphasis. The data relating to legislation enacted by the parties in power indicate that the emphasis found in the programmes is much less evident in legislation. Furthermore, these findings show that policy changes expected in the legislation enacted by the Liberal government of the Quiet Revolution as well as the two *péquiste* governments are limited. They also indicate that the UN government of 1966–1970 played a much more significant role than generally assumed in pursuing policy changes begun during the Quiet Revolution.

By basing our analysis on the frequency of references to topics of governmental interventions, it might be said that our research design provided for one hypothesis, that of competition as selective emphases, at the expense of the other hypothesis which assumes that competition is confrontational. In fact, we considered at the initial stage of our study that it would not be feasible to develop a valid and reliable coding scheme based on contrasting policies. An alternative research design is to start from the identification of the beneficiaries of state intervention. This approach is based on the assumption that policy differences between parties can be measured through variations in the frequencies with which various categories of recipients benefit from state intervention. Happily enough, the political science literature contains many such hypotheses that usually assume that the governmental interventions of left-wing or social-democratic parties favour workers, whereas those of right-wing or conservative parties favour entrepreneurs. The next issue to settle then is to classify the parties either as social-democratic or conservative. The data provided so far in this essay indicate that the PLQ of the 1960s and the PQ might be viewed as social-democratic. The UN is usually defined as the party of small business people. In the 1970s and thereafter, the PLQ has been identified more with business than labour. Thus, the hypothesis of party competition as direct confrontation would be verified if one party favoured entrepreneurs more than workers, while the other party did the opposite. The data presented in Table 5 do not support this hypothesis, as entrepreneurs are *always* the most frequent beneficiaries of state intervention, whichever party is considered. Therefore, one must return to the hypothesis of selective emphasis. Its testing requires a comparison between the proportion of state interventions offered to entrepreneurs and workers. If one considers the programmes of every party for the 25-year period, the average difference is 8.1 percent. According to this interpretation, one might assume that a party favorable to workers would score below the average difference whereas a party favorable to entrepreneurs would score above that average. This would show that the *Liberal Party* has always been relatively more favorable to entrepreneurs than to workers (but for the notable exception of its 1985 programme). Conversely, the PQ has always been relatively more favorable to workers than to entrepreneurs.

Three general conclusions emerge from this analysis. First, the notion that the PLQ has favoured organized labour, especially in its programmes of the 1960s, is untrue. Second, the notion that the PQ favours workers is mitigated somewhat. Third, the programmes of the PLQ have tended to stress workers as beneficiaries of their interventions since 1970 relatively more often, whereas the PQ programmes have evolved in the opposite direction since 1973. Indeed, the *péquiste* claim regarding its favorable prejudice toward workers does not stand up because in 1985 the PLQ offered a relatively larger fraction of its propositions of state interventions to workers (20.2 percent) than did the PQ (13.7 percent). This is an astonishing finding indicating that the PLQ is trying to invade a symbolic area that the PQ had thought was exclusively its own.

The data on the public acts adopted by the Quebec National Assembly from 1960 to 1985 indicate once more that, no matter which party is in power, the most frequent beneficiaries of state interventions are entrepreneurs (Table 6). The average difference in the frequencies of benefits offered to workers and entrepreneurs amounts to 8.8 percent. Therefore, a governing party favorable to workers would score below 8.8 percent whereas one favorable to entrepreneurs would score above that average. The data of Table 6 show that the PLQ governments of the 1960s were less favorable to workers than expected, for if the 1960–62 Liberal government was relatively more favorable to workers than to entrepreneurs, the

TABLE 5 **Beneficiaries of Governmental Intervention, 1960–1985 (in percentages)**

Category of Beneficiaries	Party	Year							
		1960	1962	1966	1970	1973	1976	1981	1985
Entrepreneurs	PLQ	33.0	22.2	20.4	32.1	23.8	26.0	23.2	24.4
	UN	5.9	23.9	21.3	23.1				
	PQ				19.4	20.2	20.1	18.3	20.1
Workers	PLQ	12.8	11.1	9.9	6.7	9.5	9.3	13.8	20.2
	UN	0.0	11.4	7.1	9.9				
	PQ				15.1	16.5	16.1	15.8	13.7
Difference Between Workers and Entrepreneurs	PLQ	20.2	11.1	10.5	25.4	14.3	16.7	9.4	4.2
	UN	5.9	12.5	14.2	13.2				
	PQ				4.3	3.7	4.0	2.5	6.4

Notes: 1) The percentages of the columns do not add up to 100 percent because the table does not include: (1) other categories of beneficiaries such as consumers and owners of houses making up an average of 40 percent over the period; (2) state interventions for which information provided is insufficient to determine unambiguously the beneficiaries; these undetermined cases add up to an average of 24.5 percent of the interventions over the 25-year period.
2) The absolute frequencies of governmental interventions are not reproduced here as they are identical to Table 3.

1962–66 administration was relatively much more favorable to entrepreneurs than to workers. Contrary to expectations, the UN government was relatively more favorable to workers than to entrepreneurs. Finally, much as expected, the two *péquiste* governments were relatively more favorable to workers than to entrepreneurs. The standard deviation of the frequencies of workers as beneficiary targets of state interventions is smaller than that concerning entrepreneurs. This might indicate that parties are less able to manoeuvre legislation for workers than for entrepreneurs.

TABLE 6 **Beneficiaries of Legislation Enacted by the Quebec National Assembly, 1960–1985 (in percentages)**

Category of Beneficiaries	Party in Power and Period						
	PLQ 60–62	PLQ 62–66	UN 66–70	PLQ 70–73	PLQ 73–76	PQ 76–81	PQ 81–85
Entrepreneurs	19.0	30.1	22.2	26.6	30.1	21.6	23.7
Workers	14.3	14.0	16.8	18.8	14.6	16.9	16.4
Difference Between Workers and Entrepreneurs	4.7	16.1	5.4	7.8	15.5	4.7	7.3

Notes: 1) The percentages do not add up to 100 percent due to the exclusion of other categories of beneficiaries such as consumers, owners of houses, etc., as well as to cases of undetermined beneficiaries.
2) The absolute frequencies are not reproduced here as they can be found in Table 4.

One can compare the data on the programmes, which are actually promises, with the data on legislation, which correspond to accomplishments of state intervention. This comparison produces an astonishing finding: the workers and the entrepreneurs are more frequently targeted as beneficiaries in the legislation than promised in the programmes of the parties. In this respect, the PQ tends to target the workers slightly more often in its legislation than in its programmes, whereas the PLQ tends to target the workers much more frequently than expected by its pledges. On the other hand, the PQ always delivers benefits to entrepreneurs at a frequency higher than promised, whereas the Liberal governments failed to deliver as many benefits as promised on two occasions (for the periods 1960–1962 and 1970–1973). This means that workers can expect more benefits than promised from the Liberals whereas entrepreneurs can expect to receive more benefits than promised from the PQ. This finding might be attributed to some kind of compensation process: the PQ attempts to compensate for its alleged favorable prejudice toward workers by giving entrepreneurs more frequent benefits than promised, whereas the PLQ tries to compensate for its alleged favorable prejudice toward business by giving workers more frequent benefits than promised in its programmes.

Conclusion

The provincial political parties have played a very active role in the debates that have taken place in Quebec with respect to the distribution of powers between the federal and the provincial governments, the protection and promotion of the French language and the role of the state in the fostering of economic growth. As a consequence, common sense inclines us to conclude that direct confrontation constitutes the major form of party competition. This conclusion is based on limited evidence as it relies on the analysis of three broad categories of issues, whereas the actual scope of issues on the agendas of the political parties is much larger. Moreover, this interpretation of party competition does not sufficiently take into account that small or moderate changes in voting behavior are often drastically amplified by the biases of the electoral process.

A content analysis of the official programmes of the parties and the public acts enacted between 1960 and 1985 demonstrates that selective emphasis constitutes the major form of party competition in Quebec. An analysis based on the topics of the governmental interventions shows that the PLQ lays more stress than the PQ on interventions related to economic issues whereas the PQ emphasizes more than the PLQ state interventions relating to social issues.

Furthermore, an examination of the data concerning the beneficiaries of governmental intervention promised in the programmes or enacted in legislation demonstrates even more convincingly that the major form of party competition is selective emphasis. We found that, whatever they preach, political parties always provide entrepreneurs with more frequent benefits than workers. This is so even for the PQ, although they emphasize state interventions targeting workers as beneficiaries more than the PLQ.

Party competition is a dynamic process. Our data show that the PQ is becoming less committed to workers whereas the PLQ is becoming more committed to them. On the other hand, the PQ tends to favour entrepreneurs as beneficiaries. In other words, the PLQ has attempted to invade policy areas that the PQ thought it owned, whereas the PQ has tried to invade policy areas in which the Liberals were thought to be the only credible party. *competitive*

In short, party competition is selective rather than confrontational. Moreover, parties tend to converge because they tend to increasingly consider the same issues and to increasingly agree on them.

In theory, parties could change their programmes radically after each election. They do not. In theory, a new governmental party could repeal the established commitments of its predecessors and implement its own programme, but it does not. This is because past laws create expectations and rights on the maintenance of the status quo that organized interests use to sustain the previous commitments of governments. Since the 1960s, the commitments of governments have increased drastically with the expansion of the role of the state. Consequently, a newly elected government can at best alter in a piecemeal fashion the previous commitments of its predecessors if it wants to avoid creating chaos.

Party competition as direct confrontation might correspond to politics as it is presented in the media. However, party competition as selective emphasis is how political parties develop their political programmes and enact legislation.

ENDNOTES

1. I. Budge and D.J. Farlie, "Party Competition: Selective Emphasis or Direct Confrontation? An Alternative view with Data," in H. Daalder and P. Mair, eds., *Western European Party System* (Beverly Hills, Ca.: Sage Publications, 1983), pp. 267–305.
2. I. Budge and D.J. Farlie, *Voting and Party Competition* (New York: John Wiley, 1977); I. Budge, "The Internal Analysis of Election Programmes," in I. Budge, D. Robertson and D. Hearl, eds., *Ideology, Strategy and Party change: Spatial Analyses of Post-War Election Programmes in 19 Democracies* (Cambridge: Cambridge University Press, 1987), pp. 15–38; A. Downs, *An Economic Theory of Democracy* (New York: Harper and Row, 1957); P.C. Ordeshook, "The Spatial Theory of Elections: A Review and a Critique" in I. Budge, I. Crewe and D. Farlie, *Party Identification and Beyond Representations of Voting and Party Competition* (New York: John Wiley, 1976).
3. H. Guindon, "Social Unrest, Social Class, and Quebec's Bureaucratic Revolution," *Queen's Quarterly* (Summer 1964), pp. 150–162; K. McRoberts, *Quebec: Social Change and Political Crisis* (Toronto: McClelland and Stewart, 1988).
4. W. Coleman, *The Independence Movement in Quebec, 1945–1980* (Toronto: University of Toronto Press, 1984).
5. R. Landry, "Biases in the Supply of Public Policies to Organized Interests: Some Empirical Evidence," in W. Coleman and G. Skogstad, eds., *Policy Communities and Public Policy in Canada* (Mississauga: Copp, Clark, Pitman, 1990).
6. D. Robertson, *A Theory of Party Competition* (New York: John Wiley, 1976).

30 The Pattern of Prairie Politics

NELSON WISEMAN

Canadian historians and social scientists have usually depicted Prairie politics as a response to externally imposed conditions: the tariff, the withholding of authority over natural resources by the federal government, discriminatory transportation policies, etc. This approach tells us substantially about east-west Canadian relations. By itself, however, it tells us little about the diversity of political traditions *on* the Prairies. What is needed is an interpretive analysis which comes to terms with intra-regional differences. Why, until 1969, was Manitoba so dominated by Liberal and Conservative regimes? Why was Saskatchewan so receptive to the CCF-NDP? Why did Alberta spawn such a durable and unorthodox farmers' government (the UFA) and then, overnight, become the bastion of an equally unorthodox Social Credit regime before continuing its tradition of one-party dominance by stampeding to the Conservatives?

The answers to these questions do not lie (although some clues do) in an analysis of the east-west relationship. Nor do the answers lie in analyses which focus strictly on party systems or economic conditions. An economic analysis may be used to explain why, in the landmark federal election of 1911, Saskatchewan and Alberta endorsed the Liberals and freer trade, but it will not explain why Manitoba endorsed the Conservatives and protectionism. An analysis of party systems may be used to explain why, at the provincial level, Saskatchewan and Alberta rejected the two older parties in favour of third parties. It will not explain, however, why those two third parties are at opposite poles of the Canadian political spectrum. Identifying and accounting for the differences among the three Prairie provinces, therefore, is essential. But this too is insufficient because striking diversities are to be located not only among but also *within* the provinces. By the 1890s, for example, Manitoba had been remade in the image of western Ontario. Yet in 1919, Winnipeg exhibited a level of class consciousness and class conflict that was decidedly more European than North American. In Saskatchewan, until 1945, the federal Liberal party was consistently stronger than in any

Nelson Wiseman, "The Pattern of Prairie Politics," originally published in *Queen's Quarterly*, Vol. 88, No. 2 (Summer 1981). This version has been revised and updated especially for this edition.

other English Canadian province. But it was this same province that returned North America's first social democratic government, the CCF, whose ideology was rooted in the British Labour party. Inconsistent political patterns seem no less profound in Alberta where governing parties that are defeated at the polls have faded almost immediately.

The analysis employed here utilizes the concepts of ideology and ethnicity. Elements of Canadian toryism, liberalism, and socialism[1] have been present in varying proportions in each province. Political representatives of these ideological tendencies on the Prairies include men as diverse as Rodmond Roblin, John Diefenbaker, Charles Dunning, J.W. Dafoe, J.S. Woodsworth, Tommy Douglas, Henry Wise Wood and William Aberhart, none of whom were born on the Prairies. Because the Prairie provinces and their societies were moulded in the late nineteenth and early twentieth centuries this is not surprising. Ideas and ideologies first appeared on the Prairies as importations.

It is very unlikely that a Roblin or a Douglas, preaching what they did, could have become premiers of Alberta. Aberhart would not likely have succeeded in Manitoba or Saskatchewan. Politicians are reflectors of their society, their environment, their times. They may be examined in terms which transcend quirks of personality. Their ideas and actions may be seen as reflections of the popular and ideological-cultural basis of their support.

The key to Prairie politics is in the unravelling of the dynamic relationship between ideological-cultural heritage and party. In Manitoba, the imported nineteenth-century Ontario liberal party tradition (with "a tory touch") maintained political hegemony until 1969. In Saskatchewan, the dominant tone of politics reflected a struggle between Ontario liberal and British socialist influences. In Alberta, American populist-liberal ideas gained widespread currency beginning in the very first decade of that province's existence. In all three provinces minorities of non-Anglo-American origins helped make and break governments. These minorities, however, did not determine the ideological coloration of any major party.

Prairie political culture is best seen as the product of the interaction of four distinct waves of pioneering settlers. The first wave was a Canadian one. More precisely, it was largely rural Ontarian. This wave was a westward extension of English Canada's dominant charter group. Ontarians were a charter group in each Prairie province but their impact was greatest in Manitoba. It seemed both fitting and telling that one of Manitoba's premiers (Hugh John Macdonald) was the son of Canada's first prime minister. Tory-touched Canadian liberalism was the ideological core of nineteenth-century Ontario and its Prairie offshoot.

A second distinct wave in Prairie settlement was a new, modern, British group. Coming near the turn of this century, it was largely urban and working class. Transformed and battered by nineteenth-century industrialism, Britain's working class had begun to turn to socialism. Despite the cultural and ideological differences between the Ontario and new-British waves, their social status in the west was roughly equal, both groups being British subjects and Anglo-Saxon pioneers in British North America. The new-British wave had its greatest impact in the cities, most powerfully in the largest Prairie city, Winnipeg. In Saskatchewan relatively large numbers of new British and European-born immigrants settled in rural areas and produced Canada's most successful provincial social democratic party. It seemed appropriate that Saskatchewan's premier in this labour-socialist tradition—Tommy Douglas—was British-born and grew up and was politically socialized in Winnipeg's new-British, labour-socialist environment.

The third wave in Prairie settlement was American. More specifically it was midwestern, great plains American. Like the Ontario wave, but unlike the new-British wave, it came out of an agrarian setting with deeply rooted agrarian values and settled, in overwhelming numbers, in rural areas. American Anglo-Saxons became for the time being the only non-Canadian, non-British charter group on the Prairies. The dominant ideological strain carried by the American wave was similar but not identical to that carried by the Ontarians. It was, to be sure, liberal, but its liberalism was devoid of toryism. It was a radical "populist" liberalism that stressed the individual rather than the community or the state as a tory or socialist would. This wave's greatest impact was in rural Alberta, the continent's last agricultural frontier. Populist liberalism expressed itself both in an unconventional farmers' movement and government known as the United Farmers of Alberta (UFA) and in the long tenure of Social Credit. This wave's leading representative was a veteran Missouri populist (Henry Wise Wood).

The fourth and last wave of Prairie settlement consisted of continental Europeans. Because of their numerous national origins, they were the most diverse of the four waves. They were, however, neither a charter group nor did they have a significant ideological impact (the eastern European and Finnish influences in the Communist Party being a minor exception). The non-Anglo-Saxons were "alien" and suspect in the eyes of the other three groups, and at times their very presence was attacked and challenged; at best they were tolerated. The ideological and political role of the continental wave became largely one of deference. The continental wave had its greatest urban impact in Winnipeg and its greatest rural impact in Saskatchewan. These areas were also those in which the new-British wave had its greatest impact. The combined voting strength of these two waves was to lead to CCF-NDP victories in Manitoba and Saskatchewan in later years. The Old World ideological attributes of the continentals were dismissed as illegitimate on the Prairies. Thus, continentals deferred to the parties based on the other three groups; but the continentals represented the largest swing factor in voting of the four waves. They helped elect and defeat parties anchored by the other waves; they neither anchored nor led a major party.

The foregoing description of the four distinct waves of Prairie settlers is not intended to imply that all Ontarians were tory-touched liberals, that all new Britons were labour-socialists, that all Americans were populist-liberals and that all continentals deferred ideologically and politically. Furthermore, it should be understood that not all Ontarians voted for the Liberals and Conservatives, not all new Britons voted CCF, and not all Americans voted UFA-Social Credit. The contention here, simply, is that without the new-British impact the CCF would never have attained the stature it did (indeed, it might not have been created at all); similarly, without the American impact the UFA-Social Credit phenomenon in Alberta would not have been anything like what it was; and without the Ontarians, Prairie Liberal and Conservative parties would not have gained early hegemony. The conceptual framework underlying this analysis is that Manitoba, Saskatchewan and Alberta were most influenced in their formative years by the political cultures of early twentieth century Ontario, Britain and the American midwest respectively. What we have here is a bare and simple macrocosmic sketch of the ethno-cultural and ideological bases of Prairie politics in the first half of this century.

The evidence for the interpretation presented here is to be found in Prairie historiography, but it is generally disregarded. The notion that Ontario, British, American and continental European people and influences have helped shape Prairie politics is not a new idea. But it might as well be, because it is an idea that has never been developed. There are 10 excellent books in a series titled "Social Credit in Alberta: Its Background and Development." Not one of these books, however, devotes one paragraph to the American impact on Alberta, an impact unparalleled in Canada.

The impact of transplanted ideas was greater in Canada's west than in the United States because the physical impact of immigrants was greater. In 1914, for example, the year of greatest immigration to the US in the decade, one immigrant arrived for every 80 in the population. In Canada, in contrast, one immigrant arrived for every 18 in the population in 1913. The bulk of these immigrants, whether from Britain, continental Europe or the United States, went west. Moreover, Canada's frontier experience was different from that of the US. South of the border, a soft frontier meant immigrants acculturating as settlement spread slowly westward. North of the border, a hard frontier meant getting off a boat and immediately boarding a transcontinental train. Immigrants and their ideas appeared more suddenly and in greater relative proportions on the Canadian Prairies than in the American west.

Initially, Ontarians prevailed on the Prairies. They occupied the best agricultural lands and secured homesteads along the new Canadian Pacific Railway. Their power was most profound in Manitoba which, having entered Confederation in 1870, offered the most accessible frontier. The Ontarians were soon followed by waves of Britons, Americans and continentals. The British came from the most urbanized industrial society in the world, but one that offered no rise in real wages between 1895 and 1913. More than a century of slowly developing working-class consciousness was represented by this new-British group. The American settlers, in contrast, came largely from the rural midwest. The Jeffersonian physiocratic notion that the soil was the sole source of wealth guided their thinking. Their interest in the Canadian frontier was fueled by Canadian government propaganda which invoked the agrarian ideal, the Horatio Alger tradition and the log cabin stereotype, all prominent features of American liberal mythology. The continental immigrants were largely from eastern and central Europe, where land tenancy systems were in some cases only a half-century removed from feudalism. Of these three groups the Americans were the most likely and the British the least likely to homestead. Many Britons and continentals were to find their way into the new and growing Prairie cities: Winnipeg, Regina, Calgary and Edmonton.

In addition to differences in immigrant distribution among the provinces there were differences within each province. Although there were equal numbers of Americans and Britons in Alberta, for example, in the 1920s Americans outnumbered Britons in all 15 of Alberta's rural census divisions, by a ratio of two to one. In a province where the rural MLAs prevailed this meant an extraordinary American political influence. In 12 of the 15 rural census divisions in Alberta Americans also outnumbered continental-born settlers. All three exceptions were in the northeast—that part of the province that provided the strongest rural opposition that both the American-influenced United Farmers of Alberta and Social Credit encountered.

In Saskatchewan, in the 1920s, Britons only slightly outnumbered Americans. The relative rural homogeneity of Saskatchewan, however, produced a dramatically different equation than in Alberta: the overwhelming majority of Britons settled in rural areas. Paradoxically, Saskatchewan had fewer Britons than either Alberta or Manitoba, but the Britons it did have penetrated rural Saskatchewan in a way that the Britons in neighbouring provinces did not. Furthermore, in Alberta the majority of American settlers were Anglo-Saxons; in Saskatchewan Anglo-Saxons were in a minority among Americans. This was important because a condition for political success was an Anglo-Saxon background. The largest number of Britons who entered Manitoba and Alberta generally headed for the cities; in Winnipeg population quadrupled between 1901 and 1915.

The four distinct waves of immigrants differed in religion as well as political ideology. Methodists and other social gospellers had their greatest impact in places like Winnipeg where the British-born labourist wave was particularly strong. Catholicism, brought over by many continental Europeans, was strongest in Saskatchewan and contributed to the Liberals' long hold on power there. Anglicans, with roots in both Ontario and Britain, reinforced Conservative tendencies in all three provinces. Many fundamentalists—and they represented an exceptionally high 20 percent of Alberta Protestants—came to that province as American Bible Belt populists.

Ethnic voting studies have not been able to provide a coherent interpretation of Prairie politics because studying "ethnic" voting by listing "Anglo-Saxons" as separate from Germans, Ukrainians, French, etc., fails to appreciate that some "Anglo-Saxons" were from the "Red" Clyde of Glasgow, others from Perth County, Ontario and still others from the populist state of Kansas. Different types of divisions of course existed within other ethnic groups. Between the 1920s and 1950s the key distinguishing features in Anglo-Saxon voting in Winnipeg were class status and birthplace. For example, in one part of Winnipeg represented almost continuously between the 1920s and 1980s by MPs J.S. Woodsworth and Stanley Knowles, large numbers of British-born, low-income residents voted overwhelmingly CCF. The city's highest-income Anglo-Saxon area with relatively fewer British-born, in contrast, voted overwhelmingly Liberal and Conservative.

In both areas Canadian-born Anglo-Saxons far outnumbered other Anglo-Saxons. This revealed that second and third generations reflected inherited ideological-cultural traditions which continued to be expressed in party voting.

Although their demographic impact was great, continental immigrants did not play a leading role in early political developments. Rather, they yielded to the politics of the charter groups. Large numbers of them were isolated in rural ethnic colonies; many were in marginal farming areas where federal agents had directed them. In response to their new opportunity, and in their related effort to prove their loyalty to their new country, these minorities voted Liberal in Alberta from 1905 to 1921, and Liberal in Saskatchewan from 1905 to 1944. In Manitoba too the Liberals were the main beneficiaries of this vote although occasionally, as in 1914, proof of loyalty expressed itself in a Conservative vote. Winnipeg was an exception to the rest of the Prairies only in that its working-class continentals were sufficiently numerous, concentrated and class-conscious to form a vibrant Communist party after 1920. The politics of deference, however, did little to raise the status of the European minorities. Racist prejudice against the continentals was widespread.

Ontarian influence seemed dominant in all three provinces until at least 1921. During World War I, for example, all three provincial premiers, their ministers of agriculture and a majority of MLAs were Ontarians. In Manitoba the grit agrarianism of Ontario expressed itself in the selection of every premier from the 1880s until Ed Schreyer in 1969. Its distinct mark was reflected in the transplantation of the Ontario municipal system and in the School Question. In Saskatchewan this same, essentially Protestant and English grit outlook dominated the Saskatchewan Grain Growers Association (SGGA), the province's federal and provincial Progressives and the Liberal party. But in Saskatchewan, unlike Ontario and Manitoba, the dominance of this liberal grit tradition was dependent on support from other elements in the population, specifically non-Anglo-Saxons, of which Saskatchewan had English Canada's highest percentage. Moreover, Saskatchewan's version of grit agrarianism was to encounter a powerful ideological competitor in the form of British-style socialism. The votes of the continentals helped elect a Prairie version of the British Labour party in 1944.

American populist influences were greater in Saskatchewan than in Manitoba but they were secondary and not nearly as significant as in Alberta. In Alberta, the American-style populist UFA determined the complexion of successive provincial governments for years. Alberta populism, like American populism, attracted some socialists, but it rejected socialist ideology. CCF socialism, embraced in Saskatchewan, was rejected by Alberta farmers on the peculiarly American grounds that it represented a repudiation of their "rugged individualism."

Manitoba: the Ontario of the Prairies

Manitoba was the province most true to the values of rural Ontario. In the language rights debates it was more Orange than Ontario. Manitoba imported its early American-inspired farm organizations—the Grange and the

Patrons of Industry—only after they had become established in Ontario. Manitoba's tory farmers rejected any suggestion of possible secession from Confederation and American annexation in the 1880s.

A good representative of Manitoba's tory-touched liberalism was Rodmond Roblin, premier from 1900 to 1915. His toryism was reflected in the debate over direct legislation, an idea brought to the Prairies from the United States. Every political party on the Prairies supported the proposal except Roblin's Conservatives in Manitoba. Roblin attacked direct legislation on the basis that it was "A Socialistic and Un-British Plan." This permitted him to appeal to a fundamentally liberal but tory-touched rural Manitoba. According to Roblin, direct legislation represented a form of "degenerate republicanism," much too strong a phrase to use successfully in Alberta, but not in Manitoba.

T.A. Crerar was a typical Ontarian in rural Manitoba. As a member of the dominant charter group on the Prairies, Crerar became a spokesman for the West but remained a product of the East. Between 1919 and 1922 he was offered the premierships of both Ontario and Manitoba. Crerar's liberalism was expressed in his leadership of the Progressive party and in his role as the architect of federal Liberal-Progressive rapprochement. He insisted that his party was not appealing to any specific class in society. Alberta's Henry Wise Wood, by contrast, insisted that it must make a class appeal to farmers by demanding occupational representation or what became known as "group government." Wood's approach was typical of the American left and was within the confines of monolithic American liberalism, defining class in liberal (equality of opportunity) rather than socialist (equality of condition) terms. Crerar's liberalism, closer to British liberalism, denied any connection with class politics. Crerar represented the tory-touched rural liberalism of Manitoba; Wood reflected the radical populist liberalism of Alberta.

Although Manitoba Liberal and Conservative governments relied on rural support from continental-born immigrants, few Europeans, of either British or continental origins, were to be found in the higher echelons of either of these parties. Nor were many to be found in the United Farmers of Manitoba (UFM). "Canadian Ukrainians do not have any influence," declared one Ukrainian paper in 1932, the year of the CCF's birth. "We are poor and need political help. Ukrainian farmers and workers depend for their livelihood on the more powerful. This forces us to support a politically influential party. Affiliation with small radical parties brings Ukrainians only discredit and ruin." Such deference, however, did little for continental immigrants in the city. In the 1930s none of Winnipeg's banks, trust companies, or insurance firms would knowingly hire a Jew or anyone with a Ukrainian or Polish name. Nor would Anglo-Saxon premiers pick them for their cabinets.

Labour-socialist politics in Manitoba were as much determined by newly arrived Britons and Europeans as agrarian politics were determined by Ontarians. Winnipeg became the home of Canada's first Independent Labour party (ILP) and, by 1899, 27 separate unions appeared at the May Day parade. A year later, the editor of Winnipeg's labour newspaper, *The Voice,* was elected to the House of Commons.

Within a decade the labour-socialist sectarianism of Europe was reproduced in Winnipeg. Two groups working outside of the dominant ILP influence were the Social Democratic party and the Socialist party of Canada. By 1920–21 the two permanent parties that emerged were the British-led labourist ILP and the continental-based Communist party. Every imprisoned 1919 strike leader, except one, came from Britain to Winnipeg between 1896 and 1912. So too did most of the ILP leadership. The Communists, on the other hand, drew their inspiration from the Russian Revolution and scientific socialism. A small and insignificant British minority including strike leader R.B. Russell of the One Big Union, stayed out of both camps. In Manitoba, as in Britain, labourism won over Marxism and syndicalism. By 1923, when the Ontario ILP was falling apart, the Manitoba ILP could boast that it held more than two dozen municipal and school board seats, the mayoralty of Winnipeg and representation in both federal and provincial parliaments. This modern, turn of the century British labourist tradition had its greatest Canadian urban impact in Winnipeg and Vancouver and, thus, the strength of the CCF-NDP in these cities.

Until at least 1945 much of the politics of the large Ukrainian community in North Winnipeg were still tied to the Russian Revolution and its aftermath. Those against the Revolution supported the Liberals. The CCF, for many virulent anti-communists, was a socialist step in a hated communist direction. Those supporting the Revolution embraced the Communist party. The CCF, for many communist sympathizers, was a naive, liberal, social democratic, reformist gang. Since World War II, however, ethnic assimilation has contributed to strengthening the CCF-NDP position within both the former Liberal and Communist Ukrainian groups. An example of the shift from the CP to the NDP is the contrast between Jacob and Roland Penner, father and son. The former was for decades Winnipeg's leading Communist, the latter became the NDP's attorney general in 1981. The CP withered because the older continental-born generation died and the party lost its base. The ideology of British labourism, in contrast, in the form of the ILP-CCF, survived and took root. Other socialist traditions among British and continental immigrants either accommodated themselves to this dominant influence on the left or they generally faded, as did the SPC and CP.

Liberal, Conservative and Farmer governments dominated provincial politics. Winnipeg counted for little in the government's considerations and centre and north Winnipeg, where the British and European-born had settled, counted for less. It was unpenalized neglect because a rurally biased electoral map ensured agrarian dominance. Between 1920 and 1949, for example, Winnipeg had only 10 seats in a 55 seat Legislature. In the 1922 election labour votes equalled those for 27 non-labour MLAs, but Labour won only six seats. In 1945 the CCF received as many votes as the Liberal-Progressives and almost double the Conservative total, but the CCF won only 10 seats to the Liberals' 24 and the Conservatives' 13.

Successive Manitoba governments reflected an alliance of Anglo-Saxons in the southwestern wheat belt and in south Winnipeg. This alliance went under various labels at different times: Liberal, Conservative, United Farmers of Manitoba, Progressive, Liberal-Progressive, Brackenite, Coalition, and even Non-Partisan.

What distinguished it from its main ideological opponent was class and heritage, not ethnicity. In 1919 the warring Strike Committee and Citizens Committee had one feature in common: Anglo-Saxon backgrounds. In working-class Winnipeg the European minorities lined up behind the British-born Strike Committee because the Citizens Committee gave them little choice, condemning them as alien radicals. In rural Manitoba these minorities deferred to the established Canadian-born anti-strike forces.

These divisions were reflected in voting patterns. There seemed little basis for farmer-labour cooperation in Manitoba. They shared little in common. Labour issues, such as the eight-hour day, were ridiculed in the countryside, and every rural newspaper in Manitoba condemned the 1919 strike. Labour's attitude to Manitoba's farmers was also one of suspicion and, until 1927, UFM members were ineligible to join the ILP.

Manitoba's farm leaders went the way of Ontario's. Alberta's UFA, Saskatchewan's UFC (SS) and even Ontario's UFO affiliated with the federal CCF in 1932 (although the latter disaffiliated in 1934). The UFM, like its forerunners a half-century before, was true to the values of rural Ontario and remained aloof. In the late 1940s agrarian politics in Manitoba began to shift somewhat with the rise of the Manitoba Farmers Union (MFU). The MFU's membership came largely from more northerly, less prosperous, continental-born, and second generation Canadian farmers. By the 1950s, ethnic interaction over the course of 40 years made possible the viability of such an organization. To the MFU leadership the Manitoba Federation of Agriculture, like its UFM predecessor, represented the wealthier, established, Anglo-Saxon Liberal farmers. After Diefenbaker and Conservative Premier Roblin left their respective leadership posts in 1967, the provincial NDP capitalized on gaining informal MFU support in certain rural areas. It was a breakthrough that helped the NDP win enough rural seats to form a government in 1969. For a combination of reasons, including the fact that he was the son-in-law of the first president of the MFU, Ed Schreyer was the only figure in the Manitoba NDP who could attract such support.

In 1969 Manitoba was ripe for an NDP victory in a way that Ontario was not. In Ontario the impact of Anglo-Saxon voters, most of them long established in Canada, was more powerful than in Manitoba. This is another way of pointing out that Ontario is ideologically older than Manitoba in its conservatism, particularly in the rural areas, but in the cities too. There was a significant new British labourist impact in Ontario (e.g. Toronto mayor Jimmie Simpson in the 1930s) but, because of Ontario's relative oldness, it was not as profound as it was further west.

Manitoba had enough of Ontario in it to have sustained the only provincial Conservative party west of Ontario that has never collapsed. But it also had enough of modern Britain and continental Europe to provide CCFer J.S. Woodsworth and provincial Communist leader Bill Kardash with parliamentary seats between the 1920s and 1950s. Manitoba also had enough of the Prairies in it to produce national and provincial Progressive parties in the 1920s. Their Ontario-born liberal leadership, however, led both of them back to the Liberal party.

Saskatchewan: British Labourism on the Prairies

As in Manitoba, provincial politics in Saskatchewan initially meant transplanting Ontarian politics. The provincial Liberal government operated at the pleasure of the Saskatchewan Grain Growers Association, the dominant political and economic organization in the province. Both the Liberals and the SGGA were led by the same figures, most of whom had Ontario roots. The Progressive debacle in Ottawa, however, and the inability of the SGGA to break with the Liberals fuelled the formation of a rival agrarian organization: the Farmers Union of Canada. It was founded and first led by L.B. McNamee, a former British railway worker and trade unionist. This difference between the SGGA's Ontarian leadership and the Farmers Union British leadership broadly represented the difference between Ontario liberal and British socialist influences. The division became a central feature of Saskatchewan politics.

The success of the Farmers Union led to the formation of the United Farmers of Canada (Saskatchewan Section) and that, in turn, led directly to the Farmer-Labour party, led by British socialists and Canadians sympathetic to socialism. It then took three elections and 10 years, from 1934 to 1944, to catapult this party to power under a CCF label. This became possible because enough continental-origin voters transferred their preferences from the Liberals to the CCF.

Liberalism at first seemed unbeatable in Saskatchewan. Although it came later than in Manitoba, the Ontarian impact was the first in Saskatchewan and it was, as in Manitoba, generally Liberal. While the national, Manitoba, and Alberta Liberal parties were rejected in the early 1920s, the Saskatchewan Liberals carried on. All six of Saskatchewan's daily newspapers supported them. A key factor for the Liberals in Saskatchewan was the province's large numbers of Catholics and eastern and central Europeans. In the European rural districts the provincial Liberals reaped the rewards of the federal government's immigration programme.

In Saskatchewan, however, unlike Manitoba and Alberta, there was a significant new-British *rural* presence. Although Saskatchewan attracted fewer Britons than either Manitoba or Alberta, it had almost as many British-born farm operators as the other two provinces combined. This British influence, coming later than the Ontario influx, took a longer time to assert itself. The farmer-labour connection in the Farmers Union was unique among Prairie farm organizations of any significant size. Much of its support came from farmers in continental-based areas, areas that switched from the Liberals to the CCF between 1934 and 1944. The SGGA, like the neighbouring UFM and UFA, had largely ignored the non-Anglo-Saxon farmers and had almost no following in areas settled by Europeans. All three organizations were rooted in the oldest and most established areas.

The United Farmers of Canada (Saskatchewan Section), a product of a merger of the growing Farmers Union and the declining SGGA in the mid-1920s, was socialist in a way that no other Canadian farm organization had ever been. That socialism, like Saskatchewan's early made-in-Ontario liberalism, was imported.

The two most important permanent officials of the new UFC (SS) were former members of the British Labour party and the Socialist party of the United States. The UFC (SS)'s socialist, British, labourist and agrarian heritages could be summed up by isolating two planks in its 1930 platform: "Abolition of the competitive system and substitution of a cooperative system of manufacturing, transportation and distribution," and "Free trade with the mother country." The UFC (SS) endorsed a land nationalization scheme, one patterned on the British Labour party's rural programme. The UFC (SS) also forged a political alliance with the Saskatchewan Independent Labour party. Formed in the late 1920s, the ILP was largely composed of teachers, some unionists and British socialists. It was patterned on the successful Manitoba ILP. When the UFC (SS) and the ILP came together in 1932 they formed the Farmer-Labour party and elected a British-born Fabian, M.J. Coldwell, as their leader.

A contributing factor to the rise of socialism in Saskatchewan was that the cooperative movement was stronger there than in any other province. Moreover, Saskatchewan's cooperators were more socialist than their provincial neighbours. The cooperative movement became an integral part of the CCF's constituency in Saskatchewan and the movement's growth in the province was aided by a provincial government branch headed by a British immigrant experienced in the British cooperative movement. This British link reappears often in Saskatchewan history.

The story of the CCF's success in Saskatchewan need not involve, as most sources do, a discussion of the Depression. When the Farmer-Labour (CCF) party ran in 1934 it was largely an unknown entity in politically cautious and deferential continental-origin areas. It had to contend, moreover, with the Catholic Church. Catholic opposition to the CCF was important in Saskatchewan because it was the most Catholic of the Prairie provinces. A papal encyclical and a 1934 statement by the Archbishop of Regina attacking socialism as contrary to the Catholic faith aided the Liberals. The Liberals swept both the Ontario-anchored regions and the continental, particularly Catholic, areas. Voting among Anglo-Saxons was divided, however, between areas that were largely Ontarian in origin and areas that contained large numbers of British-born. In both the 1934 and 1938 elections cultural rather than economic factors provided the clues to unravelling voting patterns.

The CCF succeeded because it was British-led and ideologically British-based. The CCF's Britishness, its cultural acceptability, made it difficult to attack as alien, and its cultural legitimacy made it politically acceptable. It could therefore become an alternative to the Liberals for Saskatchewan's continental-origin citizens. Even more than in Manitoba, continental-origin citizens represented a large potential swing factor in voting. This helps explain why the CCF-NDP's success in Saskatchewan came 25 years before it did in Manitoba and why it was more profound in terms of votes and seats. The large rural British presence, combined with a large rural continental presence relative to Manitoba and Alberta, made it easier for continental-origin citizens in Saskatchewan to attach themselves to the CCF. This was further facilitated in 1943 when another barrier to CCF aspirations was lowered: the Catholic Church declared its support for the cooperative movement, expressed concern respecting social welfare and told its members they were free to vote for any party that was not communist. The CCF victory in 1944, therefore, was no surprise.

The surge in CCF support in 1944 was most dramatic in the previously Liberal, continental-origin areas. Many CCF rural leaders were of non-Anglo-Saxon origins, a dramatic contrast to the overwhelming Anglo-Saxon character of the Liberal and Conservative leaders. The swing among continentals from the Liberals to the CCF was no less pronounced in urban areas. Between 1934 and 1944, for example, support for the CCF rose 218 percent in the most European part of Regina.

American influences in Saskatchewan were secondary to the Ontario and British influences. In contrast to Alberta, however, the Americans in Saskatchewan tended to help the fortunes of British-led anti-Liberal organizations such as the Farmers Union and the CCF. In Saskatchewan, unlike Alberta, the majority of Americans were non-Anglo-Saxons. Moreover, fewer of the Americans in Saskatchewan had English as a mother tongue. Among these European-Americans in Saskatchewan were large numbers—larger than in Alberta—of Scandinavians. European and American Scandinavians in Saskatchewan were much more receptive to socialism than Anglo-Saxon Americans—the majority American group in Alberta. Therefore, European-Americans, such as Scandinavians, encountered a powerful, legitimate and culturally acceptable ideological ally in Saskatchewan in the form of the British-influenced CCF. In Alberta, in contrast to Saskatchewan, there were both fewer British farmers and fewer European-Americans. British labour-socialism, moreover, was not a leading ideological force in rural Alberta as it was in Saskatchewan. In Alberta, European-Americans represented a minority among Americans in rural areas. Moreover, they had no corresponding powerful rural British labour-socialist strain to attach themselves to. Thus, in Alberta, there never arose a socialist agrarian rival to the UFA as there was to the SGGA in the form of the Farmers Union.

The connection between British birth and labour-socialist politics has been demonstrated in Manitoba. It was also reflected, as late as 1942, in Alberta where four of five CCF provincial executive members were British-born, and in British Columbia where nine of the 14 CCF MLAs were British-born. In Saskatchewan, in slight contrast, there were four Americans yet only three Britons among the 11-member British-led CCF caucus. Some of the Americans elected as CCF MLAs in 1944 had voted for Socialist Eugene Debs in the United States. In the United States, as the Socialist party withered, socialist supporters of European origins on the American great plains returned to the established American parties. In Saskatchewan, by contrast, as the socialist-farmer-labour movement grew, American socialist sympathizers of European ancestry, not overwhelmed by American liberalism as they were in the United States, had alternatives not restricted to the established parties.

In the late 1950s Saskatchewan produced another political phenomenon, John Diefenbaker, who made it possible for the Conservatives to become a national party for the first time since 1935. In the 1940s, Manitoba preferred the Liberals, Saskatchewan the CCF, and Alberta Social Credit. Diefenbaker, unlike other national leaders, was neither Anglo-Saxon nor was he identified with central Canadian financiers. This made it possible for European-origin farmers to flock, for the first time, to the Conservative banner. Ethnic interaction and the passing of earlier prejudices no longer crippled the Conservatives in Saskatchewan's European-origin areas. At the same time, Diefenbaker's toryism and commitment to agricultural interests made him equally acceptable to rural, Anglo-Saxon, Prairie farmers. They recognized him as an established, Ontario-born Canadian and not as a European, naturalized one. Diefenbaker's populist image, another side of this phenomenon, helped him in Alberta where agrarian populism, as in the United States, eased its way into agribusiness. The Prairies could therefore embrace the federal Conservative party after the 1950s because it was a qualitatively different party under Diefenbaker than it had been under Arthur Meighen, R.B. Bennett, John Bracken, and George Drew.

Seymour Lipset's *Agrarian Socialism* is something of a misnomer in reference to Saskatchewan. The Saskatchewan CCF-NDP consistently fared better in cities than in the countryside. More precisely, it had been a case of British-style socialism succeeding in an unexpected agricultural setting. M.J. Coldwell, Tommy Douglas, Woodrow Lloyd, and Allan Blakeney were never farmers. Nor was British-born and longtime Toronto MP Andrew Brewin who drafted Saskatchewan's "showpiece" labour legislation in the 1940s. Saskatchewan did produce one British-born non-socialist premier: Charles Dunning. But he represented an older part of Canada's British heritage. Dunning succeeded as easily in Prince Edward Island, which he went on to represent as finance minister in Mackenzie King's Cabinet. The only part of the Maritimes that would have sent a Tommy Douglas to Ottawa was Cape Breton because it had been subject to the same type of new British influx as Saskatchewan. This connection between British-birth and socialist inclinations was revealed in the 1970s when Douglas represented Nanaimo, British Columbia as an MP. In the 1920s, Nanaimo was the most British city in Canada, almost half its residents having been born in the British Isles. The British labourist-socialist connection became, paradoxically, most successful in Canada's most agrarian province.

By the late 1970s, the Liberals disappeared from the Saskatchewan legislature for the first time. Liberals defected in droves to the Conservatives who went from 2 percent of the vote in 1971 to 54 percent in 1982. This represented no ideological realignment; the Conservatives, who were by now free-enterprising liberals indistinguishable from the Liberals, merely replaced the latter as the preferred anti-socialist standard bearer in Saskatchewan's bipolar political system. Saskatchewan's Liberals, like their Manitoba and Alberta cousins, suffered from their identification with the federal Trudeau Liberals with the result that there was only one elected provincial Liberal in all of western Canada in the late 1970s. More than ever, the Saskatchewan NDP appeared as an unmistakable urban party. As such it lost power, its rural weakness becoming the major impediment to its return to office. The provincial Conservatives, moreover, had been remade and recast, calling themselves populists and opening their membership so that they were no longer an anathema to the ethnic minorities.

Alberta: the American Midwest on the Prairies

The politics of rural Alberta were as much influenced by the values of the American great plains as the politics of rural Manitoba were influenced by the standards of rural Ontario. In Alberta the various cultural waves—from Ontario, Britain, continental Europe and the United States—came closest to arriving simultaneously. Early Ontario settlers in rural Alberta, as in Saskatchewan, encountered another ideological strain. It was not, however, a socialist challenge as it had been in Saskatchewan. It was, rather, a more militant, more radical, less tory form of petit-bourgeois liberalism, than was the Canadian norm. It was not so much a challenge as a reinforcement of the natural liberalism of transplanted Ontarians. There seemed little need, as there had been in Saskatchewan, for two rival agrarian organizations or for an ideologically distinct opposition party. The older parties simply re-oriented themselves. The Liberals and Conservatives became competitors vying for support from the American-influenced UFA. An MP remarked in the House of Commons that Alberta, "from the border northward to Edmonton, might be regarded as a typical American state."

American populism pervaded Alberta politics. Many Canadian- and British-born settlers, to be sure, were found in the vanguard of the agrarian movement. But Americans and American ideas played an influential role in Alberta that was unparalleled in Canada. An early example of this in the UFA was that both sides in the debate over whether or not to enter electoral politics argued their cases with reference to experiences south of the border, one side referring to the sad end of the People's party and the other side pointing to the Non-Partisan League's success in North Dakota.

When Social Credit came to power in 1935 there was no significant shift of ideological allegiance in rural Alberta. UFA members had been nurtured on inflationary monetary theories in the United States and at UFA conventions throughout the 1920s. The overwhelming majority of UFA supporters found socialism alien and voted for a technocratic, "pragmatic" remedy in Social Credit. It was a response with American (Free Silver, Greenbackism), not Canadian, antecedents. Social Credit had much in common with American monetary reform schemes like the Townsend Plan which, in 1936, claimed over three million adherents. Although the Social Credit label originated in Britain, Alberta's version of Social Credit had stronger material links to the United States. In Britain, Social Credit's appeal was strongest among the Catholic, the urban and the cosmopolitan. In Alberta, by contrast, Social Credit was viewed most suspiciously in Catholic areas and was most popular in the rural and Protestant, particularly American fundamentalist, areas.

The American influence in rural Alberta expressed itself in many ways. In sheer numbers, more than one in five Alberta residents at one point was American-born while the national ratio was less than one in 25. Canadian branches of the American Society of Equity, containing large numbers of transplanted Nebraskans and Dakotans, were the core of the UFA when it was formed in 1909, and about one half of the directors on the UFA's board were American-born, outnumbering both British- and Canadian-born.

In sharp contrast to T.A. Crerar and Manitoba's farmers, Henry Wise Wood and the UFA's break with the Liberals was to be final and complete. The division between the UFA brand of third-party populism and the Manitoba brand of third-party parliamentarism, the latter longing for a reconciliation with the Liberals, appeared at the founding convention of the national Progressives in 1920. Wood intended that the UFA govern Alberta with no reference to the older parties. This never happened in Ontario-anchored Manitoba. This difference meant that the Liberal party was doomed in Alberta. In Ontario, Manitoba and Saskatchewan, in contrast to Alberta, most of the federal Progressives who had been elected to replace Liberals became Liberals.

American-style populism prevailed in Alberta because a rurally oriented electoral map, like Manitoba's, meant agrarian dominance. The new British labour-socialist impact in Calgary and Edmonton was insufficient to offset American populist-liberal dominance in the rural areas. Although one third of Calgary was British-born, and it served as the site of the founding conventions of both the OBU and the CCF, as well as being the constituency of Labour MP William Irvine, Calgary was in the largely rural province of Alberta and was thus also subject to an American impact: it became the headquarters of the Society of Equity, the Non-Partisan League, the UFA, Prairie evangelism and Social Credit, all of which had American roots.

Alberta's preoccupation with monetary theories was a result of the American influence. Low agricultural prices in the United States led American farmers to fight for the free coinage of silver and an inflation in the money supply. When J.W. Leedy, the former populist governor of Kansas, American credit expert George Bevington and many other Americans emigrated to Alberta, they brought their monetary theories. Throughout the 1920s and 1930s UFA conventions became debating forums for the monetary theorists. The monetary issue was second to none. In Manitoba and Saskatchewan, by contrast, it was rarely debated. When C.H. Douglas's Social Credit theories appeared they had much in common with notions already present in the UFA. The UFA had contributed to this link by distributing Douglas's books throughout the 1920s. Social Credit, therefore, could be regarded as a supplement rather than as an alternative to UFA thinking.

Wood's retirement from the UFA presidency led to a crystallization of the majority and minority positions in the UFA. The American-influenced majority was occupied with monetary reform; a British-influenced minority was more interested in socialist efforts at the national level. Both positions gained recognition at the 1931 UFA convention: Bevington's annual inflationary money resolutions were endorsed and British-born, socialist leaning Robert Gardiner became the new UFA president. Gardiner led his federal Ginger Group caucus into an even closer working arrangement with Woodsworth's Labour group. When the UFA's federal leadership in 1932 took the UFA into the CCF, Gardiner's caucus in Ottawa became isolated from the majority sentiment in rural Alberta. Neither Wood, nor UFA Premier Brownlee, nor his cabinet ever endorsed the "farmer-labour-socialist" alliance as the CCF described itself.

Social Credit was the political heir of the American-influenced monetary reform wing of the UFA. William Aberhart succeeded only because the monetary reformers in the UFA had tilled the soil so well for him. It was the UFA, he continually reminded his audiences, that had introduced Social Credit thinking into Alberta. By 1935 UFA locals throughout the province were clamouring for some form of Social Credit. During the election campaign Social Credit was really not a partisan issue: few dared attack it. It became, rather, an assumption. Even the Liberals promised Social Credit and the Alberta Federation of Labour indicated enthusiasm as well. Aberhart's Social Credit message was consistent with Alberta's populist history. The American monetary reformers had done their work well. Social Credit's sweeping victory in 1935 was therefore no surprise. Had Social Credit not appeared, another party would have arisen preaching much the same gospel.

American analogies are logical in Alberta. There is something to the argument that Aberhart came closest among Canada's premiers to looking and sounding like a radical, populist, American governor. Many of his supporters referred to him as Alberta's Abraham Lincoln. But no one could compare Prairie CCF leaders such as Douglas, Coldwell or Woodsworth to American populists. One could identify them with a Norman Thomas but, to be more accurate, one would have to look to a Briton like Ramsay MacDonald, Labour's first prime minister.

Alberta's voting patterns may be related directly to the patterns of settlement and to the ideological-cultural heritages of the settlers. Initial Ontario settlers in the south, particularly those who came before 1896 and settled along the CPR line, voted for the party of the railroad, the federal Conservatives. The early twentieth-century American influx altered this. The American impact was most pronounced in southern and eastern Alberta, an area representing the key to political power in the province just as the southwest represented that key in Manitoba. The southern, American-settled parts of Alberta which were most favourable to prohibition in 1915 became the most favourable to the UFA from 1921 to 1935 and to Social Credit from 1935 to the early 1970s. Those areas in northern Alberta that tended toward the UFA were those whose population most closely resembled the American-anchored south.

Continental-origin and French Canadian voters in northern Alberta represented a Liberal electoral base for the same reasons as in Saskatchewan and Manitoba: the Liberals were the party of immigrants and Catholics. The UFA, in contrast, was overwhelmingly Anglo-Saxon, composed of Canadian-, American- and a sprinkling of British-born farmers. UFA and Social Credit majorities were produced by an electoral map which ensured that the party that swept the south was the party that won elections. UFA and Social Credit vote totals were never as high in the continental and French Canadian north as in the Ontarian and American south. These patterns reflected how much the UFA and Social Credit had in common with each other and how little either had in common with the CCF.

The new British labour-socialist element in Alberta was largely isolated in the urban centres. Consequently, the CCF floundered. The British-anchored provincial CCF never managed to win more than two seats in Alberta. Significantly, both CCF MLAs in the 1950s were from the north and were second generation Ukrainians, as were large numbers of their constituents. These northeastern areas were among the very few where, in the 1920s, continental-born farmers outnumbered American-born ones. The CCF success here confirmed the shift, in a much less dramatic fashion than in Saskatchewan, from the Liberals to the CCF among non-Anglo-Saxons of continental, particularly eastern European, origin. In Saskatchewan, large numbers of rural continentals had swung their votes to support the party of large numbers of rural Britons, the CCF. In Alberta, however, there were both fewer continentals and fewer rural Britons. Thus, the CCF was a relatively minor force in Alberta's rural areas.

Manifestations of the American influence in Alberta abound. One example of a republican liberal tendency was the Alberta government's refusal to appear in 1938 before the Royal Commission on Dominion-Provincial Relations, addressing its comments instead to "the Sovereign People of Canada." Parliamentary government was described as a form of state dictatorship. Another example was the complaint of a Nebraska-born MLA who called the caucus form of government undemocratic and criticized the Speech from the Throne for making more of the 1937 coronation festivities than of Social Credit. Could such a sentiment respecting the coronation have been expressed at Queen's Park or in any other English Canadian provincial legislature? Solon Low, Alberta's treasurer and then the national Social Credit leader in the 1950s was the son of Mormon immigrants from Utah. In the 1980s, when the Western Canada Concept elected an MLA in the constituency of the departing Social Credit leader, that MLA was a graduate of Utah's Brigham Young University.

Conclusion

Although Prairie politics continue to be tied to Prairie history as the twentieth century draws to a close, the passage of time has brought changes. In the late 1980s, Conservatives formed the governments of all three Prairie provinces. Once the anti-immigrant party, they refashioned themselves over time and have succeeded among many of the grandchildren of the ethnic pioneers. As ethnic differences count for less in Prairie politics, other cleavages, such as class, may count for more. The politics of deference on the part of the ethnic minorities are no longer practised nor anticipated. The European-origin minorities became established economically, culturally and politically. In the 1970s, for example,

Jews served as leaders of Manitoba's Conservative and Liberal parties and as the provincial chief justice. When the latter retired, he was replaced by a Franco-Manitoban. This would have been inconceivable in the 1950s and unlikely in the 1960s. Slavs made up one third of Howard Pawley's first NDP government and were present, in increasing numbers and in influential positions, in the administrations of all three provinces. One became the leader of the Saskatchewan NDP and another was the runner-up for the Alberta Conservative leadership and the premiership. One served as a lieutenant governor, another became the deputy prime minister and, in 1988, Manitobans elected a Conservative premier of Romanian-Ukrainian heritage.

The increasingly active role of those from the ethnic minorities was fostered by their integration, acculturation and assimilation. Urbanization and mobility, as well as changes in laws, education and values, have also played a role. "Multiculturalism" became part of the national constitutional fabric with all the parties courting rather than excluding minorities from active participation. The older British or Anglo-Saxon charter group, moreover, decreased in relative numbers, making up just over a third of the populations of Manitoba and Saskatchewan in the 1980s. Today's new ethnic minorities include diverse groups of Asians and Native peoples who are not as numerous or as established as the European-origin minorities. Nevertheless, they too have today relatively easy access to the political system, contesting and winning ridings for all three parties. In the 1980s, unlike the 1920s, it is Ontario and not the Prairies that is home to most new immigrants. Ethnicity and foreign birth are today perhaps more clearly expressed as factors in party politics in metropolitan Toronto than on the Prairies, where a population that was once more than 40 percent foreign-born is now overwhelmingly Canadian-born and socialized. The ethnic minorities are in the mainstream, rather than at the periphery, of Prairie politics.

Ideological differences among the parties continue to be reflected symbolically and in public policy agendas. Although parties of different stripes behave similarly once in office, differences in nuance, style and substance persist. In 1980 Sterling Lyon, for example, exhibited a trace of toryism in objecting to a revised constitution that entrenched individual rights at the expense of parliamentary sovereignty. Peter Lougheed, in contrast, offered historically more populist and liberal Alberta a referendum bill in 1980 that could be used to settle constitutional as well as non-constitutional matters. Allan Blakeney's career as a civil servant and then as a socialist politician in Saskatchewan reflected the NDP's ideological concern with building a professional civil service, one sensitive to social democratic values.

The successful persistence of the social democratic NDP has sustained a continuing ideological fissure in a way that is absent, by contrast, in Atlantic Canada. Lyon regularly referred in the 1970s to the need to "throw out the socialists who follow alien doctrines laid down in Europe in the nineteenth century," and the Manitoba Legislature in 1983 became the unlikely venue for a debate on American policy in Nicaragua. In the context of Alberta's more radical liberal environment, the Western Canada Concept (WCC) depicted the reigning

Conservatives as crypto-socialists. And, in an echo of Aberhart's Social Credit, the WCC's leader suggested that all who voted for his party would receive $1000 from a WCC government.

Protest parties continue to sprout on the Prairies, but they may not flourish or establish a secure beachhead. The Reform party (led by the son of a Social Credit premier), the WCC and the Confederation of Regions party, which ran second in a number of Manitoba's federal ridings, are likely to fail and fade. In part this is due to the institutionalization of the established parties through new rules that range from party finance legislation to free access to broadcasting. But it is also a product of changes in the constituencies that once fed and sustained protest. Rurally based and led parties, once the driving forces in Prairie politics have bleak prospects because electoral maps have become more representative and because farmers are fewer and count for less: Saskatchewan, for example, had 170 000 farms in the 1950s, but only 70 000 in the 1970s. Today there are more university students than farms in Manitoba, more government employees than farmers and one city, Winnipeg, has as many ridings as the rest of the province. Prairie politics are, like Prairie society and economy, in continuing flux.

ENDNOTE

1. See Gad Horowitz, "Conservatism, Liberalism, and Socialism in Canada: An Interpretation," *Canadian Journal of Economics and Political Science*, Vol. 32, No. 2 (May 1966). A short version of this work appears as essay 14 of this volume.

31 Grits and Tories on the Prairies

DAVID E. SMITH

In her book *Survival*, Margaret Atwood describes the motif of early Prairie fiction, where man kills nature in his attempt to control it, as "straight line wins over curve."[1] It is an evocative theme for westerners, whose vulnerability to external forces has driven them to seek protection through political and social experiments. In this region too, line has another meaning, quite a different context, for here the development of Canada is seen as moving over two centuries from Atlantic to Pacific with the Prairies locked in direct relationship to central Canada: "Not western development," wrote Vernon Fowke, "but western development exclusively integrated with the St. Lawrence economy, was the national policy of the Fathers of Canadian Confederation."[2]

Thus, in fiction and in history, as in geography, the Prairie perspective is linear. Yet that plane has distinct physical boundaries: east of Winnipeg, west of Calgary and north of the Saskatchewan River basin. (Prairie residents have never fully adjusted to the fact that more than half of the region is neither plain nor parkland, but pine.) Only to the south is there no break in topography, yet the 800-mile border with some of the least populated of the American states has acted quite as effectively as a regional boundary. Nowhere else is the United States more accessible yet less pervasive.

Except for the brief but dizzy optimism reflected in the boom before World War I, the mood of the Prairies has alternated between latent and overt resentment of its position in Confederation. Its natural resource economy (which includes the most famous staple of all, wheat), reliant on external capital and cooperative federal legislation, created a dependence the West found difficult to accept or to break.

The federal government's retention, until 1930, of the Prairies' natural resources indicated that provincial autonomy for Manitoba, Saskatchewan and Alberta was to be different from that enjoyed elsewhere. The resources were judged too important to the national interest for equality of treatment. Thus the centre dominated and the frontier, which in the United States became a vital

This is a revised and updated version of the essay that appeared in the previous edition of this book.

influence in that nation's development, was never "allowed free expression" in Canada.[3] Limited freedom transformed rare concessions into inalienable rights, as the modern history of the grain industry bears witness.

Natural gas, oil and potash are glamorous newcomers, developed in the period after World War II, whose future is inextricably linked to the region's, but whose combined impact can never approach that of grain. Because grain came first, its roots are the Prairies' roots, for it determined the settlement pattern and transportation network, and on these bases all else rested. But wheat is hauled over rails laid three quarters of a century ago, at rates only recently allowed to rise to cover costs, and under direction of the Canadian Wheat Board, now in its fifth decade. Economic dependence has forced the Prairies to rely upon shibboleths like freedom of choice, orderly marketing and, of course, the family farm to guard its major industry against external attack, traditionally depicted as coming from central Canada but more recently from multinational corporations as well. Advocates of change pose a threat to the western farmers, who can marshall evidence to support the view that the change initiated from outside the region has been detrimental to their interests.

Since Sir Clifford Sifton's time, a distinctive characteristic of Prairie society has been its ethnic heterogeneity. As with Quebec, the Prairie provinces have a large minority population, but unlike elsewhere that minority is neither English nor French. There is a French population but nowhere on the Prairies is it the second or even third largest of the ethnic groups. Whether or not the existence of minorities "contributes to a sense of self-conscious identity for all groups,"[4] Prairie leaders from the beginning of this century were keenly aware of the "non-English." For some, ethnic diversity was a problem to be solved through "Canadianization"; for others cultural assimilation was less important than the immigrant's vote. Either directly or subsumed under the provincial versus minority rights debate, the ethnic question provided a cleavage around which parties formed, and in the heated exchanges that followed some participants forgot to distinguish between the French and the other non-English.

This insensitivity to Canada's dual ethnic origins can be traced in the main to the region's English-speaking settlers: especially those from Ontario, who viewed the West as a preserve, and those from the British Isles, who sought to save Canada for the Empire. Both expected British institutions to prevail. Nonetheless, parliament had provided for denominational education rights in the three provinces and, then as now, religion and language became confused. By 1900, the battle for publicly supported Roman Catholic schools had been lost in Manitoba but flared up in Saskatchewan and Alberta in 1905, and was revived once more in Saskatchewan in the 1920s by the Ku Klux Klan. The bicultural cleavage, which had originated in central Canada, persisted in Prairie politics as long as these denominational disputes lingered. When the ethnic debate subsided, another cleavage, economic in character, replaced it and "has dominated politics in western Canada since."[5] The succession did not occur at the same time in each of the three provinces. Because of the Klan's racism, it came last in Saskatchewan where the Liberal party, with its bicultural reputation strengthened after World War I, continued to function as a partisan force long after its counterparts in Alberta and Manitoba had all but disappeared.

The Trudeau government's language policies resurrected an issue that was thought to have been laid to rest. The emphasis upon French as an official language does not conform to the view those of British origin have of their history, while it is interpreted by the descendants of the non-English as devaluing their status as well as their contribution to Canada. Whether one argues that the West is a mosaic, with a variety of cultures of which French is only one, or a melting pot in which there are no "hyphenated Canadians," the indisputable fact remains that the frame or mold of Prairie culture today is of English Canadian design. The Canadianization of the non-English did succeed: line was imposed on curve. If this explanation is correct, then it is not difficult to understand hostility toward an official policy that promotes linguistic distinctiveness. This recognition of French is a daily reminder of the price paid by others who conformed to the English culture.[6]

In the 1980s all three Prairie provinces had to deal with bilingualism as a result of decisions by the Supreme Court of Canada which found existing provincial laws invalid because they were enacted only in English. Unilingualism in Manitoba had resulted from provincial legislation in 1890 which repealed a guarantee of bilingualism in the Manitoba Act of 1870, a statute of parliament. After the Supreme Court found that legislation *ultra vires* in 1979, the NDP government of Howard Pawley sought to work out an accommodation with Franco-Manitobans which opposition in and outside the legislature eventually thwarted. This led to a second Supreme Court judgment that imposed official bilingualism on the province and set a timetable for its accomplishment. A different case emerged in Saskatchewan and Alberta, where in 1988 the Court found unilingual laws invalid because territorial law requiring bilingualism, from the period before the provinces' creation in 1905, had never been repealed. Unlike the Manitoba judgment, the Court allowed these two provinces to determine their linguistic future. Both opted for one official language—English—with promises of expanded services in French and selective translation of laws and documents. All three Prairie provinces received extensive financial help from the federal government to implement their new language regimes. As news accounts of these emotive events reveal, the failure of the three provinces to implement bilingualism of their own accord is explained by the latent and overt opposition to French expressed by selective segments of the non-French Prairie population.

Of course western grievances did not begin with bilingualism and biculturalism. In fact, they predate the first shipment of wheat from the region in 1876. The seed of discontent was sown early by the federal government's practice of ignoring local opinion and experience in almost all matters affecting the region.[7] Acquiescence in western demands, such as the Macdonald government's granting of provincial status to a diminutive Manitoba, was a rare event and, in this particular case, one which encouraged later generations of exasperated westerners to transform Louis Riel from rebel to regional hero.

The character of the Prairies is defined not only by grievances but by innovation. The settlement pattern fostered a recognition of societal dependence rather than a spirit of rugged individualism. Westerners were never loathe to experiment together, for example in the provision of health care or the establishment of farmers' cooperatives or in sparking the creation of the United Church. Equally distinctive were their pragmatic politics. No party on the current scene has failed to tap a significant portion of the region's electoral support at some time or other. In fact, kaleidoscopic partisanship holds out hope to those parties now out of favor, as well as to those who would begin anew with yet another party, movement or league.

It is beyond the scope of this essay to recount in detail the party history of the Prairies. That the region was fertile ground for the founding of third parties is well known and documented. Less frequently remembered, however, is the continuing claim of the two old parties on the loyalties of westerners. In this century, except for 1921 when the Progressives captured 38 of the Prairies' 43 seats, the Liberals and Conservatives have won a majority of Manitoba's seats at every federal election except 1980, and a majority of Saskatchewan's in all but five (1945, 1953, 1957, 1980 and 1988). Their record in Alberta was poor, however, failing to capture a majority of that province's seats from 1921 through 1957. In terms of a popular vote, though, the Liberals and Conservatives have always won a majority in Manitoba, 50 percent or better in Saskatchewan, and failed to garner at least 50 percent in Alberta only in the federal elections of 1935 and 1945.

In the last 30 years some of the most intriguing questions about party politics on the Prairies centre on the fluctuating fortunes of the Liberal and Progressive Conservative parties. In that period in only one province (Saskatchewan) and in one election (1988) has the NDP won a majority of seats. The liaison with the Progressive Conservatives has matured into what appears to be a lasting union, while the rejection of the Liberals appears equally emphatic. Between these extremes the other parties have fared poorly in federal politics, although the ill effects have not been transmitted so clearly into the provincial sphere, where partisan fortunes have become compartmentalized, as has the federal system itself.

Liberal Dominance and Decline

Between the elections of 1958 and 1980 Liberal unpopularity became legend but it was not always so: in the decades before the Diefenbaker sweep, the Grits in Saskatchewan and Manitoba (but neither of the old parties in Alberta) were almost as unassailable as the Tories today. The switch in voter allegiance, which continued even after the Liberals returned to power nationally in 1963, meant the region was excluded from the councils of the governing party. That the cost proved intolerable for neither the West nor the Liberals indicated the gap that had come to exist between regional interests and influence on the one hand, and Liberal interests and power on the other.

At one time the Liberal party's claim on the West was indisputable. Identified with prosperity before World War I and racial tolerance during it, the Liberals' new leader after 1919 healed the intraparty schism, inherited from the fight over Union government, and reined in the agrarian revolt after its first success. One characteristic of Mackenzie King's leadership, evident from his first administration when he sought to reduce the Progressives' threat, was his ability to co-opt into his Cabinet powerful regional spokesmen like Thomas Crerar from Manitoba, Charles Dunning and James G. Gardiner from Saskatchewan and Charles Stewart from Alberta. Indeed King became the most skilful practitioner of this Canadian variant of consociational democracy. But his accommodation went beyond mere obeisance to the traditional federalized Cabinet. It extended to sub-groups of the executive like the Wheat Committee of Cabinet and to individual ministers like Gardiner to whom King frequently deferred in western matters: "Gardiner . . . seemed to feel that he was right in his own judgment. He is not only Minister of Agriculture but a former Premier in a Western province, and I think he knows the West as well as anyone. I feel, in such a situation, there is nothing left to do but to accept this advice and let him proceed."[8]

Accommodation was neither the sole reason for Liberal supremacy nor was it equally successful in each Prairie province. It worked best where there was a strong, stable party organization on which a minister could depend. In Saskatchewan, problems were few, but in Manitoba, where the Liberal battalion was divided into federal and provincial companies, much time was taken with intraparty negotiation, while in Alberta, guerrilla skirmishes over patronage made accommodation impossible and truces temporary. Accommodation was important for what it symbolized—a provincial representative among the mighty—but also for what it presumably caused to happen: policies favourable or at least not detrimental to the region. Cause without effect would give the lie to accommodation as a political technique and for this reason King had to acquiesce occasionally in a minister's desires even when, as in the case of Gardiner, they might strike him, a number of other ministers and a significant section of caucus as profligate, political rather than principled and in conflict with the party's national interest.[9]

The touchstone of Liberal fortunes on the Prairies during the King period was the government's wheat policy. Briefly, the policy was one of reluctant intervention. Except in response to wartime disruptions, the Canadian federal government had largely stayed clear of involvement in the industry other than to set the ground rules early in the century. Significantly, the Liberal party had not been in power at any time that departures from the open-market system were deemed necessary, and when in office during the 1920s the King government had had the good fortune of coexisting with the Pools, whose determination to remain independent of government was welcomed by all elected officials. Thus it was only in the chaotic economic conditions of 1935 that the Liberals were forced to determine their government's position towards the country's chief export.

Their immediate dilemma arose from the Bennett government's creation, during its last weeks in office, of the Canadian Wheat Board, which the Liberals had supported once compulsion was removed (although even then they found the principle of state intervention repugnant to their *laissez-faire* sensibilities).

Liberal history and ideology ranged from the progressivism of Dunning's Saskatchewan to the conservatism of Gouin's Quebec, but it did not countenance interference that smacked of "socialism." While there were strong opponents in the party who wanted to scrap the Wheat Board, others accepted the need on emergency grounds and in preference to increased relief payments to destitute western farmers.

Before the end of the decade, the Liberals discovered that they could not backtrack even when they were united and economic conditions had improved. Western grain farmers had fought unsuccessfully in the 1920s for the reinstitution of a board like that of 1919–20, which was given credit for the record high prices that year. Constitutional barriers and the King government's philosophical reluctance had pushed farmers into cooperative Pools, which had prospered until the market collapsed in 1930. Later in the decade, Gardiner proposed that the Pools resume their marketing responsibilities but the farmers were not convinced and, as a result, the Pools' energies to the present day have been devoted solely to the elevator business. The board's lure was that it replaced the peaks and troughs of the futures market with the assurance of an advance initial payment based on projected sales of wheat, and a final payment calculated on the pooling of returns from actual sales. Orderly marketing in fact meant the removal of domestic competition and thereby the realization of the western farmer's dream of first-line protection in the tumult of the international market. The board was truly a "steward of producers' interests" and the fervor with which the vast majority of farmers has defended it reveals how great was the need it satisfied.

The board created by Bennett was voluntary and thus the open market, in the form of the Winnipeg Wheat Exchange, continued to function. But in 1943 the press of war demands on limited wheat supplies threatened the government's price control policy and, "to arrest an advance rather than a decline in the price of wheat," the board was given monopoly control.[10] This action, earnestly sought by generations of western farmers, signalled both the end of Exchange trade in wheat and the further entanglement of government.

The ardent attachment to the board among farmers, and the government's treatment of it as an affair of convenience, were part of the explanation for the Liberal's spectacular losses on the Prairies in the general election of 1945. In Saskatchewan, the citadel of wheat and Liberal strength, the party's popular vote fell 10 percentage points to the lowest level since 1921, and its seats were reduced from 12 to two. Mackenzie King lost Prince Albert, which he had held since 1926, and Gardiner squeaked through in Melville with a majority of 28 out of 20,162 votes cast. These results gave added urgency to the government's, and especially to Gardiner's, search for markets in the postwar period in the hope, thereby, of protecting the farmer from a repetition of the disastrous drop in price experienced after World War I.

As with everything else associated with the board's history, this initiative was viewed in the West as a precedent which bound successive governments. And this presumption of government responsibility determined the course of later events: for those in power it meant they should try to sell wheat, while for the producers it meant government should be concerned about their welfare. Conflict over the meaning of responsibility ultimately defeated the Liberals in the 1950s and firmly joined farmer to Tory in the 1960s.

The Wheat Board originated in a concern about scarcity of income and crops. But the intractable problem of the postwar period had been recurring surpluses which, according to some observers, so distorted the grain-handling system 35 years ago that the effects still remain.[11] When the Liberals were defeated in 1957, a record volume of unsold wheat (640 million bushels) was piled on the Prairies, although the average annual marketing of all grain between 1945 and 1950 was only 458 million bushels. As a consequence, the huge carryover was the principal cause of the St. Laurent government's unpopularity on the Prairies. The *Western Producer* commented:

> We do not say that the manner of financing pipelines is not important nor do we suggest that all the sound and fury has been inspired by political motives. But we do state that at the time when the failure of agriculture may be at stake it is sheer madness—a modern version of fiddling while Rome burns—to devote the time of the government and Parliament to what in comparison are minor matters.[12]

But it was less the government's inability than its apparent disinclination to move wheat that angered the farmers. Economic orthodoxy on the part of the Liberals once again proved the stumbling block. This time the lightning rod for discontent was C.D. Howe, minister of trade and commerce since 1948, whose formidable talents and energy in different portfolios had piloted Canada's expansion for two decades (coincidentally up to the pipeline legislation itself) but whose knowledge of the grain trade, as engineer of most of the country's terminal elevators, was even older. Anxious to increase sales, western farmers and farm organizations pressed the government to grant easy credit and accept cheap money. Howe would do neither, arguing instead that sales on credit or for foreign currency would discriminate against and lose old customers. He did think the price of wheat might have to be reduced, as long as a "fetish" were not made of holding the line, but the farmers were unwilling to carry the cost despite the government's claim that they were better off than at any time in the last 25 years.[13] Cynics among them noted that the last quarter century began in the early 1930s.

A related issue, which harmed Liberals most, was the debate over advance payments. Since farmers got paid only for wheat delivered to elevators, and since this was regulated by quotas which, because of the glut, were low or nonexistent, they argued for some payment in advance of delivery. The suggestion was not new. It had been made at the beginning of the war, before there were quotas on deliveries and where congestion had occurred. After investigating the initial proposal the Liberals had decided the scheme could not be administered efficiently or fairly, since it did not get to the root of the problem of income disparity between rich and poor farmer. It would also impose on the Wheat Board, the only feasible administrative agent, a relief function that would conflict with its primary job of selling wheat. Thus, in the mid 1950s, the Liberals rejected the resurrected proposal with a finality that implied they knew better and, perhaps more inflammatory to westerners, that the problem was not as serious as claimed. Both Howe and St. Laurent reminded Prairie audiences that they should be thankful, not critical of "Providence's bounty."[14]

Eventually the government did respond with a scheme for low-interest bank loans, but farmers everywhere rejected this alternative, claiming that it meant they had to "pay" for their own money. The episode of the advance payments had serious repercussions for the Liberals beyond contributing to their defeat at the next election. First, it exacerbated relations between federal and provincial Liberals across the Prairies. In Alberta, already, the feeling was abroad among local Grits that the St. Laurent government, especially Howe and the Alberta member, George Prudham, minister of mines and technical surveys, were too friendly with the Socred government in Edmonton and the oil industry in Calgary while they let the provincial group languish.[15] In Saskatchewan, where dissension was widespread, the provincial leader "Hammy" McDonald described the loan plan as "less effective than a stirrup pump at a forest fire."[16] The Manitoba Liberals, led by Douglas Campbell and still disguised as Liberal-Progressives, were the most conservative of the provincial parties. They criticized the loan scheme, the Liberals' wheat sales record (which the Manitoba minister of agriculture said he would improve by selling "to the devil himself" on easy credit) and the St. Laurent government's health and welfare programmes, which the premier described as "socialistic."[17]

But the loan scheme was equally significant for its effects upon Liberal relations with organized farm groups, particularly the three Prairie Pools. They were held in the highest esteem by leading Liberal politicians and by senior public servants who looked upon these organizations as indispensable to the grain trade and as allies. Relations with the United Grain Growers were similarly close, stretching back to Crerar's agrarian leadership days. For the other farm organizations, especially the Farmers' Union, there was not such sentiment, although the Liberals sought not to antagonize even these groups, who they saw as CCF-inspired.

The debate over cash advances created a division between the Pools and the Liberal party which never disappeared. Ultimately they found themselves aligned with the CCF and the Farmers' Union in support of cash advances. Unlike these organizations the Pools did not condemn the bank loans, but persisted in arguing that the scheme was insufficient. They had disagreed with federal legislation before but always there had been compromise leading to a reconciliation of positions. In alienating this traditionally friendly behemoth the government convinced many westerners, in the clearest possible way, that it was inept and remote, which were frailties not previously associated with the Liberal party.

The Diefenbaker Revolt

The Progressive Conservatives formed their government in June 1957 mainly as a result of a large shift in voter support in the Atlantic provinces and Ontario; Quebec and the Prairies followed suit nine months later. Time was needed to shatter Grit bedrock in those parts of the country used to seeing Progressive Conservatives as enemies, if they saw them at all. In the West the adjustment was helped by the new government's quick action on two pressing matters: early passage of the Prairie Grain Advance Payments Act, assented to less than a month after parliament opened in October 1957 and, the following January, the appointment of John Bracken, former Liberal-Progressive premier of Manitoba and later Progressive Conservative national leader, as a one-man royal commission to inquire into the distribution of boxcars.

The latter initiative signalled federal sympathy for a grievance that had aroused farmers but not Liberals for four years. Boxcars, like "crow rates," are one of those incendiary subjects which kindle western wrath with remarkable regularity. In the battle with the CPR and the elevator companies early in this century the farmers won the Sintaluta case, which upheld the individual producer's right to equality of treatment by the railroads in the distribution of cars needed to transport grain to lakehead terminals. The first-come, first-served principle in allocating boxcars was a vital part of the farmer's much-vaunted freedom of choice. But 50 years later when the cooperatives owned the majority of elevators, a large percentage of which were filled with wheat, that freedom seemed illusory. Equality of boxcar distribution did not help clear a system whose member companies were unequal nor did it guarantee individual producers the right to patronize their own companies. Complaints which accompanied congestion increased in the wake of the Liberals' ineffectual responses.

Under Diefenbaker the Tories responded to western grievances in a manner different from their predecessors. It was not that they were initially more successful at dealing with the old problems—they were not—but their publicized open-door to farmers, leading directly to the prime minister who was himself a westerner, assuaged the Prairies' desire for attention, which in the 1950s the Liberals seemed more often to withhold than to give.

Regional demands were often rejected by Liberals because they *were* regional: "[Howe] raised the question as to whether we could expect special treatment in Western Canada. Did we know that the fishermen at the Eastern Coast may be worse off than the wheat growers of the West?"[18] The invocation of other interests to deflect Prairie demands was not unique to C.D. Howe: Mackenzie King had done it years before and Pierre Trudeau, during another unmanageable wheat surplus, was to remind farmers of the same fishermen.[19] Liberal rejection of narrow regionalism was belied, westerners thought, by the friendly reception given to demands from the business interests of central Canada. As a result, Liberal pleas for economic flexibility and regional balance were interpreted more and more by westerners as a cavalier rejection of their interests.

The Diefenbaker government's disagreement with western demands which, after 1958 and in response to the ever-bulging granaries, took the form of petitions and delegations in support of deficiency payments, was never viewed in the same light. Deficiency payments were subject to wide interpretation but their irreducible minimum was a commodity support price which gave some surety of income. The familiar argument against the proposal, which the government employed, was that it favoured the large and prosperous over the small and marginal farmer. Although the Tories' alternative—acreage payments of up to $200 per farm—did not meet demands for income security, it was welcomed as an income supplement scheme and, most of all, as an indication of government responsiveness.

The claim of the Progressive Conservatives on the loyalties of the West was nurtured by the change in government attitudes, but it took root and flourished because of two events that occurred early in the 1960s. One was the sale of massive quantities of wheat to Communist China. The sale meant a dramatic rise in income for Prairie farmers and the onset of the greatest wave of prosperity in memory. But equally important was the buoyancy of spirit which followed. For the first time in 10 years delivery quotas were removed and Alvin Hamilton, the minister of agriculture and minister responsible for the Wheat Board, called on farmers to grow all the wheat they could. While the Diefenbaker government had not been responsible for the Chinese crop disasters that led to the demand, they did claim credit for Canada's being chosen supplier of the needed wheat. The purchase had been promoted through the introduction of new credit arrangements that later become acceptable practice but at the time, because they were seen as unorthodox, earned the Tories lasting gratitude in the West.

The other event was really not a single happening but a series of governmental moves which together indicated confidence in the region's traditional institutions and way of life. Among these was the decision to go ahead with the South Saskatchewan River Dam, a project which had been promoted for a quarter century by Saskatchewan politicians of all stripes including M.J. Coldwell, T.C. Douglas, John Diefenbaker and J.G. Gardiner, the last of whom, however, had to acquiesce in a Royal Commission recommendation and a governmental decision in 1956 not to proceed with construction. Although the plan's irrigation scheme made diversification of agriculture a possibility, the project was seen, by supporters and detractors alike, as a rehabilitation undertaking which would increase grain productivity. Thus, for those who wanted to see wheat farmers more secure in their livelihood, the dam was a vote of confidence in Prairie life.

So too was ARDA (Agriculture and Rural Development Act, 1961), which was intended to bolster the bases of rural society. The Act was associated with Alvin Hamilton and it reflected that minister's "rural fundamentalist faith in the rejuvenation of the farmer."[20] Any politician determined to protect the region against hostile economic forces, of international or domestic origin, was bound to win strong support. But Hamilton's "grass roots" appeal struck another responsive chord when he defended the farmer against government bureaucrats as well. Always wary of planners, he was especially scornful of politicians who listened to them or, as he later said, who "sold their soul to the mandarins."[21]

Indeed, after the Liberals returned to power in 1963 the emergence of far-flung plans and planners destined to renovate the wheat industry multiplied the fears and complaints about anonymous advisers first articulated by the Tories nearly 30 years ago. The "big magician in the east" became synonymous with "the backroom boys drafting policy" since both were viewed as being engaged in "an academic exercise" unrelated and often in defiance of the realities of grain farming.[22] Because the New Democrats gave free rein to boards and planners in the provinces where they exercised power, they too were held culpable by Tory critics.

This was a major theme of the Saskatchewan Progressive Conservatives in the provincial election of 1982, when they attacked the socialists' "family of crown corporations." In that campaign, the local Tories annihilated the ruling NDP and set the stage for their counter-attack later in the decade on behalf of "privatization."

The most remarkable feature of the Tory revolt on the Prairies was its entrenchment after the party moved into opposition. If anything, that hold grew as the Progressive Conservatives intoned their past accomplishments. During the Pearson years, when there was no western minister of long standing in cabinet, the Liberals were ridiculed as ignorant about wheat and this ineptness (which overshadowed a very creditable sales record) was used to counteract tales of Tory debacles in Ottawa. During the Trudeau period when one minister, Otto Lang, was identified for nearly a decade with the industry and attempts to modernize it, the Tories criticized Liberals not for ignorance but for being insensitive to the region's way of life based on the traditional institutions of the wheat economy.

Some western Tories have also challenged the government's policy on bilingualism and biculturalism. That policy has never been popular and in 1969 when the Official Languages Act was before parliament, the Prairie premiers of the time (Harry Strom, Social Credit, of Alberta; W. Ross Thatcher, Liberal, of Saskatchewan; and Walter Weir, Progressive Conservative, of Manitoba) talked about but did nothing to challenge its constitutionality. Whatever the philosophical base for this dissent, of which "unhyphenated Canadianism" is certainly an important element, it has been transmitted effectively through Progressive Conservative ranks. The breaking of party discipline by Diefenbaker and 16 other Tories—all but one westerners—on the passage of the Official Languages Act thwarted Robert Stanfield in his attempt to open wider the party's doors to Quebec; while nearly two decades later, under a prime minister from Quebec who had led the PCs to their greatest victory in Canadian history, opposition from western Tory Caucus members forced the Mulroney government to amend its national language legislation to guarantee the new law would not hurt unilingual anglophones.

Return of the Liberals

If Liberal success in the old days could be attributed to those provincial chieftains who sat in the federal cabinet but held sway over local tribes, so too could Liberal failure in 1957 and 1958. In the aftermath of defeat the Liberals set about constructing a new organization centred in Ottawa which assumed as its primary task the promotion and, it was hoped, eventual return of a federal Liberal government. Pursuit of this objective required that power over nominations and patronage, traditionally exercised in and for the Liberals of each province, be transferred to federally designated officials. Not only the conduct of campaigns but their focus was altered as well, first as part of a grand design "to win over to the Liberal party" CCF supporters in central Canada and, second, "to enforce[e] our strength in what might be described as the middle class group of people, particularly in Ontario."[23]

These changes in direction and strategy guaranteed conflict with areas like the Prairies, whose interests and political complexion were not those of the centre. Compounding these problems, if not resulting from them, was the inability of Prairie Liberals to get elected and stay elected. Relations between Ottawa and the region deteriorated after the victory of 1963 secured for the foreseeable future the new organization's permanence. Each of the Prairie provinces presented special problems, but it was in Saskatchewan where the flame of dissent burned brightest. There the provincial Liberals defeated the CCF in spite of tepid federal support and for the next seven years the fire of intraparty controversy was stoked by a series of policy disagreements as well by the constant irritant of organizational strife. Across the Prairies the refusal of the federal Liberals to treat with their established provincial numbers was interpreted as bad faith and poor politics which would ultimately hurt all Liberals, even the strong Saskatchewan Grits who found themselves being held responsible for federal Liberal actions and policies they stoutly opposed.

The federal organization scheme introduced in the early 1960s was scrapped later in the decade when it failed for a third time to give the Liberals the majority they wanted in 1965. After 1968 the party entered on yet another organizational venture, this time in response to the then popular principle of participatory democracy. The call for the democratization of party structures and the abandonment of élite control from the centre as well as the periphery, required a bridging of the organizational gap that had antagonized Prairie Liberals for nearly 10 years. The problem remained, however, that any structure, especially one claiming to be democratic, required cooperation to make it work. This was difficult to achieve when provincial Liberals were fighting for their lives and losing, which was the case in each of the three Prairie provinces from the mid-1960s to the mid-1980s: the last election in the 1960s saw Liberal percentages of the popular vote in Manitoba, Saskatchewan and Alberta stand at 34 46 and 11 respectively, while at the first election in the 1980s Liberals in each of the same provinces won 7, 5 and 2 percent of the vote. Since then Liberal fortunes have risen dramatically in Manitoba (35 percent in 1988) and Alberta (29 percent in 1989) but far less so in Saskatchewan (10 percent in 1986). Whether that change can be translated into a permanent Liberal revival in federal contests in the first two of those provinces remains to be seen; in the general election of 1988 Liberal candidates won 14 percent of the vote cast in Alberta and 37 percent in Manitoba.

One symptom of a party in decline is preoccupation with the subject of organization. The Alberta Liberals, whose demise has been frequently predicted, have made more fresh starts with charts, zones and chains of command than any party in power. The same was true of the Saskatchewan Liberals in the 1950s when they alternated between blaming "Jimmy" Gardiner for their plight and reorganizing themselves. For federal Liberals on the Prairies the debate over organization, once it progresses beyond patronage matters, assumes an air of unreality; they think they have little influence on the outcome which, in any case, they consider relatively unimportant. Policies and personalities win elections, they argue, as they look to Tory precedent and the Diefenbaker organization which defied description.[24]

Despite the efforts of the party hierarchy, the breakthrough was not to be the result of personality. A legion of unsuccessful Liberal candidates whose personal attractiveness seemed hard to improve on and a succession of local notables, enticed by the prospect of a Cabinet portfolio, proved no match for the Tories. If candidates who were eminently regional failed, then policies made in Ottawa for consumption in the St. Lawrence valley were unlikely to succeed. The reception given the federal government's language legislation has been discussed; in the 1960s there was also the Carter Commission's recommendations and the subsequent white paper whose contents the West considered inflammatory. Changes in estate tax and the introduction of a capital gains tax, as well as the inclusion of all increases in economic gain as taxable income, were interpreted as threats to the family farm, which passed from generation to generation as a gift or through inheritance. Proposed changes in tax exemptions on mineral exploration raised the cry of regional discrimination; for Ottawa seemed ready to close the door to investors in western Canada now that Quebec and Ontario had their mining industries. That at least was the view of a number of Prairie politicians, especially Liberals, who had spent a good part of the decade fighting Walter Gordon's nationalist economic policies.

In the 1970s the natural resources of Saskatchewan and Alberta became the subject of another dispute with Ottawa, this time over pricing. As the international price of oil soared the two provinces were urged to think of the national interest, have compassion for their less fortunate partners in Confederation (including Manitoba) and accept a negotiated increase. Exhortation proved fruitless however, and a tortuous series of events ensued before an energy accord could be reached in 1981. The defeat of the Liberals at the polls in 1979, their defeat of the Progressive Conservatives in parliament and the Liberal win in the subsequent general election were only part of the story. The debate over the retention of Petro-Canada as a public corporation had a differential impact on Canadian attitudes not least between Saskatchewan and Alberta with their NDP and PC governments. But intraregional differences were papered over when the federal government announced its National Energy Policy. For here again appeared the familiar devil of federal intrusion: more than a century had passed since parliament had created Manitoba but retained her natural resources, yet in spite of the transfer of 1930 the avarice of federal authorities seemed never to wane.

In fact the provinces were already primed to react negatively by two Supreme Court of Canada decisions in 1978 and 1979. In the first (*Canadian Industrial Gas and Oil Ltd. v Government of Saskatchewan, et al.*) a provincial royalty tax to limit windfall gains accruing to petroleum producers was declared to be an indirect tax and therefore *ultra vires* the provincial Legislature. In the second (*Central Canada*

Potash Co., Ltd., et al. v Government of Saskatchewan, et al.), in which the federal government had entered as a co-plaintiff, the provincial government's attempt (begun by the Thatcher Liberals and continued by the NDP) to control potash production experienced the same fate, for it was seen as an interference with interprovincial and international trade. Prairie, indeed provincial, sentiment on the matter of local control of resources proved so intense that constitutional discussions at the beginning of the decade led to a new section (92A) being incorporated in the Constitution Act. This section confirmed the provinces' exclusive legislative authority over non-renewable resources, granted them jurisdiction over the indirect taxation of resources (provided these taxes did not discriminate between provinces) and recognized concurrent jurisdiction over interprovincial trade in resources (with federal paramountcy and, again, in the absence of discrimination).[25]

Wheat, as usual, received great attention. The Pearson years had been prosperous for the Prairies but the Trudeau administration opened with a market slump that caused a drastic fall in farm income and an unmanageable surplus to clog the system. The federal government's remedy was LIFT (Lower Inventories for Tomorrow), a scheme that paid farmers not to grow wheat. Historically, acreage reduction had never been popular on the Prairies because, in effect, it put farmers on the dole. In the Canadian system farmers produce all they can, the Wheat Board sells it and any restriction placed on the activities of either is blamed on the federal government. At its most popular, the LIFT program had a mixed reception but it was later roundly criticized as evidence of the Liberal government's lack of confidence in the farmers and in its own ability to get the system moving again.

The emotion triggered by the programme was a measure of its impact. LIFT was an unprecedented break with traditional government wheat policy. In the face of surpluses the St. Laurent government had waited and then provided low interest loans to help pay storage costs; the Diefenbaker government had also waited after giving cash advances on farm stored wheat, but the Trudeau government did not wait—it legislated the surplus out of existence by curtailing production. For an industry whose structure and function were imperceptibly different from a half century before, LIFT was a portent that aroused concern and even alarm.

In the swift and sweeping programme that followed the temporary acreage reduction, the government had two broad goals: to provide security of income for the region and to make the grain industry more efficient. Major legislation to achieve the first objective was a grain income stabilization plan based on contributory payments by producers and government from which western farmers as a group would benefit when income on the Prairies declined. The original legislation, introduced in 1970, had to be withdrawn because of prolonged opposition; it was eventually passed in amended form early in 1976. Significantly, the plan did not insure individual incomes—that would have conflicted with the government's belief that the grain industry had to become more, not less, responsive to change. In their desire for efficiency the Liberals thus opened themselves to the old charge that they would sacrifice the "family farm" and in turn those community institutions that depend on it.

The government's reply was to note that an industry so vital to Canada and in a competitive international market could be preserved in its original state but must be modernized if it was to be profitable. As a major wheat exporter Canada is in a unique situation—its grain is grown over a vast area and collected at thousands of delivery points, hauled a thousand miles or more to only three seaports (Vancouver, Thunder Bay and Churchill), the last two of which are ice-locked for more than half the year. The Crow Rates, the ancient roadbeds and the hundreds of antiquated elevators were seen in Ottawa as serious liabilities to achieving efficiency.

The government appointed commissions of inquiry to study the first two (the last depended on action by the elevator companies). During the past 15 years federal research and policy advisers had demonstrated why changes should be made, but their exhaustive findings still were not convincing to the large body of western opinion, which feared change, especially when it was recommended by outside experts. Therefore, with the federal government (for so long synonymous with the Liberal party) depicted as insensitive and the federal bureaucracy unresponsive, the possibility of popular reform to this major industry seemed dim.

After the Liberals came back into power in 1980, with only two seats of 77 in the four western provinces, they appeared committed to changing the ground rules of the grain industry. During the campaign Trudeau had talked of doubling Prairie trackage and thereby speeding grain haulage. Later, after concerted consultation with farm groups, it was announced that the Crow Rates would be abolished. Notwithstanding differences in Cabinet over how this should be done, opposition from the Saskatchewan and Manitoba governments at both the principle and the terms of the change, alarm from Quebec meat producers about the effect of change on their livelihood and obstruction of parliamentary debate by the NDP and PC parties to highlight the significance of the changes, parliament passed legislation late in 1983 to end the historic rates. Debate lingered, however, for western farmers remained suspicious that their interests would be adversely affected despite federal government promises to the contrary and despite a huge payout to the railways in the form of a transportation subsidy. By the end of the decade, a more efficient industry had begun to emerge, as grain was transported in less time than ever before. But with both trackage and the number of grain farmers in decline, it was a mute point for many westerners whether the end of the Crow did not also mean the end of "the way of life" the wheat economy had supported for almost a century.

Plus Ça Change...

For Alberta and Saskatchewan the 1980s began with the promise of fundamental change. A dramatic increase in revenue from oil and natural gas offered escape from dependency on a fluctuating economy based on grain.

Equally attractive, the new wealth seemed likely to force a change in the economic terms of Confederation, thereby reducing another form of dependency—the West's subservience to central Canada's financial and commercial institutions. That at least was the hope at the decade's outset; but the federal government's National Energy Policy (NEP), with its strictures on so-called windfall profits going to the oil-producing provinces, and a rapid decline in the world price for oil destroyed the West's recent dream of economic diversification. A world-wide decline in wheat prices and a series of poor crops drove Prairie incomes even lower. By the decade's end, the region's economy had slumped precipitously, whether compared to the optimism of 10 years before or to the continuing prosperity of central Canada. Not since the boom of the late 1920s had expectations reached such heights only to be deflated so quickly. This sequence of anticipated growth followed by stagnation contributed to the sense of frustration evident among Prairie voters as the decade progressed.

NEP lost the Liberals western support which the NDP did not capture. The Progressive Conservatives were the big winners in the election of 1984, picking up seats from the NDP in Manitoba and Saskatchewan, while retaining once again all of Alberta's seats. For the first time since 1958, a majority of Prairie MPs found themselves in government and not in opposition ranks; the opportunity had finally come to make the region's voice heard where it counted. That did not happen or, if it did, it was not perceived to noticeably affect the federal government's procurement, language or monetary policies, or the decisions of its regulatory agencies. Western complaints about the federal government's sensitivity to central Canadian concerns and insensitivity to those of the other regions continued to be heard after 1984, only now they were directed at Tory and not Liberal ministers. In the 1988 election the Tories lost five seats in Saskatchewan, four in Manitoba and one (but the first in 20 years) in Alberta. After only four years of a national Tory government, the much-vaunted Conservatism of Prairie voters appeared to be on the wane, replaced by a growing disenchantment with the institutions of the central government itself.

Evidence to support that conclusion could be found in the West's (and especially Alberta's) new infatuation with constitutional reform, in particular Senate reform. Of the region's many political flirtations in this century, constitutional reform is the latest; and except for Quebec's promotion of the subject after 1960, no area of the country has been more intoxicated by its potential than the West in recent years. It is no coincidence that western enthusiasm for this cause mounted at the very time the party it overwhelmingly supported formed the government, for the PCs after 1984, like the Liberals before them, seemed unable to deliver what the West wanted.

Provincial political developments in the 1980s accentuated Prairie voter frustration. Despite Tory regimes in Alberta for all of the decade and in Saskatchewan for eight years, discontent with the federal party intensified in both provinces after mid-decade. By way of contrast, hostility to the federal Tories in Manitoba contributed to the provincial political stalemate in 1988 which saw the formation of a minority PC government. The federal policies noted above, plus the Meech Lake Accord and the Mulroney government's Free Trade Agreement with the United States, helped wrench apart federal and provincial Conservatives on the Prairies, just as the Trudeau government's energy and grain policies, among others, handicapped Prairie Liberals. The presence of the same party in power at both levels of the federal system had a deleterious effect on the fortunes of each: in Saskatchewan the provincial Conservative vote fell from 54 percent in the election of 1982 to 45 in 1986, while in Alberta it slumped from 63 percent in the election of 1982 to 51 in 1986 to 44 in 1989. The Manitoba Tories found it politically desirable to repudiate the Meech Lake Accord (the only Conservative government in Canada to do so), while the Saskatchewan Tories laboured to support the intensely unpopular free trade policy of its federal counterparts.

The most remarkable feature of Prairie politics in 1990 is its similarity to Prairie politics in 1980; only the party labels of the protagonists have changed. The two old parties continue to dominate federal politics in the region and as long as the Liberals continue to rule, the region will find satisfaction in aligning itself with the principal opposition party. Unhappiness with the federal Progressive Conservatives, in power since 1984, is evident across the Prairies at the beginning of the 1990s. Improved Liberal fortunes in Manitoba and Alberta might presage a revival of the other "old party" on the Prairies, but the strength of NDP support in Saskatchewan and the continued activity of the Reform party in Alberta (in the 1988 federal general election it won 15 percent of the vote cast in that province) make any prediction of regional voter behaviour a dangerous enterprise. However, it is safe to venture the following judgment: if the Progressive Conservatives succeed in capturing a majority of seats in the first general election of the new decade, it will not be due to bedrock Prairie support but because they have held on to Ontario and Quebec voters. No other prediction could illustrate more acutely the turnabout in Liberal and Conservative party fortunes or the quandary it presents Prairie voters.

ENDNOTES

1. Margaret Atwood, *Survival: A Thematic Guide to Canadian Literature* (Toronto: Anansi, 1972), p. 123.
2. Vernon C. Fowke, "National Policy and Western Development," *Journal of Economic History*, Vol. XVI, No. 4 (December 1956), p. 476.
3. W.T. Easterbrook, "Recent Contributions to Economic History: Canada," *Journal of Economic History*, Vol. XIX, No. 1 (March 1959), p. 99.
4. Mildred A. Schwartz, *Politics and Territory: The Sociology of Regional Persistence in Canada* (Montreal: McGill-Queen's University Press, 1974), p. 102.
5. Jane Jenson, "Aspects of Partisan Change: Class Relations and the Canadian Party System," Unpublished paper prepared for the Conference on Political Change, Saskatoon, March 1977, p. 17.
6. See J.E. Rea, "The Roots of Prairie Society," in David P. Gagan, ed., *Prairie Perspectives* (Toronto: Holt, Rinehart and Winston, 1970) pp. 46–55, and "My mainline is the

kiddies . . . make them good Christians and good Canadians, which is the same thing," in W. Isajiw, ed., *Identities: The Impact of Ethnicity on Canadian Society* (Toronto: Peter Martin Associates, 1977) pp. 3–11. See, as well, "Separate Statement," by J.B. Rudnyckyj in Canada, *Report of the Royal Commission on Bilingualism and Biculturalism.* Book I (Ottawa: Queen's Printer, 1967), pp. 155–69.

7. Lewis Herbert Thomas, *The Struggle for Responsible Government in North-West Territories, 1870–97* (Toronto: University of Toronto Press, 1956), ch. 2.

8. King Diary, 21 March 1939, quoted in C.F. Wilson, *A Century of Canadian Grain: Government Policy to 1951* (Saskatoon: Western Producer Prairie Books, 1978), p. 596.

9. King Diary, 20 April 1939 and 5–7 March 1941, in Wilson, *A Century of Canadian Grain,* p. 680.

10. Vernon C. Fowke, *The National Policy and the Wheat Economy* (Toronto: University of Toronto Press, 1957), p. 276.

11. United Grain Growers Limited, "Submission to the Grain Handling and Transportation Commission (Hall Commission)," 24 October 1975.

12. *Western Producer* (editorial), 24 May 1956, p. 6.

13. *Ibid.* 17 June 1954, p. 4.

14. *Ibid.* 15 May 1957, p. 6.

15. Interview with Nick Taylor, leader and past president of the Alberta Liberal Association, December 1976; taped interview with J.C. Gardiner by Una Maclean Evans, 29 December 1961–5 January 1962, tape No. 6. These tapes are deposited in the Glenbow Alberta Institute. For a general discussion of the period, see John Richards and Larry Pratt, *Prairie Capitalism: Power and Influence in the New West,* (Toronto: McClelland and Stewart, 1979), chs. 3 and 4.

16. *Western Producer,* 27 October 1955, p. 1.

17. *Ibid.* 15 November 1955, p. 1 and *Winnipeg Free Press,* 26 June 1957, p. 1.

18. *Ibid.* 3 December 1953, p. 1 (magazine).

19. King Diary, 24 April 1939 quoted in Wilson, pp. 600–01 and *Western Producer,* 31 July 1969, p. 5.

20. Anthony G.S. Careless, *Initiative and Response: The Adaptation of Canadian Federalism to Regional Economic Development* (Montreal: McGill-Queen's University Press, 1977), pp. 75–6.

21. Canada, *House of Commons Debates,* 3 May 1977, p. 5257.

22. *Western Producer,* 14 January 1971, p. 8 and 11 November 1971, p. 13.

23. National Liberal Federation Papers, Public Archives of Canada, W. Ross Thatcher to Lester Pearson, 24 February 1960 and D.K. McTavish (NLF President) to J.J. Connolly, 27 February 1958.

24. Interviews with A.R. O'Brien (National Director of the Liberal Party, 1966–69), January 1977 and Senator H.W. Hays (Minister of Agriculture, 1963–65), February 1977.

25. J. Peter Meekison, Roy J. Romanow and William D. Moull, *Origins and Meaning of Section 92A: The 1982 Constitutional Agreement on Resources* (Montreal: Institute for Research on Public Policy, 1985).

32 Alberta Politics: The Collapse of Consensus

ALLAN TUPPER

The results of the 1986 and 1989 provincial elections in Alberta demand innovative interpretations of politics in this often politically anomalous province. The advent of relatively large legislative oppositions, fierce interparty competition in Edmonton and Calgary and the entrenchment of the New Democrats as the official opposition mock the conventional interpretations of Alberta as a bastion of conservative politics, one-party dominance and feeble opposition parties.[1] As we move into the 1990s, Alberta politics are more complex, more competitive and more stimulating. Questions about the province's place in Canadian Confederation, while still important, are now taking second place to debates about such explicitly provincial matters as the role of the provincial government, the relative political power of urban and rural areas and the province's economic prospects.

This often speculative essay reviews recent political developments in Alberta, to suggest an explanation for the weakening of the Conservatives' electoral hegemony and to demonstrate the increased complexity of politics in this changing Prairie province. My theme is that the Conservatives' electoral stranglehold is loosening because the party has not adapted to the province's changing economic, social and political landscape in the 1980s. Its policies, its view of the electorate and its political *modus operandi* are rooted in the circumstances of the 1970s. More specifically, the provincial Conservatives have adapted neither to the lessened economic and political significance of oil and natural gas, nor to the changes wrought by the election in 1984 and 1988 of federal Progressive Conservative majority governments with strong Albertan representation. Moreover, the economic boom of the 1970s followed by the province's economic weakening in the 1980s produced an insecure and volatile electorate which has not been soothed by Conservative slogans about the province's potential.

In the midst of significant economic and political uncertainty, the governing Tories also face challenges that flow from their own political style and their own experiences as a governing party since 1971. Like the successful federal Liberal

---

This is an original essay written especially for this volume.

party of the postwar period, the Alberta Conservatives have cultivated an image of extraordinary administrative competence. They maintain that they alone possess the talent, the experience and the managerial capacity to direct provincial affairs. But the events of the last five years have shattered this image, thereby dislodging a pillar of Tory strength. To make matters worse, the government's secretive, high-handed approach to governing, its failure to experiment with new forms of citizen participation and its refusal to take its critics seriously have created new political problems. The flaw of arrogance is now combined with evidence of administrative ineptitude. Put differently, the Conservative style is as much an obstacle to its renewal as is its position on various controversial policy issues.

This essay briefly reviews the economic and political landscape that forms the backdrop for the 1986 and 1989 elections. It then probes the election results, paying particular attention to the increase of party competition, to the growing strength of the New Democrats and Liberals and to the erosion of the Conservatives' urban support. It examines the campaigns themselves in order to highlight Tory decline. Our conclusion raises several questions. Are more competitive electoral politics now an ingrained feature of Alberta politics, or will one-party dominance return, possibly under Liberal control? And have Alberta politics lost their traditional distinctiveness in the face of economic and social change?

Alberta at the Polls: 1986 and 1989

Contemporary Alberta is a diverse and rapidly changing society. The past two decades have witnessed the impact of three intertwined forces— rapid urbanization, economic boom and bust, and an expanded role for the provincial government—which have combined to condition the political environment and to set the stage for the political changes of the late 1980s.

The lingering image of Alberta as a rural and agrarian province is now completely at variance with the province's reality. In the late 1980s, a mere 8.7 percent of Albertans lived on farms, while 77 percent were urban dwellers. Noteworthy as well is the remarkable growth of the province's two major cities, Edmonton and Calgary, which in the past two decades have grown to the point where nearly 60 percent of Albertans reside in the two cities. As Roger Gibbins notes, modern Alberta is "urban and technocratic."[2] An explicitly political consequence of such rapid urbanization is the resurrection of perennial questions about the political power of urban and rural areas in the provincial Legislature. But in a deeper way, the province's rural-urban transformation has altered the political parties' styles, their communications techniques and their policy making.

Alberta experienced unprecedented prosperity in the 1970s. Propelled by spectacular increases in the price of oil and natural gas, the province enjoyed a decade of growth, low unemployment and substantial in-migration. Indeed, as measured by most economic indices, Alberta was the envy of other provinces throughout the decade. A freewheeling indigenous business class emerged and rose to prominence often with the overt assistance of the provincial state. And at the height of the boom, provincial boosters even claimed that economic and ultimately political power would shift toward Alberta, thereby altering Ontario's traditional dominance.

Such heady optimism was shattered in the early 1980s when the global recession hit Alberta severely. The collapse of commodity prices later in the decade dealt a further blow to a staggering economy. Unemployment rose sharply, business and personal bankruptcies soared while real estate values plummeted, prompting a rash of foreclosures. Particularly depressing was the collapse of several Alberta-based financial institutions, a development which shook confidence and destroyed the dream of the emergence of major, Alberta-based banks. The cumulative impact of such economic woes was to reinforce Albertans' traditional anxieties about their economic future and to highlight the province's vulnerability to severe and unpredictable economic changes. The provincial government, which took credit for the boom in the 1970s, was now expected to find solutions to the problems posed by relative economic decline.

The 1970s also witnessed an expansion of the provincial government's role. Under Premier Peter Lougheed, Progressive Conservative governments rhetorically preached the virtues of free enterprise and unfettered markets, but intervened extensively in the economy and society. There was a significant expansion of the provincial welfare state and increased funding for education, health care and the economic infrastructure. A number of aggressive and controversial interventions were undertaken to enhance local control over economic development and to lessen the impact of indifferent or hostile federal policies on provincial resource industries. Moreover, the government undertook policies designed to diversify the economy before the depletion of the province's non-renewable resource base. Armed with substantial resource revenues, the provincial government was able to fund such activities, to maintain low tax rates and to accumulate significant surpluses. Indeed, the Lougheed governments stressed that their careful stewardship of provincial affairs resulted in Albertans enjoying the best public services in the country while shouldering the lightest tax burden.

Such claims were challenged in the mid-1980s when the persisting economic slowdown, combined with low commodity prices, caused the 1986 Getty government to raise taxes, to cut expenditures and to run a deficit. These unpopular measures focused the electorate's attention on such questions as the size of the provincial public sector, the present and future capacity of the provincial Treasury to maintain services and the province's fiscal situation given the decline of resource royalties as a source of revenue. Alberta budgets suddenly became much more like those of the other provinces as citizens—through taxation—shouldered the burden of paying for provincial services. In both the 1986 and 1989 elections, government finance emerged as a paramount issue notwithstanding the Conservatives' desire to campaign on other questions. The rapid growth and subsequent contraction of the provincial state, like the rise and fall of the overall economy, created complex questions which Alberta's political parties have proved ill-equipped to handle.

These broad political and economic forces combined to change Alberta's political landscape, as the results of the 1986 and 1989 provincial elections indicate. Analysis of the outcomes highlights two major developments: the election of a significant legislative opposition with the New Democrats forming the official opposition on both occasions and a significant drop in the popular vote won by the governing Conservatives. In 1986, the combined opposition was 22 (16 New Democrats, four Liberals and two Representatives) as compared with 61 Conservatives, while in 1989 the combined opposition totalled 24 (16 New Democrats and eight Liberals). Residents of other provinces, curious about the fuss, are reminded that the Alberta elections of 1975, 1979 and 1982 yielded oppositions of six, five and four members respectively.

The last two elections also witnessed a precipitous drop in the ruling Conservatives' share of the vote. As Table 1 indicates, the Tories have lost nearly 18 percent of their 1982 popular vote over the last two elections. Also noteworthy is the changing distribution of the opposition vote. In 1986 and in 1989, the New Democrats formed the official opposition but in 1989 their share of the vote was surpassed by the rejuvenated provincial Liberals, led by former Edmonton mayor Laurence Decore. Described only a decade ago as "the most impotent party in Alberta provincial politics," the Liberals have increased their share of the vote from the dismal 1982 level of 1.8 percent to nearly 29 percent in 1989.[3]

While it is important to note such general trends, particular attention must be paid to the character of electoral competition in Alberta's cities where the Tory decline has been spectacular. As Table 2 indicates, the Conservatives have lost 22 percent of their vote in Edmonton since 1982. Indeed, after the 1989 election the once-dominant Tories held only two of Edmonton's 17 seats. In 1982 they held 16 of the 17 seats. Particularly startling was the defeat of Premier Donald Getty by a Liberal in an affluent southwest Edmonton riding. And in six Edmonton ridings, the Conservatives ran third behind Liberals and New Democrats. More interesting still is the remarkable distribution of the Edmonton vote in 1989 when the Conservatives, New Democrats and Liberals won 32.9 percent, 33.8 percent and 32.9 percent of the vote respectively. Such a dead heat is hardly characteristic of a one-party dominant system!

As Table 3 reveals, voters in Calgary also exhibited diminished confidence in the Conservatives although the Tory decline there is less dramatic than in Edmonton. The 1989 election yielded the Liberals three seats, a gain of two from 1986, while the New Democrats retained their two seats and the Conservatives won the remaining 13 seats. But in 1989 the Tory share of the vote slumped to 43.3 percent, down from 56.5 percent in 1986 and the spectacular 1982 total of 73.2 percent. In contrast, the Liberal vote grew from 2.5 percent in 1982, to 16.3 percent in 1986, to 33.4 percent in 1989. Such Conservative losses in Alberta's major cities point to a weakening of the coalition of "indigenous business entrepreneurs, urban professionals and state administrators" that Larry Pratt convincingly demonstrated to be the cornerstone of Conservative strength.[4]

Another interesting manifestation of the Conservatives' diminishing urban appeal is the fact that in only one urban riding held by the Tories in 1986 did the

TABLE 1 **Party Standings—Alberta General Elections**
Seats/(percentage of vote)

	1982	1986	1989
Progressive Conservative	75 / (62.2)	61 / (51.1)	59 / (44.4)
New Democrat	2 / (18.8)	16 / (29.1)	16 / (26.4)
Liberal	0 / (1.8)	4 / (12.2)	8 / (28.6)
Representative party	2 / (5.0)	2 / (5.0)	0* / (0)
Western Canada Concept	0 / (11.8)	0 / (2.5)	0* / (0)
Other	0 / (0.4)	0 / (0.1)	0 / (0.6)

*party did not contest election

party increase its share of the vote in 1989. In 11 other ridings, urban Conservatives retained their seats while losing more than 10 percent of the vote. Analysis of the vote in rural Alberta reveals a much stronger Conservative presence, although the party's popular vote was reduced in every region of the province. Southern Alberta's 16 primarily rural ridings are the bastion of Tory support, with the party managing to win all the seats and nearly 57 percent of the vote. Central Alberta remained strongly committed to the governing party. The Tories also held most of their seats and an absolute majority of the votes in the rural northern part of the province. Such results yield a significant political irony. In 1967 when they formed the official opposition and in 1971 when they defeated

TABLE 2 **Party Standings—Edmonton**
Seats/(percentage of vote)

	1982	1986	1989
Progressive Conservative	16 / (54.6)	4 / (40.0)	2 / (32.9)
New Democrat	1 / (30.7)	11 / (41.2)	11 / (33.8)
Liberal	0 / (1.6)	2 / (15.3)	4 / (32.9)
Other	0 / (13.1)	0 / (3.5)	0 / (0.4)

TABLE 3 **Party Standings—Calgary**
Seats/(percentage of vote)

	1982	1986	1989
Progressive Conservative	18 / (73.2)	15 / (56.5)	13 / (43.3)
New Democrat	0 / (12.3)	2 / (24.6)	2 / (22.7)
Liberal	0 / (2.5)	1 / (16.3)	3 / (33.4)
Other	0 / (12.0)	0 / (2.6)	0 / (0.6)

Social Credit to form a government, the fledgling provincial Conservatives stressed their appeal as a progressive urban party in contrast to the old fashioned, increasingly rural Social Credit dynasty. For the Conservatives, urban success therefore preceded rural hegemony. In 1989, however, the party is sustained by strong rural support and in turn by a distribution of legislative seats that favours rural areas. Premier Getty's decision to run in a by-election in a safe rural seat reflects the Tories severely weakened position in Alberta's cities.

The results of the last two provincial elections also suggest that Albertans are entrusting their political fortunes to the three established parties. In 1989, 67 of 83 seats were contested only by the Conservatives, Liberals and New Democrats. And despite the province's reputation for supporting "fringe" parties, no minor party played a significant role in the 1986 or 1989 elections, although diehard Social Crediters mounted a feeble effort in a handful of rural ridings in 1989. Also noteworthy in 1989 was the absence of an explicitly "right-wing" party. By contrast, in 1982 and 1986, two parties—the Western Canada Concept (WCC) and the Representatives—presented themselves as "limited government" alternatives to the statist, "socialistic" tendencies of the established parties. The WCC is also noteworthy for its advocacy of an independent western Canada. But neither party played a significant role in either election although two Representatives were elected on both occasions. This small party, which consists of the remnants of Social Credit, contested and won two seats because of the commitment and personal popularity of its candidates. In 1989, it finally folded with one of its members winning a rural seat under the Tory banner.

A final issue is voter turnout in Alberta, which on average is the lowest in postwar provincial politics and among the lowest in federal elections. In 1986, turnout was a mere 47.5 percent while in 1989 it increased to a still low 57 percent. Curiously, this aspect of Alberta's politics has seldom been seriously analysed. Some analysts attribute low turnout to a non-participatory political culture which is rooted in the authoritarian style of early Social Credit governments.[5] Others see low turnout as a vicious circle that results from, and sustains, the province's unhealthy traditions of limited electoral competition, strong governments and weak oppositions. And in an obviously partisan argument, detractors of the Lougheed governments argue that the Tories' "overwhelming" majorities were sustained by only a quarter of the eligible voters.

Since 1986, the issue of turnout has been more widely discussed simply because the governing Conservatives emphasized it. According to Tory strategists, the party's urban fortunes declined in 1986 because committed Conservatives, satisfied with the quality of their governance and confident about the election's outcome, simply stayed home. But this self-serving argument oversimplifies the issue. For one thing, why did Conservative voters remain at home in 1986 but not, for example, in 1982? Moreover, is it not plausible that many non-voters were Conservatives who had lost confidence in the government but were ideologically hostile to the New Democrats, and not yet willing to support the rising Liberals? Regardless of the 1986 phenomenon, Tory strategists argued in 1989 that turnout was "key" to the result, thereby implying that a higher turnout would benefit the Conservatives. However, a 10 percent increase in turnout, far from working to the government's advantage, resulted in a further loss of Tory seats and votes.

On the Campaign Trail: 1986 and 1989

The main features of the 1986 Alberta election are now well known and will only be briefly summarized here.[6] At the centre of the Conservative campaign was Premier Donald Getty who returned to provincial politics after a six year absence, having been a senior minister in Peter Lougheed's governments of the 1970s. Led by an obviously rusty Getty, the Conservatives' lacklustre campaign ignored widespread anxiety about collapsing prices for Alberta's oil and natural gas. The opposition parties, especially the New Democrats, feasted on Tory indifference to economic decline and ran effective campaigns that stressed the need for an active government effort to rejuvenate the economy. Prominent Conservatives put the best light on their electoral setbacks, arguing only about low voter turnout and the inevitability of some anti-government sentiment after 15 years of uninterrupted rule and in the face of economic decline. The operative assumption was that voters, not the Conservative party, should change their ways, abandon their flirtations with opposition parties and return their allegiance to the "government party." And after all, they did win the election.

Three years later Tory strategists seized the moment in February 1989 and called an early election, and hence broke an Alberta tradition of having general elections at four year intervals. Their rationale for this unorthodox manoeuvre was complex and rooted in several assumptions. First, while by no means robust, Alberta's economy had stabilized after its 1985–86 crisis. Second, the government had for the first time in its mandate increased expenditures on health and education while proposing no further tax increases. Third, in a pre-election cabinet shuffle, Getty appointed several young, progressive ministers to key Cabinet portfolios in an attempt to assure voters that he recognized the need for Tory renewal. Finally, and perhaps most importantly, the early election was an effort to catch the opposition parties off-guard and ill-prepared to campaign, both organizationally and financially. Of particular concern were the reborn Liberals who in a well-attended convention in October 1988 selected Laurence Decore as their leader. A successful businessman of Ukrainian descent with strong connections in other northern Alberta ethnic groups and a former Edmonton mayor, Decore entered provincial politics with a reputation as a skilled manager and political organizer. He emphasized Tory vulnerability in urban areas and cast the Liberals as a pro-business alternative to the declining Conservatives. The Conservatives feared his appeal and called an early election to abort a Liberal renaissance.

The Conservatives' 1989 campaign rested on two pillars, the first being the need to nurture stronger family units. The precise means to achieve this end were never specified but a winter holiday to encourage family activities and drug abuse prevention programmes were announced. To the extent that provincial economic affairs were addressed, the focus was on several pulp and paper mill projects in northern Alberta. Portrayed as evidence of successful policies of economic diversification, the mills were to give the provincial economy a boost. The other key ingredient was the traditional Albertan call to endorse the provincial government's position in its struggles with Ottawa. In 1989, Getty sought support for his plans for a reformed Senate, for his opposition to a proposed national sales tax and for his continuing criticism of the Bank of Canada's high interest rate policy which he claimed sacrificed Alberta's lagging economy merely to arrest inflation in booming southwestern Ontario. Regarding Senate reform, Getty wanted a mandate to pursue legislation which allowed for the replacement of future Alberta senators by election. While the Meech Lake Accord allowed premiers to provide Ottawa with names of acceptable replacements when a Senate vacancy occurred Alberta proposed to advance only the winner of a provincially supervised election.[7] The strategy was designed to force the federal government to accept Alberta's cherished objective of a Triple E (elected, equal and effective) Senate.

Very early in the 1989 campaign it was apparent that the Conservative message was not engaging the electorate.[8] Many voters objected to the idea of an early election ostensibly designed to send Ottawa a message but clearly engineered to catch the Liberals off guard. But the Tory campaign came off the rails completely when, in an effort to gain new momentum, Getty promised several new programmes, each involving substantial expenditures. Particularly controversial were a scheme which promised to pave the province's entire network of secondary roads, and a complex programme whereby the province would "shield" homeowners whose current or future mortgage rates exceeded 12 percent. The controversy surrounding these initiatives was heightened by the government's confusion about their costs and administration. The policies were hastily prepared, ill conceived and poorly communicated.

Getty's extravagant promises caused the government to lose control of the electoral agenda. The election, far from being about sending Ottawa a message, came to focus on the government's tax and expenditure policies, the quality of public management, the size of the provincial deficit and the government's capacity to strike priorities. The opposition parties, and presumably the electorate as well, wondered how a government which since 1986 had been unable adequately to fund provincial health and education programmes could now pave every road in the province, pay a chunk of many residential mortgages, maintain taxes at existing levels and reduce the mounting provincial debt.

The opposition parties were delighted by the campaign's growing preoccupation with explicitly provincial concerns. The Liberals' initially lacklustre campaign was given new life as the party mocked the government's fiscal confusion and promised a return to more rational public sector decision making. The New Democrats were also buoyed by the unexpected shift of the agenda but their fortunes were changed less dramatically than the Liberals'. The Alberta New Democrats, in pursuit of their particularly mild version of Prairie social democracy, stressed the indifference of both the Liberals and Conservatives to the needs of "ordinary" Albertans. The party's policies emphasized the need for a more active role for the provincial state and argued that the Conservatives, if re-elected, would implement a "secret," right-wing agenda.[9]

The Conservative Decline: Some Observations

Most election post-mortems stressed the quality of Getty's leadership as the prime cause of the Tories' weakened condition. After all, it was his choice of the issues, his decision to call an early election and his competence that became an issue. To some observers, Getty's leadership was analogous to that of Harry Strom's. Strom, an affable farmer, succeeded Ernest Manning as premier and leader of the Social Credit party in 1968 only to lose power in 1971 to the rejuvenated provincial Conservatives led by Peter Lougheed. In some eyes, Getty was a weak leader who, like Strom, was unable to maintain the electoral base inherited from a powerful predecessor. Viewed from this perspective, the Tory problem is at heart one of leadership.

While it is tempting to blame Getty for his party's poor showing, such a focus is ultimately too narrow. For the 1989 Conservative campaign, far from being a break from past campaigns, was if anything rooted in the assumptions of the 1970s. The campaign's key elements—the need for a mandate to fight Ottawa, economic development through resource mega-projects, a policy of shielding residents from high interest rates and a refusal to debate the opposition—were taken directly from successful Tory campaigns of the 1970s and 1982. Seen in this light the 1989 campaign was a study in continuity, not in contrast. While perhaps poorly executed, the campaign was a *party* campaign whose basic principles and assumptions were not seriously questioned or debated by Tory strategists. Its flaws are much deeper than acknowledged by a focus on leadership.

The Conservatives' demise is partially rooted in the party's failure to come to grips with the changed federal-provincial balance since the 1984 and 1988 elections of the federal Progressive Conservatives. Ken Norrie and Terry Levesque argue that an Alberta government will win massive legislative majorities if it follows the "rational" strategy of pursuing a credible "anti-Ottawa" campaign.[10] Such a campaign will force the opposition parties either to agree with the governing party's position and hence become irrelevant or to dissent from the current "provincial" stance thereby exposing themselves to the devastating criticism that they are "anti-Albertan." There is obvious force to this general argument but it does not reveal the circumstances under which a party is able to employ intergovernmental issues to control the agenda and to gain partisan advantage. One prominent Tory problem in 1989 was simply that the "anti-Ottawa" issues were different in character from those prevailing in the turbulent 1970s. The 1989 issues—high interest rates, Senate reform and opposition to a new national sales tax—had two common denominators which made them difficult to manage electorally. First, each issue involved the exercise of federal authority in areas where Ottawa enjoyed an unquestioned constitutional capacity to act. It was difficult therefore to claim that the federal government was "interfering" in some area of long-standing provincial competence. Second, none of the issues, unlike the bitter resource policy controversies of the 1970s, had a distinctly Albertan dimension. Senate reform in its Triple E guise, while clearly a concern of many Albertans, is also a concern of thoughtful Canadians in other parts of the country. Similarly, all Canadians have a stake in resisting "unfair" federal fiscal or monetary policies.

A more profound change is the very different political character of the federal government in the 1980s as contrasted with the 1970s.[11] For with the election of the Mulroney Conservatives in 1984, Alberta found itself on the winning side of a federal majority government for the first time since the Diefenbaker landslide of 1958. Moreover, the Mulroney governments, particularly the 1984 version, have support in all regions of the country and can legitimately call themselves "national" governments. In policy terms, the Mulroney governments have been receptive to western interests as indicated by their prompt dismantling of the remnants of the hated National Energy Program, by their striking a new energy pricing agreement with the producing provinces and by their establishing the Western Economic Diversification programme. More importantly, the success of the Mulroney Conservatives broke down the image of the federal government, carefully cultivated by Peter Lougheed during the Trudeau years, as a remote, indifferent institution which harassed and exploited the western region from which it had no representation. Through the election of the Mulroney Conservatives, Alberta became a part of a broadly based national coalition whose existence makes difficult the collapse of provincial politics into a simplistic "us versus them" mould. No longer can it be assumed that Albertans must act *en masse* to save themselves from an insensitive federal authority.

Since the 1988 federal election, the Reform party has added a new dimension by portraying the Mulroney Conservatives as mere carbon copies of the much-despised Trudeau Liberals. The Reformers lament the allegedly statist, interventionist stance of the governing Tories and characterize the federal Tory government as being biased, like its predecessors, toward central Canadian interests and as being indifferent to its strong Albertan support. The proposed GST and the Meech Lake Accord are seen as particularly odious federal initiatives. To date, the Reform party has won a by-election in rural Alberta but observers are uncertain about its prospects and influence. Its populist, anti-statist and pro-Albertan rhetoric is much more popular in rural Alberta, the bastion of federal Tory strength, than in the province's major cities. The party's very existence reflects, however, the continuing, albeit muted, political viability of the traditional themes of western alienation.

The Alberta Progressive Conservatives have had particular problems adjusting to the new realities of national politics. Unable to decide whether the federal government is a friend or a foe, the provincial Tories have vacillated. For example, on such vital federal initiatives as the Free Trade Agreement and the Meech Lake Accord, the Alberta government has been a staunch supporter. On the other hand, a mere four months after the 1988 federal election, Getty tried to run an election campaign against Ottawa and has even resorted to occasional rumblings about the possible return of western separatism if the federal government is not more responsive. Getty's ambivalence is illustrated by his activities in the May 1989 Stettler by-election where he campaigned to win a seat in the Legislature. On the one hand, he requested a strong mandate in his struggles with Ottawa, while on the other hand he acquiesced in reduced federal transfers to the province.

The literature on the Canadian political economy stresses the impact of dominant resource industries on provincial politics. Alberta is no exception to such analyses as the province's politics are frequently seen to revolve around the fortunes of its oil and natural gas industries. Such industries are very significant for the provincial economy. In 1987, for example, oil and natural gas contributed 18.2 percent of Alberta's domestic product compared with 8 percent for manufacturing and a mere 3.7 percent for agriculture.[12] Moreover, oil and natural gas development contributes significantly to other provincial industries, notably in the service, financial and legal sectors. But the growth of the oil and gas industries has tapered off. Their economic contribution has dropped marginally for three consecutive years and is now at a level around that of the early 1970s. More significantly, recent price declines mean that resource royalties constitute a much smaller share of overall provincial revenue. In 1988, for example, non-renewable resource revenues accounted for around 23 percent of total provincial revenues compared to 46 percent in 1982 and nearly 51 percent in 1981. Such data dramatically reveal the impact of oil's decline on Alberta's public sector. As well, many oil companies radically "downsized" their staffs in response to the price collapse of the mid-1980s. Such actions were painful for many Albertans and made the industry appear like other employers in a market economy, thereby robbing it of the mystique it had cultivated over many years in Alberta. More speculatively, Albertans have adjusted to the transformation of crude oil from its status as a commodity of extraordinary significance in world affairs to its much less exalted position as a market-traded good whose supply exceeds demand, whose value has dropped sharply and whose future is uncertain.

A key political consequence of oil's relative decline is to raise to new prominence questions about the provincial government's expenditure and taxation policies. For as resource royalties decline, the province has resorted to tax increases and expenditure cuts. Who pays for and who benefits from provincial expenditures are now important political questions in a province where, for nearly four decades, resource revenues allowed governments to provide high quality public services. The weakening of oil's economic hegemony also increases political conflict in another way. For as oil declines, governments are less able to convince citizens that their interest in the dominant commodity is so great as to transcend other political cleavages. Slowly but perceptibly, Albertans are defining themselves politically in such terms as gender, age and social class.[13] Such affiliations will strengthen if oil continues to wane and as citizens see less need to define an overarching interest in the fortunes of a natural resource.

The decline of oil is problematic for the Conservatives. The party's approach to governing, as established in the 1970s, assumes the continuing economic and political pre-eminence of oil and gas. Its budgetary philosophy, its view of the determinants of provincial economic growth and its future vision remain rooted in an oil-dominated economy. Moreover, the Conservatives' primary response to the collapse of prices has been to predict an eventual upturn and hence a return to prosperity. Such a stance combined with rhetoric about Alberta's economic potential has not inspired an anxious electorate.

Can the Conservatives rejuvenate themselves in office, or is a period of opposition required? Can the party recover in the cities while maintaining its rural strength? Can it respond to a provincial political agenda characterized by environmental concerns, debates about minority rights and vexing questions about the province's financial status? No easy answer emerges to these questions as democratic politics, unlike physics or mathematics, are not governed by universal laws or principles. This having been said, our analysis will now shift from such broad themes as Alberta's place in the Canadian community and the political and ideological significance of oil to a focus on factors peculiar to the governing Tories.

Even before their first electoral victory in 1971, the Conservatives made much of their managerial ability and technical competence. The party's standard campaign portrayed it as a repository of modern management techniques, an image carefully cultivated by Peter Lougheed who emphasized the party's capacity to provide effective governance under his "chairman of the board" style. And as successes mounted, the Conservatives came to claim that they alone were qualified to preside over Alberta's public affairs. The electorate was warned not to trust the reins of government to amateurish opposition parties who had no governing experience.

The Tories' reputation as a party of extraordinary administrative competence was challenged in the mid-1980s and by the end of the decade was in tatters. Unable to buy its way out of trouble after 1985, the government clumsily handled a number of important initiatives, including revisions to the province's labour code and substantial reductions in the education, health and social services budgets. The government's use of patronage became an issue and the 1989 election campaign was flawed by policy confusion, poor logistics and the unprecedented spectacle of ministers publicly contradicting each other. But the firmest spike in the Tory coffin was hammered into place by the Code inquiry into the failure of the Edmonton-based Principal Group, a once-significant financial intermediary that collapsed in 1987. Widely reported testimony before the Code inquiry provided unprecedented glimpses into policy making within successive Alberta Conservative governments. The resultant picture was discouraging. A sorry story emerged of weak and poorly administered securities regulation, of confused, inept or indifferent ministerial supervision and of a bureaucracy that was either sycophantically subordinate to, or bullied by, ministers.

The collapse of the Conservatives' reputation as effective administrators further weakened their electoral position and opened new avenues for opposition attacks. The party lost the opportunity to argue, when all else failed, that a Liberal or New Democratic vote was a call for reckless, inept and inexperienced government. The Tories' diminished administrative capacity is, moreover, a liability in an anxious, insecure political culture that places a premium on governments' capacity to provide coherent leadership.

My final argument concerns the Conservatives' style, their political *modus operandi* which in my view is an obstacle to the party's renewal.[14] The Alberta Conservatives now seem to believe that they are a natural governing party endowed with a superior sense of the public good, a view that they are beyond criticism and the belief that their opponents are inherently unworthy. Such attitudes were either ignored or tolerated during the booming 1970s but are now a liability in a competitive political system. Moreover, the flaw of arrogance, once ingrained, is remarkably difficult to remove from a political party.

Conservative arrogance is rooted in the party's "executive" orientation to government and politics. That is, Conservatives place a premium on ensuring that the state has an unfettered capacity to act, while downplaying the need for citizen input or wide-ranging debate. Such a view is seen in the party's obsession with administrative secrecy, an intolerance of internal dissent and a contempt for all forms of opposition. Other Tory views include the notion that voting in an election every four years is enough citizen involvement, and the idea that the public interest is served by a servile Legislature that must never compromise the government's capacity to act.

The hardening of such Tory views is demonstrated by the government's campaigns and its response to the electoral setbacks of 1986 and 1989. On both occasions, the government dredged up every conceivable scapegoat including the media and the National Energy Program. Senior ministers insulted voters by implying that the electorate was simply confused in its growing support for opposition parties. Some senior Conservatives even spoke publicly about depriving voters in dissident ridings of the full range of public services. More interestingly, no senior Conservative attributed any part of the electoral setbacks to any government act or omission. And during both campaigns, Premier Getty and most other Conservative candidates refused to participate in public debates. Ignoring the different political economy and much more competitive politics of the mid-1980s, the Tories pursued their time-honoured strategy of ignoring the opposition, downplaying serious policy discussions and relying heavily on media advertising. The province was once again conveniently divided into two camps—the "doers" (those who uncritically accepted government policy) and the "knockers" (everyone else). Such undertakings reveal a party rooted in its past successes and in the view that the electorate is an object to be manipulated rather than responded to. Rather ironically, the party's intolerance of dissent makes unlikely the emergence of internal critique.

The Future of Alberta Politics

As we enter the 1990s, Alberta's politics are in flux. But a paramount question arises about their future character. Will competitive party politics remain, or is the current situation merely a transitional period before the return of one-party dominance with a single powerful party ranged against a substantial but divided opposition? No clear answer emerges to this complex question. Future Alberta politics, like past ones, will be shaped by such unpredictable forces as the domestic and international political economy and the character of federal governments. The political skills of the contending parties will also be tested. Each will be pressed to demonstrate administrative competence, leadership capacity and responsiveness to a restless electorate. In future political conflicts in Alberta, effective strategy and traditional political arts will be at a premium.

The present competitive situation will likely remain for the foreseeable future although each party's precise strength is unpredictable. At the heart of this assertion is the view that each of the established parties—the Progressive Conservatives, the Liberals and the New Democrats—has adequate support and a strong enough political appeal to be a contender for power. As a corollary, no party possesses the political equivalent of a knockout punch that can render its rivals quickly helpless. The governing Tories, despite their myriad problems of adjustment, remain the dominant party of rural Alberta and a weakened, but still formidable, force in the cities. And for their part, the New Democrats have built bastions of support in Edmonton, in parts of the rural north and to a lesser degree in Calgary. The party's appeal as the representative of the underdogs and "ordinary" Albertans is aided by the declining significance of intergovernmental concerns on the provincial political agenda, and the increasing importance of such provincial issues as the burden of taxation, environmental matters and human rights.

The Liberals are almost unanimously seen as the party with the greatest growth potential and as the party most likely to achieve an electoral stranglehold. According to conventional wisdom, the Liberals are well placed to present themselves as a rejuvenated, pro-business alternative to the fading Tories. A similar notion is that the Liberals can balance fiscal conservatism with a progressive posture on such questions as human rights and the welfare state and thereby snatch votes from both the Tories and the New Democrats. Such a scenario, however, oversimplifies the matter and is too optimistic. Why, in the face of relative economic decline and limited fiscal resources, might the electorate think that the Liberals will implement more effectively than the Tories a strategy of reconciling economic renaissance with the achievement of social justice? Can Liberals easily convince New Democratic voters that the party is something more than an up-tempo version of the once dominant Tories? Moreover, the party is a weak presence in rural Alberta with no obvious prospects for a breakthrough. Finally, a key Liberal premise is that Alberta business will quickly disassociate itself, after nearly two decades, from its close partnership with the Conservatives and align itself with the ascendant Grits. While possible, a more likely scenario sees business carefully sizing up the fluid situation, possibly beginning to distance itself from the waning Tories but, given present uncertainties, refusing to support wholeheartedly either pro-business party. And as is widely noted, business is heterogeneous in its ideological and political interests, giving rise to the possibility that different elements of Alberta business will support different parties.

Are Alberta politics losing their distinctiveness in the face of such homogenizing forces as technological change, urbanization, the rise of transnational capital and powerful communications technologies?[15] In the era of the welfare state and managed economy, do Alberta politics differ in kind or merely in degree from those prevailing elsewhere in Canada and for that matter in the rest of the industrialized world?

It appears that Alberta politics are increasingly like those of other jurisdictions. The province's party politics are more competitive and are dominated by admittedly local variations of Canada's three major parties. Oil's loosening grip on the province is reducing Albertans' traditional tendency to see themselves as stakeholders in the prospects of a dominant commodity, thereby allowing other political cleavages to emerge. And if resource royalties continue to comprise a diminishing share of provincial revenues, a key element of Alberta's political uniqueness is removed. The province must now raise revenue and spend money like other provincial governments, giving rise to disputes about the burden and benefit of state activity which, while commonplace elsewhere, have been largely absent from Alberta's political discourse. Gone too, or at least substantially tempered, is the aggressive restlessness that characterized Alberta's stance on federal-provincial questions during the oil boom of the 1970s. As argued earlier, the election of Progressive Conservative federal governments eased the province's bellicose stance and integrated its residents into a broad national political coalition. The Lougheed governments' aggressive and controversial economic interventions of the 1970s, often based on partnerships between public and private capital, have also faded into obscurity. Debates about the state's economic role in Alberta are characterized by orthodox arguments about deficit reduction, privatization and the need to lessen government's role. Such debates are more influenced by the contemporary experiences of the United States, Britain and other Canadian jurisdictions than by the unique circumstances and political culture of a Prairie hinterland. Weakly counterpoised against such forces are the province's relatively strong support, at least in national politics, for the fledgling Reform party and its continuing tradition of low voter turnout.

A final question is whether Alberta politics are "better" given the rise of more intense electoral competition. Obviously no objective answer to this paramount question is possible and readers will and should differ on the criteria to be employed in evaluating a democratic political system. But on the positive side it can be said that Alberta politics are now more interesting than traditionally, although this has not yet resulted in greater voter turnout. Moreover, the increase in party competition has produced a Legislature with a better balance between government and opposition and therefore with some improvements in governmental accountability. On the other hand, the three contending parties are, despite much contrary rhetoric, distressingly similar in their policy positions. This is particularly true of the Liberals and the Conservatives, but neither have the New Democrats veered far from the track of political orthodoxy. No party seems interested in articulating a compelling alternative interpretation of Alberta's political future. And all three parties, not just the governing Tories, are enamored with such techniques as polling, the widespread use of media advertising and the "packaging" of leaders, all of which exert a cumulatively debilitating influence on the quality of democratic politics. As a result, contemporary Alberta politics, while more competitive, still manifest most of the unpleasant aspects of modern electoral politics.

ENDNOTES

1. For a valuable review and critique of the literature on political parties and voting in Alberta see Peter McCormick, "Voting Behaviour in Alberta: The Quasi Party System Revisited," *Journal of Canadian Studies*, Vol. 15, No. 3 (1980–81), pp. 85–97.

2. Roger Gibbins, "Alberta: Looking Back, Looking Forward," in Peter M. Leslie, ed., *Canada: The State of the Federation* (Kingston: Institute of Intergovernmental Relations, 1985), p. 124.

3. J. Anthony Long and F.Q. Quo, "Alberta: Politics of Consensus," in Martin Robin, ed., *Canadian Provincial Politics* 2nd ed. (Scarborough: Prentice-Hall Canada, 1978), p. 9.

4. For details see Larry Pratt, "The State and Province-Building: Alberta's Development Strategy," in Leo Panitch, ed., *The Canadian State* (Toronto: University of Toronto Press, 1977), pp. 133–64.

5. Rand Dyck, *Provincial Politics in Canada* (Scarborough: Prentice-Hall Canada, 1986), p. 452.

6. For details see Allan Tupper, "New Dimensions of Alberta Politics," *Queen's Quarterly*, Vol. 93, No. 4 (1986), pp. 782–791.

7. For details see Alberta, Department of Federal and Intergovernmental Affairs, "Senatorial Selection Act Introduced," 17 February 1989.

8. A poll undertaken during the campaign revealed that only five percent of respondents saw the quality of family life as an issue, with even fewer citing Senate reform. For voters, the paramount issue was the provincial deficit. For details see Roy Cook, "Tories well ahead in Edmonton: But voters cool to Getty's issues," *Edmonton Journal*, 11 March 1989, p. A1.

9. For an overview and critique of the Alberta New Democratic party's development see Larry Pratt, ed., *Socialism and Democracy in Alberta: Essays in Honour of Grant Notley* (Edmonton: NeWest Press, 1986).

10. Kenneth H. Norrie and Terrence J. Levesque, "Overwhelming Majorities in the Legislature of Alberta," *Canadian Journal of Political Science*, Vol. 12, No. 3 (1979), pp. 451–470.

11. For a thoughtful elaboration of this theme see Roger Gibbins, "Alberta: Looking Back, Looking Forward."

12. Alberta, Provincial Treasury, Bureau of Statistics, *Alberta Economic Accounts 1987* (Edmonton: Provincial Treasury, 1989).

13. For a detailed and provocative development of this theme see Gurston Dacks, "From Consensus to Competition: Social Democracy and Political Culture in Alberta," in Larry Pratt, ed., *Socialism and Democracy in Alberta: Essays in Honour of Grant Notley* (Edmonton: NeWest Press, 1986), pp. 186–204.

14. This argument is influenced by John Meisel, "Howe, Hubris and '72: An Essay in Political Élitism," in John Meisel, *Working Papers on Canadian Politics* (Montreal: McGill-Queen's University Press, 1975), pp. 217–252.

15. For an excellent general development of this theme see Gerald Friesen, "The Prairie West since 1945: An Historical Survey," in R. Douglas Francis and Donald B. Smith, eds., *Readings in Canadian History: Post-Confederation* 2nd ed. (Toronto: Holt, Rinehart and Winston, 1986), pp. 606–616.

33 Socialism, Federalism and the B.C. Party Systems 1933–1983

ALAN C. CAIRNS AND DANIEL WONG

During the past 40 years, British Columbia's federal and provincial party systems have moved increasingly apart. Since World War II the federal arena has displayed an evolving mix of voter support and representation for the Liberals, Conservatives and NDP—supplemented by a brief Social Credit appearance of strength in the 1950s—while provincially the two old parties have faded badly and today have been all but completely displaced by Social Credit and the NDP. Thus of the four parties which compete for the favour of the electorate, only one—the NDP—now operates with reasonable strength at both levels. The old parties, which jointly accounted for almost two thirds of the B.C. federal vote in 1980, received only 5.5 percent of the vote in the provincial election of the previous year, and only 3.9 percent in 1983. Conversely, Social Credit, which has held provincial office for all but three years in the past three decades, has ceased to exist as a federal contender.

The divergence of British Columbia's party systems is part of a more general tendency toward federal-provincial party system asymmetry. The federal system itself is obviously open to distinctive party system complexes in the federal and provincial arenas of each province. However, the divergence of the two party systems does not always happen. When it does, the primary explanation is found in the interaction of the structural features of federalism and parliamentary government with political phenomena operating in the province.

At the onset of the depression of the 1930s, Liberals and Conservatives dominated B.C. politics both federally and provincially. However, their control was effectively challenged by the arrival of a new socialist party, the Co-operative Commonwealth Federation (later the NDP) in 1933. Suddenly both party systems had to accommodate themselves to a strong new contender dedicated to the eventual downfall of the free enterprise system, support for which had long been a hallmark of both Liberals

This article is a shortened version of a paper written for the University of Victoria, B.C. Project funded by the Social Sciences and Humanities Research Council of Canada.

and Conservatives. Moreover, the CCF's attempts to construct a mass party, stressing membership control over policy and leaders, contrasted sharply with the cadre structure and basic political style of the old parties.

The two party systems ultimately reacted to this challenge differently. Although both were affected by the CCF's presence, they were prompted down separate evolutionary paths. The provincial system was transformed radically, with the CCF and its chief adversary, Social Credit, almost completely supplanting the old parties. In contrast, the B.C. federal party system adjusted much more easily, quietly incorporating the CCF into a competitive multiparty system.

We argue that the divergence of the party systems can be traced to the different response of the party élites in the two arenas to the presence of a viable left-wing movement in the province. While voters have the final say in the development of party systems, the catalytic function is located elsewhere. In this study we argue that the voters' choice can only be understood in the context of the prior structuring of electoral choices by party élites.

The practical problem of containing an electorally formidable left-wing party has been a dominant concern in B.C. provincial politics since World War II. It has not been a significant problem in the B.C. federal arena. The different significance of the left in the two arenas of B.C. politics drove the province's party systems along divergent paths.

The polarized politics of the provincial party system has often been explained in terms of class divisions inherent in B.C. society. Yet the B.C. federal party system, which is presumably influenced by that same class divided society, has not been similarly polarized. Since the same society, therefore, is capable of simultaneously supporting two very different party systems, the explanation of either party system or of the differences between them cannot be found exclusively in the provincial society and economy.

The explanation lies in Canadian federalism, which requires the electorate as well as the party élites to respond consciously to different sets of issues, processes, and events at each level.

Provincial politics in B.C. became polarized as a result of complex interactions involving the parliamentary system of government, with its bias toward executive stability based on secure legislative majorities, the strength of the provincial left, and the political manoeuvres of a succession of party leaders from John Hart and R.L. Maitland to Bill Bennett. No similar polarization occurred in B.C. federal politics, not because the left was weaker, which until recently was not the case, but because the potential consequences attributed to left wing provincial strength were not attributed to similar left wing federal strength in the province.

Background: The British Columbia Party Systems to 1933

In order to fully appreciate the CCF's impact upon party politics in British Columbia, it is worth noting that from 1903 to 1933 the federal and provincial party systems of the province were both dominated by Liberals and

TABLE 1 **Liberal and Conservative Strength in B.C. Federal Elections 1896–1930 (percent of vote)**

Year	Liberal	Conservative	Total
1896	49.1	45.0	94.1
1900	45.9	40.9	86.8
1904	49.5	38.8	88.3
1908	35.9	46.8	82.7
1911	37.5	58.8	96.3
1917	25.6 (a)	68.4 (b)	94.0
1921	29.8	47.9	77.7
1925	34.7	49.3	84.0
1926	37.0	54.2	91.2
1930	40.9	49.3	90.2

(a) Opposition
(b) Government

Conservatives. They monopolized the party systems at both levels, rarely capturing less than 80 percent of the popular vote between them.

From 1896 to the depression of the 1930s there was a consistent, but fluctuating, left wing presence in the B.C. federal party system in the form of Socialist, Labour, Progressive, Communist, and Independent candidates, but they were typically more of an irritant than a threat to Liberal and Conservative supremacy.

Throughout this period provincial politics housed a vigorous but small left wing presence. However, the left did not constitute a serious challenge to the Liberal-Conservative party system. It was wracked by internal divisions, and torn by the staple controversy of all democratic socialist movements, the relative significance to be accorded electoral competition as opposed to socialist education. Further, the left often found itself undercut by the governments' generally progressive welfare and labour policies. While both the Liberals and the Conservatives were basically sympathetic to state-aided capitalist expansion, they were also successful in courting the labour vote, and by the late 1920s had put B.C. in the vanguard of welfare state development in Canada.

Peaceful Accommodation of the Left in the Thirties

The emergence of the CCF in 1933 did not immediately result in a divergence of party systems in British Columbia. The new party was incorporated with a minimum of difficulty, and by 1940, three-partyism was established at both the federal and provincial levels. There was little evidence, even in the provincial arena, of the intensely polarized politics that were to appear in the next decade.

The CCF was not the central issue in either federal or provincial politics in the province throughout the 1930s. Provincially it could not have been so as long as a

TABLE 2 **Liberal and Conservative Strength in B.C. Provincial Elections 1903–1928 (percent of vote)**

Year	Liberal	Conservative	Total
1903	38.5	46.4	84.9
1907	38.0	47.0	85.0
1909	33.8	53.3	87.1
1912	19.4	64.6	84.0
1916	50.9	41.3	92.2
1920	36.9	32.8	69.7
1924	32.5	31.6	64.1
1928	40.9	52.4	93.3

three-party system survived; federally it was unlikely to be the central issue as long as it was a weak contender in the country as a whole.

The weakness of the CCF in the 1930s further minimized the incentives for old-party collaboration against the left. Throughout this period the CCF was hindered by its own disunity as it struggled to bring together the divergent factions huddling uneasily beneath its banner. In addition, the party's representation in the Legislative Assembly and in the House of Commons was proportionately much less than its share of the popular vote.

However, with three strong contenders, provincial party politics in British Columbia were potentially unstable. The CCF had outdistanced both its major competitors in votes in the province in the 1935 federal election, a performance which, if duplicated in a provincial contest, was unlikely to be treated casually.

Coalition: The Simplification of Provincial Politics and the Ascendancy of the Anti-Socialist Issue

The era of Liberal dominance under Duff Pattullo crumbled when the 1941 provincial election, a quiet election fought in the shadow of World War II, produced only a shaky Liberal minority government. The CCF, with the largest share of the vote at 33.4 percent, received 14 seats; the Liberals won 21 seats with 32.9 percent of the vote, and the Conservatives 12 seats with 31 percent.

TABLE 3 **Three Partyism in Federal and Provincial Elections, British Columbia, 1933–41 (percent of vote)**

Year	Liberal	Conservative	C.C.F.	Other
1933 (Provincial)	41.7%	—	31.5	26.7
1935 (Federal)	31.8	24.6	33.6	11.1
1937 (Provincial)	37.3	28.6	28.6	5.5
1940 (Federal)	37.4	30.5	28.4	3.7
1941 (Provincial)	32.9	30.9	33.4	2.8

In the 1941 election, the CCF was clearly a factor, but not the major campaign issue. The election was generally low key. In the context of World War II—at a time when France had fallen, Europe had been overrun, Nazi forces were advancing rapidly on the Russian front, and the position of the Allies provided few grounds for optimism—purely provincial issues paled in importance. The chief election issue was Pattullo's leadership following his much criticized provincialist hard-line stand against federal proposals at the 1941 Dominion-Provincial Conference on the Rowell-Sirois Report. While the CCF was clearly not viewed as just another party at this time, it had not yet become the catalyst to unite the non-left and to make socialism and its containment the overriding issue in B.C. electoral politics.

Pressures for coalition were generated by the failure of the 1941 election to produce a single party majority at a time when strong and stable leadership in government seemed to be required by the wartime situation. The possibility of all three parties joining together foundered on the unwillingness of the CCF to participate. Consequently, after a complicated series of negotiations a Liberal-Conservative coalition was put together with former Liberal finance minister John Hart as Premier and Conservative leader R.L. Maitland as Attorney-General.

The uniting of Liberals and Conservatives launched B.C. provincial politics on a distinctive evolutionary path and disrupted the symmetry of the two party systems operating in the province. Coalition at the provincial level was not duplicated in federal politics at the national level. When the coalition broke up in 1952, both parties found themselves in weak positions vis-à-vis the CCF, whose provincial electoral strength had improved as a consequence of coalition, and Social Credit, which was to be the main beneficiary of old-party decline.

Coalition made a major contribution to the ideological polarization of provincial politics. While the elementary left-right struggle, which was to become the animating theme in subsequent provincial elections, dates partially from the inception of the CCF province, and has roots in earlier rhetoric, its full-blown expression dates from the coalition period.

The transformation of coalition into an engine of anti-socialism had several causes. First, the CCF's independent stance on the war issue provided ammunition for a Liberal-Conservative coalition regime charged with seeing the province through a national emergency as a loyal member of the Dominion and as an agent of the Allied effort.

Second, a wartime increase in CCF support both within and without British Columbia fed coalition fears that neither the Liberals nor the Conservatives could win the next provincial election alone.

Third, various international factors contributed to ideological polarization in B.C. during the coalition era. The victories of social democratic parties in the United Kingdom, New Zealand and Australia helped to structure the B.C. debate by providing external models in which similar confrontations were taking place. Such external events also muted any suggestions that the forces of democratic socialism were either ephemeral or idiosyncratically confined to the west coast environment. The emergence of the Cold War carried this polarizing trend one step further, for the pro-Soviet sympathies of a handful of CCF officals accentuated the ideological rift in B.C. politics.

Finally, the coalition's strident postwar response to the growing strength of the left was spurred on by the changes of leadership within both of its constituent parties. When Maitland died in 1946 his place as Conservative leader and as number two man in the cabinet was taken by Herbert Anscomb, a staunch defender of the right, who viewed the CCF as a cancerous growth and who, from his position as finance minister, launched polemical attacks on the left. In the election campaign of 1949 Anscomb vowed, in collaboration with the new Liberal leader and Premier Byron Johnson, to "carry on the coalition for the duration of the emergency, the emergency caused by the spread of the evil of communism, and its brother, socialism."[1]

As the war moved to its conclusion, British Columbia found itself with a de facto two-party system in which the contestants had come to define themselves in terms of a grand competition between the free enterprise of the coalition and the democratic socialism of the CCF.

For the coalition, socialism was a compelling and useful election issue. Both the 1945 and 1949 elections were fought as principled crusades between the rising tide of socialism and the hallowed forces of capitalism, and in both contests the left was convincingly defeated. With some 55.8 percent of the popular vote in 1945 and 61.4 percent in 1949, the coalition partners came to believe that the CCF, powerful as it may have been, might be contained by methods other than coalition.

Yet despite its apparent success, the coalition proved to be more damaging to its Liberal and Conservative components than to the CCF. Although the CCF would not win a provincial election in B.C. until 1972, long after its transformation into the New Democratic party, from the middle of the coalition era onward its role as one of the driving forces in west coast provincial party politics was firmly established. It survived as the second party in the system, while the Liberals and Conservatives never recovered from the break-up of the coalition.

As a result of their resounding victories in 1945 and 1949, the Liberal and the Conservative coalitionists felt able to relax their anti-socialist stance and turn their political attentions elsewhere. In the absence of additional unifying factors, the magnitude of the coalition victories, especially in 1949, eroded the two parties' willingness to sacrifice their separate political identities. Differences of opinion over the perquisites of office and personal acrimony between Anscomb and Johnson were symptoms of a growing coalition malaise. The incompleteness of the merger, with both parties keeping separate organizations, holding separate conventions, and even meeting in separate caucuses, meant that at any time either partner could terminate the arrangement. The continuing submergence of Liberal-Conservative tensions had depended on the widely held perception of a left-wing threat incapable of containment as long as the coalition partners acted alone. The 1949 election results deeply demoralized the CCF, and its apparent foundering fed beliefs that the sacrifices coalition imposed upon the Liberals and Conservatives might no longer be necessary.

Moreover, at the federal level there was no pressure for anti-socialist unity between Liberals and Conservatives, for the CCF's weakness did not require it. Further, the federal wings of both parties were dismayed by the B.C. coalition, which they saw as damaging both old party machinery and voter loyalties. By the decade's end, both coalition partners were under heavy pressure from their federal wings to end the alliance, and in 1952 the arrangement was terminated with Johnson's firing of Anscomb.

The Search for Alternative Strategies to Contain the Left

Two new approaches surfaced to combat the CCF in the wake of Liberal-Conservative disengagement. The first was an ingenious new electoral system employing the single transferable ballot. The second was a new, or effectively new, third party in the form of Social Credit, which was to become the bastion of anti-socialist politics in British Columbia for the next two decades.

The single transferable ballot (STB) was explicitly designed to prevent a minority socialist victory. It was an electoral experiment intended to provide the traditional parties with the opportunity to vie for increased shares of the non-socialist vote, without paying the price of having the CCF win office with only minority voter support.

Behind the experiment was the implicit belief that a minority socialist victory was not only undesirable on practical grounds, but was unacceptable on democratic grounds. The former raised the exaggerated spectre of a root and branch socialism destroying the B.C. way of life. The latter was based on the assumption that an anti-socialist, or at least a non-socialist, majority clearly existed in the province and that it was a denial of democracy to allow secondary divisions within that majority to frustrate its rightful claim to power. Electoral reform was thus an idiosyncratic reversal of the old "divide and conquer" strategy wherein parties and governments keep the opposition weak by playing on its internal divisions. In this case, the proponents of electoral reform sought not to divide their opponents but to prevent their own divisions from allowing the left to rule.

The electoral experiment presupposed a three-party contest in which Liberals and Conservatives would trade second place votes with each other and thus forestall minority socialist victories by aggregating old party voters behind the strongest old party contender in each constituency. Assuming that the voters shared, or could be induced to share, the old party strategists' perceptions of the party spectrum, the CCF could win only where it had majority support on the first count.

However, the STB was not, and could not have been, more than a partial and short-term response to the dilemmas implicit in the various competing purposes of the major non-left actors in the party system. It was inherently unlikely to produce a stable, practical reconciliation, lasting over several elections, of the simultaneous desire to return to a multiparty system and to generate the electoral outcomes of an enduring non-left government, which presupposed one single overriding division in the electorate. Although the STB facilitated electoral competition on the non-left, it could not guarantee a single party majority. It could not therefore guarantee against the recurrence of post-election coalitions as a means of ensuring government stability and keeping the left out, nor therefore against future federal-provincial intraparty tensions such as those which had hurt the Johnson-Anscomb regime. Further, if it had produced a majority Liberal or Conservative government, such a government might return to the first-past-the-post system in an attempt to consolidate its hold on power, thus potentially reinstating those instabilities of a multi-party system which had required coalition in the first place. Finally, the successful operation of such an electoral system required a high degree of political skill and discipline by Liberal and Conservative politicians, for it was necessary, simultaneously, to attack one's former coalition partner while pursuing the even more fundamental consideration of blocking the left by strategic second place voting. The danger clearly existed that the secondary battles between Liberals and Conservatives might deflect attention away from the primary task.

An alternative strategy for containing the left had slowly crystallized in the mind of W.A.C. Bennett, a coalition backbencher since 1941. From Bennett's perspective, the wartime alliance of Liberals and Conservatives had provided B.C. with its best government ever, but it had major structural weaknesses which made it an imperfect vehicle for the long run: first, the alliance was only temporary and partial—neither the Liberals nor the Conservatives had intended to be united indefinitely, and neither wished to sacrifice its party identity for the sake of a more complete merger. Coalition was not a step in the direction of a new party, but a marriage premised on the ever present possibility of a quick and easy divorce. Second, both parties were insufficiently divorced from their federal counterparts to devote themselves exclusively to the needs of the province. Bennett wished to have a purely provincial party controlling the government, unhindered by the ties of federal party labels and wholly dedicated to the related tasks of containing the left and developing the provincial economy. He became convinced that the Hart and Maitland coalition, in spite of its virtues, was not the best vehicle to perform this task. His tenure as a Conservative coalition MLA was marked by repeated efforts to create a lasting, tighter coalition party devoid of old line party differences. In 1946 he set up a coalition organization in his home constituency of South Okanagan. In addition, in pursuing his personal political career, he twice ran unsuccessfully for the leadership of the provincial Conservative party, unsuccessfully made a bid in federal politics in a 1948 by-election, and returned to the provincial Legislature as a coalition MLA in 1949. By this time he was convinced that it would be impossible to weld the Liberals and the Conservatives into a permanent coalition, and in March 1951, in the midst of heated controversy over the hospital insurance issue, he crossed the floor of the Legislature and proceeded to consider the possibilities of forming a new party.

Implausibly, the appropriate candidate turned out to be Social Credit, which had wielded only a sectarian influence in B.C. provincial politics since 1937, never capturing more than 1.4 percent of the vote, and was still heavily dependent on Alberta sponsorship. Yet Social Credit was to prove an ideal vehicle for W.A.C. Bennett. From its roots in Alberta, the party was clearly anti-socialist in principle. Moreover, it had a weak federal existence, and as the Alberta experience had indicated, was capable of rapid growth and was favourably disposed to a decentralized federal system with strong provincial rights and powers. To Bennett, it had the additional advantage that, although growing, it was devoid of experienced politicians; hence a takeover might not be too difficult.

The Social Credit Era Under W.A.C. Bennett

The unexpected 1952 victory of Social Credit under the new electoral rules has been analysed elsewhere. The electoral system proved to be incapable of reinvigorating the Liberals and Conservatives as separate provincial parties and producing a stable traditional party government. If the Liberals and Conservatives were to exploit the new electoral system to their separate partisan advantage and still keep the left out of office, their rivalry with each other had to be muted. They had to compete with each other while keeping alive the larger issue of containing the left. They had to operate a multiparty system and stress a single cleavage appropriate to a two-party system.

The degree of mutual animosity engendered by their acrimonious separation made this difficult. Their bitterness toward one another undoubtedly repelled many voters, deflected attention away from the left, and thus minimized the incentives for voters to view them as a team that was split for electoral competition, but was otherwise united behind the goal of an efficient non-socialist government.

The transitional election of 1952, like that of 1941, was not fought on ideological grounds. The Social Credit party, which unexpectedly surfaced as a strong contender, did not single out the left as the enemy as it would in future campaigns. The Liberals and the Conservatives committed extensive resources to battling one another. More generally, the multiparty context in which the election took place, as in the previous multiparty contests of 1937 and 1941, was hostile to a polarized rhetoric of free enterprise versus democratic socialists.

Social Credit won a minority government in 1952 and consolidated its position with a majority victory in a general election the following year. The 1952 and 1953 provincial elections were not only contests between parties, but also contests between alternative ways to structure the future party system of the province. The STB was a device to combine multipartyism in elections with non-left legislative majorities. The major alternative was a new two-party polarization, structured around competing "isms,"and sustained by the traditional British single member electoral system.

With the minority Social Credit victory in 1952 and its majority in 1953 the latter vision triumphed. From Bennett's perspective, multipartyism simply meant an undesirable fragmentation of the non-left, and worked against the consolidation of the non-socialist vote under the Social Credit banner. Further, the consolidation he sought was better designed to transform the non-left into the anti-left than was multipartyism.

By the 1953 election Bennett had realized the kind of party system he deemed appropriate for British Columbia. He had become leader of Social Credit and Premier of the province, and with great political skill had parlayed an inexperienced minority government—only one of whose 19 members besides himself had ever sat in the Legislative Assembly before—into a clear majority with 27 seats. The process of undermining the traditional parties was well under way. The premier had cut the party ties with Alberta Social Credit and thus ended the curious position of semi-tutelage under which the B.C. party had been held for almost two decades. He eliminated the STB electoral system and returned to the first-past-the-post system which was more likely to consolidate Social Credit in power. He was now ready to embark on a programme of massive development projects unmatched by any other government in B.C. history.

The rhetorical contest between free enterprise and socialism dominated elections for the two decades of Bennett's rule. As early as 1952, Henry Angus, a keen student of B.C. politics, noted that "In addition to its other sources of strength, Social Credit has shown itself a more effective anti-socialist machine than either of the other two non-socialist parties."[2] By 1972 the party's strategy was virtually unchanged, with provincial elections still depicted as struggles between the virtues of capitalism and the evils of socialism.

Bennett's continuous success in exploiting the free enterprise/socialism cleavage sustained Social Credit in a variety of ways. By encouraging the polarization of B.C. politics, he managed to keep both the provincial Liberals and the provincial Conservatives very weak, especially the latter. From 1952 up to the election of 1972 the old parties' share of the popular vote steadily decreased.

Throughout this era, British Columbia's economic élites had little choice but to support Social Credit. In a province where labour was highly organized and extremely militant and where strikes could easily cripple key sectors of the economy, Bennett's policy of provincial economic development, coupled with his unabashed use of government power to control industrial conflict, was obviously attractive to managers, entrepreneurs and investors. By engaging in a symbolic war with the unions, the premier was able to mobilize the business community and the vast pools of capital it controlled behind his government and thus make it extremely difficult for his opponents not to appear to be pro-union and hence anti-development.

Social Credit lost the 1972 provincial election because the issue of combatting socialism temporarily lost its salience as other issues surfaced. While Bennett continued to insist on the dangers of splitting the free enterprise vote, fewer of the electorate listened as disillusionment with the Social Credit government grew. By 1972 the highways had been paved and the dams had been built. The positive province-building component of Social Credit's appeal seemed to be more of an achievement of yesterday than a future goal still to be struggled for, with a resultant decline in the voter appeal of the anti-socialist syndrome with which it had been inextricably linked.

Equally important, the NDP downplayed the socialist issue. This low-profile strategy, which might be called a reverse band-wagon campaign, was used to deny the incumbent party an election issue upon which to mobilize support, rather than to mobilize the NDP's own supporters behind the prospect of a party victory. As a campaign strategy, it proved to be less durable than the anti-socialism issue which resurfaced in 1975, but in 1972, when age and party decay had finally caught up with Bennett and his party, it was sufficiently effective to place the NDP in power for the first time in British Columbia.

The election of 1972 demonstrated that although skilful exploitation of the anti-socialist issue and an unflagging commitment to provincial economic development were effective strategies for keeping the left out of power for many years, they could not succeed indefinitely. Social Credit had benefitted from the histrionics of a polarized politics and the ubiquitous fear of splitting the non-socialist vote. Yet the Social Credit solution to containing the left, like the earlier coalition solution, had its limitations.

In the first place, the leader grew old, the party organization became decrepit, and the government's capacity for policy innovation declined. Unless they constantly renew themselves, government parties fall prey to scandals, to organizational malaise and to electoral disenchantment. They are always, potentially, their own worst enemy.

In the second place, the continuous replaying of the socialist/free enterprise game required the cooperation of the left. Should the left catch on and refuse to play the game, the capacity of the government to polarize the electorate by exploiting fears of a left wing victory would be reduced. Although the NDP had adopted this approach without success in previous elections, in 1972 it worked.

Further, in the long run polarization strengthened the left by increasing its share of what had become a veritable two-party vote. Thus the more successful Social Credit was in polarizing the electorate, the more it ensured that its eventual defeat would be at the hands of the NDP. These developments invited the left to moderate its socialist rhetoric and become a competitor for the centre vote in traditional omnibus fashion. Thus the polarization designed to keep the left out had the paradoxical effect of strengthening the left, moderating its radicalism—thus partly denying the necessity of further polarization against it—and virtually ensuring that it would become the government should the incumbent administration founder. In the 1972 election, Social Credit lost part of its middle of the road support to the NDP and was further weakened by a fragmented vote shared with the Liberals and Conservatives.

The NDP Interregnum and the Return of Polarization

The 1972 NDP victory created an opportunity for British Columbia's federal and provincial party systems to re-converge. If the Social Credit decline continued, as most experts predicted it would, then the Liberals and the Conservatives were likely to recover and the trend toward party system differentiation would be reversed.

This did not happen. Instead, provincial politics became polarized once again, thus reinforcing differences between the federal and provincial party systems. The performance of Dave Barrett's NDP government created a sense of urgency and fear on the non-left. At the same time, under the leadership of Bill Bennett, the remarkable ability of Social Credit in consolidating the non-left through co-optation meant that two-partyism would continue to be a hallmark of B.C. provincial politics. The Liberals and the Conservatives, who still held 29 percent and 33 percent of the B.C. federal vote respectively, were unable to assert themselves as leaders of the non-socialist camp provincially, and thus found themselves drifting even further off the provincial political scene.

The NDP government under Dave Barrett was characterized by the populist oratory of the premier and a blizzard of legislation which, regardless of its individual merits, did little to support the traditional claim that the left was wedded to and capable of coherent planning. The B.C. NDP was far removed from the cool, technical competence of the Blakeney regime in Saskatchewan, or the restrained, cautious administration of the Schreyer regime in Manitoba. Neither did it combine populist appeals with technical competence, as had the Douglas/Lloyd governments in Saskatchewan from 1944 to 1964. Barrett's skills were electoral rather than managerial, a fact that made his decision to assume the finance portfolio along with the position of premier little short of disastrous. The government's public image was tarnished, particularly by the press, which depicted the premier and his cabinet as a group of inexperienced left wing bunglers whose goodwill far outran their capacity to govern.

Like the Conservatives in federal politics, the NDP suffered from a "minority party syndrome" when it assumed provincial office in 1972. A lengthy and frustrating period of almost 40 years in opposition constituted poor preparation for the task of wielding government power. The new government lacked a unifying vision of the goals it hoped to attain. The long history of socialist movements and parties in British Columbia, extending back to the nineteenth century, had contributed very little in the way of theoretical applications of democratic socialism to the very specific circumstances of the B.C. polity and economy. Paradoxically, the party of planning had a much less developed vision of the future, and a much weaker conception of the socio-economic transformations it sought for the province, than had the Social Credit government which it replaced.

Against this backdrop, three years of NDP rule widened the rift between left and right in British Columbia as never before, and precipitated a crucial competition between the three provincial opposition parties to determine who would emerge as the strongest anti-socialist representative. The outcome of the contest was not predetermined. In fact, there was a strong possibility that no one would succeed, and the NDP, aided by a revived multiparty system, would be re-elected. What was clear was that the situation was fluid, and that any one of a number of possibilities for combatting the NDP government might be employed

TABLE 4 **CCF-NDP Federal-Provincial Vote 1952–83 (percent of vote)**

Federal		Provincial	
1953	26.6	1952	30.8
1957	22.3	1953	30.9
1958	24.5	1956	28.3
1962	30.9	1960	32.7
1963	30.3	1963	27.8
1965	32.9	1966	33.6
1968	32.7	1969	33.9
1972	35.0	1972	39.6
1974	23.0	1975	39.2
1979	31.9	1979	46.0
1980	35.3	1983	44.9

in the next election. There was vague talk of a unity movement; there were proposals that opposition forces unite behind the strongest non-left candidate in each riding after joint nominating meetings; there were suggestions that the old single transferable ballot be reintroduced.

Ultimately, however, the response to the challenge of restructuring the party system was left to a Darwinian competition between the three opposition parties, which competed against one another for the privilege of championing the free enterprise vote. Partly because it was unhampered by ties with a Social Credit federal party, Social Credit emerged as the clear frontrunner in this competition, thus engineering one of the greatest comebacks in the history of Canadian politics. Having successfully erased the tired image of W.A.C. Bennett and his aging government, the party embarked on a massive membership drive and media campaign for its new leader, the son of the former premier who, to the surprise of many, became a formidable politician. Also significant in both symbolic and functional terms was the party's successful recruitment of three of the five provincial Liberal caucus members, and one Conservative member.

TABLE 5 **Social Credit Federal-Provincial Vote 1952–83 (percent of vote)**

Federal		Provincial	
1953	26.6	1952	30.2
1957	24.2	1953	45.5
1958	9.6	1956	45.8
1962	14.2	1960	38.8
1963	13.3	1963	40.8
1965	17.4	1966	45.6
1968	5.8	1969	46.8
1972	2.7	1972	31.2
1974	1.2	1975	49.2
1979	0.2	1979	48.2
1980	0.1	1983	49.8

Subsequently, in the provincial election of December 11, 1975, the "new" Social Credit received 49.2 percent of the popular vote, its highest figure ever, and obtained a decisive majority of 35 seats. Much of this renewed support came at the expense of the Liberals and Conservatives, who received their smallest ever share of the vote, a combined total of only 11 percent, and won only one seat apiece. Widespread reaction to the left on the part of the right, and even among some who had supported the left in 1972, evoked a right wing Social Credit populism with which the more traditional Liberals and Conservatives could not compete. The possibility of escaping from polarization opened up by the 1972 election was lost.

The polarization pattern continued in the elections of 1979 and 1983. In both campaigns a frequently heard claim in the Social Credit camp was that NDP victory would simply return to power the same group of inexperienced socialists who had allegedly wreaked havoc upon the province's balance sheets from 1972 to 1975. Social Credit mobilized the vote in its favour—48.2 percent in 1979 and 49.8 percent in 1983 by painting the NDP as a group of idealists who would mortgage the province's economic future for questionable short-term social benefits. Given the Social Credit government's own less than enviable record, this strategy testified to the government's capacity to mould the electorate's perceptions of political choice.

Socialism, Federalism and the National Party System in British Columbia

The federal party system in British Columbia underwent a different evolution. The B.C. federal party system is part of a countrywide party system and is therefore constantly influenced, directly or indirectly, by external party developments. Foremost among these extraprovincial factors is the relative weakness of the CCF-NDP in national politics. The left has never threatened to form the national government. Notwithstanding occasional surges of support, the CCF-NDP has never captured more than 20 percent of the vote in a general election, nor held more than 11.7 percent of the seats in the House of Commons.

In B.C. provincial politics, manipulation of the free enterprise versus socialism issue proved an effective device for mobilizing the non-left vote. The CCF-NDP was strong enough to challenge the parliamentary ideal of having a stable governing executive as long as its opponents were divided among two or more evenly matched parties. By raising the spectre of socialism, the non-left could be united to produce a majority government, whether in the form of a Liberal-Conservative coalition or a new third party such as Social Credit.

A similar strategy was not seriously considered at the federal level. It would have made little sense for either of the traditional parties to turn their strategic efforts away from one another in order to combat a socialist phantom. A more effective strategy was simply to deflate the left by co-opting its most popular policies, not in the name of socialism, but rather in the name of progressive, Keynesian reform.

The Effect of the CCF/NDP on National Political Parties in British Columbia in the 30s and 40s

The CCF's entry into national politics spelled the end of the old party monopoly in British Columbia, but did not lead to a dramatic change of the federal party system in the province as it had with the provincial party system. Instead, it produced a highly competitive three-party arrangement that preserved the Liberals and the Conservatives. In the four federal elections held between 1933 and 1951, for example, none of the major contenders—Liberal, Conservative, or CCF collected less than 25 percent of the B.C. vote; none collected more than 34 percent, and not once did the difference between first and third place finishers surpass 9 percent. The CCF's performance in these elections roughly approximated its performance in the five provincial elections held during the same period.

Yet despite its internal competitiveness, the federal party system in British Columbia did not witness the kinds of strategic manoeuvres that were taking place in the provincial arena. Coalition against the left was unnecessary at the national level and meaningless with respect to federal party competition in the province. Countrywide electoral reform to combat the left in the several provinces where it had federal strength was unnecessary. More generally, polarization to keep the left out was irrelevant at the national level, with the possible exception of the 1945 federal election, and pointless at the B.C. federal level where the strength of the left could not be translated into the possession of a government. Thus, the issue of socialism in B.C. federal politics did not attain the significance it had in the provincial arena. In short, British Columbia's party systems moved apart in this period because the powerful inducements which led to the simplification of the provincial party system had no counterpart either at the national level, or within the B.C. component of the national party system.

British Columbia's Federal Party System in the Social Credit Era

Twenty years of Social Credit populist democracy transformed British Columbia's provincial party system. But the Social Credit impact on federal politics in the province was much weaker and shorter lived. When W.A.C. Bennett's provincial Socreds were defeated in 1972, their federal counterparts, who had temporarily challenged the three major contenders for ascendancy in B.C. during the 1950s, had long since been reduced to insignificance.

Like the CCF, Social Credit's entry into B.C. politics was not restricted to the provincial arena. The party made an auspicious debut in B.C. federal competition in the general election of 1953 by collecting 26.1 percent of the vote and sending four representatives to the House of Commons. In 1957, it took 24.2 percent of the vote, won 6 of the province's 22 seats, and ran ahead of the Liberals in both categories. Unlike the CCF, however, Social Credit proved to have limited staying power in federal politics. It was hurt badly by the Diefenbaker landslide in 1958, and after making a partial comeback in the 1960s, it virtually disappeared from the political scene. In 1980 the party captured only .1 percent of the B.C. federal vote, while the provincial party was stronger than ever with 48.2 percent of the vote in 1979, and 49.8 percent in 1983.

Although W.A.C. Bennett launched several "on-to-Ottawa" campaigns in the hope of influencing federal politics through his influence on Social Credit MPs in Ottawa, and for a time was a strong supporter of Réal Caouette, the British Columbia Social Credit party was essentially a provincial creature. Unlike its Alberta counterpart, the B.C. party was not a protest movement against a distant, exploiting federal government. It had negligble interest in being part of a broad national movement to acquire national power. Indeed, a strong national party would have produced those same intraparty complications between federal and provincial party wings which Bennett felt had prevented the provincial Liberal and Conservative parties from devoting their undivided attention to provincial development. Unlike the CCF-NDP, the B.C. Social Credit vision of social change did not extend beyond the provincial scene, and after Bennett assumed the leadership in 1952, Social Credit monetary policy was cast aside as an irrelevancy, inapplicable to the provincial scene to which the party's efforts were directed. Finally, the antisocialist role which Social Credit performed so effectively in provincial politics did not have to be carried out at the B.C. federal level, where the strength of the left, while deplorable to free enterprise believers, was not threatening.

Recent Developments in the B.C. Federal Party System: The Decline of the Liberals

From the birth of the CCF in national politics to the Trudeau landslide in 1968, British Columbia's federal party system was marked by close competition between three evenly matched contenders—the Liberals, the Conservatives and the CCF-NDP, with a brief four party interlude before Social Credit faded from the federal scene. Only recently has this pattern begun to change, with the new order manifest most clearly in the decline of the Liberals and the accompanying strengthening of the Progressive Conservatives. Since the election of 1968, when the B.C. Liberal vote reached 42 percent, its highest level since 1904, the party's support has fallen off precipitously. It has constantly lagged behind the Tories in both votes and seats and in the 1980 federal election it ran a distant third at the polls, sending no representatives to the House of Commons for the first time since 1958.

Conclusion

The divergence of federal and provincial party systems in British Columbia was neither accidental nor inevitable. It resulted primarily from the differential consequences attached to left wing strength in the federal and provincial arenas, and from the different party strategies those consequences elicited. These strategies were never responses to the brute fact of CCF-NDP strength *per se*; rather, they derived from the interaction between the institutional incentives which parliamentary government holds out for majority government, and from real and manipulated fears in a divided society over the prospect of a left-wing government.

The parliamentary system of government, which stresses executive stability preferably based on single party majorities, created severe pressures to simplify the provincial party system. As long as that system housed three or more reasonably close competitors, the likelihood of a majority government situation arising was significantly reduced. The same pressures for simplification did not, however, operate in British Columbia's federal party system. The fact that the province's federal party system was a multiparty system which more often than not failed to produce a majority of B.C. seats for any one party was only an interesting oddity. Multipartyism at the B.C. federal level, even when election results produced no single party majority of federal seats from the province, was tolerable. Similar results at the provincial level, as in 1941 and 1952, had convulsive effects. These differential consequences attached to multipartyism, quite independently of the socialist issue, tended to drive the two party systems apart.

Further, it was possible for the CCF-NDP to be a powerful actor in British Columbia's federal party system without disturbing the sleep of economic élites. The very concept of socialist victory, which at the provincial level had a galvanizing effect on the non-left, had no meaning for that segment of the national party system which functioned in B.C. In the B.C. federal arena, the sudden appearance of the CCF had the effect of reducing the Liberal and Conservative vote, but it did not drive the old parties together, nor did it set in motion any tendencies for their elimination, whether jointly or separately. The left was too weak nationally to have been perceived as sufficiently threatening to justify extraordinary strategies for its defeat or containment in those parts of the country where it had federal strength.

At the provincial level, the pressures to overcome multipartyism came not only from the parliamentary system, but also from the existence of a powerful left wing party. The CCF-NDP's consistent capacity to deliver one third of the vote posed a serious challenge to political and economic élites on the old party side, and thus generated powerful pressures to simplify and consolidate the non-left. In contrast to the B.C. federal arena, where the concern aroused by actual or possible CCF-NDP victories was negligible, similar possibilities in provincial politics produced deep alarm. This differential response was not attributable to differences in left wing strength, but to differences in the expected consequences of left wing strength when control of a government was at stake.

Since the early years of the provincial coalition there has been constant pressure for political actors outside the left to counter the possibility of a CCF-NDP government. In these circumstances anti-socialism has been the obvious rhetorical tool for overcoming fragmenting tendencies on the non-left. Anti-socialist mobilization at the provincial level, whether in the form of coalition or of Social

Credit, inevitably drives the B.C. federal and provincial party systems apart, and produces serious intraparty tensions between the federal and provincial wings of the same party.

The enduring strength of the provincial left contributed to the continuation of the coalition, and to the ideological polarization so successfully manipulated by subsequent Social Credit governments. The free enterprise versus socialism dichotomy brandished by W.A.C. Bennett was explicitly hostile to any multi-party tendencies which might have allowed the left to slip into office with less than 50 percent of the votes. Social Credit's success was built on the failure of Liberals and Conservatives to establish themselves as credible anti-socialist alternatives, and on its ability to structure the terms of debate so that the business and non-left vote generally would have no real choice but to follow Bennett's anti-socialist forces. The reception and success of the same strategy by the Social Credit party of Bill Bennett was testament to powerful strains in the political culture, in the context of provincial politics, to which the responses of successive B.C. governments have both been an acknowledgement and a powerful rein-forcement.

The coexistence of federal and provincial party systems in British Columbia constitutes a kind of natural experiment which allows the student to isolate the effects of institutional context on party system evolution. Explanations of the provincial party system focusing on class, economy and society are clearly inade-quate since B.C. federal politics interacts with the same class system, economy, and society but with very different consequences.

Differences of party system context exerted an institutional bias in favour of party system asymmetry. The playing out of these differences over half a century has destroyed the provincial multiparty system, allowed the federal multiparty system to survive, and thus has driven the two party systems progressively apart. Institutional factors, then, ought not to be ignored by students seeking to understand party systems. The interaction of one common B.C. society with two separate and distinct institutional contexts has resulted in two very different party systems.

ENDNOTES

1. The Vancouver *Sun*, 1 June 1949.
2. H.F. Angus, "The British Columbia Election," *Canadian Journal of Economics and Political Science*, Vol. 18 (June 1952), p. 525.

34 Ontario's Party Systems: Under New Management

ROBERT J. WILLIAMS

In August 1983, the Ontario Progressive Conservative party quietly marked the 40th consecutive year of its control over the provincial administration. Less than two years later, however, the party was defeated on a vote of confidence in the Legislative Assembly after the two opposition parties formally agreed to cooperate to that end. The PCs relinquished office in June 1985 to David Peterson and the Liberals. In the September 1987 general election, after winning at least a plurality of the seats at stake in 13 successive elections, the Progressive Conservatives plummeted to a third place finish in the Legislature and the popular vote. This complete reversal of fortunes by the PCs' was followed three years later by the sudden demise of their Liberal successors. To suggest that provincial party politics in Ontario is in a state of flux may be the political understatement of the 1990s!

In federal politics the long-dominant Liberal party was abruptly displaced from government by a rejuvenated Progressive Conservative party under the leadership of Brian Mulroney. Its landslide national victory of 1984, in which PC candidates captured 75 percent of the seats in the House of Commons and 50 percent of the popular vote, was only marginally less decisive in Ontario where they captured 71 percent of the seats with 47 percent of the popular vote. Indeed, the Liberals in 1984 held only one more seat in Ontario than the New Democrats (14 and 13 respectively).[2] In the 1988 election, large numbers of Ontario voters swung back to the Liberal party; as a result, Ontario contributed fully two thirds of the increase in the Liberal caucus.[3] However, Ontario's ambivalence on the free trade question led to a virtual "saw-off" between the Liberals and PCs in both the popular vote and seats, with the NDP remaining a distant third. Fluctuations in electoral fortunes are not unknown in federal party politics in Ontario, but the dramatic changes which occurred in the 1980s are remarkable nonetheless.

This essay will concentrate on the patterns of party politics up to the late 1980s in Ontario, with most of the attention centred on the provincial scene. It is too soon to offer considered analysis of the 1990 provincial election and it remains to

---

This is a revised and updated version of the essay that appeared in the previous edition of this book.

be seen how much politics have altered in Ontario, even though the major actors have reversed their long-standing roles in federal politics and the provincial legislature is under completely new management.

Dominant Themes in Ontario Politics

Congruence

Foremost among the perennial features of Ontario politics is the apparent congruence of the federal and provincial party systems, in both of which a three-party configuration involving the Liberals, Progressive Conservatives and CCF-NDP has been maintained since the mid-1940s. In this respect, "Ontario is the only province to mirror the national party system" at the provincial level.[4]

Yet, the Canadian national party system is not a large-scale version of the provincial party system in Ontario. Nor is the provincial party system to be understood as simply a miniature version of the national party system.[5] There are, indeed, many parallels in the dynamics of the two systems, the most obvious of which is the fact that one party dominated government after 1945 primarily because the opposition to it was split between its competitors.[6] Beyond that, however, the two party systems are distinctive and this latter feature will be discussed in a subsequent section of this essay. Furthermore, the relationship between the federal and provincial organizations is complex and varied. This, too, will be discussed later.

Stability

A second feature of Ontario politics is an apparent long-term stability, especially in provincial politics. First, the parties have tended to be fairly persistent in the level of voter support they have achieved. As Peter McCormick has noted,

> the CCF-NDP has spent the entire postwar period oscillating within the 15–30 percent zone, never rising above 30 percent and never falling below 15 percent for even a single election. No other provincial party system has anything comparable.[7]

Moreover, the long-term competitiveness of the three parties and the fairly solid bases of support they continue to enjoy give little indication that any one of them will collapse in the near future.[8]

The stability of voter support for the two major parties in federal elections is much less pronounced; after 1935, "Ontario has swung back and forth, often dramatically, and since 1968 the province has switched parties at each successive election."[9] But Ontario has actually become a "swing province" only as far as the Liberals and PCs are concerned; the New Democrats have finished within about two percentage points above or below 20 percent in each election since 1965. This still means that there is a form of stability in that the non-NDP forces are competing for a fairly constant proportion of the electorate.

Stability has also been evident in Ontario's support for the governing party, of whatever stripe. All students of Canadian party politics are aware of the pattern of one-party dominance which has characterized national politics since 1867: for long periods of time the 'normal' alternating of power between one party and another has been supplanted by a period of monopoly of office by one party.[10] The successive victories of the Conservative governments of Macdonald and the Liberal governments of Laurier, King and St. Laurent, and Trudeau (despite an anomaly in 1979) are evidence of this feature of Canadian political life. Barring the Laurier years, when Conservative loyalties prevailed in Ontario in the face of a national preference for the Liberals, Ontario voters have played a significant part in sustaining this process of one-party dominance. However, despite its size, Ontario has not always been able to determine the outcome of federal elections for "in 1945, 1962, 1972 and 1979, the opposition won more seats in Ontario than the government."[11]

At the provincial level, a pattern of one-party dominance has also been evident. The Liberals governed from 1871 to 1905 (some 24 of those years under Sir Oliver Mowat) and, as noted at the outset of this discussion, the Progressive Conservatives (who had never really governed before 1905) maintained a dynasty for 42 years in the middle of this century, which "established a modern day record for political longevity in Canada."[12] The journalist Eric Dowd once described the modern Ontario PCs as "the Harris tweed of political parties," a phrase which reflects this durability.

Another way to look at the same phenomenon is to note that "changes in government in the province have been a comparatively rare occurrence" in this century, happening "less than [in] any other province with a history of party competition during the same period."[13] Moreover, once a competitive party system evolved, only one Ontario provincial government (that of the United Farmers of Ontario) has ever failed to be re-elected after its initial victory. After Rosemary Speirs chronicled the self-inflicted wounds to the Miller government in 1985, she concluded that "the traditional stability of Ontario politics has meant that incumbent governments could count on re-election unless they defeated themselves by serious blunders."[14] Despite a second incumbent government meeting the same fate within about five years, stability remains the long-term pattern in the Ontario provincial party system.

Pragmatism

A third feature of politics in Ontario is the emphasis on pragmatism rather than partisanship as the basis for party support, and the development of party organizations geared to capitalize on this condition.

Brokerage or consensus politics seems to be the watchword for all three provincial parties. The Tories in the early 1980s were "a patchwork coalition of right-wing Conservatives, moderate Tories of the Davis ilk, and many who were really Liberals but gravitated to the party in power"[15]; one insider asserts that this result was quite deliberately cultivated.[16] The style "presented a problem for the Liberal party in Ontario. It often found difficulty in staking out an alternative stance when the Conservatives seemed to be all over the ideological map." The Liberals developed a reactive mentality, apparently taking whatever position had not been espoused by the government; thus "the party has sometimes been to the left and sometimes to the right of the Conservatives." The NDP "has clearly been on the left in its emphasis on social issues" as well as certain economic issues, although it "aims for a 'pragmatic radicalism'" which led it to expel the more extreme left-wing movement, the Waffle, in the 1970s. Thus, Dyck concludes,

> . . . it could be said that all three Ontario parties have a progressive and a conservative element, or that all three try to operate within a fairly narrow progressive conservative ideological range.[17]

References to "brokerage" and "consensus" parties are frequent in studies of federal politics; Hugh Thorburn has even suggested that a "habit of pragmatic moderation, used to appeal to a majority, was formed well before Confederation."[18] There is no point in reproducing the same analysis here. It is sufficient to remember that the style of federal parties in Ontario is consistent with these labels, especially the Liberals and Progressive Conservatives who "have historically been broadly based centrist parties competing in elections for wide and shifting coalitions of support."[19] Recent elections have been marked by "abrupt and dramatic" shifts in the issues considered of greatest importance to the electorate but the "ability of a party to link itself to a particular issue or set of issues in the mind of the electorate has been a crucial element of political party strategy. . . ."[20]

One key to the longevity of the Progressive Conservatives was the development of a formidable party apparatus. The legendary "Big Blue Machine" was pragmatic to an extreme. Certainly it "repeatedly proved itself to be the most professional, innovative and successful organization in the election business."[21] In a 'requiem for the Big Blue Machine,' PC activist Eddie Goodman confirmed the party's formula:

> Through a mixture of progressive, centrist policies, good management, and sophisticated electoral strategies, the machine became well-nigh invincible in its determination to provide Ontarians with solid Tory government.[22]

The success of the Big Blue Machine was achieved by a blending of well-honed electoral skills with moderate partisanship and an emphasis on good leadership. The critical distinction between the government and the opposition was not what the PCs believed in or where they were going but what they had delivered. "Good politics" was equated with "good management" and material well-being. Challenges to Ontario's economic dominance and relative affluence had become more frequent in the 1980s; the replacement of William Davis by Frank Miller raised questions within the electorate—and, more importantly, within the PC party—about the leadership-management issue. The rationale for continued support for the party was threatened by these flaws. The up-shot, according to Rosemary Speirs, was that in 1985 Ontario "voters lost faith in the province's long-time managers and began to look elsewhere."[23]

Ironically, that collapse was accelerated by the success of the PCs in the federal arena and an "inheritance" from the Big Blue Machine itself. The link was the move of "the guru of the Ontario Big Blue Machine, Norman Atkins" from the provincial to the federal scene. His presence was of great importance to the success of the 1984 federal campaign and his absence "was undoubtedly a factor in the party's ill-fated 1985 provincial effort."[24] Essentially, the party machinery was driven off its long-established course in 1985 and broke down completely in 1987.

Competitiveness in Ontario Party Politics

The notion of pragmatism obscures the fact that Ontario voters do make choices and are disposed to spread their support unevenly among the three major parties. In recent federal elections, as Joe Wearing pointed out, there has been a tendency to switch support between the two larger parties. In provincial politics, the Tories exercised a monopoly over governmental office from 1943 to 1985, but only in the elections of 1951, 1955 and 1963 did they even come close to capturing one half of the popular vote.[25]

The consistent success of the provincial PCs in retaining government was, then, really only part of the picture of political life in Ontario. "Notwithstanding the Tories' stranglehold on power before 1985," Peter McCormick noted, "Ontario elections have always been competitive and increasingly so in recent decades."[26]

When the rankings of the major parties over the last three federal and provincial elections are considered, some perspective on competitiveness is possible. For example, in the 1984 federal contest, the Liberals and NDP won 14 and 13 seats respectively; in 1988 they won 43 and 10 respectively. This apparently dramatic shift is less surprising when it is realized that the Liberals were second in 62 seats in 1984 while NDP candidates were second in only 12. The three elections in the 1980s indicate that the NDP is "competitive" (that is, finishing first or second) in only about one third of the Ontario federal seats, while the Liberals have actually been "competitive" in more seats than the PCs over the same period.

In provincial politics, the aggregate rankings clearly demonstrate the inconclusiveness of the 1985 election (both Liberal and PC third-place finishes actually increased and one New Democrat finished fourth), as well as the extent of the Liberal triumph in 1987 (no Liberal candidate even finished third). The extent of the collapse of the Progressive Conservatives is stark, especially compared to its 1981 record, although its position is slightly better than that of the NDP on the simple measure of competitiveness used here (combined first and second place finishes). When the bloom wore off the Peterson rose in 1990, however, the dynamics of a three-party system led to an unpredicted outcome: more than two dozen NDP candidates leapfrogged from third place to first place.

**TABLE 1.1 Aggregate Electoral Results in the Province of Ontario
Federal Elections 1980–1988**

Year	Party	Popular Vote	Seats
1980	Liberal	41.7%	52
	NDP	21.8%	5
	PC	35.4%	38
	Total Seats		95
1984	Liberal	29.8%	14
	NDP	20.8%	13
	PC	47.6%	67
	Other	1.8%	1
	Total Seats		95
1988	Liberal	38.9%	43
	NDP	20.1%	10
	PC	38.2%	46
	Total Seats		99

Sources: Chief Electoral Officer, *Report of the Chief Electoral Officer, 32nd/33rd/34th General Election* (1980/1984/1988).

**TABLE 1.2 Aggregate Electoral Results in the Province of Ontario
Provincial Elections 1981–1987**

Year	Party	Popular Vote	Seats
1981	Liberal	33.7%	34
	NDP	21.1%	21
	PC	44.4%	70
	Total Seats		125
1985	Liberal	37.9%	48
	NDP	23.8%	25
	PC	37.0%	52
	Total Seats		125
1987	Liberal	47.3%	95
	NDP	25.7%	19
	PC	24.7%	16
	Total Seats		130

Sources: Chief Election Officer of Ontario, *Election Summaries with Statistics from the Records*, 1981, 1985 and 1987 General Elections.

Recent Party Politics in Ontario

A further examination of the results of the three federal elections and three provincial elections between 1980 and 1988 reveals two additional points about the character of recent party politics in Ontario.

TABLE 2.1 **Aggregate Ranking of Parties in Federal Elections in Ontario**
            1980–1984–1988

Year (Seats)	Party	First	Second	Third	Fourth
1980 (95)	Liberal	52	38	5	0
	NDP	5	23	67	0
	PC	38	34	23	0
1984 (95)*	Liberal	14	62	19	0
	NDP	13	12	69	1
	PC	67	21	7	0
1988 (99)	Liberal**	43	51	4	0
	NDP	10	13	76	0
	PC	46	35	18	0

*Major party first-place finishes add up to 94 because 1 independent was elected.
**One Liberal candidate had to withdraw from the election; therefore only 98 Liberal candidates appear in the Table and there are a total of only 98 third-place finishers among the parties represented here.
Sources: Based upon Chief Electoral Officer, *Report of the Chief Electoral Officer, 32nd/33rd/34th General Election* (1980/1984/1988).

Regionalism

First, Ontario has had a highly regionalized party system. The comparative strength of the three parties has historically been significantly different in various corners of the province in both electoral arenas.[27] If we divide the Ontario constituencies into five geographic regions (Table 3), the aggregate picture of party strength—which is usually taken as the measure of party success (as in Tables 1 and 2)—is seen to mask patterns of perceptible strengths and weakness in the three parties.

For this purpose, the Municipality of Metropolitan Toronto will be considered one region containing 23 federal seats and 29 provincial seats (30 in 1987). Northern Ontario, the entire territory north of the French River, is treated as another region with 11 federal seats and 15 provincial seats. Eastern Ontario is the area from east of Oshawa, north through the Kawarthas, Haliburton and Parry Sound to the Quebec border; it contained 18 federal seats (19 in 1988), five (then six) of which were in the Ottawa metropolitan area, and 24 provincial seats, seven of them in the Ottawa area. The Golden Horseshoe region contains the largely urbanized (or urbanizing) territory running from Oshawa on the east, north of Metropolitan Toronto, around the western end of Lake Ontario and the Niagara peninsula. The region contained 17 federal constituencies (20 in 1988), and 23 provincial constituencies (27 in 1987). Finally, western Ontario will be considered to be the remaining area: it stretches from Lake Simcoe on the northeast down to Windsor and Essex County on the southwest. This region could easily be subdivided further, but the patterns would not be substantially altered. There were 26 federal ridings in the federal elections of the 1980s and 34 provincial ridings.

TABLE 2.2 **Aggregate Ranking of Parties by Region in Federal Elections in Ontario 1980–1984–1988**

Region	Year (Seats)	Party	First	Second	Third	Fourth
Eastern	1980 (18)	Liberal	7	11	0	0
		NDP	0	0	18	0
		PC	11	7	0	0
	1984 (18)	Liberal	3	14	1	0
		NDP	1	0	17	0
		PC	14	4	0	0
	1988 (18)	Liberal	13	6	0	0
		NDP	0	1	18	0
		PC	6	12	1	0
Horseshoe	1980 (17)	Liberal	5	10	2	0
		NDP	2	2	13	0
		PC	10	5	2	0
	1984 (17)	Liberal	1	19	16	0
		NDP	2	4	10	1
		PC	13	3	1	0
	1988 (17)	Liberal	6	13	1	0
		NDP	1	2	17	0
		PC	13	5	5	0
Metro	1980 (17)	Liberal	17	5	1	0
		NDP	2	7	14	0
		PC	4	11	8	0
	1984 (17)	Liberal	6	15	2	0
		NDP	3	3	17	0
		PC	14	5	4	0
	1988 (17)	Liberal	12	10	0	0
		NDP	2	4	17	0
		PC	9	9	5	0
Northern	1980 (11)	Liberal	11	0	0	0
		NDP	0	10	1	0
		PC	0	1	10	0
	1984 (11)	Liberal	3	3	5	0
		NDP	4	2	5	0
		PC	4	6	1	0
	1988 (11)	Liberal	6	4	1	0
		NDP	4	4	3	0
		PC	1	3	7	0
Western	1980 (26)	Liberal	11	13	2	0
		NDP	1	4	21	0
		PC	14	9	3	0
	1984 (26)	Liberal	1	20	5	0
		NDP	3	3	20	0
		PC	22	3	1	0
	1988 (26)	Liberal	6	18	2	0
		NDP	3	2	21	0
		PC	17	6	3	0

TABLE 3 **Electoral Regions in the Province of Ontario**

Region	*Fed. Seats*	*Percentage Fed. Seats*	*Prov. Seats*	*Percentage Prov. Seats*
Eastern	18	19	24	19
	19 (1988)	19 (1988)		18 (1987)
Horseshoe	17	18	23	18
	20 (1988)	20 (1988)	27 (1987)	21 (1987)
Metro	23	24	29	23
		23 (1988)	30 (1987)	23 (1987)
Northern	11	12	15	12
		11 (1988)		11 (1987)
Western	26	27	34	27
		26 (1988)		26 (1987)
Total	95		125	
	99 (1988)		130 (1987)	

Tables 3 and 4 provide the results of this re-examination of the fortunes of the three major parties. They show evidence of a regional variation in electoral support, leaving aside the complications caused by the landslides in the 1984 federal and the 1987 provincial elections.

The federal PC party won an overwhelming victory in 1984 and had a less dramatic margin in Ontario in 1988, but turned in a rather unremarkable performance in northern Ontario in the three general elections of the 1980s. With 33 seats to be won (11 in each of three elections), Tories captured a total of only five, and four of them came in its 1984 sweep. Metropolitan Toronto has been another area in which the party has fared relatively poorly over the years. Again, the 1984 surge brought it a windfall of about 60 percent of the seats in the region, but the 1988 results dropped it back to its recent average level of success (about 40 percent of the seats). Conversely, in the eastern and western regions (barring the Ottawa and Windsor seats) the PCs have been the dominant political force for some years.[28] The federal PCs have been the most successful party in the urbanized belt around the western end of Lake Ontario in the 1980s, as well.

The federal Liberal party has a more mixed record in the 1980s than previously.[29] In part, this is a result of the widespread collapse it suffered in 1984: in its areas of greatest strength, northern Ontario (where it held a monopoly in 1980) and Metropolitan Toronto (where it held three quarters of the seats in 1980), it was only able to retain about one quarter of the seats. The Liberals nevertheless recaptured about half of them in 1988 and avoided third place completely in Toronto. Their fortunes in eastern Ontario rose in 1988 to levels not seen in 20 years, primarily (but not exclusively) by sweeping the Ottawa area and francophone seats. In western Ontario the party was successful in some rural seats, in contrast to its recent reliance on more urbanized seats within this region.

The New Democrats in Ontario have had little to be happy about in federal

TABLE 4.1 **Aggregate Ranking of Parties in Provincial Elections in Ontario 1981–1985–1987**

Year (Seats)	Party	First	Second	Third	Fourth
1981	Liberal	34	63	28	0
(125)	NDP	21	21	83	0
	PC	70	41	14	0
1984	Liberal	48	47	30	0
(125)	NDP	25	20	79	1
	PC	52	58	15	0
1987	Liberal	95	35	0	0
(130)	NDP	19	43	67	1
	PC	16	52	61	1

Sources: Based upon Chief Election Officer of Ontario, *Election Summaries with Statistics from the Records*, 1981, 1985 and 1987 General Elections.

elections, capturing a high of 13 seats in 1984, only to drop back to 10 in 1988. Combining first and second place finishes as a measure of competitive strength, the regionalized nature of Ontario politics re-emerges. NDP candidates tended to be most successful, relatively speaking, in the north and in scattered urban constituencies in 1984 and 1988 (based in Oshawa, Brantford, central Toronto, Windsor and Hamilton). Eastern Ontario continues to be a scene of desolation to federal NDP candidates. Only one person finished higher than third in the three elections: Michael Cassidy, a former provincial leader, who captured Ottawa Centre in 1984 but lost it in 1988.

In federal politics in Ontario, the Liberals and PCs are the major protagonists throughout most of the province, although Liberal-NDP contests have been found in the north and in certain urban constituencies. Indeed, some of the evidence suggests that not only does Ontario have regions, it has sub-regions. The overall picture of Ontario as a three-party system federally is, then, a function of these more regionalized patterns of competition.

In provincial politics, the Liberal landslide of 1987 and the collapse of 1990 confound some generalizations about regional support. In any event, the Liberals have historically relied on western Ontario as the building block of the caucus at Queen's Park. As the party's total of seats tripled from 1981 to 1987, the proportion elected from this region declined. Its dominance within the region was, however, clear: it won 56 percent of the seats in 1981, 68 percent in 1985 and 82 percent in 1987. In eastern Ontario and the Horseshoe the Liberals were fairly competitive, even before 1987. The record of the Liberals in Metropolitan Toronto is quite extraordinary: in 1981 it won two seats (about 7 percent of the total), but in 1987 it won 24 (80 percent of the total), shutting the PCs out completely. Despite jumping from one to seven seats in the north between 1985 and 1987, and from 12 third-place finishes to none, the region actually rewarded the Liberals less

TABLE 4.2 **Aggregate Ranking of Parties by Region in Provincial Elections in Ontario 1981–1985–1987**

Region	Year (Seats)	Party	First	Second	Third	Fourth
Eastern	1981 (24)	Liberal	6	16	2	0
		NDP	2	0	22	0
		PC	16	8	0	0
	1985 (24)	Liberal	8	14	2	0
		NDP	1	2	21	0
		PC	15	8	1	0
	1987 (24)	Liberal	18	6	0	0
		NDP	0	6	17	1
		PC	6	12	6	0
Horseshoe	1981 (23)	Liberal	6	13	4	0
		NDP	4	3	16	0
		PC	13	7	3	0
	1985 (23)	Liberal	7	13	3	0
		NDP	5	2	16	0
		PC	11	8	4	0
	1987 (27)	Liberal	18	9	0	0
		NDP	5	6	16	0
		PC	4	12	11	0
Metro	1981 (29)	Liberal	2	17	10	0
		NDP	9	7	13	0
		PC	18	5	6	0
	1985 (29)	Liberal	9	11	9	0
		NDP	10	7	12	0
		PC	10	11	8	0
	1987 (30)	Liberal	24	6	0	0
		NDP	6	12	12	0
		PC	0	12	17	1
Northern	1981 (15)	Liberal	1	6	8	0
		NDP	5	4	6	0
		PC	9	5	1	0
	1985 (15)	Liberal	1	2	12	0
		NDP	7	5	3	0
		PC	7	8	0	0
	1987 (15)	Liberal	7	8	0	0
		NDP	6	5	4	0
		PC	2	2	11	0
Western	1981 (34)	Liberal	19	11	4	0
		NDP	1	7	26	0
		PC	14	16	4	0
	1985 (34)	Liberal	23	7	4	0
		NDP	2	4	27	1
		PC	9	23	2	0
	1987 (34)	Liberal	28	6	0	0
		NDP	2	14	18	0
		PC	4	14	16	0

Sources: Based upon Chief Election Officer of Ontario, *Election Summaries with Statistics from the Records,* 1981, 1985 and 1987 General Elections.

generously than any other.[30] On election night 1990, the shattered Liberal caucus was still regionally skewed: western Ontario now provided less than 10 percent of its members, but eastern Ontario MPPs constituted about one third of the whole group. The Metro and Horseshoe regions provided one quarter each and the north remained relatively weak.

The provincial New Democrats have traditionally two areas of consistent strength: Metropolitan Toronto and northern Ontario. In each of the three elections detailed here, about two thirds of all NDP MPPs were elected in these two regions. The party had some modest success in eastern Ontario in 1981 (two seats) and 1985 (one seat plus two second-place finishes); thus, six second-place finishes in 1987 constitute a remarkable increase. The 14 second-place finishes in western Ontario in 1987, perhaps an artifact of the PC collapse in this region, were an omen of change. The NDP's 1990 majority rested on that foundation plus a breakthrough in western Ontario constituencies such as Oxford, Lambton and Middlesex where 1987 support had been less than 20 percent of the popular vote. Eastern Ontario and the Horseshoe regions provided some satisfying results, but—building upon its recent electoral record—a majority of northern and Metro Toronto constituencies endorsed NDP candidates.

For the provincial Progressive Conservatives, the three elections of the 1980s brought a steady decline in fortunes. The party dominated eastern Ontario, and was very strong in the Horseshoe, Metropolitan Toronto and the north up to 1981. The 1985 results show that the east remained loyal, but modest slippage started in the Horseshoe and the north. The drop in the west and Metro was more dramatic. By 1987, three quarters of the seats in the east and the Horseshoe went Liberal and the Tories were completely unsuccessful in Metro. Only two former Cabinet ministers were returned in the northern region. The extent of the party's losses were so severe in 1987 that nothing resembling a regional stronghold remained. In the slight recovery of 1990, the PCs made more gains in the Metro area and in western Ontario, but remained weak in the Horseshoe and northern Ontario where only the party leader, Mike Harris was elected.

Provincial aggregate figures, despite these circumstances, mask an element of regionalism. The more traditional PC-Liberal contests in the east and much of western Ontario co-existed with PC-NDP battles in the north and Metro Toronto, and all three parties have made good showings in different parts of the Golden Horsehoe.

Ontario is not electorally homogeneous, but is large and complex enough to house various combinations of two-party (and occasional three-party) contests. The aggregate results might determine the composition of the party caucuses at Queen's Park and in the House of Commons, but in recent years the regional results provide a more insightful picture of the nature of the Ontario party systems.

Symmetry and Asymmetry

The second point to observe in the examination of the regional support for Ontario's parties is implicit in the first. As far as the two larger parties are concerned, the regional support patterns noted above are not identical in the federal and provincial arenas. In other words, areas of persistent strength in federal politics are not necessarily areas of strength in provincial politics, and vice versa. This suggests that, although the same three parties are successfully electing MPs and MPPs in Ontario, the relationship of the parties to each other and to the electorate is different in the federal and provincial systems.

At the constituency level, there are some unusual cases. The provincial constituency of Perth, for example, long stood among the safest Liberal seats in Ontario, giving the incumbent a minimum of 61.2 percent of the popular vote over the five elections from 1975 to 1987 before falling to the NDP in 1990. The federal constituency of Perth returned a PC candidate with a comfortable plurality in 1974, 1979, 1980 and 1984. When it was redrawn as Perth-Wellington-Waterloo in 1988, it re-elected the PC incumbent, but only by a narrow margin. In the east end of Hamilton, the provincial constituency has been a safe CCF-NDP seat since 1959, while Liberal John Munro was elected to the House of Commons continuously from 1962 to 1980 in much the same area and Sheila Copps retained the seat for the Liberals in the 1984 and 1988 elections. It is harder to find comparable evidence in Metropolitan Toronto, where electoral boundaries have recently changed at both levels and the 1984 and 1987 landslides have disrupted longer-term patterns of support. The best evidence for the argument being made here is perhaps the case of the provincial constituency of Eglinton which returned PCs in 1981 and 1985 and the federal constituency of Eglinton-Lawrence (admittedly a larger and more diverse area) which elected Liberals in 1980, 1984 and 1988.

On the regional level, northern Ontario and Metropolitan Toronto were areas dominated by the federal Liberal party in the 1980 election results, but were fairly poor areas for the provincial Liberals in 1981. As the provincial Liberals rose to dominate the Golden Horseshoe in the 1980s, the federal PCs established predominance in the same region. Western Ontario showed a marked tendency to favour provincial Liberal candidates over PCs throughout the 1980s, but in federal politics the relationship is the reverse.

On the broadest level, there is a significant difference in the types of constituencies from which the parties draw their electoral support.[31] This is implicit in the evidence presented here about the Liberals and PCs. The NDP is, however, unique since it has been most successful in similar constituencies in both arenas, namely those which are urban and/or heavily unionized. In the mid-1970s, its fortunes rose dramatically in provincial politics as it began to acquire sustained support in Metro Toronto, northern Ontario and portions of the Golden Horseshoe. In this same period, the federal NDP was most successful in northern Ontario and Metro Toronto. It has struggled hard, with only intermittent success, to expand its appeal to the rural and more middle-class constituencies, but has been thwarted by the strength of the ties of those sections of the community to the two traditional parties.

The contemporary relationship between the Liberals and the Progressive

Conservatives in the two electoral arenas is curious, since longevity in office for one wing of each party affected the political dynamics of Ontario for a lengthy period. Before 1984–85, the federal Liberals and the provincial PCs were "both leader-oriented, broker, middle-of-the-road parties, pursuing essentially similar interests"; there has also been evidence of deliberate cooperation between them which would promote the other's re-election.[32] Moreover, the demise of one was followed shortly after by the collapse of the other. The question is whether this is a cause-and-effect relationship or, as seems more likely,[33] merely two parallel reactions by Ontario voters to long-entrenched incumbent governments.

As the "government party" for so long, the federal Liberals exercised electoral dominance over the PCs through the judicious application of government programmes, the momentum of power and the promise of reward. This forced the federal PCs to play the politics of reaction and frustration in Ontario, often leaving it with a caucus composed largely of rurally based MPs from eastern and southwestern Ontario. That pattern changed in 1984, so that the federal Liberals have now acquired "loser-party status."[34]

In provincial politics, the long-term roles were established after the PC victory over a divided and directionless Liberal party in 1943. The provincial PCs honed the strategic application of the powers of government for electoral purposes from a blunt weapon to a precision instrument. They had, moreover, a strong urban core of voter support throughout this century[35] and combined this with effective links to the rural community. Thus, the provincial PCs were not a party of the margins, but a party which drew continued support throughout the province. The Ontario Liberal party, as noted earlier in this essay, was unable to achieve consistent support outside of its rural southwestern base, despite the optimistic forecasts which appeared after its occasional electoral upswings. In the early part of the century it was obsessed by a crusade against drink. In the 1930s and early 1940s it suffered under questionable leadership, and from 1943 to early 1985 it was simply outperformed by the PCs.[36] Once again, the pattern changed sharply and the two parties found themselves in unfamiliar roles. It is too soon to tell how well—or for how long—those new roles will be played.

The significant point is that the status of the Liberals in federal politics, from 1935 to 1984 with two interruptions, and that of the PCs in the provincial field from 1943 to 1985, were actually symmetrical and it was this configuration of a dominant party (or 'power party'[37]) facing two smaller opposition parties which gave a measure of similarity to the two Ontario party systems. The achievement of government and the winning of convincing majorities by the two former opposition parties within a short period of time is itself another form of symmetry in the two systems.

Yet, the federal and provincial wings of each party did not necessarily win seats in the same regions nor even necessarily appeal to the same voters; more importantly, the relationship of the parties to each other and to the electorate was different in the federal and provincial systems. These dissimilarities point towards Ontario being characterized by two distinctive party systems.

The Distinctiveness of Federal and Provincial Politics in Ontario

The final aspect of political life in Ontario to be considered is the distinctiveness (or separation) of federal and provincial politics.

The long-term success of the federal Liberal party gave it a dominant place over its provincial counterpart. From the mid-1940s, when the provincial party lost control of Queen's Park, to the mid-1980s the major organizational and individual focus of most Ontario Liberals was the House of Commons. The positive side of that situation was that some of the success rubbed off on the provincial party and its continued existence was assured by the needs of the federal party.[38] The negative side was that federal politics tended to attract most of the energy, resources and talents of Ontarians who regarded themselves as Liberals,[39] leaving the provincial party with far less support than was necessary to win a provincial election. In fact, as has been noted, even the party's ultimate victory in 1985 was as much a result of the failure of the PC government as it was of the Liberal's own efforts. It is ironic that as late as the summer of 1984 this attraction to federal politics persisted: David Peterson lost four prominent members of his caucus who resigned provincial seats to contest the federal election. Two of them were successful, but, of course, continued to be members of an opposition whereas their colleagues who stayed at Queen's Park found themselves in government some nine months later.[40] When the provincial party was actually in a position to make a strong effort to help its federal colleagues in 1988, it failed to "make up for the inadequacies of the federal party's weak organization."[41]

During the provincial PC hegemony, the federal PCs had nothing remotely resembling the Big Blue Machine. At times, it did not even have the benefits which one might assume could accrue to another wing of the same party. It is widely believed that the commitment of the provincial electoral organization to the federal party "depended entirely on the provincial leader's relationship with his federal counterpart. . . . Davis did all he could to help Mulroney get elected in 1984 [including the move of Norm Atkins to the federal campaign] . . . whereas he was conspicuously unhelpful to Joe Clark in 1980."[42]

By contrast, the NDP has long prided itself on a strong organizational base, one which serves both federal and provincial causes without prejudice. In practice, however, the provincial field has been a more attractive and successful target and the party's provincial office has devoted most of its resources to that cause except during federal elections, when it operates as part of the national campaign apparatus.

In structural terms, the NDP's integrated federal-provincial party structure is an anomaly in Ontario. The PC party office in Toronto serves the provincial party alone (although there is a regional office of the federal party), while the Liberals have operated two parallel structures in Toronto since 1976, one for the federal party—the Liberal party of Canada (Ontario)—and the other for the provincial party—the Ontario Liberal party.[43] These practices reflect both competitive and operational priorities among the three parties and also demonstrate that two of the Ontario parties have chosen to develop overt signs of independence between their federal and provincial organizations. As Wearing has suggested, a close relationship between federal and provincial parties may not necessarily be an advantage when it comes to attracting voters who are disaffected by one level of government or the other.[44]

Another dimension of the distance between federal and provincial politics in Ontario is evident in the experiences of party candidates. Surveys of major party candidates in the federal election of 1974 and the provincial election of 1975 demonstrated that there is very little movement between the two electoral are-nas.[45] A more recent review of the successful candidates in the 1987 provincial and 1988 federal elections shows only one former MP at Queen's Park (NDP leader Bob Rae) and three former MPPs in Ottawa (Liberals Don Boudria and Sheila Copps and New Democrat Iain Angus). As noted earlier, former provincial leader Michael Cassidy sat in the 33rd parliament. Considering the number of seats at stake in Ontario in the two electoral arenas, the proportion of candidates who have been nominated to run at both levels is actually quite small. A more comprehensive analysis of MPs concluded that "provincial legislative experience has been even rarer among MPs of central Canada than it has been among MPs elected from the regional peripheries." Indeed, only 3.3 percent of Ontario MPs elected between 1958 and 1984 had served in the Ontario Legislature.[46]

There has been considerable debate over whether Ontario voters distinguish between federal and provincial issues when casting their ballots,[47] but it appears that many party activists and the party organizations themselves base their actions upon a recognition of the independence of the two areas and have worked towards sustaining the separateness of federal and provincial politics in Ontario.

Conclusion

Ontario is the only Canadian province in which the three major national parties are also the major competitors in provincial politics. This overt congruence between the two party systems has masked a number of features of party politics in Ontario.

First, one must remember that each party is not a significant force across the entire province. It has been demonstrated here that the aggregate support figures are less revealing of the nature of the province's political preferences than are the regional patterns where quite different patterns of party support prevail.

Second, one must set aside the notion that, because the same three parties are competing for and winning seats, the two arenas are essentially the same. It has been demonstrated here that, at least for the Liberals and PCs, the patterns of success and even the overall roles played by the parties in the electoral arenas are quite different.

Third, one should avoid thinking of the Liberals or the Progressive Conservatives as integrated competitive entities in Ontario. Evidence on party organizations and practices and, to some extent, on candidates and elected representatives, suggest that the provincial and federal wings of these parties are quite distinct structures that happen to share a common label. This condition contributes to the separation of federal and provincial politics in Ontario.

Fourth, Ontario voters seem to prefer pragmatism to ideological posturing in both federal and provincial politics. Ontario's record in federal politics is, however, coloured by a measure of ambivalence about which party is most capable of looking after Ontario's interests, as observed in the mixed signals coming out of the 1988 election. Part of this dilemma stems from an uncertainty over what Ontario's interests really are. From the beginning, Ontario governments have fought with national governments in the cause of provincial rights, to keep the provincial administration independent enough of federal control to do what it determined was properly in Ontario's interests. Yet, at the same time, many Ontarians have identified themselves first with Canada and have seen the federal government as contributing to Ontario's well being.[48] As such, they want a strong government in Ottawa. This ambiguity has influenced the choices made by Ontarians in many federal elections.

In the provincial sphere, Ontarians experienced more than four decades in which politics had actually been de-politicized! Most electoral and governmental strategies since 1945 have been driven by the desire to isolate the opposition parties on the margins of the political spectrum, but this is done by trying to avoid ideological labels altogether. Moreover, this tendency did not end with the defeat of the Progressive Conservatives in 1985. If anything, it continues unchanged. Both Davis and Peterson are "fundamentally pragmatic politicians" and both "claimed that attempts to classify them on the political spectrum were fruitless, because they would respond to practical needs as they arose."[49] Larry Grossman, PC leader in the 1987 election, went so far as to observe that "Peterson and former Tory Premier William Davis were cut from the same mould—and out of date." Grossman, however, failed to convince very many Ontario voters that "That competent, confident style of management is not what is needed now."[50] It is also not unreasonable to speculate that David Peterson's failure to maintain a "competent, confident style of management" led to his party's demise in 1990.

Finally, the long tenure in office by the provincial PCs led commentators "to regard them as inevitable governors of a cautious and unimaginative people."[51] The fact that the dynasty came to an end weakens the validity of that view of the Ontario electorate. The majority of Ontarians—who knew no other governors in their lifetime— are now actually coming to grips with a second change in five years.

Ontario may be on the brink of a new political era. This is not as much of a cliche as it might sound, for Ontario political history has not witnessed much in the way of dramatic changes this century. The last Liberal majority before 1987 was 50 years earlier, when Mitch Hepburn repeated his success of 1934. Although the early indications in the 1930s were that the Liberals had revived their glory days under Mowat, they crumbled under administrative ineptitude and succumbed in 1943 to the slow, careful reconstruction of the Conservative party under George Drew who laid the foundations for the Tory dynasty. It took more than 40 years for the Liberals to recover.

One key question now is why David Peterson reprised the meteoric rise to and fall from power of Mitch Hepburn (albeit without the chaos which surrounded that premier) rather than enjoy the opportunity to dominate Ontario politics for a generation.

One explanation may be that the Liberals brought change to the Ontario political scene but not to the dynamics of the party system. The reality of three-way competition in a regional context is continuing vulnerability. In the 1990 election the New Democrats were able to achieve what their competitors had taken for granted: majority government built upon an electoral plurality. That was a neat trick, to be sure, but repeating it will be an even greater challenge.

ENDNOTES

1. An overview of the provincial Liberal party's return from the political wilderness can be obtained in Rand Dyck, *Provincial Politics in Canada* (Scarborough: Prentice-Hall Canada, 1986), pp. 289–307.

2. Ironically, this smaller Ontario group still constituted 35 percent of the Liberal MPs elected in 1984, virtually identical to Ontario's relative strength in the 1980 majority caucus.

3. The national total rose from 40 to 83, an increase of 43. Ontario Liberal MPs rose from 14 to 43, an increase of 29.

4. Peter McCormick, "Provincial Political Party Systems, 1945–1986" in Alain G. Gagnon and A. Brian Tanguay, eds., *Canadian Parties in Transition: Discourse, Organization and Representation* (Scarborough: Nelson, 1989), p. 158.

5. The overt similarity of the two systems has sometimes led to the conclusion that they are one and the same; some 30 years ago, Dennis H. Wrong asserted that the "politics of Ontario are a microcosm of the federal politics of Canada, except that the Conservatives rather than the Liberals are the dominant party." This study disagrees with Wrong's assessment of the dynamics of the two systems. Wrong, "Ontario Provincial Elections, 1934–55; A Preliminary Survey of Voting", *Canadian Journal of Economics and Political Science*, Vol. XXIII, No. 3 (August 1957), p. 402.

6. One of the implications of this situation is to give the party winning the popular vote a disproportionate share of the seats in Ontario. When the system operates with a different split of the vote-share, the distribution of the seats may vary. The federal situation is noted in Richard Johnston, "Federal and Provincial Voting: Contemporary Patterns and Historical Evolution," in David J. Elkins and Richard Simeon, *Small Worlds: Provinces and Parties in Canadian Political Life* (Toronto: Methuen, 1980), pp. 135, 138.

7. McCormick, "Provincial Political Party Systems, 1945–1986", p. 158. His examination of volatility among all provincial voters since 1945 (p. 164) revealed the net movement has been over 10.1 percent ("at least one voter in 10 switching from one party to another in subsequent elections"); in Ontario, however, the net movement has been above 10 percent on only three occasions (of the 12 considered from 1945 to 1986) and "usually it has been much lower."

8. Rand Dyck also reached this conclusion between the 1985 and 1987 elections. See *Provincial Politics in Canada*, p. 308. This view differs from that taken by John Wilson and David Hoffman in "Ontario: A Three-Party System in Transition," in Martin Rubin, ed., *Canadian Provincial Politics: The Party Systems of the Provinces*, 1st ed. (Scarborough: Prentice-Hall Canada, 1972).

9. Joseph Wearing, *Strained Relations: Canadian Parties and Voters* (Toronto: McClelland and Stewart, 1988), p. 46. Note that this pattern was partially disrupted in the 1988 federal election when Ontario voters switched back (albeit by a narrow plurality) to the Liberals while the PCs were repeat winners in the seat count (again by a narrow plurality).

10. See the discussion of this pattern in John Meisel, "The Decline of Party in Canada" in the previous edition of this book.

11. *Ibid.*

12. Dyck, *Provincial Politics in Canada*, p. 307.

13. John Wilson, "The Red Tory Province: Reflections on the Character of the Ontario Political Culture," in Donald C. MacDonald, ed., *Government and Politics of Ontario*, 2nd ed. (Toronto: Van Nostrand Reinhold, 1980), p. 212.

14. Rosemary Speirs, *Out of the Blue: The Fall of the Tory Dynasty in Ontario* (Toronto: Macmillan, 1986), pp. 223–224.

15. *Ibid.*, p. 22.

16. Eddie Goodman, *Life of the Party: The Memoirs of Eddie Goodman* (Toronto: Key Porter Books, 1988), p. 240, writes that Bill Davis "was a pragmatist who did not approach government in an inflexible philosophy of the right or the left." Rosemary Speirs notes that Bill Davis was once quoted as rejecting "the ideological prisons of right and left". Speirs, *ibid.*, p. 234.

17. Dyck, *Provincial Politics in Canada*, pp. 315–316.

18. H.G. Thorburn, "The Development of Political Parties in Canada," in this volume.

19. Lawrence LeDuc, "The Flexible Canadian Electorate" in Howard Penniman, ed., *Canada at the Polls, 1984: A Study of the Federal General Elections* (Durham, North Carolina: Duke University Press, 1988), p. 40. A similar appraisal is found in another essay in the same collection: John C. Courtney, "Reinventing the Brokerage Wheel: The Tory Success in 1984," p. 198.

20. Lawrence LeDuc, "The Changeable Canadian Voter" in Alan Frizzell, Jon H. Pammett and Anthony Westell, *The Canadian General Election of 1988* (Ottawa: Carleton University Press, 1989), p. 107.

21. Dyck, *Provincial Politics in Canada*, p. 308.

22. Goodman, *Life of the Party*, p. 271.

23. Speirs, *Out of the Blue*, p. xv.

24. Rand Dyck, "Relations Between Federal and Provincial Parties" in Gagnon and Tanguay, *Canadian Parties in Transition*, p. 200. For a discussion of Atkins' role in the 1984 campaign, see George Perlin, "Opportunity Regained: The Tory Victory in 1984" in Penniman, *Canada at the Polls, 1984*, pp. 84–85 and Val Sears, "The Buttery-Smooth Conservatives" in Alan Frizzell and Anthony Westell, eds., *The Canadian General Election of 1984: Politicians, Parties, Press and Polls* (Ottawa: Carleton University Press, 1985), pp. 28–36.

25. See the figures presented by Robert J. Drummond in "Voting Behaviour: Counting the Change," in Graham White, ed., *The Government and Politics of Ontario*, fourth edition (Toronto: Nelson, 1990), p. 243 and in John Wilson and David Hoffman, "Ontario: A

Three-Party System in Transition," in Martin Robin, ed., *Canadian Provincial Politics: The Party Systems of the Provinces* (Toronto: Prentice-Hall Canada, 1972), pp. 204–205.

26. McCormick, "Provincial Political Party Systems, 1945–1986", p. 160.
27. Some earlier observations on these patterns may be found in Wrong, "Ontario Provincial Elections, 1934–55", pp. 402–403 and in Lawrence S. Grossman, "'Safe' Seats: The Rural-Urban Pattern in Ontario," *Canadian Journal of Economics and Political Science*, Vol. XXIX, No. 3 (August 1963), 368.
28. See Wearing, *Strained Relations*, pp. 46–47 and Maps 1.1 and 1.2 in which Conservative strength in rural seats in these areas is discussed.
29. See Robert J. Williams, "Ontario's Party Systems: Federal and Provincial" in the previous edition of this book.
30. See also Speirs, *Out of the Blue*, pp. 222–223.
31. See Wrong, "Ontario Provincial Elections, 1934–55", pp. 397–400.
32. Rand Dyck, *Provincial Politics in Canada*, p. 311. On the cooperation question, see Speirs, *Out of the Blue*, p. 66.
33. This is the view, for example, of Rand Dyck, *Provincial Politics in Canada*, p. 311.
34. Stephen Clarkson, "The Liberals: Disoriented in Defeat" in Frizzell, Pammett and Westell, *The Canadian General Election of 1988*, p. 40.
35. The best discussion of the emergence of the pattern of party support in the first three quarters of this century is found in Charles W. Humphries, "Sources of Ontario 'Progressive' Conservatism, 1900–1914," in the *Canadian Historical Association Annual Report, 1967*, pp. 118–129.
36. The (mis)fortunes of the Ontario Liberals from the 1920s to the 1970s can be traced, in part, in Peter Oliver, "The Ontario Liberal Party in the 1920s: A Study in Political Collapse" in his *Public and Private Persons: The Ontario Political Culture, 1914–1934* (Toronto: Clarke-Irwin, 1975), pp. 127–154; in Neil McKenty, *Mitch Hepburn* (Toronto: McClelland and Stewart, 1967); and in Jonathan Manthorpe, *The Power and the Tories* (Toronto: Macmillan, 1974). See also Rosemary Speirs, *Out of the Blue*.
37. The term is used in John McMenemy, "Party Organization" in David J. Bellamy, *et al.*, eds., *The Provincial Political Systems: Comparative Essays* (Toronto: Methuen, 1976), p. 114.
38. See Wilson and Hoffman, "Ontario: A Three-Party System in Transition", p. 203.
39. See Speirs, *Out of the Blue*, p. 66 and Dyck, *Provincial Politics in Canada*, p. 312.
40. The prospects of a Liberal victory in 1985 were not shared by other members of the Liberal caucus who had served many years in opposition. Two who were senior enough to have been shoo-ins to the first Peterson Cabinet (Pat Reid and James Breithaupt) left politics before the election. See Speirs, *Out of the Blue*, p. 69 and Sherri Aikenhead, "Building a Remarkable Image," *Maclean's*, 21 September 1987, pp. 18–19.
41. Clarkson, "The Liberals: Disoriented in Defeat," pp. 39–40.
42. Dyck, *Provincial Politics in Canada*, p. 312.
43. Dyck, "Relations Between Federal and Provincial Parties," in Gagnon and Tanguay, eds., *Canadian Parties in Transition*, pp. 188–190, 198–200, 207–209. Also see Joseph Wearing, "Political Parties: Fish or Fowl?" in MacDonald, ed., *Government and Politics of Ontario*, 3rd ed. pp. 294–296.
44. Wearing, *ibid.*, p. 295.
45. Williams, "Ontario's Party Systems: Federal and Provincial," in the previous edition of this book, pp. 312–313.
46. Doreen Barrie and Roger Gibbins, "Parliamentary Careers in the Canadian Federal State," *Canadian Journal of Political Science*, Vol. XXII, No. 1 (March 1989), p. 144.

47. See Wearing, *Strained Relations*, pp. 79–81 and Dyck, *Provincial Politics in Canada*, pp. 310–311.

48. Dyck, *ibid.*, p. 269.

49. Speirs, *Out of the Blue*, pp. 234–235.

50. Mary Janigan, Sherri Aikenhead, *et al.*, "The Big Red Wave," *Maclean's*, 21 September 1987, p. 14. Rosemary Speirs wrote about some of Grossman's earlier attempts "to occupy the moderate middle" when he found that "David Peterson already inhabited much of it." Speirs, *ibid.*, pp. 225–226.

51. Speirs, *ibid.*, p. xviii.

35

Party Politics in Atlantic Canada: Still the Mysterious East?

AGAR ADAMSON AND IAN STEWART

Dalton Camp, in his book *Gentlemen, Players and Politicians*, made the following observation:

> Politics is largely made up of irrelevancies. Politicians, when they have nothing else to do, immobilize themselves and everyone near them, obsessed, like Spanish border guards, with the continuous assertion of their authority. It is a mechanism for self-preservation.[1]

Camp's observation can be used to summarize the nature of politics in Atlantic Canada. In other sections of the country, politics is a part of life to be endured, but in Atlantic Canada it might be called the bread of life. Nowhere else in Canada are politics followed from the cradle to the grave as they are in these four provinces.

If it is true that federal structures are largely the result of regional differences, it is equally true that, once established, these same federal institutions tend to engender further regional diversity. It seems apparent, for example, that there was little sociological justification in 1905 for dividing the new provinces of Alberta and Saskatchewan along a meridian of longitude (110 West); neverthe-less, the pattern of party politics in these two artificially separated political communities quickly diverged. After two centuries of institutional distinctive-ness, therefore, one might expect to find many significant political differences within Atlantic Canada.[2] While some do exist, this essay will demonstrate that the party politics of Nova Scotia, New Brunswick, Prince Edward Island, and even Newfoundland and Labrador continue to be notably similar. Underlying this partisan similarity is a manifestly regional political culture. Because many residents have been tied to a subsistence economy of renewable staples, because both federal and provincial governments have been consistently

---

This is a revised and updated version of the essay that appeared in the previous edition of this book.

unable to alleviate the extensive poverty, because the sea to the east and the more developed economies to the west and south have served as channels for dissatisfaction[3] and because immigration was essentially completed by the middle of the nineteenth century, the dominant political orientations of all four Atlantic provinces have historically revolved around the twin elements of traditionalism and cynicism.

There is, of course, disagreement as to whether or not Newfoundland's political culture should be grouped with that of the three Maritime provinces.[4] Every Newfoundland government since Confederation, and particularly those Tory administrations which succeeded the Smallwood regime, has stressed that Newfoundland is not one of the Maritime provinces and that there remains a considerable difference between Newfoundland and the other three provinces. Witness, for instance, the behaviour of the Peckford government with respect to the cod fishery, Clyde Wells' position on the Meech Lake Accord, the various stands taken at other federal-provincial conferences, and Newfoundland's 1983 decision to withdraw from the Atlantic Provinces Economic Council. Nevertheless, the gradual demise of the outports has eroded many of the distinctive aspects of the Newfoundland political culture, while integration into the Canadian political community has simultaneously reinforced the pervasive traditionalism and cynicism of Newfoundlanders. In short, Newfoundland's political culture has recently been converging with that of the three Maritime provinces. It should also be stressed that the relative importance of the United Empire Loyalists to the region's political culture has probably been exaggerated. The fact that the bulk of the region's Loyalists settled in New Brunswick and Nova Scotia does not seem to have made traditionalism any more potent in these provinces than in Newfoundland or Prince Edward Island.

Of course, there will always be room for some debate over both the precise composition of and the extent of homogeneity within the Atlantic political culture. Political values and orientations cannot be directly observed; instead, they must be inferred from the presence of more tangible phenomena. In this respect, the position of the contemporary political scientist is not too dissimilar from that of the sixteenth century marine biologist who was forced to deduce from such indirect evidence as air bubbles and wave patterns that something portentous was lurking unseen under the water's surface.

Fortunately, the "air bubbles and wave patterns" in Atlantic Canada unambiguously point to a traditionalistic and cynical political culture. The former attribute can be readily inferred. Dale Poel, for example, discovered that the region's provincial governments have not been major policy innovators,[5] and others have noted that, despite equalization payments and other grants from the federal government, the Atlantic provinces have historically been welfare state laggards.[6] Nor have these elite activities been inconsistent with mass desires, for Simeon and Blake observed that, in comparison to other Canadians, residents of the Atlantic provinces have been the least supportive of an expanded role for government, the least supportive of progressive social policy, the least permissive on moral issues and the most interested in maintaining ties with Great

Britain and the monarchy.[7] Finally, that Newfoundland kept the Union Jack as its provincial flag until 1980, that the last two dual-member federal constituencies were in Atlantic Canada, that Prince Edward Island retained alcoholic prohibition until 1948 and that the retention of the monarchy was an issue in the 1978 Nova Scotia provincial election all bespeak a traditionalistic political culture.[8]

The evidence is similarly voluminous with respect to cynicism. Residents of the Atlantic provinces are typically more politically informed than are other Canadians; indeed, even at a relatively young age, this phenomenon is apparent.[9] Moreover, with the exception of Newfoundland, Atlantic Canadians have far higher political participation rates than the national average and voting turnouts for both provincial and federal elections are consistently the highest in the country.[10] Yet notwithstanding these apparent indicators of a "civic culture," Atlantic Canadians have historically been distinguished from other Canadians by their relative lack of both political efficacy and political trust.[11] In other words, there have been curious contradictions in the Atlantic provinces' political culture. Despite the fact that they have both distrusted politics and politicians and felt incapable of effecting political change, Atlantic Canadians have continued to invest in politics high amounts of physical, intellectual, and, as we shall subsequently see, emotional resources. The result of these tensions has been a political culture characterized, in the words of former New Brunswick Premier Richard Hatfield, by an "unhealthy cynicism."[12] Of course, as Hatfield was to discover firsthand, there are limits to the electorate's cynicism. Referring to a series of scandals which bedevilled Hatfield's last term of office, one bitter Tory backbencher summarized the electoral whitewash of 1987 thus: "The premier raped the principles and morals of the people of New Brunswick and they decided to do something about it."[13]

What, then, has been the impact of this political culture on the party politics of the region? Not surprisingly, the traditionalist orientations of Atlantic Canadians have served to maintain a traditional party system. Perhaps the most obvious manifestation of this phenomenon has been the stability and intensity of party attachments. Data from one study revealed that whereas 59 percent of Atlantic Canadians claim always to vote for the same party at federal elections, the comparable figure for other Canadians is only 45 percent.[14] In fact, party loyalties can seemingly become matters of heredity in the Atlantic provinces as entire families can remain either Liberal or Conservative for generations. Typifying this phenomenon is the Maritimer who said:

> Yes, we have been Liberals since before Confederation. . . . Well, it was something like your religion. It was emotion really. . . . We would feel that we would be disloyal. . . . It was a certain loyalty. I would feel that I was disloyal to Father. . . .[15]

A respondent to a questionnaire sent to delegates at the 1971 Nova Scotia Progressive Conservative leadership convention answered the question, "When did you become a member of the Progressive Conservative party?" with, "At conception."[16]

It is important to note, however, that at least at the elite level, Newfoundland constitutes an exception to the regional norm of stable party attachments. Some of the most prominent Newfoundland politicians of the modern era (including Leo Barry, Walter Carter, John Crosbie, William Rowe, Richard Cashin, Brian Peckford and Tom Rideout) have switched parties *after* entering public life. One Upper Canadian editorialist has sardonically noted not only that the Newfoundland "ship of state carries as many defectors as a Polish ocean liner," but also that "there is probably no more moving experience in politics than holding office in Newfoundland."[17]

It is clear that the region's traditionalist predispositions have undercut those parties which have periodically challenged the Grits and the Tories. Unlike in many other parts of Canada, third parties have found the political soil in Atlantic Canada to be extremely barren and strewn with rocks. PEI affords probably the most dramatic instance of this phenomenon. In this century, the only non-Liberal, non-Conservative elected to either federal or provincial office was J.A. Dewar, an independent MLA between 1919 and 1923. The New Democratic party and its predecessor, the CCF has never received more than 8 percent of the vote on the Island and in the 1989 provincial campaign obtained only 4 percent of the popular vote.

Third parties have been only slightly more successful in New Brunswick and Nova Scotia. In 1920 a temporary coalition of radical workers and reformist farmers managed to elect nine MLAs in New Brunswick and 11 in Nova Scotia, but dissension stemming from the perceived incompatibility of the component wings caused these movements to disintegrate quickly. Since that time, in New Brunswick both Social Credit and the Parti Acadien have made ineffective electoral forays. In 1978 the Parti Acadien captured 4.8 percent of the popular vote; however, as so often happens with third parties, the major parties moved quickly to answer the discontent which had given rise to the Parti Acadien. Hatfield's unprecedented victory, particularly in the Acadien constituencies in 1982, attested to the success of his attack on the root causes of Parti Acadien support; in the Liberal sweep of 1987, the Parti Acadien was not a factor. One must suspect that the Parti Acadien, if not dead, is at least comatose.

Only the New Democratic party and its predecessor, the Co-operative Commonwealth Federation, have made perceptible inroads into the support of the two traditional parties. In both New Brunswick and Nova Scotia, the CCF-NDP's share of the popular vote peaked initially at the end of World War II,[18] retreated through the 1950s and 1960s, and then rose to new highs in the late 1970s and early 1980s. Yet although the party did manage to win 16.2 percent of the popular vote in New Brunswick and 20.9 percent in Nova Scotia in the 1980 federal election, they won no seats in either province. By 1988 the NDP popular vote had fallen to 9.3 percent in New Brunswick and 11.4 in Nova Scotia. The bastion of CCF-NDP support in Nova Scotia had always been in industrial Cape Breton where they have elected federal and provincial members periodically since 1939, but none since 1981. In New Brunswick, on the other hand, the party has never elected a federal member and did not elect a provincial member until the 1982 success of Robert Hall in Tantramar. Hall's election can perhaps be credited more to his own personality and popularity than to any perceived attributes of his party. He was defeated in 1987. The NDP also won a second seat in a 1983 by-election but the member soon defected to the Liberals.

In Nova Scotia, the party has always been split between Cape Breton and the mainland. As David Lewis has written:

> One thing I learned from my many visits to Nova Scotia during the years following 1938 and 1939 was the difficulty in persuading the Cape Bretoner to accept a person from the Nova Scotia mainland as his spokesman.... The attitude of Cape Bretoners led to considerable difficulty in setting up a provincial headquarters, in appointing the occasional organizer, ... and in electing officers for the provincial party.[19]

This enmity between the two major geographic regions of Nova Scotia continues to the present day. In the 1981 provincial election, the NDP was for the first time able to elect a member on the mainland (though here again the circumstances were similar to those of New Brunswick, with the victory more attributable to the calibre of the candidate, provincial party leader Alexa McDonough, than to the party's programme). In the same election, however, the NDP lost its two seats in industrial Cape Breton. At the present time, the Nova Scotia NDP is still recovering from the 1980 expulsion of Paul McEwan, the MLA for Cape Breton-Nova Scotia since 1970. McEwan, a "maverick," charged that the NDP was being infiltrated by Trotsky-ites.[20] McEwan subsequently formed and then disbanded the Cape Breton Labour party. In the election of 1984 the CBLP received two percent of the popular vote, but in industrial Cape Breton it obtained twelve percent. McEwan was re-elected as an Independent in 1988 and has now joined the Liberals. The demise of the CBLP should have been an electoral blessing for the NDP in 1988. It was not, for in 1986 the Liberals selected Vince MacLean of Sydney as their new leader. In 1988, the Liberals swept all but two of the Cape Breton seats. The allure of a native son premier was stronger than party loyalty and once again the NDP were shut out in Cape Breton, running third in all their old strongholds. However, they managed to hold two of the three mainland seats they won in 1984, their share of the provincial popular vote rising from 15.9 to 16.1 percent.

Finally, despite their relatively recent integration into the Canadian political community and despite being without party politics during the 15 years of Commission government (i.e. under direct British control), Newfoundlanders have also rarely deserted the two traditional parties. At first, the basis of support for the two major parties revolved around the issue of Confederation. Those who supported Confederation joined J.R. Smallwood in the Liberal party and those who were opposed became members of the Progressive Conservative party. When the union with Canada proved to be an economic blessing, the Tories' initial anti-Confederation stance became a profound electoral hindrance. Over the years, those third parties which have challenged the dominance of the Liberals and Conservatives have been "fragment" parties,[21] originating not out of social protest, but rather out of conflict within the political elite. Hence, the United Newfoundland party, which won two seats in the 1959 provincial election, reflected a split in the Conservative caucus over the relative generosity to Newfoundland of the Diefenbaker administration in Ottawa and Diefenbaker's handling of a woodworkers' strike. Both the New Labrador Party, which won a single seat in the 1971 provincial election (holding the balance of power), and the Liberal Reform party, which won four seats in the 1975 provincial election, largely reflected splits over leadership within the Liberal caucus. The CCF-NDP has never been a strong force in provincial politics. It did not win its first seat until a 1984 by-election, and in 1986 gained a second seat in a subsequent by-election. However, they lost both in 1989 and saw their percentage of the popular vote drop by 10 percent from 1985 to just under 5 percent. The party has managed to win two federal by-elections (1978, 1987) but lost both seats shortly thereafter. In short, the distribution of party strength in Newfoundland bears a strong resemblance to that already observed in Nova Scotia, New Brunswick and Prince Edward Island; in all four provinces, the Liberals and Progressive Conservatives have been and continue to be the only serious contenders for political office.

It is tempting to ascribe the preference of Atlantic Canadians for the two traditional parties to the traditionalist orientations which have already been shown to exist in the region's political culture. A brief, pan-Canadian scrutiny of third parties suggests, however, that the cynicism of Atlantic Canadians is also significant. To understand the nature of Canadian third parties, two premises must be accepted: first, that national integration (in both its territorial and ethnic manifestations) constitutes the dominant sociopolitical cleavage of this country; and second, that the Liberals and Conservatives have not completely fulfilled the role of "brokerage parties" assigned to them in popular mythology. At times, the types of policy compromises required of brokerage politics have been logically impossible. How, one wonders, could all recognised interests have been successfully accommodated on such matters as the hanging of Louis Riel or the imposition of conscription? At other times, certain structural constraints (both economic and electoral) have strongly encouraged policy makers to discard the role of "honest broker." What is significant in the present context is that, when faced with such situations, both Liberal and Conservative administrations in Ottawa have generally favoured the interests of the heartland over the peripheries (in, for example, tariff, tax, transportation, budgetary and resource matters) and of anglophone Canada—at least until the 1970s—over francophone Canada (in, for example, the Riel Rebellion, a variety of educational disputes, two conscription crises and, most recently, the patriation of the Constitution). The result of these systemic biases has been latent resentment—in the peripheries against the heartland, and in francophone Canada against anglophone Canada. Such latent resentment constitutes one of the preconditions of successful third-party gestation in Canada.

One should not necessarily fault the national parties for their lack of interest in Atlantic Canada. When one looks at the number of seats available in the four Atlantic provinces (currently 32) and compares this with the number of seats available in the Golden Horseshoe around Lake Ontario and, furthermore, if one compares the traditional voting patterns of the residents of Atlantic Canada with those of the industrial heartland of Ontario, one can see why policies have not been developed to obtain electoral support in Atlantic Canada. To put it another way, representation by population in the House of Commons and the lack of an effective regional voice in the upper chamber have worked to the disadvantage of the region.

In any event, this latent resentment against the heartland does exist in Atlantic Canada. Irrespective of Confederation, the region's golden era of "wood, wind and water" would obviously not have outlasted the nineteenth century. Nevertheless, the union with the Canada's has been blamed (and not always inaccurately) for much of the Atlantic region's subsequent economic ills. Nova Scotia, for example, was considered by many to be a "have" province in 1867. Today, of course, it is labelled along with the rest of the region as a "have not" province. It is also true that Atlantic Canada has suffered from the lending policies of Canadian banks; that the region has received only a minimal return on its share of the investment to open up the West; that its industries, in the age of protectionism, were often unable to bear the high costs engendered by tariffs designed to protect central Canadian enterprise; that it was not compensated for the alienation of Dominion lands to Quebec, Ontario and Manitoba; and that it has been relatively disadvantaged in the disbursement of federal monies, and so on.[22] With the accumulation of these grievances has come a "huge reservoir of anti-Upper Canadian feeling which rests near the surface of the collective psyche of Nova Scotia" (and, one might add, of New Brunswick, Prince Edward Island and Newfoundland).[23]

But if Atlantic Canada has one of the two preconditions for successful third-party activity, it clearly lacks the other. In order to galvanize this "huge reservoir" of latent resentment into political action, people must have a high sense of either individual or regional efficacy. Yet, as was pointed out earlier, Atlantic Canadians have felt notoriously inefficacious; they have believed that neither individually nor collectively can they be politically influential at the national level. As a result, the region's latest resentment has not been tapped by protest parties; Atlantic Canada has remained a dispirited hinterland.

In any case, even where the two preconditions exist, there must be a precipitating factor for the formation of a successful third party. That is to say, there must be some crisis, strain or dislocation (however elastically defined)[24] to catalyze the latent resentment and the high feeling of efficacy into third-party activity. In Atlantic Canada there have been remarkably few such dislocations. The contrast between the wild fluctuations in the economic health of western Canada and the relative stagnation of the Atlantic Canadian economy is particularly instructive. Uncertainty, rising expectations and relative deprivation are all far more likely to engender some form of "strain" than a grinding and omnipresent poverty. In short, not only does Atlantic Canada lack one of the two preconditions for successful third-party activity, it may also lack that seemingly most common of political phenomena—a precipitating factor.[25]

Yet even if the Liberals and Conservatives continue to dominate Atlantic Canadian politics, the relative strength of these two parties has changed over time. Residents of the Atlantic region have shown a historic preference for the Liberal party; twentieth century provincial election results across the region reveal that the Liberals have held office over 60 percent of the time. Nevertheless, after the mid-1950s there was a resurgence in the strength of the Progressive Conservative party so that, during the mid-1980s, there were Conservative administrations in all four provincial capitals. Although three of these governments have since returned to the Liberal fold, the result of this perceptible shift in voter allegiance over the past three decades has been to transform the region from one which might have been categorized as one-party dominant to one in which there are now two equally prepared competing political parties.

Because the level of party system symmetry is so high in Atlantic Canada (that is to say, because the Liberals and Conservatives are still dominant at both levels), the region's political parties are far more integrated than are those found in the remainder of the country. For both the provincial and national wings of the two major parties, the same organization is responsible for raising funds, recruiting candidates, fighting elections and so on.[26] As a result, provincial administrations pay close heed to the results of federal campaigns and it is instructive that many observers regard the 1968 setback of the federal Liberals in Newfoundland as the beginning of the end for J.R. Smallwood's provincial Liberal government.[27] As both a cause and a consequence of this relatively high degree of party integration across levels of government, voters in Atlantic Canada are far more likely than their counterparts in the rest of Canada to support the same party in both federal and provincial politics. One recent study of Canadian partisanship revealed that while 86 percent of Atlantic Canadians are consistent identifiers across the two levels, the corresponding figure for the other six provinces is only 65 percent.[28]

Even if it may be losing some of its importance as an electoral determinant, the region's traditionalism is also apparent in the lingering impact of religion. It is not a coincidence, for example, that the Halifax-Cornwallis provincial constituency has elected only one Protestant (George Mitchell, 1970–1978). In fact, the Smallwood government kept sectarianism alive with elaborate religious gerrymanders and with promises to maintain Protestant denominational schools.[29] The religious cleavage was also institutionalized in Prince Edward Island, where for many decades, the two parties would run one Roman Catholic and one Protestant candidate in nine of the 15 dual-member ridings, and two Protestants in each of the other six constituencies. The result was that, irrespective of its partisan composition, the provincial Legislature would contain 21 Protestants and nine Roman Catholics. In fact, in the 1986 provincial election, Liberal candidate Michael Gallant was prevented by his party from challenging the "Protestant" nominee on the Tory ticket because, although he was divorced and had not been to church in a decade, he had a "Catholic" name! As Gallant complained: "It's bizarre, it's Stone Age, but it's true."[30] Whether such norms have served to perpetuate or defuse the religious cleavage is unclear, but concern over sectarian tensions was sufficient to ensure that clergymen were banned from elected office in the province until 1967.[31]

Finally, Atlantic Canada's traditionalism is manifested in the overwhelming preponderance of white males in the party élites. The region has been particularly slow to accept women in politics. For example, Nova Scotia has only had a single woman Cabinet minister, while Prince Edward Island waited until 1970 to elect its first female to the Legislature. Politics remains such a male bastion in the region that one prominent Nova Scotia Conservative spoke out strongly within party circles against running women in the 1981 provincial election. Similarly, the black and Native populations have not been successful in having members of their groups elected to the provincial Legislatures. It is true that there have been black and Native candidates, but they have usually run for the New Democratic party and thus have suffered the same fate as has the party generally.

Cynicism is also readily apparent in the region's party system. In particular, despite their aforementioned lack of political trust, the historically low feeling of efficacy among Atlantic Canadians has permitted the many oligarchical features of the region's party politics to go unchallenged. The role and function of the party leader has always been of great importance in all four provinces. Writing of Nova Scotia and Robert Stanfield, Dalton Camp stated:

> In Nova Scotia, politicians are either looked up to or looked down upon, and it was clear that most Nova Scotians looked up to Robert Stanfield. They admired his calm, and they respected him for his presumed financial independence—for they felt that a man's honesty was assured if he was rich in the first place, and thus more likely beyond temptation. And they liked Stanfield's plain, unostentatious manner. The quality of the chieftain matters a good deal to Nova Scotians.[32]

Such successful politicians as Angus L. Macdonald, Louis Robichaud, J.B. McNair, Alex Campbell, and J.R. Smallwood all exhibited these qualities and were consequently able to influence election results by their personal popularity. Nova Scotians in particular have a tendency to loathe an opposition leader until he becomes premier, when of course he is lionized as having chieftain qualities. Once again, Stanfield was an example, as was John Buchanan until just before the end of his tenure as premier.

Certainly, the position of the party leader and other senior members of the party is more exalted in Atlantic Canada than in other areas of the country. It has been alleged, for example, that nominating conventions in New Brunswick are of only ritualistic import, with the victorious candidate having already been ordained by the party leader.[33] Moreover, the Nova Scotia Conservatives did not even have a party constitution until 1975, while the Newfoundland Liberals lacked even the most rudimentary elements of a formal party organization until the late 1960s.[34] In fact, with the partial exception of Prince Edward Island, where delegates to the Conservative and Liberal conventions each number in excess of 1500, surveys conducted at leadership contests in the region have revealed that the party rank and file have exceptionally little opportunity to participate in meaningful party dialogue.[35] Finally, it has proven to be very difficult for political newcomers to rise quickly in these cadre parties; rather, they are expected to go through the normal channels and climb the ladder as did their elders.

Their approach to the electoral process also reveals the cynical orientations of Atlantic Canadians. Elections are not designed to provide the voter with a choice between competing world views; on the contrary, provincial party platforms are "remarkable more for their similarities than their differences."[36] At the outset of the 1984 provincial campaign, Premier Buchanan of Nova Scotia announced that "I don't believe elections should be fought on issues";[37] two weeks later he made the equally extraordinary assertion that "I don't think political parties should run on their records."[38] Perhaps not surprisingly, voters in Atlantic Canada have been found to be much less likely than their counterparts in the rest of the country to have an "issue" basis for their selection.[39] Why, therefore, do Atlantic Canadians still continue to invest such heavy resources in the political game? Why do they continue to participate in politics more extensively than other Canadians? Part of the answer lies in the age-old practice of patronage.

Two types of patronage are apparent. The first concerns jobs and services (such as road-paving) for the friends of the party, while the second is the use of money and rum on election day. With respect to the first, it is perhaps no worse than that which exists in other provinces, except that in Atlantic Canada it is an openly accepted part of the political process. Hence, former Newfoundland Premier Brian Peckford once acknowledged that since he was "living in the real world," he was not "squeaky clean" on patronage,[40] while New Brunswick Premier Frank McKenna recently asserted that "patronage is a way of life" in his province.[41] Because of the relative smallness of the population of the four provinces, patronage is much more noticeable than it would be in a larger province. Also, at least in the recent past, governments tend to change frequently in these four provinces and when they do, the friends of one party are replaced by the friends of the other. Hence, at the 1978 Prince Edward Island Liberal leadership convention Premier Bennett Campbell's floor demonstration was led by two patronage-appointed provincial employees; one drove a school bus and the second operated a snow-plough. In fact, in the 1981 provincial election the Conservative member for Hants East, Nova Scotia, was defeated by members of his own party because he had refused to fire the Liberal-appointed highway workers. Voters in this constituency had to witness the ludicrous situation of a former Conservative member working to defeat an incumbent Conservative. In other words, party members expect to receive the spoils of office.

There has been little attempt by any of the political parties to come to grips with patronage. In part, this reflects the region's poverty; it has been persuasively argued that in an expanding economy, governments are more likely to concentrate on production, while in a stagnant economy, they turn to "parasitism."[42] Nevertheless, one cannot ignore the reciprocal relationship that exists between cynicism in the political culture and corruption in the party system; as a *Toronto Daily Star* reporter noted in 1967:

It does not matter much whether the stories of election bribery, corruption, and patronage that one hears everywhere are true or not, the fact is the people believe them and there is this universal cynicism about all things political in this area of Atlantic Canada.[43]

As for election day "treating" as it is described, an effort was made, particularly in the late 1960s and early 1970s, to stamp out these practices. The catalyst for this move was another article in the *Toronto Daily Star* which was entitled, "Dollars and Rum Still Buy Votes in Nova Scotia." In that article, the reporter quoted now Senator Findlay Macdonald:

It is a practice . . . which will be followed by all three political parties. It is also a practice that should of course be stopped and one that Stanfield is doing his best to end. But it's a part of the political scene here and we have to do it because the others will even if we don't. And it probably works out pretty even in the end anyway.[44]

The upshot of these two articles (note that the paper which raised the issue was not one in the region) was the appointment of a Royal Commission and subsequent legislation to reform the Nova Scotia political system. Yet such legislation, both in Nova Scotia and elsewhere in Atlantic Canada, may have had relatively little impact on the region's political practices. A few party workers have actually been convicted of vote-buying in the 1980s,[45] but it is possible that the vast majority of such occurrences go undetected (especially the practice of bribing probable opponents not even to go to the polls). In short, while there is some evidence to the contrary,[46] many continue to echo the words of the premier of Prince Edward Island, Donald Farquharson, who observed in 1900 that "it is simply a matter now of who will buy the most votes and the man who works hardest and is prepared to use means fair or foul will get in."[47]

Those who decry these practices (and most of them are in academia) are criticized for not understanding this system and for being naive about the political process.[48] Furthermore, Atlantic Canadians wonder whether it has been any worse to buy votes with rum and money than to promise new highways, bridges, school cafeterias, oil sands plants and hockey rinks. They, of course, have a point; bribery at election time has always existed in one form or another throughout the country.

What, then, can one conclude about politics in Atlantic Canada? Politics in Atlantic Canada has a greater social significance than is found in the rest of the country; indeed, one might refer to politics as "the national sport" of Atlantic Canada. Furthermore, as befits a dependent hinterland, parties are more closely aligned to their federal counterparts than is the case in other regions of the country. One also notes that only the two old-line cadre parties have been successful in Atlantic Canada. Finally, one can detect not only extensive patronage and corruption, but also, notwithstanding the current RCMP investigation of the Nova Scotia Conservative government, an apparent lack of will to reform and cleanse the political process. In short, Atlantic Canada's traditionalist and cynical political culture (the existence of which was earlier inferred from indicators not directly related to the operation of political parties) is clearly reflected in the region's party system.

Nevertheless, there is reason to suspect that Atlantic Canadian party politics will be somewhat less distinctive in future years. While the national election surveys of 1965, 1968 and 1974 uncovered clear regional differences with respect to political trust and political efficacy (with Atlantic Canadians scoring significantly lower than the national norm), these discrepancies disappeared in the surveys of 1979 and 1984. Although some lag time is likely, eventually political practices should reflect this attitudinal convergence. On some dimensions, the change is already apparent. Pollsters for the New Brunswick Liberals altered their strategy in the 1987 provincial campaign after discovering a significant generational cleavage in the electorate. In clear contrast to their elders, the under-40 New Brunswick voters did not differ by ethnicity and had no strong partisan ties.[49] Moreover, Atlantic Canadians are apparently becoming less concerned with maintaining friendly relations with the national government. Three of the region's four Conservative provincial governments have been defeated since 1984, when Brian Mulroney first assumed office in Ottawa. The case of Prince Edward Island is particularly instructive in this context. In 15 consecutive campaigns between 1927 and 1979, Islanders ensured that their provincial governments would be the same partisan stripe as the government in Ottawa; the likelihood that this occurred randomly (that is, independently of any inter-level effects) is just under one in 33,000.[50] The provincial elections of 1982, 1986 and 1989, however, all deviated from this established tendency; Islanders, it would seem, have belatedly discovered the joys of "fed-bashing."[51] In short, while Atlantic Canadian party politics remain distinguishable from those elsewhere in the country, those wishing to book passage to the mysterious east should not tarry unduly.

ENDNOTES

1. Dalton M. Camp, *Gentlemen, Players and Politicians* (Ottawa: Deneau, 1979), p. 284.
2. For a discussion of the cultural impact of one such provincial boundary, see Ian Stewart, "More Than Just a Line on the Map: The Political Culture of the Nova Scotia-New Brunswick Boundary," *Publius*, Vol. 20 (Winter 1990), pp. 99–111.
3. It has been demonstrated that, at least for Nova Scotia, out-migrants come disproportionately from the more educated sector of the community. See J.R. Winter, *Net Migration Rates by County for the Maritime Provinces* (Wolfville: Acadia University, 1970), p. 78.
4. David Bellamy, "The Atlantic Provinces," in David J. Bellamy, Jon H. Pammett, and Donald C. Rowat, eds., *The Provincial Political Systems: Comparative Essays* (Toronto: Methuen, 1976), p. 3.
5. Dale H. Poel, "The Diffusion of Legislation Among the Canadian Provinces: A Statistical Analysis," *Canadian Journal of Political Science*, Vol. 9 (1976), pp. 605–626.
6. See, for example, Marsha A. Chandler and William M. Chandler, *Public Policy and Provincial Politics* (Toronto: McGraw-Hill Ryerson, 1979), p. 193.

7. Richard Simeon and Donald E. Blake, "Regional Preferences: Citizens' Views of Public Policy," in David J. Elkins and Richard Simeon, eds., *Small Worlds: Provinces and Parties in Canadian Political Life* (Toronto: Methuen, 1960), pp. 84–103.

8. Prince Edward Island even banned automobiles in 1908; eventually, they were permitted on the Island, but those in operation had to be preceded by an individual on foot carrying a red flag! See Marlene-Russell Clark, "Island Politics," in Francis W.P. Bolger, ed., *Canada's Smallest Province: A History of P.E.I.* (Charlottetown: The Prince Edward Island 1973 Centennial Commission, 1973), p. 319.

9. Alan Gregg and Michael Whittington, "Regional Variation in Children's Political Attitudes," in Bellamy, Pammett, and Rowat, eds., *The Provincial Political Systems*, pp. 76–85.

10. See, for example, Allan Kornberg, William Mishler, and Harold D. Clarke, *Representative Democracy in the Canadian Provinces* (Scarborough: Prentice-Hall Canada, 1982), pp. 99–103.

11. See Kornberg, Mishler, and Clarke, p. 80, and especially, Richard Simeon and David J. Elkins, "Provincial Political Culture in Canada," in Elkins and Simeon, eds., *Small Worlds*, p. 346.

12. J. Murray Beck, "Elections in the Maritimes: The Votes Against Have It," *Commentator*, Vol. 17 (Dec. 1970), p. 7. One recent survey discovered that although Maritimers are generally cynical, this is especially noticeable with respect to Nova Scotians. See *The Halifax Chronicle-Herald*, 16 February 1989, pp. 1–2.

13. *The Vancouver Sun*, 15 October 1987, p. B1.

14. Mildred A. Schwartz, *Politics and Territory: The Sociology of Regional Persistence in Canada* (Montreal: McGill-Queen's University Press, 1974), p. 148.

15. D. Campbell and R.A. MacLean, *Beyond the Atlantic Roar: A Study of the Nova Scotia Scots* (Toronto: Macmillan, 1974), p. 236.

16. Agar Adamson, "The Nova Scotia Progressive Conservative Leadership Convention: How Representative?", paper presented to the annual meeting of the Canadian Political Science Association, 1972.

17. *The (Toronto) Globe and Mail*, 20 February 1985, p. 6.

18. Despite electing only two MLAs, the CCF even constituted Nova Scotia's official opposition after the 1945 provincial election.

19. David Lewis, *The Good Fight* (Toronto: Macmillan of Canada, 1981), p.160.

20. For details on this rift in the Nova Scotia NDP, see Agar Adamson, "Does MacEwan's Real Ale Give the NDP Heartburn?", paper presented to the 11th annual meeting of the Atlantic Provinces Political Studies Association, 1985.

21. See John McMenemy, "Fragment and Movement Parties," in Conrad Winn and John McMenemy, eds., *Political Parties in Canada* (Toronto: McGraw-Hill Ryerson, 1976), pp. 29–48.

22. See Bruce Archibald, "Atlantic Regional Underdevelopment and Socialism," in Laurier LaPierre, Jack McLeod, Charles Taylor, and Walter Young, eds., *Essays on the Left* (Toronto: McClelland and Stewart, 1971), pp. 109–111; and David Alexander, "New Notions of Happiness: Nationalism, Regionalism, and Atlantic Canada," *Journal of Canadian Studies*, Vol. 15, No. 2 (1980), p. 36.

23. G.A. Rawlyk, "The Farm-Labour Movement and the Failure of Socialism in Nova Scotia," in LaPierre, McLeod, Taylor and Young, p. 37.

24. For an example of employing "strain" as an explanatory variable without first defining its meaning, see Maurice Pinard, *The Rise of a Third Party: A Study in Crisis Politics* (Englewood Cliffs: Prentice-Hall, 1975).

25. Because the preconditions to successful third-party gestation exist only in Quebec and the West, these two regions have historically been the most politically turbulent in Canada. From the former have come the Nationalistes, the Union Nationale, and the Parti Quebecois; from the latter have emerged the Progressives, the CCF-NDP, and Social Credit. In all cases, it is an easy, but relatively unrewarding, task to discover the dislocation which precipitated their emergence.

26. For a more detailed discussion of relations between the federal and provincial wings of the major parties, see Rand Dyck, *Provincial Politics in Canada* (Scarborough: Prentice-Hall Canada, 1986), pp. 71, 95–96. A former co-chairman of the Liberal national campaign and principal secretary to Premier Gerald Reagan, Senator Michael Kirby recently confirmed the closeness of federal-provincial party links in the Atlantic region (interview, March 1989).

27. See, for example, Peter Neary, "Politics in Newfoundland: The End of the Smallwood Era," *Journal of Canadian Studies*, Vol. 7, No. 1 (1972), pp. 9–16. One might similarly argue that the 1988 defeat of the federal Conservatives in Newfoundland signalled the downfall of their provincial counterparts six months later.

28. Harold D. Clarke, Jane Jenson, Lawrence LeDuc, and Jon H. Pammett, *Political Choice in Canada* (Toronto: McGraw-Hill Ryerson, 1980), p. 97. See also Schwartz, pp. 154–155.

29. See Peter Neary, "Democracy in Newfoundland: A Comment," *Journal of Canadian Studies*, Vol. 4, No. 1 (1969), pp. 37–45. Smallwood's open support for Protestant groups, in conjunction with the St. John's-Outport cleavage at the time of Confederation, has meant that the Progressive Conservative party of Newfoundland, like that in P.E.I., but unlike those in the other eight provinces, has historically received the support of Roman Catholics.

30. *The (Toronto) Globe and Mail*, 5 April 1986, p. A8.

31. See Clarke, pp. 299–301. It is also interesting to note that denominational schools were the catalyst for Prince Edward Island's only coalition administration (1876–1879) in which Protestants from both parties formed the government with the Roman Catholics from both parties in opposition.

32. Camp, p. 213.

33. P.J. Fitzpatrick, "New Brunswick: The Politics of Pragmatism," in Martin Robin, ed., *Canadian Provincial Politics*, 2nd ed. (Scarborough: Prentice-Hall Canada, 1978), p. 124.

34. See S.J.R. Noel, *Politics in Newfoundland* (Toronto: University of Toronto Press, 1971), pp. 283–285; and George Perlin, "Patronage and Paternalism: Politics in Newfoundland," in D.I. Davies and Kathleen Herman, eds., *Social Space: Canadian Perspectives* (Toronto: New Press, 1971), pp. 192–194.

35. Agar Adamson and Marshall W. Conley, data from unpublished leadership delegate surveys.

36. Hugh G. Thorburn, *Politics in New Brunswick* (Toronto: University of Toronto Press, 1961), p. 114. Nevertheless, one should note the existence of the Red Tory phenomenon. Such people as Robert Stanfield, Gordon Fairweather, and David MacDonald historically ensured that the Conservative party in the Atlantic provinces would remain to the left of its counterparts in the rest of the country. Flora MacDonald once summarized her belief in Red Toryism when she stated: "I could bring myself to vote for an NDP candidate, but I never vote for a Liberal." (In an address to students at Acadia University, 1976).

37. *The (Toronto) Globe and Mail*, 3 October 1984, p. 5.

38. *The (Toronto) Globe and Mail,* 10 October 1984, p. 5. In a similar vein, Newfoundland premier Clyde Wells refused to discuss policy matters in the period before the Liberal convention at which he was elected leader. *The (Toronto) Globe and Mail,* 6 June 1987, p. A6. Buchanan has not changed his views on campaigning. In 1988 he refused to unveil a campaign platform, but rather from time to time "released details of 'renewable ideas' focusing on education, business, industry and social issues." He also refused to run on his record (*Halifax Chronicle-Herald,* 4 August 1988, p. 1).

39. Kornberg, Mishler and Clarke, p. 124.

40. *The (Toronto) Globe and Mail,* 2 January 1986, p. A4.

41. *The (Toronto) Globe and Mail,* 1 September 1987, p. A10.

42. Ralph Matthews, "Perspectives on Recent Newfoundland Politics," *Journal of Canadian Studies,* Vol. 9 (1974), pp. 20–35.

43. The *Toronto Star,* 29 May 1967.

44. The *Toronto Star,* 26 May 1967.

45. See, for example, *The (Toronto) Globe and Mail,* 27 November 1984, p. 5 and *The (Toronto) Globe and Mail,* 7 April 1989, p. A5.

46. See, for example, Ian Stewart, "On Faith Alone: Petty Electoral Corruption on Prince Edward Island," a paper presented to the annual meeting of the Atlantic Provinces Political Science Association, 1990.

47. Wayne E. MacKinnon, *The Life of the Party* (Summerside: Prince Edward Island Liberal Party, 1973), p. 73.

48. This conforms with Kenneth Gibbons' speculation that the dominant orientation of Atlantic Canadians towards political corruption is one of "blamelessness." See Kenneth M. Gibbons, "The Political Culture of Corruption in Canada," in Kenneth M. Gibbons and Donald C. Rowat, eds., *Political Corruption in Canada: Cases, Causes, and Cures* (Toronto: Macmillan, 1976), pp. 231–250.

49. *The Vancouver Sun,* 17 October 1987, p. B2. Following the October 1987 provincial election, the Confederation of Regions party (COR) has begun operating in New Brunswick, particularly at the provincial level. COR's strength amongst unilingual anglophones could hurt the Conservatives in southwestern New Brunswick, which historically has been their bailiwick.

50. Ian Stewart, "Friends at Court: Federalism and Provincial Elections on Prince Edward Island," *Canadian Journal of Political Science,* Vol. 19 (1986), pp. 127–150.

51. One might also note that certain "modern" issues have recently forced their way on to the region's political agenda. During the 1988 provincial campaign, Nova Scotia Premier John Buchanan emphatically stressed his concern for environmental issues, while in the 1986 PEI campaign, Jim Lee was widely perceived to have bungled the issue of equal pay for work of equal value (which he dismissed as merely "something fashionable"). See *Maclean's,* 5 May 1986, p. 14.

Federal Election Results 1878–1988

APPENDIX A

I am indebted to Professor Howard A. Scarrow who provided most of the data that follow[1]. The results after and including 1962 are taken from the preliminary results issued by the Chief Electoral Officer and published in the daily press. The information relating to the distribution of seats is taken from the Canadian Press summary. The papers from which the results are cited are the *Toronto Daily Star* and the Kingston *Whig-Standard*. The results of 1988 were supplied by the Chief Electoral Officer of Canada.

NEWFOUNDLAND

Election Year	Party Forming Federal Government	Total Seats	Conservative Seats	Conservative Votes (%)	Liberal Seats	Liberal Votes (%)	Other Seats	Other Votes (%)
1949	Lib.	7	2	28	5	72		
1953	Lib.	7	0	28	7	67		5[1]
1957	Con.	7	2	38	5	62		
1958	Con.	7	2	45	5	54		1
1962	Con.	7	1	36	6	59		5[2]
1963	Lib.	7	0	30	7	65		5[3]
1965	Lib.	7	0	32	7	64		4[4]
1968	Lib.	7	6	53	1	42		4[5]
1972	Lib.	7	4	49	3	45		5[6]
1974	Lib.	7	3	44	4	47		10[7]
1979	Con.	7	2	31	4	38	1	31[8]
1980	Lib.	7	2	36	5	47		17[9]
1984	Con.	7	4	57	3	36		6[10]
1988	Con.	7	2	42	5	45		13[11]

1. Including 4 percent CCF.
2. Including 5 percent NDP.
3. Including 4 percent NDP.
4. Including 1 percent NDP and 2 percent Social Credit.
5. Including 4 percent NDP.

6. Including 5 percent NDP.
7. Including 10 percent NDP.
8. Including 31 percent NDP.
9. Including 17 percent NDP.
10. Including 6 percent NDP.
11. Including 12 percent NDP.

ENDNOTE

1. Complete details can be found in his book *Canada Votes: A Handbook of Federal and Provincial Election Data* (New Orleans: Hauser Press, 1962).

NOVA SCOTIA

Election Year	Party Forming Federal Government	Total Seats	Conservative Seats	Conservative Votes (%)	Liberal Seats	Liberal Votes (%)	CCF-NDP Seats	CCF-NDP Votes (%)	Other Seats	Other Votes (%)
1878	Con.	21	14	52	6	44			1	4
1882	Con.	21	14	55	7	45				
1887	Con.	21	14	50	7	47				3
1891	Con.	21	16	54	5	45				1
1896	Lib.	20	10	50	10	49				1
1900	Lib.	20	5	48	15	52				
1904	Lib.	18	0	44	18	55				1
1908	Lib.	18	6	49	12	51				
1911	Con.	18	9	49	9	51				
1917	Con.[1]	16	12[2]	48	4	46				6
1921	Lib.	16	0	32	16	53				15
1925	Lib.	14	11	56	3	42				2
1926	Lib.	14	12	54	2	43				3
1930	Con.	14	10	53	4	47				
1935	Lib.	12	0	32	12	52				16
1940	Lib.	12	1	40	10	51	1	6		3
1945	Lib.	12	2	37	9	46	1	17		
1949	Lib.	13	2	37	10	53	1	10		
1953	Lib.	12	1	40	10	53	1	7		
1957	Con.	12	10	50	2	45	0	5		
1958	Con.	12	12	57	0	38	0	5		
1962	Con.	12	9	47	2	42	1	10		1
1963	Lib.	12	7	47	5	47	0	6		
1965	Lib.	12	10	49	2	42	0	9		
1968	Lib.	11	10	55	1	38	0	7		
1972	Lib.	11	10	53	1	34	0	12		
1974	Lib.	11	8	48	2	41	1	11		
1979	Con.	11	8	45	2	36	1	19		
1980	Lib.	11	6	39	5	40	0	21		
1984	Con.	11	9	51	2	33	0	15		
1988	Con.	11	5	41	6	47	0	11		1

1. Wartime Coalition.
2. Including three Liberal Unionists.

NEW BRUNSWICK

Election Year	Party Forming Federal Government	Total Seats	Conservative Seats	Conservative Votes (%)	Liberal Seats	Liberal Votes (%)	Other Seats	Other Votes (%)
1878	Con.	16	5	45	11	55		
1882	Con.	16	9	55	7	45		
1887	Con.	16	10	51	6	49		
1891	Con.	16	13	59	3	38		3
1896	Lib.	14	9	49	5	44		7
1900	Lib.	14	5	48	9	52		
1904	Lib.	13	6	49	7	51		
1908	Lib.	13	2	46	11	54		
1911	Con.	13	5	49	8	51		
1917	Con.	11	7[1]	59	4	41		
1921	Lib.	11	5	39	5	50	1[2]	11
1925	Lib.	11	10	60	1	40		
1926	Lib.	11	7	54	4	46		
1930	Con.	11	10	59	1	41		
1935	Lib.	10	1	32	9	57		11
1940	Lib.	10	5	43	5	55		2
1945	Lib.	10	3	38	7	50		12
1949	Lib.	10	2	39	8	54		7
1953	Lib.	10	3	42	7	53		5
1957	Con.	10	5	49	5	48		3
1958	Con.	10	7	54	3	43		3
1962	Con.	10	4	46	6	45		9[3]
1963	Lib.	10	4	40	6	47		13[4]
1965	Lib.	10	4	43	6	47		9[5]
1968	Lib.	10	5	50	5	44		6[6]
1972	Lib.	10	5	45	5	43		11[7]
1974	Lib.	10	3	33	6	47	1	20[8]
1979	Con.	10	4	40	6	45		15
1980	Lib.	10	3	33	7	50		17[9]
1984	Con.	10	9	53	1	32		15[10]
1988	Con.	10	5	40	5	45		15[11]

1. Including four Liberal Unionists.
2. Progressive.
3. Including 5 percent NDP and 5 percent Social Credit.
4. Including 4 percent NDP and 9 percent Social Credit.
5. Including 9 percent NDP.
6. Including 5 percent NDP and 1 percent Social Credit.
7. Including 6 percent NDP and 6 percent Social Credit.
8. Including 9 percent NDP, 8 percent independent and 3 percent Social Credit.
9. Including 16 percent NDP.
10. Including 14 percent NDP.
11. Including 9 percent NDP.

PRINCE EDWARD ISLAND

Election Year	Party Forming Federal Government	Total Seats	Conservative Seats	Conservative Votes (%)	Liberal Seats	Liberal Votes (%)	Other Seats	Other Votes (%)
1878	Con.	6	5	57	1	43		
1882	Con.	6	1	48	5	52		
1887	Con.	6	0	46	6	54		
1891	Con.	6	2	48	4	52		
1896	Lib.	5	3	49	2	51		
1900	Lib.	5	2	48	3	52		
1904	Lib.	4	3	51	1	49		
1908	Lib.	4	1	50	3	50		
1911	Con.	4	2	51	2	49		
1917	Con.[1]	4	2	50	2	50		
1921	Lib.	4	0	37	4	46		17[2]
1925	Lib.	4	2	48	2	52		
1926	Lib.	4	1	47	3	53		
1930	Con.	4	3	50	1	50		
1935	Lib.	4	0	39	4	58		3[3]
1940	Lib.	4	0	45	4	55		
1945	Lib.	4	1	47	3	49		4[4]
1949	Lib.	4	1	48	3	49		3[5]
1953	Lib.	4	1	48	3	51		1
1957	Con.	4	4	52	0	47		1
1958	Con.	4	4	62	0	38		
1962	Con.	4	4	51	0	44		5[6]
1963	Lib.	4	2	51	2	47		2[7]
1965	Lib.	4	4	54	0	44		2[8]
1968	Lib.	4	4	52	0	45		3[9]
1972	Lib.	4	3	52	1	41		8[10]
1974	Lib.	4	3	49	1	46		5[11]
1979	Con.	4	4	53	0	40		7[12]
1980	Lib.	4	2	46	2	47		7[13]
1984	Con.	4	3	52	1	41		7[14]
1988	Con.	4	0	41	4	50		9[15]

1. Wartime Coalition.
2. Including 12 percent Progressive.
3. Including 3 percent Reconstruction party.
4. Including 4 percent CCF.
5. Including 2 percent CCF.
6. Including 5 percent NDP.
7. Including 2 percent NDP.
8. Including 2 percent NDP.
9. Including 3 percent NDP.
10. Including 8 percent NDP.
11. Including 5 percent NDP.
12. Including 7 percent NDP.
13. Including 7 percent NDP.
14. Including 7 percent NDP.
15. Including 7 percent NDP.

QUEBEC

Election Year	Party Forming Federal Government	Total Seats	Conservative Seats	Conservative Votes (%)	Liberal Seats	Liberal Votes (%)	Other Seats	Other Votes (%)
1878	Con.	65	45	56	20	40		4
1882	Con.	65	52	59	13	41		
1887	Con.	65	36	51	29	49		
1891	Con.	65	29	52	34	45		3
1896	Lib.	65	16	46	49	54		
1900	Lib.	65	8	44	57	56		
1904	Lib.	65	11	43	54	56		1
1908	Lib.	65	11	41	54	57		2
1911	Con.	65	27	49	38	51		
1917	Con.[1]	65	3[2]	25	62	73		2
1921	Lib.	65	0	18	65	70		12
1925	Lib.	65	4	34	59	59	2	7
1926	Lib.	65	4	34	60	62	1	4
1930	Con.	65	24	45	40	53	1	2
1935	Lib.	65	5	28	55	54	5	18[3]
1940	Lib.	65	1[5]	20	61	63	3[4]	17
1945	Lib.	65	2[7]	8	53	51	10[6]	41
1949	Lib.	73	2	25	68	60	3	15
1953	Lib.	75	4	29	66	61	5[8]	10
1957	Con.	75	9	31	62	58	4[9]	11
1958	Con.	75	50	50	25	46		4
1962	Con.	75	14	30	35	40	26[11]	30[10]
1963	Lib.	75	8	20	47	46	20[11]	34[12]
1965	Lib.	75	8	21	56	46	11[13]	33[14]
1968	Lib.	74	4	21	56	53	14	26[15]
1972	Lib.	74	2	17	56	49	16[17]	34[16]
1974	Lib.	74	3	21	60	54	11[19]	25[18]
1979	Con.	75	2	13	67	62	6[21]	25[20]
1980	Lib.	75	1	13	73	70		17
1984	Con.	75	58	50	17	35		15[22]
1988	Con.	75	63	53	12	30		17[23]

1. Wartime Coalition.
2. Including one Liberal Unionist.
3. Including 9 percent cast for Reconstruction party.
4. Independent Liberals.
5. Independent Conservative.
6. Six Independents, one Independent Liberal, two Bloc Populaire Canadien, one Labour Progressive.
7. Including one Independent Conservative.
8. Three Independents and two Independent Liberals.
9. Two Independents and two Independent Liberals.
10. Including 26 percent Social Credit and 4 percent NDP.
11. Social Credit.
12. Including 27 percent Social Credit and 7 percent NDP.
13. Including nine Créditistes, one Independent Progressive Conservative and one Independent.
14. Including 18 percent Créditiste and 12 percent NDP.
15. Including 16 percent Créditiste and 8 percent NDP.
16. Including 24 percent Social Credit and 6 percent NDP.
17. Including 15 Social Credit and 1 Independent.
18. Including 17 percent Social Credit and 7 percent NDP.
19. Social Credit.
20. Including 16 percent Social Credit and 5 percent NDP.
21. Social Credit.
22. Including 9 percent NDP and 2 percent Parti nationaliste du Québec.
23. Including 14 percent NDP and 1 percent Rhinoceros party.

ONTARIO

Election Year	Party Forming Federal Government	Total Seats	Conservative Seats	Conservative Votes (%)	Liberal Seats	Liberal Votes (%)	Progressive Seats	Progressive Votes (%)	CCF-NDP Seats	CCF-NDP Votes (%)	Other Seats	Other Votes (%)
1878	Con.	88	62	52	26	47						1
1882	Con.	92	54	51	38	49						
1887	Con.	92	54	51	38	49						
1891	Con.	92	48	49	44	49						2
1896	Lib.	92	43	45	43	40					6[1]	15
1900	Lib.	92	56	50	36	50						
1904	Lib.	86	48	50	38	50						
1908	Lib.	86	48	51	37[2]	47					1[3]	2
1911	Con.	86	73[4]	56	13	43						1
1917	Con.	82	74[5]	62	8	34						4
1921	Lib.	82	37	39	21	30	24	28				3
1925	Lib.	82	68	57	11	31	2	9			1[6]	3
1926	Lib.	82	53	54	26[7]	39	2	4			1[8]	3
1930	Con.	82	59	54	22	44	1	1				1
1935	Lib.	82	25	35	56	43					1[9]	22[10]
1940	Lib.	82	25	43	57[11]	51						6
1945	Lib.	82	48	42	34	41				14		3
1949	Lib.	83	25	37	56	46			1	15	1[12]	2
1953	Lib.	85	33	40	51	47			1	11		2
1957	Con.	85	61	49	21	37			3	12		2
1958	Con.	85	67	56	15	33			3	11		
1962	Con.	85	35	39	44	42			6	17		2
1963	Lib.	85	27	35	52	46			6	16		3[13]
1965	Lib.	85	25	34	51	44			9	22		
1968	Lib.	88	17	32	64	46			6	21	1	1
1972	Lib.	88	40	39	36	38			11	22		1
1974	Lib.	88	25	35	55	45			8	19		1
1979	Con.	95	57	42	32	37			6	21		1
1980	Lib.	95	38	36	52	42			5	22	0	7
1984	Con.	95	67	47	14	30			13	21	1	2
1988	Con.	99	46	38	43	39			10	20		3

1. Three McCarthyite, two Patrons of Industry, one Independent.
2. Including one Independent Liberal.
3. Independent.
4. Including one Independent Conservative.
5. Including twelve Liberal Unionists.
6. Independent Liberal.
7. Including two Liberal Progressives and one Independent Liberal.
8. Independent Liberal.
9. United Farmers of Ontario-Labor.
10. Including 12 percent for Reconstruction party.
11. Including two Liberal Progressives.
12. Independent.
13. Including two percent Social Credit.

MANITOBA

Election Year	Party Forming Federal Government	Total Seats	Conservative Seats	Conservative Votes (%)	Liberal Seats	Liberal Votes (%)	Progressive Seats	Progressive Votes (%)	Labor-CCF-NDP Seats	Labor-CCF-NDP Votes (%)	Other Seats	Other Votes (%)
1878	Con.	4	3	50	1	50						
1882	Con.	5	2	47	3	53						
1887	Con.	5	4	51	1	49						
1891	Con.	5	4	53	1	47						
1896	Lib.	7	4	47	2	35					1[1]	18
1900	Lib.	7	3	48	4	52						
1904	Lib.	10	3	42	7	55						3
1908	Lib.	10	8	52	2	45						3
1911	Con.	10	8	52	2	45						3
1917	Con.[2]	15	14[3]	80	1	20						
1921	Lib.	15	0	24	1	11	12	44	1	6	1[4]	15
1925	Lib.	17	7	42	1	20	7	27	2	11		
1926	Lib.	17	0	42	11[5]	38	4	11	2	9		
1930	Con.	17	11	48	4[6]	37		4	2	11		
									CCF			
1935	Lib.	17	1	27	14[7]	41				2	19	13[8]
1940	Lib.	17	1	26	15[9]	48				1	19	7
1945	Lib.	17	2	25	10	35				5	32	8
1949	Lib.	16	1	22	12	48				3	26	4
1953	Lib.	14	3	27	8	40				3	24	9[10]
1957	Con.	14	8	36	1	26				5	24	14[11]
1958	Con.	14	14	57	0	22				0	20	1
									NDP			
1962	Con.	14	11	41	1	31				2	20	8[12]
1963	Lib.	14	10	42	2	34				2	17	7[13]
1965	Lib.	14	10	41	1	31				3	24	4[14]
1968	Lib.	13	5	31	5	41				3	25	3[15]
1972	Lib.	13	8	42	2	31				3	26	1
1974	Lib.	13	9	48	2	27				2	24	
1979	Con.	14	7	44	2	24				5	31	1
1980	Lib.	14	5	38	2	28				7	33	1
1984	Con.	14	9	43	1	22				4	27	
1988	Con.	14	7	37	5	36				2	21	6[16]

1. McCarthyite.
2. Wartime Coalition.
3. Including six Liberal Unionists.
4. Independent Liberal.
5. Including seven Liberal Progressives.
6. Including three Liberal Progressives.
7. Including two Liberal Progressives.
8. Including 6 percent Reconstruction party.
9. Including one Liberal Progressive.
10. Including 6 percent Social Credit.
11. Including 13 percent Social Credit.
12. Including 7 percent Social Credit.
13. Including 7 percent Social Credit.
14. Including 4 percent Social Credit.
15. Including 2 percent Social Credit.
16. Including 3 percent Reform party.

SASKATCHEWAN

Election Year	Party Forming Federal Government	Total Seats	Conservative Seats	Conservative Votes (%)	Liberal Seats	Liberal Votes (%)	CCF-NDP Seats	CCF-NDP Votes (%)	Progressive Seats	Progressive Votes (%)	Other Seats	Other Votes (%)
1908	Lib.	10	1	37	9	57						6
1911	Con.	10	1	39	9	59						2
1917	Con.	16	16[1]	74	0	26						
1921	Lib.	16	0	17	1	21			15	61		1
1925	Lib.	21	0	25	15	42			6	32		1
1926	Lib.	21	0	27	18[2]	57			3	16		
1930	Con.	21	8	38	11	47			2	12		3
1935	Lib.	21	1	19	16	41	2	21			2[3]	19[4]
1940	Lib.	21	2	14	12	43	5	29			2[5]	14
1945	Lib.	21	1	19	2	33	18	44				4[6]
1949	Lib.	20	1	14	14	44	5	41				1
1953	Lib.	17	1	12	5	38	11	44				6[7]
1957	Con.	17	3	23	4	30	10	36				11[8]
1958	Con.	17	16	51	0	20	1	28				1
1962	Con.	17	16	50	1	23	0	22				5
1963	Lib.	17	17	54	0	24	0	18				4[9]
1965	Lib.	17	17	48	0	24	0	26				2[10]
1968	Lib.	13	5	37	2	27	6	36				
1972	Lib.	13	7	37	1	25	5	36				2[11]
1974	Lib.	13	8	36	3	31	2	32				
1979	Con.	14	10	41	0	22	4	37				1
1980	Lib.	14	7	40	0	24	7	36				
1984	Con.	14	9	42	0	18	5	38				
1988	Con.	14	4	36	0	18	10	44				1

1. Including seven Liberal Unionists.
2. Including two Liberal Progressives.
3. Social Credit.
4. Including 16 percent Social Credit.
5. One Unity, one Unity Reform.
6. Including 3 percent Social Credit.
7. Including 5 percent Social Credit.
8. Including 10 percent Social Credit.
9. Including 4 percent Social Credit.
10. Including 2 percent Social Credit.
11. Including 2 percent Social Credit.

ALBERTA

Election Year	Party Forming Federal Government	Total Seats	Conservative Seats	Conservative Votes (%)	Liberal Seats	Liberal Votes (%)	Progressive Seats	Progressive Votes (%)	Social Credit Seats	Social Credit Votes (%)	Other Seats	Other Votes (%)
1908	Lib.	7	3	44	4	50						6
1911	Con.	7	1	43	6	53						4
1917	Con.[11]	12	11[1]	61	1	36						3
1921	Lib.	12	0	20	0	16	11	57			1[2]	7
1925	Lib.	16	3	32	4	26	9	32				10
1926	Lib.	16	1	32	3	24	11	39			1[2]	5
1930	Con.	16	4	34	3	30	9	30				6
1935	Lib.	17	1	17	1	21			15	48		14[3]
1940	Lib.	17	0	13	7	38			10	35		14[4]
1945	Lib.	17	2	19	2	22			13	37		22[5]
1949	Lib.	17	2	17	5	35			10	37		11[6]
1953	Lib.	17	2	15	4	35			11	41		9[7]
1957	Con.	17	3	28	1	28			13	38		6[8]
1958	Con.	17	17	60	0	14			0	22		4[9]
1962	Con.	17	15	43	0	19			2	29		9[10]
1963	Lib.	17	14	45	1	22			2	26		7[12]
1965	Lib.	17	15	47	0	22			2	23		8[13]
1968	Lib.	19	15	50	4	35			0	2		12[14]
1972	Lib.	19	19	57	0	25			0	4		13[15]
1974	Lib.	19	19	61	0	25			0	3		11[16]
1979	Con.	21	21	66	0	22			0	1		11[17]
1980	Lib.	21	21	66	0	21			0	1		12[18]
1984	Con.	21	21	69	0	13						18[19]
1988	Con.	26	25	52	0	14					1	34[20]

1. Including four Liberal Unionists.
2. Labour.
3. Including 13 percent CCF.
4. Including 13 percent CCF.
5. Including 18 percent CCF.
6. Including 9 percent CCF.
7. Including 7 percent CCF.
8. Including 6 percent CCF.
9. Including 4 percent CCF.
10. Including 9 percent NDP.
11. Wartime Coalition.
12. Including 7 percent NDP.
13. Including 8 percent NDP.
14. Including 9 percent NDP.
15. Including 13 percent NDP.
16. Including 9 percent NDP.
17. Including 10 percent NDP.
18. Including 10 percent NDP.
19. Including 14 percent NDP.
20. Including 17 percent NDP and 15 percent Reform party.

BRITISH COLUMBIA

Election Year	Party Forming Federal Government	Total Seats	Conservative Seats	Conservative Votes (%)	Liberal Seats	Liberal Votes (%)	CCF-NDP Seats	CCF-NDP Votes (%)	Social Credit Seats	Social Credit Votes (%)	Other Seats	Other Votes (%)
1878	Con.	6	6	89	0							11
1882	Con.	6	6	83	0	11						6
1887	Con.	6	6	87	0	13						
1891	Con.	6	6	72	0	28						
1896	Lib.	6	2	51	4	49						
1900	Lib.	6	2	41	4	49						10[1]
1904	Lib.	7	0	39	7	49						12[2]
1908	Lib.	7	5	47	2	36						17[3]
1911	Con.	7	7	59	0	37						4[4]
1917	Con.	13	13	68	0	26						6[5]
1921	Lib.	13	7	48	3	30					3[6]	22[7]
1925	Lib.	14	10	49	3	35					1[8]	16[9]
1926	Lib.	14	12	54	1	37					1[10]	9[11]
1930	Con.	14	7	49	5	41					2[12]	10[13]
1935	Lib.	16	5	25	6	32	3	34			2[14]	9[15]
1940	Lib.	16	4	31	10	37	1	28			1[16]	4[17]
1945	Lib.	16	5	30	5	28	4	29		2	2[18]	11[9]
1949	Lib.	18	3	28	11	37	3	31		1	1[20]	3
1953	Lib.	22	3	14	8	31	7	27	4	26		2
1957	Con.	22	7	33	2	21	7	22	6	24		
1958	Con.	22	18	49	0	16	4	25	0	10		
1962	Con.	22	6	27	4	27	10	31	2	14		1
1963	Lib.	22	4	23	7	33	9	30	2	13		1
1965	Lib.	22	3	19	7	30	9	33	3	17		1
1968	Lib.	23	0	20	16	42	7	33	0	5		
1972	Lib.	23	8	33	4	29	11	35	0	3		
1974	Lib.	23	13	42	8	33	2	23	0	1		
1979	Con.	28	19	45	1	23	8	32				
1980	Lib.	28	16	42	0	22	12	35				1
1984	Con.	28	19	47	1	16	8	35				
1988	Con.	32	12	34	1	21	19	37				8[21]

1. Labour.
2. Including 4 percent Socialist, 8 percent Independent.
3. Including 7 percent Socialist and 10 percent Independent.
4. Including 3 percent Socialist.
5. Including 5 percent Labour.
6. Two Progressives and one Independent.
7. Including 9 percent Progressive; 5 percent Labour; 5 percent Socialist; 2 percent Independent.
8. Independent.
9. Including 6 percent Labour and 6 percent Progressive.
10. Independent.
11. Including 7 percent Labour.
12. One Independent; one Independent Labour.
13. Including 6 percent Independent Labour.
14. One Reconstruction; one Independent.
15. Including 7 percent Reconstruction.
16. Independent.
17. Including 3 percent Independent.
18. One Independent CCF; one Independent.
19. Including 5 percent Labour Progressive.
20. Independent.
21. Including 5 percent Reform party.

THE TERRITORIES

Election Year	Party Forming Federal Government	Total Seats	Conservative Seats	Conservative Votes (%)	Liberal Seats	Liberal Votes (%)	Other Seats	Other Votes (%)
1887	Con.	4	4	69	0	31		
1891	Con.	4	4	81	0	19		
1896	Lib.	4	1	44	3	46		10[1]
1900	Lib.	4	0	45	4	55		
1904	Lib.	11	4	43	7	57		
1908	Lib.	1	0	11	1	40		49[2]
1911	Con.	1	1	61	0	39		
1917	Con.[9]	1	1	54	0	46		
1921	Lib.	1	1	51	0	48		1[3]
1925	Lib.	1	1	59	0	41		
1926	Lib.	1	1	56	0	44		
1930	Con.	1	1	60	0	40		
1935	Lib.	1	1	56	0	44		
1940	Lib.	1	1	54	0	46		
1945	Lib.	1	1	40	0	0		60[4]
1949	Lib.	1	0	0	1	49		51[5]
1953	Lib.	2	0	27	2	54		19[6]
1957	Con.	2	0	41	2	59		
1958	Con.	2	1	49	1	50		1[7]
1962	Con.	2	1	47	1	46		7[8]
1963	Lib.	2	2	54	0	42		4[10]
1965	Lib.	2	1	45	1	52		3
1968	Lib.	2	1	47	1	48		5[11]
1972	Lib.	2	1	39	0	30	1	30[12]
1974	Lib.	2	1	39	0	28	1	33[13]
1979	Con.	3	2	37	0	33	1	30[14]
1980	Lib.	3	2	32	0	37	1	31[15]
1984	Con.	3	3	47	0	25	0	28[16]
1988	Con.	3	0	30	2	30	1	40[17]

1. Independent.
2. Independent.
3. Independent.
4. Including 28 percent CCF and 32 percent Labour Progressive.
5. Including 17 percent CCF and 34 percent Independent.
6. Including 14 percent Social Credit.
7. Including 1 percent Independent Progressive Conservative.
8. Including 7 percent Social Credit.
9. Wartime Coalition.
10. Including 4 percent Social Credit.

11. Including 5 percent NDP.
12. Including 30 percent NDP thereby winning one seat.
13. Including 33 percent NDP thereby winning one seat.
14. Including 29 percent NDP thereby winning one seat.
15. Including 31 percent NDP thereby winning one seat.
16. Including 24 percent NDP.
17. Including 37 percent NDP thereby winning one seat.

COMBINED ELECTION RESULTS

Election Year	Party Forming Federal Government	Total Seats	Conservative Seats	Conservative Votes (%)	Liberal Seats	Liberal Votes (%)	Progressive Seats	Progressive Votes (%)	CCF-NDP Seats	CCF-NDP Votes (%)	Social Credit Seats	Social Credit Votes (%)	Reconstruction / Créditiste Seats	Reconstruction / Créditiste Votes (%)	Other Seats	Other Votes (%)
1878	Con.	206	140	53	65	45									1	2
1882	Con.	211	138	53	73	47										2
1887	Con.	215	128	51	87	49									2	2
1891	Con.	215	122	52	91	46									7	9
1896	Lib.	213	88	46	118	45										1
1900	Lib.	213	81	47	132	52										1
1904	Lib.	214	75	47	139	52									1	2
1908	Lib.	221	85	47	135	51										1
1911	Con.	221	134	51	87	48										3
1917	Con.[1]	235	153[2]	57	82	40										6
1921	Lib.	235	50	30	116	41	65	23							4	5
1925	Lib.	245	116	46	99	40	24	9							6	4
1926	Lib.	245	91	45	128	46	20	5							6	3
1930	Con.	245	137	49	91	45	12	3							5	3
1935	Lib.	245	40	30	173	45			7	9	17	4	1	9	7	3
1940	Lib.	245	40	31	181	51			8	8	10	3			6	7
1945	Lib.	245	67	27	125	41			28	16	13	4			12	12
1949	Lib.	262	41	30	193	49			13	13	10	4			5	4
1953	Lib.	265	51	31	171	49			23	11	15	5			5	4
1957	Con.	265	112	39	105	41			25	11	19	7			4	2
1958	Con.	265	208	54	49	34			8	9	0	2				1
1962	Con.	265	116	37	100	37			19	14	30	12				1
1963	Lib.	265	95	33	129	42			17	13	24	12				1
1965	Lib.	265	97	32	131	40			21	18	5	4	9 (Créditiste)	5		1
1968	Lib.	264	72	31	155	45			21	17	0	1	14 (Créditiste)	5	2	1
1972	Lib.	264	107	35	109	38			31	18	15	8			0	1
1974	Lib.	264	95	35	141	43			16	15	11	5			1	1
1979	Con.	282	136	36	114	40			26	18	6	5			1	1
1980	Lib.	282	103	33	146	44			32	20	0	1			0	2
1984	Con.	282	211	50	40	28			30	19					1	2
1988	Con.	295	169	43	83	32			43	20					0	4

1. Wartime Coalition.

Leaders of Major Federal Political Parties

APPENDIX B

Conservative Party Leaders

Sir John A. Macdonald, 1867–91
*PM July 1867 – Nov. 1873;
Oct. 1878 – June 1891*

Sir John J.C. Abbott, 1891–92
PM June 1891 – Nov. 1892

Sir John Sparrow Thompson, 1892–94
PM Dec. 1892 – Dec. 1894

Sir Mackenzie Bowell, 1894–96
PM Dec. 1894 – Apr. 1896

Sir Charles Tupper, 1896–1900
PM May 1896 – July 1896

Sir Robert Laird Borden, 1901–20
*PM (Conservative Party) Oct. 1911 –
12 Oct. 1917; PM (Unionist Party)
Oct. 1917 – July 1920*

Arthur Meighen, 1920–26
*PM (Unionist Party) July 1920 – Dec.
1921; PM (Conservative Party) June
1926 – Sept. 1926*

Hugh Guthrie, 1926–27

Richard Bedford Bennett, 1927–38
PM Aug. 1930 – Oct. 1935

Robert James Manion, 1938–40

Richard Burpee Hanson, 1940–43

Gordon Graydon, 1943–45

John Bracken, 1945–48

George Drew, 1948–56

John Diefenbaker, 1956–67
PM June 1957 – April 1963

Michael Starr, 1967

Robert Stanfield, 1967–76

Charles Joseph Clark, 1976–83
PM June 1979 – March 1980

Martin Brian Mulroney, 1983–
PM Sept. 1984–

Liberal Party Leaders

Alexander Mackenzie, 1873–1880
PM Nov. 1873 – Oct. 1878

Edward Blake, 1880–1887

Wilfrid Laurier, 1887–1919
PM July 1896 – Oct. 1911

William Lyon Mackenzie King,
1919–1948
PM Dec. 1921 – June 1926;
Sept. 1926 – Aug. 1930;
Oct. 1935 – Nov. 1948

Louis St. Laurent, 1948–1958
PM Nov. 1948 – June 1957

Lester Bowles Pearson, 1958–1968
PM Apr. 1963 – April 1968

Pierre Elliott Trudeau, 1968–1984
PM Apr. 1968 – June 1979;
Mar. 1980 – Mar. 1984

John Napier Turner, 1984–1990
PM June 1984 – Sept. 1984

Jean Chrétien, 1990–

CCF Leaders

J.S. Woodsworth, 1932–1942
M.J. Coldwell, 1942–1960
Hazen Ague, 1960–1961

NDP Leaders

Tommy Douglas, 1961–1971
David Lewis, 1971–1975
Ed Broadbent, 1975–1990
Audrey McLaughlin, 1990–

Canadian Political Party Leadership Conventions

APPENDIX C

Liberal Party

1919

Candidates	First ballot	Second ballot	Third ballot
W.L. Mackenzie King	344	411	476
W.S. Fielding	297	344	438
George P. Graham	153	124	—
D.D. McKenzie	153	60	—

1948

Candidates	First ballot
Louis St. Laurent	848
James Garfield Gardiner	323
Charles G. "Chubby" Power	56

1958

Candidates	First ballot
Lester B. Pearson	1 074
Paul Martin	305

1968

Candidates	First ballot	Second ballot	Third ballot	Fourth ballot
Pierre Elliott Trudeau	752	964	1 051	1 203
Robert Winters	293	473	621	954
John Turner	277	347	279	195
Paul Hellyer	330	465	377	—

J.J. Greene	169	104	29	—
Allan MacEachen	165	11	—	—
Paul Martin	277	—	—	—
Eric Kierans	103	—	—	—

1984

Candidates	First ballot	Second ballot
John Turner	1 593	1 862
Jean Chrétien	1 067	1 368
Donald Johnston	278	192
John Roberts	185	—
Mark MacGuigan	135	—
John Munro	93	—
Eugene Whelan	84	—

1990

Candidates	First ballot
Jean Chrétien	2 662
Paul Martin	1 176
Sheila Copps	499
Tom Wappel	267
John Nunziata	64

Progressive Conservative Party

1948

Candidates	First ballot
George A. Drew	827
John G. Diefenbaker	311
Donald M. Fleming	104

1956

Candidates	First ballot
John G. Diefenbaker	744
Donald M. Fleming	393
E. Davie Fulton	117

1967

Candidates	First ballot	Second ballot	Third ballot	Fourth ballot	Fifth ballot
Robert Stanfield	519	613	717	865	1 150
Duff Roblin	349	430	541	771	969
E. Davie Fulton	343	346	361	357	
Alvin Hamilton........	136	127	106	167	—
George Hees	395	299	277	—	—
John G. Diefenbaker ...	271	172	114	—	—
Donald M. Fleming	126	115	76	—	—
Wallace McCutcheon ...	137	76	—	—	—
Michael Starr..........	45	34	—	—	—
John P. McLean........	10	—	—	—	—
Mary Walker Sawka	2	—	—	—	—

1976

Candidates	First ballot	Second ballot	Third ballot	Fourth ballot
Joe Clark	277	532	969	1 187
Claude Wagner	531	667	1 003	1 112
Brian Mulroney	357	419	369	—
Jack Horner	235	286	—	—
Flora MacDonald................	214	239	—	—
Paul Hellyer	231	118	—	—
Patrick Nowlan	86	42	—	—
John Fraser	127	34	—	—
Sinclair Stevens	182	—	—	—
James Gillies....................	87	—	—	—
Heward Graftey.................	33	—	—	—

1983

Candidates	First ballot	Second ballot	Third ballot	Fourth ballot
Brian Mulroney	874	1 021	1 036	1 584
Joe Clark	1 091	1 085	1 058	1 325
John Crosbie....................	639	781	858	—
David Crombie	116	67	—	—
Michael Wilson	144	—	—	—
Peter Pocklington................	102	—	—	—
John Gamble	17	—	—	—
Neil Fraser	5	—	—	—

New Democratic Party

1961

Candidates	First ballot
Tommy Douglas	1 391
Hazen Argue	380

1971

Candidates	First ballot	Second ballot	Third ballot	Fourth ballot
David Lewis	661	715	742	1 046
James Laxer	378	407	508	612
John Harney	299	347	431	—
Ed Broadbent	236	223	—	—
Frank Howard	124	—	—	—

1975

Candidates	First ballot	Second ballot	Third ballot	Fourth ballot
Ed Broadbent	536	586	694	984
Rosemary Brown	413	397	494	658
Lorne Nystrom	345	342	413	—
John Harney	313	299	—	—
Douglas Campbell	11	—	—	—

1989

Candidates	First ballot	Second ballot	Third ballot	Fourth ballot
Audrey McLaughlin	646	829	1 072	1 316
Dave Barrett	566	780	947	1 072
Steven Langdon	351	519	393	—
Simon de Jong	315	289	—	—
Howard McCurdy	256	—	—	—
Ian Waddell	213	—	—	—
Roger Lagasse	53	—	—	—

Source: "Canadian Political Party Leadership Conventions," *The Canadian World Almanac & Book of Facts 1991* (Toronto: Global Press, 1990), pp. 73–74. Reprinted with the permission of Global Press.

INDEX